Hegel's Trinitarian Claim

Hegel's Trinitarian Claim
A Critical Reflection

Dale M. Schlitt

Published by State University of New York Press, Albany

Second Edition © 2012 State University of New York
First Edition © 1984 E. J. Brill

All rights reserved

Printed in the United States of America

No part of this book may be used or reproduced in any manner whatsoever without written permission. No part of this book may be stored in a retrieval system or transmitted in any form or by any means including electronic, electrostatic, magnetic tape, mechanical, photocopying, recording, or otherwise without the prior permission in writing of the publisher.

For information, contact State University of New York Press, Albany, NY
www.sunypress.edu

Production by Eileen Nizer
Marketing by Anne M. Valentine

Library of Congress Cataloging-in-Publication Data

Schlitt, Dale M.
  Hegel's Trinitarian claim : a critical reflection / Dale M. Schlitt.
    p. cm.
  Includes bibliographical references (p.   ) and index.
  ISBN 978-1-4384-4375-1 (hardcover : alk. paper)
  ISBN 978-1-4384-4374-4 (pbk. : alk. paper)
  1. Hegel, Georg Wilhelm Friedrich, 1770–1831—Religion. 2. Trinity—History of doctrines—19th century. I. Title.

231'.044092—dc23   2011045577

10 9 8 7 6 5 4 3 2 1

Contents

Preface — ix

Abbreviations of Works by Hegel — xv

Introduction: Hegel's Trinitarian Claim — xix

Part One
Logic—Hegel's Reformulation of the True Content of Trinity

1 Logic as Movement of Trinitarian Divine Subjectivity — 3
   1. Logic—the Movement of Pure Thought — 3
   2. The Movement of Self-determining Subjectivity — 8
   3. The Self-determining of the Divine Subject — 14
   4. The Necessarily Triadic Structure of the Self-determining Divine Subject — 19
   5. The *Logic* as Elaboration of Hegel's Trinitarian Claim — 21

2 Hegel's Logic of Pure Thought — 25
   1. Through *Etwas* to Being — 25
   2. The Primordial, Elementary Movement of Pure Thought — 29
   3. Summary Remarks on the Structure of Hegel's Dialectic — 35
   4. Critique of the Primordial, Elementary Movement of Pure Thought — 41
   5. The Determinate Nature of Any Beginning—Implications for Trinity — 47

Part Two
Hegel's Explicit Trinitarian Texts

3 Overview of Hegel's Explicit Trinitarian Thought and a Criterion for the *Phenomenology*   57
   1. Transition to Hegel's Explicit Trinitarian Texts   57
   2. Hegel's Syllogistically Structured Explicitly Trinitarian Thought   59
   3. Guiding Concerns in Approaching the *Phenomenology*   70
   4. Toward a Criterion for Critiquing the *Phenomenology*   73
   5. A Criterion for Hegel's Argument in the *Phenomenology*   79

4 The Incarnational Immediacy of Trinitarian Reconciliation in the *Phenomenology*   83
   1. Preliminary, Contextualizing Remarks   83
   2. Reconciliation in Its Incarnational Immediacy and Trinitarian Explicitation   85
   3. Critique of Trinitarian Reconciliation in Its Incarnational Immediacy   92
   4. Implications for Trinity and for the Self   111

5 Trinitarian Reconciliation in Hegel's Philosophy of Religion *Lectures*   121
   1. Introduction and Context   121
   2. Syllogistically Structured Trinitarian Divine Subjectivity in the 1827 Lectures   124
   3. Critique of Trinitarian Reconciliation as Spiritual Community   140
   4. The Formal Triadic Structure of Becoming   149

Part Three
Reconstructing Hegel's Trinitarian Envisionment

6 From Finite to Infinite   159
   1. Recapitulative Overview   159
   2. The Contours of Hegel's Finite "and" Infinite   162
   3. From Finitude to Triadically Structured Inclusive Infinite   174
   4. Toward a Reformulation of Hegel's Trinitarian Claim   181

Postscript: From Thought to Experience	183
Notes	193
Bibliography	349
Index of Names	371

Preface

I would like to thank the State University of New York Press for the gracious offer to make this study available again, and now more widely, with a paperback printing. I am especially grateful to Mr. Andrew Kenyon, Assistant Acquisitions Editor, for his encouragement of this project and for his wise counsel and helpful guidance in carrying it out.

I believe the present study has stood the test of time over the years since its first publication in 1984. Between then and now many excellent studies have appeared on Hegel's philosophy of religion and, more specifically, several on Hegel's philosophical reading of Trinity, including what would today in theological circles be distinguished as "immanent" and "economic" Trinity. Still, I would suggest that the presentations made and argumentation carried out in the present study have not been superseded in the intervening years since its first publication. Today I would, though, after decades of pondering Hegel's brilliant thought, probably have written in a kinder and gentler tone. In line with my overall reading of the continuing relevance of the present study, I in fact took as something of at least a partial compliment the oral remark by a respected Hegel scholar who, after reading the book, said that he disagreed with my argument but could not point out any passages from Hegel which I had misread or misrepresented.

Fortunately I was able, when carrying out this study, to profit from the pioneering research of Reinhard Heede and especially that of Walter Jaeschke in preparation for a critical text of Hegel's *Lectures on the Philosophy of Religion*, which he subsequently edited. I profited as well from Peter C. Hodgson's publication of a trustworthy and insightful translation of parts of these *Lectures*. Luckily, Chapter Five of the present study works with Hegel's more fully developed lecture series of 1827 as represented in the then available Lasson edition. This Lasson text is the one which ended up serving as primary reference for the 1827 lecture series in Jaeschke's German edition and its full English translation edited by Hodgson.

I remain convinced Hegel was right in claiming that to think God as Subject and as personal one must think of God as Trinity. Given his own criteria for making his case, though, he was not able to defend that claim successfully in the public realm of thought and discourse, at least not in the way in which he argued it. In carrying out this study, it seemed strategically wise and indeed necessary not only to treat Hegel's reading of Trinity more indirectly in his *Phenomenology of Spirit* and directly in his *Encyclopedia* and *Lectures on the Philosophy of Religion*, but also to consider seriously his *Science of Logic*. For Hegel's entire mature encyclopedic system is a form of argument in favor of his trinitarian claim. So, working with his *Logic*, the presentation of incarnation in the *Phenomenology*, and his development of the idea of community in the Christian religion proved to be a good way to cover in this critical reflection all three of Hegel's "trinitarian" moments.

While, then, the original study seems to me to maintain its relevance, republishing it now provides a welcome occasion to make it more readily available and to enhance the text in several ways. For example, this Preface is new, as is the Postscript. The Bibliography has been updated to include references to works which have come to my attention especially, but not only, concerning Hegel on Trinity. Some of them may touch rather tangentially the question of Trinity and are included more because they caught my philosophical fancy. Perhaps, though, at a certain point in life after longer reflection and study, this more serendipitous approach will have some value. In light of suggestions and remarks made over the years, I have here and there added a short phrase in the text itself or in notes to help clarify a particular point. This new printing provides as well an opportunity to correct some of the typographical and stylistic errors found in the first, hardcover edition.

There are, however, several points raised by reviewers and others over the years which I would like to address more directly here in the Preface since these points have to do with the overall approach the present study takes and the argumentation it presents. Addressing these points will help underscore, at least indirectly, my ever-increasing admiration for Hegel's extraordinary genius, permit highlighting one or the other aspect of my overall reading of Hegel, and further clarify my argument concerning his philosophical interpretation of Trinity and the way in which it unfolds.

The first of these points is the proposal that my criticism of Hegel is based ultimately on comparison with some "elusive theological orthodoxy."[1] To proceed in such a comparative mode was not at all my intention. In fact I did try to make it clear that my criticism took the form of an immanent critique of Hegel's thought, a critique based on and working with his own criteria for successful argumentation. The text reads, for example, at the beginning of Section Four in Chapter Three: "Criteria for an internal critique of Hegel's works in general must arise out of what Hegel in fact wrote, from the project he proposed to carry through and what he understood himself to be doing at the time of the writing itself." Hence the study was meant first and foremost as a philosophical exercise. If Hegel was not successful in arguing his position on Trinity in the way in which he did, and if in fact his position could not be argued in the way in which he propose to do it, then there would be little need to consider introducing it, at least as he argued it, directly into theological discourse.

With reference to this immanent critique, we could well note another approach William Desmond has brilliantly worked out at some length over the years. He writes: ". . . one cannot judge Hegel just in terms of the immanent coherence of his claims. . . . Rather, one must have dwelled in the ambiguous plurivocity of being religious, enacted philosophical reflection about the ultimate astonishments and perplexities there occasioned, strained one's soul to the utmost to remain true to the God that is God . . . While internal instabilities and even incoherencies in Hegel are not unimportant, there is something more important—fidelity to the 'matter itself.' "[2] Though this abbreviated quotation cannot begin to do justice to Desmond's thought, it does give a taste of his approach. I would myself, however, give more weight to an immanent critique, at least as a first step in a process of working with and beyond Hegel, since such a critique, among other considerations, allows us to learn from him and his brilliant proposal rather directly while then working to go beyond him. After all, as just mentioned in a similar vein, if Hegel were able to argue successfully in the public realm his trinitarian position in the way in which he presented it, it would seem hard to resist embracing that position, especially since he claimed his position was in principle inclusive and to have left nothing outside its purview.

Several eminently qualified reviewers of the hardcover edition of the present volume have raised various points whose consideration will help us clarify certain aspects of the argument presented in the present study.

Emilio Brito[3] has suggested that carrying out an immanent critique of Hegel and concluding that his theory led to untenable contradictions seemed a little naive, given the extraordinary coherence of Hegel's speculative thought. Brito suggests, rather, that it would be better to appeal to an alternative experience whose intelligibility can be shown. However, I would hold that one is in fact being more faithful to Hegel in pursuing, perhaps inevitably a bit naively, an immanent critique of his thought. After all, an immanent critique is at least in part the way in which Hegel approached the thought of his predecessors. To exemplify this we can note his treatment of Kant's philosophy, in which he finds so much to admire and yet where he points to contradictions not resolved in that philosophy.[4]

In Chapter Three of the present study, I understand Hegel, in his 1830 *Encyclopedia*, §§ 567–571, to be describing the three "trinitarian" moments in terms of syllogisms. Brito argues that, contrary to my interpretation, those moments prior to that of individuality, but especially the moment of "immanent" Trinity, are only virtually syllogistic.[5] It is true that the first sentence in § 571, speaking of three syllogisms constituting one syllogism, is varyingly interpreted to indicate either all three moments of the concept—namely, universality, particularity and individuality—or merely the three syllogisms constituting the moment of individuality. On the basis of a consideration of the overall structural dynamic of Hegel's thought, of the immediate context, and of other descriptions of Trinity by Hegel as syllogism, I interpret the disputed phrase to refer directly to the three syllogisms making up the moment of individuality and, through them, as well all three moments of the concept. The development toward further explicitness from Hegel's logically speaking earlier forms of the syllogisms to the later forms takes sufficiently into account both the movement, in the consummate religion, from more implicit to more explicit and the realization that Hegel is already working with God as absolute subjectivity from the beginning of the *Encyclopedia* presentation of the consummate religion. In fact Hegel stated explicitly, though parenthetically, in an 1829 book review that his thought on Trinity (*Dreieinigkeitslehre*, as the author of the book in question had referred to Hegel's thought) was a "syllogism of absolute self-mediation, which [syllogism] is made up of three syllogisms."[6] In any case, all would surely agree that the last "trinitarian" moment, namely, that of individuality, is syllogistically structured, and this moment is the one more immediately relevant for my critique, in Chapter Five, of Hegel's syllogistic structuring of his thought on Trinity.

Merold Westphal interestingly identifies what he sees to be certain parallels between my criticism of Hegel and that carried out by Kierkegaard. In this regard, Westphal refers to the unavailability of a system of pure thought to human thinkers, the impossibility of seeing the historical contingency of the incarnation in terms of conceptual necessity, and the inability to perceive immediately a divine-human unity.[7] Though I do not recall being aware of possible affinities with the thought of such a creative philosopher when writing the present study and though the reasons why I find Hegel's argumentation problematic may differ at least to some extent from those of Kierkegaard, it would be a singular honor to be associated even modestly and indirectly with such an outstanding thinker.

Jean-Pierre Labarrière has, in a dense and particularly focused review,[8] helpfully raised a number of points deserving further attention. As he points out, in the Introduction to my study I write: "Systematically speaking, Hegel argues this [his] trinitarian claim as a movement from infinite to finite to inclusive or affirmative infinite with infinite understood as inclusive totality." He draws attention to what could be considered the ambiguous character of the phrase, "Systematically speaking," which he translates as "to say it in a systematic way" ("*Pour le dire de façon systématique*"). Labarrière would seem to be indicating that the phrase could be taken simply to mean, "to say it in a summary or orderly, systematic fashion." In fact, in using this phrase, "systematically speaking," I meant to say "from the point of view of Hegel's system." What has become clearer to me is that it is important to stress the word "speculative" so as to indicate clearly that the reference is to the speculative formulation of Hegel's dialectic as a movement from an initial moment of immediacy. I should say more exactly, "speaking from the perspective of the speculative formulation of Hegel's thought."

More substantively, Labarrière argues that my view of Hegel's thought as a movement from initial infinite to finite to true or inclusive infinite is reductionist, since with Hegel reflection takes off as much from the exterior as from the interior.[9] He further recalls, and this I much appreciate, that there are binary, ternary, and even quaternary "schemas" of thought in Hegel's presentation of the movement of Spirit. Therefore, to say that Hegel's thought, presented simply as one of a movement from infinite to finite to inclusive infinite, is an adequate "systematic" or organized summary of Hegel's thought is of course not true. However, I would want to remain with the fundamental affirmation that, from the point of view of Hegel's systematic or "mature" thought in its speculative formulation, for Hegel it is the movement from being to nothing to becoming/*Dasein* which, in its forward moving and retroactively grounding dialectic, underlies and makes possible the other structural movements. It is this speculative movement, as movement, which is very important here, and which comes to the fore particularly in the philosophy of religion. Hegel himself is concerned to establish the speculative dialectic of "in itself," "for itself," and "in and for itself," a dialectic which is the grounding movement making possible the often more phenomenologically expressed move from finite to infinite. The speculative dialectic of "in itself," "for itself," and "in and for itself" expresses the grounding movement of identity and difference, of subjectivity, freedom, and Spirit. I would argue that, from the point of view of his speculative presentation, for Hegel the movement of Spirit does not begin equally from finite and from infinite. The speculatively presented movement of Spirit (and for Hegel presentation is argumentation) begins in and with pure being. Any other more multiple beginning to his speculative system would no longer allow Hegel to escape from what would then seem to be an antinomical situation. It would ultimately be a denial of the idealist solution to the overcoming of alienation, namely, that one begins from an initial unity of thought and being.

The present reprinting provides the occasion to thank those who have commented on this study and to express my gratitude for their insightful questions and helpful remarks which have provided the opportunity to clarify various aspects of this critical reflection on Hegel's trinitarian claim. In the Postscript I will take up further questions concerning why we should study Hegel, but especially his thought on Trinity, if he was not able to argue his trinitarian claim successfully, what we have learned from this critical reflection, and where it may well lead us in subsequent, more constructive reflection.

Abbreviations of Works by Hegel

AR　　*Vorlesungen über die Philosophie der Religion.* Philosophische Bibliothek. Vol. 63: *Die absolute Religion.* Edited by Georg Lasson. Hamburg: Felix Meiner, 1974.

BDG　　*Vorlesungen über die Beweise vom Dasein Gottes.* Philosophische Bibliothek. Vol. 64. Edited by Georg Lasson. Hamburg: Felix Meiner, 1973.

BR　　*Vorlesungen über die Philosophie der Religion.* Philosophische Bibliothek. Vol. 59: *Begriff der Religion.* Edited by Georg Lasson. Hamburg: Felix Meiner, 1974.

CR　　*The Christian Religion. Lectures on the Philosophy of Religion. Part Three. The Revelatory, Consummate, Absolute Religion.* Translation of AR by Peter C. Hodgson. Ann Arbor, MI: Scholars, 1979.

E　　*Enzyklopädie der philosophischen Wissenschaften im Grundrisse.* Third original edition 1830. Philosophische Bibliothek. Vol. 33. Edited by Friedhelm Nicolin and Otto Pöggeler. Hamburg: Felix Meiner, 1969. § = paragraph. R = Remark.

GI　　*Vorlesungen über die Philosophie der Religion.* Philosophische Bibliothek. Vol. 61: *Die Religionen der geistigen Individualität.* Edited by Georg Lasson. Hamburg: Felix Meiner, 1974.

GL　　*Hegel's Science of Logic.* Translation of L 1 and 2 by A. V. Miller. New York: Humanities, 1969.

GW 9   *Gesammelte Werke*. Vol. 9: *Phänomenologie des Geistes*. Edited by Wolfgang Bonsiepen and Reinhard Heede. Hamburg: Felix Meiner, 1980.

GW 11   *Gesammelte Werke*. Vol. 11: *Wissenschaft der Logik. Erster Band. Die objective Logik (1812–1813)*. Edited by Friedrich Hogemann and Walter Jaeschke. Hamburg: Felix Meiner, 1978.

GW 12   *Gesammelte Werke*. Vol. 12: *Wissenschaft der Logik. Zweiter Band. Die subjektive Logik (1816)*. Edited by Friedrich Hogemann and Walter Jaeschke. Hamburg: Felix Meiner, 1981.

ILT   *Religionsphilosophie*. Vol. 1: *Die Vorlesung von 1821*. Edited by Karl-Heinz Ilting. Naples: Bibliopolis, 1978.

L 1, 2   *Wissenschaft der Logik*. Philosophische Bibliothek. Vols. 56 and 57. Edited by Georg Lasson. Hamburg: Felix Meiner, 1975.

LPR 3   *Lectures on the Philosophy of Religion*. Vol. 3. Translation of BDG (according to the second Friends edition) by E. B. Speirs and J. Burdon Sanderson. New York: Humanities, 1962.

NR   *Vorlesungen über die Philosophie der Religion*. Philosophische Bibliothek. Vol. 60: *Die Naturreligion*. Edited by Georg Lasson. Hamburg: Felix Meiner, 1974.

Phän.   *Phänomenologie des Geistes*. Philosophische Bibliothek. Vol. 114. Edited by Johannes Hoffmeister. Hamburg: Felix Meiner, 1952.

Phen.   *Phenomenology of Spirit*. Translation of *Phän.* by A. V. Miller. New York: Oxford University Press, 1977.

PM   *Hegel's Philosophy of Mind*. Translation of E, Part Three, by William Wallace. Oxford; Clarendon, 1971. § = paragraph. R = Remark.

SL   *Hegel's Logic*. Translation of E, Part One, by William Wallace. Oxford: Clarendon, 1975. § = paragraph. R = Remark.

WS 16, 17   *Werke. Theorie Werkausgabe.* Vols. 16 and 17: *Vorlesungen über die Philosophie der Religion.* Edited by Eva Moldenhauer and Karl Markus Michel. Frankfurt am Main: Suhrkamp, 1969.

*Some sources cited by page and then line from the top.

Introduction

Hegel's Trinitarian Claim

G. W. F. Hegel is one of the greatest thinkers of the Greek-Western trinitarian tradition. He said that the theologians of his day had effectively abandoned the doctrine of the Trinity so that it was up to him as a philosopher to recoup the trinitarian tradition.[1] Though Hegel left to posterity a brilliant, philosophically informed trinitarian argument, it is not philosophers so much as theologians who have profited from his efforts. By way of example, Hegel's radical restructuring of the general trinitarian dogma into the dialectical movement of a triadically structured divine self-development finds a striking structural parallel in the positions of Karl Barth and Karl Rahner, perhaps the two most significant Western trinitarian thinkers in the first three quarters of the twentieth century. Consistent with their respective Christian traditions, Barth[2] understood the trinitarian God as a movement of self-revelation and Rahner[3] as a movement of self-communication. Both have, each in his own way, elaborated parallels to Hegel's trinitarian divine self-development from infinite to finite. What is for Hegel more radically a trinitarian divine self-othering becomes for Barth a trinitarian self-revelation and for Rahner a trinitarian self-communication.

Hegel's trinitarian envisionment can be intimated by quoting briefly from what Hegel wrote in the manuscript for his 1821 philosophy of religion lectures on the absolute religion:

> God is *Spirit—that* is, that which we call the *triune God*; . . . God is Spirit, *absolute activity, actus purus*, i.e., *subjectivity, infinite personality*, infinite distinction of oneself from oneself,

generation. However, this process of distinguishing is contained *within the eternal Concept,* . . . i.e., [within] *universality* as *absolute subjectivity.*⁴

This reference to God as triune is primarily and immediately concerned with what would today, when properly nuanced in view of Hegel's complex treatment, be referred to as "immanent" Trinity. Nevertheless, the very use of the term "Spirit" (*Geist*), which is ultimately for Hegel the totality of his philosophical system inclusive of its self-determining development, clearly implies as well what would today, again when properly nuanced, be referred to as "economic" Trinity. As an 1824 philosophy of religion lecture transcript records in the context of a discussion on the suffering and death of the Mediator, "God is the true God, Spirit, because God is not merely Father, enclosed within Self, but rather because God is Son, becomes the other and sublates this other."⁵ For Hegel this reference to Trinity is not, however, a mere description of the divine but a claim to be argued in the public realm. For Hegel, God can be Subject, Person and Spirit only to the extent that the divine is trinitarian in structure, to the extent that a movement of self-othering and return is verified in God and, here very generally stated, in God as inclusive of the world. In his philosophy of history lectures Hegel claims, "God is only then recognized as Spirit to the extent that God is known as triune."⁶ And using the term "personhood" (*Persönlichkeit*) as particularly appropriate to his *Outline of the Philosophy of Right*, Hegel wrote in the margin, "One may define believing in God how one will, but if personality is not there, the definition is inadequate."⁷ Finally, as representative of Hegel's clear trinitarian claim in the various philosophy of religion lectures:

> God is however to be grasped only as Spirit, and this is no empty word, no superficial determination. But if God is not to be for us an empty word, then God must be grasped as triune God; this is that through which the nature of Spirit is made explicit . . . Only the Trinity is the determination of God as Spirit; without this determination Spirit is an empty word.⁸

There is a particular earnest with which Hegel makes his claim that only if God is known as what would today be termed "immanent" and "economic" Trinity can God be known as Spirit, that is, that there can be established in God inclusive subjectivity becoming absolute Spirit finally as philosophical Concept. This earnest is indicated both by the consequences Hegel draws from the successful or unsuccessful establishment of that trinitarian structure and by his consistently maintained systematic position on the identity of content but difference of form between religion and philosophy. In trinitarian divine self-othering and sublation of that otherness Hegel sees the principle or axis upon which world history turns.[9] World history is for Hegel a history of God.[10] This trinitarian dialectic is equally for Hegel the principle of freedom,[11] the source of community,[12] the reason why God can be known[13] and the justifying content of Christianity's distinctive truth claims[14] as the religion of absolute subjectivity[15] and freedom.[16] Trinity, the content of the true religion, is for Hegel divine self-revelation.[17] According to Hegel, without a trinitarian structure to the divine there would be no true reconciliation in Christ.[18] God would be an empty name, one-sided and finite rather than inclusive and infinite.[19] There could be no truth as mediation for there would be no possibility of a transition from religion with its true content but representational form to philosophy where form and content would be identical as absolute Spirit in the philosophical Concept as Self.

For Hegel religion and philosophy have the same true content but differ in form.[20] Whereas in religion alienation overcome by reconciliation is realized representationally in the trinitarian God, in philosophical thought that same content was to have been expressed in its necessity, that is, to have received its adequate form as a mediation which was to have been the identity of thought and Spirit, Concept and Self.[21] In his system, logic and philosophy become for Hegel respectively the appropriate logical and philosophical reformulations of this true content which has been expressed religiously as Trinity, God as reconciliation or absolute subjectivity. In this sense, Hegel's famous claim in the Preface to the *Phenomenology*, "everything turns on grasping and expressing the True, not only as *Substance* but equally as *Subject*,"[22] becomes an appropriate philosophical reformulation of his trinitarian claim. So too Hegel's insistence that truth can only be mediated by a content which is itself. "The only content which can be held to be the truth is one not mediated with something else, not limited by other things: or, otherwise expressed, it is one mediated by itself."[23] Or again, a logical reformulation in the *Logic* where Hegel describes the true infinite as the mediation of infinite and finite, thus as inclusive totality.[24] Hegel's logic and philosophy, his system as a whole, are the example of that self-mediation[25] which is expressed for Hegel on the level of religion as trinitarian divine reconciliation—absolute subjectivity. Hegel's system as a whole is the fullest philosophical expression of his trinitarian claim. As Hegel was recorded to have said in more explicitly religious language with reference first of all, but surely finally not only to, "immanent" Trinity, "God eternally begets God's Son, . . . But at the same time we ought to know that God Self is this entire activity. God is, the beginning, God acts thus; but God is likewise the end, the totality, and it is as totality that God is Spirit."[26]

Systematically speaking, that is, from the point of view of his system and especially in its speculative formulation, Hegel argues this trinitarian claim as a movement from infinite to finite to inclusive or affirmative infinite with infinite understood as inclusive totality. This self-positing movement from infinite to finite is witnessed to by his systematic beginning ever with the immediacy of an originary unity positing itself as otherness which is in turn sublated in a return to enriched immediacy. In the *Logic* and *Encyclopedia* this originary unity is pure being,[27] in the *Phenomenology* sense certainty,[28] in the *Lectures on the Philosophy of Religion* as a whole the Concept of religion[29] and in the lectures specifically on the absolute religion "immanent" Trinity as religiously represented.[30]

Though there is no end to the literature on Hegel,[31] and sufficient research would probably show that most everything possible has already been said about him in one way or other, apparently only two monographs have been published so far specifically on his trinitarian thought. Neither of them has directly challenged the particular direction or way in which Hegel tries to establish his trinitarian claim. Johannes Hessen's 1922 volume, *Hegels Trinitätslehre. Zugleich eine Einführung in Hegels System*,[32] is far too brief (45 pages) to provide an adequate summary and critique of Hegel's trinitarian thought. In *Die Trinitätslehre G. W. F. Hegels*,[33] Jörg Splett intended to fulfill Hessen's original proposal.[34] Splett gives a considerably more thorough and helpful overview of Hegel's widely scattered writing on Trinity. By gathering many of Hegel's texts and students' lecture transcripts on Trinity, Splett has verified the central import of this topic for any serious study of Hegel's thought. Splett closes with several points of discussion and critique.

The present study has as its purpose a critical reflection on Hegel's trinitarian claim. Its basic thesis is that Hegel cannot establish his trinitarian claim as he intended to, namely, on the basis of an argumentation in the public realm from infinite to finite. Hegel's argument always presupposes a prior movement from finite to infinite. In Part One of this study, Chapter One presents the *Logic* as an appropriate text to be examined, and Chapter Two critiques the movement of logic or pure thought in its primordial, elementary instantiation, being/nothing/becoming. In Part Two, Chapter Three provides an overview of the syllogistic structure of Hegel's explicit trinitarian thought on the basis of the *Encyclopedia* and works out a criterion for evaluating Hegel's argument in the *Phenomenology*. Chapter Four contains a critique of Hegel's trinitarian argument in its incarnational immediacy as presented in the *Phenomenology*. Chapter Five forms a critical reflection on Hegel's trinitarian thought in its final communitarian and syllogistic structure.

Strictly speaking, the immanent critique presented in the context of this overall critical reflection applies directly only to Hegel's thought. However, it should be noted that Hegel is one of the most significant representatives of those who have developed a trinitarian position from infinite to finite. To the extent that others, whose trinitarian thought parallels or is dependent on Hegel's, may not themselves have been able to resolve the contradictions or ones similar to those which will have become apparent in Hegel's position, they too would be susceptible to this critique.

Finally, it is most important to distinguish between Hegel's general conception of a triadically structured inclusive infinite and the specific way in which he argued his claim to its necessity. The present critique is aimed primarily at the way in which Hegel argues his claim, namely, as self-determining movement of conceptual thought from infinite to finite. When freed of certain limitations, his general envisionment of the divine as a triadically structured inclusive infinite, God inclusive of world, remains unchallenged. Rather, when seen in proper correlation with Hegel's understanding of self-contradictory finitude, this trinitarian envisionment will be employed in Part Three, Chapter Six, of this study to build on the Conclusions especially to Chapters Two, Four and Five in an attempt at a first sketching of an alternative trinitarian argument from finitude to triadic inclusive infinite.

PART ONE

LOGIC—HEGEL'S REFORMULATION OF THE TRUE CONTENT OF TRINITY

1

Logic as Movement of Trinitarian Divine Subjectivity

1. Logic—the Movement of Pure Thought

The widely differing contexts within which Hegel referred to Trinity and within which he articulated his trinitarian claim indicate not only the importance attached to this claim[1] but, more profoundly, the multiple problematic to which his attempt to establish God as trinitarian responded. He saw that the orthodoxy of his day with its supernaturalistic theology tended to reduce God to an object and that its otherworldliness could lead to a this-worldly atheism. He realized as well that the developing bourgeois society might easily set itself over against the unified state and fragment it. This double estrangement in religion and society was for Hegel expressed in Kant's philosophical dualism. Together with that dualism this estrangement formed the Enlightenment-grounded alienation which Hegel proposed to overcome by adopting, but more so deeply adapting, Fichte's notion of the positing Ego. In order to acknowledge the necessary passage through alienation as the way to integral and integrating Selfhood, Hegel employed a dialectic of trinitarian self-revelation speculatively interpreted as self-positing Subject and philosophically reformulated as absolute reconciling Spirit.[2] He conceived of the trinitarian God as a movement of absolute logic[3] constituting the triadic structure of inclusive subjectivity. This "inner trinitarian God" or inclusive Subject was for Hegel equally the structure of absolute Spirit, although not as yet its realization. The Subject needed an other to come to itself as Spirit.[4] For Hegel the final reconciliation of Subject and object, religiously speaking, of God and world, was to be attained by the mediation of both Subject and object in true philosophical thought, in the movement of absolute Spirit.[5]

Hegel's understanding of triadically structured subjectivity and its realization as absolute Spirit are to be explored and critiqued by means of an examination of appropriate texts. First, this present chapter argues on a more general level that the *Science of Logic*[6] is a study of logically reformulated trinitarian divine subjectivity. Chapter Two will concentrate on specific texts in the *Logic* in order to analyze and challenge the structure and movement of Hegel's overall response to philosophical alienation. Chapter Three turns to texts from the *Encyclopedia*[7] to present an overview of the syllogistic structure of Hegel's explicitly trinitarian thought and then to Hegel's more general hermeneutic texts from the *Phenomenology of Spirit*[8] in order to set the stage in Chapter Four for an examination of Hegel's systematic breakthrough within the specific context of the distinction between consciousness and its object. Chapter Five focuses on particularly relevant references in the *Lectures on the Philosophy of Religion*[9] to investigate Hegel's further argumentation in the appropriate "realphilosophical" (*realphilosophische*)[10] spheres. Finally, Chapter Six will work toward a reconstruction of Hegel's trinitarian envisionment and a reformulation of Hegel's trinitarian claim on the basis of insights gathered from a critique of the explicitly trinitarian texts and from the *Logic* itself.

Beginning with the Logic brings advantages and disadvantages, both of which are rooted in the depth and complexity of Hegel's multidirectional, many-leveled thought.[11] The advantages are both practical and systematic. Practical, in that starting with the Logic allows for an initial, clarifying stance and briefer argumentation vis-à-vis Hegel's overall proposal while, early in this study, acknowledging a critical dependence on a particular interpretation and critique of Hegel's notion of God.[12] Systematic, in that it respects and generally follows[13] the encyclopedic ordering Hegel himself most fully develops.[14] Argued internally, that is, from within the framework of the Hegelian systematic, logic is the structure and movement of reality in its universal truth,[15] so that an adequate treatment of Hegel's systematic realphilosophy inevitably involves reference to the *Logic*. To approach his thoughts without some understanding of the *Logic* would be to proceed naively.[16] Discussing his notion of God without immediate reference to the *Logic* borders on the impossible.

Working first with the *Logic* does bring with it certain disadvantages. Systematically considered, the most serious of these is the danger of underrating logic's multiple significance for Hegel. This could be done either by inordinately stressing any one of its functional aspects or by implicitly isolating it from the realphilosophy. However, the centrality of the subject matter here in question, coupled with its being handled further in the following chapters, should help correct any tendency toward a one-sided treatment.

More practically considered, an additional disadvantage is the difficulty involved in beginning with a relatively unknown or at least misunderstood and historically disputed text. The *Logic* develops neither formal logic in the traditional sense of the word nor modern logistic, but the logic of absolute form and the science of pure thought. Logic grounds the further development of the Hegelian system, and yet is itself grounded by the systematic return to it in the form of philosophy. It forms for the mature Hegel the first as well as the last science.[17] A brief overview will facilitate further specific reference to and interpretation of this central Hegelian text.[18] For present purposes the survey remarks found in the *Logic*'s "Introduction"[19] plus supplementary observations in what might be termed a second introduction[20] supply a sufficient basis for this overview.[21]

Without intending either to follow the *Logic*'s Introduction in detail or provide a direct commentary, it can be pointed out that Hegel initially posits logic as a fundamentally presuppositionless science.[22] He criticizes the general understanding of logic as a merely formal science of thought, devoid of specific content,[23] and whose categories are usually treated statically and without internal reference to one another. The correction of this latter, logically isolationist attitude toward the categories of thought constitutes the basis of Hegel's own conception of logic and for Hegel addresses the root cause of the misunderstanding of logical categories as empty forms.[24] It is this question of category content which first explicitly occupies Hegel's attention and in response to which he develops his own original conception of logic.[25]

Hegel stresses that even the older "formal" logic had its own content in the sense of rules and forms studied.[26] But while appreciative of Kant's giving logic a place of honor,[27] he opposes Kant's reduction of thought's revelatory validity to the realm of the phenomenal and to a subjectivist position.[28] With brief reference to the incompleteness of Fichte's attempt to establish the positing ego,[29] Hegel describes logic as the pure science of self-determining thought. For Hegel this pure science both presupposes and itself establishes the overcoming of the Subject-object opposition characteristic of consciousness, a task accomplished according to Hegel's view at the writing of the *Logic* in the

Phenomenology.[30] Logic, this pure thought, constitutes of itself its own objective content:

> It [the pure science of logic] contains *thought in so far as this is just as much the object in its own Self, or the object in its own Self in so far as it is equally pure thought* . . .
> This objective thinking, then, is the content of pure science. . . . Accordingly, logic is to be understood as the system of pure reason, or the realm of pure thought.[31]

Further, the objective content, which thought itself is, constitutes the true "matter" of pure science, "but a matter which is not external to the form, since this matter is rather pure thought and hence the absolute form itself."[32] Logic is for Hegel the science of pure thought, which is its own objective content and is therefore absolute form.[33]

No external, mathematical, quantifying methodology is applicable to this pure science of absolute form.[34] The only adequate philosophical method is that found in the *Logic*, "for the method is the consciousness of the form of its inner self-movement."[35] This self-movement is a speculative dialectical method, of which the *Phenomenology* is a concrete example.[36] Method could be described for Hegel as:

> . . . the recognition of the logical principle that the negative is just as much positive, or that what is self-contradictory does not resolve itself into a nullity, into abstract nothingness, but essentially only into the negation of its *particular* content, in other words, that such a negation is not all and every negation but the negation of a specific subject matter which resolves itself, and consequently is a specific negation, . . . Because the result, the negation, is a *specific* negation it has a *content*. It is a fresh Concept but higher and richer than its predecessor; for it is richer by the negation or opposite of the latter, therefore contains it, but also something more, and is the unity of itself and its opposite. It is in this way that the system of concepts as such has to be formed—and has to complete itself in a purely continuous course in which nothing extraneous is introduced.[37]

The method is the content itself, the true dialectic,[38] which contains the negative within itself and which progresses by means of this negative, by means of necessary contradiction.[39] Since the dialectical method consists in the grasping "of opposites in their unity or of the positive in the negative,"[40] logic can be described as the speculative dialectical method in and through which the Concept[41] determines itself as a non-temporal movement of thought categories.[42] These categories progress immanently and consistently[43] on the basis of self-contradiction according to a triadic rhythm describable on the widest level of logic as a movement from being to essence to Concept (*Sein-Wesen-Begriff*).

Considering logic or pure thought as absolute form has enabled Hegel, especially later on in the *Logic*, to describe pure thought as its own objective content. This total correspondence of form and content allows him to speak of pure thought as the truth.[44] Hegel's seeing logic as absolute form grounds his relating of logic to the other sciences of nature and Spirit, the latter two seen in terms of "reality," "realization," "realized content."[45] Logic does not contain the reality, "which is the content of the further parts of philosophy, namely, the philosophical sciences of nature and of Spirit."[46] The relationship between logic and the spheres of nature and Spirit remains mutual, in that logic both is and contains the spheres of nature and Spirit in as it is their "archetype" (*Vorbildner*) and the latter spheres in turn are and contain logic as their "inner formative principle" (*innern Bildner*).

> As contrasted with these concrete sciences (although these have and retain as their inner formative principle that same logical element, or the Concept, which had served as their archetype), logic is of course the formal science; but it is the science of the absolute form.[47]

This identification of content with the self-development of absolute form[48] roots already within the *Logic* the relationship of logic to the other concrete sciences by providing the presence of an "other" totally mediated within this realm of pure thought. The self-development of the Concept is ultimately conceived as pure self-mediation. Without this objective content which thought is, thought itself would be empty and unmediated; there would be no other to immediacy. Thought is therefore for Hegel always already mediated. As such thought always brings with it mediation, or better, always mediates. Already from this introductory survey of logic as pure self-determining and self-mediating thought it can be seen how Hegel's understanding of logic proposes to provide the structure of his response to philosophical alienation with implications as well for the overcoming of alienation in religion and society.

2. The Movement of Self-determining Subjectivity

For simplicity's sake the introductory description of logic as system of reason and realm of pure thought temporarily bracketed Hegel's reference to "subjectivity" (*Subjektivität*).[49] In the context of his discussion on the identity of thought (*Gedanke*) and object (*Sache*) Hegel had included in the *Logic*'s first edition: "Or it is the Concept of the science of logic that truth is pure self-consciousness and has the shape of the Self, so that *the truth of being is the Concept* and the Concept *is the truth of being*."[50] Or as in the second edition where Hegel more straightforwardly stresses the identification of Concept with the shape of the Self, the developmental character of self-consciousness and the logical completeness of the Concept: "As science, truth is pure self-developing self-consciousness and has the shape of the Self, so that *the absolute truth of being* is the *known* Concept and the Concept as such is *the absolute truth of being*."[51] This assertion of the Concept-Self identity is often indicated by Hegel's stringing together various combinations of terms like Individual, Concept, Person, the Free, the Subject, the True.[52] At least for Hegel this apparently unnuanced if not haphazard juxtaposition was, while admitting the need for further determinations, justifiably grounded in the structural identity of Concept and subjectivity as self-thinking Idea which is self-positing, self-developing method. The "self" in these expressions bears with it a triple connotation: first, the inner spontaneity and lack of external influence characteristic of a necessitarian activity now redefined as "free"; secondly, the absence of any substratum or presupposition underlying the Concept; and thirdly, the inclusive end-result of the process as absolute Idea which is Subject, Self and "I."[53]

What this Concept in the shape of the Self consists in as a movement of self-determining subjectivity can be further explained by again considering Hegel's notion of method. His specific presentation in the *Logic*'s last section on the absolute Idea forms an anchor text.[54] For Hegel, the absolute Idea is the Concept free, subjective and rational.[55] It is the Concept inclusive of both subjectivity and objectivity. Method is the movement of this Concept itself. It "has emerged as the *self-knowing*

Concept that has itself, as the absolute, both subjective and objective, *for its subject matter*, consequently as the pure correspondence of the Concept and its reality, as a concrete existence that is the Concept itself."[56] As self-knowing Concept, the speculative dialectical method is equally and culminantly movement of subjectivity.

> The richest is therefore the most concrete and most *subjective*, and that which withdraws itself into the simplest depth is the mightiest and most all-embracing. The highest, most concentrated point is the *pure personality* which, solely through the absolute dialectic which is its nature, no less *embraces and holds everything within itself*.[57]

This speculative dialectical method is structured movement[58] of the Concept from beginning (*Anfang*) as immediate and universal through dialectical progression (*Fortgehen*) as negation of the beginning on to result (*Resultat*) as negation of the first negation. This result is enriched return to the beginning, consequently positive immediacy inclusive of immediacy and mediation.[59] The triadically structured movement of self-mediation occurs already in its immediacy in the logic of being as "transition into another"[60] or, better, "having gone over into another."[61] Therefore, Hegel can already speak of *Etwas* ("something") as the first concrete negation of negation and the beginning of the Subject. "The negative of the negative is, as *Etwas*, only the beginning of the Subject."[62] Implicit self-mediation can be traced on, logically speaking, farther back to becoming (*Werden*), with its moments of being (*Sein*) and nothing (*Nichts*), although this mediation is for Hegel not yet posited as in *Etwas*.[63]

Whereas with *Etwas* and the logic of being in general the arising of thought determinations is described in terms of transition, in the logic of essence with its relative determinations of reflection the dialectical method's progression takes place as "appearance in the other."[64] In the logic of the Concept, the resultant third moment of logic as a whole, Hegel characterizes the dialectical movement as development (*Entwicklung*)[65] in which each category is explicitly the totality of the Concept.[66] Hegel labels this third logical sphere "subjective" logic,[67] in contradistinction to the "objective" logic of the spheres of being and essence. In this third sphere, the logic of the Concept, Hegel treats subjectivity thematically; it forms the logic of the Concept's first moment.

This first moment consists in the dialectical development from beginning as Concept (*Begriff*) through judgement (*Urteil* with the connotation of "othering" or "separating") to syllogism (*Schluß*) as perfect self-mediation through the concrete universal as middle term.[68] As is characteristic of all initial moments or beginnings in the *Logic*, the logic of the Concept's initial moment of subjectivity in general and this moment's culmination, syllogism, in particular present the structure of the further development in the logic of the Concept through objectivity (*Objektivität*) to the result, absolute Idea. The absolute Idea is dialectical method in its enriched return both to the logic of the Concept's initial moment of subjectivity and to the immediacy of being, the initial moment of logic. Logic, the movement of pure thought, is in the entirety of its development a movement of subjectivity.

This sketching of Hegel's structural identification of Concept with Self and then application to the logic of pure thought as movement of subjectivity has already given a sense of the complexity of Hegel's usage of the term "subjectivity."[69] In the *Logic* Hegel refers especially to Kant's and Fichte's philosophies as one-sidedly subjective. But the term's two uses of interest here are Hegel's labeling the logic of the Concept's first moment "subjectivity" and his understanding of the absolute Idea as "inclusive subjectivity."[70] The logical moment of subjectivity does not yet for Hegel contain posited objectivity, and is therefore in a sense still one-sided. Nevertheless, this moment of subjectivity is already the totality, the self-knowing Concept and self-mediating subjectivity because syllogism contains as moment the otherness of judgement and thus displays its infinity.[71] This understanding of subjectivity as syllogism finds its fulfillment in the absolute Idea, which as method is realization of syllogism's full self-mediation. In the absolute Idea, the objectivity consequently posited by syllogism is seen to bear the structure of the Self.[72] In formulating the absolute Idea as mediation of subjectivity and objectivity, Hegel has taken up the one-sided and therefore inadequate Kantian notion of subjectivity and transformed it into an infinite moment in his notion of inclusive subjectivity.

It is now important to characterize further Hegel's structuring of inclusive subjectivity in terms of speculative dialectical method as beginning, progression and result.[73] Beginning, the first moment in Hegel's theory of subjectivity, refers most importantly to being as the absolutely initial moment of pure thought but also to all other beginnings or first logical moments, whether they be essence or universality (*Allgemeinheit*) or so forth.⁷⁴ The content of any beginning is immediacy, which has the meaning and form of abstract universality. It is, Hegel would say, *Ansichsein ohne Fürsichsein*. On account of this poverty of determination, the beginning or first moment is always "lacking." "Hence the beginning has for the method no other determinateness than that of being simple and universal; this is itself the *determinateness* by means of which it is deficient."⁷⁵ Since it is here a question of objective, immanent Form, the beginning is, on the one hand, in its very immediacy already of itself lacking and characterized by an inner drive to self-development.⁷⁶ On the other hand, the beginning is likewise seen as inadequate or incomplete from the wider point of view of method or truth.⁷⁷ The beginning is the universal which is the objective concrete totality as yet unposited, still *an sich*.⁷⁸

This implicitly concrete totality, beginning, is likewise the beginning of the Concept's progression and development which, as the moment of mediation through differentiation, is according to Hegel the most difficult to describe.⁷⁹ Unlike with finite knowing, absolute knowing contains the determination of universality within itself so that the appearance of difference, that is, judgement or determination arises analytically and synthetically out of the immediacy of the first moment. Analytically, in that determination is founded in the Concept's universality alone, and this is the absolute objectivity of the Concept. Synthetically, in that the method's object, which first bears the determination of simple universal, is then through the determination contained in this object able to show itself as an "other."⁸⁰ This transition or progression from beginning to other by judgement is called by Hegel "dialectic." "This no less synthetic than analytic moment of *judgement*, by which the universal of the beginning out of its very self determines itself as the *other of itself*, is to be named the *dialectical* moment."⁸¹

In a particularly tightly drawn summary of the dialectical progression from beginning as immediacy to the second moment as mediated, that is, referred or related to an other,⁸² Hegel speaks of the universal becoming a particular in such a way that the second is the negation of the first. In view of further development of the Concept, progression is the first negation. This negation is not empty since the immediate has gone over into this other, which is the other of the first, the negation of the immediate, and thus the mediated containing the determination of the first within itself. This mediated (*vermittelte*) is furthermore that which mediates (*vermittelnde*) the first moment, since it includes this first moment within it.[83] This determination is a relationship, the negation of the positive. This negation is the other for itself, but equally the other of an other and therefore includes its own other within itself. As this contradiction, the second moment is "the posited dialectic of itself."

> It [the second determination] is therefore the other, but not the other of something to which it is indifferent—in that case it would not be an other, nor a relation or a relationship—rather it is the *other in its own Self*, the *other of an other*, therefore it includes *its* own other within it and is consequently *as contradiction*, the *posited dialectic of itself*.[84]

The difference which is only *an sich* or implicit in immediacy is explicit (*gesetzt, für sich*) in this moment which, as the determined, is difference, relationship and inclusive, mediating other.

On any level, then, the moment of difference is the beginning now as mediated. It is the determination or content as an apparent other through which the beginning returns to itself as result and newly enriched immediacy of beginning.[85] This resultant return arises out of what is for Hegel the essential moment of the Concept, the thinking of contradiction. Thinking this dialectical moment of difference or progression results in the explicitation or positing of the unity already contained in the Concept's self-contradictory second moment or determination. In one of the most important sentences in the *Logic* Hegel writes, "The second, on the contrary, is itself the *determinate* moment, the *difference* or relationship; therefore with it the dialectical moment consists in positing the *unity* that is contained in it."[86] In what is almost a hymn to negativity, Hegel describes this depth of thought contradiction as the source of all activity and that through which the opposition between Concept and reality is overcome.[87] This turning point in the movement of the Concept, the thinking of contradiction, results in a second negation, the overcoming of contradiction, a negation of negation. It is absolute negativity, the moment of absolute mediation, the unity which is inclusive subjectivity.[88]

> Now more precisely the *third* is the immediate, but the immediate *resulting from sublation of mediation*, the simple resulting from *sublation of difference*, the positive resulting from sublation of the negative, the Concept that has real-

ized itself by means of its otherness and by the sublation of this reality has become united with itself, and has restored its absolute reality, its *simple* relation to itself. . . . As that with which we began was the *universal*, so the result is the *individual*, the *concrete*, the *Subject*.[89]

The result is negation of negation, enriched immediacy, the formation of a "new" beginning. In this way the Hegelian dialectic is to advance immanently and consistently in establishing the ever richer, ever more concrete content of pure thought until reaching the unity of the absolute Idea.[90]

The absolute Idea is end result and enriched return to the immediacy of beginning, to being. Its unity includes the Subject-object distinction negated, taken up and transformed (*Aufheben*).[91] This one movement of the Concept from being to Idea and grounding return from Idea to being[92] is for Hegel the transition from substance to Subject. Such development is partially but inadequately illuminated by reference to the structure of a judgement expressed in the form of a sentence, where the grammatical Subject is conceived in terms of immediacy or mere name. This grammatical Subject receives, for Hegel, its content from the predicate as that which mediates and is mediated. The predicate itself contains the Subject. But such sentences, and for example, "The finite is infinite," betray of themselves the emptiness of the unmediated copula and their inability to express speculative truth.[93] According to Hegel, only the syllogistic form of inclusive subjectivity as total self-mediation[94] is able explicitly to overcome the Subject-object dichotomy. For Hegel this dichotomy paradigms the alienation of philosophical from positive, with the latter prephilosophically and therefore provisionally understood as that which is not universally concludable on the basis of reason.

On the level of an absolute logic Hegel has constructed a triadically structured understanding of true or inclusive subjectivity: immediacy of beginning; progression through mediation; and enriched return as resultant unity of the two.[95] In order to do this Hegel has redefined the notion of positivity as negation, that is, the negativity of otherness in relation to a beginning which by definition is simple immediacy. His conception of positivity as related, inclusive negation allows him to conclude to a unity of immediacy and difference, a unity as total self-mediation. In this way objectivity, reestablished as the negation or otherness of subjectivity, is integrated as logically momentary totality in the self-development of inclusive subjectivity. In the movement of logical thought as absolute form the relationship between Subject and object is now in a sense that of form to content.[96] As content is present in pure thought in the form of thought, so objectivity bears in pure thought the form of subjectivity. Absolute form is inclusive subjectivity.

3. The Self-determining of the Divine Subject

The onesidedness characteristic of finite thought[97] is overcome in the absolute Idea, which is for Hegel the *an sich* unity of thought and being or, more exactly, of Concept and reality in the form of pure thought, and therefore truth (*Wahrheit*).[98] It is not just abstract universality (*Allgemeinheit*), but individuality (*Einzelheit*) inclusive of universality and particularity (*Besonderheit*), therefore individual (*das Einzelne*).[99] The absolute Idea is for Hegel not just a theory of subjectivity, but the unity of Subject and object in the form of inclusive subjectivity as already, in logic, resultant concrete totality, that is, "personal" and "free" Subject.[100] Since in its development the absolute Idea is method, it is already in its beginning the Absolute[101] as yet not posited, not explicit, and therefore not absolutely absolute.[102] The Idea's methodic progression, the showing and self-manifestation of the Absolute, pertains to the essence of the Idea as initially the Absolute one-sidedly conceived.

> Hence the advance is not a kind of *superfluity*; this it would be if that with which the beginning is made were in truth already the absolute, the advance consists rather in the universal determining itself and being *for itself* the universal, that is, equally an individual and a Subject. Only in its consummation is it the Absolute.[103]

The Absolute is the Idea, the absolute Idea. It is the true, individual, concrete, that is, Subject. It is the truth (*das Wahre*).[104]

Since for Hegel truth or the absolute Idea contains the particularity of otherness within its own immediacy, it can function as initial, positing moment of the non-logical or realphilosophical spheres of nature and Spirit.[105] This transition from logic to nature and Spirit is a transition systematically speaking necessitated by the renewed and enriched immediate subjectivity constitutive of the absolute Idea but described by Hegel as "free self-release."¹⁰⁶ It covers a multitude of functions to be performed by Hegel's absolute logic. Logic is to be a post-Kantian replacement for traditional metaphysics, in that it reveals the inner structure of the movement of all reality, whether non-temporal or historical.¹⁰⁷ Logic is also both to reflect and further to enable the movement of thought from historical to non-temporal, from finitude to infinity.¹⁰⁸ Systematically considered, that is, from the point of view of the system, absolute logic serves both as initial moment and philosophic thought's point of final return. The movement of pure thought is that from substance to Subject, a movement whose final return through the realphilosophical spheres in philosophy is seen to be the realization of absolute Spirit.¹⁰⁹ The sweeping significance of Hegel's logic hints at some of its many epistemological, logical and metaphysical functions. This logic provides the dynamic structure inherent in the philosophies of nature, art, history, society and religion. It develops for Hegel the series of determinations structuring the movement of absolute Spirit coming to itself in philosophic thought. Absolute logic is capable of such multiple functioning precisely because for Hegel it is the movement of pure thought, the inclusive, self-positing totality constituting the Subject. It is truth.

Hegel's conception of pure thought as truth and resultant Subject is the logical reformulation of what is for him the true content expressed on the level of religion by the name or term "God."¹¹⁰ Just as with truth, so too God is individual, concrete, absolute, Subject, personal and Spirit.¹¹¹ God is for Hegel the self-determining Concept, the self-thinking Idea, which as logic occurs only in and through human thought while grounding and sublating that thought. In his 1829 lectures on the proofs for the existence of God, Hegel spoke of logic as metaphysical theology in so far as logic consisted in the elevation of finite thought determinations to the infinite.

> Logic is to that extent, metaphysical theology, which treats of the evolution of the Idea of God in the ether of pure thought, and thus concerns itself with this [Idea] which is in and for itself perfectly independent.¹¹²

Hegel has taken up and transposed "God" in logic to self-positing resultant Subject and in the final systematic moment, philosophy, to absolute Spirit with the identification of Concept and Self. In both logic and philosophic thought, form and content are identical and therefore adequate.[113] Not to acknowledge this transposition would amount to failing to come to grips with Hegel's logic in its totality, significance and functioning as he intended it.[114] Not to recognize the essential continuity between the manifestation of the Absolute as God on the level of religion and appropriately as Subject in the sphere of logic is to miss the inner dynamic of Hegel's thought. It would, furthermore, amount to ignoring Hegel's radical situating of his thought within the western metaphysical tradition where God is generally conceived of in terms of thought[115] and form.[116] However, the movement of logic must be seen as speculative theology not only to characterize correctly Hegel's total view, intention, inner continuity and context. More importantly, unless logic be understood as the self-development of the concrete, the individual, that is, Subject, the movement of pure thought could not for Hegel in and of itself ground the positing of otherness, of the world. Merely abstract or even theoretical universality could not give rise to particularity.[117] But to speak of logic as concrete, individual and so resultant Subject is for Hegel to speak logically correctly of the Absolute, known in the sphere of religion as God.[118] Logic functions for Hegel in many ways, but foundationally as Hegel's initial, systematic form of speculative theology.[119]

Although Hegel's logic can accurately be described as speculative theology or "*Onto-theo-logik*,"[120] there remains a fundamental ambiguity in Hegel's attitude toward and usage of the term "God." On the one hand Hegel, especially in his later writings, employs the logically and philosophically clarified or reformulated notion of God as truth.[121] On the other hand, "God" is merely the contentless *name* for the self-manifestation of the Absolute on the level of religion. And since "God" is merely name, according to the Hegel of the *Phenomenology* it would be better to work philosophically with terms more directly conceptual.[122] This latter position readily reflects Hegel's preference for thought categories (*Denkbestimmung*) to express the on-going movement of the Absolute.[123] Nevertheless, there remains a tension between these two views. It is only partially resolvable in terms of Hegel's apparent shift through the years to a more positive interpretation of the perduring role of religion and to a more explicit reference to God.[124] This tension is ultimately rooted in Hegel's somewhat unnuanced position that the content and goal of art, religion and philosophy are the same, although the ways of realization are different with philosophy's being the highest, that of the Concept.[125] As it stands, Hegel's claim to difference of ways, that is difference in form, but identity of content among the spheres of art, religion and philosophy does not adequately take into account his own analysis of form and content, in which content is itself "formed matter."[126] To change form involves a change in "formed matter." It involves at least a purification of content through a realized adequacy between form and content in philosophy. In the transition from religion to philosophy where, finally, form and content coincide as they had for Hegel initially in logic, there results a change in content in so far as Hegel asserts again in philosophy the logically necessitarian character of divine self-development through a self-othering.[127]

Hegel's double usage of "God" is still reflected a century and a half later in a vague tendency especially but not only in Germany for some members of departments of philosophy to deemphasize the significance of the divine for an interpretation of Hegel's philosophy in comparison with the attitude found among members of university departments of theology.[128] Hegel does himself refer to the "divine Concept." While describing the incompleteness of logic vis-à-vis the sciences of nature and Spirit, he writes, "the science only of the divine Concept."[129] In stressing the fundamental totality and logical completeness of the absolute Idea, Hegel refers to "divine knowing": "but in the Idea it [the *form* of its determination, its *externality*] remains essentially and actually the totality of the Concept, and science in the relationship of divine cognition to nature."[130] In fact, the entire Hegelian system begins in the *Encyclopedia* with God.[131] Hegel's system comes at the end of the *Encyclopedia* under the interpretative standpoint of the Aristotle quote on God as self-thinking thought.[132] Though by introducing potentiality and movement or activity into the divine, Hegel transformed the Aristotelian understanding of God as unmoved mover, he ultimately identified his entire system with the self-development of God in logic as Subject and finally in the philosophy of Spirit as absolute Spirit.[133]

Hegel would ultimately dismiss as arguing over a name the discussion about whether or not to refer to the pure thought of logic as "divine" or God conceived in terms of self-determining infinite thought. Hegel himself did not hesitate to speak of categorical determinations of pure thought as metaphysical definitions of God.

> Being itself and the special sub-categories of it which follow, as well as those of logic in general, may be looked upon as definitions of the Absolute, or *metaphysical definitions of*

> *God*; . . . For a metaphysical definition of God is the expression of his nature in thoughts as such; and logic embraces all thoughts so long as they continue in the thought form.[134]

The careful wording ("can . . . be looked upon") points to Hegel's reserve concerning the inadequacy of the structural form of "definition" as sentence.[135] It also presumes his critical presentation of definition (*Definition*) in the movement of logical thought, where definition is the first moment of synthetic thinking.[136] As first moment, definition is characterized by immediacy and universality. However this immediacy appears in the realm of objectivity;[137] its content is taken from an object, from *Dasein*. Therefore its immediacy is definite and determinate. On the basis of this immediacy's determination, definition develops into its other, division (*Einteilung*).[138] So definition alone cannot express completely what something or someone is. Yet it does function in the movement of logical thought as the momentary totality of the Concept.[139] Definition indicates correctly, though of course finally inadequately, that to which it refers.[140]

Despite Hegel's hesitation concerning definition's form, whose inadequacy is grounded in its determinate immediacy, Hegel in the case at hand still sees logical determinations as varyingly adequate expressions of the divine, of the Absolute, with Idea as absolute definition of the Absolute.[141] True, when Hegel calls logical determinations "definitions of the Absolute," he at first exempts the second moment, that of difference, because, so he claims, second moments are definitions of the finite.[142] Nevertheless, in fact he also speaks of nothing, a second moment, as definition of the Absolute.[143] Otherness and negation are found within the divine, in God,[144] and indeed in the initial reformulation of the divine as pure thought. Hegel failed fully to correlate his varying references to the moment of negation. This tension can be partially resolved by recalling that the second moment of any logical triadic does serve for Hegel as the expression both of content and of finitude, but always of both of these in the form of pure thought.[145] The logical moment of otherness or negation, i.e., of contradiction, is for Hegel in fact the central moment[146] in the self-positing development of the Subject, a movement occurring in and through while grounding and for Hegel sublating human or finite thought. This Subject is, for Hegel, the appropriately reformulated true content of "God" on the level of logic,[147] a true content whose final logical expression is the absolute Idea.

4. The Necessarily Triadic Structure of the Self-determining Divine Subject

The self-determining of the divine Subject is for Hegel the triadically structured movement of the Concept.[148] This rhythmic pulsation moves from beginning as the simple immediacy of subjectivity through progression as the mediated and mediating negativity of reflection constitutive of the otherness of objectivity to result as the enriched immediacy of return to the beginning. Result is, logically considered, finally the inclusive subjectivity of the absolute Idea in which objectivity is seen to bear the structure of the Self. In his development of this notion of method, Hegel flirts briefly with a quadruplicity. And in this connection he underscores the doubled self-contradictory nature of method's second moment, which negates the original immediacy as well as its own negativity in return to the beginning. However, more generally, Hegel's remarks display an ongoing disdain for directly mathematical or numerical considerations since these inevitably remain on the level of understanding which separates (*Verstand*). He then returns to, and works definitively with, a triadically structured dialectical movement.[149]

In Hegel's intended ever triadically structured logic, each of the Concept's non-temporal moments or thought determinations is the momentary whole or totality of the Concept.[150] In the logic of being and of essence, each moment is implicitly totality because its other is contained within it in an as yet unposited manner. The other into which a given category in the logic of being "has gone over" or in the logic of essence "appears in" is not yet posited as particular and individual, Subject and "free."[151] In the logic of the Concept, each moment which develops into its other is the posited totality or whole (*das Ganze*) since each explicitly contains for Hegel the determination of its other within it. Each is concrete totality.[152] Within this third sphere, each moment is in its own way the full mediation of thought and being, of Concept and reality, pure self-mediation coming to clear expression in the triadic form of syllogism.[153] "Every moment of the Concept is itself the whole Concept (§ 160), but the Individual, the Subject, is the Concept posited as totality."[154] As with most Hegelian conceptualities, "totality" is verified in a variety of ways on different levels, with its logically later form explicitating what was previously only implicit.[155]

That each logical moment is in its own way the totality of the Concept and that each moment is for Hegel only conceivable in terms of the triadically structured dialectical method—these are the two characteristics which fundamentally justify the identification of Hegel's logic as a philosophically transposed and, in the form of pure thought, for Hegel adequately formulated trinitarian movement of divine self-constituting subjectivity.[156] However, "immanent" Trinity in its logical reformulation is not to be explicitly and adequately thought in the Hegelian system only on the level of the logic of the Concept.[157] Rather, it is the movement of pure thought taken as a whole which constitutes Hegel's full logical reformulation of "immanent" Trinity, because logic is characterized throughout by identity of form and content, where each thought determination is on its own level and in its own way the momentary totality of the Concept.[158] From the very beginning in pure being to absolute Idea the movement of pure thought, of the Concept, is method.[159]

To qualify this triadically structured method as divine trinitarian subjectivity, it would theoretically and even perhaps in view of the diverse Christian trinitarian traditions more practically speaking not be necessary to speak of "tripersonality."[160] Nevertheless, in addition to the logically preferable and here preferentially employed terms "subjectivity" and "Subject" Hegel does speak in the *Logic* of "personhood" and "Person" (*Persönlichkeit, Person*).[161] His understanding of personhood and its concretization in Person could, where used in Hegel's reconstructed sense of self-donation or becoming, further gather together in one the various affirmations concerning totality, triadicity, method and identity of form and content. It would as well contextualize Hegel's thought in relation to Fichte's understanding of Person as necessarily finite and in relation to the question of the personhood of God as raised by those who followed after Hegel. Though Person in its later actualization beyond logic tends, for Hegel, to be a richer notion than Subject,[162] what is of concern here is the underlying structure common to subjectivity and to personhood, that of inclusive subjectivity.[163] Both personhood and subjectivity are structurally a movement of "going over into" (*Übergehen*) or "giving to" (*Hingabe*), a realizing of Self in the other. Yet this "going over into" is at the same time realized in varying ways in the arising of each thought determination, that is, in the way appropriate both to each thought determination's position in its contextual triadic and also to the logical sphere in which it arises.[164] This "going over into" is explicitly and adequately established as development of one thought determination into its other in the logic of the Concept on the level of the individual.¹⁶⁵ To the extent, then, that the structure of "going over into" or self-donation is constitutive of all logical moments, Hegel's ever triadically structured movement of pure thought from being to absolute Idea is the self-development of the divine Subject in what is for him a necessarily though reconstructedly "tripersonal" way. At the same time the movement of absolute logic goes for Hegel beyond considerations of numbers to an inclusive notion of personhood or subjectivity.¹⁶⁶ It is for Hegel the appropriately formulated triadically structured "inner" trinitarian development of divine self-constituting subjectivity. This movement of absolute logic is equally the structural form or inner image¹⁶⁷ of the "economic" trinitarian self-realization of divine absolute Spirit in the realphilosophical spheres.¹⁶⁸

5. The *Logic* as Elaboration of Hegel's Trinitarian Claim

Since Hegel distinguishes "inner" or "immanent" and "economic" Trinity clearly in terms of modes of realization but not in terms of differing structural dynamics,¹⁶⁹ it will be possible already in Chapter Two to make a fundamental examination and critique of the viability of Hegel's understanding of Trinity, an examination and critique to be made on the basis of the movement of pure thought or logic. That Hegel's logically reformulated trinitarian thought does not escape a certain ambiguity is initially indicated by two problem areas. First there is the way in which Hegel tries to integrate finitude into infinity, the ambiguity of which appears as the difficulty of considering the second or dialectical moment a metaphysical definition of God.¹⁷⁰ Secondly, one senses a residual ambiguity in the relationship between "immanent" and "economic" Trinity. In regard especially to this second question, Hegel has already placed within "immanent" Trinity the logical structural movement of creation and crucifixion by positing otherness as negation. However brilliant this move may be, the positing of otherness as negation fails fully to resolve the ambiguity, even tension, caused in the first problem area by the proposed sublated presence of finitude in the form of absolute thought.¹⁷¹ It might be helpful to note that from the standpoint of Christian theology, this doubled tension has been consistently criticized in terms of a criticism of the necessitarian character of the divine self-othering (*Selbstentlassung*) into the finitude of nature and Spirit, with this necessity rooted in the divine as an expression not simply of overflowing fullness but of implicitness as lacking.[172] The necessity characteristic for Hegel of "economic" trinitarian self-othering is systematically grounded in Hegel's reformulation of Trinity within the realm of pure thought, that is, in his identification of Subject with the self-determination of the Concept,[173] and more specifically with the Concept as absolute Idea which is itself for Hegel renewed and enriched immediacy requiring an other. Since triadically conceived logical self-mediation is for Hegel internal self-determination, he labels it "free."[174] Yet the basic philosophical question remains whether or not Hegel has falsely located the source of any necessity in the relationship between infinite and finite within the divine, that is, within infinity, rather than first and foremost within finitude.[175]

Despite these tensions and given Hegel's starting point in immediacy, it is essential to Hegel's system that he establish otherness from within the logical structure of the Self or Subject, an otherness logically speaking initially internal to the Self. Otherwise, Hegel believed he could not provide a view of mediation which could avoid collapsing into the one-sidedness of finitude.[176] Otherness recognized as Self provides the included content without which inclusive subjectivity would for Hegel be reduced to mere finite subjectivity, to opinion. So, on the one hand, less than a triadic conceptualization of inclusive subjectivity would fail to provide absolute mediation. On the other hand, the movement from immediacy to mediation in terms of otherness and then to unity of the two was to be an exhaustive analysis and synthesis of reality as thought. In this sense and on this level there was to be no need of or possibility for a fourth, whether that be a presupposed substratum or a further synthetic moment. The triadically structured movement of pure thought was for Hegel to constitute the paradigmatic and constitutive structure of all reality as taken up into thought.

Hegel's paradigmatic, logically necessarily triadically conceived movement of self-mediation does not even in itself remain merely abstract and is for Hegel no longer a mere theory of subjectivity. It is in its own immediacy the concrete universal containing particularity within it, inclusive subjectivity which is individual, the Absolute as Subject. This Subject is not related to the Christian dogma of Trinity merely on the basis of some external analogy, but is for Hegel the logically reconstructed adequate content of that dogma presented in the appropriate form of pure thought.[177] These constitutive characteristics of Subject and likewise Hegel's concern to retain the content of the basic Christian dogmas are felicitously underscored by the term "Trinity." Though "Trinity," as is the case also with the term "God,"[178] as such originates on the level of religion and is not a logical category, it is always handled by Hegel already from a philosophical perspective.[179] In philosophical thought, the "inner" trinitarian structure of logical Subject becomes the "economic" trinitarian structure of explicitly posited absolute Spirit. With the positing of this development of Subject as Spirit, Hegel gives his final trinitarian response to philosophical alienation, with implications for the religious and socio-political levels as well.

The *Logic* both provides the immediate structure of inclusive subjectivity, i.e., the logical Subject, and therewith the structure common as well to the logical Subject's realization as absolute Spirit in the realphilosophical spheres. Hegel has in fact, appropriate to his system, treated of "immanent" Trinity in two places: logically reformulated as the movement of pure thought culminating in the absolute Idea; and, in the realphilosophical sphere of the absolute or consummate, revealed and revelatory religion as the first or "immanent" moment in the appearance of the divine Idea to religious consciousness.[180] Among Hegel's various treatments of "immanent" Trinity, that of the *Logic* surely forms his strongest and most prolonged argumentation that concrete subjectivity can be established in God only when God is conceived of as Trinity.[181] Hegel's famous reference to logic as the presentation of God before the creation of the world is no mere religious slip of the pen but, with the use of philosophically reinterpreted representational language, a valid description of logic:

> Accordingly, logic is to be understood as the system of pure reason, as the realm of pure thought. This realm is truth as it is without veil and in its own absolute nature. It can therefore be said that this content is the presentation of God as God is in God's eternal essence before the creation of nature and a finite Spirit.[182]

2

Hegel's Logic of Pure Thought

1. Through *Etwas* to Being

Understanding logic, the movement of pure thought, as logically formulated "immanent" trinitarian divine self-positing subjectivity provides the fundamental justification for first examining the *Logic* and then Hegel's explicit trinitarian texts. It grounds earlier methodological considerations,[1] where the term "methodology" unfortunately but initially almost inevitably rings of externality and merely generalized applicability not only for moderns conditioned by bureaucratizing technology[2] but already for Hegel almost 200 years ago.[3] This examination of logic, whose inner movement itself constitutes for Hegel its method, is therefore to be carried out internally on the general basis of thought's inherent capabilities and limitations.[4] This chapter's examination and critique progress in five somewhat overlapping steps: first, a focus on the primordial, elementary movement of logic or pure thought and its context; second, a summary of Hegel's presentation of this elementary movement; third, several more general remarks on Hegel's absolute dialectic; fourth, a detailed critique of Hegel's argumentation to establish logic in its primordial movement; fifth, a conclusion to the determinate nature of any beginning.

Any examination of the *Logic* should pay attention both to the total movement of self-positing, self-determining thought and to the specific categorical moments constituting that movement. The necessity for these two focuses of attention is rooted in Hegel's very conception of logic as distinguishable difference within unity, as the dynamic of pure thought or absolute form wherein each category is dialectically the non-temporal momentary totality.[5] The prior imperative, never to lose sight of the total movement of thought, arises out of each category's being momentary totality first of all in so far as each logical moment must be thought through to the point of transition into its categorical other, whether that transition be realized within the logic of being as the immediacy of "having gone over into," within the logic of essence as the reflective form of "appearance in the other," or within the logic of the Concept as "self-development into the other."[6] Therefore, this and the earlier description of Hegel's logical dialectic as pure form and method[7] establish the constantly presumed context within which specific thought determinations are to be analyzed. These remarks concerning total movement, form and method should not give the vague impression of some deeper dialectic underlying or independent of the movement realized in each category or in each major logical sphere. Rather, they represent an attempt to capture the sense of wholeness Hegel himself stresses by elaborating on method in the final, inclusive logical moment, the absolute Idea.

The second focus and imperative, to think through and examine the logical moment of the absolute Idea itself or any other specific moment, is likewise rooted in the same category characteristic of non-temporal momentary totality. Each of the logical determinations is in its own way the totality of the Concept. There is for Hegel simply no substratum underlying the thought category, nothing else to think through beyond the immanent arising of the specific categories. Furthermore, the immanence demanded by Hegel's method means that the specific categories have to justify their own coming into being. They have to arise out of one another both without appeal beyond the inadequacy of the previous category and within the context of the movement of thought itself.[8] On the basis of the characteristic of momentary totality, it is necessary to keep sight of the overall context while always examining particular moments or categories.[9] This double focus both justifies and necessitates the study of specific logical moments in order to understand and critique the *Logic* as a whole.

Two specific moments come to mind immediately in regard to Hegel's triadically structured presentation of logic as self-positing divine subjectivity: *Etwas*[10] and syllogism (*Schluß*).[11] *Etwas* or "something," but without emphasis on "thing" (*Ding*), which is itself a thought determination in the logic of essence,[12] is according to the second edition of the "Logic of Being" "only the beginning of the Subject"[13] but is nevertheless a beginning. Characteristic for the logic of being, Hegel's brief discussion of the arising of this logical category presents the total movement of the Concept in a logical nutshell, in the form of immediacy. Because position, content and significance are inseparable in Hegel's *Logic*, *Etwas*'s importance is mirrored by its early position as result and beginning within the overall logical movement of pure thought. *Etwas* is result or synthesizing third moment of "*Dasein* in general" (*Dasein überhaupt*) and quality (*Qualität*). Through them it grounds,[14] and so opens the way to a critical analysis of, the complex structure of Hegel's method in its initial, therefore simplest and most immediate development: being/nothing/becoming (*Sein/Nichts/Werden*).[15] As beginning *Etwas* leads for Hegel through other (*Anderes*) into a discussion of thought's movement to true infinity.

Similarly to *Etwas*, the positioning of syllogism as third moment of the logic of the Concept's first major triadic, subjectivity, indicates its significance for Hegel's overall conception of inclusive subjectivity or Subject.[16] The role of syllogism in its renewed immediacy as beginning—objectivity or object—[17] is of less immediate direct interest in this study than its functioning as synthesizing result and return from the self-othering of the Concept in judgement. Fully realized syllogism is for Hegel, in terms of structure, complete self-mediation with the concrete universal for middle term and provides the structure of the logically later and culminating absolute Idea, method. Syllogism will be treated in Part Two of this study in connection with its concrete realization in the realphilosophical sphere of religion.[18] *Etwas* itself will serve briefly now as a representative text and thought determination giving a sampling of the complexity of Hegel's thought and illustrating major moves in his dialectic. However, *Etwas* is of primary concern here precisely in so far as it provides a context for and gives an opening to the movement of pure thought in the immediacy of its initial moments. *Etwas* and syllogism form axial moments on which Hegel's whole theory of inclusive subjectivity as Subject turns—and depends.

A closer scrutiny of the five paragraphs[19] in which Hegel initially discusses the axial category, *Etwas*, reveals a distinct movement of thought. He argues from the first paragraph, in which the sublation of the differentiation of quality[20] as the determination and negation[21] of *Dasein* is accomplished in view of its being, of its containing *Dasein*, on through to paragraph five, which provides the transition to finitude. This transition occurs on the basis of *Etwas*'s being a concrete becoming whose moments are themselves now both seen to be *Etwas*, that is, *Etwas* and other. This establishment of other will in Chapter Six below lead into a consideration of Hegel's notion of the true infinite. Of present interest are several remarks in the three middle paragraphs. Although it is not necessary here to summarize adequately or really exegete Hegel's many complex moves in these middle paragraphs, it is important to continue giving a brief taste of how Hegel in fact proceeds. Highlighting a few of the significant points made in this section so thoroughly consistent with Hegel's overall thought will lead into a discussion of the initial logical categories of being, nothing and becoming.

Etwas is merely the first posited negation of negation, only the beginning of the Subject. With the situating of this concrete category within the movement of thought, Hegel illustrates logic's critical function. His taking up of *Etwas* into logic recognizes its superficial character while establishing what for Hegel is the category's true content.[22] Hegel's positioning of *Etwas* as mere beginning or first concrete negation of negation means that for Hegel it underlies and grounds the more abstract and logically immediately prior determinations of *Dasein* and *Dasein*'s determination of quality differentiated as reality (*Realität*) and negation (*Negation*). *Etwas* grounds as well the categories logically preceding *Dasein*, the earliest, empty categories of being and nothing. As paragraph four indicates, since *Etwas* is (*seiend*), it is simple relation to itself but equally mediation of itself with itself. This self-mediation is already abstractly present in becoming. In fact the moment of mediation is found in every thought determination. *Etwas* as self-mediating negation of negation and categorical beginning of the Subject necessarily refers to the earliest logical categories without which it, the structure of subjectivity in general and the movement of logic as such, could not for Hegel be adequately understood, interpreted and justified.

Together the previously mentioned first and now the second paragraphs present *Etwas*'s arising, which later comes explicitly to be seen as a moment in the overall self-determination of the Concept. In this second paragraph Hegel underscores the continuing availability of "*Dasein* in general," difference to it and the sublation of this difference, which difference cannot be left aside since it is. So *Dasein* is *Daseindes*, *Etwas*. Paragraphs three and four contain reflections on and implications of *Etwas* as the first more concrete negation of negation. In paragraph three Hegel stresses the importance of *Etwas*, but more so the notion of negation of negation in general. In this structure can be recognized the self-determination of *Dasein* or *Leben* to "that which is" (*Daseindes*) and "that which lives" (*Lebendiges*), even of divinity (*Gottheit*) to God

(*Gott*). This self-determination as manifest in *Etwas* is the beginning of the concrete and individual, of the Subject. Later in the *Logic* the Subject's structure comes to be seen as the recognition that the other, the object, bears the very structure of the Subject itself.[23] The other or object is then for Hegel not merely the abstraction of a first negation, but has become negation of negation, the structure of true subjectivity.

It is characteristic of the *Logic* that once a thought determination is appropriately introduced and its true content therewith determined, it may be used to describe later moments, a usage based in the continuing negated presence of the logically earlier categories in any subsequent movement of thought. Hence the continuing reference to being, nothing, becoming.[24] These are the primordial, elementary categories, whose transitions will shortly be seen to present, in the form of absolute immediacy, the fundamental structure of the Hegelian dialectical method, the self-determination of the Concept as Subject. It is a question of the viability of the difference of the immediacy of the first three categories within the unity of the overall self-determination of the Concept.[25] Now to turn from *Etwas*, the beginning of the Subject, to subjectivity's absolute beginning.

2. The Primordial, Elementary Movement of Pure Thought

"*Being, pure being*,—without any further determination." This is the phrase or anakoluth with which Hegel avoids even the form of a full sentence in presenting being, the initial category of thought.[26] It and the subsequent categories, in particular of nothing but also in its own way of becoming, arise within the sphere of absolute immediacy, which necessarily further cramps Hegel's already somewhat labored style.[27] Hegel's historically so disputed presentation of pure being is short enough to be quoted fully in a schematized fashion in order visually and in a preliminary way to highlight his determined attempts to ward off any internal differentiation of external relationship:

Being, pure being,
—without any further determination.
    In its indeterminate immediacy it is
        equal only to itself
        and also not unequal over against an other;

> it has no diversity
> within itself
> nor with any reference outwards.
>
> Through any determination or content,
> which could be distinguished in it,
> or through which it could be distinguished from an other
> were it so posited,
> it would not be held fast in its purity.
>
> It is pure indeterminateness and emptiness.
>
> —There is *nothing* to be intuited in it,
> if one can speak here of intuiting;
> or, it is only this pure, empty intuiting itself.
> Just as little is there anything to be thought in it,
> or it is equally only this empty thinking.
>
> Being, the indeterminate immediate, is in fact *nothing*,
> and neither more
> nor less
> than nothing.[28]

Even a cursory reading of this text on being immediately reveals that after the initial, positive formulation, "*Being, pure being*," all the following remarks are in one way or another negative. Particularly striking are the first three assertions: indeterminate immediacy; no differentiation; and, necessary absence of determination or content. Each is, furthermore, applied internally and externally. Even the first sub-qualification, "equal only to itself," which might at first appear to be a positive assertion, is dependent on "indeterminate immediacy." First then, immediacy means for Hegel that which has not yet won itself, a first which is therefore simple.[29] Being is the simple unity of Subject and object,[30] the first moment of truth, whose objective being *Sein* expresses. So being can be described as the simplest definition of the Absolute[31] and, because it is "equal only to itself and also not unequal over against an other," as that through which all exists, or better "is."[32] Being is singular. Secondly, being is characterizable neither within nor without in terms of differentiation. It is the primordial, as yet undeveloped (*an sich*) concrete totality of the Concept,[33] as yet without differentiation. Thirdly, any such determination or content differentiatingly established in being would constitute it as *Dasein* and *Etwas*.[34] Its only acknowledgeable determination is its very indetermination,[35] so that for Hegel its *Was* or "what" is simply its *Daß* or "that."[36] Being lies within the realm of absolute form.[37] Hegel's presentation of pure being climaxes half way through the paragraph: "It is pure indeterminateness and emptiness."

A second reading of Hegel's presentation of being reveals a double movement from the opening "pure being" to the latter half of the paragraph. First, by using dashes Hegel binds his insistence in the first half of the paragraph on the determinationlessness of pure being with the opening phrase, "pure being," in such a way as at the same time to subordinate it to a direct move from that opening phrase to the absence of content for thought. Secondly, at the end of the section enclosed in dashes, the assertion of the pure non-determination and emptiness of being forms the point and means of transition to nothing by way of the all-important reference to thought: there is nothing in being to intuit, nothing to think. In Hegel's text the hesitation about mentioning intuition (*Anschauen*) should be noted. Intuition recalls that in the *Logic* the movement is one of pure thought already beyond any separation of form and content, Subject and object, thought and being.[38] Toward the end of the *Logic*[39] Hegel explains it is really a question of thought which can also be called an inner intuiting because of the intended immediacy characteristic of the unity being is. Thought not only finds in being nothing to think, but being as such is simply this empty thinking, pure thought.[40] Within the realm of logic it is equally correct to refer to pure empty thought or pure being.[41] Both logic as a whole[42] and being in particular are pure thought, with being as the totality of the one pure thought in its initial moment. Being is the one beginning[43] and therefore "the *first* in the *process* of thought."[44] It is the abstract beginning, the abstract moment of the Concept,[45] abstract not in the sense of extracted from something but as lacking in determination, that is, still undeveloped.[46] Being is for Hegel the one absolute beginning because it is blind facticity of initial unity, pure indeterminate thought and non-dependence upon what follows.[47]

The transition from being as beginning to nothing occurs or, better, has already occurred by the end of the paragraph on being. In Hegel's view, to ask what sets this transition in motion would be to misunderstand both the dialectical nature of thought in general and specifically the immediacy of this transition as already having occurred.[48] Obviously there could be no recourse to consciousness over against an object, nor to the spontaneity of a positing ego. Further, for Hegel there is no need to refer to any more concrete form of being, nor to compare being with "that which exists" (*das Seiende*) or with the whole, nor again to appeal to a prior intuition or to some teleological orientation of the categories. This transition or any other in the *Logic* can for Hegel have occurred strictly speaking only by the category's having been thought through to its end, by having thought what it is and what it expresses.[49] In the case of being the transition to nothing has occurred in the very thinking of being as indeterminate immediacy.[50]

The absence of the term "immediacy" (*Unmittelbarkeit*) in Hegel's presentation of nothing[51] is the first and most prominent difference between the texts on being and nothing. This absence is already hinted at by "*das*" in the opening phrase, *Nichts, das reine Nichts*, more determinate than being's opening phrase, *Sein, reines Sein*. The further references or descriptions of nothing generally reproduce those of being: simple equality with itself; perfect emptiness; absence of determination and content; non-differentiation within itself. Though, like being, nothing is indeterminate simplicity,[52] it is not itself the immediacy of an absolute beginning, for its simplicity is not that of a first which has not as yet won itself. Rather, nothing brings the negation, that is, the emptiness and determinationlessness of being, to explicit expression. It is not *reines Nichts* but *das reine Nichts*, and with this explication already difference and progression.[53] As with being, Hegel moves the consideration of nothing along by reference to intuition or thought, both of which are now treated practically speaking as referring to the same reality. Hegel argues, it counts as a difference if something or nothing is thought.[54] Thinking nothing has a meaning, so nothing *is* in thought, "so nothing *is* (exists) in our intuiting or thinking."[55] Hegel's presentation of nothing as logical category climaxes in establishing this moment of contradiction: nothing is.

Nothing is of course not yet "nonbeing" (*Nichtsein*), the explicit assertion of being and nothing in one, which would in fact be nothing as it is in becoming.[56] Whereas in the immediately preceding discussion on being reference was always made to thought as such, here the argumentation refers to "our" thought, a move in line with Hegel's general attitude of referring particularly the second member of any triadic to finitude.[57] Hegel's attempt to express the as yet unreflected contradiction[58] "nothing is" recalls his more general remarks stressing the difficulty involved in presenting the second member of any triadic.[59] These remarks are particularly applicable here, where Hegel tries to establish the total differentiation of being and nothing within the overall framework and limitations of immediacy and of the specific problematic of abstractness as contentlessness.[60] The tension, or more correctly the contradiction, that nothing is, formulates both the disappearance of being and its having been taken up into the totality of the Concept, which nothing is. As Hegel writes, nothing is "empty intuition and thought itself." Here the same terminology is used to describe nothing as had been used earlier concerning being.

It is, however, important to call attention to Hegel's slight adaptation of the phrases at the beginning of the presentation on nothing. "Equality with itself" is not complemented by being's "not unequal over against an other." "Undifferentiatedness in itself" is no longer further applied by "nor with any reference outwards." From the more concrete moment of becoming on, Hegel will speak of being and nothing as "other."[61] In the discussion of the second moment of method in the absolute Idea, otherness is constitutive of progression.[62] Yet Hegel likewise insists that the immediate transition from being to nothing, as then too the transition from nothing to being, is to be grasped without further determination, "—the transition is not yet a relation."[63] Though it is here a question of a relationless negating,[64] Hegel leaves the text on nothing open to the logically later acknowledgement of the otherness which nothing is then seen to be. At the present moment he intends to establish otherness and difference only as the logically immediate form of the pure posited emptiness or determinationlessness of pure thought, nothing as "empty intuition and thought itself." This Hegel can accomplish only by insisting that before[65] the consideration of becoming both being and nothing are, to use a logically later phrase, in their determinationlessness the totality of the Concept first *an sich* or simply as immediacy. Secondly, nothing is the progression of posited or explicitated determinationlessness, which is (i.e., *für sich* or for itself). For Hegel this logical distinction of unposited and posited, implicit and explicit, *an sich* and *für sich* is constitutive of being and nothing, which are worlds apart and yet the same.[66] It thereby provides, in the form of immediacy, the structure of all further logical differentiation. Negation, determination, otherness, contradiction, mediation—all these characteristics and functions of progression, the second moment of method, are to be seen as developments rooted in, conditioned and structured by the primordial appearance of nothing, the posited emptiness of being.[67]

Being and nothing are the totality of opposition in its immediacy.[68] The return from nothing to being occurs, or better, has already occurred by the end of the paragraph on nothing. In Hegel's view, nothing is (exists) in our thinking, or rather is the empty thinking itself, the same empty thinking which being is. This thinking to its end the contradiction that nothing is has shown nothing to be the same determinationlessness as being and therefore in its positedness the same as pure being.

The explicitation of this unity of being and nothing, a unity already contained implicitly in the contradiction that nothing is, constitutes the arising[69] of the category of becoming (*Werden*),[70] the immanent synthesis[71] of being and nothing. The thematization not of contradiction but of unity, that being and nothing are not without one another, forms the newness of this higher and richer category.[72] Unlike with the previous two categories, Hegel presents becoming in three paragraphs: the unity of being and nothing; the moments of becoming; and the sublation of becoming. The opening sentence of the first of these paragraphs, "*Pure being* and *pure nothing* are, therefore, the same,"[73] attempts to indicate with its singular verb the unity within which being and nothing take on a more determinate character. In the second paragraph Hegel will go on to speak further of this determinate unity within which being and nothing are, and within which they are unseparated from their other.[74] But here the truth is neither being nor nothing, nor again their lack of difference. The truth is that they are absolutely different and yet disappear into their opposite. Both points are given sharper focus in the second edition: "But it is equally true that they are not undistinguished from each other, that, on the contrary, they are *not the same*, that they are *absolutely distinct*, and yet that they are unseparated and inseparable and that *each* immediately *vanishes in its opposite*."[75] The truth of being and nothing is this movement of immediate disappearance of one in the other; it is becoming, in which both remain different, but on the basis of a difference immediately resolved. Becoming is, to use determinations thematized later on in the *Logic*, the immediacy of identity in difference.[76] It is the transcendent truth of being and nothing. In view of its positive character it forms a third, an other,[77] over against being and nothing and in which according to Hegel these two continue as moments: negated, taken up and given their true meaning.[78]

Yet as Hegel's second paragraph on becoming underscores, becoming is for Hegel likewise the immanent unity or identity in the difference which being and nothing are. Becoming is this identity in so far as the transitions both from being to nothing (disappearance, *Vergehen*) and from nothing to being (rising, *Entstehen*) are the same. They are both a going over into the opposite; both are becoming. "They [being, nothing] are not reciprocally sublated—the one does not sublate the other externally—but each sublates itself in itself and is in its own self the opposite of itself."[79] The restlessness of becoming, emphasized in Hegel's second paragraph on becoming, settles in his third paragraph into restful unity on the basis of the paralyzing counterbalance of becoming's doubled determination as arising and disappearing. Becoming is the disappearance of disappearing itself. "Becoming is an unstable unrest which settles into a stable result."[80] This result is disappearance (*Verschwundensein*) not as a simple falling back into nothing, but the unity of being and nothing come to restful simplicity, which is being, but being which is (*seiend*), *das Dasein*.[81]

In the move from becoming to *Dasein* Hegel distinguishes more clearly than with most later "results" or third categories between restlessness and coming to rest, a distinction indicated by the very use of two categories.[82] The closest parallel and equally or more difficult to interpret would be Hegel's treatment of the absolute Idea as return to the immediacy of being, a return in which the Idea remains Concept while freely releasing itself[83] as total immediacy in the form of Nature. One difference in Hegel's handling of becoming and Idea is of course that great effort is made on the one hand to present *Dasein* as the very settling of becoming itself, which disappears.[84] On the other hand, for any number of possible reasons including Idea's being Subject, Hegel refuses to speak of the Idea's simply settling into the immediacy of nature. Nevertheless with becoming, as finally with the absolute Idea, the recurrent pattern of result as enriched return to the immediacy of new beginning is clearly asserted, if not so clearly argued. Becoming is always at hand as the positing ground of being and nothing, just as on its own level the absolute Idea in the fullness of its posited subjectivity is the enriched resultant return to the beginning, which is being.[85]

3. Summary Remarks on the Structure of Hegel's Dialectic

This enriched return to being on the part of the absolute Idea completes for Hegel the methodological circle constituting the logic of pure thought. The initial logical categories were sketched against the background of this cyclic development with the intention of allowing for and even stressing their immanent arising. Here this meant respecting the immediacy characteristic of the methodic movement, the dialectic of these first thought determinations, without uncritically importing logically later categories. Yet it likewise involved coming to the recognition that these first categories do instantiate method itself in its immediacy.[86] As there is for Hegel but one Idea,[87] so too is being in its immediacy the single absolute beginning of logical thought, the originary unity of thought and being and, in this sense, the beginning of Hegel's entire encyclopedic system and of all philosophical thought.[88] It will shortly be argued that the viability of Hegel's entire systematic philosophy, in the form in which he conceived it, depends ultimately on his ability to establish this beginning as the available identity of pure being.

Though this absolute beginning or being is the absolutely immediate, it is for Hegel likewise in at least two senses mediated:[89] first by its origin in the phenomenological sublation;[90] and, secondly, by the grounding presence of the absolute Idea. However, *as first moment* of pure thought pure being is sheer immediacy.[91] Realized self-mediation is the function of result and is result. Mediation as such is the function of progression. This progression as negation in the nakedness of immediacy is nothing[92] arising out of pure being. When seen in its truth, in becoming, nothing is literally the presentation of positivity as otherness in the form of pure negation.[93] Since it is the negation of being, it is mediated otherness. Since it is the other of its own other, and includes its other within itself, it is mediating otherness.[94] Nothing is. Such mediated and mediating otherness finds its truth, as mentioned immediately above in a qualifying sense, now as result or in a resultant sense in becoming, because both being and nothing are seen as transition into the other, as being in the process of becoming. In so far as becoming forms the truth of being and nothing, it becomes the interpretative category through which being and nothing are to be understood.[95]

As moment of truth, becoming bears for Hegel within it the fundamental dialectical structure of self-mediation which the Concept shows itself to be in coming to itself through its posited other.[96] However for Hegel becoming paradigms this structure in the form of logical instability. It sinks again into the immediacy of being, which as enriched by the sublated presence of nothing is now the logical category of determinate being, *Dasein*. The final realization of the structure of self-mediating truth, the absolute Idea, is becoming in its full logical concreteness. It is the full truth of the self-mediating Concept in its return within the sphere of logic to the enriched immediacy of initial being and in the sphere of external otherness to the immediacy of nature. From becoming to Idea all logical determinations, and especially third members of logical triadics, are in their own way and on their own levels increasingly concrete forms of becoming.[97] The first of these increasingly concrete becomings qualifying for Hegel as true negation of negation is *Etwas*, a becoming whose sublated moments of *Dasein* and quality are both themselves concrete in contrast to the abstractness of being and nothing. These latter constitute special categories[98] whose immediate abstractness is to be appreciated within the context of the overall logical movement of pure thought, of absolute form.[99] The axial moment making possible this differentiation within continuity is becoming. The ultimate grounding of the unity of the movement of pure thought is the return of the absolute Idea to being, the initial moment of the Concept itself.

The dialectic of being and of nothing both coming to the concreteness of *Dasein* through becoming gives clearest access to the dynamic of Hegel's logic. This dialectic is pure thought in its primordial and elementary structure and movement. It is primordial, that is, first in the deepest possible sense of being originary. It is the origin giving rise to and being transformed by all which originates in and out of it. It has universal signiftcance.[100] "Elementary" picks up on these themes and stresses both the basic simplicity of the initial dialectical triadic and the fact that being, nothing and becoming are the logical "elements" with which and according to whose rhythm the Concept further determines itself.[101] Their negated and transformed but ever recurrent presence[102] is exemplified in their continued usage by Hegel as explanatory categories throughout the rest of the *Logic*.[103] This dynamic, which pulsates through the *Logic* and which is the pulsation of pure thought itself, is finally primordial and elementary in the sense that a critique of it is as well a critique of Hegel's conception of the movement of an absolute logic as a whole and as such.

A critique of the triadic, being/nothing/becoming, is a critique of the overall structural dynamic of Hegel's logical dialectic in the immediacy of its initial moments, which lay bare the basic moves of Hegel's thought. This dialectical movement from positive to negative to negation of negation and thus to positive[104] bears a striking preliminary resemblance to analogy's general form: positive statement; negation of the assertion; and reassertion on a higher level.[105] However, for Hegel the dialectical movement is totally immanent,[106] self-grounding, and occurs not only between the various spheres of logic, nature and Spirit but also within the realm of pure thought itself. For Hegel the initial positive is an immediacy with a content and determination as yet an sich, a unity unposited, still only implicit and therefore not yet available to itself. In this sense the initial, positive beginning is characterized by a lacking, the thinking of which gives rise to the negation of that beginning. Negation's arising remains immanent; this thinking is the movement of thought itself. The motivating force for Hegel lies in the inability of immediacy to rest in its lacking, to be thought through adequately without a transition to the negative of itself, which is its other inclusive of itself, *für sich*.[107] This other, established on the basis of the internal inadequacy constitutive of immediacy is difference, the other of initial identity[108] and identity's determinate negation through which indeterminate identity becomes determinate. So Hegel can speak highly of Spinoza's "*Omnis determinatio est Negatio*," rendered in the *Logic*'s second edition, "Determinateness is negation posited as affirmative."[109] In the first logical triadic, being becomes determinate through nothing in that becoming, that is, the explicit, positive thought that nothing is, settles into determinate being, *Dasein*. This immediate dialectic and Hegel's general dialectical thought of as a whole is so constructed that immediacy requires a mediated and mediating difference arising out of itself in order to come to itself, to be an and für sich what it was originally only implicitly. Thinking through the contradiction constitutive of difference overcomes that contradiction by bringing to expression in thought the unity already contained in the contradiction itself. The result is self-mediation, in which immediacy and difference, positive and negative, *an sich* and *für sich*, implicit and explicit arrive at a higher unity containing them as its moments.

Along with being/nothing/becoming, the most famous formulation of this immanent dialectic is found at the beginning of the logic of the Concept's moment of subjectivity, where being, nothing and becoming have been negated, taken up and transformed in the self-development of the Concept as universality (*Allgemeinheit*), particularity (*Besonderheit*) and individuality (*Einzelheit*).[110] In the logic of the Concept each of these three moments is explicitly the totality of the Concept[111] with concrete individuality as unity of universality and particularity, its moments.[112] This threefold self-development of the Concept gives clear expression to the overall structural dynamic of Hegel's logical dialectic, the immanent self-development of the Concept as subjectivity from the initial, universal moment of identity. Any successful critique of the first three logical categories becomes as well a critique of Hegel's conception of logic as a whole in terms of the viability both of that logic's immanent dialectic and the nature of its starting point.

In the immanent development of Hegel's dialectic of pure thought, otherness defined as the negation of initial identity and therefore as difference plays the central role. It is the mediated and mediating other. The thinking of its self-contradiction serves for Hegel as logical driving force and essential moment in absolute thought's self-positing, the Concept's self-determination.[113] Without this included other, the movement of logic could not be considered pure thought, absolute form, inclusive Subject.[114] Immediacy or initial identity considered by itself and without its included other would for Hegel remain one-sided. In the *Encyclopedia*, within the context of a critique of three possible positions thought could take vis-à-vis objectivity, Hegel criticizes the form of immediate knowledge for leaving truth abstract and therefore finite or not inclusive.

> We have still briefly to indicate the general nature of the *form of immediacy*. It is indeed the form itself, which, because it is *one-sided*, makes its content itself one-sided and therefore finite.[115]

The condition of the possibility of an absolute logic is therefore a movement of necessary self-othering within the realm of pure thought. This necessary self-othering allows Hegel to establish a movement of nonfinite self-mediating, that is, self-positing and self-determining inclusive subjectivity. Such necessary self-othering is already initially established in the logical impossibility of thinking pure being without having gone over into the thought of nothing.[116]

In a remark on the unity of being and nothing, Hegel introduces into the second edition of the *Logic* a sentence which somewhat disturbs the flow of the paragraph, but which brings together in a reference to God the establishment of an other both within pure thought and in the spheres of nature and finite Spirit: "Thus in God Self quality (*activity, creation, power* and so forth) involves the determination of the negative—they are the bringing forth of an *other*.[117] "Activity," but especially "creation" and "power," evokes in reference to God the otherness of a finite world, whereas "quality" as such is internal to the movement of logical thought, i.e., determination which is,[118] and mediating moment between *Dasein* and *Etwas*. In God, then, there is both the necessary internal and external bringing forth of an other to immediacy. Without an internal, mediated and mediating other, God would remain in Hegel's view abstract, one-sided[119] and would not function as absolute truth. Without an other recognized as other of the divine Self and therefore reconciled, God would not be acknowledgeable as Spirit.[120] In the case as well of an externalized but included other, which is ultimately structurally the same as the immediate internal other, the absence of an included other would amount to a finitized God over against a finite consciousness.[121] This is in effect a radical statement of Hegel's claim that God must be triadically conceived to be concrete, living Spirit.[122] In fact, for Hegel God must be thought as "immanent" and "economic" Trinity to be truly infinite. Trinity is for Hegel the question of reconciled otherness in God, the triadically structured movement of divine subjectivity, finally the realization of absolute Spirit. This construction by Hegel of "immanent" Trinity in the form of absolute logic as thinkable (*begreifbar*) inner pulsation constituting the divine Subject and the "economic" Trinity as the reconciled otherness of nature and finite Spirit in absolute Spirit stands or falls with his ability to establish mediating and mediated otherness in the immanent dialectic of pure thought. That immanent dialectic stands or falls with its primordial, elementary movement.

Hegel's establishment of logically reformulated trinitarian otherness remains problematic. His understanding of otherness as negation does enable him to overcome the dichotomy between Subject and object and, by implication, alienation in its various forms to the extent that such are subsumable under this "dichotomy." Yet, rather ironically, the very burden which otherness is made to bear[123] renders Hegel's understanding of it particularly vulnerable to critique. Concretely, despite some clarification there remains a certain ambiguity surrounding the finitude and/or infinity of the moment of otherness in the realm of space and time and, more to the point at present, within the realm of pure thought.[124] Historically the fundamental theological objection to Hegel's conception of God was the necessitarian character of the transition to finitude as other of God, a necessity rooted by Hegel both in the nature of logical thought and in the need for an other if God were through self-development to come to be absolute Spirit.[125] Perhaps, however, necessity in the relationship between God and the world finds its proper rootage in finitude, with God then conceived as inclusive other of the world.[126] In a more explicitly philosophical vein, the important role attributed to otherness is counter-balanced by its ultimately logically momentary character.[127] It could be asked if the unfinished nature of Hegel's complex notion of negation[128] might not be an indication of deeper difficulties in the way he sets up his dialectic? Could negation really exhaust the meaning of otherness?[129] Has difference no content of its own?[130] Even given the specific characteristics attributed by Hegel to "moment," does not the definition of finitude as moment reduce its inherent importance and proper sharpness?[131] These various difficulties and questions revolving around Hegel's conception of otherness lead back to the fundamental question of the viability of Hegel's immanent dialectic. Although otherness itself is here problematic, more importantly, it appears as symptom of a deeper philosophical malaise, the difficulty of thinking the immanent dialectic in its primordial and elementary instantiation with the absolute beginning in pure being.

4. Critique of the Primordial, Elementary Movement of Pure Thought

Hegel's immanent dialectic with its absolute beginning in being and logical result in absolute Idea has been summarized so far as movement of absolute form, the triadically structured self-positing and self-determining of inclusive subjectivity, logically reformulated divine trinitarian Subject. The methodic movement of self-developing subjectivity was presented in its immediacy by means of reference through *Etwas* to the first logical categories arising out of pure being. Such a prolonged engagement with Hegel's circular progression can be justified in view of the respect demanded by his masterful systematic construction, by the necessity to establish the *Logic* as appropriate object of a study on Trinity and, given the brilliant ambiguity of Hegel's thought, by the need to avoid as much as possible merely reacting to a straw Hegel. But the lulling effect of the ever-recurrent triadic progression, both here in this study's multi-leveled presentation and in Hegel's writing in general, can obscure the need for a more consciously critical approach toward the beginning and immanent dynamic of his dialectic. This critique will progress from a brief reference again to thought (*Denken*) as absolute form and its relation to human thought on to argue the unavailability to thought of the initial dialectical moments in the form proposed by Hegel.[132]

The pure thought of logic is for Hegel absolute form because it gives rise to, and is, its own object, which it contains within the unity that it is.[133] This pure thought is unifying or reasoning thought (*Vernunft*, *vernunftiges Denken*) in contradistinction to the inadequacy of understanding (*Verstand*). The latter remains for Hegel uncritically on the level of opposition between Subject or finite self-consciousness and existing object, between finite and infinite, between world and God.[134] Hegel's unifying thought or reason stresses thinking's creative role in line with the spontaneity of the Kantian principle of the transcendental ego, but proposes to avoid Kant's unresolved dilemma between spontaneity and receptivity.[135] This absolute thought both expresses itself and is expressed in logical determinations. Hegel speaks in terms of a thought or the thought (*Gedanke*),[136] of Concept (*Begriff*) and of Idea (*Idee*). His concern is with a thought which not only reaches the unifying moment of truth[137] but which grasps the truth and gives expression to it, or better, to a thought in which truth expresses itself.[138] His intention is to go beyond meaning or opinion to the public realm.[139]

In modern German, Hegel's *Denken* would be expressed especially as Begreifen, conceptually grasping or comprehending.[140] As with the mediation of the opposition between Subject and object in general, the notion of sublation (*Aufhebung*) is for Hegel likewise the key to an understanding of the relation between finite human thought and the one, infinite movement of pure thought or *Vernunft*. The raising of finite thought to the level of logic was the function of the *Phenomenology*[141] and is the systematic task of the *Logic* itself,[142] where the self-positing and self-determining of the Concept are critiques of the thought determinations through which it develops as the Absolute. Negation, preservation and elevation,[143] the three moments constituting the movement of sublation, structure and characterize the dialectical relationship between the pure thought of logic and finite thought. Finite thought is negated in so far as it remains on the level of opposition, preserved in that the movement of thought as such is a movement from manifold to universal where manifold remains a moment of the universal,[144] and elevated or moved forward in that pure thought expresses itself in transformed human thought.[145] This movement of absolute thought does not for Hegel destroy human thought but fulfills it,[146] so that he can describe a human person as essentially thought and speaks of finding one's own infinity in thought.[147] Since this sublation is to fulfill and not to destroy, it must be available to transformed human thought which remains dialectically moment in pure thought as well as the locus of pure thought's self-development. In either criticizing or defending Hegel's view of logic, it is necessary to examine whether such proposed transformed human thought, as taken up into absolute thought, can in any real sense of the word think the Hegelian structuring of being, nothing and becoming.

Being/nothing/becoming is for Hegel the initial dialectic of thought as absolute form, with form and content totally adequate to one another in the immediacy of their identification. The mutual adequacy of form and content is more explicitly expressed, according to Hegel, in the course of the self-determination of the Concept, a progression from being to absolute Idea with the latter's full explication of the unity of form and content in terms of the mediation of Subject and object. In this overall progression, content (*Inhalt*) is used in two distinguishable but ultimately reconciled ways. First, content refers to the self-enrichment of the immediacy of the Concept. This enrichment takes place through immediacy's negation in the second moment of the dialectic and its reappearance in the reuniting of the two through negation of the negation.[148] Thought gains in concreteness and determination through the overcoming of this posited otherness or difference conceived as negation. In this sense it can provisionally be said that form itself posits content. However, secondly, in the realm of logic content is ultimately identified by Hegel with form. This is so because the thought determinations are themselves the content of objective thought. It is a question of absolute form.[149] Here, therefore, all three moments of the Hegelian dialectic can explicitly, though in varying ways, be referred to in terms of content. This second use of "content" includes the first. The reconciliation of these two usages of the term "content" is made explicit by the reflexive form in Hegel's summary of the way in which the Concept determines itself. Form itself determines itself as content:

> The form, when thus thought out into its purity, will have within itself the capacity to *determine* itself, that is, to give itself content, and that same indeed in its necessity—as a system of thought determinations.[150]

"Self-determining" (*Sich-bestimmen*)—the question of a double understanding of content is for Hegel at the same time the problem of determinateness (*Bestimmtheit*) and determinate, logical thought. The two ways in which content is employed by Hegel highlight two of the ways in which he speaks of determinateness. First, all logical thought is inherently concrete in its very abstractness, since absolute thought is from its initial moment in pure being negation of negation and logically later seen to be concrete universal.[151] Pure thought is ever determinate, even in the first moment whose determinateness is its determination-lessness (*Bestimmungslosigkeit*).[152] Secondly, the Concept's dialectical self-development occurs through a positing of explicit content as negation of immediacy and through the following negation of this negation. Such self-development is determination through negation.[153] With the double use of the notion of determination, in which the first use logically includes the second, Hegel proposes to retain and give proper context and meaning to Spinoza's axiom, "all determination is negation."[154]

The first dialectical moment is determinate but in such a way that as first and in the order of being it is not limited. The second moment, negation, is likewise determinate. But it is both infinite as momentary totality of pure thought and other inclusive of its other and likewise the form of finitude or limitation in that it expresses its content.[155] The third or unifying moment is determinate but not limited, that is, spared of being reduced to the form of finitude supposedly because it is enriched return to immediacy. But is such a dialectical interrelationship and multiple usage of the notion of content and determination available to human thought? Is such available to thought at all? It could be suggested that even to raise such a question is to slip back into metaphysical thinking, into understanding. Such an early retort is in order as a warning. It can be considered a valid defense of Hegel only if his proposal is presupposed. In fact, asking this question is an attempt to think through the categories and thought determinations Hegel presents. In the *Logic* he tries to make these categories available to the realm of public discourse, to determinate human thought, by transforming (*Aufheben*) such thought in the process. But here lies the philosophical rub. How can either a proposed pure thought or any other form of thought think through one or more logical categories whose content is in its own order effectively determinationlessness and contentlessness? How could they be thought precisely as logical categories and momentary totalities in the self-development of the Concept? How could such a position ever be truly defended?

Hegel tried valiantly to defend pure being as the one, necessary and absolute beginning of logical thought and of philosophy as a whole.[156] It was a beginning forced upon him by the demands of consistency in a systematically speaking deductively constructed and argued immanent dialectic whose beginnings are characterized by lacking.[157] The absolute beginning had to be the absolutely immediate unity of Subject and object. But try as Hegel might to justify this determinationless first moment of logical thought,[158] he failed to make such a beginning effectively available to that thought, which always remains determinate, or is no thought at all.[159] Therewith Hegel was unable to make such a beginning really thinkable at all, given his requirement of *begreiffendes Denken* (comprehending/grasping thought).[160]

Hegel's most significant attempt to establish pure being within the realm of thought consisted in his indirect acknowledgement of thought's determinate nature by insisting that the determination of being was its determinationlessness.[161] This does not at all solve the problem of how to think being.[162] Secondly, Hegel attempted to embrace being's lack of determination by making it the very driving force moving thought forward to the expression of this determinationlessness, to nothing.[163] This is an example of Hegel's bold genius, his tendency to set in center stage what others would hide as weakness. Here such a move simply gives up thinking pure being and raises the question again in terms of nothing. A third and far more complex proposal by Hegel for establishing pure being was by means of either an indirect or direct attempt to express it in thought and language. "Being equal to itself, simplicity, purity, immediacy, that which is wholly empty, the most universal, perfect abstraction, indeterminateness"[164] are representative of the terms used to refer to pure being. As with expressions in the initial presentation of being[165] these are all in one way or another negative terms inevitably referring to their other.[166] Hegel acknowledges this with regard to the exemplary expression "immediacy" (*Unmittelbarkeit*). "*Simple* immediacy is itself an expression of reflection and contains a reference to its distinction from what is mediated. This simple immediacy, therefore, in its true expression is pure being."[167] The phrase following this second edition text has been expanded by Hegel to include a comparison to the immediacy of pure knowing. Since being is the being of pure knowing, both are in question, and even this comparison leaves unanswered why being as immediacy can be exempted from a reference to otherness and therefore not be finite.[168] In an extreme form of indirect reference Hegel speaks of being as "unexpressible."[169] In the course of the logically later presentation of the universal he writes of being: "*Being* is simple as *immediate* being; for that reason it is only something *meant* or *intended* and we cannot say of it what it is."[170] An unexpressible as beginning of grasping or comprehending thought ultimately leaves such thought without a beginning in its own realm.

In contradistinction to these attempts to express indirectly the initial moment of pure thought, Hegel makes one positive statement. "Being, pure being."[171] The trouble with "being" however is that, as with any other term (*Ausdruck*) either of thought or of speech, determinateness is immediately and inevitably present even before the transition to nothing simply because it is thought or spoken.[172] Hegel's many attempts to work around this fact are themselves a witness to the determinate character of thought. Such statements as these last two might at first sight appear merely to presume what is under discussion. But on closer examination both thought and any possible expression of thought remain determinate, meaning in this case, limited, and therefore in Hegel's understanding finite.[173] This remains the case whether such thought be a proposed absolute thought as subsumed human thought or any other form of thought. To speak of a thought which does not remain determinate is to speak equivocally of thought so as ultimately to destroy human thought. A totally indeterminate moment of thought could not be the self-expression of the Absolute in human thought. Innumerable alternative ways could be piled up to defend Hegel's dialectic of pure thought, but they would remain inadequate until they have fully responded to the problematic surrounding the impossibility of really thinking the initial moment of pure thought.

The same insoluble difficulty arises more glaringly in any attempt to establish pure nothing as non-temporal moment of absolute thought in sublated human thought:[174] In order to posit progression, to avoid an antinomy situation in which logic could equally begin with either being or nothing, Hegel had to insist that nothing is. Nothing is therefore for Hegel the other of its own other and inclusive of its other. With "nothing is" Hegel means to express the dialectical moment of contradiction in its absolute immediacy. But in fact nothing is always the other of something and not of pure being as grasped in thought.[175] As with being so too with nothing, speaking of determinationlessness as determination fails to make nothing truly graspable in comprehending thought.

Reflexive terms functioning nominally or in a merely indicatory fashion are likewise inadequate. Perhaps nothing is conceptually unexpressible. Hegel had so referred to being.[176] However this would form for Hegel's system a disastrous dichotomy between thought and its expression. It would not only make pure thought nothing but would leave it nowhere. In fact, when expressed conceptually, the "is" (*ist, existiert*) in "nothing is" inevitably gives expression to determination and therefore finitude. At least for being it could be argued that being was a border conceptuality,[177] which cannot be said of nothing. Hegel's systematic consistency forced him to argue to a dialectical moment of pure contradiction, a momentary totality not really graspable in conceptual thought.

Thinking the contradiction that "nothing is" was in Hegel's mind to give rise to becoming.[178] Becoming was to be the thematic expression of the unity of being and nothing already contained in this contradiction. Logical consistency forced Hegel to posit becoming as this immanently arising immediacy of identity inclusive of difference. In Hegel's methodic self-development of the Concept this identity or third moment was to be enriched return to the immediacy of beginning. Becoming was to be the grounding return to being, a return enriched by the sublated presence of nothing and therefore settling into *Dasein*.

In view of the argumentation concerning being and nothing, Hegel's notion of becoming flounders on two accounts. First, because neither being nor nothing can be established in thought as indeterminate momentary totalities in the movement of absolute thought.[179] Being cannot provide the necessarily indeterminate initial identity. Nothing cannot serve as an indeterminate moment of pure contradiction needed to engender the immediacy of mediation which becoming is meant to be.[180] Second, because becoming qua concept always remains itself determinate and therefore limited.[181] For Hegel becoming sinks into *Dasein* because it is unstable. In fact, however, this is due to the inherent determinateness of thought, a determinateness made clear by what Hegel calls becoming's necessarily having settled with *Dasein*.[182]

5. The Determinate Nature of Any Beginning— Implications for Trinity

Despite what has at times been perceived as significant ambiguity in Hegel's thought and phrasing, embracing the Hegelian synthesis in its rhythmic regularity might temptingly appear to provide philosophical satisfaction and even soothe personal insecurities. Hegel's astonishing complexity of thought, scope of vision and brilliance of insight could easily lead to the conclusion that any negative critique of his fundamental position should be countered by an appeal to further complexities in that very position. Specifically, an attempt might be made to cover the Achilles heel, namely, the initial moment of pure being, in Hegel's absolute logic by appealing to the grounding role of the absolute Idea in its return to this beginning. But such a grounding could never free thought from the impossible, though for Hegel necessary, task of comprehending the determinationless immediacy of pure being as lacking and of grasping nothing as pure contradiction. Becoming itself as moment of unifying mediation is simply not available to thought in Concept. What cannot be established in its immediacy could not for Hegel be merely retroactively justified in logically later and more complex instantiations. Though Hegel's logic is not to be conceived of as merely deductive in a simplistic sense of the term, it is to be argued as arising immanently and consistently out of pure being. Systematically speaking, Hegel's argumentation itself is a deductively argued dialectical movement.[183] That Hegel's monumental philosophical system depends on so fragile a basis as the dialectic of being, nothing and becoming and in particular on the establishment of pure being in thought is both a tribute to his genius and a warning to beware. It is as if it would take a "will to believe" in order to accept this initial moment of pure being and, logically speaking, move on from there.

Hegel cannot argue convincingly to his overall conception of absolute logic because any beginning conceptually graspable in thought which as beginning is not the being of pure thought is in fact *Dasein*, finitude or even more specifically the *Dasein* of finite thought.[184] It can furthermore provisionally be stated here[185] that Hegel's formulation, "nothing is," expresses not pure thought's abstract moment of contradiction, but what will come to be seen as the self-contradictory character of *Dasein* considered in and for itself. Again provisionally stated, with becoming Hegel has not gasped in thought the initial, paradigmatic instance of the Absolute's self-mediation but the restless and tentative developmental character of finite thought or even of finitude as such.[186] Therefore Hegel's magistral post-Kantian reinterpretation of the Western philosophical tradition in the logical nutshell, being/nothing/becoming, cannot instantiate his posited movement of absolute method. Beginning, progression and result cannot immanently arise from one another as immediacy, otherness as negation, and enriched return to resultant, inclusive immediacy. They cannot adequately structure the Concept as self-positing and self-determining subjectivity. Hegel's overall self-positing dialectical movement was to have been one from implicit to explicit, from *an sich* to *für sich*, from immediacy to otherness, from positive to negative. These two moments were to have been mediated by an immanently developed return to the enriched immediacy of beginning, negation of negation. Logical consistency forced Hegel to posit the pattern of this dialectical self-mediation in an initial triadic whose naked and so more vulnerable immediacy set forth the structural movement of the totality of his thought. The implicit contradiction of pure being was to have been made explicit in "nothing is" and both implicit and explicit were to have been mediated in becoming. Systematically necessary as the positing of this primordial, elementary triadic of self-positing pure thought was for Hegel, it forced him valiantly but unsuccessfully to defend the conceptually graspable character of these essentially ungraspable moments. Pure being was to have been the first moment *in* and of the movement of pure thought, whose culmination in the absolute Idea was itself to have been grounding return to the immediacy of being. Consistent with his own criteria, not only could Hegel not argue an adequate case for this initial and therefore paradigmatic triadic, but in not establishing logic's absolute beginning he could not defend the movement of self-mediating logical thought as he had conceived of it.[187]

The fundamental flaw in Hegel's self-positing and self-determining mediation or triadically structured absolute idealism lies in his misreading of subjectivity as a lacking which can be absolutized.[188] That such a lacking cannot be absolutized is exemplified in Hegel's comparison of the comprehension of a child who already understands a proverb to the enriched meaning that proverb has for the same person after a lifetime of experience.[189] The notions of progression and enrichment are important and valid insights, but they are always progression from a determinate beginning. Neither such an appeal merely by way of illustration (from which Hegel would of course not argue) to such a concrete experience of understanding the proverb nor Hegel's argumentation for the establishment of pure being as the beginning of pure thought can justify Hegel's unwarranted ontotheological extrapolation to subjectivity as initially determinationless. To claim that the determination of pure being is its determinationlessness attempts in fact to acknowledge this determinateness of all beginnings graspable in conceptual thought. However, as has been argued [190] this still fails to make pure being identifiable as first moment in and of conceptual thought. All beginnings are, in the public realm of thought, irrefutably determinate and particular, not universal.[191]

If beginnings as graspable in human thought are always irrefutably determinate, it is now possible to make a further attempt at unraveling the moves in Hegel's unsuccessfully deductively argued and retroactively grounded movement of absolute thought, which was for Hegel to have been the ontotheologically constitutive structural movement of reality.[192] With the use of thought determinations of reflection (*Reflexionsbestimmung*) treated by Hegel in the logic of essence,[193] his system can be summarized as an immanently developed movement from initial, positive moment of identity conceived as lacking to difference as negation of that lacking, to renewed and enriched identity containing the previous two as its moments. Hegel had tried systematically to begin with the indeterminate identity of the pure being of absolute thought. Such an attempt would indeed be ironically predictable, given the post-Kantian[194] philosophical climate rejecting the thing-in-itself, but a climate also conditioned especially by Fichte and Schelling. In fact this fundamentally flawed move to establish self-determining inclusive subjectivity out of an initial, determinationless moment was an unwarranted, though for Hegel systematically necessary, projection back to a logically prior and abstractly formulated originary unity as beginning. Hegel's projection back was an attempt to formulate in Concept and present in the public realm of discourse that unity or identity without which concrete difference could not, as he accurately saw, be adequately thought, that is, could not be truly mediated. But difference's not being able finally to be conceived without reference to some identity neither requires nor justifies positing an initial determinationless identity as logical momentary totality of the Concept. Beginning and *sine qua non* are not necessarily the same and in this case cannot be identified.

Once Hegel had proposed an initial moment of total determinationlessness, it was necessary for him to reestablish the determinateness from which he had abstracted in trying to identify the initial moment of lacking as first, determinationless moment of pure thought. Hegel's attempted reestablishment or as he called it positing (*Setzen*) of determinateness can be illustrated in its immediacy by calling to mind nothing, the explicitation of the determinationlessness of pure being. What

Hegel here in his retroactive evaluation viewed as the Concept's self-positing and self-determining was really the inevitable reacknowledgment of the determinateness of thought.[195] The moment of unity, now misplaced by Hegel in an initial and initiating originary position and positing role, needed then necessarily to posit an other defined as the negation of itself in order to reestablish by means of a logically sequential progression that from which Hegel had attempted to abstract.[196] In a general sense Hegel had correctly identified the "second" moment or difference as contradiction. But this contradiction will be seen to be not a self-positing but the self-contradiction of determinate being or finitude whose self-contradictory being would, when adequately thought through, lead to some resolution.[197] The third moment, the necessary, resultant negation of negation or Subject, was to be available as Concept. Here again Hegel mislocated in conceptual thought that mediating unity or identity without which he rightly felt difference could not be finally adequately thought. Neither the initial identity of pure being nor the first inclusive identity of becoming nor again the finally retroactively grounding absolute Idea is conceptually graspable in Concept, and certainly not in the way in which Hegel wanted and his system demanded. They cannot provide the self-mediation he proposed.

Hegel's structuring of an initial identity positing difference in pure thought seemed to permit him to integrate positivity into his understanding of the universal character of logical, conceptual thought. But this he accomplished only at the price of a necessitarian self-othering on the part of universality and a denigration of the finitude so evidently characteristic of thought. Hegel has not been able to conceptualize appropriately and convincingly that infinite truth without which he correctly saw that the finitude of human thought and its finite enrichment could not be fully grounded. Hegel's deductively argued trinitarian, triadically structured overall dialectical mediation from infinite to finite to infinite in fact presupposes an unthematized prior movement from finitude to infinity. Hegel's or any other attempt to build up a deductively argued system would first have to come to terms with this more fundamental movement of thought from finite to possible infinite. Deductively argued positions involving an infinite represent a second level of argumentation. They can function valuably as handy, often clearly statable summary expressions of what has been previously concluded to on the basis of the movement of thought from finitude to infinity. Arguing directly from a deductive position[198] not only presupposes a prior argument, but often runs the risk of distracting from and tending to obfuscate the original concern out of which and in response to which a position or system arose in the first place. Hegel's absolute logic, which would seem to be the most exhaustively developed and brilliantly constructed, systematically speaking deductively argued Western philosophical position, is particularly susceptible to this critique and risk.

The implications[199] of this critique of Hegel's logically reformulated triadically structured divine subjectivity and of the subsequent conclusion to the determinate nature of any beginning graspable in thought[200] for a theory of Trinity are immense. First, it is necessary to examine any trinitarian theory which begins from the infinite to see if that theory does not in fact either presuppose a prior argument and argumentation or if it simply settles for an unargued initial moment taken for granted. Or again it might simply presuppose an unthematized experience. In any of these cases there is the danger that such a trinitarian theory eventually will lapse into irrelevance because it does not subject itself to discussion in the public realm. Secondly, beginning from finitude opens the way to a resolution of the tension in Hegel's thought where he ultimately identifies freedom and necessity. The necessity that God be conceived by us in trinitarian fashion would lie in finitude's onesidedness and inability to ground itself, not in the need for the universal to other itself in order to come to itself in fullness. Third, establishing the beginning as *Dasein* or finitude or even more specifically the finitude of thought will later allow for an understanding of becoming as growth or development, as qualitative increment, and consequently eventually open the way for a more appropriate conception of development in the divine. Otherness would not be conceived primarily as negation but as occasion for enriching growth. Fourth, such a beginning opens up new perspectives out of which to use Hegel's convincing insights concerning God as inclusive totality in order to attempt to reconstruct Hegel's claim that God must be conceived as Trinity to be Spirit. Hegel's mistake lay not in envisioning God as inclusive totality or Spirit but in attempting to formulate this unity as a beginning graspable in conceptual thought. He erred in trying to establish a beginning whose determinateness was its being determinationless and which could as such posit itself as determinate.

Before working more directly in Part Three, Chapter Six of this study toward the sketching of a tentative reconstruction of Hegel's trinitarian claim on the basis of an elaboration of the argument presupposed by Hegel's systematic position, it is important to turn now to Hegel's texts dealing explicitly with trinitarian divine subjectivity. It is necessary to turn to these phenomenotheological texts because logic can no longer stand as initial positing moment in the encyclopedic system as Hegel meant it to. Logic must be returned to its finite context. Philosophical theology will arise then out of a reintegration of Hegel's logic and realphilosophical spheres.

Part Two

Hegel's Explicit Trinitarian Texts

3

Overview of Hegel's Explicit Trinitarian Thought and a Criterion for the *Phenomenology*

1. Transition to Hegel's Explicit Trinitarian Texts

A critique of the *Logic* already constitutes an examination of Hegel's logical reformulation of his understanding of the Christian doctrine of "immanent" Trinity.[1] Since this logical reformulation itself is equally the structure both of Trinity's "economic" self-realization in the sphere of religion and of "economic" Trinity's true philosophical expression in the form of the Concept as Self, this critique of Hegel's absolute logic is in principle as well a critique of these "economic" trinitarian developments. This is witnessed to by the very structure of the pedagogically oriented systematic outline Hegel presents of his thought in the various editions of the *Encyclopedia* and especially, for present purposes, by the last and fullest edition, that of 1830.[2] In the *Encyclopedia* absolute Spirit as Idea develops from the immediacy of logic to its self-othering in nature and finite Spirit and returns in philosophic thought to the renewed and enriched immediacy of the logical Idea.[3]

Nevertheless, the developmental structure of Hegel's encyclopedic system makes it equally imperative to turn directly to Hegel's "realphilosophical"[4] texts in order to effect an adequate critique of the particular form of Hegel's claim to a necessarily trinitarian divine subjectivity. The realphilosophical texts here in question are ones representative of those treating explicitly of Incarnation and Trinity. They are texts which themselves present, implicitly or explicitly, trinitarian reconciliation as an already philosophically informed representation (*Vorstellung*) of philosophical mediation.[5] The critical examination of explicit texts on

Incarnation and Trinity serves as a direct critique of Hegel's understanding of absolute Spirit on the level of religion. But in view both of this philosophical reinterpretation on the level of religion and of Hegel's overall proposal of a dialectical development from religion to philosophy characterizing variously the *Phenomenology*, *Lectures*[6] and *Encyclopedia*, this critical examination functions already equally as an indirect, though sufficient, evaluation of Hegel's final philosophical formulations on condition that Hegel has been unsuccessful in his logical argumentation as it appears on the level of religion.

The critical turn to specific realphilosophical texts is necessary on grounds internal to Hegel's own system, where truth is the movement of Spirit taken as a whole.[7] Truth is for Hegel fully realized only in the final moment of self-actualization, philosophic thought, which includes in sublated form the entire logical and "realhistorical" movement of self-positing and self-determining thought.[8] This final moment of philosophic truth arises already in terms of content in Hegel's earlier work, the *Phenomenology*, as revelatory religion (*die offenbare Religion*), in the philosophy of religion *Lectures* primarily as absolute or consummate religion (*die absolute, vollendete Religion*) and in the *Encyclopedia* as revealed religion (*die geoffenbarte Religion*).[9] For Hegel, through an appropriate interpretation on the level of religion and a fully adequate reformulation on the level of philosophy, "economic" Trinity contains "immanent" Trinity as sublated initial positing momentary totality. At the same time "economic" Trinity constitutes through philosophic thought a grounding return to that same "immanent" Trinity both in its realphilosophical elaboration and in its logical form, the dialectical identity of Subject and object, of form and content. Therefore, not only the external demands of a reasonably comprehensive examination of Hegel's mature thought but that very thought itself, as a progressive, teleological and circular movement constituting truth, requires a turn from logic to *Phenomenology* and especially philosophy of religion. That thought itself in its encyclopedic formulation *is* a movement from logic through philosophy of religion to the truth of philosophical thought where form and content are the same. There is for Hegel but one divine trinitarian Subject whose full self-realization both in finite Spirit and through finite Spirit's sublation in philosophic thought is absolute Spirit.

The teleological and circular, that is, syllogistic character of this movement of Spirit as Idea out of logic by way of understanding both justifies above in Part One (Chapters One and Two) the prolonged study of Hegel's *Logic* and now in Part Two calls for an examination of Hegel's explicit or realphilosophical trinitarian texts. The previous critique of Hegel's logic will, in these Chapters Three, Four and Five of Part Two, be applied from different points of view and with necessary adaptations and supplementation to Hegel's argumentation in selected realphilosophical texts. The present Chapter Three will, with reference to Hegel's *Encyclopedia*, underscore the consistent and constant syllogistic structure of Hegel's trinitarian speculation[10] from the *Phenomenology* of 1807[11] to the 1821-1831 Berlin philosophy of religion *Lectures*, while summarizing Hegel's specific distribution of *theologoumena* in the *Encyclopedia*. This Chapter Three will, secondly and more specifically, focus upon the nature of Hegel's first mature systematic work, the *Phenomenology*, in order to draw up an appropriate criterion for testing Hegel's argument in the *Phenomenology* which, as the first mature presentation of his formulation of syllogistic thought, constitutes for Hegel a trinitarian breakthrough. This criterion will be further adapted and applied in Chapter Four to Hegel's trinitarian position as argued in its incarnational immediacy. Chapter Five will zero in on Hegel's explicit syllogistic formulation of Trinity in a text representative of the various Berlin philosophy of religion *Lectures*. These Berlin *Lectures* are themselves not only representative of references to Trinity found scattered throughout Hegel's many other lectures but constitute the most appropriate level on which to examine that syllogistic formulation.[12] Phenomenotheological texts and, indirectly through them, the scientific philosophical texts in these particular works will be studied for two reasons: first, to see if Hegel brings in further arguments and argumentation to defend his trinitarian claim in the way in which he structures it; and, secondly, to gather information and conceptualities helpful for Chapter Six's initial attempt at reconstructing that claim.

2. Hegel's Syllogistically Structured Explicitly Trinitarian Thought

The self-development of the Idea to absolute Spirit is presented in the *Encyclopedia* as a syllogism whose members, namely, logic, nature, finite and absolute Spirit, are themselves each in their own way syllogisms so that philosophy in its encyclopedic presentation is "a circle of circles."[13] In its encyclopedic formulation, Hegel's philosophy of Spirit in particular appears, in its third and final overall totalization, as absolute Spirit, that is, as the unity of subjective and objective Spirit.[14] This highest sphere, absolute Spirit, can in general be termed "religion,"[15] though absolute Spirit is itself moreover the movement of the Concept first as art, then religion, specifically the revealed or Christian religion,[16] and philosophy as unity of art and religion, "the thinking and known Concept of art and religion."[17] Revealed religion, as moment of absolute Spirit, is presented by Hegel in schematic fashion in the form of a syllogistically structured "immanent" and "economic" self-revelation and self-development of trinitarian divine subjectivity.[18] With a properly nuanced understanding of Hegel's conception of God as the totality which is truth,[19] it can be said that, from the *Encyclopedia*'s first moment in the pure being of logical thought through to posited trinitarian divine subjectivity and this subjectivity's true formulation as Concept, the *Encyclopedia* presents for Hegel a movement of speculative theology.[20]

a. Aspects of Hegel's Notion of Syllogism

Before sketching Hegel's presentation of revealed religion as the syllogism of trinitarian divine subjectivity, it will be helpful to gather and highlight several aspects of Hegel's notion of syllogism (*Schluß*) itself.[21]

Already from the *Phenomenology* of 1807 on through to the *Encyclopedia* of 1830, that is, in the overall period of Hegel's mature system, there were no fundamental changes of direction but, rather, developments and clarifications in Hegel's essential conception and structuring of syllogism. Syllogism remained a triadically constructed progressively more adequate movement of self-mediation.[22] The position of syllogism in the larger and smaller *Logics* remained the third moment in the subjective logic, following Concept and judgement. Syllogism was, therefore, the unity or truth of Concept and judgement,[23] grounded judgement[24] and the fulfilled or completed self-grounding Concept.[25] Already on the basis of position it can be said that for Hegel syllogism expressed the full structure of inclusive subjectivity.[26] Its middle term was the empty "is" (*ist*) or copula of judgement now made explicit, full and given content.[27] Specifically, syllogism was for Hegel both a thought determination and equally a series of thought determinations or syllogisms, each made up of three "sentences" in the form of sublated judgements.[28] For Hegel syllogism consisted of three terms: the two extremes, namely a major and a minor,[29] plus a unifying middle term repeated in major and minor premises. The progressively more explicit interrelationship of the two extremes by means of the three possible middle terms and the progressively more explicit inclusion of extremes in the middle terms express for Hegel various possible configurations of Subject and object.[30] This increasingly adequate mediation or inclusion of the extremes in the middle term arrives for Hegel in the final and fullest syllogistic figure, the disjunctive syllogism, at the moment of complete self-mediation where there is "a coupling of the Subject not with an *other*, but with a *sublated* other, with *itself*."[31] Thus Hegel's theory of subjectivity comes to full structural expression in the disjunctive syllogism logically speaking before its ceasing to be syllogism in the renewed immediacy of its self-othering as object (*Objekt*).[32] Position and "what" cannot be distinguished in the movement of absolute logic. Position and content of syllogism are so important for Hegel that for him everything rational is ultimately a syllogism. "The syllogism is the *reasonable*, and *everything* reasonable."[33] So the totality of Hegel's thought is in one way or another contained in his notion of syllogism, a totalizing moment in the movement of absolute thought and not merely a theory of formal syllogistics. Hegel's syllogism was to be a tri-membered movement of becoming, a negation of negation, absolute negativity.[34] For Hegel syllogism without a third or middle term inclusive of the other two would remain unmediated judgement or difference, mere negation, and not the enriched reestablishment of the positive, that is, of the initial identity of the Concept. As completed syllogism, the Concept was for Hegel to grasp or comprehend itself as Subject.[35]

The Concept's comprehending itself as Subject occurred for Hegel in and through a dynamic and necessarily irreversible progression of ever more inclusive or more fully mediating middle terms.[36] In a progressively arranged series of syllogisms Hegel cast and recast the major, minor and middle terms, each in turn in terms of universality (*Allgemeinheit*, A), particularity (*Besonderheit*, B) and individuality (*Einzelheit*, E). A quick review of this series of syllogisms[37] reveals three genera or types (*Gattung*)[38] of syllogisms developed by Hegel in a specific order. First, the qualitative syllogism of *Dasein*, whose basic structure or common schema is E-B-A.[39] The syllogism of *Dasein* develops as a progression of three[40] syllogisms wherein each term successively functions as middle term in the order pervasively characteristic of Hegel's general presentation of middle terms as progressively more explicit instantiations of the concrete universal, B→E→A. As seen in the syllogism of *Dasein*'s general schema (E-B-A), in the syllogism of *Dasein* mediation occurs by means of an abstract particularity, so that "in this way the extremes are put as independent and without affinity either towards one another or towards the mean."[41] Secondly, the quantitative syllogism of reflection, whose overall schema is B-E-A.[42] The syllogism of reflection develops as a progression of three named syllogisms of allness, induction and analogy. Again in this second series each term successively plays the role of middle term in the characteristic order of B→E→A. In the syllogisms of reflection, mediation does not any longer occur by means of an abstract particularity. "Now it [the middle term] is posited as the *totality* of the determinations; as such it is the *posited* unity of the extremes."[43]

The third type of syllogism is the relational syllogism of necessity, whose basic structure or general schema is E-A-B.[44] The syllogism of necessity develops as a final progression of three named syllogisms, the categorical (E-B-A),[45] the hypothetical (A-E-B)[46] and the disjunctive (E-A-B),[47] which is finally no longer a syllogism. In the syllogism of necessity in general, but explicitly in the disjunctive syllogism, full mediation occurs by means of a fulfilled universality or middle term. "But the middle term is the *universality* that is *pregnant with form*; it has determined itself as *totality*, as *developed* objective universality. Consequently the middle term is not only universality but also particularity and individuality."[48] Again, in the overall syllogism of necessity the order of progression of middle terms is B→E→A, as is the case with the overall progression from one to another of the general schemas of the three types of syllogisms, namely of *Dasein*, reflection and necessity, as a whole. It is this middle term and its progressively more explicit inclusiveness or mediation of the extremes which is essential to Hegel's understanding of syllogism. This progression is consistent and constant among Hegel's various direct and indirect presentations of syllogism in *Logic*, *Phenomenology* and *Encyclopedia*. The extremes in turn are for Hegel both theoretically[49] and in practical working out[50] less fixed. They can be interchanged quite easily, even without changing the basic figure of an individual syllogism.[51] These syllogisms of *Dasein*, reflection and necessity and equally the three syllogistic figures constituting them can, then, in the richness of Hegel's thought be legitimately described or referred to in various ways. Taking their identification from the middle terms, both the three syllogisms of *Dasein*, reflection and necessity and their individual figures can respectively be spoken of as particularity (B), individuality (E) and universality (A).[52] From the perspective of the *specific characteristics* of these middle terms in each of the types of syllogisms and in each of the individual syllogism figures, the types and figures of syllogisms can each respectively be spoken of likewise as universality (A), particularity (B) and individuality (E). In this latter perspective, the ordering of syllogisms corresponds to Hegel's development of logical thought as a whole.[53] Then again, in line with the overall dialectical movement of Hegel's thought, the three types and three figures of syllogisms can each as well be referred to respectively as beginning, progression and result.[54] Or again, specifically in line with the movement of Hegel's logic of subjectivity, they can be referred to as Concept, judgement and syllogism.[55] With this richness and complexity of thought Hegel has proposed a necessarily triadic and syllogistically structured subjectivity. It is a subjectivity equally necessarily developed in an irreversible succession (B→E→A) on the basis of a progressively developed finally total interchangeability of mediating and mediated middle terms.[56]

b. Syllogistic Trinitarian Structure of Revealed Religion in the 1830 Encyclopedia

Now to sketch[57] Hegel's presentation of revealed religion in the 1830 *Encyclopedia*[58] as a series of self-mediating syllogisms, namely a movement of syllogistic trinitarian divine subjectivity. In eight extremely tightly constructed paragraphs[59] Hegel develops his understanding of the true religion on the basis of the interrelationship between the notions of revelation and of true religion's content being absolute Spirit. "It lies essentially in the notion of true religion,—the religion, i.e., whose content is absolute Spirit—that it be *revealed*, and, what is more, revealed *by God.*"[60] For Hegel true content and revelation merge in that for God as Spirit revelation becomes divine self-revelation.[61] Substance determines itself as Spirit; that is, absolute Spirit manifests itself.[62] Though for Hegel the content of revealed religion is true, namely, absolute Spirit, "in point of form absolute Spirit exists first for the subjective knowing of *representation.*[63] This means that for religious representation the moments of absolute Spirit take on an independent and sequential character. Though these characteristics are, even on the level of religion, already sublated in faith and cult,[64] nevertheless the representational form involved results in the presentation of these moments as particular spheres or elements. After summarizing in more conceptual terms the three spheres in which absolute Spirit reveals itself,[65] Hegel employs a more explicit, religiously representational but nevertheless always conceptually informed language[66] to lay out the three moments of universality (A), particularity (B) and individuality (E) in their corresponding spheres.[67] Finally, by means of an enriched understanding of revelation as the mediated resultant return of Spirit to itself, Hegel concludes to a return not only to the simplicity of faith and cult but now to that of thought (*Denken*). The true content of God as mediated and mediating, reconciling Spirit in revealed religion advances to the enriched simplicity of the Subject as self-determining philosophical Concept. "In this form of truth, truth is the object of *philosophy*."[68]

This transition from religion to philosophy was for Hegel one to the resultant simplicity of the philosophical Concept, a transition from the religious syllogisms of reason.[69] Hegel himself is cited in his *Lectures on the History of Philosophy* as saying concerning God, "But the concrete is, that God is a syllogism, which brings itself together with itself."[70] Hegel stated explicitly though parenthetically in an 1829 book review that his thought on Trinity (*Dreieinigkeitslehre*, as the author of the book in question had referred to Hegel's thought) was a "syllogism of absolute self-mediation, which [syllogism] is made up of three syllogisms."[71] In the last paragraph on revealed religion in the 1830 *Encyclopedia* Hegel uses basically the same expression as he had in the 1829 book review to summarize the trinitarian movement of divine self-revelation. In the *Encyclopedia* Hegel explicitly refers to the three syllogisms of individuality[72] and through them to the overall syllogistic trinitarian movement from universality through particularity to individuality.[73] "These three syllogisms, constituting the one syllogism of the absolute self-mediation of Spirit, are the revelation of that Spirit, whose life is set out as a cycle of concrete shapes in representational thought."[74]

Hegel's encyclopedic presentation of revealed religion, as syllogistically structured phenomenotheological spheres of universality, particularity and individuality,[75] progresses according to Hegel's characteristic pattern of syllogisms in general (A-B-E [E-B-A], B-E-A, E-A-B)[76] and especially of middle terms (B→E→A) in particular. These syllogistically structured spheres are, each in its own way, the true content of absolute Spirit present in revealed religion as absolute divine Subject.[77] They are such in a general sense similarly to the way in which each thought determination in the movement of logic or absolute thought is itself, on its own level, the momentary totality of that movement.[78]

In the Introduction to the *Logic* Hegel had spoken of the mutuality between the formal structure of logic and the reality of the concrete sciences or realphilosophical spheres. The realities or realizations in these spheres contain the logical thought determinations as "inner formative principle" (*innern Bildner*). These logical thought determinations in turn constituted for Hegel the non-temporal "archetypes" (*Vorbildner*) of the realities in the realphilosophical spheres.[79] Appropriately, syllogism serves for Hegel as the overall logical determination arising out of, realized in and therefore structuring, on the level of revealed religion, the spheres of universality, particularity and individuality as the movement or self-revelation of absolute Spirit as Subject—God. More specifically, these three spheres on the level of religion are best seen neither merely as realizations of the general progression of Hegel's overall syllogistic schema,[80] nor of the wider syllogistic types of *Dasein*, reflection and necessity.[81] Rather, because of the explicit presence in each religious sphere of the true content of revealed religion, that is, of absolute Spirit as Subject or totality, it is more accurate to consider these trinitarian spheres in general, and the three syllogisms structuring the sphere of individuality in particular, as the realizations or instantiations of the three named syllogisms of necessity, namely, successively categorical, hypothetical and disjunctive syllogisms.[82] In these three syllogisms of necessity the middle term more adequately expresses and more correctly corresponds to the true content of revealed religion, Spirit as absolute subjectivity. This is so because each of the middle terms is in its own way in the progression B→E→A already explicitly totality or concrete universality inclusive of the extremes,[83] and thus for Hegel the true structure of subjectivity.

Further summaries of the specific and somewhat varying religiously represented content of extremes and middle terms of Hegel's syllogistically structured understanding of Trinity and reconciling or mediating middle terms will be given later on, and this on the basis of Hegel's first fully developed presentation in the 1807 *Phenomenology* and Hegel's philosophy of religion *Lectures*.[84] Of present interest is the sketching of the *Encyclopedia*'s overview primarily of the syllogistically structured progression of mediating middle terms in the three religious spheres of universality, particularity and individuality.[85]

Hegel describes the first sphere, that of universality, or more explicitly theologically speaking "immanent" Trinity, as a self-contained movement in which "the absolute content presents itself, a) as eternal content remaining with[in] itself in its manifestation."[86] As realization of the first or categorical syllogism of necessity,[87] the sphere of universality appears as the syllogistically structured movement A-B-E.[88] The first extreme is universality (A) because absolute Spirit as presupposed (*das Vorausgesetzte*) is precisely the indeterminacy of an as yet unposited universality. Absolute Spirit "in this eternal sphere . . . only begets *itself* as its Son"[89] (particularity B). Absolute Spirit, however, in this differentiation as Son "eternally sublates itself and through [this self-mediation] the first substance is essentially as *concrete individuality* and subjectivity—is the *Spirit*"[90] (individuality E). This syllogistically structured movement of "immanent" Trinity both reveals the logical foundation *for* and summarizes the phenomenological progression *from* eternal essence to real or externalized self-othering and consequent reconciliation.

The transition from the sphere of universality to that of particularity, from "immanent" Trinity to the self-externalization of creation and "in principle" redemptive Incarnation, makes manifest the inner self-othering within the sphere of universality. This transition from the sphere of universality to that of particularity equally results out of sublation of this inner self-othering into individuality, with individuality as enriched resultant return to the immediacy of universality.[91] (This is a sublation into individuality, which had of course occurred initially within the sphere of universality.) For Hegel, absolute content now presents itself in the sphere of particularity "as differentiation of the eternal essence from its manifestation, which by this difference becomes the phenomenal world into which the content enters."[92] As realization of the second or hypothetical syllogism of necessity, this sphere of particularity conforms to the syllogistically structured movement A-E-B[93] or better, A-E/E-B, with the doubled middle term indicating the hypothetical syllogism's openness to the multiplicity characteristic of individuality as middle term.[94] This doubling of the self-othering or middle term is always the distinguishing structural characteristic of the second moment in Hegel's mature formulation of his dialectical movement.[95] The first extreme is the sphere of universality;[96] "it is this concrete eternal being which is presupposed."[97] The doubled middle terms are "the breaking down . . . of the eternal Son into the independent opposition on the one hand . . . of . . . concrete nature, [and] on the other hand . . . of *finite* Spirit"[98] (individuality E/E). Spirit is finite indeed because of this opposition to nature. By defining evil as finite Spirit's both making itself and remaining independent[99] over against nature "and existing through its own therewith posited naturalness, yet amid that naturalness it [finite

Spirit] is, when it thinks, directed towards the eternal."[100] This reminder, that finite Spirit is "when it thinks, directed towards the eternal," taken together with the entrance of true content into the world of appearance[101] provides or indicates thought and therefore in principle the overcoming of the opposition to nature as second extreme (particularity B). In principle, redemptive incarnation occurs for Hegel in the *Encyclopedia* already in absolute Spirit's return to itself in finite Spirit as thought.

Though finite Spirit, as that which thinks, establishes in principle the overcoming of self-independent otherness or evil, as a relating to the eternal, this same finite Spirit remains external in the moment of particularity.[102] In the 1830 *Encyclopedia* the life, death and resurrection of the mediator are in fact and explicitly presented by Hegel in the third moment, that of individuality.[103] Stated in more conceptual terms, in this moment absolute content appears "c) as infinite return and reconciliation of the externalized world with the eternal being, the returning of the eternal from appearance into the unity of its fullness."[104] This third moment, individuality, is itself the unifying ground of universality and particularity,[105] internal reconciliation. For Hegel the moment of individuality is itself a movement of three syllogisms with middle terms sequenced B→E→A, a tri-syllogistic structure recapitulating, completing and grounding the movement of divine self-revelation.[106] Thus the extreme importance of this third moment for any critique of Hegel's thought on Trinity.[107]

This third moment, individuality, is in the *Encyclopedia* the concrete universality of the Concept realized progressively more inclusively and concretely in three stages.[108] Hegel gives each of these stages or realizations of individuality an appropriate syllogistic structure. The first bears the structure again of the categorical syllogism (E-B-A). The first extreme in this categorical syllogism is the sensible immediacy of the Mediator (individuality E): "as *presupposition* the *universal* substance . . . actualized into an *individual* self-consciousness."[109] The mediating middle term is particularization of the Mediator carried even to the negativity of death (particularity B): "this . . . sensible existence . . . placing itself in judgement and expiring in the pain of negativity."[110] The second extreme is the universalization of this particular self-consciousness in the moment of death, a movement from immediate Self to Spirit (universality A): "it [the absolute concrete] as infinite subjectivity identical with itself . . . as *absolute return* . . . has realized its being *for itself*,—the idea of Spirit as eternal but alive and present in the world.[111] With this first absolute return, mediating concrete universality has exhibited the characteristic of, and in fact is, an immediate individual consciousness, that is, particularity (B), so that this first syllogism bears the overall characteristic of particularity.

The second of these three syllogisms constituting the overall moment of individuality is structured as the movement of a hypothetical syllogism (A-E-B). The first extreme (universality A) is the life, death and resurrection-to-Spirit of the Mediator as an other over against and intuited by the finite immediacy of the individual: "his objective totality [the Idea of the eternal, but . . . present Spirit] is the *presupposition* existing in itself for the *finite* immediacy of the individual subject, for which [it exists as] an *other* and *intuited*, but the intuition of truth existing *in itself*."[112] The middle term is this finite Subject, which perceives itself first on the basis of its immediacy as evil and then as believer in view of the example of the Mediator, dies to itself (individuality E):[113]

> it [the finite subject], on account of its immediate nature, at first characterizes itself as nought and evil, and further according to the example of its truth, by means of faith . . . is also the movement to throw off its immediate determination as nature and . . . to close itself in unity with that example in the pain of negativity.[114]

By means of this second use of death or the pain of negativity as middle term, that is, the identification in faith of the finite individual with the death of the Mediator, the finite individual is the movement "thus to recognize itself as united with the essential being"[115] (second extreme, particularity B). With this second return, mediating concrete universality has progressed to exhibit the characteristic of and occur in the immediate individual consciousness of the believer qua individual, that is individuality (E), so that this second syllogism bears the overall characteristic of universality as individuality.[116]

The final reconciling syllogism of the moment of individuality bears the structure of the disjunctive syllogism (B-A-E), in which universality, as explicitly posited mediating and mediated middle term, indicates the sublated presence of otherness. The other is now the Self posited as other, that is, the sublation of mediation,[117] still of course for Hegel within the realm of religious representation. The first extreme (particularity B) is the mediation attained in the Mediator and available to the individual believer: "through this mediation."[118] The middle term or reconciling and mediating universality (A) is the indwelling effected by absolute Spirit (here *Wesen*) in self-consciousness: "which [being] brings about its own indwelling in self-consciousness."[119] Finally, the second extreme is the concrete universal as totality, inclusive individuality (E): "which [being] . . . is the actual presence of Spirit which exists in and for itself as the universal."[120] With this return of absolute Spirit to itself, that is, both the third return in the moment of individuality and the final return on the level of religion, revelation has come to be seen as the effective self-revelation of absolute Spirit in and through finite Spirit in community.[121] Mediating universality has come to posit itself as the totality which is concrete universality, so that this third syllogism bears, from the point of view of its middle term, the overall characteristic of universality.[122]

The universality of this disjunctive syllogism of community represents the final moment of syllogistically structured divine trinitarian self-revelation, the movement of self-positing divine subjectivity as yet not explicitly established as the absolute Self or Concept in philosophic thought. Hegel has here, on the level of religion, proposed what he considered to be a necessarily triadic and syllogistically structured divine trinitarian self-revelation. This divine self-revelation was for Hegel a progressively more explicit movement of reconciliation, a tri-membered negation of negation or movement of becoming in which alienation was to be overcome appropriately in each third moment of each of the divine spheres of universality, particularity and individuality. Without this multiple return there would for Hegel have been no true inclusion of extremes in a final, mediated and mediating middle term, that is, no recognition of God as Subject, of finite Spirit as in principle reconciled and, finally, of absolute Spirit coming through the death of the Mediator to itself in and through community. This reconciling divine self-revelation was for Hegel a movement of triadically structured self-positing and self-determining divine Subjectivity necessarily developed in an irreversible succession (B→E→A) on the basis of a progressively developed total interchangeability of extremes and mediating and mediated middle terms. In the *Encyclopedia* these middle terms structure the progression (B→E→A) Hegel consistently follows throughout his realphilosophical texts. According to their religious representation in the *Encyclopedia* these middle terms were successively the eternal Son, the doubled reality of nature and individual finite consciousness, and the triply staged universalization of that finite consciousness in the death of the Mediator, the individual believer's identification in faith with that death and the community's being constituted by Spirit present in self-consciousness.

This progression of mediated and mediating middle terms in the syllogistically structured moments of universality, particularity and individuality provides, from the point of view of the *Encyclopedia*, an overview of Hegel's philosophically informed presentation of "immanent" and "economic" Trinity. Chapter One and especially Chapter Two above have already appropriately laid out a critique of Hegel's understanding of the moment of universality as "immanent" Trinity in its logical reformulation. Chapter Five will provide an assessment of Hegel's development of "economic" Trinity in the extremely important final moment, that of individuality, by critiquing its explicitly syllogistic formulation as disjunctive syllogism of the community. In Chapter Five this will be done appropriately on the level of religion by approaching a specific text in Hegel's 1827 philosophy of religion lectures. Chapter Four will assess Hegel's presentation of the "economic" trinitarian moment of particularity in the directness of its presentation in the *Phenomenology*, an especially appropriate text, as the implicit syllogism (A-E-B) of incarnational immediacy. However, it will now be helpful in the next sections of this present Chapter Three first to set the stage for Chapter Four by focusing on what the *Phenomenology* is in order to draw up an adequate criterion for then evaluating in Chapter Four the success of Hegel's argument to the incarnational immediacy of the divine as finite Self, an argument to the implicit syllogism of incarnational immediacy.[123]

3. Guiding Concerns in Approaching the *Phenomenology*

The *Phenomenology*[124] can broadly be described as Hegel's initially intended history of the experience of self-consciousness (*Selbstbewußtsein*). It is a history which itself in the course of its writing evolved for Hegel necessarily,[125] without denial of its fundamental purpose, into an explicit phenomenology of Spirit. In the "Introduction," written before the body of the *Phenomenology* (that is, about 1805), Hegel had spoken of the "science of the *experience of consciousness*."[126] In the "Preface," written probably in early 1807 and certainly after the *Phenomenology* text itself was completed, Hegel described the *Phenomenology* as follows:

It is this coming-to-be of *Science as such* or of *knowledge*, that is described in this *Phenomenology* of Spirit. Knowledge in its first phase, or *immediate Spirit*, is the non-spiritual, i.e. *sense-consciousness*. In order to become genuine knowledge, to beget the element of Science which is the pure Concept of Science itself, it must travel a long way and work its passage.[127]

The *Phenomenology* can for present purposes be considered a basically unified text presenting the course of the phenomenological appearance of Spirit as self-positing movement of thought in the form of a history of the experience of consciousness rising to self-consciousness, a form continuing through to and including the moment of absolute knowledge.[128] In this way the *Phenomenology* presents absolute Spirit's consciousness of itself.[129]

Hegel's *Phenomenology* forms the first clear and developed statement of his mature dialectic. It shares in all the strengths and ambiguities attendant upon what was, in a real sense, a "first work"[130] written in trying circumstances.[131] It represents for Hegel a breakthrough in that here for the first time he came truly to center upon negativity as motivating dialectical force.[132] With his understanding of determinate negation, that is, negation as other of the other, Hegel was then able clearly to articulate the triadically structured movement of self-determining syllogistic[133] subjectivity[134] understood as absolute negativity[135] and self-mediation.[136] Already in the *Phenomenology*'s Introduction Hegel had written what was as negation of negation to become the mature *Logic*'s methodological clarion call:[137]

> However nothing is in fact the true result only when it is taken as the nothing of that out of which it has emerged; it is itself thereby *determinate* and has a *content*. . . . When . . . the result is conceived as it is in truth, as *determinate* Negation, a new form has thereby immediately arisen.[138]

Self-positing and self-determining trinitarian subjectivity syllogistically structured according to this notion of determinate negation will be seen to be for Hegel revelatory religion's true content expressed in the inadequate and even hindering form of representation.[139] This content will find immediate expression in the Incarnation and explicit development in Hegel's "immanent" and "economic" trinitarian thought.[140] Content and form become according to Hegel truly mutually adequate in absolute knowing (*das absolute Wissen*), where Self, Concept and content are identical. The object is recognized as Self, and the Self as Concept.

> This last shape of Spirit—the Spirit which at the same time gives its complete and true content the form of the Self and thereby realizes its Concept, while remaining in its Concept in this realization—this is absolute knowing; it is the Spirit knowing itself in the shape of Spirit, or comprehensive knowing.[141]

In this final and inclusive moment of absolute knowing Hegel will have stated his basic systematic response to the earlier mentioned problem of alienation.[142]

After Hegel's death the *Phenomenology* with its response to the problem of alienation became the most disputed of his works.[143] The *Phenomenology* is of present concern here only in regard to the possible viability and value of that response or answer which, according to Hegel, took the form of an appropriation and philosophical reformulation of the Christian doctrines of Trinity and Trinity's phenomenological presupposition, Incarnation. Other much discussed questions will remain in the background. Among these: the *Phenomenology*'s historico-systematic composition and development;[144] its relationship and comparison to other contemporary attempts to develop a history of consciousness;[145] its relation as well to the encyclopedic system including the *Logic*;[146] the detailed argumentation concerning the *Phenomenology*'s internal unity, a unity increasingly acknowledged in Hegel scholarship and here accepted;[147] the historically typical variant interpretations of the *Phenomenology*;[148] Hegel's own varying attitude toward the *Phenomenology*.[149] Such questions as these will be referred to only obliquely and to the extent that such might be necessary to critique the pertinent Hegelian texts on revelatory religion. Here, as with this study's concern in approaching "realphilosophical" texts in general,[150] there is a double interest. First, to evaluate in this breakthrough text the viability of Hegel's argumentation for his trinitarian claim and, secondly, to garner from this first work hopefully more easily available insights of value for a later initial restatement and reconstruction of that claim in Part Three, Chapter Six.

4. Toward a Criterion for Critiquing the *Phenomenology*

Criteria for an internal critique of Hegel's works in general must arise out of what Hegel in fact wrote, from the project he proposed to carry through and what he understood himself to be doing at the time of the writing itself. Applied specifically to the *Phenomenology*, this mandates reference to what Hegel wrote in the texts immediately to be studied, to the project proposed in the *Phenomenology*'s Introduction and to his own reflexive self-evaluation in the Preface taken together with the concluding chapter, "Absolute Knowledge," which the Preface presupposes. Criteria must arise out of the *Idee* of the *Phenomenology*.[151] This focusing is especially important for the argument which constitutes the *Phenomenology* both in order to address Hegel's real position from within and because of his shifting attitude through the years toward the *Phenomenology* and its significance. This "first work" and breakthrough text had taken on for Hegel many of the characteristics of a first love. Though he could both reinterpret its function and significance and distance himself somewhat from the text, he still referred to it time and again at least for examples.[152] He could never forget it. At the end of his life in the Fall of 1831, Hegel had come so far as to write in preparation for a second edition, "Characteristic earlier work, do not rework,—relative to the time during which it was composed—in Preface: *the abstract Absolute* ruled then."[153]

Reference now to the *Phenomenology*'s Introduction and Preface, along with its last chapter, "Absolute Knowledge," will eventually facilitate more focused and restricted treatment of pertinent texts in the body of the *Phenomenology* itself. But first it can be helpful to compare quickly the *Phenomenology* with the already critiqued *Logic* in order to highlight the distinctive considerations required by what the *Phenomenology* was generally meant to be.

Summarily stated, the *Logic* was intended to be and was written as a movement of pure thought, as a logical progression of thought determinations, each of which was the momentary totality of that pure thought.[154] The internal criterion for critiquing the movement of absolute logic was, then, whether or not such thought determinations and in particular the first moment of pure being could be conceptually grasped in sublated but not annihilated human thought.[155]

When compared with that of the *Logic*, internal criteria for judging the success or failure of Hegel's argumentation in the *Phenomenology* prove somewhat more complex. The *Phenomenology* has been preliminarily described[156] as the history of consciousness coming to self-consciousness, a history recognized as a phenomenology of Spirit, and thus the *Dasein* of absolute Spirit's self-development.[157] It is the movement of thought not in its logical purity but in the form of a logically structured development of self-consciousness.[158] Correspondingly then, whereas in the *Logic* Hegel spoke of the development of thought determinations as pure, non-temporal "moments," in the *Phenomenology* he generally refers to a phenomenologically observed and varyingly, from the points of view of absolute knowledge and of the phenomenologist, logically necessary[159] succession of "shapes" or "figures" (*Gestalt*) of consciousness.[160] These as wider configurations in turn contain moments within them.[161] Parallel to the momentary totalities of logic, these shapes of consciousness are successive totalizations of the entire phenomenological movement. They can, however, be adequately defined only in relation to the *Phenomenology*'s other shapes of consciousness.[162] In contradistinction to the identity of form and content in the logical moments,[163] in these shapes of consciousness content and form[164] are adequate to one another only in the enriched immediacy of the final shape or figure, that of absolute knowing where content, Concept and Self are the same.[165] Broadly stated, then, any criteria as to the viability of Hegel's specific argumentation in the *Phenomenology* must of necessity refer to the interplay[166] between object (*Gegenstand*) and consciousness in the increasing mutual adequacy of content and form. Such criteria must include reference to the relationship in consciousness between content and form as this relationship expresses in any given shape and in a way appropriate to that shape the there realized logical form or structure of the Self as Spirit.[167]

a. The Introduction: The Science of the Experience of Self-consciousness

More specifically, criteria are to be established on the basis of Hegel's own understanding of consciousness and its development. This understanding is expressed in a more systematic-logical and reflexive vein by Hegel in the post-*Phenomenology* Preface together with the *Phenomenology*'s last chapter, but especially and first of all in the second half of the Introduction, the whole of which was written before the *Phenomenology* itself and from a more hermeneutic or "epistemological" perspective.[168] Here Hegel begins from, and in the *Phenomenology* then deals with, the structure of "consciousness as such" (*Bewußtsein überhaupt*).[169] He argues in the Introduction from what he considers to be the indisputable phenomenal characteristic of consciousness as that which distinguishes and relates. "Consciousness *distinguishes* itself from something, and at the same time *relates* itself to it."[170] Hegel's very discussion of this consciousness shows that even from the beginning, in the immediacy of sense certainty,[171] he is handling consciousness as available to or taken up into discursive thought. In this handling, which is the *Phenomenology*, there are for Hegel then three distinguishable instances of consciousness.[172] First there is that of natural consciousness, which represents any given era's level of education. It is an understanding rather than a reasoning consciousness,[173] and is often indicated by "for it[self]" (*für es*) in Hegel's *Phenomenology* text. Second, that of the phenomenologist or reader who sees but does not add to the necessary movement from one shape or moment of consciousness to the next. This is at times explicitly indicated by "for us" (*für uns*) in Hegel's text.[174] Thirdly, there is that of the author of the *Phenomenology*, the point of view of absolute knowledge.[175] To each of these instances corresponds a particular logicity: immediate; phenomenological; and speculative.[176] Hegel's goal in the *Phenomenology* is to reconcile and unite these three instances of consciousness and their corresponding logicities.[177]

Hegel's Introduction insufficiently stresses that the uniting of these three instances of consciousness has, in an as yet unreflected manner, already taken place[178] in the immediacy of the Subject-object unity which constitutes for Hegel the initial moment of consciousness as sense certainty.[179] Within the dynamic progression of distinguishing and relating, that is, within consciousness from sense certainty on, Hegel somewhat surprisingly terms that to which consciousness is related, or conversely that which is related to consciousness, "knowing" (*Wissen*). This is his famous "for itself" (*für sich*, or also *für es*),[180] and is also called "for a consciousness" or "for an other."[181] Consciousness as it is distinguished from this "knowing" is referred to by Hegel as "in itself" (*an sich*) or "truth" (*Wahrheit*).[182] So truth is both the "in itself" and also most properly the correspondence between knowing and the truth of consciousness or the "in itself," that is, "in and for itself."[183] This dynamic correspondence takes place for Hegel totally within consciousness. "Consciousness provides its own criterion from within itself, so that the investigation becomes a comparison of consciousness with itself; for the distinction made above falls within it."[184]

As can already be gathered from this preceding quote, there are three implications flowing from the locating of this distinction within consciousness itself: first, the particular type of object (*Gegenstand*) in question, consciousness itself;[185] second, the establishment of a measure or criterion of truth within consciousness itself; third, the question as to whether this distinction within consciousness can, as Hegel proposes, ground a real unity of Subject and object.[186] In response to this last point, Hegel argues not at first sight fully convincingly that such is only an apparent problem. The distinction between knowledge and essence or criterion falls within the unity of consciousness. With the acknowledgement of an initial unity of consciousness, natural consciousness comes to be seen as the same as consciousness *für uns*, as our phenomenological consciousness or even equally consciousness as such (*überhaupt*). It is eventually as well for Hegel to be seen to be the speculative consciousness of the author. Supposedly, then, the phenomenologist or reader can and need merely see and adds nothing to the movement of consciousness itself.[187]

Hegel terms this dialectical[188] movement of consciousness "experience" (*Erfahrung*). "*Inasmuch as the new object issues from it*, this *dialectical* movement which consciousness exercises on itself, on its knowledge as well as on its object, is precisely what is called *experience*."[189] The dynamic structure of this movement giving rise to new content in the form of more adequate shapes of consciousness, this movement of consciousness itself, is described in the Introduction as the realization that negation is always negation of something. For Hegel result is determinate negation. This dialectical structure of determinate negation is the dynamic which powers and is in itself "The Progression to True Knowledge."[190] So determinate negation is for Hegel the dynamic of the dialectical movement of consciousness's self-experience in the arising of new objects.[191] As was the case with logical thought,[192] so too this self-movement of content[193] is characterized by immanence and consistency. Immanent in that the shapes of consciousness are actually to arise out of one another without either external addition or assistance.[194] Consistent in that the new content as resultant shape is to be accounted for only by its determination through the realization that negation is negation of something, through determinate negation. This immanent and consistent dialectic of the experience of consciousness is the underlying reason why for Hegel consciousness can have its own measure within itself.[195] Not only does this presence of an adequate measure within consciousness reduce the role of phenomenologist to that of "observer,"[196] but this role of the phenomenologist is so circumscribed ultimately by the very nature and functioning of the dialectic of determinate negation itself.

b. Preface and Last Chapter: The Phenomenological Self-manifestation of Absolute Spirit

Hegel discusses this immanent and consistent dialectic of the experience of consciousness again in the Preface,[197] a pivotal text pointing back to the *Phenomenology* and forward both to Hegel's envisioned system and in particular to the future *Science of Logic*. In the Preface Hegel again takes up the Introduction's important points concerning the development of consciousness.[198] Though the two treatments are clearly in basic agreement as to the structure and dynamic of consciousness, the Preface is written from and handles consciousness and knowing from the point of view of a more developed speculative dialectic.[199] This is witnessed to by the very terminology Hegel employs in the Preface, with special emphasis on such terms as "form" (*Form*) and "content" (*Inhalt*).[200] This Preface has indeed profited from being written after the *Phenomenology*'s last chapter, "Absolute Knowledge," which it presumes. In the Preface, texts treating directly of consciousness place greater emphasis on the phenomenon of the self-development of shapes of consciousness precisely as successive concrete realizations of specific logical categories.[201] For Hegel this succession of figures of consciousness now clearly constitutes the logically structured self-development of absolute Spirit in the *Dasein* of its existing phenomenal immediacy, consciousness.[202] They are now shapes of Spirit in the form of figures of consciousness.[203]

It is important again to recall that in the *Phenomenology*'s final shape of Spirit, that is in absolute knowledge, content and form, object and Subject are one in the dialectical identity of the Concept, which is Self.[204] This is important because Hegel's understanding of the relationship between form and content in the *Phenomenology* is ultimately dependent on this identification. The identity of Self is in fact for Hegel an enriched return to the originary simplicity and immediacy of sense certainty.[205] The progression from sense certainty, the initial shape of consciousness or Spirit, to absolute knowledge consists in the recurrent arising within consciousness of otherness as negation and the sublation of that otherness in the realization that it is negation of its other, that it is determinate negation.[206]

This dialectic of determinate negation has already been discussed with reference to the pulsation of pure or logical thought.[207] In logical thought, on the one hand, this is a movement of pure or absolute form which for Hegel can equally be referred to as content. The thought determinations themselves are content, so that their logical development can in its entirety be described also as content. Secondly and more specifically, content refers to the Concept's self-othering or the second moment, that of negation, taken together with the enriched return to immediacy through negation of negation. Since for Hegel logical thought as such is not characterized by opposition, this second meaning or use of content need be considered only implicitly twofold. Such does not deny that the second and third moments are logically fully distinct, but rather indicates that content is properly established in the dialectical move from second to third moments.[208] On the other hand, in consciousness, which is for Hegel characterized by opposition, this second meaning of content is to be distinguished explicitly. Second and third dialectical moments are each in their own way to be spoken of as content. This, coupled with Hegel's final identification of form and content in Concept or Self, results in an at least threefold predication of content in reference to the movement of consciousness. First of all, what Hegel has termed the object, the "for itself" and knowledge is content because it is that which is related, what is known.[209] Second, content is what can best be expressed as objectivity.[210] This is the third dialectical moment, what Hegel refers to as "in and for itself," truth (*Wahrheit* as correspondence), determinate negation or result. This third moment constitutes the arising of a new and inclusive shape of consciousness.[211] Third, content refers to the absolute Self, the unity of Subject and object, the true content in its true form.[212]

The absolute Self is the true content in its adequate form. Technically speaking, Hegel always uses the term "form" in reference to Self.[213] But for present purposes it can be said that there are two important senses in which form is verified or realized in the *Phenomenology*. First, form refers to the absolute Self, which is the pure form of the Concept.[214] Secondly, form can be used to indicate the immediacy of Self or certainty in its experience of opposition, which latter is then for Hegel the negativity characteristic of otherness.[215] This second use of form, the initial dialectical moment of immediacy, is described by Hegel as "in itself," truth and measure. It is related to its object as form is to content. These two distinguishable, but ultimately for Hegel in absolute knowledge reconcilable, uses of form recall Hegel's double relationship of form *to* content and form *within* content developed in the *Logic*.[216]

However, whereas in logical thought content is subsumed in form, which is its own content, in consciousness it is content which for Hegel is to be given priority until the final figure. For natural consciousness and phenomenological knowledge, form is dependent on content, although to scientific knowledge, that of the author, content is form as yet simply inadequately mediated. Content is then given a priority, first, in that each figure as totality is for consciousness not as such a new form but a new content.[217] Secondly, it is content which, qua other of form, provides the dialectical force in the changing relationship of opposition between "in itself" and "for itself."[218] The new object changes consciousness "in itself"; it thus according to Hegel calls forth a more adequate form, since a change in what is known requires a change in that which knows. So each new object or content gives rise to a new figure of consciousness, a new objectivity. This objectivity in turn contains form within it as the moment of immediacy though, until the moment of absolute knowledge, consciousness remains unaware of this as the still implicit presence of absolute Self as Self. For Hegel the figures of consciousness succeeding one another are increasingly adequate configurations of and interrelationships between form and content. Form and content are related in each figure according to the logical structure of Spirit appropriate to the specific figure in question.

5. A Criterion for Hegel's Argument in the *Phenomenology*

These remarks concerning the interrelationship of form and content are based on Hegel's Introduction and Preface taken in conjunction with the *Phenomenology*'s last chapter, "Absolute Knowledge." This doubled survey acknowledges Hegel's development from his intended science of the experience of consciousness to a phenomenology of Spirit, that is, Spirit whose appearance occurs in a series of ever more adequate shapes of consciousness. At the same time, it becomes clear that Hegel's basic intention remains the same throughout the *Phenomenology*: to argue to a necessary elevation of natural consciousness, characterized for Hegel by opposition, to the overcoming of that opposition in the self-relatedness of absolute knowledge.[219] This basic intention and the *Phenomenology*'s consequent overall unity ground the possibility of a fundamental and fair general criterion with which to evaluate the success of Hegel's argumentation. The immanent and consistent dialectic constituting the dynamic appearance of Spirit in consciousness as ever more adequate configurations of form and content forms the material out of which such an internal criterion is to be formulated.

On the basis of Hegel's intention to establish an immanently and consistently developed dialectic of the phenomenological appearance of Spirit in the form of successive figures of consciousness, it is now possible to draw up an internal criterion. This criterion can be stated in the form of a question, and first very generally: Is it possible to argue convincingly in discursive[220] thought on the basis of content alone to a necessary movement from natural consciousness to absolute knowledge? This general question can be further specified with reference to the three levels of consciousness functioning for Hegel in the *Phenomenology*. Since for natural consciousness content as object is simply to appear and is experienced without reference to movement or origin,[221] the more loosely stated criterion can be further nuanced by asking if in fact the object to have arisen does indeed bear the characteristics required of it by Hegel at a particular level to effect a change in the relationship between consciousness and object, here form and content? Secondly, since phenomenological consciousness is for Hegel simply to observe the necessitarian character of the arising of the new object and consequently of the new figure of consciousness,[222] it should be asked whether in a given figure this necessity can be adequately argued on the sole basis of the nature of the specific object of consciousness as compared with the previous object of consciousness and without presuppositions concerning the nature of absolute knowledge? Can this necessity be established without appeal to the explicit fullness of form, wherein form and content are for Hegel adequate as Self?[223] Thirdly, in view of the knowledge available to the *Phenomenology*'s author, it should be asked if both the varying configurations of form and content and the necessity characteristic of the movement from one of these figures to another and from one moment to another within a given figure can be justified in terms of the movement of the logical thought determinations appropriate to the figure(s) in question?

The internal criterion adequate to Hegel's complex argument in the *Phenomenology* can be summarily stated in the following question: Is it possible to argue in discursive thought[224] merely on the basis of the proposed coming into consciousness of a specific object to the necessary transition from natural consciousness to absolute knowledge through a succession of specific shapes of consciousness, each of which can be sufficiently structured and consequently argued according to logical categories appropriate to the shapes of consciousness in question?

The criterion for evaluating the success of Hegel's project in the *Logic* was the possibility of thinking the logical categories as Hegel proposed to do. The criterion for assessing the *Phenomenology*'s argument becomes the possibility[225] of arguing in discursive thought to the immanent and necessary arising of successively more adequate shapes of consciousness on to absolute knowledge. In each case it is a question of thought; Hegel is of course always doing philosophy. Still, this distinction between thinking and "arguing in discursive thought" is rooted in and partially reflects Hegel's own on-going, though at times somewhat differently and surely over-evaluated, distinction between reason (*Vernunft*) as unifying thought and understanding (*Verstand*) as distinguishing or more analytical thought.

Hegel's attempt to move by means of the *Phenomenology*, his first "systematic" work, along the road from understanding to reason, from the distinguishing and relating for Hegel characteristic of consciousness to the self-relating unity of the Concept as absolute knowledge, forms the context within which Hegel treats the implicit mediation attained in the reconciling incarnational immediacy of a divine-human Self and that implicit mediation's explicitation as reconciling trinitarian divine subjectivity. In the *Phenomenology*, Hegel's trinitarian breakthrough[226] is a treatment of implicitly syllogistically structured incarnational immediacy and explicitly syllogistically structured trinitarian development of that immediacy. This treatment constitutes for Hegel the final shape of consciousness characterized by continuing opposition between Subject and object. It is equally the penultimate shape of absolute Spirit. In this penultimate shape Hegel argues to a syllogistically structured trinitarian conception of divine reconciliation which remains for Hegel consistent on through to the 1830 *Encyclopedia* presentation. This latter, consequently, has in the first half of the present chapter provided a convenient overview of the consistent and constant syllogistic structure underlying Hegel's trinitarian thought. This preliminary, encyclopedic overview will in turn allow for a more focused concentration on specific *Phenomenology* texts in Chapter Four and on specific philosophy of religion texts in Chapter Five. The summaries of Hegel's trinitarian thought in these two following chapters will help corroborate and nuance the present positing of a consistent and constant underlying syllogistic structure and movement to Hegel's mature trinitarian thought.[227] The more general treatment of the *Phenomenology* in the second half of this present Chapter

Three should allow for a sharper focusing in Chapter Four on Hegel's pertinent argumentation in directly relevant and limited *Phenomenology* texts. In the last analysis, Hegel's *Phenomenology* argument depends on what he presents in particular shapes of consciousness.

4

The Incarnational Immediacy of Trinitarian Reconciliation in the *Phenomenology*

1. Preliminary, Contextualizing Remarks

Informed selectivity has always been a major characteristic of good scholarship. The current flood of publicly accessible information and analysis in all areas of research and in Hegel studies in particular mandates such selectivity. In recent decades selectivity has been raised to the level of an explicit methodological principle, the appreciation of and appeal to "classic texts."[1] As has already been mentioned with regard to the *Logic*,[2] in Hegel's own thought the focus on specific works and more especially within these works on determinate texts or passages bearing the weight of his argumentation finds an internal, systematic grounding. Now, more specifically regarding the *Phenomenology*, it should be observed that there is in its movement of phenomenological consciousness no substratum underlying the succession of ever-more internally adequate shapes of consciousness. The intended immanent and consistent arising of each shape or figure and each figure's being the totality of the movement on the level in question call for the study of particular shapes of consciousness argued to in specific, distinct *Phenomenology* texts.

In terms of content the immediately obvious texts to be considered are found in the last two chapters of the *Phenomenology*, Chapter Seven, "Religion,"[3] and Chapter Eight, "Absolute Knowledge."[4] There specifically in the shapes or figures of "revelatory religion,"[5] which is the third subdivision of Chapter 7, and of "absolute knowledge" Hegel concretely formulates his trinitarian claim within the framework of an attempt to overcome alienation as philosophically paradigmed in the Kantian estrangement of Subject and object.

Hegel's response in the *Phenomenology* to this alienation can be contextualized by a quick reference to three reconciliations or mediations of the opposition characteristic of consciousness. Phenomenologically prior to, but interpreted from the point of view of the final mediation in, absolute knowledge, Hegel claimed to establish two reconciliations of Subject and object. The first occurs at the end of Chapter Six, a chapter itself entitled "Spirit," where Spirit gains "existence" in morality or moral philosophy[6] and is then considered by Hegel "actual Spirit," Spirit "for itself."[7] But since actual Spirit remains in the realm of consciousness rather than self-consciousness,[8] it is phenomenologically and logically inadequately developed and therefore of less direct interest for investigating Hegel's trinitarian argumentation. The second of these reconciliations prior to absolute knowledge is that of religion or "religious Spirit,"[9] which is *an sich* already the reconciliation of actual and religious[10] or theoretical Spirit.[11] This *an sich* reconciliation in religion climaxes for Hegel in Christian or revelatory religion, itself the synthesis of natural religion[12] and art religion.[13] But revelatory religion remains for Hegel, as religion, on the level of representation. It is, therefore, as far as content is concerned a true reconciliation but as far as form is concerned still inadequate. It is an *an sich* reconciliation in which the reconciliation of Subject and object in Trinity remains the *object* or other of Christian religious consciousness.[14] In absolute knowledge, which is the mediation of these two reconciliations (actual Spirit and religious Spirit),[15] Hegel claims to arrive at the explicit (*an und für sich*) identity of Subject and object in Concept. From the point of view of Hegel's intended elevation of natural consciousness to that of absolute knowledge, however, the mediation posited by Hegel in absolute knowledge is dependent on the successful argumentation of the *an sich* mediation already to have been achieved phenomenologically in revelatory religion. Therefore revelatory religion, and then absolute knowledge indirectly through revelatory religion, is the text to be studied to evaluate further Hegel's trinitarian claim. The critical analysis primarily of the argument in revelatory religion texts provides the opportunity for the necessary shift from logic qua logic to logically informed religion and indirectly thereby on to philosophy.[16] This analysis is implicitly a critique of Hegel's whole project especially as he conceived it from the point of view of the *Phenomenology*'s Preface, namely, the *Phenomenology* as the concrete manifestation (*Erscheinung*) of a philosophically reformulated movement in consciousness of trinitarian divine subjectivity and finally as explication of this subjectivity as a proposed absolute knowledge.

A somewhat lengthier overview of the movement of Hegel's argument for trinitarian divine subjectivity in the *Phenomenology* is warranted not only by the *Phenomenology*'s being a breakthrough first work with a more rigorously developed argument, but also because this helps to illustrate that the fundamental syllogistic structure of that subjectivity remains generally the same throughout Hegel's mature writings already from 1807 in the *Phenomenology* on to and including the 1830 *Encyclopedia* and the 1821–1831 Berlin *Lectures on the Philosophy of Religion*.[17] This longer treatment provides the earlier mentioned opportunity[18] to examine the logic of Hegel's syllogistic theory in its realphilosophical realization first in its incarnational immediacy as the logic of self-manifestation (*Erscheinungslogik*) developed especially in the text on revelatory religion.[19] Despite its complexity and at least apparent ambiguity, the *Phenomenology* is a published text whose rigorous presentation[20] of syllogistically structured divine subjectivity merits considerable attention.

2. Reconciliation in Its Incarnational Immediacy and Trinitarian Explicitation

Hegel's argument in the *Phenomenology*'s Chapter Seven, "Revelatory Religion," progresses through four major stages developed in the chapter's four main sections or subdivisions.[21] Hegel composes his argument with a minor climax in the second section on Incarnation and a major climax in the fourth section on Trinity. The first section serves as lead into the chapter as a whole and movement in particular to the second section, the moment of Incarnation. The third section in turn elaborates on the previous moment of Incarnation and presents the structure according to which the fourth and final movement, Trinity, is unfolded.[22] In the first[23] of these major sections Hegel recapitulates the previously presented and now gathered concrete conditions for revelation. The first of these conditions is the movement characteristic of religion and particularly of art religion to an externalization of substance as Self. The second condition is the corresponding movement of actual Spirit, which Spirit had originated historically in art religion and moved beyond through Stoicism and Skepticism to their truth in the "unhappy consciousness," constituted by a sense of loss because Self has become essence, and here absolute esence.[24] The third and proximate condition is now the combination of these two conditions in that same unhappy consciousness, which longs for "the simplicity of the pure Concept, which contains those shapes as its moments."[25] As is generally the case with recapitulation or repetition in the *Phenomenology*, Hegel employs this recapitulative reinterpretation of the conditions for revelation to move his argument forward here from art religion's result in "comic consciousness" to the simple content of the Concept, that is, to revelation's immediacy or *Dasein*.

Hegel presents this immediacy as revelation's simple content in Chapter Seven's second[26] of the four larger discernible subdivisions. Already the first paragraph of this second section or subdivision[27] contains the essence of Hegel's move from the longing of the unhappy consciousness to the Concept's entrance into immediate existence. The double divestment of Self to substance in actual Spirit and substance to Self in religion establishes a mutuality in which each (substance and Self) becomes the other such that Spirit "comes into existence as this [its] unity."[28] This entrance into determinate existence must for Hegel, to overcome the subjectivity of mere imagination, appear "as immediate being itself,"[29] as a human being who can be seen and felt and heard.[30] "This incarnation of the divine Being, or the fact that it essentially and directly has the shape of self-consciousness, is the simple content of the absolute religion."[31] Already with the Incarnation it can be seen why Hegel calls the Christian[32] religion "revelatory"[33] and "absolute." In it God's revelation is self-revelation, as God really is, Spirit.[34]

In the third section[35] of Chapter Seven Hegel reflects on the limitations of the immediacy constitutive of the previous moment, Incarnation.[36] In so doing he draws out and gives expression to the three stages of consciousness according to which he will structure the developed presentation of Trinity in the fourth and final part of Chapter Seven.[37] The three stages of consciousness or thought (*Denken* in a wide sense)[38] are succinctly sketched in the penultimate paragraph of this section,[39] where Hegel speaks of "thought," of "representation" and of "the element of self-consciousness itself" as three moments (*Moment*) or circles (*Kreis*).[40]

In this second last paragraph,[41] in a manner reminiscent of his various reflections on method,[42] Hegel in effect develops the third level of consciousness (that of the community or *Gemeinde*) as a recapitulation of the previous two, of which the first is (pure) thought still on the level of representation. "Spirit is the content of its consciousness at first in the form of *pure substance*, or is the content of its pure consciousness. This element of thought is the movement of descending into existence or individuality."[43] This abstract thought corresponds to and is for Hegel an implication of the Incarnation as immediate existence and consciousness's sense certainty of that immediacy. The second level of consciousness is representation. "The middle term between these two [thought, individuality] is their synthetic connection, the consciousness of passing into otherness, or representation as such."[44] As Hegel had said earlier in similar fashion, representation is "the synthetic connection of sense immediacy and its universality or thought."[45] The third element is "the return from representation and otherness, or the element of self-consciousness itself."[46] This recapitulative return out of and to self-consciousness, a return in which the first two levels of consciousness are seen as "moments" constitutive of Spirit,[47] is here in fact the enriched return to the simplicity of the immediacy constitutive of Incarnation. Now, however, the simple immediacy is no longer that of sense consciousness as verified on the level of revelatory religion in the Incarnation but of absolute Spirit represented in revelatory religion as "substance *in the element of pure thought*,"[48] eternal essence,[49] the movement of trinitarian divine subjectivity *an sich* or in itself.

Taken in itself, this eternal essence is for Hegel the totality of divine self-revelation in the element of pure thought, "immanent" Trinity. Still it is in truth but the first of three moments developed by Hegel in the fourth, larger section or subdivision of revelatory religion.[50] Hegel argues in five paragraphs[51] that this eternal essence[52] is Spirit and thus self-differentiation and reconciliation. Its moments are those of essence (*Wesen*), being-for-itself (*Fürsichseyn*) and being-for-itself (*Fürsichseyn*)[53] or its knowledge of itself in the other.[54] True to the terminology established long before in the *Phenomenology*'s Introduction,[55] Hegel terms this second being-for-itself "*essence's knowledge of its own Self*,"[56] the word immediately spoken and taken back. This difference within (pure) thought remains unposited, takes on various inadequately determinate characteristics,[57] since it occurs in (pure) thought as yet still in the realm of representation, and, finally, calls for real exteriorization. This "being other" (*Andersseyn*) is found within the Concept, within Spirit itself.[58] For Hegel this "immanent" Trinity in the form of (pure) thought is "this immanent circular movement."[59] This circular or syllogistic movement from essence or universality (*Allgemeinheit*, A) through otherness or particularity (*Besonderheit*, B) to Self or Concept, that is, individuality (*Einzelheit*, E) forms for Hegel what can be identified as a categorical syllogism (A-B-E).[60] The syllogistic structure of "immanent" Trinity again here in the *Phenomenology*[61] both reveals the logical foundation for and summarizes the phenomenological progression from eternal essence to externalized self-othering and consequent reconciliation. The divine as moment of abstract universality contains mediating particularity within it. This implicit otherness gives rise to actual otherness. In the language of representation, God *"creates then a world."*[62]

Representational language is for Hegel most appropriate to the second sphere of divine self-revelation, the one in which absolute Spirit's actual self-othering takes place first in the arising of the immediacy of a world whose being is "for an other"[63] and, then, on the basis of this world's being the very immediacy of Spirit, in finite Spirit.[64] In the course of seven paragraphs[65] Hegel develops the contradiction constitutive of the middle term:[66] world/finite Spirit; thinking consciousness which in becoming aware of itself as otherness loses its innocence and gains "the self-opposed thought of *Good* and *Evil*."[67] In the opposition evil/good, evil arises first. It is the thinking of otherness qua otherness,[68] but the good consciousness[69] or that which is selfless simplicity[70] is equally already on hand or present.[71] The opposition good/evil takes place in the arena of the human being in such a way that "just as Evil is nothing other than the self-centeredness of the natural existence of Spirit, so, conversely, Good enters into actuality and appears as an existent self-consciousness."[72] Spirit's self-alienation is this separation of the Self of Spirit and its simple thought.[73]

The overcoming of this separation or opposition between good and evil occurs when both are treated as thoughts (*Gedanke*) opposed to one another. Good and evil are opposed, but at the same time equally being-in-itself (*Ansichseyende*) each over against the other.[74]

That which is being-in-itself is determined only in opposition and therefore goes over into its other. So

> it is therefore that side which has . . . simple being as its essence that alienates itself from itself, yields to death, and thereby reconciles absolute essence with itself. For, in this movement, it manifests itself as *Spirit*; abstract essence is alienated from itself, it has natural existence and self-like actuality;

this its otherness, or its sensuous presence, is taken back by the second othering and posited as superseded, as *universal*. . . . This death is, therefore, its resurrection as Spirit.[75]

In this hypothetical syllogism (A-E/E-B),[76] God as moment of abstract thought (A) becomes other as world. This otherness is doubled individuality in the opposition of nature taken for itself as evil (E) and good overcoming the isolatedness of evil in the death of the Savior (E),[77] which is resurrection to Spirit,[78] the self-consciousness constituting community (B).[79] For Hegel the syllogism A-E-B reveals the structure of divine self-othering in a world itself sublated through finite consciousness into human history. History, focused in a determinate death, gives rise to the universalized self-consciousness of the Christian community. This communal self-consciousness is, still in representational thought, the inclusive third moment of God's self-revelation as Spirit.

"Spirit is thus posited in the third element, in *universal self-consciousness*; it is its community."[80] With this sentence Hegel announces the appearance of the last and inclusive moment of reconciliation in revelatory religion[81] where spirit as abstract divine essence has come to itself as Subject.[82] This movement of universal self-consciousness or community is an explicitation of what the death of the divine man (*göttliche Mensch*) or human God (*menschliche Gott*) was implicitly or *an sich*.[83] In six paragraphs[84] Hegel moves his argument along from the death of the Mediator (*Mittler*)[85] to Spirit's becoming Subject by a complex interweaving of at least three themes. The first of these is the explicitation of what is for Hegel implicit in the death of the Mediator, an explicitation made on the basis of the triadic structure of self-consciousness.[86] Second, Hegel works through this explicitation by comparing the structural moments of self-consciousness with their counterparts in representation and more specifically in relation to the Mediator represented. The third theme is the integration of the individual sinful or evil consciousness (the sinner) into the reconciling community.[87] This integration is the concern with which Hegel first works to develop what was implicit in the Incarnation.[88] Spirit is at first natural Spirit[89] and must come to realize that its arising out of nature is evil. At the same time, however, the arising is the overcoming of evil. After recalling that in representational consciousness evil was presented as existent, Hegel points out that in self-consciousness representational thinking has taken on the form of a sublated moment.⁹⁰ In self-consciousness the knowledge of evil takes on the form of the thought of evil and is thereby already the abandonment of evil (nature). This is the first moment (the "in itself") of reconciliation and death to sin.⁹¹ However, this first moment in the movement of self-consciousness requires the continued presence of the representation of this reconciliation for fear it will fall into subjectivism (the "for itself" or self-consciousness). Reconciliation so represented then always remains an object for Christian consciousness and therefore still over against it.⁹² Of course, whereas specifically in representation Spirit was grasped as an individual, or as Hegel now says, "rather *qua* particular,"⁹³ in self-consciousness it is a question of the particularity of the particular person dying in its universality.⁹⁴ It is this dying in which the individual believer takes part daily, the individual whose presence in the community is mediated by the Spirit, "who lives in its community, dies and rises in it every day."⁹⁵

The daily dying and rising of the individual into the universality of the community is the movement of consciousness through which absolute Spirit moves from being the abstract divine essence of mere thought to itself as actual Spirit and Subject.⁹⁶ As mentioned,⁹⁷ Hegel argues to this complex movement of consciousness on the basis of explicitation, comparison and integration. His argument and its complexity are based in and bear the structure of Hegel's disjunctive syllogism of necessity (B-A-E). The divine-human Christ (B) has become the universal self-consciousness of the community (A) in which the individual comes to consciousness of reconciliation (E).⁹⁸ "The death of the Mediator as grasped by the Self is the sublation of his objective existence or his particular being-for-self; this being-for-self has become a universal self-consciousness."⁹⁹ In this disjunctive syllogism universality (A), the middle term, contains both extremes, that of the deceased Mediator (B) and of the individual believer (E). Likewise here in Hegel's syllogistic theory, the middle term itself (A) is mediated by the two extremes or other terms (B, E).¹⁰⁰ This syllogistic structuring of religious self-consciousness expressed not only the result of the death of the Mediator but that of the death of the abstract God as well.¹⁰¹ God or absolute Spirit is actual Spirit, self-consciousness as Subject constituted by the moments "in itself," "for itself" and "in and for itself."¹⁰²

> This it is [Spirit is *actual Spirit*] because it runs through the three elements of its nature; the movement through its own phases constitutes its actuality. It is that which moves itself;

it is the Subject of the movement and is equally the *moving* itself, or the substance through which the Subject moves.[103]

In the fullness of revelatory religion God is truly revealed as Spirit and inclusive Subject. *An sich* the sublation of the opposition between actual and absolute self-consciousness,[104] between essence and Self,[105] has already taken place in the reconciliation of the three moments of self-consciousness: universality, particularity and individuality. The disjunctive syllogism with its universal middle term is, in this realization, for Hegel in and as the sphere of individuality an enriched but as yet still inadequately reconciling return to the phenomenologically and logically prior sphere of universality, "inner" Trinity. True, the "immanent" and "economic" trinitarian reconciliation so far realized in and through full divine self-revelation is structured overall according to the inner trinitarian movement, A-B-E. But according to Hegel this true content, reconciliation in absolute Self, remains for the devout consciousness an other,[106] as yet distanced from the Self.[107] At the heart of trinitarian reconciliation there occurs the reinforced reappearance of the unhappy consciousness.[108]

Hegel ends this intensely orchestrated[109] phenomenotheological presentation of absolute Spirit's overall trinitarian self-movement from essence to Subject with a long paragraph[110] on what had served as leitmotiv throughout revelatory religion, namely, the nature of representational thinking. Here he emphasizes representation's (its inadequacy's) dual function of hindering and effecting the transition to mediation "in and for itself" in absolute knowledge,[111] where form and content are truly adequate in the Concept as Concept, which is self-determining inclusive Subject. Hegel indicates that representation impedes true mediation when he speaks in this paragraph of the community's actual spirituality being burdened with the representational form.[112] The community consciousness still treats of representations,[113] in which Spirit gains pure negativity, but without the religious consciousness being able to express pure negativity's positive meaning.[114]

> The action of the Self retains . . . towards it [religious consciousness] this negative meaning because the externalization of substance is taken by the Self to be an action implicit in the nature of substance; the Self does not grasp and truly comprehend it, or does not find it in its own action as such.[115]

Hegel underscores the longing by indicating that consciousness attains the satisfaction of the positive meaning of this pure negativity, the unity of Self and essence, only externally.[116] He evidently stresses the hindering effect of distanced reconciliation in representation especially at this point in the *Phenomenology* in order to enhance the need for the transition to absolute knowledge.[117] According to Hegel reconciliation has been effected in the heart, which longs for the true mediation not yet attained in self-consciousness as such.[118] The implicit or *an sich* reconciliation in revelatory religion has not yet achieved the explicitness of absolute knowledge.[119]

The dynamic transition from implicit to explicit mediation is for Hegel rooted in the very inadequacy of representation to express true mediation. This inadequacy is the perduring presence of the inadequately sublated historical, which hinders the realization of the Concept qua Concept,[120] and thereby at the same time grounds the dissatisfaction of religious consciousness with an external reconciliation. Since the historical remains inadequately sublated, representation can for Hegel both impede and move ahead, a double functioning which reflects representation's being for Hegel the synthetic construction binding together sense immediacy and its universality or thought.[121] This representational thought or, more widely speaking, consciousness as available to thought, is then first of all the mode in which religious consciousness functions.[122] Representation is, secondly, the way of thinking characterizing properly the second dialectical moment in Hegel's treatment of religion.[123] In the *Phenomenology* Hegel conceives of the hindering and longing constitutive of religion (especially of revelatory religion) and based in the nature of representation as something to be overcome. However, it is important to ask whether this hindering and this dynamic longing are not in fact a dialectic much more fundamentally and perduringly characteristic and constitutive of consciousness than Hegel envisioned.[124]

3. Critique of Trinitarian Reconciliation in Its Incarnational Immediacy

Hegel proposed to achieve the mediation of consciousness and self-consciousness explicitly in absolute knowledge, but *an sich* or implicitly already in religion in general and revelatory religion in particular. His argument to a reconciliation achieved in necessarily trinitarian divine subjectivity can be effectively evaluated by examining one specific text[125] while also referring to and quoting as helpful other texts concerning its content.[126] The specific text in question is Hegel's development of the true content of revelatory religion in terms of its immediacy in Incarnation. This text summarizes the arising of revelatory religion as a new shape of consciousness in which the absolute essence reveals itself as Spirit in a finite Self. This text makes available for review in an immediate form the totality of Hegel's argument on the level of revelatory religion, an argument which is conceived by Hegel as the total movement of self-revelatory absolute Spirit in its immediate realization. Incarnation is the simple content of what comes later in the presentation on revelatory religion to be seen as the syllogistically structured trinitarian flowering of that argument in the explicit expression of consciousness as the reconciling self-consciousness of the community. This incarnational immediacy encapsulates the whole movement of the *Phenomenology* prior to final mediation in absolute knowledge. It is likewise the *Dasein* of as yet undeveloped absolute knowledge.

a. The Incarnational Immediacy Hegel Argues To

In order to present and make a critique of the movement of mediation implicit in the reconciliation of divine and human in incarnational immediacy, it will be helpful to recall the threefold criterion previously drawn up.[127] This not only allows for a recall of the natural, phenomenological and logical[128] instances of consciousness, but also provides a framework both for summarizing and criticizing Hegel's interpretation of Incarnation. When these criteria are applied specifically to the "Incarnation of the divine essence,"[129] the overall question becomes: Is it possible to argue convincingly in discursive thought on the basis of content alone to a necessary movement from art religion and specifically from comic consciousness to the implicit reconciliation to be effected in revelatory religion in and as the immediate appearance of a concrete, individual divine-human Self, namely, to an immediate divine self-revelation? In regard to the appearance of this Self to natural consciousness, does this "object" in fact bear the characteristics of the as yet undeveloped but true content[130] proposed by Hegel to effect the advance to the more adequate relationship of form to content in revelatory religion as trinitarian divine self-revelation? Is the necessity of this advance justified for phenomenological consciousness solely on the basis of the arising of the "object" which de facto appears, and this, without presuppositions concerning the nature of absolute knowledge? From the point of view of the author of the *Phenomenology*, can both the new configuration of form and content, that is, of an immediate Self as reconciling other to religious consciousness, and this new configuration's necessary arising be seen as actualization, in religious consciousness, of the logical categories of immediacy, categories themselves constituting an internally coherent and consistent movement of absolute knowledge?

Hegel's proposed answer to these questions is in fact his presentation of what is for him the logically structured and phenomenologically necessary appearance of the divine-human Mediator as immediate Self. This answer, Hegel's presentation, can be analyzed and submitted to critique on the basis of an examination and expansion of points made in the first paragraph of Hegel's treatment of the simple content of absolute or revelatory religion:

> [17] Spirit has in it the two sides which are presented above as two converse propositions: [18] one is this, that *substance* alienates itself from itself [19] and becomes *self-consciousness*; the other is the converse, that self-consciousness [20] alienates itself from itself and gives itself the nature of a Thing, or makes itself a universal Self. [21] Both sides have in this way encountered each other, and through this encounter their [22] true union has come into being. The externalization (or kenosis) of substance, its growth into [23] self-consciousness, expresses the transition into the opposite, the unconscious [24] transition of *necessity*; in other words, that substance is *in itself* self-consciousness. [25] Conversely, the externalization of self-consciousness expresses this, that it is *in itself* [26] the universal essence, or—since the Self is pure being-for-self which [27] in its opposite communes with itself—that it is just because substance [28] is self-consciousness *for the Self*, that it is Spirit. Of this Spirit, [29] which has abandoned the form of Substance and enters existence in the shape of self-consciousness, [30–31] it may therefore be said—if we wish to employ relationships derived from natural generation—that it has an *actual* [32] mother but an *implicit* father. For *actuality* or [33] self-consciousness, and the *in-itself* as substance, are its two [34] moments through whose reciprocal externalization,

each becoming the other, Spirit [35] comes into existence as this their unity.¹³¹

This paragraph illustrates Hegel's concern here not with the death of the Mediator as is more the case in his later *Phenomenology* development of trinitarian divine self-othering¹³² but with the appearance of the mediator as an immediate self-consciousness. This entrance of Spirit into existence (*Dasein*) gives rise to revelatory religion, the new shape of consciousness in which the presence of the immediate concrete Self is the simple but true content of consciousness still in the form of representation. Spirit, as this immediate form of self-consciousness, is the unity of two previous shapes of consciousness, those of comic consciousness and unhappy consciousness.¹³³ Here Hegel universalizes these shapes of consciousness, so that comic consciousness becomes the movement from substance to self-consciousness and unhappy consciousness that from self-consciousness to substance. Comic consciousness is the first of the two movements which have become moments in existing Spirit. It is, therefore, implicit or simply positive and structures the overall movement inaugurating the specific shape of consciousness which is revelatory religion. Unhappy consciousness is the second movement, a negation forming the dialectical mid-point (*Mittelpunkt*) in the birth or appearance of Spirit as self-consciousness.¹³⁴ In their own ways each of these self-disposings is a becoming which exercises a dialectical priority in the entrance of Spirit into existence as self-consciousness. The Incarnation is thus, as the unification of the unhappy consciousness and the happy or comic consciousness, the *an sich* reconciliation of actual Spirit and religious Spirit.¹³⁵

A reading of the paragraph under review shows that Hegel argues the unity of the shapes of comic and unhappy consciousness in seven steps. First, there is the programmatic statement that these two converse or opposite movements are the two sides of Spirit (lines 17–18). Second, Hegel sketches these two in such a way as to highlight their reverse movements (lines 18–20). Third, for Hegel the two movements have, in the acknowledgement of their converse character, come together in a true unification (lines 21–22). Fourth, Hegel analyzes the implicit and explicit terms of each of these two movements or becoming in order to ground the unity of the two movements in the fact that each movement terminates in what the other explicitly already is. Each movement begins from what the other already is implicitly (*an sich*) (lines 22–26). Fifth, therefore the Self remains itself in its other so that substance is self-consciousness and then by definition[136] Spirit (lines 26–28). Sixth, Hegel illustrates Spirit's abandoning its form as substance and entering into existence as self-consciousness by an allusion to the virgin birth (lines 28–34).[137] Seventh, there is the concluding statement that, through and as the unity of this double becoming, Spirit enters into existence (lines 34–35). This argumentation of Hegel's and the paragraph as a whole are based in a delicate use of the often philosophically slippery word unit *an sich*, which usually for Hegel means "implicit" and/or "in itself." It also carries with it here the presently unexpressed connotation of objectivity within the unity of consciousness.[138] In this paragraph's argumentation, which is rooted in the movement from implicit to explicit, the elements of critical concern are: first, the existence or *Dasein* of Spirit or absolute essence in religious consciousness[139] as immediate Self; second, the necessary and immediate appearance or arising of this Self; third, the underlying essential logical structure of the movement from becoming (*Werden*) to existence (*Dasein*) occurring for Hegel in the realm of religious consciousness.

"Spirit comes into existence as their unity."[140] Twice in the paragraph here in question[141] Hegel states that Spirit enters into *Dasein*, into concrete and immediate existence, in the shape of self-consciousness. By this appearance Hegel means to refer to a unique[142] historical fact, an intention indicated by his repeated reference to a "real individual human being,"[143] whom equally as this divinity (*Göttlichkeit*) "the believer . . . *sees, feels* and *hears*. Thus, this self-consciousness is not imagination, but is actual in the believer."[144] The very immediacy of this having entered into existence will become the basis on which Hegel will argue to the passing of this appearance, which as immediate being becomes a "having been,"[145] and therefore past and remote.[146] Yet the Incarnation is for Hegel an historical reality taken up into and here discussed in relation to consciousness.[147] Clearly Hegel continues to work out of the same general framework of the structure of consciousness sketched in his Introduction,[148] though now in the Incarnation it is absolute Spirit which comes to the shape of immediate self-consciousness as a Self which is object to religious consciousness. The shape of religious consciousness constituting revelatory religion in its simple content is, therefore, in no sense peripheral to the *Phenomenology* and its interests. Rather, in the *Phenomenology* Incarnation is the movement of what came to be Hegel's explicitly stated central theme, the transition from substance to Subject,[149] a movement actualized in the immediacy of the self-consciousness of a particular historical human being. The Incarnation is for Hegel the immediate self-revelation of divine subjectivity, an immediacy shortly to be developed by him into the full self-revelation of trinitarian divine subjectivity.[150]

In regard to Incarnation it is possible to elaborate on Hegel's reference to *Dasein* in this paragraph in question[151] by distinguishing three interrelated ways in which Hegel uses "immediacy." First, it refers to the manner in which the Self in question arises, a usage to be discussed separately below.[152] In view of the distinction still appropriate to this stage in the development of phenomenological thought, Hegel speaks of immediacy, secondly, in reference to "form" and, thirdly, in referring to content. Immediate describes the "form" or way according to which this Self stands related to an object directly present to consciousness, in this case to an intuiting sense consciousness[153] on the level of religion. The existing individual Self is an object posited "neither as something thought or imagined, nor as something produced."[154] "The Self of existent Spirit"[155] has become a "*simple* positive Self"[156] and "has, as a result, the form of complete immediacy."[157] Immediacy refers as well to and describes the content of Incarnation, namely, the simple[158] appearance in history, effectively the later Bultmannian *Daß* or "that" of absolute substance's becoming Subject, a Subject which is concrete, historical Self.[159] Immediacy describes the Self as yet not truly owning itself, not yet having posited itself in the form of Self as Concept[160] and in this sense remaining abstract. The Concept has as yet the mere shape of immediacy, which on the earlier level of sense consciousness was sheer contentlessness.[161] This undeveloped or *an sich* content of the Concept on the level of religion is a divine-human Self. "Spirit is known as self-consciousness and to this self-consciousness it is immediately revealed, for Spirit is this self-consciousness itself. The divine nature is the same as the human, and it is this unity that is beheld."[162]

"This incarnation of the divine Being, or the fact that it essentially and directly has the shape of self-consciousness, is the simple content of the absolute religion."[163] This simple content, the *Daß* or "that" of the appearance of the divine-human Self is not directly and explicitly claimed by Hegel to be contentless, although each of the senses in which the Incarnation is for Hegel immediate point to and insist on the totally undeveloped and *an sich* character of the Incarnation as event and as content. Hegel means effectively to establish an appearance of a *Dieses* ("this") which is a divine-human Self contentless beyond the mere appearance of this divine-human Self to consciousness. Nevertheless, despite this insistence of Hegel's on sheer immediacy, this content is surprisingly rich and elaborated. Hegel is able to say so much about the Incarnation because there is in his thought an underlying interplay of sense consciousness, the logical categories of being realized in the shape of sense consciousness and Hegel's developing understanding of a movement of absolute or pure thought as self-positing subjectivity.[164] A representative listing (as they appear in Hegel's text) of more important expressions used by Hegel to describe this Incarnational immediacy will recapitulate what has been said thus far and allow for an appreciation of Hegel's own elaboration: immediate consciousness; existing object; Spirit which knows itself; Concept; the immediate in itself; the immediate in-itself of Spirit; the existing necessity; knowledge of itself; truth; the shape of consciousness in itself; a real man; this divinity; the Self of existing Spirit; form of full immediacy; this God; self-consciousness; essence/ Spirit; Subject or Self; the inseparable unity with itself; the immediate universal; the pure Concept; pure thought; being-for-itself; immediate being; being-for-an-other; that which is alone truly revelatory; this pure universal; the revelatory; the unity of divine and human nature; this being; absolute essence; the absolute abstraction; the pure individuality of the Self; the immediate; being; an existing self-consciousness; this immediate *Dasein;* immediacy; absolute essence in pure thought; the unity of being and essence, of thought; the thought of this religious consciousness; mediated knowledge; immediate knowledge; the unity of being and thought; the unity which is thought; thought; pure essence; concrete existence; the negativity of itself; Self; this; universal Self; revelation; Spirit.[165] These references exemplify that for Hegel immediacy is the characteristic common to the phenomenological level of sense consciousness, to the logic of being and in general to the realm of pure thought taken in itself. Were it not for Hegel's regular reminders that this immediacy remains in the realm of religious representation and for his references to the "object of consciousness," it would be easy to mistake this treatment of divine self-revelation as Spirit in the Incarnation for a study in Hegelian logic.

In the Incarnation, revelatory religion's simple content is the immediate appearance to natural consciousness of a divine-human Self. Now for consciousness in its phenomenological instance, that is, for the reader of the *Phenomenology*, there is then as well a phenomenological "logicity" in the arising of this Self. The appearance of the divine-human Self is not only an immediate content but, equally for Hegel, movement and becoming. This appearance is to be for the reader an immediate arising out of the double becomings both of the phenomenologically previous realization of Spirit in art religion's final stage, comic consciousness, and of the movement of actual Spirit in the unhappy consciousness.[166] This immediate arising of the divine-human Self occurs according to Hegel with a necessity observable by the phenomenologist. "The externalization or kenosis of substance, its growth into self-consciousness, expresses the transition into the opposite, the unconscious transition of *necessity*; in other words, that substance is implicitly self-consciousness."[167] The Concept's giving itself the shape of an immediate Self occurs according to Hegel, "by just the same necessity of the Concept by which *being* or the *immediacy*, which is the content-less object of sensuous consciousness, externalizes itself and becomes the 'I' for consciousness."[168] Necessity becomes for Hegel so much the characteristic of this movement that he can speak of the two different moments of consciousness and object both in terms of necessity as "the knowing of necessity" and "the existing necessity"[169] or "the becoming of intuited necessity."[170] This arising, in consciousness, of the divine-human Self is according to Hegel necessary because it is a dialectically structured arising of this resultant immediate appearance, a movement from implicit to explicit. The immediate logicity apparent to natural consciousness has become for Hegel equally the phenomenological logicity of necessity. The divine-human Self is according to Hegel already the immediate and therefore necessary reconciliation of actual Spirit and religious Spirit, a reconciliation intended to become explicit on the level of religion in trinitarian reconciliation and finally adequately in the mediation which absolute knowledge is intended by Hegel to be.[171] There remains the question as to whether Hegel can argue immediacy of appearance to natural consciousness on the basis of dialectically necessitated phenomenological arising.

The immediate appearance and necessary arising of the divine-human Self occur according to a speculative logic made apparent by the terms "becoming" (*Werden*) and "concrete existence" (*Dasein*) Hegel uses in the paragraph previously quoted.[172] In this paragraph Hegel summarizes the announcement of Spirit's entrance into existence as an individual Self on the basis of a threefold analysis of the convergent movement of the conditions of Spirit's self-manifestation. These conditions constitute "the coming-to-be, the Concept or the in principle production of it [Spirit conscious of itself as Spirit]."[173] In this threefold analysis, Hegel works first from the point of view of the directions of the transitions from substance to self-consciousness and from self-consciousness to substance meeting or coming together.[174] Secondly, he works on the basis of the implicit identity of these two transitions, that is, from the point of view of the movements themselves.[175] Thirdly, he works from the standpoint of the result, in which the two becomings are seen as moments of *Dasein*.[176] This appearance of the existent Self establishes a new experience or shape of consciousness, revelatory religion, in which the movements from substance to self-consciousness and self-consciousness to substance are intended to be reconciled in the Self as determinate negation.[177] It is through the mutual divestment making up each of these moments or sublated movements, "each becoming the other," that "Spirit comes into existence as this their unity."[178] For Hegel speculative logic, grounding and enfleshed in the Incarnation, is the settling of becoming in concrete existence.[179]

b. Critique of Hegel's Proposed Incarnational Immediacy

The settling of becoming in concrete existence is for Hegel the logical structure of the threefold immediacy of the Incarnation, an immediacy of "form," of content and of coming-to-be. This threefold immediacy coalesces for Hegel in religious consciousness into the unique historical event of divine self-revelation in a concrete divine-human Self or self-consciousness. The reasons why Hegel must try to establish such an immediacy in order to achieve the mediation he seeks are phenomenological and systematic.[180] Phenomenologically considered, Hegel must opt for an initial immediacy of divine self-revelation for several reasons. First, in order to avoid a merely subjectivist, or more accurately projectionist view of revelation.[181] Secondly, Hegel's non-subjectivist position with its requirement of an immediate presence reflects the structure of consciousness out of which Hegel is working.[182] Thirdly, this "object for consciousness" must be an immediate *Self*, where form will finally be equal to content, though of course here as a re-presented presence.[183] Not the immediacy of nature but nature's having been taken up into a finite Self[184] provides the adequate *locus* of divine self-revelation as Spirit. Fourthly, from the point of the view of the structure of the *Phenomenology*, incarnational immediacy is the required response, the simplicity of the Concept, longed for by the unhappy consciousness.[185] Again, the structure of the *Phenomenology* is such that trinitarian reconciliation and, consequently, philosophical mediation arise out of and are for Hegel dependent on the lacking or inadequacy inherent in this immediacy.

Underlying the phenomenological necessity for Hegel to establish such an initial incarnational immediacy is the question of systematic necessity. In view of Hegel's overall intention of an immanent and consistent argumentation from implicit to explicit, the self-revelation of God as trinitarian divine subjectivity necessarily presupposes an initial immediate Subject or Self. Explicit trinitarian reconciliation and philosophical mediation presuppose for Hegel an implicit reconciliation of actual self-consciousness and absolute self-consciousness. Philosophically considered, this systematic transition from implicit to explicit establishes consciousness's requirement of a reconciling Self as object in order for consciousness finally to come to self-consciousness in absolute knowledge as Concept which is Self in and for itself. Logically considered, the Self in question is itself determinate negation and therefore resultant immediacy. Equally, however, this Self comes to be seen phenomenologically[186] and speculatively[187] as the dialectical moment of self-othering, of negativity, whose return in mediation is again determinate negation as absolute subjectivity. This self-othering, both as itself determinate negation and in order to function as dialectical moment in the trinitarian movement of absolute or divine subjectivity, must for Hegel appear as the immediacy of a single divine-human Self.

In order consistently to develop his proposal Hegel was, on phenomenological and systematic grounds, obliged to argue to an immediate appearance of absolute essence as an existent Self intuited by sense consciousness on the level of religion. By way of reminder that Hegel in fact attempted just this, it will be helpful to recall his own words. "Spirit comes into existence as this their [the two externalizations'] unity."[188] This *Dasein* is for Hegel meant to be a historical, existent Self "neither as something thought or imagined, nor as something produced."[189] This Self was to be the immediate unity of divine and human self-consciousness immediately intuited. "Spirit is known as self-consciousness and to this self-consciousness it is immediately revealed, for Spirit is this self-consciousness itself. The divine nature is the same as the human, and it is this unity that is beheld."[190] Necessary as it may have been for Hegel so to present and argue incarnational immediacy if he was to carry out his phenomenological program, such an immediate presence of a historical divine-human Self to and within religious consciousness is simply not available, given Hegel's continuing goal of the elevation of natural consciousness to absolute knowledge.

To sharpen the critique of Hegel's proposed intuition of a historical divine-human unity as finite Self it will be helpful first to state in global fashion what Hegel has really done. He correctly saw that faith perceives some divine-human unity in the Mediator. However, this perception of such a unity is itself the result of further reflection on the finite Self which has thereby come to be perceived as a divine-human unity. Hegel has effectively replaced the original historical and finite Self with an already interpreted or developed divine-human unity. The original historical event has been replaced by a unity which was supposed to be immediately intuitable but the intuition of which is in fact the result of further development beyond the historically intuitable finite Self. Hegel apparently tries to cover this by speaking of a divine-human unity immediately available to the *religious* consciousness,[191] but this does not in any way free the proposed intuition of an immediately appearing historical Self from the conditions of contingency. Rather, with this proposed divine-human unity Hegel is, practically speaking, beginning with a dogma. He is with such a notion of Incarnation effectively and not just implicitly already at Trinity. However Hegel cannot interpret the finite Self from Trinity but is supposed to be proceeding from the finite Self to Trinity. The immediate presence Hegel proposes is simply not available as he intended it to be and as it was necessarily to have appeared if his program were to succeed. It will be seen that such an immediate presence or appearance is impossible, first, on the basis of the nature of historical events which are inherently contingent in their immediate appearance, secondly, from the point of view of the nature of sense consciousness qua sense consciousness and, thirdly, from the perspective of the object of religious consciousness in question, namely, from the very nature of the finite Self as self-consciousness.[192]

Before presenting these arguments against Hegel's position, it is important to underscore and clarify two points: the nature of the unity supposedly immediately available to consciousness and the "consciousness" to which this unity is related. First then, surely Hegel's references to the unity occurring in the Incarnation are to a dialectical unity,[193] that is, to distinction-within-unity. There are two senses in which the incarnated historical Self is for Hegel a unity containing difference within it. First, in terms of origin, the Self is the unity of the two becomings of the unhappy and the comic consciousness, the *an sich* unity of actual Spirit and religious Spirit.[194] Second, in terms of result, the unity in question is that of human self-consciousness and divine self-consciousness.[195] On the surface, this acknowledgement of a dialectical unity might appear to mitigate the arguments shortly[196] to be presented against Hegel's position. But in fact, though the distinction remains in this incarnational unity, it is precisely the sheer appearance to natural consciousness of the new, unified object which is to give rise to the new shape of consciousness.[197] In reference to both meanings of dialectical unity, it is the immediate appearance of the unified divine-human Self that provides Hegel with the proposed *an sich* reconciliation in religion of actual consciousness and religious consciousness needed by Hegel in order to progress through Trinity to absolute knowledge.[198] This unity is to have been an immediate divine self-revelation.[199] As witnessed to by Hegel's repeated insistence on immediacy[200] and without denying that the two sets of distinctions are present, it is the unity qua unity of the new object (whether in regard to its origin or to it as result) which is for Hegel operative and to be made available to natural consciousness on its journey to absolute knowledge.[201]

The second point to be clarified before actually critiquing Hegel's position is to identify the consciousness to which the divine-human Self is related. Hegel intended to make available to natural consciousness the divine-human Self as the object giving rise to revelatory religion,[202] the penultimate shape of Spirit as consciousness. This intention of Hegel recalls that, both at this level in the phenomenological development of consciousness and from the very beginning in sense certainty on, Hegel was never concerned merely with the movement of an individual finite consciousness as individual.[203] Rather, from the very beginning in sense certainty on through to revelatory religion and absolute knowledge, Hegel tried to elaborate the very structure of consciousness becoming self-consciousness. As in the *Logic* so in the *Phenomenology* Hegel worked in the public realm of discourse, namely, with consciousness as available to thought.[204] True, in the second half of the *Phenomenology* the structure of consciousness became explicitly a movement of Spirit becoming absolute self-consciousness. Still, throughout the *Phenomenology* the development of self-consciousness, its structure and movement, was always for Hegel to be analyzed as occurring in and through finite human consciousness, which, from the perspective of the Preface, was for Hegel the *Dasein* of absolute Spirit.[205] The basic indication for this continuity is Hegel's goal both before writing the *Phenomenology* and after, the goal of elevating natural consciousness to the systematic point of view of the author, to the realm of absolute knowledge.[206] In fact, either the movement of Spirit as consciousness takes place for Hegel in and through finite consciousness or it does not take place at all as far as finite consciousness and more specifically natural consciousness are concerned. This occurrence of Spirit coming to self-consciousness in and through finite consciousness is meant by Hegel to move along, to sublate, but not destroy, finite consciousness. Consequently, the objects in general and the incarnational immediacy of the divine-human Self in particular to which Hegel argues must be able to be made available to finite consciousness characterized for Hegel by distinguishing and relating.[207]

In view of the movement of Spirit as consciousness in and through the development of finite consciousness to self-consciousness, it can be said that for Hegel there are three senses in which the divine-human Self is immediate object of consciousness. First, absolute Spirit becomes present to or conscious of itself, becomes self-consciousness, in and as a finite Self.[208] Second and correlative with the first sense, the divine-human Self is object to itself. The object in question is an individual *self*-consciousness.[209] Third, as an individual Self this self-consciousness is the object of sense consciousness on the level of religion, where it is seen, heard and felt by the religious consciousness.[210] It is to this dialectical unity in these three senses immediately present on the level of religion to natural consciousness that Hegel cannot argue in view of the nature of historical events, of sense consciousness and of the individual Self as self-consciousness.

The contingency (*Zufälligkeit*) essentially characterizing historical events cannot be established by Hegel in regard to the immediacy of content in the Incarnation if Incarnation is, as he claims, to be considered the immediate appearance to consciousness of the dialectical unity of a divine-human Self. This Self was intended by Hegel to be the immediate appearance to natural consciousness of what he refers to variously as essence, Concept, substance, self-consciousness or Spirit,[211] all of which from specific perspectives refer to and indicate the infinite as totality or truth.[212] Hegel tries to account for contingency by positing this immediate appearance in the form of a finite Self. But such a proposed immediately intuitable appearance of the infinite as a divine-human Self could not be qualified as an historical event characterized and constituted by contingency, when contingency is understood as that which is, or is such and such, but could be or have been otherwise.[213] For Hegel essence, Concept, substance, true self-consciousness and Spirit bespeak a necessity which has overcome the doubled presence of possibility and actuality. They bespeak a necessity which has overcome exactly that which constitutes contingency and which contingency itself thematizes.[214] Indeed it was Hegel's intention in the *Phenomenology* to avoid the contingent character of this event[215] and in his philosophy in general, to situate contingency within its necessary and necessitarian context.[216] Laudable in itself as Hegel's intention to identify contingency's necessary (but not necessitarian) context may be, and without needing for present purposes to develop the here implicit critique of Hegel's understanding of history in general, it is now being argued that his specific attempt to establish an immediate appearance of a divine-human Self does not sublate, but rather destroys, the radical contingency of this supposedly truly historical event occurring within consciousness. It is not, then, the question of merely pitting one view of an historical event over against another, but rather that Hegel's positing of an immediate appearance of a divine-human Self qua divine-human unjustifiably sacrifices to systematic interests[217] the contingency of a specific historical event occurring in space and time. On the basis of the radical contingency of events in their occurrence in history, consciousness taken as phenomenologically characterized by distinguishing and relating[218] requires a further mediation or reflection in order to posit the divinity of a specific finite human Self.

Hegel argues that the coming into consciousness of the supposedly historical event of a divine-human Self is an immediate appearance to sense consciousness on the level of religion. It was to be the immediate appearance of an object whose givenness to consciousness was to have established a new shape of consciousness, an advance in the movement of Spirit from substance to Subject as self-consciousness. The *Daß* or givenness of this event was an immediate content or *Was*, this Self as self-consciousness, a *Dieses*.[219] With this conceptual framework Hegel remained surprisingly faithful[220] to what he had written so much earlier at the very beginning of the *Phenomenology* concerning sense certainty.[221] However, in his discussion of sense certainty Hegel was as yet indeterminately dealing with an object of consciousness, consciousness "for itself."[222] It was an object unavoidably distinguishable in terms of time and space. "Here and now" were for Hegel the necessary conditions for, and even more so that which constituted, sense certainty[223] beyond its originary unity. On the level of religion, sense certainty as sense consciousness remains totally conditioned by time and space.²²⁴ But such a spatially and temporally constituted consciousness could not be immediately related to an immediate and as yet *an sich* or still to be explicitated reconciliation of actual Spirit and religious Spirit in a divine-human Self. Hegel does not argue merely that what immediately arises in consciousness is a finite human Self, but the divine-human unity of a Self as self-consciousness.²²⁵ It is this divine-human unity which cannot be made available in its immediacy to sense consciousness, since such a unity could not qua divine-human meet the spatio-temporal requirements of sense consciousness. Such a divine-human unity would effectively mean the immediate spatial and temporal availability of essence, substance, Concept and Spirit, that is, an (not *the*) individual essence, substance, "concept" and finite Spirit. This would be a finitization which would result only in the immediate appearance of a human Self and not of a divine-human Self.²²⁶ As concluded so far²²⁷ on the basis of the nature of an historical event, so too here on the basis of sense certainty on the level of religion, the divine would be in some sense or other "object" to consciousness only by means of a further mediation or reflection needed in order to posit the divinity of a specific finite human Self.²²⁸

Not only is Hegel unable to argue to the appearance of an immediately intuitable divine-human unity in view both of the real contingency of historical events and of what is for Hegel the spatio-temporal constitution of sense consciousness, but the very conceptuality of a Self as divine-human unity of self-consciousness cannot survive critical scrutiny. Basically, this conceptuality is not tenable because the specific object in question is itself a self-consciousness, which nevertheless as movement of consciousness remains characterized most fundamentally for Hegel by distinguishing and relating.²²⁹ Therefore, as movement of consciousness this individual Self in question must be able to distinguish within itself and from itself the divine self-consciousness as well as be related to that self-consciousness. Otherwise the Self in question would fall below the level of religious consciousness already reached in this phenomenological development of consciousness. This distinguishing and relating in the individual self-consciousness in question results in the anomaly that for the individual Self the acknowledgement of itself as divine-human unity would require further mediation or reflection, whereas to religious consciousness as such that unity would be immediately intuitable and intuited. In the last analysis, Hegel's conception of an immediately intuitable divine-human unity is self-contradictory. If, on the one hand, there is a moment of mediation within the Self in question, there is then no immediate unity to be intuited. If, on the other hand, there is posited an immediate unity of divine and human as self-consciousness, this negates the essential characteristic of consciousness as that which distinguishes and relates.

In view of what is for Hegel the characteristic structure of consciousness and in view of the nature both of sense consciousness and of historical events, it is not possible for Hegel to establish the divine-human unity of self-consciousness as immediate object to consciousness, an object giving rise to the new shape of revelatory religion. Underlying the various arguments presented so far against Hegel's position and operative in these arguments is the fact that Hegel's goal of the elevation or sublation of natural consciousness had to occur in and through finite consciousness.[230] But, with the immediate intuiting of a divine-human unity of self-consciousness, Hegel proposed an object which could not be related to finite consciousness without destroying rather than sublating that finite consciousness. Before drawing further conclusions, however, it is necessary to turn briefly to the question of the proposed necessity of the arising of the divine-human unity and to a consideration of the logical structure of this appearance.

Hegel asserts that the arising of the divine-human unity is one whose necessity is observable by the phenomenologist or reader.[231] He makes this observation implicitly concerning the transition from Self to "being a thing" (*Dingheit*) or universal Self.[232] This necessity characterizing the Concept's giving itself the shape of an immediate Self occurs for Hegel as an absolute necessity, "by just the same necessity of the Concept by which *being* or the *immediacy*, which is the contentless object of sense consciousness, externalizes itself and becomes the 'I' for consciousness."[233] Necessity is, given Hegel's overall logico-ontological framework, the identity of possibility and actuality,[234] a logico-ontological interrelationship verified in Hegel's structuring of and argumentation for the dialectical arising of the divine-human unity as a Self out of the movements of comic and unhappy consciousness. In both of these movements there is verified the transition from potentiality or *an sich* in this case to the convergent unity of actuality or *Dasein*. This movement from potentiality to actuality was intended by Hegel to result in an immediate Self, whose arising was to be observed as absolutely necessary.[235] But since, as has been argued,[236] the divine-human unity in question neither in fact does arise in consciousness nor can do so without destroying consciousness itself, there can be no argument to such an object's necessary arising.[237] To rephrase Hegel's own logico-ontological position, what cannot be and is not need not occur. Therefore, the proposed necessity of the advance to revelatory religion is not justifiable for phenomenological consciousness solely on the basis of the appearance of the object in question and without presuppositions concerning the nature of absolute knowledge.[238]

Not only is the dialectical arising of the *Dasein* which is a divine-human unity of self-consciousness not characterized by necessity, but such an arising is, in the way Hegel wants it, impossible. It is impossible not only from the point of view of the finitude of consciousness, but most fundamentally now also from the vantage point of the author. That is, it is impossible from the very structure of the speculative logic realized in the becoming which is a coming into existence as the incarnational immediacy of the divine-human Self. That structure, stated in its logical formulation as thought determinations, is *Werden im Dasein* or the settling of becoming into concrete existence.[239] Though this structure is presented on the level of religion as the movement of the logic of appearance (*Erscheinungslogik*),[240] the structure is finally that of *Werden im Dasein*,[241] as indicated by the very terms, movements and arguments Hegel employs.[242]

These terms, movements and arguments found in Hegel's presentation of the entrance of Spirit into concrete existence[243] present a concretization very closely reproducing in consciousness much of what Hegel later was to write in the *Logic* concerning the move from becoming to *Dasein*.[244] While critical concern earlier[245] focused on the transitions from being to nothing and vice versa giving rise to becoming, here it is more a question of the doubled becoming resulting in *Dasein*.[246] On the one hand, the movement of comic consciousness from substance to Self realizes in consciousness on the level of religion the ceasing-to-be or disappearance (*Vergehen, Verschwindensein*), the becoming, which is a transition from being to nothing. On the other hand, the movement of unhappy consciousness realizes the becoming which is a transition from nothing to being, the transition of coming-to-be or arising (*Entstehen*). In both cases, the individual Self in question is the moment of negativity and then as result or *Dasein* is determinate negation. As Hegel would later write, "Both [coming-to-be, ceasing to be] are the same, *becoming*, and although they differ so in direction they interpenetrate and paralyze each other. . . . Becoming is an unstable unrest which settles into a stable result."[247]

The dialectical structure of determinate negation verified in the doubled becoming resulting in the *Dasein* of a self-consciousness is dependent upon the viability of the logic underlying it. This is so because this particular dialectical structure of determinate negation, incarnational immediacy, is meant by Hegel to realize in consciousness the very structure of this logic of appearance considered in this logic's immediacy, namely, becoming settling in concrete existence. Hegel's direct concern in the *Phenomenology* is of course to establish the resultant immediacy of self-consciousness in existence. Logically considered, Hegel's concern is with the move from becoming to *Dasein*. However, this resultant *Dasein* must always logically be seen as momentary totality dependent in terms of argumentation on the viability of Hegel's prior logical moves and specifically of those constituting its moments. A closer examination of this wider movement of absolute thought from being to *Dasein*, then, reveals that the various transitions involved in fact establish for Hegel two results: becoming as restless result[248] and *Dasein* as restful result.[249] According to Hegel's own overall understanding of his dialectical method,[250] becoming should have itself constituted the immanent and consistent resultant unity as return in a renewed immediacy, and therefore a new "first moment." Instead, these characteristics are attributed by Hegel to *Dasein*.[251] That Hegel does in fact delineate two results is indicated by his trying to introduce "between" becoming and *Dasein* an additional movement of doubled becoming (*Entstehen, Vergehen*), each of which is dialectically related and thus results in *Dasein*, or as Hegel says, "they mutually paralyze each other."[252] Even though this is for Hegel meant to be a doubled movement of becoming, it is indisputably set up and structured as a second dialectical movement or triadic.[253]

This second dialectical triadic in the movement from being to *Dasein* is necessitated by Hegel's inability to establish the needed "restful unity" directly in becoming. Becoming is simply unable to function adequately for Hegel as mediating third moment and resultant immediacy without introducing a second result.[254] This particular form of restlessness in view of which becoming cannot function for Hegel as resultant immediacy indicates again an unjustified abstraction[255] by Hegel from the immediate content of an initial subjectivity and from the determinateness of all thought.[256] To reintroduce such determination Hegel finds himself obliged to establish a second, more clearly determinate result in *Dasein*. This need draws attention immediately to another reduplication, that of the doubling of the moments of becoming: being and nothing;

coming-to-be and ceasing-to-be.[257] It is precisely here in these moments of becoming or equally of *Dasein*[258] that Hegel's unwarranted and unwarrantable logical reduplication can best be brought to light.[259] To get from being to *Dasein* in pure thought, Hegel was obliged to argue twice on the basis of being and nothing. True he regularly enough uses being and nothing as helps to explain and make explicit certain logical movements or transitions. But in this case being and nothing are first treated as the initial moments of pure thought, then as sublated moments of becoming and, what is unwarrantable, again reintroduced as moments of becoming itself in its logical advance to *Dasein*.[260] The transition from being to nothing and vice versa has already occurred for Hegel in the very thinking of being and nothing.[261] They are therefore the same, and this realization is becoming.[262] Hegel's restatement of the dialectic as the doubled determination of becoming does not give rise even according to Hegel to coming-to-be and ceasing-to-be as graspable advancements in the movement of pure thought, that is, as new momentary totalities of the Concept. They are rather simply becoming considered from the point of view of being and nothing. There is nothing which they make explicit beyond becoming, nothing logically new to justify Hegel's move to *Dasein*.

> Becoming is in this way in a double determination. In one of them, nothing is immediate, that is, the determination starts from nothing which relates itself to being, or in other words changes into it; in the other, being is immediate, that is, the determination starts from being which changes into nothing: the former is *coming-to-be* and the latter is *ceasing-to-be*. Both are the same, becoming.[263]

Even if Hegel's reduplication or at least second appeal to being and nothing as "moments" could be justified, then, given the added dialectical triadic of *Entstehen* and *Vergehen* that Hegel tries to insert, it would still have to be admitted that becoming does not meet Hegel's own requirement of a resultant return to immediacy. The speculative logical movement from becoming to *Dasein*, the logic operative in Hegel's notion of the arising of incarnational immediacy, is not viable.[264] It cannot be argued in thought, and consequently cannot be argued in terms of consciousness as available to discursive thought. And so from the speculative point of view of the author of the *Phenomenology*, neither the new configuration of form and content characteristic of the content of revelatory religion in that content's immediacy, that is, of a divine-human Self as reconciling other immediately present to religious consciousness, nor this new configuration's necessary arising can be seen as actualization in religious consciousness of the logical categories of immediacy. This is so because these categories themselves do not constitute an internally coherent and consistent movement of absolute knowledge in its development as pure thought.

4. Implications for Trinity and for the Self

a. Implications for Hegel's Explicit Theory of Trinity

The logical categories constituting the arising of *Dasein* were meant by Hegel to structure the immediate appearance of the Redeemer or Mediator as divine-human unity of self-consciousness. This Self was to be the immediate presence of God, the fulfillment of sense certainty on the level of religion. As Hegel himself writes in the course of his own reflections[265] on the limitations of this Self in its incarnational immediacy, "This individual man, then, which absolute Being has revealed itself to be, accomplishes in himself as an individual the movement of *sensuous Being*. He is the *immediately* present God."[266] This God sensuously present as a proposed divine-human unity in the form of a finite self-consciousness was to have been a resultant immediacy. This divine-human unity was to have been a determinate negation in which comic consciousness and unhappy consciousness were to perdure as sublated shapes of consciousness. However, psychologically powerful as this uniting of comic and unhappy might be, it was not possible[267] for Hegel to conclude on the basis of the character of a new content, of an immediate divine-human Self, to a necessary phenomenological development from art religion to the implicit or *an sich* reconciliation of actual and religious Spirit achieved in revelatory religion.

In regard to this revelatory religion in particular and the *Phenomenology* in general, Hegel had intended to argue in the public realm and not on any merely subjectivist basis[268] to an immediately intuited divine-human unity. This immediate unity of self-consciousness was further intended by Hegel to be a phenomenologically higher return to the immediacy of the originary unity of sense certainty. In view then of

Hegel's intention to argue in the public realm, that is, responsible to the conditions he rightly saw as constitutive of thought and consciousness, and despite his hope of establishing a return on the level of religion to the immediacy and immediate unity of sense certainty, it can be said that in any[269] theory of a divine self-revelation the divine must always be mediated through and by the truly finite.[270] This finite serves as first point of departure for any further logical or phenomenological movement to a divine or infinite presence.[271] Unfortunately, Hegel's theory of incarnational immediacy does not adequately take into account the immediacy of a truly finite Self. Rather it short-changes the Redeemer or Mediator's true finitude by insisting on an intuition of a divine-human unity.[272] Hegel's theory replaces the real intuition of a historical Self with the proposedly sensible perception on the level of religion of what may in its own way be an equally real but nevertheless further interpreted and developed dogma of faith.

By so short-changing finitude Hegel nullifies his own argumentation from the lacking constituting the implicitness of the Concept as simple content to the developed Concept in representation as syllogistically structured content of Trinity.[273] Hegel's failure to establish an intuitable divine-human unity of self-consciousness means that the simple content of revelatory religion is, as Hegel proposed it, simply not available to be developed.[274] The implicitly syllogistic structure of incarnational immediacy,[275] namely, the divine-human Self, cannot be expanded to explicitly syllogistically structured Trinity.[276] Given the nature of consciousness, Hegel cannot argue to the incarnational immediacy which his intended phenomenological movement would necessitate. That is, Hegel cannot conclude to the appearance of a finite Self which, as such and without further mediation, constitutes the initial external revelation of God as Self, Subject and Spirit.[277] In the *Phenomenology* Hegel cannot implicitly and therefore cannot explicitly in the way in which he argues establish his claim to a necessarily trinitarian divine subjectivity.[278]

Hegel intended with the establishment of explicitly trinitarian divine subjectivity to elaborate in representational form a syllogistically structured reconciliation of Subject and object, of *an sich* and *für sich*, of consciousness and self-consciousness, of religious Spirit and actual Spirit. This reconciliation was, from the point of view of the *Phenomenology*'s last chapter, "Absolute Knowledge,"[279] to be the *an sich* mediation[280] overcoming in a phenomenological formulation the alienation characteristic of the modern world.[281] From the perspective of the *Phenomenology*'s

The Incarnational Immediacy of Trinitarian Reconciliation 113

last chapter, the earlier reconciliation achieved by "Spirit that is certain of itself"[282] as the unity of theoretical and practical knowledge in the finite idea of morality was intended by Hegel to be the *für sich* mediation of consciousness and self-consciousness.[283] Hegel attempted to move from the representational form of "immanent" and "economic" Trinity to what was for him the true form of absolute knowledge where form and content were to be adequate to one another because Concept and Self were the same. The object of consciousness was to be seen as posited by itself and therefore itself, hence true self-consciousness,[284] the *an und für sich* mediation of the two reconciliations.

> This reconciliation of consciousness with self-consciousness thus shows itself as brought about from two sides; on one side, in the religious Spirit, and on the other side, in consciousness itself as such [Spirit that is certain of itself]. The difference between these is that in the former this reconciliation is in the form of *being-in-itself*, and in the latter in the explicit form of *being-for-self*. . . . The unification of the two sides has not yet been exhibited; it is this that closes the series of the shapes of Spirit, for in it Spirit attains to a knowledge of itself not only as it is *in itself* or as possessing an absolute *content*, not only as it is *for itself* as a form devoid of content, or as the aspect of self-consciousness, but as it is *in and for itself*.[285]

Since this *an und für sich* mediation was to occur as immanent and consistent transition from religion[286] to absolute knowledge, the self-consciousness to have been achieved was an absolute self-consciousness, absolute subjectivity, self-conscious and self-certain absolute Spirit as "grasping" knowledge (*begreiffendes Wissen*), the equality of certainty and truth, science.[287] However, this elevation from natural consciousness to scientific knowledge cannot be argued by Hegel even an sich on the level of religion. A fortiori he does not and cannot conclude from the syllogistically structured true object of revealed religion to absolute knowledge.[288] This absolute knowledge was supposed to be both the explicitation of the originary unity of sense certainty and the enriched return to it.[289] It was likewise to be an enriched return to that unity's reappearance as a finite self-consciousness (as a divine-human unity, that is) on the level of revelatory religion. Absolute knowledge was to be the logical moment of pure being considered as culmination of the phenomenological elevation from natural consciousness to science. It was likewise to function equally as first moment of pure thought and as the complete movement of that thought, that is, science.[290] Hegel cannot establish an incarnational immediacy which, by means of explicitation in Trinity, would then come to itself in the renewed immediacy of absolute knowledge. This absolute knowledge can, therefore, be justified neither from the phenomenological perspective, as has been argued here in Chapter Four, nor from the logical perspective, as was concluded in Chapter Two above.[291] So, neither on the level of representation nor doubly on the level of reason can Hegel argue convincingly to an absolute knowledge where Concept and Self are the same, the absolute negativity of absolute subjectivity. In the way in which Hegel argues in the *Logic* itself and in the self-othering of logical thought in the immediacy of nature, ultimately from infinity to finitude, and in the *Phenomenology* presupposing such an argument, he cannot maintain his claim to the necessarily trinitarian structure of divine subjectivity in its logical or, finally, philosophical reformulations.

b. The Self as Finite Becoming

Hegel is able to argue to the trinitarian structure of divine subjectivity neither in its incarnational immediacy nor consequently in its logico-philosophical reformulation as the renewed immediacy of absolute knowledge. His inability to justify both this intended incarnational immediacy and its supposed true form of Concept as Self in absolute knowledge necessarily raises the question of his misreading the admittedly fundamental and constitutive character of consciousness as distinguishing and relating. True, this doubled movement remained for Hegel, from the *Phenomenology*'s Introduction[292] on, the basic movement structuring the development of consciousness. Again, it was this movement of distinguishing and relating speculatively formulated as the dialectical movement of determinate negation which finally allowed for the acknowledgement of the *Phenomenology*'s being, as a specific work, basically unified and so intended by Hegel.[293] This unity in turn allowed for speaking of the *Phenomenology*'s argument and justified an overall criterion according to which that argument could be evaluated. Nevertheless, despite what Hegel intended and the consequent justification of an overall criterion, he failed to take seriously and radically enough the ever-present movement of distinguishing in consciousness and the equally ever-present but radically inadequate movement of relating of any consciousness which is to occur in and through finite consciousness without destroying that finite consciousness.

This misreading of the fundamental, perduring and even constitutive presence of distinguishing and relating flaws and finally nullifies Hegel's argumentation concerning the unity to have been achieved first in incarnational immediacy and consequently at the ultimately dialectically identified beginning and result of the phenomenological movement of consciousness as form of thought. Hegel's presentation of the object giving rise to revelatory religion, namely, the divine-human unity of self-consciousness, failed to provide and could not allow for the necessary mediation between human self-consciousness and divine self-consciousness. Hegel's positing of a divine-human unity immediately intuitable could not meet the criteria of time and space conditioning such an intuition on the level of religious consciousness. Since in religion the object is for Hegel representationally present, it cannot correspond to this proposed originary unity of sense certainty but must even for Hegel fall under the conditions of space and time as applicable to consciousness. As historical appearance, this object could not, without further mediation, make present essence, Concept, substance and absolute Spirit.[294] In each of these three questions, namely, concerning the object itself, the nature of sense consciousness and the nature of historical events, Hegel has failed adequately to account for the primordial and perduring radical distinguishing constitutive of consciousness qua consciousness if such distinguishing is to be available to and occur in and through finite consciousness. Conversely, Hegel too facilely posited the relating of divine and human in a unity of self-consciousness immediately intuitable as divine-human on the basis of the unity's supposing to appear on the level of religion.

Hegel's under-appreciation of distinguishing and overestimation of relating consequently extends from the progression he tried to establish in incarnational immediacy to the movement of consciousness in its proposed resultant absolute knowledge and in its initial moment, the originary unity of sense certainty, to which absolute knowledge was for Hegel to have been an enriched resultant return. On the basis of his failure to argue to incarnational immediacy, it must be said that Hegel unwarrantedly extrapolated to an absolute negativity as absolute subjectivity, to Concept as Self.[295] His identification of Concept and Self, therefore, amounted to an unjustifiable transfer from the ever-present real distinction constituting any movement of consciousness to a proposed realm of merely ideal distinguishing in absolute knowledge.[296] This resulted effectively in an ungrounded leap reducing the significance of distinguishing and over-evaluating the movement of relating characteristic of consciousness.

The misreading by Hegel of this possibility of elevating natural consciousness to an absolute knowledge without destroying that natural consciousness necessitates for present purposes a brief though critical return to the originary unity of sense certainty. Hegel had proposed a "knowledge of the immediate or of what simply is,"[297] a sense certainty which appears at first as the richest and truest form of knowledge but which is in fact the most abstract and poorest, since it only affirms that the object is.

> All that it [this sense certainty] says about what it knows is just that it *is*; and its truth contains nothing but sheer *being* of the thing (*Sache*). Consciousness for its part, is in this certainty only as a pure 'I'; or I am in it only as a pure 'This,' and the object similarly only as a pure 'This.'[298]

Hegel protests that "I" and "this" are not distinguished in the original shape of sense certainty.[299] He then claims that it is the realization that "an actual sense-certainty is not merely this pure immediacy, but an *instance* of it,"[300] which gives rise to distinction. Despite both the protest and this appeal to "instance" or "example," there is in fact already in sense certainty a phenomenologically available distinguishing of "I" and "this." Hegel attempted even before his reference to "example" or "instance" to ward off the inevitable distinguishing present from the very beginning in sense certainty as available to the public realm. His very attempt to avoid this distinguishing indicates how necessary it is to distinguish "I" and "this" even in the initial moment of a phenomenology of consciousness as thought, a distinguishing Hegel himself could not avoid.[301] Sense certainty is always already from the beginning an "instance." Hegel has both underestimated the presence of distinguishing and overestimated the relating movement of consciousness even in the first moment of consciousness. From the very beginning, consciousness is characterized by a "here" and a "now." Without a logically adequately founded[302] initial unity of consciousness, Hegel cannot establish a movement of distinguishing and relating immanently and consistently argued and developed out of itself, a development to have been argued only on the basis of the arising of new content.

The proposed immediate appearance of a divine-human Mediator, its explicitation in absolute knowledge and its presupposition, sense certainty, are all characterized in such a way by a radical distinguishing and real but inadequate relating that the Self Hegel posits in the *Phenomenology* remains ever a finite, that is, limited and one-sided Self as existent becoming (*daseiendes Werden*). In the *Phenomenology* Hegel has not established an accomplished triadically structured reformulation of trinitarian divine subjectivity as absolute knowledge but, rather, a development from consciousness to an ever-renewably mediated real consciousness of Self, the finite Self as becoming. This movement or experience of the coming into being or becoming of self-consciousness is a movement of relating of Subject and object which truly occurs but which out of itself alone cannot explain and justify the Subject's own enriching relationship with object or other. Not only then is any beginning necessarily finite;[303] here in the context of the *Phenomenology* it is seen to be the beginning of a finite becoming or progression as well. The Self as finite becoming is the true realization of the distinguishing and relating constitutive of consciousness.[304] It is truly a movement of the enriching development or growth of self-consciousness in that there occurs an interrelationship with the other. However, in this very relating in which consciousness is that to which the object is related and the object is that which is related to consciousness there remains the inevitable and immediately recurrent distinguishing of Subject and object. The Self arrived at remains finite, ever renewedly limited and one-sided.[305] Despite his original intention to raise natural consciousness to the level of absolute knowledge or science, Hegel has, rather, in the *Phenomenology* established consciousness as the interplay of Subject and object, a finite and not finally self-explanatory or self-arguable dialectical interrelationship between ever-renewedly distinguished Subject and object. Hegel has established this interplay between Subject and object as the experience of the development from consciousness to an ever-to-be renewed and reintegrated Self as self-consciousness, the reality of qualitative increment or enriching growth. It is this enriching becoming which is allowed to come to the fore when Hegel's thought is freed of the constraints imposed by the insistence on beginning with the infinite. The reality of enriching becoming is the valid insight latent in Hegel's reference to a child's and an older person's understandings of a proverb.[306] It is equally the insight latent in Hegel's insistence on the dynamic character of logical categories.[307]

It would be important at another time to elaborate further the implications of this Subject-object interplay for a truly dialogically developed and thereby renewedly important phenomenological experience of self-consciousness. It could as well be helpful on another occasion to work out a monologically developed movement of finite objective logic. These two formulations, the monological and the dialogical, would each be dialectically speaking the total formulation of the structure of finite qualitative increment. They would each in their own way be the totality of the movement from finite to true infinite.[308] Each would also ground the other, and together they would constitute a more detailed argumentation for a truly inclusive infinite.[309] However, what is of present concern is only the formal structure of any finite becoming as qualitative increment, whether dialogically or monologically formulated, whether expressed as a finite movement of consciousness or of thought. This formal structure is, in turn, of concern primarily in so far as it opens the way in Part Three, Chapter Six, to a first sketching of a reconstruction of Hegel's trinitarian claim in terms of a movement from finitude to a triadically structured true or inclusive infinite.

Whether the argument from finite to triadically structured and appropriately conceptualized true infinite were to be developed in its dialogical or monological interdependently totalizing instantiations, what is most important for the discussion at hand is the acknowledgement, in either form, of the incontestable reality of enriching movements of becoming, that is, of qualitative increment as coming to be more than what there was before. In both of these finite developments, the dialogical and the monological, finite becoming would be freed of the constraints imposed by Hegel's need to establish an immanently grounded movement from Subject to object in which the pluriform interrelationality of the two is reduced to a logically sequenced movement of negation and then resultant third as negation of negation or positive. Brilliant as this dialectic was, it is based on an overly simplified constituting of the relationship between object and Subject as one of opposition,[310] if one might broach the word "simple" with reference to anything Hegel has written or argued. Rather, now freed of the constraints of a conceptually available and merely immanently motivated dialectic, it is possible again to acknowledge that otherness is co-constitutively[311] and in non-prioritizable fashion[312] negation and positive, whether in a phenomenological or in a logical framework. More psychologically expressed, otherness both attracts and threatens. It is the complexity of this interrelationship between Subject and object with otherness as co-constitutively negative and positive which is, on the finite level, the source of real enrichment. However, this movement is neither a fully achieved nor finally a self-explanatory mediation. The enrichment cannot be grounded in its own immanent dialectic.[313]

As was argued in Chapter Two above, Hegel was not able to establish the mediation which was to have been a movement of self-positing and self-determining inclusive subjectivity in the form of pure thought. Here it has been proposed that Hegel could not argue alone on the basis of the arising of a new object for consciousness to the elevation of natural consciousness to an absolute knowledge wherein Concept and Self were identified. He has not been able appropriately to conceptualize that inclusive truth without which the enrichment or becoming of finite self-consciousness or its monological structure could not be fully explained and grounded. Before turning in Chapter Six to proposing a rudimentary reconstruction of Hegel's trinitarian claim and thereby indicating a conceptually more appropriate grounding to finite qualitative increment, it will be helpful to make a critique of Hegel's proposal again in the public realm of discourse but now on the explicitly communitarian level. Chapter Five will hone in on Hegel's philosophy of religion lectures and their presentation of the communitarian experience of a triune God. Of special concern will be the explicitly syllogistic, triadic structure of that proposed communitarian experience which is for Hegel Spirit. This will help explore further the in principle formal triadic structure of becoming as enrichment.

5

Trinitarian Reconciliation in Hegel's Philosophy of Religion *Lectures*

1. Introduction and Context

In his Berlin lectures[1] of 1821, 1824, 1827 and 1831 on the philosophy of religion, Hegel characteristically begins his philosophical presentation of the communitarian[2] experience of God by positing an originary unity or totality. Similarly to the way in which he had begun the *Phenomenology* with "sense certainty"[3] and the *Logic* and consequently the *Encyclopedia* with "pure being,"[4] in these lectures Hegel proposes a Concept of religion as totality. As appropriate to the realphilosophical sphere of religion, he speaks of religion as a totality inclusive of two moments or sides, namely of God as the object of religious consciousness, on the one hand, and religious consciousness itself, on the other. In his 1821 manuscript Hegel writes simply:

> [We treat first of all of the] Concept of religion as such. This Concept [is known to us] from representation; [so] we know first of all, that religion [is] as such the consciousness of God, . . . But the object, which we are treating of, is religion itself; in it however we at once meet two moments, the object in religion and the consciousness, Subject, the human being who relates him- or herself to it, the religious feeling, intuition and so forth.[5]

By the 1824 lectures Hegel had drastically revamped the first main section, the "Concept of Religion," and spoke as well more explicitly and complexly of a structured totality, the speculative Concept of religion, as "the *infinite negativity*, the affirmative consciousness, which exists only as the negation of a finite, as of a negative."[6] This negation of negation, a movement from finite as negative to inclusive infinite knowing itself in and through the finite, took on for Hegel a more integrated and explicitly triadic structure as the moments of the Concept, of God as this inclusive infinite.[7] In this first main section of the 1824 lectures, the "Concept of Religion," Hegel spoke briefly of three forms in the Concept of religion: "substantial unity"; "diremption"; and "absolute affirmation."[8] He had provided an Introduction preceding this section, the "Concept of Religion," in each of the lecture series. In the 1824 Introduction he more clearly than in the following section, "Concept of Religion," developed this triadic by establishing first the pure thought itself as yet of course here in religion still on the level of consciousness. Second, Hegel spoke of the differentiation of consciousness into finite knowing Spirit and Spirit as object of this knowing. Third, then however, both in the Introduction and "Concept of Religion" Hegel for the first time developed cult as pertaining to the Concept of religion itself.[9] He posited cult as the reconciliation of Spirit previously differentiated as knowing and known.[10] By the 1827 lectures and presumably for the 1831 series as well[11] the section "Concept of Religion" itself took on an even more definitive and simplified[12] triadic structure on the basis of the logical moments of the Concept: universality, where Hegel treats of the problem of beginning with God; particularity, where he examines various forms of religious consciousness; individuality, where he very briefly discusses cult.[13] As moments of the Concept of religion these present the development of God Self. Hegel is recorded to have said at the beginning of the 1827 lectures, "first the philosophy of religion is the scientific development, the knowledge of that which God is, through which one experiences by way of recognition what God is."[14]

After the Introduction and "Concept of Religion" in each of the lecture series Hegel continued with the second major section of the lectures, "the Determinate Religions," and ended each lecture series with the third major section, "the Absolute Religion," which was Hegel's interpretation of what was for him, historically speaking, the Christian religion.[15] In the section "the Determinate Religions," Hegel worked out over the years what, given the beginning phase of their study in his day, could only be considered a marvelous analysis and serially developed integration of world religions.[16] It was however for Hegel the absolute religion, in its "immanent" and inclusively "economic" trinitarian structure,[17] which was the religion of absolute subjectivity[18] and consequently constituted the fulfillment of the very Concept of religion as consciousness of God.[19] In the 1821 lectures Hegel had treated the absolute religion as last of the determinate religions, while from 1824 on he placed it more independently and prominently as third, unifying moment bringing to fruition the initial unity of the Concept of religion and the reality already achieved in the second moment, that of the determinate multiplicity of world religions.[20] By 1827 Hegel had clearly set up the overall lecture subdivisions according to the logical determinations of the Concept: universality ("Concept of Religion"); particularity ("the Determinate Religions"); individuality ("the Absolute Religion").[21] In addition, Hegel referred to the necessary progression constitutive of the development of the philosophy of religion, with terms from the logic of the subjective Concept, as a movement from Concept to judgement to syllogism.[22] Other triads more or less explicitly operative in the lectures already from 1821 on are: taken from the logic of being, "in itself" (*Ansich*[*sein*])—"*in* existence" (*Dasein*)—"existing for itself" (*Fürsich*[-*sein*]); taken from the three main sections of the logic of the Concept, "Concept" (*Begriff*)—"objectivity" (*Objektivität*)—"*Idea*" (*Idee*).[23] Hegel further claims that these triads are likewise "operative"[24] on each level in the philosophy of religion and in each religion.[25] In fact, in typical fashion Hegel proposes already in 1821 that each of the progressively more developed and adequate determinate religions and, finally, the absolute religion as fulfillment of the Concept of religion and of the strivings of each of the previous determinate religions contain in their own way all the determinations of the Concept of religion.[26] From 1824 on each religion clearly embodies in its own way all the determinations of the divine, so that each religion is on its own level the progressively more adequate realization of the Concept, of God.

Specifically regarding the absolute religion, Hegel's overall conception remained the same in underlying logical structure, and even somewhat in regard to the distribution of content, throughout the various lectures. Changes involved more corrections, more tightly drawn thought and enrichments.[27] Nevertheless, in the 1821 lectures Hegel had not as yet managed to work out his later, more straightforwardly trinitarian structure for the absolute religion. Rather, he had developed the absolute religion according to its abstract Concept, then, secondly, concrete representation which itself was triadically subdivided according to the moments in the Idea of God and, thirdly, community or cult.[28] By the 1824 lectures, in which Hegel had identified the development of the Concept of religion with that of God, he simplified the previously doubly triadic structure of the absolute religion into a single triadic of the three elements (*Element*) in the development of the Idea of God.[29] This resulted in a return to the exact structure of the revelatory religion as found in the 1807 *Phenomenology*,[30] a structure followed again in the 1827 lectures.[31]

2. Syllogistically Structured Trinitarian Divine Subjectivity in the 1827 Lectures

Hegel's philosophy of religion was, in typical Hegelian fashion, meant to be an immanent and consistent philosophically informed communo-historical progression of determinate religions as successively more adequate realizations of the consciousness of God as Subject and finally as absolute Spirit. It was for Hegel a progression culminating in the revealed, revelatory, consummate (*vollendete*) religion of absolute subjectivity.[32] Hegel situated this progression on the level of what he called thinking representation as compared with intuition, which was the form of knowing proper to art, and as compared with the conceptual thought of philosophy.[33] In the lecture Hegel de facto values representation more positively than in the *Phenomenology*. By the time of the lectures, representation was for Hegel perduring vehicle of truth. He wrote, "Religion is the truth *for all people*."[34]

This truth in its fullest manifestation as the consummation of the Concept of religion is in each of Hegel's lecture series the reconciliation representationally available as self-positing trinitarian divine subjectivity. In 1821, in the context of the Concept of God in and for itself, Hegel wrote what can also be taken as representative of his later lecture series on the "first element":

> God is Spirit—that is, that which we call the *triune* God, + [a] purely speculative content, i.e., [the] *mystery* of God. + God is Spirit, *absolute activity, actus purus*, i.e., *subjectivity, infinite personality*, infinite distinction of oneself from oneself, generation. However, this process of distinguishing is contained *within the eternal Concept*, + divinity standing over against itself and objective to itself, + i.e., [within] *universality* as *absolute subjectivity*.[35]

Trinitarian Reconciliation in Hegel's Philosophy of Religion *Lectures* 125

In the 1824 lectures, within the context of the "second element" and specifically with regard to reconciliation, Hegel gives expression to his trinitarian claim: "God is the true God, Spirit, because God is not merely Father, enclosed within Self, but rather because God is Son, becomes the other and sublates this other. This negation is perceived as a moment of the divine nature; therein all are reconciled."[36] The 1827 transcripts present a vintage Hegel summarizing in the "third element's," that is, community's second subsection the overall "economic" trinitarian divine self-realization from universality to particularity to individuality:

> The community itself is existing Spirit, Spirit in its existence, God existing as community. The first moment in the Idea in its simple universality for itself, having not yet progressed to judgement, other-being, not yet being disclosed—the Father. The second moment is that of particularity, the Idea in appearance—the Son. In so far as the first moment is concrete, other-being is indeed already contained in it; the Idea is eternal life, eternal bringing-forth. But the second moment is the Idea in its externality, such that the external appearance when inverted becomes the first moment and is known as the divine Idea, the identity of the divine and the human. The third moment, then, is this consciousness of God as Spirit. This Spirit as *existing* and *realizing* itself is the community.[37]

Religion, the consciousness of the all-encompassing object or God, has become for Hegel the fully inclusive self-consciousness of absolute Spirit,[38] of trinitarian divine self-positing subjectivity. It is in, through and for finite consciousness or Spirit[39] a movement of "immanent" and "economic" reconciliation through divine self-othering and return.

Though Hegel lectured four times on this "immanent" and "economic" trinitarian realization of religious reconciliation, there are good reasons in the present instance for concentrating attention on his 1827 lectures. Without intending to undervalue the intrinsic worth of each lecture series, it can be observed that many texts in Hegel's 1824 and especially in the 1827 lectures were more speculatively elaborated and developed than in the 1821 lectures.[40] Choosing to work primarily with the 1827 lectures, then, respects and follows Hegel's own specific and for him quite typical interest not primarily in the history of religions as such but in a philosophy of religion exposing the conceptual necessity with which, according to Hegel, the determinate religions and especially the consummate religion develop,[41] namely, a *Phänomeno-theo-logik*.[42] While this choice will not allow here for a longer and more explicit study of the development of Hegel's trinitarian thought throughout the Berlin period,[43] it does, by working mostly with a later lecture series, in principle acknowledge such a shifting and refinement. The basically similar structures of trinitarian subjectivity in the 1824 and presumably in the 1831 lectures are for present purposes adequately covered by an examination of the available 1827 lecture material. Hegel's first attempt to lecture on the philosophy of religion, as found in his 1821 manuscript, will be referred to in footnotes where appropriate.[44] In fact, studying the 1827 lecture series does nevertheless constitute an indirect examination of the structural movement of trinitarian divine subjectivity as found in the other lecture series as well, since even a cursory examination reveals an overall continuity.[45] This continuity is indicated by the fact that in each of the lecture series the first or paradigming moment of "immanent" Trinity is the same both in terms of structure and even of distribution of content.[46]

Although it could not be argued that the 1827 consummate religion texts as available in Lasson's edition are a complete transcript of the 1827 lectures themselves, Lasson's text is conveniently available and what it does contain can be considered, as far as possible with transcripts, a reliable and accurate source for the 1827 lectures on the absolute religion.[47] Summarizing and then critiquing Hegel's realphilosophical trinitarian thought by focusing on the 1827 lectures integrates the present concern for the inner viability of Hegel's interpretation, Hegel's own interest in the conceptual necessity of absolute trinitarian subjectivity, the development and formal relationships among the various lecture series and the intrinsic worth of the gathered 1827 lecture transcripts themselves. It is these 1827 transcripts which clearly structure the absolute religion more speculatively in three "elements" according to the overall logical moments of the Concept: universality; particularity; individuality.[48]

a. *The First Element—"Immanent" Trinity*

In the 1827 lecture transcripts the appearance of the divine Idea in the element of universality is presented with a particularly striking use of logical terminology.[49] Hegel expresses his disdain for traditional trinitarian terminology concerning Father and Son, the numbering of three units and the reference to "Persons" in as these are conceived of as discrete units as opposed to the self-emptying characteristic of true personhood.[50] Logically expressed, the first element is the treatment of God "in God's eternal Idea . . . on the whole in the abstract element of thinking—the abstract Idea of thinking, not of conceptualizing."[51] This sphere or element of universality,[52] this eternal Idea is "expressed in terms of the holy *Trinity*: it is God Self, eternally triune."[53] It is the whole Idea but only *an sich*,[54] the divine Concept[55] which is concrete universal containing otherness within itself.[56] As concrete universal this speculative Idea is rational.[57] It is phenomenologically available pure thought and truth.[58] The speculative Idea as concrete universal contains a moment of judgement, the particular over against the universal.

> In this judgement or separation [*Urteil*] the other is found, the opposite of the universal, the particular as distinguished from God, but in such a way that this distinguishing is the entire Idea in and for itself, so that these two determinations are also one and the same for each other, an identity.[59]

This circular dynamic from universal to particular and then by means of the particular to what can only be termed the reconciliation of both in the individual is in this first element for Hegel a self-enclosed establishment and sublation of otherness.

Hegel insists upon the self-contained character of this mediated progression by reference here in an exemplary way to the movement as love which is only "a play of distinguishing,"[60] and by an essential reference to the realm of pure thought wherein Hegel proposes the establishment of an ideal (*ideell*) other as opposed to the world seen as realized finite other of God.[61] This "immanent" trinitarian dialectic characterized by the immediacy of its transitions and by particularity functioning as mediating totality inclusive of the extremes of universality and individuality[62] reveals in itself the triadic structure of inclusive and here absolute subjectivity in the form of Hegel's categorical syllogism (A-B-E).[63] But the eternal Idea remains as such unrealized. It is perfected (*vollkommen*) only in its final realization as Spirit in community having risen to thought.[64]

b. The Second Element—Diremption and Reconciliation

Spirit rises to thought in community according to Hegel by means of the divine Idea's self-othering in what Hegel terms the second element.[65]

In characteristic Hegelian fashion, this is most properly the sphere of representation,[66] the appearance of the divine Idea in the doubled movement of diremption and reconciliation.[67] It is the sphere of particularity and objectivity,[68] the movement of judgement in which the divine Idea comes into existence "for itself."[69] It is appropriately the element of consciousness,[70] and so characterized by opposition not only in terms of the overall doubled movement of diremption and reconciliation, but as well by an almost stylized progression by means of a series of alternative and even opposed reflections.[71] Hegel treats of the divine Idea in this second element "in so far as it [the Idea] emerges out of its universality and infinitude into the determinacy of finitude."[72] This universality of God is initially referred to by Hegel religiously as the presupposition of divine omnipresence.[73] From this beginning Hegel proceeds with his doubled progression by, on the one hand, observing that the appearance of the Idea must take place for the thinking subject and, on the other, that it must from the point of view of the Idea itself go beyond difference (the eternal Son) to real differences.[74] So the divine Idea others itself in judgement as an independent world,[75] out of which there arises finite Spirit distinguishing itself from nature and from its own nature. Consequently there exists in finite Spirit the exigency for reconciliation with the truth.[76] These real differences constitute the doubled individuality of nature and finite Spirit.[77]

Hegel concentrates on the second of these, finite Spirit, in its identification and estrangement from its own nature.[78] Finite Spirit is for Hegel by nature, then, both good and evil, a contradiction sustained in the unity of the subject itself.[79] The intensity of Hegel's elaboration can presently only be hinted at by recalling the analyses of other great thinkers such as Augustine and, following Hegel, Kierkegaard. The opposition giving rise to the need for reconciliation with the truth, for the overcoming of the evil which finite Spirit perceives itself to be, is to be probed to its final depths.[80] This basic need of Spirit to fathom the depths of its own self-constituting opposition or contradiction is to be carried through in order that finite Spirit might become conscious of the implicit condition (goodness) for reconciliation found within itself and likewise conscious of the determinate form of the necessarily exclusive individuality (*ausschließende Einzelheit*) in which this reconciliation has to occur.[81] Hegel establishes the appearance of this exclusive individuality, "the unity of divine and human nature . . . in *a single man*,"[82] in terms generally reminiscent of his earlier argumentation found in the *Phenomenology*'s[83] doubled presentation of incarnation. This argumentation refers to the need for human certainty, a certainty for Hegel requiring immediacy.[84] By means of a two-part consideration first of the life and then of the mediating[85] death of Christ, Hegel has concluded to the kingdom of God as most fundamentally the presence of God.[86] Finitude and human death have become a moment in the very life and nature of God.[87] This renewed establishment of what was God's omnipresence now as the presence of God recognized by the community in a finite individual is the reconciliation with truth, namely, of all with God.[88] In the second element, this reconciliation continues to be presented in the particularity of the community's consciousness of an immediate existence spiritually interpreted as the risen Christ,[89] whose death forms for Hegel the transition to and restoration of an original glory. The history of resurrection and ascension begins in the religious interpretation of this death, an interpretation giving rise to the community.[90]

The objective reconciliation already realized[91] in this second element of the communitarian history of God was characterized by Hegel as a mediation of religious consciousness in the doubled mode of representational thought. In a reference both to the moment of universality or "immanent" Trinity and to God's externalized and reconciled self-othering, Hegel claims (specifically here in reference to this second element) that the community's awareness of God's being triune arose on the basis of and indeed out of the overall divine history. In the new context of his ontological position Hegel here echoes ancient patristic concerns in claiming that were God not triune there would be no reconciliation.

> For the community, this is the history of the appearance of God. This history is a divine history, whereby the community has come to the consciousness of truth. Out of this there arises the consciousness, the knowledge, that God is triune. The reconciliation believed in as being in Christ has no meaning if God is not known as the triune God, if it is not recognized that God *exists*, but precisely *as the other*, as self-distinguishing, so that this other is *God Self*, having implicitly the divine nature in it, and that the sublation of this difference, this other-being, the return, this love is God. This consciousness involves the fact that faith is not a relationship to any other, but *a relationship to God Self*.[92]

This historical appearance of the divine Idea occurs as a triadically structured movement from God as presupposed universality to the particularity of the community's spiritual consciousness of the risen Christ by means of mediating individuality culminating in the death of Christ. The doubled individuality of nature and finite Spirit, its giving expression to the multiplicity inherent in finite individuality, its mediating of universality and particularity, its incarnation in the *Dasein* of sense certainty and result in a sublated *Dasein* as second extreme[93] reveal for the philosophically informed religious consciousness the triadic structure of the absolute Subject in the form of Hegel's hypothetical syllogism (A-E/E-B).[94] There remains as yet for Hegel the need to realize this objective reconciliation in the individual subject who is a member of the believing community.

c. The Third Element—Spiritual Community

The objective reconciliation achieved in Christ has for Hegel in the third element, community (*Gemeinde*),[95] become the subjective relationship[96] of the individual Subject to this objective reconciliation with the truth. This relationship is one in which God is present "for feeling, for subjectivity and in the subjectivity of Spirit, in the innermost being of subjective Spirit."[97] Prior to this third element or move to subjectivity and on the basis of his empirical analysis of the overall threefold movement of thought, Hegel had first identified the relationship of finite consciousness to the truth as one of thought in the first element or eternal divine Idea as "immanent" Trinity. Secondly, he had identified this relationship as representation in the second element or appearance of the eternal Idea in the finitude of an individual human Self. However, these three progressively more adequate relationships (thought, representation, subjectivity) of the finite Subject to reconciliation with the truth[98] are not the mere result of an empirical analysis. They are for Hegel most significantly the very progression of the idea of God,[99] the absolute eternal Idea in itself, for itself and now in and for itself. They are the very life and activity of God[100] now in the third element consummated as the community or unity of the individual empirical Subjects who are filled by the Spirit of God,[101] individuals who live in the Spirit of God and with whom the Spirit of God is dialectically identified.[102] "This third moment, then, is the consciousness of God as Spirit. This Spirit as *existing* and *realizing* itself is the community."[103] God existing in and as the community of finite Subjects is the very realization of God as Spirit,[104] the Holy Spirit or reconciling return of the divine Idea out of the self-othering of judgement.[105] This third element is, therefore, from the point of view of its dynamic reconciling function clearly identifiable as syllogism.[106] It is the reconciliation of particularity and individuality by means of universality. It is equally the divine Idea in the overall determination of individuality.[107] It is above all in this third element that God exists as absolute Spirit.[108] This third element is the final reconciling moment in the religion of absolute subjectivity, the moment thereby giving fullest expression to what Hegel has called the Christian principle or the idea of Christianity as the self-consciousness of freedom or the freedom of selfconsciousness.[109]

In his development of this final reconciling moment of inclusive and now explicitly realized absolute subjectivity, Hegel proposes to establish the reconciliation of the individual believer with the life, death and resurrection of Christ in three stages or subsections: the origin (*Entstehung*) of the community; the realization (*Realisierung*) of the community; and, "the realization of the spirituality of the community in universal actuality."[110] These three stages are contained in the three subsections discernible in Lasson's compilation of 1827 transcripts on this third and final element of absolute religion.

An initial reading of this third, subjective element of absolute religion and its three progressive stages or subsections results in the at first glance rather surprising recurrent emphasis on the objective. In the first subdivision, the origin or coming into existence of the community,[111] Hegel recapitulates the prior element's second extreme, namely, the objective reconciliation now present as the spiritual consciousness of the risen Christ. It is an objective reconciliation to be participated in by other finite Subjects.[112] The origin of the community in this objective reconciliation now present as shared spiritual consciousness is in religious terms phrased as the resurrection, ascension[113] and "the outpouring of the Holy Spirit."[114] This outpouring is the immediate rising to consciousness of "a sensible human appearance"[115] now present in a spiritual way.[116] Appropriately then this objectively realized and now spiritually interpreted reconciliation is available to the individual finite Subject first in the immediate knowledge of faith (*Glauben*).[117] The confirmation of this faith and of this consciousness of the spiritual must itself be spiritual and could not be accomplished in sense immediacy.[118] This first moment or subsection, the origin of the community, is then the particularity of objective reconciliation as an originary, unitary spiritualized consciousness immediately available to the individual Subject in the form of thought which is faith.[119]

In this third overall or major element of Hegel's development of the absolute or consummate religion, that is, community, Hegel comes now to treat faith as the presupposition[120] out of and as explication of which he elaborates this third element's second subsection, the realization of the community.[121] By what can only be called a stroke of systematic genius Hegel proposes an understanding of faith as the originary unity of the act of believing (immediate knowledge) and that which is believed (the spiritualized presence of objective reconciliation).[122] He points out that this immediacy of faith overcomes the difficulty of the separation between individual Subject and absolute Spirit. That is, religiously expressed, God sees the heart and the inner, true, "earnest willing,"[123] which will later become the rational will.

Properly speaking, Hegel begins the development of the second subsection, the realization of the community, with the insistence that this initial and undeveloped faith as "felt, flash-like witness of the Spirit"[124] must be developed or made explicit in the arena of representation. So Hegel is recorded as making the transition with the help of a similarity in German theological terms from the internality of an already available and presupposed teaching (*Lehre*) as faith (*Glauben*) to the externality of the mixed form of thought, doctrine (*Glaubenslehre*).[125] For Hegel doctrine reestablishes otherness out of the unity of faith. Doctrine is already at hand, a given, not as sensible realities are externally available, but as that which is taught in the Church. The individual Subject is born into this doctrine and participates at first unconsciously therein (Baptism).[126] Truth as doctrine comes to the Subject "necessarily . . . at first . . . in the form of *authority*."[127] Truth or doctrine, that is, the rational as spiritual, exists then for the Subject as something valid, as something to be learned in the Church and assimilated or made one's own.[128] That which was originally at hand as the inner Spirit corresponding to this rational content or doctrine has become an object for that consciousness. In the Church, then, education, practice and formation constitute for the Subject the "becoming acclimated to the good and the rational."[129] The Subject (or here the child) is therefore born into freedom in so far as when it is born into the Church it comes to know itself in and through this other, namely, doctrine whose otherness is already present as having been overcome. There is, Hegel continues, no question of overcoming evil, since evil has already been overcome by Spirit as, now, "intrinsically a nullity."[130] The Church is to make sure that the truth of this objective overcoming of evil becomes ever more identified with the Self, with the human will.¹³¹ In this identification with the overcoming of evil, the community becomes real. It is no longer a question of the community in its arising, but in its continuing in existence as Church. "The real community is what we generally call the *church*."¹³²

Hegel brings this second subsection, the realization of the community, to a close by positing the Church as the institution by and in which the individual Subject comes to the truth of reconciliation. The Holy Spirit is then present in the individuals so that they exist in the participatory enjoyment of the truth, of the Spirit. The truth, the doctrine of reconciliation, is no longer available merely as the pouring forth of the Spirit but as the enjoyment of the presence of God, of unity with God. Surprisingly enough for a Protestant, Hegel refers at this point to this unity's beginning with the Host.¹³³ Hegel gives his interpretation of the Catholic position on transubstantiation and of the reformed position on presence in memory. But it is really by means of his interpretation of the Lutheran position wherein God is present not in externality but in Spirit and faith, in the believer, that Hegel concludes to the enjoyment of the presence of God, "the partaking of the presence of God in the self-preservation of the community."¹³⁴ In each of these moments, that is, out of presupposed faith through doctrine, Church and sacrament it has always been for Hegel a question of the reconciling activity of the Spirit, of the objectively presented universality of truth mediating the objective reconciliation in Christ to the individual Subjects, so that the presence of God in Christ is now subjectively available to the individual Subjects as the conscious enjoyment in community of the presence of God.¹³⁵

In the 1827 lectures absolute religion's third main section, community, concludes with a terse but complex third subsection, "the realization of the spirituality of the community in universal actuality."¹³⁶ This third subsection is for Hegel the movement from the shared conscious inner enjoyment of the presence of God to a claimed adequate mediation in self-knowledge, in philosophy. The 1827 transcripts convey the sense of a three-step development: first, from the positing of this interior enjoyment's need to be realized in exterior life, secondly, to a triply developed objective realization culminating in ethical life and, thirdly, to the fulfillment of that inner peace or enjoyment of the presence of God in an again triply developed movement to the adequacy of philosophical thought.¹³⁷ In the first of these three steps¹³⁸ Hegel proposes that the inner enjoyment of the presence of God must find its externalization in secular reality for two reasons. First, on the one hand, because the pure heart, which has attained reconciliation, remains abstract over against the world. The Self here reconciled interiorly is still only universal spirituality.[139] On the other hand, secondly, this inner reconciliation is equally that of a Subject having a developed worldliness already at hand. Inversely, "the truth for the worldly is the spiritual."[140] In his elaboration on this principle, Hegel moves from the Subject as object of divine grace, to the establishment of the Subject's infinite worth, on the basis of which then the Subject recognizes itself as Spirit's certainty of itself. This knowledge is the eternity of Spirit, the freedom with which the Subject as free Person relates to the world. This liberation (*Befreiung*) or being at home in the world has arisen according to Hegel out of religion itself.[141] "This freedom, which has the impulse and determinacy to realize itself, is rationality."[142] Thus Hegel is recorded at this point as stating two principles: truth for the secular is the spiritual, and, freedom is to be interpreted as rationality.

In the second of these three steps[143] Hegel develops three ways in which the Subject moves freely to realize reconciliation in secular life. The first way[144] is for Hegel the untrue mode of immediacy, an asceticism maintaining a negative relationship of the community with and against the world. This undeveloped spirituality or reconciliation is untrue because it pertains to Spirit to differentiate into worldliness.[145] The second of these ways[146] is that in which Church and world, religiosity and worldliness remain external to one another, "a relation in which one dominates over the other, and thus there is no reconciliation at all."[147] The domineering Church takes the secular up into itself while leaving the secular itself unreconciled.[148] In this relationship of un-freedom (*Unfreiheit*), a spiritless worldliness enters into the Church. In this Church the human is at odds with itself, in slavery. Such a reconciliation with secular life is exactly the opposite of reconciliation.[149] This rupture so carried out is the corruption of the Church, "the absolute contradiction of the spiritual within itself."[150] What makes this grouping of objective realizations for Hegel no mere list[151] but, rather, a grouping to be systematically interrelated is his insistence that the third of them, ethical life (*Sittlichkeit, das Sittliche*),[152] is the resolution of this contradiction found within the domineering Church, the second of these objective realizations. Ethical life is inner reconciliation's true and objective realization in secular life since ethical living introduces the principle of freedom into the worldly itself.[153] In as the worldly now in ethical life has been formed in accord with reason, it is "freedom that has become concrete and will that is rational."[154] The earnest will of faith[155] has for Hegel become the rational will in the ethical. Reconciliation with the worldly is realized in a movement from immediate to domineering to ethical.[156] That is, in view of the available terse transcript text, in a general way from universal to particular to individual, from positive but as such untrue to negative to negation of the negation.[157]

Hegel's identification of freedom with rationality was here first developed in what could only be described as the "real" (*reell*) or objective side of realized reconciliation, though Hegel himself does not use this term. Since Hegel is still working on the level of representation, he now appropriately sketches as third step in the realization of the spirituality of the community in universal actuality a second, that is, "ideal" (*ideell*) or inclusively subjective side[158] emerging in and out of religious consciousness. This second side, the truth of the "real" side, consists in three subjective attitudes logically speaking structurally parallel to the prior movement of the three objective realizations of inner reconciliation culminating in ethical living.[159] Following the reconciliation of spiritual and worldly in ethical life, Hegel begins this last step in the third subsection with a reference back to the Subject's *knowledge* (*Wissen*) of its inner peace *with itself*.[160] Whereas in the prior parallel development of the three objective realizations of inner reconciliation the stress was on the presence of developed worldliness to the Subject,[161] now Hegel emphasizes that the Subject knows this reconciliation of Spirit as reconciliation with itself. "Inwardness knows itself to be present to itself precisely in the reconciliation of Spirit with itself; and this knowledge of being present to Self is precisely thinking."[162]

This knowledge of being present to oneself, of being at peace with oneself remains according to Hegel abstract and undeveloped.[163] This freedom of reason as reconciliation or liberation opposes itself now after the reconciliation in ethical life to any merely spiritless externality.[164] Hegel identifies this attitude, first, with the concrete form of the Englightenment.[165] He treats the Enlightenment with respect by insisting that it has maintained the freedom of spirit[166] and retains the principle of freedom, though as only abstractly grasped.[167] Hegel, secondly, identifies this attitude of thought opposing itself to any spiritless externality with the attitude of pure subjectivity,[168] historically speaking, Pietism.[169] This attitude stays with the determination of the good as pure but abstract freedom. In an intriguing analysis Hegel interprets this position as one of caprice and contingency, a subjectivity abandoning truth.[170] Though this pure subjectivity or Pietism, which Hegel treats less respectfully than the Enlightenment, denies any doctrine, it does retain a relationship of mere feeling with Christ.[171] Not only is Pietism, therefore, for Hegel a self-contradiction in the way in which it tries to realize reconciliation, but Enlightenment and Pietism find themselves to be "the two extremes opposing each other in the development of the community."[172] Despite their mutual opposition, these two have according to Hegel the same catastrophic result: the refusal of truth, an unfreedom due to there being no included objective content.[173]

The third of these three attitudes or posturings of thought vis-à-vis objective content is philosophy, which is for Hegel knowledge or subjectivity developing out of itself and reconciling content according to the necessity to be found in the content itself.

> The third stage consists in the fact that subjectivity develops the content out of itself, to be sure, but in accord with necessity, that it knows and acknowledges this content as necessary and as objective, existing in and for itself. This is the standpoint of *philosophy*, according to which the content takes refuge in the Concept and obtains its justification by thinking.[174]

Philosophy is comprehending thought (*Begreifen*) which as essentially concrete "determines itself to its totality, to the Idea."[175] In and with philosophy thought has become independent, free reason.[176] As subjective freedom it produces the truth, and yet acknowledges this truth from an objective standpoint as existing in and for itself.[177] The Concept is the justification of religion because it both recognizes the limitations of the forms of the content of religion and sees beyond their finitude, whereas the Enlightenment only knew of negation, and Pietism needed no content.[178] Philosophy reconciles the forms or ways in which God has appeared in as it is these forms themselves which are to have arrived at universality, at thought.[179] As "third" over against Enlightenment and Pietism philosophy has now more proximately reconciled the opposition between the extremes of Enlightenment abstract thought and Pietist feeling as well as the contradiction inherent in Pietism itself. Thought accomplishes this for Hegel in so far as it is the very process of thought, once it has begun to set itself against the concrete, "to carry through this opposition until it arrives at reconciliation."[180] This process of thought, the acknowledgement of necessity in religious forms and of their limitation, is what Hegel calls the witness of the Spirit, thought (*Denken*) itself.[181] The reconciliation of thought with the concrete, a reconciliation posited by Hegel in the arrival at self-positing objective thought, is philosophy. So, "philosophy is to this extent theology."[182] Philosophy has reconciled God, nature and finite Spirit. "This reconciliation is the peace of God."[183]

The individual Subject's knowledge or conceptual awareness of its inner peace with God and therefore with itself has now for Hegel become as philosophy the reconciliation which is the very peace of God. Hegel's move in this third and last step, the "ideal" side to the realization of the spirituality of the community in universal actuality, is the freedom of a self-development[184] out of the pure heart or immediacy posited previously at the beginning of this third subsection in the transition from the realization of the community to the realization of the spirituality of the community.[185] However, not only is this third and last step culminating in philosophy for Hegel such a self-development, but it is as well the synthesis of the initial immediacy of the pure heart with ethical living, that is, with the actualization of this inner reconciliation in the external world. The synthesis or reconciliation of spiritual, meaning here, inner reconciliation, and worldly achieved finally as philosophical thought has for Hegel arisen by means of a (repeated) dialectic of negation of negation (with one exception, the three interpretations of eucharistic presence). This progression from the immediacy of pure heart to philosophy has occurred according to Hegel through ethical living with this latter, in turn, itself as result in relation to the opposition of asceticism and dominating Church. The realization of the spiritual in objective reality is in its result, ethical living, equally the means to the renewed immediacy of the pure heart now as Concept become Idea which is for Hegel the unity of Concept and reality. Finally, this realization of the spirituality of the community as philosophical Concept is as well in terms of logical structure an enriched return to the immediacy previously identified on the level of absolute or consummate religion as "immanent" Trinity. The objective realizations of inner reconciliation with the worldly occur successively as asceticism, the ruling Church and ethical life, in a movement identifiable as one from universality to particularity to individuality. The ideal side moves from abstract thought or Enlightenment to a self-contradictory feeling or Pietism on to their fulfillment or adequate form in philosophy, again universality, particularity, individuality.[186] As enriched return to the immediacy previously identified on the level of absolute religion as first element or "immanent" Trinity, these two realizations repeat the logical structure of "immanent" Trinity.[187] Their result is for Hegel realized inclusive absolute subjectivity, the Self as Concept and the Concept as Idea.[188]

This transition from the abstractness of the pure heart to philosophy, namely, to absolute Spirit as the Concept, self-positing and self-determining absolute subjectivity, represents for Hegel the final moment of reconciliation between the objective reconciliation already achieved in Christ and the individual Subject. With philosophy this mediation takes on the final form of universal reality, the Concept, as concrete universal, as totality and therefore as inclusive, developed individuality.[189] This process of universality's concrete realization as individuality is described in the 1827 transcripts as "the realization of the spirituality of the community in universal actuality."[190]

The transition to this realization of the spirituality of the community in philosophy is the end result of the progression Hegel posits in community, the third element of the absolute religion in the 1827 lectures. This progression is for Hegel, in the form of thought, the realization in the individual Subject of the reconciliation between divine and human objectively established in the death and resurrection of Christ. This transition occurs as the presence of God established in Christ, realized in the individual Subject as member of the spiritual community and then enjoyed and become conscious of by that member. This conscious enjoyment of the presence of God becomes for Hegel the inner peace of the individual Subject with God and, finally, the very peace of God. This transition takes place for Hegel within the third element as one from immediate faith as witness of the Spirit to thought again as witness of the Spirit and from sincere will to rational will to thought. From the point of view of the dynamic development or internal progression out of primordial and presupposed faith through doctrine, Church and sacrament to realization of the individual Subject's inner reconciliation first with the worldly in ethical life and then culminantly in philosophy as the concrete universality which is individuality, this development corresponds to and arises first out of empirical observation. More fundamentally it is the very development of the idea of God itself. It is a movement from beginning through progression to result, from universality to particularity to individuality.

More importantly, however, from the point of view of religious reconciliation and philosophical mediation the third element is structured as a movement from particularity by means of objective universality to inclusive individuality (B-A-E). The first stage or subsection[191] in this third element, in community, is the origin of the community, a moment identifiable as particularity. It is the presence of God as Spirit or objective universality in the spiritual form of crucified and risen Christ, a spiritual presence immediately available in faith. In the second subsection,[192] the realization of the community, the objectivity Hegel regularly stresses throughout the third element and here in his discussion of presupposed faith, of doctrine, Church and sacrament is the mediating presence of God as Holy Spirit. This mediating presence is objective universality inclusive of the particularity of the spiritually interpreted objective reconciliation in Christ and the individual Subjects in whom the philosophical Concept is to arise.[193] From the point of view of reconciliation, the second stage or subsection is identifiable as objective universality filled with content. In the third stage,[194] the realization of the spirituality of the community in universal actuality, objective universality becomes the concrete reconciliation of spiritual and worldly in ethical life and, finally, for Hegel the free, concrete individuality of the self-knowledge of the sublated finite Subject in the philosophical Concept. The structure (B-A-E) of mediation as religious reconciliation in the third element or community develops as that of the disjunctive syllogism.[195] The middle term, universality, appears as universality, particularity and individuality. This middle term is characterized as objective universality inclusive of the two extremes, a filled (*erfüllte*) universality. There occurs here a mediation in which each of the moments mediates the other two. Universality as explicitly posited mediating and mediated middle term has indicated the sublated presence of otherness. The other is now the Self posited as other, that is, the sublation of syllogistically structured trinitarian reconciliation. This has resulted according to Hegel in the transition from a reconciliation characterized by the continuing presence of the reconciling other to the immediacy of the philosophical Concept as self-mediation.

Though the absolute religion develops for Hegel as this self-mediation as yet on the level of religious representation, it does for Hegel contain the true content of self-mediating absolute Spirit. In "immanent" and "economic" syllogistically structured trinitarian reconciliation absolute religion has shown itself to be the religion of absolute subjectivity, the self-consciousness of freedom in which Subject has recognized itself in its other. The absolute or consummate religion, Hegel's interpretation of Christianity, has for Hegel shown itself to be the fulfillment of the Concept of religion and of the (other)[196] determinate religions. The 1827 transcripts have provided an overall systematically complete presentation of the trinitarian development of the consummate religion despite the possibility that the transcripts gathered in Lasson might not contain a full record of all Hegel had said during the 1827 lectures on absolute religion.[197] In these 1827 lectures, the three elements of absolute religion progress according to Hegel's understanding of the truth of the syllogism.[198] That is, each of the determinations of the Concept has functioned successively as middle term in the progression of the syllogisms of necessity: "immanent" Trinity as categorical syllogism A-B-E (universality-particularity-individuality); diremption and reconciliation as hypothetical syllogism A-E-B (universality-individuality-particularity); spiritual community as disjunctive syllogism B-A-E (particularity-universality-individuality). Hegel's overall inferential argumentation has here exhibited an intended necessary progression of middle terms B→E→A. Even allowing then for the doubled syllogistic development in the Encyclopedia,[199] Hegel's presentation of trinitarian reconciliation has, in its syllogistic structure and progression of middle terms, remained constant and consistent from the 1807 *Phenomenology*[200] on through to the various editions of the *Encyclopedia*[201] and to the philosophy of religion *Lectures*.

3. Critique of Trinitarian Reconciliation as Spiritual Community

a. Concentration on the Third Element as Syllogism

The examination and critique of specific texts from Hegel's *Logic* in Chapters One and Two above have in effect served as a critique of "immanent" Trinity, which Hegel by the 1827 philosophy of religion lectures referred to as the "first element" of absolute or consummate religion. This critique concluded to the finitude of any beginning available to human thought. The examination and critique of portions of Hegel's *Phenomenology* in the second half of Chapter Three and in Chapter Four above have in principle, though in the context of the *Phenomenology*'s specific character as a theory of self-consciousness, treated diremption and reconciliation, referred to by Hegel in 1827 as the "second element" of absolute religion. Any finite beginning was seen to be the beginning of a finite but real progression or enrichment, a growth as qualitative increment. It is now necessary to concentrate on Hegel's understanding of the culmination of trinitarian reconciliation in and as spiritual community, what Hegel calls in the 1827 lectures the "third element" of consummate religion. It will be concluded that finite progression or for that matter any enrichment bears a specific, in principle, triadic structure.[202]

This concentration on the "third element" of consummate religion in Hegel's 1827 lectures[203] is important not only from the perspective of methodological and systematic completeness, but more particularly in view of this third element's significance on the level of Hegel's philosophy of religion. The third element, spiritual community, is culminating moment of the absolute religion, which itself is in turn consummation of the Concept of religion[204] and, especially by the 1827 lectures, synthesis of that Concept with the prior, determinate religions.[205] Community, and more specifically its third subsection, "the realization of the spirituality of the community in universal actuality,"[206] presents in Hegel's thought the transition[207] to philosophical mediation in the Concept as Self. Community, the third element, is itself for Hegel unquestionably the movement of absolute Spirit in its true content as absolute divine self-determining subjectivity, God existing as Spirit in the community of finite Subjects.[208]

The movement of Spirit in its true content as absolute divine self-positing and self-determining subjectivity is for Hegel the movement of the consciousness of God, with this genitive functioning typically for Hegel as both objective and subjective. Spirit is the self-consciousness of God.[209] As is indicated particularly clearly in the 1824 lectures, Spirit is for Hegel a movement of self-differentiation and sublation of that difference.[210] In the consummate religion in general,[211] and particularly in this third element, community, and its third subsection or movement to universal actuality, Hegel synthesizes the notions of Spirit, the living God, the Holy Spirit, Trinity, absolute subjectivity, Concept as Idea and truth into one dynamic of self-othering and sublation of that otherness.[212] This dynamic is for Hegel the movement of rational thought or rationality, which he identifies as the essence of freedom.[213] So it is that, in the absolute or consummate religion in general but particularly in its third element and thematically in that third element's third subsection, Hegel sees coming to fruition what can be termed the Christian principle of the self-consciousness of freedom. "The freedom of self-consciousness is the content of religion, and this content is itself the object of the

Christian Religion, i.e., Spirit is its own object."[214] This freedom of self-consciousness is the development simultaneously of the living God as Trinity, of absolute subjectivity, of Spirit, Idea and Truth, since freedom is for Hegel rationality. As such, freedom must develop according to the inner necessity of the content involved,[215] finally the necessity of the Concept. Freedom is ultimately for Hegel necessary self-determination.

It would be possible to critique Hegel's positing of trinitarian reconciliation as spiritual community by focusing on his conception of freedom as necessary self-determination on the level of philosophy of religion. This would involve an examination of Hegel's definition of humanness in terms of rationality,[216] so that human freedom is realized to the extent that human consciousness is sublated in the movement of self-determining thought.[217] It would be necessary to ask if freedom as necessary self-determination is at all available to a finite Subject in such a way that it would not destroy rather than sublate that finitude.[218] It would, secondly, be important to ask if Hegel's understanding of freedom as necessary self-determination is not rooted in an excessively narrow characterization of otherness as negation. Freedom might take on a different structure and coloration if otherness were co-constitutively positive and negative.[219] But, rather than pursue a critique of Hegel's understanding of freedom on the level of the philosophy of religion, it will be more economical to turn directly to the logical structure Hegel has given to this freedom as trinitarian reconciliation in spiritual community. If freedom is for Hegel rationality, the most significant point at which to make a critique of the viability of his understanding of freedom as necessary self-determination will be the disjunctive syllogism.[220] This syllogism, which is for Hegel the logical structure of spiritual community,[221] is itself the last of the syllogisms in Hegel's *Logic*. It contains for Hegel its own presuppositions and is the grounding truth of all his logically prior syllogisms.[222] The disjunctive syllogism is for Hegel the posited identity of that which mediates and that which is mediated.[223] As the truth of syllogistic mediation, in the *Logic* the disjunctive syllogism is, in the very fulfillment of its structure as inclusive self-determining subjectivity, to result in the sublation of the very syllogistic form of mediation.[224] It becomes imperative to make a critique of Hegel's proposed trinitarian reconciliation, his understanding of spiritual community as the freedom of necessary self-determination, directly in the clarity and accessibility of its logically formulated proposal as disjunctive syllogism.

b. Critique of Hegel's Disjunctive Syllogism

In the 1827 lectures Hegel sketches the spiritual community as a dialectical development from its origin in the particularity of the spiritualized consciousness of Christ through the universality of the realization of the community to the realization of the spirituality of the community in universal actuality as individuality. Hegel consistently envisions the dynamic of the spiritual community as the movement, in pure thought, of the disjunctive syllogism, particularity (B)/universality (A)/individuality (E).[225] In Hegel's *Logic* the disjunctive syllogism reads:

> A is either B or C or D,
> But A is B,
> Therefore A is neither C nor D.[226]

Stated very generally,[227] Hegel claims that individuality indicated by the exclusion, "neither C nor D," is mediated with particularity indicated by the disjunction, "either B or C or D," by means of the presence of the middle term, A, as universality and functioning as Subject in both premises and in the conclusion. A is universality in the first premise, serves as particularity (is determinate) in the second premise and is posited as individuality in the conclusion. It can then for Hegel equally be said that A as universality is mediated with individuality. In the disjunctive syllogism A, or universality is for Hegel that which mediates and that which is mediated.[228]

A more careful reading of Hegel's text on the disjunctive syllogism in the *Logic* reveals that Hegel develops the essentials of his presentation of the disjunctive syllogism in a text[229] consisting of three clearly distinguishable sections. First, there is the core exposition with which Hegel attempts to establish his understanding of disjunctive syllogism.[230] Then, secondly, Hegel illustrates the structural movement of the disjunctive syllogism with two alternative formulations.[231] With specific reference to this schema of the disjunctive syllogism, Hegel then in the third section[232] repeats[233] what had been posited in the first section. By further reflection on the structure of the disjunctive syllogism, he concludes[234] that it results in the unity of that which mediates (universality) and that which is mediated (universality). So for Hegel the syllogistic form of mediation has been sublated. There is no longer any syllogism.

Before actually presenting a critique of Hegel's understanding of disjunctive syllogism by means of an examination of the first section or core exposition, it is important to underscore certain of Hegel's observations in the first half[235] of his third of the three sections developing the essentials of his view of the disjunctive syllogism. Hegel had earlier spoken of universality, A, Subject of the first premise, as genus (*Gattung*).[236] He here claims that universality is posited as particularity in the predicate of the first premise, "either B or C or D," with this predicate taken as the universal particularized into the totality of its species. In the second premise, universality is posited as determinate or as a species (*Art*). In the conclusion, universality is posited as exclusive, individual determinateness. With reference specifically to the second possible formulation of the disjunctive syllogism (but applicable in its wording to individuality in both formulations), Hegel spoke of universality's being posited as "exclusive individuality" (*ausschliessende Einzelheit*), an individuality which excludes. By "excluding individuality" Hegel means an individuality which is the momentary totality of the Concept over against but equally inclusive of itself as universality and particularity[237] as well as exclusive of "others" in the plural.[238] Individuality is for Hegel constituted by "exclusive totality," just as for Hegel particularity is "the *universal* sphere particularized into the totality of its species."[239]

At first sight it would appear strange that Hegel has spoken in the first and third sections of his development of the disjunctive syllogism in terms of the momentary totalities in the order universality/particularity/individuality (A/B/E). It would seem strange because the very dynamic of the disjunctive syllogism was to be the mediation of particularity with individuality by means of universality (B-A-E, or as in the *Logic* E-A-B). But as a closer examination of the structure of the disjunctive syllogism will show, the mediation of particularity with individuality by means of the middle term, universality, is itself dependent for Hegel on his ability to establish the predicate of the first premise ("either B or C or D") as totality of species, and therefore particularity. The inferential movement from the second premise to the conclusion is dependent upon the either/or which is predicate of the first premise.[240] In the disjunctive syllogism the mediation of particularity and individuality by means of universality and the self-determining of the momentary totality, concrete universality, as particularity and individuality are in fact the same dialectical development of self-mediating subjectivity. B-A-E stresses the resultant interrelationship of the determinations of the Concept, and

A/B/E stresses the movement or self-development of the Concept as the various thought determinations.[241] A critique of the disjunctive syllogism as the self-determining movement A/B/E is a critique of the syllogistic interrelational structure B-A-E.

A critique of Hegel's understanding of and claims for the disjunctive syllogism can best be carried out by an examination of the core exposition with which Hegel attempts to develop this syllogism. In thirteen lines he begins with the overall statement that the middle term as self-determining totality, developed objective universality, is not only universality but also particularity and individuality. He moves on to a progressive elaboration of that statement by consideration of universality and particularity respectively as genus and species. Hegel's core exposition reads:

> [123.36] But the middle term is the *universality* that is *pregnant with form*; [37] it has determined itself as *totality*, as *developed* objective universality. [124.1] Consequently the middle term is not only universality [2] but also particularity and individuality. As universality it is first the substantial identity [3] of the genus; but secondly an identity that *embraces within itself particularity*, [4] but a particularity *co-extensive with this identity of the genus*; it is therefore the universal sphere that [5] contains its total particularization—the genus disjoined into its species: *A* that is [6] *B and C and D*. But particularization is differentiation and as such is just as much [7] the *either-or* of *B*, *C* and *D*, the *negative* unity, the *reciprocal* [8] exclusion of the terms. Further, this exclusion is not [9] merely a reciprocal exclusion, or the determination merely a relative one, but is just as [10] essentially a *self-related* determination, the particular as *individuality* [11] to the exclusion of the *others*.[242]

This brief text, in which Hegel tries to elucidate the disjunctive syllogism's inferential movement in terms of the genus universality's functioning equally as particularity in the totality of the species and, finally, as exclusive individuality, constitutes a privileged point at which to make a critique of Hegel's structuring of freedom as necessary self-determination. The text on the disjunctive syllogism in general and this core text in particular[243] provides the opportunity to discuss together in one text both Hegel's formulation of disjunction, namely his "either/or" (124.7) and his proposed "excluding individuality" (124.7–11). Though there would not have been the close trinitarian tie-in, it would also have been possible, on the one hand, to challenge Hegel's position earlier in the *Logic* where he develops the Concept as particularity and individuality.[244] However, at that point Hegel is not forced to treat so explicitly of particularity as disjunctively formulated totality of the species. On the other hand, it would likewise have been possible to confront Hegel where he presents the disjunctive judgement,[245] though there Hegel is not forced to handle so clearly the viability of proposing the Concept as "exclusive individuality." For purposes of critique it will then not be necessary to summarize all the steps in this core exposition. Rather, this text provides the opportunity to highlight the weakness in Hegel's development by referring to the way in which Hegel treats of disjunction and exclusion. This can be done by reviewing the way in which he in this core text interweaves "excluding" (*Ausschliessen*) and "as well as" (*ebensosehr*) in view of "as much [one]/as [the other]" (*sowohl/als*) and "either/or" (*entweder/oder*).

On the basis of the transition from the hypothetical syllogism now to the disjunctive syllogism (123.26–124.6),[246] Hegel tries, first, firmly to establish that the predicate of the first premise ("either B or C or D") is universality as particularity, the totality of the universal sphere of species, "*A that is B and C and D*" (124.3–6). The "as much [one]/as [the other]" is meant by Hegel to indicate the positive identity of the particular with the universal.[247] Hegel, then, typically recalls that particularization (*Besonderung*) is, as differentiation, as well (*ebensosehr*) the "*either-or of B, C and D*" (124.6–8). He wants this to be a mutual exclusion of "determinations" (*Bestimmung*) not only relative to one another (124.8–9), which would amount to a finitization, but a mutual exclusion which is equally a self-related determination, and thus exclusive individuality (124.8–11). "As much [one]/as [the other]" is meant by Hegel to point out the equality and identity of universality as the identity of the genus and as the particularity which is the totality of the species. "Either/or" is used by Hegel to allow him, on the basis of the differentiation which particularization is, to establish universality now as exclusive individuality.

Despite Hegel's clear intention of establishing universality as momentary totality of particularity and as momentary totality of exclusive individuality, what actually occurs is the immediate collapse of particularity into finite individualities. Hegel proposes to establish particularity as totality of species contained in the genus (124.2–5), which itself is objective universality (123.36–124.1). Since particularization is equally (*ebensosehr*) differentiation, it is as well the reciprocal exclusion of the determinations ("*Bestimmungen*") (124.6–8). "Determinations" remains somewhat ambiguous here in Hegel's text. In other contexts it could be presumed that the term refers to the thought determinations of universality and particularity, as might at first sight be concluded on the basis of Hegel's prior use of "as well [one]/as [the other]." Hegel might have intended here to presume a logically prior exclusion between Subject and predicate in the disjunctive syllogism's first premise. But the logically first exclusion occurs among "B, C and D" as species, so that "determinations" must for the sake of disjunction be taken to refer to the other species, to the species among themselves, an interpretation confirmed by a close reading of the text itself. The logically prior, first mutual exclusion is at this point among the species and not between universality and particularity inclusive of universality.[248]

Hegel continues by saying that this exclusion is not only reciprocal exclusion but "just as" (*ebensosehr*) "essentially a *self-related* determination; the particular as *individuality* to the exclusion of the *others*" (124.10–11).[249] This subsequent linkage of exclusion with the reminder that this differentiation is just as essentially self-related so that this is an exclusion now effectively of individuality over against and inclusive of particularity and universality rushes past the problematic already raised in establishing the first or reciprocal exclusion among species on the basis of particularity as differentiation. The "as much [one]/as [the other]" is not able to cover the fact that in the disjunctive syllogism the disjunction is among discrete, mutually related others. Hegel's proposal of a reciprocally exclusive differentiation among species as means to arrive at an exclusive individuality as totality acknowledges and has already introduced into the predicate of the first premise exclusive individuality as merely finite and relative. Of course Hegel himself cannot and does not claim that this reciprocal exclusion remains on the level of species. He has acknowledged that the exclusion is mutual and the determination relative, though he adds, not only such (124.6–11). It is important to recall that exclusivity is for Hegel the characteristic of individuality, not particularity.[250] So, in establishing finite reciprocally exclusive individualities, Hegel cannot then by means of a reminder ("just as" *ebensosehr* 124.19) of a self-related determination recoup what has already been lost in the positing of a reciprocal and therefore relative differentiation among species.

This step to finite differentiation might at first have merely sounded like Hegel's expected dialectic of giving logical expression to finitude in the methodological moment of progression. However, already at this point, where Hegel claimed to be treating of particularity, he is in the realm of individuality, and more exactly of finite individualities, finite others. Hegel wanted to posit accomplished resultant mediation in the form of an exclusive individuality as inclusive totality. He had in his reflection on the disjunctive syllogism attempted to acknowledge this characteristic of individuality as excluding precisely by means of a reminder that for him individuality was as well (*ebensosehr*) excluding self-relation. The climax to this development of the disjunctive syllogism was to have been the establishment of the posited identity of mediating universality and mediated universality,[251] thus the sublation of syllogistic mediation issuing in the immediacy of objectivity.[252] Instead, what resulted was a renewed need for further mediation. Particularity as totality of species and, consequently, exclusive individuality as inclusive totality prove as moments of pure thought to be untenable conceptualities.[253]

Hegel is not able to establish necessary disjunctive self-determination in pure thought. Since he cannot develop objective universality as posited particularity and individuality, there can be no syllogistically elaborated mediation of particularity and individuality by universality such that universality itself would be mediated as well. Hegel cannot establish a movement of pure thought as self-mediation. In view of the fact that the disjunctive syllogism B-A-E cannot be defended on the level of a proposed pure thought as Hegel had intended, freedom cannot be defined as necessary self-determination of the Concept as Subject. Hegel's notion of freedom as necessary self-determination is, then, not to be repudiated so much on the basis of more traditional theological considerations as because it is itself philosophically not convincingly presentable as a movement of pure thought. It was this disjunctive syllogism as movement of necessary self-determination which was to have provided the reasoned structure of spiritual community in its development out of the particularity of its origin through the universality of its on-going existence in Spirit to the realization of that community's spirituality in universal actuality as inclusive individuality. Hegel's proposed trinitarian reconciliation in absolute religion's third element, community or absolute Spirit as absolute divine subjectivity in and through finite Subjects, presupposes for its development the viability of this self-determining dialectic as thought and, more specifically, as the disjunctive syllogism of pure thought. Therefore, Hegel's conception of community cannot be maintained as he proposed it. And to the extent that Hegel's first and second elements of consummate religion (and even his Concept of religion itself) are dependent in their trinitarian syllogistic structure on this third element, they too fall under this critique since Hegel's necessary progression of syllogistic middle terms B→E→A remains ungrounded. What Hegel terms the third element, spiritual community, is not the gathering of finite Subjects in the necessary actualization he had envisioned, but rather the ever-to-be-renewed gathering of those living in the freedom of hope.[254]

4. The Formal Triadic Structure of Becoming

Hegel had proposed a spiritual community of finite Subjects in and through which there was to occur the necessary actualization of absolute Spirit as triadically structured syllogistic self-mediation. Here in Chapter Five it has been concluded that Hegel's disjunctive syllogistic structuring of spiritual community in the realphilosophical sphere of religion was not viable ultimately because Hegel could not establish the disjunctive syllogism itself as explicit self-mediation. It was demonstrated in Chapter Two above that Hegel's understanding of pure thought was not available in that pure thought's proposed first moment as pure being. It has been argued in Chapter Four above that such a proposed pure thought could not viably structure a divine-human Self's immediate appearance to consciousness as the settling of becoming in *Dasein*. Whether Hegel treats of this settling of becoming in *Dasein*, of pure being or of the disjunctive syllogism, he has not presented, and cannot convincingly present, self-mediation as a movement of self-determining pure thought. Consequently Hegel cannot, in the way in which he wants to, either initiate an "inner" trinitarian movement or argue to divine self-revelation as the immediate unity of a divine-human Self or, again, present a spiritual community to be sublated in the philosophic actualization of the Concept. Hegel has not established and cannot establish trinitarian reconciliation on the basis of a self-determining pure thought as logically, but ultimately philosophically (conceptually), formulated self-mediating subjectivity as Spirit. He cannot equate freedom as self-determination with necessary logical self-determination of the Concept as Subject. He cannot establish his trinitarian claim in the way in which he proposed to do it.

In Hegel's trinitarian claim there lies expressed an understanding of God as inclusive and absolute subjectivity, or more to the point at the moment, as inclusive totality or whole. It is not this valuable understanding as such of God as inclusive totality which has been rejected so far. Rather, issue has been taken with the way in which Hegel set up his trinitarian claim and the specific dynamic he employed to establish it. As made particularly clear in the "economic" trinitarian divine self-othering, Hegel's working out of his trinitarian claim attempted to give expression to God as inclusive totality by proposing that God posits or others (God) Self as nature and finite Spirit. Then in and through finite Spirit God comes to (God) Self as Spirit in community and, finally, as philosophical Concept. The world as nature and finite Spirit was to have been God's own other, the self-othering of God. Nature and finite Spirit were to have become the momentary totality of finitude sublated in the philosophical Concept. Already, however, the fact that Hegel's God othered (God) Self logically speaking first in nature as the realm of unfreedom points out Hegel's more fundamental inability to establish the identification of freedom with a logically necessitated dialectical development of pure thought. The challenge, then, is to employ Hegel's envisionment of God as totality inclusive of the world in an attempt to reformulate his trinitarian claim in one way or another on the basis of the world's inability to be conceived of as a unity or to be thought finally without reference to God as inclusive other or totality.

Hegel's own trinitarian claim was that only if God were conceived of as Trinity could God be established as Spirit, that is, as concrete Subject and Person.[255] As Hegel proposed it, his trinitarian claim was to have been the expression, in philosophy of religion language, of his claim to have established a self-mediating inclusive and absolute subjectivity paradigmed in the logical progression of pure thought and finally realized as a self-positing dialectical development from originary infinite to finite as its own other on to enriched, inclusive infinite. Hegel has defined mediation most generally as "the condition of having gone out from a first to a second and a proceeding out of that which is different."[256] According to Hegel, syllogism in general gave clearest expression to this having gone out to a second and a proceeding out of that which is other. Especially his final syllogism, that of disjunction, was an unsuccessful attempt by Hegel to wed the essential role of otherness in mediation with his overall theory of self-mediating subjectivity. This integration was to have been available as a necessary logical movement of pure thought and a necessary self-actualization in philosophy as resultant, enriched return to the immediacy of logic.[257] Unfortunately Hegel's concern to proceed systematically first from an infinite, self-determining pure thought obscured the necessarily prior movement from finite becoming to the possibility of an infinite, grounding becoming. There can be discerned in Hegel's thought the correct identification of the elements of any positive mediation or becoming as Selfhood, otherness, and progression as enrichment. However, he had confused the issue, admittedly in a most brilliant fashion, by trying to proceed, systematically speaking, from the notion of a logically graspable self-mediating subjectivity.[258] Hegel obfuscated the trinitarian claim primarily by distracting from the fact that Selfhood, otherness, and progression as enrichment are constitutive aspects of *any* positive mediation or becoming available to thought as such. Finally, he obscured the question by tending to turn attention from the necessarily incomplete or finite character of any becoming initially available to thought.

At an earlier period of his life Hegel had flirted with the notion of becoming or mediation as either bad unification or good unification, but he quickly concentrated solely on mediation as positive unification.[259] As has been indicated in Chapter Four above,[260] the concern here in this study is with becoming as growth, enrichment and qualitative increment. Whether becoming as degeneration or disintegration would be sublatable into the understanding of becoming or mediation as growth, enrichment and qualitative increment need not be settled here. What is essential to the present step in this effort toward a tentative reconstruction of Hegel's trinitarian claim is the formal structure of becoming when this becoming is the inescapable fact of growth, whether that growth concretely be logical, psychological, emotional, interpersonal, or now in view of the present chapter's critique, communal and societal. What is at present essential is this becoming or mediation's structure taken formally in three senses. First, as was indicated in the conclusion to Chapter Four above,[261] the argument could under other circumstances be developed in more detail out of either the possible dialogical or monological formulations of finite becoming or out of a wider consideration of both of these dialectically identified. However here it is only the formal structure of any positive becoming which is to be treated as such. Second, formal in the sense that, though in fact reference here is made directly at first only to finite or limited becoming, the triadic formal structure finally to be indicated is in principle that of any becoming either available to and expressible in thought or in any way indicatable by thought.

To indicate the third sense in which there is concern here for becoming only in its most formal structure, it will help to recall again Hegel's response to the experience of socio-political, religious and philosophical alienation.[262] His fundamental response to this alienation had taken on the shape of a becoming as resultant, positive mediation. It was one of Hegel's great contributions not to try to explain away an apparently alienating otherness but rather to take otherness seriously enough to recast the whole relationship between Subject and object in such a way that otherness becomes essential to becoming or mediation. Unfortunately, as was mentioned earlier,[263] Hegel has oversimplified the logically speaking initial relationship between Subject and object in terms of otherness as negation.[264] Freeing finite becoming from the unjustifiable prior imposition of a necessarily self-determining movement of pure thought as self-mediation allows now for the acknowledgement of a multiple interplay and interrelationship[265] between Subject and object or otherness with otherness co-constitutively positive and negation.[266] While, then, acknowledging this multiple interplay between Selfhood and otherness, it is possible to identify the third sense in which the present concern is only with the formal structure of becoming. Of interest here is not the detailed working out of that multiple interplay,[267] but simply the indisputable reality of the interrelationship between Selfhood and otherness in any notion of becoming.

The inability of thought to remain merely with its own givenness or *Dasein* as beginning and without further enriching reflection is an irrefutable indication of the reality of finite becoming.[268] In different contexts this *Dasein* of finite thought quite appropriately has been taken to refer to beginning with finitude in various formulations. In the Conclusion to Chapter Two, *Dasein* quite naturally was taken to refer both to the givenness of a finite movement of logical thought and to the first thought determination in one possible elaboration of a movement of finite logical thought. In the Conclusion to Chapter Four, *Dasein* could equally well refer to the givenness of finite, that is, not totally inclusive qualitative increment or enriching growth. Common to any of these references is the indication of the necessary point of departure or beginning in finitude, and more specifically in a finite becoming which itself has a finite beginning. It is this givenness of finite becoming and that becoming's own finite beginning from which this study argues in its move toward a reconstruction of Hegel's trinitarian envisionment and a reformulation of his trinitarian claim.

Any finite movement of becoming as qualitative increment or progressive enrichment involves initial Selfhood, otherness, enriched Selfhood and recurrent otherness. Initial Selfhood is the determinate beginning or point of departure. Otherness[269] is the co-constitutively negative and positive to which initial Selfhood is related. Thus otherness is likewise that which is related to Selfhood. Otherness is the primary finite source of the novelty or newness which is the engendered result of the process of becoming. Enriched Selfhood is the resultant relationship between initial Selfhood and otherness. It is a resultant enriched Selfhood renewedly defined by its being related to ever-recurrent otherness. So finite becoming is the dynamic development from initial Selfhood in interrelationship or interplay with otherness to enriched resultant Selfhood ever-renewedly to be enriched in its interrelationship with recurrent otherness.[270] Though this tetradically structured finite becoming is, as far as its formal structure is concerned, a non-temporal enriching progression, it is not an immanently self-grounding qualitative increment. The "more" involved, the enriched Selfhood, can be justified by or grounded in neither the mere givenness of otherness nor consequently in the mere definitional interrelatedness as such of initial Selfhood and otherness nor again in itself as the resultant or realized relationship. Otherness taken on its own and as such cannot justify its being related to as a unity. First of all, on its own it simply dissolves into a multiplicity of others. Secondly, even as multiplicity the recurrence of otherness indicates the incompleteness or one-sidedness of the interrelationship between initial Selfhood and otherness is any movement of finite becoming. The realized interrelationship itself between initial Selfhood and otherness, in as it is the enriched Selfhood or resultant relationship of initial Selfhood and otherness, is never exhaustive, but always equally resultantly one-sided and so to be brought to further enrichment as renewedly inclusive of otherness. Since it is not truly inclusive, that is, since it is equally inclusive and one-sided, the resultant relation between initial Selfhood and otherness constantly contradicts itself. In its very enrichment it finds its limit.

Before going any further it is important again to emphasize that what is intended here is simply the establishment of the formal or it could be said structural constitution of real but not self-explanatory finite becoming. This formal constitution of finite becoming has been spoken of in the more abstract terms of Selfhood and otherness in order to bracket out a number of questions not essential to the proposed rudimentary reconstruction of Hegel's trinitarian claim. These questions include a more concrete discussion with specific philosophical or religious systems treating in more detailed fashion of the relationship between Selfhood and otherness, the way in which a Subject might perdure in time and space, and the problems of temporality and dualism. More specifically, the formulation "Selfhood" allows for setting aside the problem of the further identification of the Self. Likewise, Selfhood is to be taken widely enough to avoid any immediate identification of Concept and Self. The formulation "otherness" is meant to remove from present discussion the difficulties revolving around simultaneity in the relationship between Subject and object, the ever-recurrent epistemological question, and the discussion of internal versus external relationality. What this discussion of the formal structure of becoming is not meant to do is to abstract from the concrete reality of existent becoming (*daseiendes Werden*). The abstraction is from detailed philosophical or religious discussion of particular points, but not from becoming as existent qualitative increment. Initial Selfhood, otherness, resultant enriched Selfhood as ever renewedly initial Selfhood, and ever-recurrent otherness are the formal structural elements of real, finite becoming.

The formal structure of any finite movement of becoming as progressive enrichment is necessarily constituted by these four elements: initial Selfhood; otherness; enriched Selfhood; recurrent otherness. However, though the recurrence of otherness and enriched Selfhood's functioning anew as initial Selfhood do in fact establish a tetradically structured, non-self-grounding movement of finite becoming, in principle the formal structure of becoming qua becoming is necessarily triadic. True, in any finite becoming initial Selfhood is the necessarily determinate beginning without which there could be no finite becoming. It is the beginning of that becoming. Nevertheless, it would not be essential to initial Selfhood as such, namely, indicated by but not grasped in conceptual thought, that initial Selfhood stand over against otherness in such a way that it would by definition necessarily be finite. Initial Selfhood could simply be that without which there could be no becoming. If initial Selfhood were that which was related to a non-recurrent otherness, then this non-recurrent otherness would be that without which initial Selfhood could not be enriched. Any enrichment of initial Selfhood taken as such could occur only through some form of otherness, through otherness as such need not by definition be recurrent. Without this otherness there would be no progressive enrichment or becoming. Progressive enrichment or becoming must occur as resultant enriched Selfhood, as the "more" of qualitative increment. Selfhood as resultant enrichment is, as such, reducible neither to initial Selfhood nor to otherness. None of the three constituent elements can be reduced to one or a mere combination of the other two. Enriched Selfhood does of course function anew as initial Selfhood with the reemergence of otherness in the ever-to-be renewed process of finite becoming. Though the proposal here was initially dependent in its development on the limited character of initial Selfhood and recurrent otherness, in principle the formal structure of becoming qua becoming is necessarily triadic: initial Selfhood; otherness; enriched Selfhood. Anything less than these three elements would fail to constitute becoming. Any indication of more than the three elements is merely the observation that a specific, determinate becoming is not inclusive and not immanently self-grounding but finite. A triadically structured movement of becoming would be inclusive totality, that which could be expected to resolve the contradiction inherent in finite becoming.

Hegel had sensed the necessarily triadic formal structure of becoming qua becoming when he emphasized triadically structured syllogistic mediation, that mediation's primordial, elementary expression in the dialectic of being/nothing/becoming and its logical fulfillment in the absolute Idea as method. With his stress upon thought Hegel firmly planted the discussion of his trinitarian claim within the public realm. In his more generalized formulations of mediation he had pointed to the three elements constitutive of mediation as becoming.[271] Most importantly, despite his insistence on an originary self-mediating pure thought, Hegel had happily managed to place otherness at the center of his dialectic. The essential role of otherness becomes even clearer when the shift is made to a systematic beginning from finitude, which by definition recognizes the stubborn recurrence of otherness. Hegel's theory of self-mediation as response to alienation becomes transformed into a theory of enriching growth or qualitative increment. Pluralism, in its widest sense as the positive acceptance of otherness taken in its co-constitutively negative and positive character, becomes the condition for the possibility of becoming as progressive enrichment. There remains so far, however, the tension between becoming as in principle triadically structured and its de facto tetradic formulation as finite becoming which, in its finitude, is finally not self-explanatory. Though Hegel's notion of subjectivity has gained in interest as the dynamic becoming of progressive enrichment, it has so far not been possible to maintain that subjectivity's ultimate, finally inclusive character but only to refer to it as the in principle formal triadic structure of becoming. Chapter Six will present an initial attempt to recoup that inclusive character.

PART THREE

Reconstructing Hegel's Trinitarian Envisionment

6

From Finite to Infinite

1. Recapitulative Overview

With his claim that God could be conceived of as Subject, Person and Spirit only on the basis of an elaboration of a trinitarian divine subjectivity,[1] Hegel had stated in philosophically informed religious representational language his theory of an attained absolute self-mediation in, of and through thought. Hegel gave this self-mediating movement of absolute Spirit essentially a logical, phenomenological, philosophy of religion and philosophical formulation. It was necessary here at least in principle directly or indirectly to have made a critique of all these various formulations in order now to assert that Hegel could not establish his trinitarian claim in the way in which he had proposed it.

Stated very inadequately, Hegel had proposed to establish his trinitarian claim by means of a progression from God to world. More exactly, for Hegel the divine was necessarily[2] to have othered itself as world in the dualism of nature and finite Spirit and to have returned enriched to itself through finite Spirit's sublation in absolute Spirit as philosophic thought. The world was to have been the finite other of God.[3] Hegel's mature dialectic was to have been a movement beginning from infinity (*Unendlichkeit, das Unendliche*) as *an sich* totality to its necessary self-othering as finitude (*Endlichkeit, das Endliche*), again dialectically speaking taken as momentary totality, and then enriching return as inclusive infinite. When infinite and finite are not maintained in abstraction from one another, for Hegel

> there is this to be said about the coming or going forth of the finite from the infinite: the infinite goes forth *out* of itself into finitude because, being grasped as an abstract unity, it

has no truth, no enduring being within it; and conversely the finite goes *into* the infinite for the same reason, namely that it is a nullity.[4]

It is a logical beginning with the infinite which Hegel cannot argue to in the public realm of thought and discourse. And to the extent that other trinitarian formulations would be dependent upon or reducible to Hegel's deductively argued position or even to its structure, they would as well be vulnerable to the critique directed here specifically against Hegel's position.

That Hegel could not defend his deductively argued trinitarian claim in its directionality from infinite to finite to enriched infinite as a movement of self-positing thought has been argued in this study's preceding Parts One and Two. In a wide sense Part One, composed of Chapters One and Two, was concerned with *Etwas*, only the beginning of the Subject.[5] Chapter One sketched the seductive rhythm of pure thought with its culmination in absolute Idea as method so as to establish the *Logic* as logical reformulation of the true content of Trinity. Chapter Two worked through *Etwas* back to pure thought in its primordial, elementary instantiation as being/nothing/becoming. Out of a critique of this initial triadic, in which Hegel had unsuccessfully tried to establish subjectivity's beginning in pure determinationlessness as its determination, there flowed the conclusion that any becoming available to human thought was necessarily finite and determinate. Part Two consisted in a turn to Hegel's realphilosophical spheres. It was effectively an examination of Hegel's understanding of syllogism both in syllogism's purity as thought determination and in its realization in trinitarian reconciliation. Chapter Three provided a first, encyclopedic overview of Hegel's syllogistically structured trinitarian reconciliation and a criterion for evaluating the success of Hegel's argumentation in his breakthrough text, the *Phenomenology*. Chapter Four concentrated on an examination and critique of trinitarian reconciliation in its incarnational immediacy and concluded to the givenness of finite, determinate becoming as enriching growth and qualitative increment. Chapter Five treated of Hegel's indisputably syllogistically structured trinitarian reconciliation in the 1827 *Lectures* on the third element of absolute religion. As concluded in Chapter Five, with syllogism Hegel had correctly sensed the necessarily triadic formal structure of any becoming, though he was not able to develop that structure convincingly as an immanent and consistent self-grounding movement of self-determining pure thought. In the conclusion to Chapter Five it was proposed that the irreducible constituent elements of becoming as enriching growth and qualitative increment are initial Selfhood, otherness and enriched Selfhood.[6]

Any proposal to reestablish Hegel's trinitarian claim, whether as here on the basis of enriching growth or on any other basis, will have to begin in and with finitude if the claim is to be argued in the public realm of thought and discourse. An end-run distinction between epistemologically or noetically necessary starting point in finitude and ontologically necessary beginning in any type of initial, positing infinite would throw the whole discussion onto the level of preference or opinion. Such a proposed logically prior ontological starting point in infinity would remain merely a premise or ungrounded presupposition. Even the conclusion from finitude to needed grounding infinite could not then justify the indication of an infinite as logically or ontologically prior starting point. The argumentation for Hegel's trinitarian claim could not even with various qualifications move from infinite to finite. The in fact prior movement from finitude to infinite remains, as presupposition verifiable in the public realm of thought and discourse, always logically prior to any movement from infinite to finite. Hegel himself, admittedly in the context of his attempt to justify the logical starting point of the absolute science in pure being, insisted that a true beginning must be without presuppositions.[7] Only a beginning in and with finitude can claim that givenness or *Dasein* which is initially premised only upon its own reality and limitation. Any deductively argued position from infinite to finite would necessarily presuppose a logically prior movement from finite to infinite, and this ultimately because logic itself is finite.

The here proposed rudimentary reconstruction of Hegel's trinitarian envisionment, a reconstruction now to be made on the basis of a movement from finite to infinite, begins from that finite becoming which is enriching growth or qualitative increment. This becoming itself in turn begins in the finitude of an initial Selfhood and bears an in principle triadic formal structure of initial Selfhood, otherness and enriched Selfhood. However, though the ever-present recurrence of otherness ensures, on the level of the finite, the fundamental pluralistic basis for enriching growth, it equally establishes a de facto tetradic movement of finite or non-inclusive becoming. This tension between triadic and tetradic leads now in Part Three, Chapter Six, on into a discussion of finite and infinite, as Hegel presented them in the *Logic*, to a sketching of the reconstruction of the transition from finite to infinite and on to a closing initial reformulation of Hegel's trinitarian claim. This present Chapter Six serves as first move toward a recasting of *Etwas*, syllogism and infinite, indeed toward a reintegration of logic and realphilosophical spheres with reference to, and in terms of, the need to posit a triadically structured inclusive infinite.

2. The Contours of Hegel's Finite "and" Infinite

Etwas[8] or "something" without emphasis on "thing" was Hegel's axial category or thought determination providing access, in Chapter Two,[9] to the overall movement of logic or pure thought in its primordial, elementary instantiation as being/nothing/becoming. *Etwas* now considered as first more concrete negation of negation and "only the beginning of the Subject"[10] provides the point of departure for an overview of Hegel's understanding of finite and infinite in the *Logic* as momentary totalities of pure thought. In the first edition of the "Logic of Being" (1812),[11] Hegel had proposed to establish a transition to "other" (*Anderes*) out of *Dasein*,[12] and only then spoke of *Etwas*.[13] However, by the second edition of the "Logic of Being" (1831), Hegel had proposed a transition from *Dasein* to quality to *Etwas*, and then from *Etwas* and other on eventually to his various formulations of finitude and infinity.[14] Though Hegel did not change his basic understanding of finite and infinite from the first to the second editions of the "Logic of Being,"[15] he did elaborate, make more consistent and thereby sharpen his presentation of the movement from *Dasein* to the true infinite.[16] This sharpness and greater internal consistency as well as Hegel's fuller elaboration were the result of his many years of reflection on the relationship between finite and infinite. The following summary will therefore profit by concentrating on Hegel's presentation of finite and infinite in the second edition of the "Logic of Being."[17]

Hegel's positioning of *Etwas* in the second edition of the "Logic of Being" as result in the triad *Dasein/quality/Etwas* had allowed him to set the stage more exactly for his discussion of finite and infinite by explicitly introducing the elements with which he would work to accomplish his transition from finite to true infinite.[18] Principal among these elements are the notions of negation and negation of negation, with negation of negation being the structure of inclusive self-mediating subjectivity. "The negative of the negative is, as *Etwas*, only the beginning of the Subject."[19] Already here Hegel has clearly introduced the distinction between a first negation or negation as such and a second negation, the negation of negation; "the latter is concrete, *absolute* negativity, just as the former on the contrary is only *abstract* negativity."[20] By recalling that this negation of negation, *Etwas*, is and is *Daseiendes*, a concrete becoming which has as its moments "now determinate being, and, further, *a* determinate being,"[21] Hegel moves rather too quickly to announce the transition to "a *determinate* being, but determined as a negative of something—an other."[22] Since the moments of *Etwas* are themselves *Etwas*, Hegel proposes *Etwas* and other merely over against one another.[23] With negation of negation and initially independent otherness Hegel had established the basic parameters of his discussion of finite and infinite and laid the groundwork for his brilliant resolution of the opposition between finite and infinite.[24]

It is by means of a subtly developed and progressively more explicit series of negations of negation that Hegel moves from *Etwas* to infinite. This logically sequenced series of ever more concrete categories was for Hegel to have been the movement of pure thought as the sphere of *Dasein*. In view of the critiques in Chapters Two, Four and Five above there is here no longer a question of accepting the movement of pure thought in the way in which Hegel intended to establish it. So now it will be sufficient merely to give a resume of his presentation leading to finitude and then through it to infinity. What is of concern here is an overview of Hegel's understanding of the thought determinations "finite" and "infinite" in themselves to the extent that this is possible given Hegel's conception of them. This overview is equally concerned with them in their mutual transition to one another in order to provide access to the overall contours of Hegel's conception of finite "and" infinite. These contours will provide the general framework to be employed in a first sketching of a proposed rudimentary reconstruction of Hegel's triadically structured inclusive infinite. Finally, this will lead to a brief, closing reformulation of Hegel's trinitarian claim.

The overall elaboration of finitude as a subtle progression of negations of negation occurs in the Logic[25] by a recurrent analytic and synthetic treatment of otherness, otherness always at least implicitly and quite soon explicitly established within the movement of pure thought. Under the first subheading, "*Etwas* and an other,"[26] Hegel proceeds in three steps. First, in an initial way he in several moves indicates that

Etwas and other are the same, each is other to the other, so that in change *Etwas* remains identical with itself.[27] In a second step[28] Hegel typically progresses by presenting two opposing categories, "being-for-other" (*Sein für-Anderes*) and "being-in-itself" (*Ansichsein*). For present purposes it is important to underscore that Hegel presents otherness as both contained in *Etwas* and separated from *Etwas*.[29] However, thinking the category being-for-other immediately gives rise to or, better, has already immediately given rise to the thought determination being-in-itself. *Etwas* and other indicated independence; now being-for-other and being-in-itself are relational determinations. In a third step[30] Hegel stresses that being-for-other and being-in-itself are moments of one and the same *Etwas*. The dialectically developed resultant identity of being-for-other and being-in-itself allows Hegel to assert being-for-other's being in *Etwas*, and then, as simple being, "determination" (*Bestimmung*).[31]

From "*Etwas* and an other" Hegel progresses through the second subsection, "Determination, Condition and Limit,"[32] to the thought determination, "the finite." Determination is at hand as the "determinateness which is in itself" (*an-sich-seiende Bestimmtheit*).[33] In the first of three moves, Hegel distinguishes determination from determinateness (*Bestimmtheit*) in such a fashion as to establish determination as that which *Etwas* remains in itself in the face of its own being-for-other. In a second move, Hegel again gives expression to the arising of otherness but this time determinateness is present as that into which determination has separated itself, constitution (*Beschaffenheit*).[34] Constitution at first expresses the externally relational and changeable. But constitution is related to *Etwas* as the quality of *Etwas* so that for Hegel change now is transition internal to *Etwas* itself. Though determination and constitution are to be distinguished from one another, they are as well both mediated as the determinateness of *Etwas*. Constitution is otherness now explicitly considered with determination as co-constitutive of *Etwas*. "The *Etwas* itself is further determined and the negation is posited as immanent in it, as its developed *being-within-self*."[35] This being-within-self (*Insichsein*) is the non-being (*Nichtsein*) of an otherness contained in that being-within-self[36] and equally distinguished from it. Determination and constitution are movements of negation of negation which mutually limit *Etwas* so that *Etwas* is its limit (*Grenze*).[37] In a third move, Hegel returns to this enriched and more unified positing of *Etwas* as limit. As thought determination in the movement of pure thought, limit is developed by Hegel first as that which establishes what *Etwas* as such is not.[38]

Since limit is equally the non-being of the other, *"Etwas* at the same time *is* through its limit."³⁹ Hegel recalls therefore that limit is now the first negation and other the negation of negation, *Etwas*'s being-within-itself.⁴⁰ "Limit is the mediation through which *Etwas* and other each as well *is* as *is not*."⁴¹ Hegel, secondly, observes that the negative determinate being (*das Nichtdasein*) and the *Dasein* of *Etwas* fall outside one another. The *Dasein* of *Etwas* lies without *Etwas* and the negative determinate being as limit lies within *Etwas*.⁴² Third, Hegel slowly reintegrates the negative determinate being of *Etwas* and the *Dasein* of *Etwas* by concluding that *Etwas* and other share a common limit so that *Etwas* has its *Dasein* only in limit. But *Etwas* equally separates itself from itself and "points beyond itself to its non-being, declaring this to be its being."⁴³ *Etwas* equally then has as determination its own restlessness, which pushes it out beyond itself.⁴⁴ "*Etwas* with its immanent limit, posited as the contradiction of itself, through which it is directed and forced out of and beyond itself, is the *finite*."⁴⁵

Hegel posited the transitions from *Dasein* to the finite as a specific sequence within the overall movement of self-positing and self-determining pure thought or logic as series of ever more concrete thought determinations. In the *Logic* any specific presentation of thought determinations must be considered as taking place simultaneously on various levels. Since the series of logical transitions from *Dasein* to the finite occur within the overall logic of being, their fluidity consisted in the transition already having taken place in their being thought.⁴⁶ Methodologically speaking, these categories amounted for Hegel to an ever more explicit thinking of otherness, especially from the presentation of "*Etwas* and an other" on. Hegel had observed that the categories *Dasein*, quality (reality, negation) and *Etwas* were developed in an affirmative determination, while "*Etwas* and an other," being-for-other and being-in-itself, determination, constitution, being-within-self and limit developed the negative determination, a negation of negation with *Dasein* as a first negation.⁴⁷ By means of a growing opposition and a sense of internal contradiction contained ever more explicitly within an increasingly determinate *Etwas*, Hegel progressed to the finite and would continue through the finite to the bad infinite, infinite progression and the true infinite.

With the coming into being of the category "limit," Hegel has thematized the contradiction for him constitutive of finitude and has given initial expression to the fluidity characteristic of finitude. It is this fluidity as finitude's drive beyond itself which will allow Hegel to make the transition to a discussion of infinity. Limit is the mutual boundary between *Etwas* and other, but a boundary equally immanent to *Etwas* itself.[48] So on the basis of limit Hegel concludes that the being, or here the *Dasein*, of *Etwas* lies outside itself. Yet, with limit immanent to, *Etwas* the being (*Sein*) of *Etwas* is equally its non-being (*Nichtsein*).[49] With the thinking through of limit there arises for Hegel the thought determination "the finite." With the coming into being of the finite, Hegel has sublated into one category the crescendo of progressively more explicit internal contradiction now seen to have been characterizing the categories in the movement of pure though from *Dasein* on. In the finite, otherness is now for Hegel not only limit as such but limitation (*Schranke*).[50] However, while making thematic the being-in-itself of the finite, limitation is also inevitably taken as limit distinguishable from being-in-itself, so that limitation is ought (*Sollen*).[51] The contradiction progressively more explicitly characteristic of the categories of pure thought from *Dasein* on forms a climax in the identification of limitation and ought as moments of the finite, and therefore themselves respectively explicitly and implicitly finite.[52] "What ought to be *is* and at the same time *is not*."[53] Hegel dialectically identifies limitation and ought. As ought, *Etwas* has gone beyond its limitation, and yet only in as *Etwas* is ought does it have its limitation.[54] For Hegel ought contains limitation and limitation contains ought. They are opposed as negation over against one another. "The infinite is thus inwardly self-contradictory."[55] This negation or going over into one another results, first, not in the ceasing to be of the finite but only in another finite in an infinite progression. On closer examination, for Hegel each of the moments of ceasing to be, namely limitation and ought, goes over into an other which is really itself. "This *identity with itself*, the negation of negation, is affirmative being and thus the other of the finite, of the finite which is supposed to have the first negation for its determinateness; this other is the infinite."[56]

Before clearly establishing the infinite as a becoming[57] (*Werden*) which is an inclusive whole (*Ganze*), Hegel pursues a further elaboration of the movement of pure thought so as to heighten the contradiction between finite and infinite. After recalling that it is the very nature of the finite itself to become the infinite, the affirmative being or negation of negation which the finite truly is an sich, Hegel asserts that "what is, is only the infinite."[58] On the basis of the fact that the infinite is, Hegel proceeds to conclude that the infinite is "at the same time the negation of an other, of the finite."[59] As equally the being and the non-being of an other, the infinite has however fallen back into the finitude of an *Etwas* with a limit. The thought of the finite has gone over into the infinite and vice versa. But the two equally stand over against one another "in a qualitative relation, each remaining external to the other."[60] However, again not only are finite and infinite other to one another. Rather, finitude is posited limitation, and infinity is what the finite ought to be. The infinite as ought is again burdened with an opposition to the determinate finite as its other. The infinite is thus determined as "the indeterminate void, the beyond of the finite."[61] The infinite in these ways set over against the finite in a qualitative relationship of otherness is Hegel's well-known "bad infinite" (*das Schlecht-Unendliche*). It is the infinite of understanding, which is supposed to be the absolute truth but in fact is absolute contradiction: the infinite standing over against the finite, two worlds with the infinite as limit of the finite and so itself a finite infinite.[62] Hegel then works out this contradiction in ever more explicit fashion as the alternation of finite and infinite.[63] As separated as the finite and the infinite of understanding remain from one another, they are equally related by the very negation which separates them, the mutual limit each has against the other.[64] Finite and infinite are then equally inseparatable. "But this their unity is *concealed* in their qualitative otherness."[65] Out of this inseparability of finite and infinite there again arises limit so that the finite recurs in thought. Yet this new limit, and therefore the finite it engenders, is in turn to be gone beyond so that the infinite reappears as indeterminate void, "and so on to infinity."[66] This infinite progression is itself the bad or finite infinite pushed to its extreme self-contradiction. "The infinity of the infinite progress remains burdened with the finite as such, is thereby limited and is itself *finite*."[67] The truth or mediation of finite and infinite is for Hegel already present in this infinite progression, but remains so far obscured by understanding's insistence on a strict separation of finite and infinite to avoid contradiction rather than embrace it.[68]

It now becomes clear why Hegel proceeds not directly from finite to true infinite but, rather, from finite to infinite renewedly finitized as bad infinite and most importantly infinite progression. True to form, Hegel intends to establish the true infinite by making explicit the truth for him already implicit or at hand in the back and forth between finite and infinite. He needs the infinite progression as momentary totality in the movement of pure thought since in it "[the] truth [of the infinite progression] is already implicitly *present*, and all that is required is to take up what is before us."[69]

Hegel begins to make this truth explicit by recalling that finite and infinite are each a movement. He wants to make explicit the type of unity present in and between each of these movements or moments simply by comparing them as they have come to be seen so far.[70] Hegel examines and compares the two movements twice, each time in as they appear related and separated. In the first comparison, on the one hand when considered from the aspect of their relatedness, the infinite and the finite are defined in terms of movement beyond self (*Hinausgehen*). The infinite *is* only as movement beyond the finite; it is the negation of the finite. The finite *is* only as that which must be gone beyond. It is "the negation of itself in its own self, which is infinity."[71] In each, in the finite and in the infinite, there lies the determination of the other. Though in the infinite progression finite and infinite are held apart and presented alternately, neither can be conceived without the other.[72] On the other hand, again in this first consideration or comparison, when the two movements are considered as separated, the infinite is not seen as a whole. This infinite contains a limit over against the finite and is therefore itself finite.[73] The finite in turn becomes, as separated, a relationship to itself, gaining an independence "which the infinite is supposed to be."[74] This doubled movement gives one result: each contains the other in itself as moment. For Hegel this one result provides a new type of unity or infinite, a unity of finite and infinite and which includes infinite and finite. He now makes a second comparison of finite and infinite. In as the two must be related,[75] each moment is itself the unity of finite and infinite. Each of these two unities has in common that it posits the negation of the two determinations so that they lose their qualitative difference.[76] In as the two movements are distinct, there is in each a different determination of the unity of the infinite. The infinite determined as such is only an "in itself" (*an sich*); finitude remains mere determinateness and limit. So here the infinite is merely a finitized infinite. In the same way, since the finite as such is only the negation of the in-itself (*das Nichtansichsein*), it contains the infinite within its determination and is the infinitized finite.[77]

So far now Hegel has come to assert that finite and infinite each contains the other in its determinations. The understanding has continually failed to acknowledge this by ignoring the negation in this doubled unity of infinite and finite.[78] The unnegated infinite remains for understanding a mere *an sich* without determinateness and limitation. The unnegated finite remains merely perduring infinitized determination. According to Hegel, understanding forgets what is the very Concept of these moments, their unity. Each is in itself this unity as the sublation of itself.[79] The finite sublates itself in the infinite, which is the negation of finitude. And finitude has long since been established as non-being. So the infinite is negation of negation. But as negation of determinateness as such, "the sublating of itself in the finite is a return from an empty flight, a *negation* of the beyond which is in its own self a *negative*."[80] There is present in each the same negation of negation, affirmation as return to itself, namely mediation. In infinite progression both finite and infinite are in fact negated, but still only as following upon one another and not in their last truth.[81]

Whereas Hegel had so far considered infinite progression primarily from the perspective of finite and infinite in their separation, now, in order to arrive at their last truth, he takes a second look at that infinite progression especially in as it gives expression to the connection (*Zusammenhang*) between finite and infinite.[82] By an examination parallel to but more briefly developed than in his look at finite and infinite and then infinite progression as such, Hegel now looks at the negation of finite and infinite as the negation is posited in infinite progression. Beginning with the finite, one sees that it is negated in the transition to an empty infinite, which is then itself negated in the return to the finite. In one sense, this is merely a series of external acts but, in a deeper sense, this is "the complete, self-closing movement which has arrived at that which constituted the beginning."[83] By a similar observation Hegel posits a movement beginning from the infinite, negating that infinite and then returning to that infinite as to itself.[84] So finite and infinite are this movement of mediation, negation of negation, result. The finite is no longer merely a hardened existence over against an empty infinite and vice versa. Understanding has continued to fail to see that both finite and infinite are negated, "that they occur therein only as moments of a whole."[85] The objection that two different points of departure dictate two results does not stand since, according to Hegel, the difference in points of departure is here without significance.[86] Hegel illustrates his position with reference to infinite progression as a line wherein each moment occurs as the transition to the other. Together as moments finite and infinite are the finite. Equally, together negated in the result they are, as this result, "as negation of the finitude of both . . . with truth the infinite."[87]

For Hegel the true infinite (*wahrhaft Unendliches*) *is* the process of mediation in which the infinite, having become finite, sublates its difference or finitude into its own self-affirmation.[88] The true infinite is not to be thought of as an abstract unity of static moments, but as a more determinate becoming whose moments themselves, finite and infinite, are in the process of becoming.[89] This true infinite is for Hegel "the consummated return into self, the relation of itself to itself."[90] From the perspective of the true infinite, the unattainable (*unerreichbar*) bad infinite is only a first negation, and infinite progression appears as if it were a straight line with the infinite appearing only at both limits. The true infinite is to be pictured as a determinate circle, a line bent back upon itself without beginning and end.[91] The true infinite is for Hegel the true reality. It is negation of negation, affirmation inclusive of the finite, a finite now seen as "*das Ideelle*," namely, not as independent but as posited moment of the infinite.[92] The true infinite is for Hegel inclusive totality.[93]

The thought determinations from *Dasein* to true infinite constituted for Hegel a series of logical transitions in which each category was to have been momentary totality in the movement of pure thought. These thought determinations formed a particular segment in the movement of pure thought, which thought was to have begun in pure being and would for Hegel have continued through the transition from the true infinite to "being-for-self" (*das Fürsichsein*) on through the logic of essence and the logic of the Concept to the final logical totality, the absolute Idea. Since the absolute Idea was itself to have been an enriched return to the immediacy of pure being, Hegel's logic itself, as he intended it, can be described as a circle, so to speak, without beginning and end, an infinite or inclusive totality which was necessarily but freely to have othered itself as the immediate finitude which is nature.

With the conceptualization of the true infinite as inclusive totality (*das Ganze, die Totalität*) Hegel had made explicit use of and in fact thematized the notion of non-temporal momentary totality, which was to have been the characteristic of each thought determination in accordance with that thought determination's position in the overall movement of self-positing and self-determining pure thought.[94] Hegel's proposed establishment of a movement of pure thought proved most fruitful in that he was able convincingly to point out the self-contradictory character of the finite and to point to a brilliant resolution of the opposition between finite and infinite, a resolution which equally attempted to respect that opposition. Nevertheless, despite Hegel's so thoroughly worked out presentation of the overall movement of pure thought, that movement cannot be adequately defended as intended. His transition from becoming to *Dasein* and his theory of syllogism as giving expression to self-mediation in thought have proven untenable. With reference to the present discussion of finite and infinite, it could be asked whether Hegel has not remained too ambiguous in his description of infinite progression both as finite and yet at least implicitly infinite. For Hegel infinite progression was infinite to the point that it contained the "unity" of finite and infinite hidden within it so that its having been thought through[95] as momentary totality was to have resulted in its self-sublation into the true infinite as a becoming whose moments would themselves be the finite and the infinite.[96] In the last analysis, since Hegel cannot establish pure being as beginning of pure thought in the way in which he intended and needed to, his seminal envisionment of finite and infinite can be freed of the strictures imposed on them by their having been inserted into a movement of self-determining pure thought. Hegel's overall analyses of the contours of finite and infinite can prove renewedly available and perhaps as well renewedly fecund in a formal or meta-philosophical usage, that is, without having at least initially to tie into any specific philosophical or theological system in its historical instantiation.

Hegel had worked out his position on and understanding of finitude systematically speaking first as a momentary totality in the movement of pure thought and then as the reality of nature and finite Spirit. Now, when logic and realphilosophical spheres are at least in principle reintegrated, finitude is freed of the ambiguity inherent in the attempt to formulate it as moment of absolute form. As Hegel correctly argued,[97] when finitude is adequately evaluated, it is seen by definition to be a contradiction, even self-contradiction. Hegel has convincingly stated his contradiction in its most abstract formulation as *Etwas* which both is and is not. More determinately expressed, this contradiction arises in the fact that finitude is a limitation which ought to be gone beyond. Still more determinately expressed, finitude is the contradiction that appears to be resolvable only in an oscillation between a finite and an infinite. Hegel's finite, the bad infinite and infinite progression are all finite in that they bear within themselves their own real and recurrent limit. Hegel's definition of the finite as the self-contradiction of *Etwas* with limit immanent in it, and thus forced to go beyond itself,[98] thematizes limit as that which had finitized *Dasein* from the beginning. Whether *Dasein* now be taken as first moment of a finite movement of thought or as the *Dasein* or givenness of any becoming as finite qualitative increment, it is always limited being. *Dasein*, as made explicit in *Etwas* defined by its immanent limit, both is and is not in and through that very limit in so far as *Dasein* as *Etwas* is determinate in and through its limit always over against an other. As this self-contradiction, finitude is therefore qua finitude restless, unstable, one-sided and incomplete. It cannot resolve its own self-contradiction. It is not self-explanatory but continually points beyond itself to the possibility of an inclusive whole as the context wherein the self-contradiction inherent in recurrent limit might find resolution. To remain merely with the self-contradictory finite would ultimately imply abandoning the public realm of discourse.

According to Hegel the finite as self-contradictory was to have gone over into the true or inclusive infinite. As logical category this true infinite was the negation of finite and infinite taken as mutually independent. It was posited negation of negation. The true infinite found expression for Hegel as progressively more explicitly inclusive in the logic of self-determining inclusive subjectivity, the appearance of absolute divine subjectivity in the sphere of religion, and absolute Spirit in philosophy as Concept or enriched return to the immediacy of the absolute Idea and, thus, to pure being. Hegel's encyclopedic system as a whole was meant to present the infinite in its truth.[99]

However, with the acknowledgement that Hegel could not give expression to or, more exactly, grasp (*Begreifen*) the true infinite in either logical or philosophical thought there arises a certain sense of freedom and flexibility vis-à-vis the more restrictive aspects of his brilliant synthesis. First of all there is no longer the need to refer to the finite as implicitly infinite. Rather, what Hegel read as "at hand" (*Vorhanden*) in the finite or, more precisely, in the infinite progression was the givenness of finitude as existent contradiction which calls for and points to an infinite in which and because of which it can perdure as such real, existent contradiction.[100] There is, secondly, no longer the need to restrict the true infinite to a logically necessitated logical and realphilosophical self-othering and self-mediation as mere negation of negation. What Hegel has in fact convincingly established in his envisionment of a true or inclusive infinite is the need rooted in the self-contradictory character of finitude for an infinite which does not stand merely over against the finite and thereby remain a finite infinite.[101] The only infinite which could respectfully resolve the contradiction which finitude is must be an infinite inclusive of that finitude and yet itself not become renewedly limited by finitude. Otherwise the contradiction would simply remain unresolved. At the same time this true or inclusive infinite must be a whole or totality which allows finitude as existent contradiction to perdure since finitude is the irreplaceable beginning without which there would be no need to point to an infinite.

Hegel had characterized his notion of true infinite as posited negation of negation,[102] a doubled going beyond in which one of the two transitions, that from infinite to finite to renewedly affirmed infinite, provided the structure of the true infinite inclusive of the finite with the finite taken as the self-othered momentary totality of the infinite.[103] The essential truth in Hegel's conception of the true infinite presented by Hegel as negation of negation and, systematically speaking, later as inclusive subjectivity and absolute Spirit is the structure by which it can be finitude's required inclusive other. Since the true infinite can only be the infinite of this given finitude, it must contain that finitude within it in such a way that the infinite does not collapse into another merely finite. The infinite can be so structured not in terms of a movement of pure thought but only as the postulating of a pluralistically structured infinite context or whole. This is so because the only way to resolve the contradiction, which finitude is, is to posit a contextualizing infinite becoming which contains limit within itself but is itself not thereby limited. Hegel had rightly argued on the basis of limit to the self-contradictory character of the finite. He has equally correctly shown that, given the reality of finitude, the infinite cannot be understood without reference to and inclusion of that finitude. Just as finite as such does not exclude but requires the postulation of a true infinite, so limit as such, given finitude, pertains to the essence of true infinity. What makes limit the source of the contradictory character of finitude is the constant renewal of limit because of the constant recurrence of otherness. Within the context of the truly infinite, limit would lose the character of recurrence since otherness would ultimately be included within the infinite understood as totality. Such an infinite as inclusive whole would necessarily not only bear within it the structure of pluralism but be specifically triadically structured. Limit bespeaks a dyadic structure which remains unmediated. The resolution of the contradiction rooted in limit requires the postulating of a third moment or movement in the truly infinite. Proposing any further moment or movement in the infinite would reduce it to another finite. The true infinite is to be understood as that becoming, a triadically structured determinate whole, to which finitude as existent contradiction points. It is that self-explanatory context without which finitude would remain hardened in its own self-contradiction.

Summarizing these contours of Hegel's understanding of finite and infinite has provided a renewed view of finitude which allows it the freedom to be what it is, the existent self-contradiction rooted in the recurrence of limit and therein pointing to an inclusive infinite without which it could not be thought through. Stated in key-word fashion, finitude only becomes truly thinkable when its contradiction is mediated; contradiction cannot be thought through without reference to its resolution.[104] This summary has, secondly, provided the indication of a true infinite freed of the strictures of a grasping or comprehending thought (*begreiffendes Denken*) so that it can truly be the triadically structured inclusive totality in which the contradiction arising out of recurrent limit finds its resolution. Finite remains finite but without becoming hardened into an infinitized finite. Infinite remains infinite without collapsing into the finitude of an empty infinite over against the finite. This overall envisionment of finite and infinite, a vision originally embedded in Hegel's system, remains now one of Hegel's greatest contributions to trinitarian thought.[105] Before closing this chapter with a brief reformulation of Hegel's trinitarian claim, these contours of finite and infinite will serve in the following preliminary sketching of a reconstructed transition from finitude to triadically structured inclusive infinite.

3. From Finitude to Triadically Structured Inclusive Infinite

The intention with this positing of the transition from finitude to triadically structured inclusive infinite is not to develop in any detail either the characteristics of finitude as self-contradiction or the structured movement of the true or inclusive infinite. Rather, reference will be made to these characteristics and this movement only in as such is necessary to argue to the transition from finitude to inclusive infinite. The focus is on arguing to this needed transition, a transition now no longer to be conceived in a primordial and paradigmatic formulation as the having gone over of one thought determination into another in the "Logic of Being." Still, this transition from finitude to inclusive infinite does retain

Hegel's particular concern that it be made as an argument in the public realm. It consists in arguing, within the limitations of thought and of consciousness as available to thought, to the need to postulate a triadically structured inclusive infinite without which finitude would remain ungrounded self-contradiction.

It will be helpful to recall what was said in the Conclusion to Chapter Five concerning finitude.[106] Very generally stated, there can be discerned in Hegel's thought the correct identification of the elements of any positive mediation or becoming as Selfhood, otherness and progression as enrichment. Though finite becoming is the formal or, here, general expression for any finite enriching growth or finite qualitative increment, its indisputable reality as such growth and increment is witnessed to by the sheer inability of thought to remain in its own givenness without further self-reflection. Any finite becoming's formal structure necessarily consists of four elements: initial Selfhood; otherness; enriched Selfhood; and, recurrent otherness. Initial Selfhood is that beginning without which there would be no finite becoming. Otherness as co-constitutively negative and positive is, on the finite level, the primary source of newness or novelty. Enriched Selfhood is that "more" or resultant enriched relationship between initial Selfhood and otherness without which there could be no speaking of progression, enriching growth or qualitative increment. Recurrent otherness is that which renewedly stands over against and is related to enriched Selfhood and thus constitutes enriched Selfhood as renewed initial Selfhood. Renewedly initial Selfhood is again that which is related to a co-constitutively positive and negative otherness. This finite becoming (*daseiendes Werden*) is the existent, ongoing but formally speaking non-temporal dynamic development from initial Selfhood in interrelationship with otherness to enriched Selfhood ever-renewedly to be enriched in its interrelationship with recurrent otherness. Though this finite becoming is and is real, it is equally problematic. Its tetradic structure points out that the otherness involved is never finally inclusively or totally related to Selfhood. The collapse of otherness into the multiplicity of others and the recurrence of otherness make manifest the non-unified character of the otherness in question. The resultant relationship of initial Selfhood and this otherness is a never exhaustively realized and ever renewedly one-sided relationship. Not only is this resultant enriched Selfhood a self-contradiction in that its very realization is by definition its limit, but the entire process as finite becoming takes on the character of a self-contradiction.

In light of Hegel's presentation on finitude and on limit in particular,[107] it can be said that the most crucial question concerning the self-contradictory character of enriched Selfhood as result of finite becoming is the establishment of this enriched Selfhood as constitutively both inclusive and one-sided. A first reading of the question might tempt one to say that one-sidedness or initial Selfhood is simply logically consequent to inclusiveness as enriched Selfhood, a position then analogous to Hegel's positing of a becoming which sinks into *Dasein*. However, though the language "enriched Selfhood and recurrent otherness" might in one sense lend itself to this reading, a second look at the enriched Selfhood and recurrent otherness in question will show a much closer tie between the two.

The tetradic formal structure of finite becoming is a development from initial becoming not through but in definitional interrelationship with otherness co-constitutively negative and positive to the resultant relationship which is enriched Selfhood renewedly an initial Selfhood standing in relationship to recurrent otherness. Of present interest is the way in which enriched Selfhood as inclusive of otherness stands in relation to recurrent otherness. Initial Selfhood is enriched primarily through the inclusion of otherness. That is the very definition of enriched Selfhood without which there would be no becoming or growth. Enrichment is the inclusion of otherness. Yet, equally, enriched Selfhood is not the inclusion of otherness. It is not here a question of a logically subsequent incomplete inclusion of otherness but, by definition in finite becoming, a one-sidedness or incompleteness in the very moment of inclusion. In finite becoming, enriched Selfhood is itself renewedly initial Selfhood and is not merely from different points of view to be considered inclusive as regards otherness and one-sided as regards recurrent otherness. The very moment of inclusion or enrichment is the moment of exclusion as well since the limit identifying recurrent otherness is common to enriched Selfhood as well. The limit defining otherness as that which is related to initial Selfhood is common to enriched Selfhood, thus constituting enriched Selfhood itself as initial Selfhood. This limit or defining boundary is immanent to enriched Selfhood itself so that enriched Selfhood is self-contradictorily inclusive and one-sided in its very moment of enrichment. It is and is not inclusive. This had been indirectly indicated in earlier analyses by reference to otherness's collapsing when considered on its own into a multiplicity of others and more directly by reference to the recurrence of otherness in enrichment.

Not only is enriched Selfhood self-contradictorily inclusive and one-sided in its interrelationship with recurrent otherness, but finite becoming's tetradic formal structure as such involves self-contradiction. Initial Selfhood, otherness, enriched Selfhood and recurrent otherness constitute a process itself involving self-contradiction not only because the result is equally inclusion and exclusion, but because the process itself occurs equally as inclusion and exclusion. It is enrichment and yet at the same time and from the same perspective limitation. Tetradically structured finite becoming bears within it the doubled limit first verified in the definitional interrelationship between initial Selfhood and otherness and then verified anew in the recurrence of otherness as that which is related to enriched Selfhood. It is a process which equally establishes itself as real but limited becoming and as that which ought always to have become more and other than what it is. The tetradic formal structure of finite becoming thematizes what finite becoming is in itself, that it is an enriching growth and qualitative increment. It tries to do this however as an in principle endless progression of recurrent interrelationships between Selfhood and otherness. Despite this attempt, the sequential process taken as a whole is self-contradictorily equally inclusion and exclusion rather than the enriching inclusion of otherness as such. In its enrichment it remains one-sided. As this self-contradiction, tetradically structured finite becoming qua finite is restless, unstable, one-sided and incomplete. Neither in its result nor in its process can it resolve its own contradiction.

Neither the process of tetradically structured finite becoming as a whole nor any of its four constitutive elements can resolve the self-contradiction which finite becoming is. As enriching growth, finite becoming should in principle simply be a movement triadically structured as initial Selfhood, otherness and enriched Selfhood. But it is not simply enrichment as such. Rather, equally as enrichment and limitation, inclusion and exclusion, tetradically structured finite becoming indicates what it should have been and yet is not. By giving rise to the conception of becoming qua becoming in principle exhaustively structurable as triadically structured inclusiveness,[108] tetradically structured finite becoming indicates the only possible context within which its self-contradiction could be overcome—a triadically structured inclusive whole containing limit within it but not itself finitized by recurrent limit.

Against the background of Hegel's elaboration of the true infinite[109] it is now possible to begin to postulate that inclusive whole as the essential context without which there could be no respectful resolution of self-contradictorily inclusive and excluding tetradically structured finite becoming. This tetradic structure not only indicates but calls for and points beyond itself to that triadically structured inclusive whole wherein its self-contradictory inclusion and exclusion find resolution. The most crucial question concerning the respectful resolution of this self-contradiction constitutive of finite becoming is the resolution of recurrent limit rooted in the recurrence of otherness. Though otherness as such is not in any sense necessarily recurrent, in finite becoming it both is recurrent and collapses into a multiplicity of "others." In finite becoming this recurrent and ever-unstable otherness is on the finite level the primary source of enrichment as well as the primary source or cause of limitation. Taken together with the self-contradiction of enriched Selfhood ever renewedly equally initial Selfhood and together with the equally inclusive and excluding character of the process of finite becoming, this assertion that otherness in finite becoming is self-contradictorily the primary source on the finite level both of enrichment and limitation again verifies that tetradically structured finite becoming cannot be conceived of as an immanently self-grounding development. Of particular present concern, unstable and recurrent otherness on the level of real but finite becoming cannot, either taken on its own or in interrelationship with initial Selfhood, justify the "more" which is enriched Selfhood. This it cannot finally do since it cannot even ground itself. Finite otherness as that which is related to initial and enriched-renewedly initial Selfhood remains itself self-contradictory as source equally of enrichment and limitation.

Recurrent and multiple otherness, within the context of the tetradic formal structure of finite becoming, remains ever on the finite level primary but self-contradictory source both of enrichment and limitation. Thinking this self-contradiction through leads inevitably to a consideration of the possibility of the resolution of this contradiction. Though it is tautological, it is nevertheless here significant and true to say that to remain with the self-contradictory is simply to maintain that contradiction unresolved. It has already been argued that there can be no resolution to this contradiction on the finite level, despite the fact that finite becoming's tetradic structure itself already indicates the direction in which a resolution of its self-contradiction lies. Recurrent and multiple otherness, taken in the overall context of tetradically structured finite becoming, can be the source equally of enrichment and limitation only if otherness as such can be postulated in the context of a becoming in which it is neither multiple nor recurrent. Recurrent and multiple otherness functioning as source of enrichment and equally of limitation on the level of finite becoming requires the postulating of an otherness which functions simply as source of enrichment. If otherness were to function on the finite level merely as source of limitation there would be no need to postulate anything beyond itself. There would in fact be no becoming. However, for recurrent and multiple otherness to function in real but finite becoming understood as enrichment, it is necessary to postulate an infinite becoming, that is, a becoming which includes otherness qua otherness. This infinite becoming is the other to and of finite becoming, that other which provides the context within which finite becoming can be maintained as real but self-contradictory enriching growth or qualitative increment.

Without an infinite becoming containing otherness qua otherness within it, there would be no final justification for speaking formally of otherness as that unified actuality which is related to a necessary beginning in initial Selfhood. This infinite becoming is the totality inclusive of tetradically structured finite becoming. Were it not so inclusive, it would not be an infinite movement of becoming and could not be argued to as the necessary condition for the possibility of resolving the contradiction inherent in finite becoming. This contradiction has been verified in enriched Selfhood's being equally anew initial Selfhood, the entire tetradically structured movement of finite becoming's being equally enrichment and limitation, and recurrent and multiple otherness's being equally the source both of enrichment and limitation.

Infinite becoming is that becoming in which otherness qua otherness and without recurrence or collapse into multiplicity is fully yet respectfully contained in the possibility of a truly enriched Selfhood. This non-recurrent and non-multiple otherness is, therefore, by definition inclusive of tetradically structured finite becoming. This inclusion occurs not as the mere inosculation or unification by juxtaposition or apposition but, rather, dialectically, and this in the sense that infinite becoming in its initial Selfhood as necessary beginning is that which is in interrelationship with otherness qua otherness. From the perspective of infinite becoming, this otherness is an actual unity which, as otherness negating the multiplicity of "others" but not the reality of otherness, is related to initial Selfhood. The result is the possibility of an enriched Selfhood, an infinite enrichment without recurrent limit since there is no recurrence of otherness. This infinite becoming is the dialectically speaking inclusive other of tetradically structured or finite becoming.

Finite becoming and infinite becoming are each on their own level and in their own way totality, the finite self-contradictorily so as totality and non-totality and the infinite as that postulated but not conceptually grasped finite becoming's needed inclusive context. Infinite becoming is the context assuring that self-contradictory enriching growth or qualitative increment has an adequate framework allowing it to perdure in its real but equally immediately limited enrichment.[110] To be this inclusive context infinite becoming must necessarily be triadic in structure.

Infinite becoming must, as the inclusive other of finite becoming, be triadic in structure both in order to be enrichment and in order to provide the totality finite becoming requires to perdure as real but self-contradictory enrichment. The need to postulate a triadically structured infinite becoming lies finally not, then, as Hegel had thought in infinity's need to other itself in order to come to itself but in finitude's need to have its self-contradiction mediated or resolved. Then, not only was there latent in Hegel's thought the valid insight of enriching becoming but, when coupled with Hegel's insistence on the self-contradictory character of finitude, this insight gives rise to the postulating of an infinite becoming as a needed context for finite becoming. With the argument to the needed postulating of a triadically structured inclusive infinite, the first and most fundamental step has been taken in the move towards a reconstruction of Hegel's trinitarian envisionment. The present proposal is not meant to be more than a rudimentary sketching of that reconstruction. Such questions as the further determination of the three elements constituting the formal structure of infinite becoming as inclusive other need not be dealt with at this point. So too for the further specification of the dialectical relationship between otherness in infinite becoming and the recurrent, multiple otherness constituting finite becoming and so too as well for the further development of the point of "contact" between infinite becoming as initial Selfhood and finite becoming as process of enrichment. In a sense, "tetradic" and "triadic" have served here as a sort of meta-philosophical shorthand in this initial elaboration of the theoretically postulated transition from finitude to triadically structured inclusive infinite. That such an infinite remains only needed theoretical postulate to explain finite becoming is the final reason why one could never begin with certainty and in the public realm from infinite to finite but must always move from a necessary beginning in finitude and the actuality of otherness to the possibility of a triadically structured inclusive infinite.

4. Toward a Reformulation of Hegel's Trinitarian Claim

Hegel cannot in the public realm argue his trinitarian claim in either its explicitly religious or logically and philosophically reformulated expressions as a transition from infinite to finite. His systematically speaking deductively argued and developed position leads inevitably to untenable self-contradictions. Among these are Hegel's unsuccessful attempt to establish pure being in its determinationlessness as first moment in a movement of conceptual thought, his positing of a divine-human unity immediately intuitable by sense consciousness and his identification of freedom with logically necessary self-determination. Hegel's intended immanent and consistent deductive argument always presupposes a prior movement from finite to infinite. Any attempt to reconstruct Hegel's trinitarian envisionment and reformulate his trinitarian claim in the public realm must come to terms with the contradictions in Hegel's system by beginning always and only in and from finitude.

This prolonged critical reflection on Hegel's trinitarian claim is justified by the significant position Hegel retains in the history of trinitarian thought, by the complexity of his argumentation and by the wealth of insight he provides for any eventual reworking of that trinitarian claim. Hegel represents the epitome of traditional trinitarian thought in so far as that thought involves a movement from infinite to finite. An examination of his trinitarian thought provides the occasion for a focused critique of contradictions seen to arise out of overall traditional trinitarian thought to the extent that such traditional thought proceeds from infinite to finite. Though Hegel has been unsuccessful in his argument, the contours of finite and infinite perceivable in his complex argumentation contribute immeasurably to any alternative attempt to reestablish his overall trinitarian claim on the basis of a transition from finite to infinite. Hegel has delineated the general self-contradictory character of finitude, the necessarily inclusive structure of the true infinite and the elements constitutive of becoming qua becoming—initial Selfhood, otherness and enriched Selfhood. His insistence on the central role of otherness has opened the way to the dialectical distinction between de facto tetradically structured finite becoming and that finite becoming's triadically structured inclusive other.

The critique contained in this critical reflection on Hegel's trinitarian claim has resulted in a new point of departure for elaborating on finite becoming and the postulation of its triadically structured inclusive other. This point of departure, Selfhood as finite becoming, contrasts with Hegel's positing of nature as immediate point of divine self-othering. Taking Selfhood understood as finite, real though self-contradictory enriching growth or qualitative increment within the context of a postulated triadically structured inclusive infinite in turn constitutes the appropriate starting point for the further development of a trinitarian position in which the freedom of the human person and the freedom of God are respectfully maintained. Freedom is no longer to be understood ultimately as logically necessitarian self-determined overcoming of alienation in the form of conceptual mediation, as was the case for Hegel. Rather, freedom comes to be seen ultimately as self-determined enriching growth through included otherness. The condition for the possibility of this freedom as becoming or progressive enrichment is pluralism in its widest sense as the positive acceptance of otherness taken in its co-constitutively negative and positive character. A triadically structured inclusive infinite is itself, and particularly in as it respectfully resolves the contradiction constitutive of finite becoming, the very structure of pluralism. It is the context insuring pluralism's ultimate significance.

This critique of Hegel's trinitarian claim and this rudimentary sketching of a reconstruction of Hegel's general trinitarian envisionment necessitate a revision of the way in which Hegel's claim itself is understood. In its most general formulation, Hegel's claim that God must be known as Trinity in order to be Spirit remains valid, since Spirit is realized inclusive subjectivity or totality.[111] However, inclusive subjectivity is here no longer the mediation of logically necessary and conceptually graspable self-othering. Spirit or realized inclusive subjectivity is that triadically structured inclusive context without which finite becoming would remain unresolved self-contradiction. The necessity for a triadically structured inclusive no longer lies in infinity's need to other itself in finitude in order to come enriched to itself. That necessity is now seen to be rooted most fundamentally in finitude's need for an inclusive reconciling other.[112] God must be postulated as Trinity in order to be Spirit, the inclusive reconciling other to finite, real but self-contradictory becoming. Developing this renewed claim and avoiding simply subordinating God to a principle, namely, to the structure of becoming qua becoming, require further constructive and comparative reflection on the analogical and dialectical dimensions of the Christian experience of the trinitarian God.

Postscript

From Thought to Experience

When studying Hegel's philosophy we quickly come to appreciate the sheer scope of his vision encompassing for him every aspect of thought and reality. This appreciation extends to his insightful philosophical reading of such a key notion as Trinity. A close reading of what Hegel has written or is recorded as saying leads us to wonder at how well informed he was, to marvel at the tightness of his argumentation and to admire the incredible detail with which he presented his philosophical vision. Perhaps "vision" would not be the word we would ordinarily use with reference to his speculative encyclopedic system, but it does capture something of the grandeur of his philosophy and its programmatic importance for his own day, even though he did not want to speak of philosophy as proposing something to be done. It reminds us that his philosophy is a monumental enterprise deserving our full and careful attention. He presented with great force and assurance a philosophy whose claim to self-justifying validity remains ever anew a challenge to scholars who come after him.

A close study of his philosophy can lead to three possible attitudes toward and options concerning it. The first of these is a more sympathetic and positive reading of Hegel and the various claims that he makes, including his trinitarian claim. If we see in Hegel's overall constructive presentation of the dynamic of Spirit the appropriate, and in the public realm successfully arguable, expression of what it means to be Subject, and if we find convincing the way in which he sees that dynamic playing itself out, we can come to terms with his philosophy's historical contingencies and with what we might consider any less-than-system-threatening deficiencies.

The second of these attitudes and options is a more radically negative reading and, consequently, a rejection both of what we might call Hegel's project and of the way in which he thought it needed to be carried out. We can reject his project and argumentation for a variety of reasons, but Hegel will not permit us to do so merely for extrinsic reasons. He insists that there is nothing finally extrinsic to his understanding of Spirit. And he usually is comprehensive and clever enough already to have foreseen, at least in principle, most extrinsic argumentation with which we might respond to his challenge to embrace what he would claim to be the essentially valid and inclusive nature of his thought. So, the informed, negatively critical reader can proceed in several ways. Such a reader can of course, on the basis of serious arguments, still point to forms of thought and experience which are perhaps beyond the reach of Hegel's philosophical vision, including his reading of Trinity. Again, a reader can check out the internal dynamics of Hegel's presentation of Spirit and reject Hegel's stand on the basis of a critical analysis of these dynamics. A reader can of course also conceivably work with both of these approaches. In any of these cases, a reader may then consider setting Hegel aside in order to turn to other thinkers and other philosophical approaches, or of course to propose her or his own.

A third attitude and option possible regarding Hegel, his philosophy, and his overall understanding of Spirit as well as his philosophically infused presentation of Trinity consists in a reading of Hegel that is both sympathetic and critical. Sympathetic to his project, expressed here very inadequately as his attempt to bring finite "and" infinite into an appropriate relationship, and here, more specifically, to his claim, phrased very summarily, that to think God as personal and Subject one must think of God as Trinity. Yet critical of the way in which the project was argued, and here I myself would privilege the immanent critique as an important first step in taking up this third option. Sympathetic in principle to his notion of Spirit as movement of inclusion and integration, but critical with regard to the specific formulation of one or more basic aspects of that movement or process.

In the present study, and in the years following its first publication, I have continued to identify with this third way of working with Hegel. So many of the issues with which he struggled remain important to us today. We are still conditioned, and even constituted in our self-awareness, by a quest for social and personal meaning. Meaning, freedom, and the attainment of a richer life are for us, as they were for Hegel, fundamental social and personal goals. So many of us remain convinced that such meaning, freedom, and enrichment must be understood in terms of an appropriate theory of subjectivity. In an age of extremes, many of us appreciate Hegel's stress on wholeness, his desire to reconcile opposites, and his interest in understanding the dynamic movement of Spirit in terms of inclusive divine subjectivity. Today, however, we would hesitate to throw our lot in with such an all-encompassing view of Spirit expressed as a movement of reflexively available conceptual thought. We would recognize that in so thinking Hegel followed upon the insights of such thinkers as Kant and Fichte in a way he found appropriate for his day. To the extent that we hesitate to embrace identification of Spirit with a movement of conceptual thought, we would identify ourselves with the second, more negative attitude or option indicated above. On the one hand, then, we see that fundamental aspects of the way in which Hegel envisioned the dynamic of Spirit need to be revamped in order better to express respectful inclusion and wholeness. Yet, on the other hand, we do not want simply to pick and choose piecemeal among the many brilliant insights Hegel has brought together in systematic form. We want to maintain a critically appreciative attitude toward Hegel and his project while proposing another understanding of the dynamic of Spirit as movement of subjectivity, an understanding which will allow us to work coherently and in a more systematic way with the riches of his thought.

Among these riches we might well highlight Hegel's insistence that we begin with an initial unity of thought and being. Though his location of this initial unity as first moment of a dynamic movement of pure thought proves problematic, it should be possible to recoup his insight into the importance of an initial unity by relocating that unity. A second point to be underscored is the importance of continuing to work with an appropriately formulated notion of subjectivity. Hegel has taught that a movement of subjectivity must be dynamic and developmental. With his notions of transition to the other and of enriched return, he has at least implicitly developed the bases for a philosophy of generosity and of enrichment. He has likewise pointed out the central role of otherness in any adequate understanding of subjectivity and has worked to reconcile Selfhood and otherness when they, or otherness itself in its various forms, are expressed as opposites and extremes. He has, furthermore, stressed the importance of both spontaneity and receptivity in the relationship between Self and other. A third point is Hegel's development of the notion of the true infinite, which is the infinite inclusive of finitude. Hegel has gone a long way toward showing that finitude is self-contradictory when considered in itself and not in relation to an inclusive infinite. He has indicated the importance of working not only with an initial unity but also with a final or inclusive unity. The fourth insight on which we need to focus is Hegel's identification of the epistemological and the ontological. Now, almost two centuries since Hegel's time, there should be other ways to continue some form of identification of these two, namely, thought and being or epistemological and ontological in a more widely conceived movement of Spirit.

Our more formal presentation, in Chapter Six above, of an alternative to Hegel's move from infinite to finite to inclusive infinite was an initial attempt to take into consideration these and other important insights of Hegel. Hegel had traced a trajectory of the development of Spirit, indeed, as he would say, the cunning of reason working through history and especially the history of thought, more immediately from Descartes with his "I think, therefore I am" on to Kant and then to Fichte and his idea of the active ego positing its opposite. Hegel's presentation of Spirit climaxed in his own philosophy as a movement of self-positing and enriching return of conceptual thought. This was, for Hegel, the movement of Spirit appropriate for his time.

Today, so many years after Hegel developed his presentation of the history of the development of Spirit, we dare say that the cunning of reason has continued to work its way through history and the history of thought. Conceptual thought has, since Hegel, shown in a variety of ways that it is capable of going beyond itself in various directions, whether they be the more existentialist direction of a Kierkegaard, a materialist direction proposed by Marx, the various phenomenologies worked out since Hegel's time, the panpsychologistic philosophy of experience constructed by Whitehead who, as a colleague of mine once remarked, seemed to have developed the finite half of Hegel's thought, on to any number of other trajectories which the development of Spirit may have taken in the nearly two centuries since the death of Hegel.[1]

There is, however, since Hegel one trajectory of thought which I find particularly attractive and promising. It has in principle the ability to provide an overall structure and movement capable of bringing together in a new synthesis many of Hegel's insights in a way more acceptable to our varied experience and compatible with the triumphs and tragedies we have lived through since Hegel's time. This trajectory is one, in particular, onto which my immanent critique of Hegel's thought, and especially of the way in which he argues his trinitarian claim, opens. It is a trajectory at least indirectly indicated by Hans-Georg Gadamer[2] when he proposed to rehabilitate Hegel's concept of the bad infinite, namely, the infinite in its extreme as the notion of infinite progression, as a movement of experience, with experience however for Gadamer being understood as linguistic in character.

In referring to the notion and reality of experience, Gadamer had, perhaps without fully recognizing it, shed light on a trajectory of development of Spirit from Hegel, who had conceived that development as a movement of thought, through Josiah Royce, John Dewey and John E. Smith and of course, in Europe, Gadamer, to an understanding of Spirit as movement of experience, and I will say shortly, enriching experience. In this trajectory of development of the notion of Spirit, experience replaces Hegel's notion of conceptual thought as, so to speak, basic "metaphysical tissue" or fundamental philosophical category with and through which an effort is made to express all that there is. Each of these thinkers just mentioned was influenced by, or at least reacted to, Hegel. Royce,[3] for example, in further developing aspects of Peirce's thought, proposed what could be called a pragmatist-idealist understanding of the threefold structure of experience as a triadic process of interpretation. Dewey[4] represents a particularly important moment in this trajectory of development from Hegel's notion of Spirit as a movement of thought to an understanding of Spirit as a movement of experience. He developed a threefold understanding of experience, perhaps better three types of experience, as primary or gross experience, secondary or reflective experience, and consummate experience, with consummate experience understood as an enriched return to gross experience in light of reflected experience or thought. Dewey had effectively reinserted Hegel's concept of thought in a wider understanding of experience, with thought now seen as one form or type of experience. John E. Smith,[5] for his part, carried this move from thought to experience further when he proposed, in reaction to various more restrictive views of the nature and role of experience, an enriched understanding of experience as revelatory encounter and funded result. For Smith experience was possibly even irreducibly triadic in character.

We have, then, on the one hand, the more formally expressed structured movement of becoming presented in Chapter Six above and, on the other hand, this specific trajectory of development from Hegel's formulation of the notion of Spirit as a movement of inclusive conceptual thought to a more comprehensive understanding of experience. I would propose that we now continue along this trajectory and prolong it by bringing together that more formal understanding of becoming with the gains which have been made in the richer understanding of experience developed since Hegel's day. Ironically, given my critique, bringing formal presentation and historical development together may well remind us of Hegel's own movement from more abstract to more concrete. Bringing together, with this phrase being used rather generally here, this more formal understanding of the structured movement of becoming with our enriched understanding of experience opens for us the possibility of envisioning Spirit as a movement of enriching experience in both its finite and infinite forms. In bringing together the formal presentation of becoming and this richer notion of experience, we flesh out the previously proposed more formal presentation of becoming as we recuperate in a new way Hegel's notions both of the bad infinite as infinite progression and of the true infinite as inclusive whole.

When we bring together the formal presentation of becoming with these various understandings of experience, we come to appreciate experience as a movement of becoming and to see the formally expressed notion of becoming "taking on flesh" as a movement of experience. We recognize that in fact finite experience is a tetradically structured movement. That movement is the relationship between initial Self and other, each of which exists in this relationship for the other, a relationship resulting in a newly constituted impoverished or enriched Self that, in turn, is equally initial Self in relationship with a renewed other. Finite experience, in which there is the recurrence of otherness, is then either impoverishing or enriching, resulting in a Self that is, respectively, qualitatively less or qualitatively more than it was as initial Self. In an impoverishing experience, Self or other or both have not participated generously in the experience. In an enriching experience, Self and other have so participated, for it is ultimately only in generous self-gift on the part of the Self, and of the other especially if it is as well a Self, that the Self can paradoxically be enriched by the presence of the other while respecting the otherness of the other. This distinction of finite experience as either impoverishing or enriching provides us in principle with new resources, in an overall Hegelian vein, with which to understand, come to terms with and hopefully resolve tensions and conflicts arising so often in our age.

Such a reading, more specifically now, of enriching experience as tetradically structured finite becoming can then point, by means of an analysis reflecting on the religious dimension of experience, to the possibility of affirming a supportive context within which that experience occurs, namely, a triadically structured movement of becoming as Selfhood in relationship with otherness resulting in enriched Selfhood. We come to see experience in its finite formulation as tetradically structured movement of impoverishing or enriching becoming. Though we are not here focusing so much on impoverishing experience, we recognize that by its very nature it can to a certain extent explain and substantiate its own resultant impoverished Self, while remaining essentially self-contradictory. We realize that finite enriching experience also remains self-contradictory, among other reasons, because its resultant enriched Self is equally and at the same time initial Self in relationship with renewed and, again, immediately limiting otherness. We come, then, to affirm that the movement of Spirit as one of enriching experience is, in its paradigmatic formulation as supportive context without recurrent otherness, triadically structured movement of enriching becoming, internally structured inclusive totality. I would suggest that these respectively tetradically and triadically structured movements of becoming are, each in its own way, that of which Hegel, Gadamer, Royce, and Dewey are really speaking and that to which Smith is in fact referring when he describes experience as constitutive revelatory encounter and funded result.[6]

In partial recapitulation, then, we are replacing Hegel's concept of Spirit as a movement of dialectically developing inclusive thought with a notion of Spirit as movement of enriching experience. In contrast to Hegel's proposal to move, from the point of view of his system, from an initial or abstract form of the infinite to the finite to a renewed and inclusive infinite, a post-Hegelian approach, and here in view of our interest in Hegel on Trinity a post-Hegelian philosophical theology, moves in a wide sense from finite to infinite, which infinite comes to be seen as respectfully including the finite. In its logical formulation, such a move occurs as a multiform analysis of the movement of finite enriching experience leading to the conclusion, through further reflection on the structure and movement of that experience, that such a finite movement requires for its full comprehension the wider context of an infinite or inclusive movement of enriching experience within which it develops. In its more religious formulation, such a move occurs as a phenomenological analysis of the basic structure and movement, considered here in a Christian context, of a human experience of God. This finite point of departure, the overall Christian experience of God, then allows us to reflect as well in a further phenomenological analysis on the experience of God taken in a more subjective sense as the true infinite, with this true infinite understood as God's experience of our finite reality. We come to see that, from the point of view of our human experience of God and working with religious language, the Holy Spirit and the risen One, in relationship one to the other, lead us to God. The Holy Spirit, namely, the divine Self urging us outward, and the risen One, namely, the divine Other who includes our own finite otherness, in relationship one to the other, lead us to God, namely, the divine resultant Self, who will then be all in all.

To rehabilitate both Hegel's bad infinite, here in its form as infinite progression, and his true or inclusive infinite, it is necessary to speak of the genitive in the phrase "experience of God" as both objective and subjective, that is, to speak of our experience of God and God's experience of us through the working of the Spirit and the presence of the risen One.[7]

With regard to Hegel's philosophy more widely considered, I have argued that Hegel's placing of initial unity as first moment in a movement of self-positing thought is problematic because that "initial unity" has been misplaced. Initial unity is simply the initial given relationship between Self and other, a relationship constitutive of the first moment in a movement of experience. In this overall understanding of experience, then, epistemological and ontological are reunited. Otherness is no longer seen at first only as "momentary" negation of initial unity. It is equally primordial constitutive pole in the relationship between Self and other. Spontaneity and receptivity become, in principle at least, ways of functioning characteristic of both Self and other. As it develops, the initial relationship can become either impoverishing or enriching, with a resultant Self either impoverished or enriched. Reconciliation of opposites and extremes can in this framework take on the form of a transformation of impoverishing experience, whether potential or real, to enriching experience.

Experience, as movement of enrichment or qualitative increment, is in its finite realization a movement of becoming or enriching growth as initial Self and other in relationship resulting in an enriched Self that is equally renewedly an initial Self in relationship with a recurrent other. In its infinite realization, experience is a movement whose formal structure is a movement of becoming as enrichment: initial Selfhood and otherness in relationship resulting in enriched Selfhood.

Finite Spirit is now seen as tetradically structured movement of experience occurring as qualitative increment or enriching growth. Infinite or absolute Spirit becomes triadically structured movement of experience, pure qualitative increment or enrichment without the external limitation of recurrent otherness. In this reformulation of the notion of Spirit, experience itself, whether in its tetradically structured finite or triadically structured infinite realization, is essentially relation, process, and result. These here proposed fundamental adaptations of Hegel's concept of Spirit allow for the resituating of thought within the context of this widened notion of Spirit, with the latter understood as movement of enriching experience. Reflexive conceptual thought takes on the possibility of functioning in a variety of forms as privileged monosubjectival formulation of the structure and movement of finite experience. Thought's reflexive character allows it to provide a series of never-ending perspectival looks at, and conditioning expressions of, the wider movement of experience. When compared with this more specific understanding of thought as reflexive, monosubjectival and perspectival, finite experience itself and as such comes to be seen as manifesting more the character of an intersubjective encounter—as long as the word encounter is not taken here to imply a merely psychologizing reading of fully formed and perduring Selves entering into various relationships. The here proposed more North American and quasi-pragmatist reformulation of Hegel's concept of Spirit as movement of enriching experience acknowledges more effectively the ongoing reality of finite becoming. Finite becoming is no longer negative "moment" in the movement that Hegel called the true or inclusive infinite. It is ongoing point of departure for experience of, reference to, and reflection on, the true infinite.

Hegel had interpreted Trinity as a movement of inclusive or absolute divine subjectivity in the form of self-positing conceptual thought. Here we propose to maintain his identification of Trinity with a movement of Spirit as inclusive divine subjectivity. However, in line with our effort to work toward a reformulation of his concept of Spirit, we sketch out an interpretation of Trinity as movement of Spirit with Spirit now understood in terms of and as movement of enriching experience. It is no longer a question of interpreting divine life and love as the self-development of a conceptually transparent absolute. Rather, the divine life of the Trinity is to be understood as the less directly conceptually available movement of Spirit as movement of enriching experience in its uniquely unlimited and finally inclusive realization: the mystery of love or ongoing free self-offer, indeed, three instances, irreducible to one another, of generous self-offering.[8]

Notes

Preface

1. See discussion at http://www/listproc.bucknell.edu/archives/hegel-1/199905/msg00315.html, accessed on August 30, 2001.

2. William Desmond, *Hegel's God. A Counterfeit Double* (Aldershot, Hants, England: Ashgate, 2003) 10–11.

3. In *Revue théologique de Louvain* 17 (1986) 368–369.

4. See further on Hegel's critique of Kant in Dale M. Schlitt, *Experience and Spirit. A Post-Hegelian Philosophical Theology* (New York: Peter Lang, 2007) 32–36, 54. Also see the helpful remarks on Hegel's "immanent critique" of Kant made by Stephen Houlgate, *The Opening of Hegel's "Logic." From Being to Infinity* (West Lafayette, IN: Purdue University Press, 2006) 27–28.

5. Brito writes, "Cette solution [with reference to Schlitt's interpretation of §§ 569–570 of Hegel's 1830 *Encyclopedia*] . . . nous semble difficile à admettre: Hegel n'emploie jamais le terme de syllogisme à propos de la Trinité; et pour cause: le concept trinitaire n'est que virtuellement syllogisme; l'explicitation en syllogisme de la vie trinitaire déborde, à ses yeux, l'abstraction idéale de l'Éternel." Review of *Hegel's Trinitarian Claim*, by Dale M. Schlitt, in *Revue théologique de Louvain* 17 (1986) 369.

6. See Chapter Three, notes 70 and 71 below, with the quotation found in note 71.

7. Westphal writes, "One cannot fail to mention (since Schlitt does not) the curiously Kierkegaardian character of the critique of Hegel developed here. The three claims that 1) Hegel's system of pure thought is not available to human thinkers, 2) that the incarnation is an historical contingency that cannot be transformed into conceptual necessity, and 3) that the unity of the divine and human is not something that can be immediately perceived are precisely the three charges that Johannes Climacus levels against Hegelian philosophical theology in the *Philosophical Fragments* and *Concluding Unscientific Postscript*." *Journal of the American Academy of Religion* 58 (1990) 312–314, with the quotation taken from 314.

8. In *Archives de Philosophie* 50 (1987) 318–319.

9. Labarrière writes, "La 'thèse de base' de cette étude [*Hegel's Trinitarian Claim*] est que le mouvement de l'Esprit, chez Hegel, va toujours, primairement, de l'infini au fini. . . . C'est négliger le fait, capital, que la 'réflexion' par autant de l'extérieur que de l'intérieur."

Introduction: Hegel's Trinitarian Claim

1. See Hegel's footnote in the Preface to the second (1827) edition of the *Encyclopedia* in E pp. 13–14. See also BR 46.13–47.33. Generally no translation is indicated for BR, NR and GI. See further in Ch. 5 n. 1 below.

The philosophy of religion text cited here, BR 46.13–47.33, is probably from the 1831 or possibly from the 1827 lectures.

Identification of the lecture years 1821, 1824, 1827 and 1831 will follow Hodgson in CR for the lectures on the absolute religion (found in AR) and, for the lectures found in BR, NR and GI, will follow the indications by Walter Jaeschke in "Der Aufbau und bisherigen Editionen von Hegels Vorlesungen über Philosophie der Religion" (M.A. thesis, Die Freie Universität Berlin, 1971). Unless otherwise indicated, "1821" at the end of the reference refers to the manuscript text. The 1824 lectures are cited from the Griesheim transcript as available in Lasson unless otherwise indicated. The 1827 and 1831 lectures are from the compiled student transcripts in the Lasson edition unless otherwise indicated. The 1821 manuscript will be cited according to ILT, followed by the Lasson pagination (BR, NR, GI, AR) and the English translation in CR as possible. Occasionally reference is made to WS 16 and 17 as well.

On Hegel's reaction to the philosophy and theology of his day, see further briefly in Jörg Splett, *Die Trinitätslehre G. W. F. Hegels* (Munich: Alber, 1965) 138.

2. See by way of entry into this question Wolfhart Pannenberg, "Die Subjektivität Gottes und die Trinitätslehre. Ein Beitrag zur Beziehung zwischen Karl Barth und der Philosophie Hegels," *Kerygma und Dogma* 23 (1977) 25–40. Note also two theologians in the general Barthian tradition, Ebehard Jüngel and Jürgen Moltmann. It would be important at another time to examine in detail whether they have freed themselves of uncriticized Hegelian and Barthian presuppositions. See Ebehard Jüngel, *Gott als Geheimnis der Welt*, second edition (Tübingen: Mohr, 1977) and Jürgen Moltmann, *Trinität und Reich Gottes. Zur Gotteslehre* (Munich: Kaiser, 1980). On Moltmann see further Ch. 5 n. 267 below.

3. Attention was drawn to this structural parallel in Hegel, Barth and Rahner by Prof. Dr. Ekkehard Mühlenberg. On Karl Rahner see his *The Trinity* (London: Burns and Oates, 1970) esp. e.g. 34–38, 83–103; _____, "Trin-

ity, Divine," in *Sacramentum Mundi. An Encyclopedia of Theology*, vol. 6, ed. Karl Rahner and others (New York: Herder, 1970) 295–303 esp. 298–302. Note Splett's indication of other, directly theological parallels between Hegel and Rahner, in *Trinitätslehre* 59–60 n. 84 and p. 63 n. 86. See also Ch. 3 n. 92 below.

4. Gott ist Geist, d.i. das, was wir dreyeinigen Gott heißen;—Gott ist Geist—die absolute Thätigkeit actus purus—d.i. Subjectivität—unendliche Persönlichkeit—unendlich—Unterscheidung seiner von sich selbst—Erzeugung— aber dieses Unterschiedene ist im ewigen Begriffe d.i. [in] Allgemeinheit als absoluter Subjectivität, gehalten." ILT 527.3–8/AR 57.1–9 (CR 67–68 trans. amended). For the sake of a fluent text Hegel is quoted in the body of this study in English translation. However, the interpretation and critique are based on the German text cited or quoted in the footnotes. In the footnotes the German text is cited or quoted from one or more editions first, then where possible the source of the parallel English translation or citation is given in parentheses.

Among the manuscript and transcript texts similarly linking "God," "Trinity" and "Spirit," e.g., AR 69.20–28 (CR 78) 1824; AR 222.24–25 (CR 285) 1824; AR 74.26–28 (CR 86) 1827; AR 69.34–40 with 70.10–46 (CR 78–80) 1831?, see CR 105 n. 61. Also, E § 554 with R and § 564 with R; GW 11:368.3–4; GW 12:128.23–24. For convenience sake when referring to the *Logic* L 1 and L 2 are also cited. Except for references to the second edition of the "Logic of Being," quotes are taken from GW 11 and GW 12, and the older spelling found therein is followed in quotations. Hegel's second edition of the "Logic of Being" is quoted only from L 1 and L 2. The translation referred to is GL by A. V. Miller. Note Miller's translation of *Begriff* as "notion" has regularly been changed to "Concept." The translations of the here cited GW 11:368.3–4 and GW 12:128.23–24 are found in GL 527 and 706. The respective texts in Lasson are L 2:154 and 354.

It is not possible here in this systematically oriented critical reflection to elaborate in great detail the shifts in Hegel's terminology throughout the years. It is equally not possible to evaluate the potential influence of external social, political and religious influences on Hegel's varying choice of more or less explicitly religious terms.

5. "Gott ist der wahre Gott, Geist, indem er nicht bloß Vater und so verschlossen, sondern indem er Sohn ist, das Andere wird und dies Andere aufhebt." AR 165.13–15 (CR 210 trans. amended). See also the basically parallel statement of 1821, ILT 647.1–16, 27/AR 163.29–164.5 (CR 208). Note also the "economic" trinitarian context of AR 198.19–199.18 (CR 257) 1827. Also AR 173.33–174.4 (CR 257) 1827.

In fact when understood in the context of Hegel's system, "immanent" Trinity is the very structure of "economic" Trinity, and "economic" Trinity includes "immanent" Trinity as first moment. See Splett, *Trinitätslehre* 66.

6. "Gott wird nur so als Geist erkannt, indem er als der Dreieinige gewußt wird." G. W. F. Hegel, *Vorlesungen über die Philosophie der Weltgeschichte. Auf Grund der Handschriften herausgegeben*, Philosophische Bibliothek, vol. 17lb–d, ed. Georg Lasson (Hamburg: Felix Meiner, 1976) 722. Also, ILT 671.14–15/AR 184.8–9 (CR 240) 1821. See also Moltmann, *Trinität* 33.

7. "Man mag an Gott glauben,—bestimmen, wie man will, fehlt Persönlichkeit, so nicht genügend." G. W. F. Hegel, *Grundlinien der Philosophie des Rechts*, Philosophische Bibliothek, vol. 124a, ed. Johannes Hoffmeister (Hamburg: Felix Meiner, 1967) 324 § 35 (on the translation see Ch. 1 n. 181 below).

8. "Gott ist aber nur als Geist zu fassen, und dies ist kein leeres Wort, keine oberflächliche Bestimmung. Soll er uns aber als Geist kein leeres Wort sein, so muß er als *dreieinige Gott* gefaßt werden; dies ist dasjenige, wodurch die Natur des Geistes expliziert wird. . . . Nur die Dreieinigkeit ist die Bestimmung Gottes als Geist; ohne diese Bestimmung ist Geist ein leeres Wort." BR 41.28–42.6 (my trans.) 1824. Note the similar wording in the context of Hegel's presentation of "immanent" Trinity in the *Phenomenology*, GW 9:410.29–31 (*Phen.* 465).

9. Hegel, *Philosophie der Weltgeschichte* 722.

10. G. W. F. Hegel, *Vorlesungen über die Philosophie der Weltgeschichte. Auf Grund der Handschriften herausgegeben*, Philosophische Bibliothek, vol. 171a, ed. Johannes Hoffmeister (Hamburg: Felix Meiner, 1970) 74; WS 17.298.18–22 (CR 220) 1827. For a summary of Hegel's treatment of Trinity in the lectures on the philosophy of history, see Splett, *Trinitätslehre* 93–99.

11. E.g., AR 225.16–226.14 (CR 287–288) 1827.

12. Note the variously stated dialectical interrelationship between Spirit and community, E § 554 with R; ILT 669.2–9/AR 182.4–12 (CR 238) 1821; AR 199.10–11, 203.9–10 (CR 257, 264) 1827.

13. E.g., AR 225.35–226.14 (CR 287–288) 1827.

14. ILT 671.13–21, 673.1–2/AR 184.6–16 (CR 240–241) 1821; AR 69.20–23 (CR 78) 1824; in comparison to Islam, AR 222.13–30 (CR 285) 1824; E § 564; note also E § 384R.

15. AR 10.38–11.16 (CR 31) 1827.

16. ILT (not located) /GI 91.36–37, 1821. Also ILT 51.16–23/BR 24.20–29, 1821; ILT 499.20–21 and 28–30/AR 35.1–4 (CR 13) 1821; AR 35.36–36.35 (CR 14–15) 1824.

17. Already in the 1807 *Phenomenology*, GW 9:405.16–25 (*Phen.* 459); E § 564. On Trinity as for Hegel the true content of the Christian religion, see, e.g., Ferdinand Christian Baur, *Die christliche Lehre von der Dreieinigkeit und Menschwerdung Gottes in ihrer geschichtlichen Entwicklung*, vol. 3: *Die neuere Geschichte des Dogma, von der Reformation bis in die neueste Zeit* (Tübingen: Osiander, 1843) 891; Franz Anton Staudenmaier, *Darstellung und Kritik des*

Hegelschen Systems. Aus dem Standpunkte der christlichen Philosophie (Mainz: Kupferberg, 1844; reprint edition Frankfurt am Main: Minerva, 1966) 817.

18. AR 173.33–174.4 but see the better text in WS 17:298.18–31 (CR 220) 1827; E p. 14.

19. God as totality is Spirit, AR 70.29–34 (CR 79) probably from the 1831 transcripts. See CR 105 n. 61. In a general sense God not as Spirit of the community would be one-sided, AR 19.5–7 (CR 9) 1824; as God over against the world, AR 7.11–8.2 (CR 27) 1827. Also, BR 41.28–42.6, 1824; BR 146.33–148.39, 1824 and 1827 mixed? Similarly GW 9:410.29–31 (*Phen.* 465); and more philosophically formulated, E §§ 8, 74.

20. GW 9:410.34–36, 427.18–428.3 (*Phen.* 465–466, 485–486); GW 12:236.27–29/L 2:484 (GL 824–825); BR 29.1–29, 1827; AR 227.7–228.13 (CR 291–292) 1827; E §§ 1, 573R.

21. GW 9:427.28–31 (*Phen.* 485); E § 571 with Remark. See on Trinity in this regard by way of brief remark, Richard Crouter, "Hegel and Schleiermacher at Berlin. A Many-sided Debate," *Journal of the American Academy of Religion* 48 (1980) 39.

22. "Es kömmt . . . alles darauf an, das Wahre nicht als *Substanz*, sondern eben so sehr als *Subjekt* aufzufassen und auszudrücken." GW 9:18.3–5 (*Phen.* 10).

23. "Für das Wahre aber kann nur ein Inhalt erkannt werden, insofern er nicht mit einem Andern vermittelt, nicht endlich ist, also sich mit sich selbst vermittelt." E § 74 (SL § 74). Note the more explicit, earlier remark in this paragraph, "Geist aber kann Gott nur heißen, insofern er als *sich* in sich selbst *mit sich vermittelnd* gewußt wird" ("But God can only be called Spirit insofar as God is known as the beginning and end, as well as the mean, in the process of mediation." SL § 74 trans. amended).

Considered from another perspective, this question of content is Hegel's whole sense of the need for included otherness, negation of negation, to establish concreteness. See e.g., L 1:102.22–28 (GL 115), or also GW 9:18.29–32 (*Phen.* 10).

24. L 1:138 (GL 148).

25. E § 75.

26. "Gott erzeugt ewig seinen Sohn, . . . Aber wir müssen wohl wissen, daß Gott dies ganze Tun selbst ist. Gott ist der Anfang, er tut dies, aber er ist eben so auch nur das Ende, die Totalität: so als Totalität ist Gott der Geist." AR 70.29–34 (CR 79 trans. amended) 1831. Note again E § 1.

27. GW 11:43.20/L 1:66 (GL 82); E § 86.

28. GW 9:63.4–8, 63.18–64.4 (*Phen.* 58–59).

29. ILT (not located)/BR 156.3–6 and 9–13, 1821; e.g., BR 188.35–189.9, 1827.

30. E.g., ILT 525.12–545.15/AR 56.32–64.19 (CR 67–75) 1821; AR 74.12–77.5, 47.11–48.10, 77.6–84.7, and 237.13–14 (CR 85–89) 1827.

31. Among the many Hegel bibliographies, the following two collections, the first a series of reviews and the second a bibliography, should receive particular mention. Walter Kern, "[Neue] Hegel-Bücher. Ein Literaturbericht für die Jahre 1958–1960," *Scholastik* 37 (1962) 85–114, 550–578, vol. 38 (1963) 62–90; _____, "Hegel-Bücher 1961–1966. Ein Auswahlbericht," *Theologie und Philosophie* (formerly *Scholastik*): Parts 1 and 2, vol. 42 (1967) 79–88 and 402–418; Part 3, vol. 44 (1969) 245–267; Part 4, vol. 46 (1971) 71–87; Part 5, vol. 47 (1972) 245–276; Part 6, vol. 48 (1973) 398–409; Part 7, vol. 49 (1974) 72–92; Part 8, vol. 50 (1975) 565–581; Part 9, vol. 51 (1976) 93–114; Part 10, vol. 51 (1976) 559–570 (includes index for Parts 1–10). Kurt Steinhauer, compiler, *Hegel Bibliography-Bibliographie. Background Material on the International Reception of Hegel within the Context of the History of Philosophy/Materialien zur Geschichte der internationalen Hegel-Rezeption und zur Philosophie-Geschichte*, Keyword Index by Gitta Hausen (Munich: Saur, 1980).

On Hegel's philosophy of religion, see the references in BR 329–340 and in AR 245–256 plus the references in Ch. 5 n. 1 below and on-going in *Hegel-Studien* published out of the Bochum *Hegel-Archiv*. Further references also in Reinhard Heede, "Die göttliche Idee und ihre Erscheinung in der Religion. Untersuchungen zum Verhältnis von Logik und Religionsphilosophie bei Hegel" (Ph. D. dissertation, Philosophical Faculty of the Westfälischen Wilhelms–Universität zu Münster/Westfalen, 1972).

32. (Freiburg in Breisgau: Herder, 1922). On Hessen see Splett, *Trinitätslehre* 10–11.

33. (Munich: Alber, 1965) 160 pp. For a fuller review of this dissertation see Kurt Flasch, *Philosophisches Jahrbuch* 73 (1965/66) 422–425; L. Bruno Puntel, "Die Trinitätslehre G. W. F. Hegels. Zum gleichnamigen Buch von Jörg Splett," *Zeitschrift für katholische Theologie* 89 (1967) 203–213.

On Trinity in Hegel note also Klaus Hedwig, "Trinität und Triplizität. Eine Untersuchung zur Methode der Augustinischen und Hegelschen Metaphysik" (Ph. D. dissertation, Philosophical Faculty of the Albert-Ludwigs-Universität zu Freiburg im Breisgau, 1968); Wolfhart Pannenberg, "Die Subjektivität Gottes" 25–40; Ludger Oeing-Hanhoff, "Hegels Trinitätslehre. Zur Aufgabe ihrer Kritik und Reception," *Theologie und Philosophie* 52 (1977) 378–407; Walter Kern, "Dialektik und Trinität in der Religionsphilosophie Hegels. Ein Beitrag zur Diskussion mit Oeing-Hanhoff," *Zeitschrift für katholische Theologie* 102 (1980) 129–155. Most of the well-known studies on Hegel's philosophy of religion treat of Trinity and contain additional bibliography.

Research for the hardback edition of the present study was ended April, 1982. Regrettably, more attention could not be given to English-language Hegel literature and to the literature of the nineteenth century in the decades after

Hegel's death. On the latter see further in Hans-Martin Saß, "Untersuchungen zur Religionsphilosophie in der Hegelschule 1830–1850" (Ph. D. dissertation, Westfälischen Wilhelms-Universität zu Münster/Westfahlen, 1963).

34. Splett, *Trinitätslehre* 11.

1. Logic as Movement of Trinitarian Divine Subjectivity

1. See the general Introduction to the present study.

2. On Hegel's earlier writings, see Günter Rohrmoser, *Subjektivität und Verdinglichung. Theologie und Gesellschaft im Denken des jungen Hegel* (Gütersloh: Mohn, 1961) with explicit mention of Trinity, p. 18, and Wolfhart Pannenberg's review of Rohrmoser's book in *Theologische Literaturzeitung* 88 (1963) cols. 294–296; Günter Rohrmoser, "Die theologische Bedeutung von Hegels Auseinandersetzung mit der Philosophie Kants und dem Prinzip der Subjektivität," *Neue Zeitschrift für Systematische Theologie* 1 (1962) 87–111, esp. 105–111. On Hegel's later thought, Michael Theunissen, *Hegels Lehre vom absoluten Geist als theologisch-politischer Traktat* (Berlin: de Gruyter, 1970) esp. p. 14 n. 41, where Theunissen indicates general agreement with Rohrmoser. On the other hand, Henning Ottmann objects to the position of Rohrmoser and Theunissen, *Individuum und Gemeinschaft bei Hegel*, vol. 1: *Hegel im Spiegel der Interpretationen* (Berlin: de Gruyter, 1977) on Rohrmoser 347–354 and on Theunissen 378–387.

On a more general level, for varying attitudes toward Hegel's dependence on Christian theologoumena in Hegel's reinterpretation of Christian dogmatics, see, e.g., Reinhard Heede's "Die göttliche Idee und ihre Erscheinung in der Religion. Untersuchungen zum Verhältnis von Logik und Religionsphilosophie bei Hegel" (Ph. D. dissertation, Philosophical Faculty of The Westfälischen Wilhelms-Universität zu Münster/Westfalen, 1972) 81–86 with literature 81–83; briefly and with literature, Heinz Kimmerle, "Religion und Philosophie als Abschluß des Systems," in *Hegel, Einführung in seine Philosophie*, ed. Otto Pöggeler (Munich: Alber, 1977) 151–152. On the American scene, James Yerkes emphasizes the importance of Hegel's concern for compatibility with Christological truth claims, *The Christology of Hegel* (Missoula, MT: Scholars, 1978) e.g., 290–291, 307–316 and 1–2 with n. 2 on p. 7, where Yerkes agrees with Emil L. Fackenheim, *The Religious Dimension in Hegel's Thought* (Bloomington: Indiana University Press, 1967) on the importance of Christian theologoumena against Walter Kaufman, *Hegel: A Reinterpretation* (New York: Doubleday, 1965) esp. 271–275 and against Gustav E. Mueller, *Hegel: The Man, His Vision and Work* (New York: Pageant, 1968) 287 and 328.

In reference to Hegel primarily during the Berlin period, Walter Jaeschke speaks of Hegel's attempted reconciliation of state, religion and philosophy on the basis of the Christian principle of free subjectivity. "Christianity and Secularity in Hegel's Concept of the State," *The Journal of Philosophy* 61 (1981) 127–145. On the need to acknowledge the historical religious situation out of which Hegel's philosophy arises as "the apprehension of what is present and actual," see briefly in Jaeschke, 127–128.

3. "Absolute logic" refers to the identity of form and content characteristic of pure thought in Hegel's system. More generally and stated provisionally here, "absolute" involves inclusiveness or totality and singularity. Hegel uses "the Absolute" (*das Absolute*) both as a specific logical category and as a unique descriptive referent of Idea and then Spirit.

4. Subject is generally used here to refer to Spirit in the logical realm of universality and immediacy. Spirit generally refers here to the movement of the Absolute in its fulfillment through the mediated otherness of finitude, and more especially in the moment of total, explicit self-mediation which constitutes true philosophic thought. The Concept is for Hegel, in his post-nominalist use, Idea in logic as Subject and in philosophic thought Idea as absolute Spirit.

5. A number of these introductory remarks are argued in the course of this chapter.

6. *Logic* so italicized here in the text of this study refers to Hegel's volumes themselves. "Logic" not italicized indicates or refers to the movement of pure thought.

7. Only the single reference E plus § for paragraph and R for Remark is given when a text is not quoted but simply referred to.

8. On the *Phenomenology* see especially the literature cited in Ch. 3 nn. 124 and 128 below.

9. On the lecture texts see in the Introduction n. 1 above and Ch. 5 n. 1 below. When referred to here in the text, the philosophy of religion texts and transcripts will be abbreviated *Lectures*.

10. A term used technically in this study to indicate in the Hegelian system all spheres of philosophy other than that of logic.

11. Note also Stanley Rosen's emphasis on the *Logic*, an emphasis evolving from his reflections on the history of philosophy, in *G. W. F. Hegel. An Introduction to the Science of Wisdom* (New York: Yale, 1974) xi–xx.

12. That of Traugott Koch. This critical dependence is primarily in the areas of Koch's method of critiquing Hegel and of Koch's review of the pertinent literature. See Koch's *Differenz und Versöhnung. Eine Interpretation der Theologie G. W. F. Hegels nach seiner "Wissenschaft der Logik"* (Gütersloh: Mohn, 1967). A general overview of Koch's study: Walter Kern, "(Neue) Hegel-Bücher 1961–1971. Ein Auswahlbericht (5. Teil)," *Theologie und Philosophie* 47 (1972) 272–275. Note also the earlier critical study to which Koch (34 n. 23) is in turn indebted, Jan van der Meulen, *Hegel, Die gebrochene Mitte* (Hamburg: Felix Meiner, 1958).

13. It is not necessary here to take a final stance on the complex question of the relationship of Hegel's *Logic* to his *Phenomenology* either as philosophical moments or as specific works.

14. L. Bruno Puntel, *Darstellung, Methode und Struktur. Untersuchungen zur Einheit der systematischen Philosophie G. W. F. Hegels*, Hegel-Studien, Beiheft 10 (Bonn: Bouvier, 1973) speaks of the encyclopedic system as only one of several possible presentations of Hegel's thought (e.g., 52). Puntel posits an "ursprünglich-grundsätzliche Identität von Logik und Realsystematik" among logic, phenomenology and noology (i.e., the psychology of the third section of subjective Spirit in the *Encyclopedia* of 1830, E §§ 440–482, Puntel 132 n. 254) as *Elementarstruktur* (133, 145). It would seem best to argue the thesis of this paper on the basis of the encyclopedic systematic presentation Hegel himself worked out. Despite Puntel's very impressive familiarity with Hegel texts and his important stress on the unity of the Hegelian system, he at times gives the vague impression of a unity beyond the various moments in the self-realization of absolute Spirit. His efforts might have appeared less strained had he treated more explicitly of absolute subjectivity. Critical reviews of Puntel's book: Walter Jaeschke, *Hegel-Studien* 12 (Bonn: Bouvier, 1977) 210–214; Johannes Heinrichs, *Die Logik der "Phänomenologie des Geistes"* (Bonn: Bouvier, 1974) 73–74 n. 51 and pp. 93–96.

15. GW 11:28.35–39/L 1:40 (GL 58). Beginning with the *Logic* is also consonant with an interpretation of Hegel's mature system as most fundamentally deductively argued.

16. Hans Friedrich Fulda, "Über den spekulativen Anfang," in *Subjektivität und Metaphysik. Festschrift für Wolfgang Cramer*, eds. Dieter Henrich and Hans Wagner (Frankfurt am Main: Klostermann, 1966) 117.

17. GW 12:198.25–35/L 2:437 (GL 782).

18. See the excellent brief presentation by Friedrich Hogemann and Walter Jaeschke, "Die Wissenschaft der Logik," in *Hegel. Einführung in seine Philosophie*, ed. Otto Pöggeler (Freiburg: Alber, 1977) 75–90. For helpful access to the *Logic* by way of the encyclopedic *Logic*, see André Léonard, *Commentaire littéral de la logique de Hegel* (Paris: Vrin, 1974). On the history of the interpretation of Hegel's *Logic*, see the valuable footnotes in Koch's *Differenz*. E.g.: on neo-Kantian Hegel interpretation pp. 40–43 n. 33; on the mistaken search for a "thinker" behind the logical categories pp. 52–54 n. 51; on Trendelenburg and the tradition following his critique pp. 52–54 n. 51; on inadequate understandings of the nature of content in Hegel's logic pp. 58–62 n. 67.

19. GW 11:15.1–29.22/L 1:23–41 (GL 43–59). The text of the first edition (GW 11) is followed here. More significant changes appearing in the second edition of the "Logic of Being" (L 1) are cited in the footnotes.

20. "Vom Begriff im Allgemein," GW 12:11.1–28.24/L 2:213–234 ("The Concept in General," GL 577–595). Puntel, *Darstellung* 50–60, refers to these

two *Logic* texts: the first (cited in n. 19 immediately above) primarily in order to describe the coextensivity (*Koextensität*) of logic and whole; the second (cited here) more to describe the difference between logic and whole, that is, seeing logic as "formal" science.

21. Hegel's reserve regarding introductions is well known. E.g., GW 11:25.27–34/L 1:36 (GL 54–55). However, since this "Introduction" represents Hegel's own post-factum reflection on and presentation of logic, it in a sense shares the vantage point of one who has first read the *Logic* in its apparent dryness, studied at least provisionally the other sciences and now returned to an enriched understanding of logic. See GW 11:27.30–29.22/L 1:39–41 (GL 57–59).

22. GW 11:15.13–22/L 1:23 (GL 43).

23. Beginning with GW 11:15.28/L 1:24 (GL 43).

24. GW 11:19.24–37/L 1:28–29 (GL 47). The proper ordering of the logical categories is meant both to critique earlier theories of metaphysics and to provide a new metaphysics in the form of an absolute logic.

25. Usually in partial opposition to several philosophers and of course Kant in particular. See notes, GW 11:417–419.

26. GW 11:16.4–9/L 1:24 (GL 44).

27. GW 11:22.30–32/L 1:32 (GL 51).

28. GW 11:17.20–28 with note p. 417/L 1:26 (GL 44–45). The second edition (L 1) speaks more explicitly than the first (GW 11) of the nature of understanding as abstractive and therefore separating.

29. GW 11:19.9–16 with note p. 417/L 1:28 (GL 46–47).

30. GW 11:21.5–6/L 1:30 (GL 49). On the *Phenomenology* see, e.g., GW 11:20.37–21.6/L 1:29–30 (GL 47–48). This is Hegel's attitude toward the *Phenomenology* in 1812. See briefly Ch. 3 n. 149 below.

31. "Sie [die reine Wissenschaft] enthält *den Gedanken, insofern er eben so sehr die Sache an sich selbst ist*, oder die Sache an sich selbst, insofern sie eben so sehr der reine Gedanke ist. . . .

Dieses objective Denken ist denn der *Inhalt* der reinen Wissenschaft. . . . Die Logik ist sonach als das System der reinen Vernunft, als das Reich des reinen Gedankens zu fassen." GW 11:21.6–18/L 1:30–31 (GL 49–50. Note Miller's translation here italicizes according to Hegel's second edition [L 1]). "Objective content" used in the text of the present study's discussion of Hegel's *Logic* does not of course in any way mean independent of thought, but brings together "objective thought" (*objektives Denken*) and "content" (*Inhalt*).

32. "eine Materie aber, der die Form nicht ein äusserliches ist, da diese Materia vielmehr der reine Gedanke, somit die absolute Form ist." GW 11:21.15–16/L 1:31 (GL 50).

33. At least in the above series of references Hegel has subsumed both matter and content under form. In *Form und Grund*, *Hegel-Studien*, Beiheft

6 (Bonn: Bouvier, 1969) 188–189, Peter Rohs observes that Hegel displayed an awareness of a certain insufficiency in his intertwining of the relationship between form and content with the question of ground. In the *Logic*, esp. GW 11:301.12–302.19/L 2:75–76 (GL 455–456), Hegel treats them in the logic of essence and asserts that form is both external to content and internal to it, thus in the latter case distinguishing content from matter (see Rohs' commentary 181–195). In the Heidelberg *Encyclopedia* of 1817 the problem of form in relation to content is effectively not treated, and in this context the presentation of form is even left aside. The later editions of the *Encyclopedia* separate the presentation of form from that of ground. The question of how and where to treat form is especially complex since the science of logic as a whole is a science of form (Rohs, 188–189). On Hegel's logic as a metaphysics of form, see Rohs, 11–37.

34. GW 11:23.15–25.17/L 1:33–34 (GL 51–53).

35. "denn die Methode ist das Bewußtseyn über die Form ihrer innern Selbstbewegung." GW 11:24.37–38 (my trans.). For the point at hand the text is clear enough, although in the German it is not totally clear what the referent of "its" (*ihrer*) is. It could be "the method" (*die Methode*) or "the science of logic" (*der philosophischen Wissenschaft*). The second edition, L 1:35, reads, "denn die Methode ist das Bewußtsein über die Form der inneren Selbstbewegung ihres Inhalts." ("for the method is the consciousness of the form of the inner self-movement of the content of the logic." GL 53. Here Miller's translation takes the referent of "its" to be the science of logic).

36. GW 11:24.38–39/L 1:35 (GL 53–54).

37. ". . . die Erkenntnis des logischen Satzes, daß das Negative eben so sehr positiv est, oder daß das sich Widersprechende sich nicht in Null, in das abstracte Nichts auflöst, sondern wesentlich nur in die Negation seines *besondern* Inhalts, oder daß eine solche Negation nicht alle Negation, sondern die *Negation der bestimmten Sache*, die sich auflöst, somit bestimmte Negation ist; . . . Indem das Resultierende, die Negation, *bestimmte* Negation ist, hat sie einen Inhalt. Sie ist ein neuer Begriff, aber der höhere, reichere Begriff als der vorhergehende; denn sie ist um dessen Negation oder Entgegengesetztes reicher geworden; enthält ihn also, aber auch mehr als ihn, und ist die Einheit seiner und seines Entgegengesetzten.—In diesem Wege hat sich nun auch das System der Begriffe zu bilden,—und in unaufhaltsamen, reinem, von Aussen nichts hereinnehmendem Gange, sich zu vollenden." GW 11.25.4–17/L 1:35–36 (GL 54). Note that "content" (*Inhalt*) in GW 11:25.12 ("hat sie einen Inhalt") is italicized in the second edition.

38. GW 11:25.21–23/L 1:36 (GL 54). Slight changes in the second edition.

39. GW 11:26.18–19/L 1:27 (GL 55). Slight changes in the second edition.

40. "des Entgegengesetzten in seiner Einheit, oder des Positiven im Negativen." GW 11:27.13–15/L 1:38 (GL 56).

41. Several special Hegelian terms such as "Concept" (*Begriff*), "Subject" (*Subjekt*), "Person" (*Person*), "Spirit" (*Geist*), "Idea" (always translating *Idee*), "the Absolute" (*das Absolute*) when functioning as substantive and "Self" (*Selbst*), except when this last serves as part of a reflexive compound, will be capitalized throughout.

For the translation of specific German terms Peter C. Hodgson's practice, guidelines and privately circulated suggestions have generally been followed. Note that *Anschauung* is here generally translated by "intuition." See Hodgson, CR xxiii–xxvi and the "Glossary," CR xxxiii–xxxvi.

42. As Heede, "Die göttliche Idee" 53, points out, Hegel himself restricts the term "category" (*Kategorie*) to the determinations of the logic of being. Regarding the logic of essence Hegel speaks of "determinations of reflection" (*Reflexionsbestimmung*) and regarding the logic of the Concept "determinations of the Concept" (*Begriffsbestimmung*). For the sake of convenience, with Heede "category" will often be used to refer to thought determinations either in general or in any of the specific logical spheres.

43. Walter Jaeschke, "Äußerliche Reflexion und immanente Reflexion. Eine Skizze der systematischen Geschichte des Reflexionsbegriffs in Hegels Logik-Entwürfen," *Hegel-Studien* 13 (Bonn: Bouvier, 1978) 86: "Das Postulat der Immanenz stellt Hegel mit seiner Forderung auf, daß sich das System der Begriffe in 'reinem, von Außen nichts hereinnehmendem Gange' vollenden müsse (GW 11.25). Den Aspekt der Konsistenz formuliert sein Theorem, daß die logischen Bestimmungen aus der Negation des besonderen Inhalts der vorangegangenen Begriffe resultieren und *als Resultate* dieser internen Negationsbeziehungen von äußerlichen Zutaten—von 'Meinen' oder vom philosophischen Räsonnement—unabhängig sein müssen."

On the general problematic surrounding method and external reflection, see esp. in Jaeschke, 85–88. Jaeschke (112 and 115) describes much of the external argumentation *de facto* found in the *Logic* as "linguistic relics" of Hegel's earlier attempts to establish a logic.

44. GW 12:25.33–34, 38–26.4/L 2:231 (GL 592–593).

45. In this passage, GW 12:25.16–26.19/L 2:230–231 (GL 592), Hegel's language is not totally unambiguous. In GW 12:25.16–20/L 2:230–231 (GL 592) Hegel speaks of "that reality" (*diejenige Realität*) with reference to the sciences of nature and Spirit. In GW 12:25.34/L 2:231 he uses "reality" and "content" interchangeably concerning absolute form, that is, concerning logic: "Diese absolute Form hat an ihr selbst ihren Inhalt oder Realität" ("This absolute form has in its own self its content or reality." GL 592). In the context, however, the distinction in question becomes clear enough.

46. "welcher der Inhalt weiterer Teile der Philosophie, der *Wissenschaften der Natur und des Geistes, ist*." GW 12:25.19–20/L 2:230–231 (GL 592).

47. "Gegen diese konkreten Wissenschaften, welche aber das Logische oder den Begriff zum innern Bildner haben und behalten, wie sie es zum Vorbildner hatten, ist die Logik selbst allerdings die *formelle* Wissenschaft, aber die Wissenschaft der *absoluten Form*." GW 12:25.29–33/L 2:231 (GL 592 trans. slightly amended). See also the generally helpful introduction by W. T. Stace, *The Philosophy of Hegel. A Systematic Exposition* (New York: Dover, 1955) 60–69. Stace speaks of the logical priority of pure thought as one of reason over consequent. However it should be pointed out that Hegel never speaks of a pure or raw reality independent of thought. Hegel always does philosophy, as Stace himself later observes (71 with 297–299).

48. "Die Form, so in ihre Reinheit herausgedacht, enthält es dann in sich selbst, sich zu *bestimmen*, d.i. sich Inhalt zu geben, und zwar denselben in seiner Notwendigkeit,—als System der Denkbestimmungen." L 1:46 ("The form, when thus thought out into its purity, will have within itself the capacity to *determine* itself, that is to give itself a content, and that a *necessarily* explicated content—in the form of a system of determinations of thought." GL 63). This sentence is not found in the first edition, GW 11:30–33. Hegel brings more elements from the body of the *Logic* itself into the second edition of the "General Division of the Logic" than he had done in the first edition. One has the impression that, in addition to minor clarifications and some moderating of statements, he both in the "Introduction" and in the "Division" tended in the second edition to make more explicit the identification of Concept with its self-movement and with itself as content. Hegel in fact puts more stress on content in the second edition.

49. The reference was cut from GW 11:21.6–18/L 1:30–31 (GL 49–50), cited Ch. 1 n. 31 above.

50. "Oder der Begriff der Wissenschaft ist, daß die Wahrheit das reine Selbstbewußtseyn sey, und die Gestalt des Selbsts habe, daß *das an sich seyende der Begriffe*, und der Begriff das *an sich seyende ist*." GW 11:21.8–10 (my trans.).

51. "Als Wissenschaft ist die Wahrheit das reine sich entwickelnde Selbstbewußtsein und hat die Gestalt des Selbsts, daß *das an und für sich Seiende gewußter* Begriff, der Begriff als solcher aber *das an und für sich Seiende ist*." L 1:30–31 (GL 49 trans. amended). See explicitly GW 12:17.7–10/L 2:220 (GL 583).

52. E.g., GW 12:246.26–27, 248.14–16/L 2:497, 499 (GL 835–836, 837).

53. E § 20 with Remark. Whether Hegel correctly identifies Concept and Subject on the basis of identical structure is a question raised often enough. See, e.g., the insightful remarks by Wolfhart Pannenberg, "Die Subjektivität

Gottes und die Trinitätslehre. Ein Beitrag zur Beziehung zwischen Karl Barth und die Philosophie Hegels," *Kerygma und Dogma* 23 (1977) 25–40 esp. 35–36. Pannenberg has made his most fundamental criticism of Hegel on the basis of Hegel's identification of Concept and Subject. On Jaeschke's hesitations about a possibly overly facile interpretation of Hegel's "theology" on the basis of such an identification of Subject and logical Concept, Ch. 1 nn. 118, 133 and 147 below. More fundamental to Hegel's program, however, is to ask whether Hegel can even verify his understanding of Concept (*Begriff*) as the conceptually available structure of thinking (*Denken*).

54. Hegel's text on the absolute Idea: GW 12:236.1–253.34/L 2:483–506 (GL 824–845). This present section on subjectivity is generally dependent on the analysis by Klaus Düsing, *Das Problem der Subjektivität in Hegels Logik, Hegel-Studien*, Beiheft 15 (Bonn: Bouvier, 1976) esp. 209–288 and esp. 327–335. For brief remarks on difficulties and alternative solutions to problems involved in the functioning and verification of Hegel's method in the arising of specific thought determinations, see Jaeschke, "Äußerliche Reflexion," esp. 85–88; see also Hogemann and Jaeschke, "Die Wissenschaft der Logik" 83–88, esp. 87–88.

55. GW 12:236.8–15/L 2:484 (GL 824).

56. "ist daraus als *der sich selbst wissende, sich* als das Absolute, sowohl Subjektive als Objektive, *zum Gegenstand habende Begriff*, somit als das reine Entsprechen des Begriffs und seiner Realität, als eine Existenz, die er selbst ist, hervorgegangen." GW 12:238.2–5/L 2:486 (GL 826). See Hegel's further remarks in GW 12:238.6–10/L 2:486 (GL 826).

57. "Das Reichste ist daher das Konkreteste und *Subjektivste*, und das sich in die einfachste Tiefe Zurücknehmende, das Mächtigste und Uebergreifendste. Die Höchste, zugeschärfteste Spitze ist die *reine Persönlichkeit*, die allein durch die absolute Dialektik, die ihre Natur ist, ebensosehr *Alles in sich befaßt* und hält." GW 12:251.8–12/L 2:502 (GL 841).

58. "Structure" and "movement" as used in this study presume Puntel's distinction and linkage of the terms: "Wenn *Methode* als die *Bewegung* des Begriffs (der Idee) aufzufassen ist, so ist unter *Struktur* die *Bestimmtheit* dieser Bewegung der Idee zu verstehen. . . . In der absoluten Idee fallen Methode und Struktur schlechterdings zusammen." *Darstellung* 229, also 25 n. 20. The wider term "method" will here always include reference to both structure and movement. However, when used separately, "structure" will generally imply reference to the determinateness of the moments of the self-development of the Concept and "movement" to the dynamic transition constitutive of the determinate moments. The use by Puntel of structure and movement with regard to Hegel's thought apparently traces its origins back through Pierre-Jean Labarrière, *Structures et mouvement dialectique dans la "Phénoménologie de l'Esprit" de Hegel* (Paris: Aubier-Montaigne, 1968) e.g., 37–40, to Joseph Gauvin.

59. GW 12:239.10–249.7/L 2:487–500 (GL 826–838).
60. "übergehen in ein Anderes," E §§ 161, 240.
61. "übergegangensein," e.g., GW 11:44.24/L 1:67 (GL 83). Nevertheless, Hegel also speaks this way of the dialectical progression of the speculative method as a whole in referring to the second moment, GW 12:246.29–33/L 2:497 (GL 836).
62. "Das Negative des Negativen ist als Etwas nur der Anfang des Subjekts." L 1:102 (GL 115 trans. amended).
63. L 1:103 (GL 116).
64. "scheinen in dem Entgegengesetzten," E §§ 161, 240; see also L 1:108–109 (GL 121–122).
65. E § 161; GW 12:59.9–12/L 2:271–272 (GL 630); see Düsing, *Das Problem der Subjektivität* 331 n. 150.
66. E § 160; GW 12:16.16–18, 31.1–7/L 2:219, 238 (GL 582, 599).
67. Hegel remarks, however, that he titled this third part of the *Logic* "subjective" for the convenience of those more accustomed to treating of this particular matter in logic. Would Hegel have preferred to apply the term "subjectivity" in a positive sense to the dialectic as a whole and particularly to the absolute Idea? See GW 12:5.2–8/L 2:211 (GL 575).
68. Düsing, *Das Problem der Subjektivität* 270–273.
69. See Klaus Düsing, "Hegels Begriff der Subjektivität in der Logik und in der Philosophie der Subjektiven Geistes," in *Hegel-Studien*, Beiheft 19 (Bonn: Bouvier, 1979) 201–214. See E § 215R. Along with subjectivity Hegel speaks of Subject, Person, subjective, I, Self, and this often without nuancing. See also, e.g., the references in Ch. 1 n. 163 below. On the use of "subjectivity" prior to Hegel see Karl Homann, "Zum Begriff 'Subjektivität' bis 1802," *Archiv für Begriffsgeschichte* 11 (1967) 184–205. Meulen had himself earlier spoken in passing of the double use of "subjectivity" to indicate the first and third moment in Hegel's dialectic. *Hegel* 19. For a wider overview of Hegel's use of subjectivity see John N. Findlay, "Hegel's Concept of Subjectivity," *Hegels philosophische Psychologie, Hegel-Studien*, Beiheft 19 (Bonn: Bouvier, 1979) 13–26.
70. "übergreifende Subjektivität," E § 215 with R. In a nuanced, helpful and stimulating article Walter Jaeschke makes a number of distinctions relevant to the subject matter of this present chapter. Specifically in regard to this term "inclusive subjectivity" he forcefully argues against using the term "absolute subjectivity" (*absolute Subjektivität*), which he would reserve for reference to Idea as Spirit in the philosophy of Spirit and especially from the level of religion on, where Hegel's variously described revelatory, revealed or absolute religion is one of absolute subjectivity. "Absolute Idee—absolute Subjektivität. Zum Problem der Persönlichkeit Gottes in der Logik und in der Religionsphilosophie," *Zeitschrift für philosophische Forschung* 35 (1981) e.g., 405–406. If one were to refer to the movement of pure thought as one of absolute subjectivity, such would

of course here mean effectively inclusive subjectivity. On Jaeschke's perhaps less well grounded reservations concerning reference to the movement of pure thought as "Subject" see Ch. 1 nn. 104, 112 and 147 below.

71. I.e., its totality or inclusiveness. Summarily stated, GW 12:90.3–91.15, 125.27–126.11/L 2:308–309, 351–352 (GL 664–665, 703–704).

72. E.g., GW 12:236.3–20, 248.19–24/L 2:483–484, 499 (GL 824, 837–838). See Düsing, "Hegels Begriff der Subjektivität" 10; _____, *Das Problem der Subjektivität* 326–327.

73. Düsing points out in *Das Problem der Subjektivität* 313 with n. 87 that Hegel develops his thought on method in two sections, first in terms of form in GW 12:237.27–249.7/L 2:485–500 (GL 825–838) and then of content in GW 12:249.8–253.10/L 2:500–505 (GL 838–843). Of course content is for Hegel present in the *Logic* in the form of thought and is ultimately absolute form, that is, thought which is its own object, GW 12:237.27–238.5, 250.4–25/ 2:485–486, 501–502 (GL 825–826, 839–840). Hegel's second development of the Idea as method in terms of content is in a sense subordinated to the first and presents less of the dialectic's dynamic and more of an overview. See e.g., GW 12:249.8–28/L 2:500 (GL 838–839).

74. On beginning see esp. GW 12:239.10–241.23/L 2:487–490 (GL 827–830).

75. "Der Anfang hat somit für die Methode keine andere Bestimmung als die, das Einfache und Allgemeine zu seyn; diß ist selbst die *Bestimmtheit*, wegen der er mangelhaft ist." GW 12:240.20–22/L 2:489 (GL 828–829). However, while this lacking of determination characteristic of being, essence or universality and so forth as beginning constitutes of itself for Hegel the determination of any beginning, this determination consists in its negativity as subsumed mediation. Each beginning is beginning in a particular way. Hegel's text on this: GW 12:249.38–250.4/L 2:501 (GL 839). In this citation Hegel indicates an important implied distinction between *Besonderheit* or particularity and *Bestimmtheit* or determination. Particularity refers there to the distinction of one moment of beginning from another. Determination refers to the indeterminateness characteristic of all beginnings in themselves and in reference to progression and result.

76. GW 12:240.26–28/L 2:489 (GL 829).

77. GW 12:251.36–39/L 2:503 (GL 841).

78. GW 12:240.29–31/L 2:489 (GL 829).

79. On progression see esp. GW 12:241.24–247.6/L 2:490–497 (GL 830–836). The argumentation however is carried forward primarily in GW 12:241.24–242.13, 244.29–246.17/L 2:490–491, 494–496 (GL 830–831, 833–835). On essence in general as the most difficult section of logic, see E § 114R.

80. GW 12:241.24–242.13/L 2:490–491 (GL 830–831).

81. "Dieses so sehr synthetische als analytische Moment des *Urteils*, wodurch das anfängliche Allgemeine aus ihm selbst als das *Andere seiner* sich bestimmt, ist das *dialektische* zu nennen." GW 12:242.14–16/L 2:491 (GL 831 trans. amended).

82. "als Vermitteltes, bezogen auf ein Anderes." GW 12:244.29–245.9/L 2:494–495 (GL 833–834).

83. GW 12:245.27–31/L 2:495–496 (GL 834–835) with GW 12:247.1–2/L 2:497 (GL 836).

84. "Sie [die zweite Bestimmung] ist also das *Andere* nicht als von einem, wogegen sie gleichgültig ist, so wäre sie kein Anderes, noch eine Beziehung oder Verhältniß,—sondern das *Andre an sich* selbst, das *Andre eines Andern*; darum schließt sie *ihr* eigenes Andres in sich und ist somit *als der Widerspruch* die *gesetzte Dialektik ihrer selbst.*" GW 12:245.31–35/L 2:496 (GL 835).

85. GW 12:250.15–25/L 2:501–502 (GL 840). On result see esp. GW 12:246.18–249.7/L 2:496–500 (GL 835–838).

86. "Das Zweite hingegen ist selbst das *Bestimmte*, der *Unterschied* oder Verhältniß; das dialektische Moment besteht bey ihm daher darin, die *Einheit* zu setzen, die in ihm enthalten ist." GW 12:246.1–3/L 2:496 (GL 835).

87. "Die betrachtete Negativität macht nun den *Wendungspunkt* der Bewegung des Begriffes aus. Sie ist der *einfache Punkt der negativen Beziehung* auf sich, der innerste Quell aller Thätigkeit, lebendiger und geistiger Selbstbewegung, die dialektische Seele, die alles Wahre an ihm selbst hat, durch die es allein Wahres ist; denn auf dieser Subjektivität allein ruht das Aufheben des Gegensatzes zwischen Begriff und Realität und die Einheit, welche die Wahrheit ist." GW 12:246.18–23/L 2:496 ("Now the negativity just considered constitutes the *turning point* of the movement of the Concept. It is the *simple point of the negative relation* to self, the innermost source of all activity, of all animate and spiritual self-movement, the dialectical soul that everything true possesses and through which alone it is true; for on this subjectivity alone rests the sublating of the opposition between Concept and reality and the unity that is truth." GL 835).

88. GW 12:246.23–29/L 2:496–497 (GL 835–836).

89. "Näher ist nun das *Dritte* das Unmittelbare, aber *durch Aufhebung der Vermittlung*, das Einfache durch *Aufheben des Unterschiedes*, das Positive durch Aufheben des Negativen, der Begriff, der sich durch das Andersseyn realisirt und durch Aufheben dieser Realität mit sich zusammengegangen, und seine absolute Realität, seine *einfache* Beziehung auf sich hergestellt hat. . . . Wie das Anfangende das *Allgemeine*, so ist das Resultat das *Einzelne, Concrete, Subjekt.*" GW 12:248.5–16/L 2:498–499 (GL 837).

90. GW 12:249.8–253.10/L 2:500–505 (GL 839–843).

91. GW 12:247.18–33/L 2:498 (GL 836–837) with, e.g., GW 12:176.4–177.3/L 2:410–411 (GL 758–759).

92. See GW 12:251.14–18/L 2:503 (GL 841).
93. GW 12:245.12–26 with, e.g., 89.4–19/L 2:495 with, e.g., 307–308 (GL 834 with, e.g., 663).
94. Treated more directly in Chapters Three and Five of the present study.
95. Claude Bruaire, *Logique et religion chrétienne dans la philosophie de Hegel* (Paris: du Seuil, 1964) 84 n. 2 rightly and importantly warns against a Fichtean understanding of Hegel's method in terms of thesis, antithesis and synthesis. He correctly recalls that Hegel does not speak of a simplistic triplicity, since one can equally speak of position, the doubled middle term as negation and negation of negation, and result. However, Hegel himself almost invariably speaks of a triplicity and of a "third." Negation of negation is in its realization result. See Puntel's clarifying summary, *Darstellung* 229–235.

It can already here be indicated that a certain school of Hegel interpretation speaks in an approving way of Hegel's dialectic as tetradically structured in terms of immediacy, progression, result and then renewed immediacy. But as Koch, *Differenz* 97 n. 9, observes in regard to the attempt to distinguish becoming as result and *Dasein* as renewed immediacy, this tetradic interpretation fails to do justice to the newness and affirmative Hegel wishes to give expression to in the third moment, result. Koch is quoted in Ch. 2 n. 82 below. See also Ch. 2 n. 85 below. See on this school of tetradic interpretation of Hegel's dialectic, for example, Heede, "Die göttliche Idee" 227–231. In reference to Bruaire, Heede (284, 289) warns against being mesmerized by Hegel's triadic, a not fully justified accusation against Bruaire. Meulen in turn speaks as well of a de facto tetradic structure to Hegel's dialectic, but cites this distinction between result and renewed immediacy as evidence of the collapse of Hegel's attempt at mediation in conceptual thought. *Hegel* 12, 15 and *passim*.

96. GW 12:237.27–238.5, 249.3–7/L 2:485–486, 500 (GL 825–826, 838), but again note the qualifications in Ch. 2 n. 150 below.
97. Expressed in terms of Concept and being, L 1:75 (GL 89); also GW 12:175.15–19/L 2:409–410 (GL 757).
98. GW 12:175.14–15/L 2:409 (GI 757 trans. amended). Also, GW 12:173.3–4, 246.18–23, 248.10/L 2:407, 496, 499 (GL 755, 835, 837).
99. GW 12:248.14–17/L 2:499 (GL 837) with GW 12:49.1–52.26/L 2:259–264 (GL 618–622); concerning a possible meaning in Hegel's madness of incessantly shifting from abstract to concrete (e.g., from universality [*Allgemeinheit*] to the universal [*das Allgemeine*]) Léonard, *Commentaire* 327 n. 3, writes in a favorable interpretation, "Le passage de l'universalité' à l'universel' s'explique par la transposition habituelle de l'abstrait au concret. C'est le concept comme sujet concret que est doué d'universalité et est ainsi 'l'universel.' "
100. Stressing here inclusive totality and of course not saying "existent" Subject. "Wie das Anfangende das *Allgemeine*, so ist das Resultat das *Einzelne*,

Konkrete, Subjekt." GW 12:248.14–16/L 2:499 ("As that with which we began was the *universal*, so the result is the *individual*, the *concrete*, the *Subject*." GL 837), with GW 12:246.26–27/L 2:497 (GL 835–836). On the Idea as Person (*Person, Persönlichkeit*) and free see also summarily GW 12:236.3–20/L 2:483–484 (GL 824).

101. Hegel presents his critically corrective view of the logical category, the Absolute, in the logic of essence, primarily GW 11: 370.1–375.39/L 2: 157–164 (GL 530–536). He argues that the one-sided conceptions of Spinoza, Eastern thought and Leibniz, that is, of the Absolute conceived as simple unmoved identity, must be replaced by an understanding of the Absolute as logical unity of the reflexive determinations of inner (*das Innere*) and outer (*das Äußere*), of being and essence, GW 11:376.1–379.33/L 2:164–169 (GL 536–540). This logical unity or initial identity which the Absolute is constitutes for Hegel determination. But as such the Absolute posits itself as attribute (*Attribut*). Insofar as it is totality, attribute is *apparently* other, but *really* the determinate identity, which is the Absolute. This enriched return to the initial immediacy of the Absolute is Mode (*Modus*). The thought determination, Absolute, is transformed by Hegel to inclusive identity, parallel to his later and fuller notion of concrete universal. This triadic movement constituting the moments of the Absolute as particular category arises out of itself and is therefore showing (*Zeigen*) and self-manifestation (*Sich-manifestieren*). In view of the conclusion to this chapter it can be said that Hegel is here effectively restating his trinitarian claim in a specific logical context.

102. "nicht das Absolut-Absolute" GW 11:372.36/L 2:160 ("not the absolute absolute" GL 533), a phrase Hegel uses to describe the Absolute in its self-posited form, attribute.

103. "Der Fortgang ist daher nicht eine Art von Ueberfluß; er ware diß, wenn das Anfangende in Wahrheit schon das Absolute wäre; das Fortgehen besteht vielmehr darin, daß das Allgemeine sich selbst bestimmt und *für sich* das Allgemeine, d.i. ebensosehr Einzelnes und Subjekt ist. Nur in seiner Vollendung ist es das Absolute." GW 12:241.6–10/L 2:490 (GL 829). But recall the clearer distinctions between the various moments of the particular thought determination "Absolute" as indicated in Ch. 1 n. 101 here above. Though each moment is the Absolute, only the result is the absolute Absolute.

104. E § 213 with Remark. Hegel's post-nominalist insistence on the absolute Idea's being one, true, concrete, individual, personal and free rings of the transcendentals (being as one, true, good and perhaps beautiful) of Aristotelian-Thomistic metaphysics, a reminder that Hegel meant his logic to criticize, take up and replace metaphysics (see Ch. 1 n. 24 above) in as it constitutes a movement from substance to Subject.

Jaeschke, "Absolute Idee" esp. 402–404, argues against describing the movement of pure thought as "Subject." He (407) interprets, for example,

E § 213R where Hegel speaks of Idea, as in its reality to be Subject and Spirit, to refer only to the Idea as it appears in the philosophy of Spirit, whereas this writer sees this reference taken in conjunction with Hegel's observations in the *Logic* as applicable to the absolute Idea as Subject already at the end of the *Logic*. As Hegel remarks, "Die *Idee des Geistes* dagegen, welcher *logischer* Gegenstand ist, steht schon innerhalb der reinen Wissenschaft." GW 12:198.25–26/L 2:437 ("On the other hand, the *Idea of Spirit* as the subject matter of *logic* already stands within the pure science." GL 782). Apparently Jaeschke's objection is directed at "Subject" and especially "absolute Subject" either understood as proposed underlying or transcendent Subject or again understood as "ein in Analogie zum endlichen Subjekt gedachtes, aber 'absolut' sein sollendes Subjekt" (403). Clearly the first would represent a misunderstanding of the movement of pure thought, and the second would miss the normative and constitutive function Hegel attributes to logical thought. Here by Subject (and Hegel is quoted as using the term in the present paragraph in reference to method and result) is meant the resultant totality of the movement of logic or pure thought. Most importantly this usage acknowledges the nominalist thrust to Hegel's conception of this logic. See the further remarks in Ch. 1 n. 112 below.

105. GW 12:252.25–253.34/L 2:504–506 (GL 842–844) with E §§ 243, 244. See the more general description of logic in GW 12:25.29–34/L 2: 231 (GL 592).

106. "Das Uebergehen ist also hier vielmehr so zu fassen, daß die Idee sich selbst *frey entläßt*, ihrer absolut sicher und in sich ruhend." GW 12:253.21–23/L 2:505 ("The passage is therefore to be understood here rather in this manner, that the Idea *freely releases* itself in its absolute self-assurance and inner poise." GL 843); E § 244. On the necessary transition from logic to realphilosophical spheres, see in general GW 12:252.25–253.34/L 2:504–506 (GL 842–844).

In trying to reconcile the necessitarian character of the movement of Hegel's Absolute and the Christian insistence on divine transcendence argued in terms of God's freedom, Anselm K. Min attempts to link Hegel's understanding of *"frei-Entlassung"* with the self-diffusive character of goodness in the Western philosophic tradition. Min's generally excellent article takes into consideration totality or fullness, which is one aspect of the positing of the spheres of nature and Spirit. However, the article fails to deal adequately with the other characteristic and driving force in Hegel's *"frei-Entlassung,"* that of the absolute Idea's own need or lacking insofar as it is renewed immediacy. This latter aspect is harder to reconcile with the classical understanding of self-diffusive goodness. From the point of view of logic and philosophy and even of philosophy of religion it might additionally be asked if Min does not too easily declare, "For Hegel, then, love is the ultimate." "Hegel's Absolute. Transcendent or Immanent?" *The Journal of Religion* 56 (1976) 81. Such love would have to be love as sublated in thought.

See on the other hand Albert Chapelle's rather too strong an opposition between the more traditional communicative generosity and Hegel's "principle of lacking," in *La Dialectique. A. Dieu et la Création* (Paris: Éditions Universitaires, 1967) 106.

It is precisely in Hegel's attempted sublation of love in knowing that after valuably surveying Hegel's thought on Trinity Jörg Splett, *Die Trinitätslehre G. W. F. Hegels* (Munich: Alber, 1965) 148, finds his central point of disagreement with Hegel. Splett correctly but only in a preliminary, programmatic fashion and without more detailed argumentation observes that Hegel "hat, was eigentlich Ziel des Erkennens ist, als Schranke mißdeutet, über die er hinausmüsse (und damit schon hinaus sei)" (152, and note the similar position briefly stated by Koch on a more general level, *Differenz* e.g., 106). Citing the earlier catchword, panlogism (*Panlogismus*), of Johannes Hessen in *Hegels Trinitätslehre. Zugleich eine Einführung in Hegels System* (Freiburg in Breisgau: Herder, 1922) 8, 39, who also has not argued his position in any detail, Splett (148) accuses Hegel of a trinitarian panentheism constructed as a panlogism. Splett cites as well Franz Anton Staudenmaier, who spoke of Hegel's trinitarian panentheism in *Darstellung and Kritik des Hegelschen Systems. Aus dem Standpunkte der christlichen Philosophie* (Mainz: Kupferberg, 1844) 752–753. Splett carefully asks if this panlogistic sublation of love (*Liebe*) in thought (*Erkennen*) is not the root cause of Hegel's establishing only a diunity (*Zweieinigkeit*) or even perhaps a merely monopersonal God (an interpretation of Hegel's thought by Splett, 145–148). This sublation is likewise for Splett the source of the necessitarian character of real divine self-othering in Hegel's thought (150). On its necessitarian character Splett partially correctly but all too briefly sketches his hesitancy about this sublation of love in thought, which latter for Splett does not allow for true otherness but only an already sublated otherness (150). On Splett see further in Ch. 1 n. 160 below.

From a more philosophical perspective John Burbidge comments in preliminary fashion on the "necessary transition" from logic to nature first by shifting the locus of freedom to temporality and then secondly by asserting that "the internal structure of pure thought is isomorphic with the activity of free, self-conscious personality." *On Hegel's Logic. Fragments of a Commentary* (Atlantic Highlands, NJ: Humanities, 1981) 221–222. It would be important to ask whether it is appropriate for Hegel to try to identify freedom with the form or structure of free personality when that form or structure is realized in a logically necessitarian movement of the Concept.

107. See Ch. 1 Subsection 1 of the present study.

108. In this way revealing the true content of the traditional proofs and especially the cosmological proofs for the existence of God. See also L 1:75 (GL 90).

109. E § 574 where Hegel refers to E §§ 236, 577.

110. "Beide [Philosophie und Religion] haben die *Wahrheit* zu ihrem Gegenstande, und zwar im höchsten Sinne,—in dem, daß *Gott* die Wahrheit und er *allein* die Wahrheit ist." E § 1 ("In both philosophy and religion the object is Truth, in that supreme sense in which God and God only is the Truth." SL § 1). On Jaeschke's proposal that this reformulation takes place for Hegel only in the move from religion to philosophy, see Ch. 1 n. 147 below.

Note also Quentin Lauer's remark on the "transformed Concept of God." "Hegel on the Identity of Content in Religion and Philosophy," in *Essays in Hegelian Dialectic* (New York: Fordham, 1971) 163.

111. E.g., God is referred to in varying contexts by Hegel. To God as individual (negatively stated), GW 12:49.32–36/L 2:260–261 (GL 619). As concrete totality, E § 51R. As Absolute, indirectly, E § 85. And see within the context of a discussion of the absolute beginning of logic, the parallel "Absolute/eternal/God," GW 11:40.15–25 with additional stress on "God" in the second edition, L 1:63 (GL 78). For a listing of *Phenomenology* texts naming the "Absolute as Subject" God, see Johannes Heinrichs, *Die Logik der "Phänomenologie des Geistes"* (Bonn: Bouvier, 1974) 50, and on a more strongly theistic interpretation of the *Phenomenology* in general, Quentin Lauer, S.J., *A Reading of Hegel's "Phenomenology of Spirit"* (New York: Fordham, 1976). On God as Subject (subjectivity, eternal "personhood" [*Persönlichkeit*]), ILT 527.3–5/AR 57.1–4 (CR 67), and see Ch. 1 n. 181 below. On God as Spirit, e.g., GW 12:128.23–24/L 2:354 (GL 706), E § 564R, GW 9:407.1–4 (*Phen.* 461). God as truth, E § 1. God as absolute Idea, ILT 501.9–10/AR 38.6–8 (CR 45). God as totality, AR 70.29–34 (CR 79).

112. "Die Logik ist insofern die metaphysische Theologie, welche die Evolution der Idee Gottes in dem Ather des reinen Gedankens betrachtet, so daß sie eigentlich derselbe, die an und für sich schlechthin selbständig ist, nur zusieht." BDG 86 and also see 85 (LPR 3:235–236 trans. amended).

Jaeschke also cites Hegel here, but interprets the "Idea of God" as "die aber erst hier, in der Philosophie des absoluten Geistes, als die im realen Inhalt begährte, absolut-konkrete und allgemeine Idee gewußt wird." "Absolute Idee" 415. While it is true that Hegel's logic's being referred to as divine subjectivity is grounded by the movement of philosophic thought which is absolute Spirit and which arises in the encyclopedic system out of the philosophy of religion, it is here argued that already in the *Logic* the absolute Idea is logically formulated movement of self-positing divine subjectivity. Philosophic thought in which content and form are the same is in fact for Hegel grounding return to the absolute Idea which appears at the end of the *Logic* and is itself the inclusive, enriched return to pure being, the beginning of logical thought.

113. In regard to logic, for an extensive treatment of this abstractest definition of God as thought which is truth, that is, identity of thought and

being, see Koch, *Differenz* 29–50, esp. 40 n. 33 citing E §§ 51R, 59; L 1:75 (GL 89–90).

Many have branded this defining God as truth pantheistic. In an at least partial defense of Hegel, Koch, *Differenz* 43–47, recalls the fundamental importance of Hegel's insistence on the negated presence of finite within infinite. Hegel himself writes, "Das *Nichtseyn* des Entlichen ist das *Seyn* des Absoluten." GW 11:290.7–8/L 2:62 ("the non-being of the finite is the *being* of the absolute." GL 443).

In a particularly insightful article Wolfhart Pannenberg in turn responds to the pantheism charge by emphasizing three points: the Absolute as the negation of finitude; divine personality; and the distinction between "inner" Trinity and world. He would see the grounding of a defense of Hegel in a more accurate interpretation of the necessitarian character of the divine self-release into finitude. See "Die Bedeutung des Christentums in der Philosophie Hegels," in *Stuttgarter Hegel-Tage 1970*, *Hegel-Studien*, Beiheft 11, ed. Hans-Georg Gadamer (Bonn: Bouvier, 1974) 188–200. Note the English translation, "The Significance of Christianity in the Philosophy of Hegel," in *The Idea of God and Human Freedom* (Philadelphia: Westminster, 1973) 160–174. This particular article is generally cited according to the German.

Rather than thematically pursuing the pantheism charge, this author would with Koch (46–47) prefer to pose the deeper question of the very viability of Hegel's deductively argued system.

114. Explicitly GW 11:21.19–21/L 1:31 (GL 50). See Hogemann and Jaeschke. "Die Wissenschaft der Logik" 78–79. Interestingly, the Eastern European, Pavel Apostel, insists upon the need first to understand Hegel's logic as "*logica divina*." "Wie ist die Entwicklung einer 'Logica Humana' im Rahmen der Darlegung der 'Logica Divina' in Hegels *Wissenschaft der Logik* möglich?" in *Die Wissenschaft der Logik und die Logik der Reflexion*, *Hegel-Studien*, Beiheft 18 (Bonn: Bouvier, 1978) 37–39. Koch, *Differenz* e.g., in a general way 47–50, speaks of the *Logic*'s being considered theology as its hermeneutic aspect. On the other hand, Puntel, *Darstellung* 117, criticizes this as merely considering one aspect.

115. "Hegel radikalisiert diese Tradition [Anselm] durch den Gedanken der ursprünglichen Identität Gottes mit dem reinen Denken." Kimmerle, "Religion und Philosophie," 170. Radical in the sense both of carrying the tradition to its extreme and of incorporating the whole tradition into his system.

116. Peter Rohs, review of *Werden zu sich. Eine Untersuchung zu Hegels "Wissenschaft der Logik*," by Ute Guzzoni, in *Hegel-Studien* 4 (Bonn: Bouvier, 1967) 253; Rohs, *Form und Grund*, *Hegel-Studien*, Beiheft 6 (Bonn: Bouvier, 1969) 31–36.

117. Summarily on concrete universality, Léonard, *Commentaire* 326–327.

118. Heede, "Die göttliche Idee" 266–268, goes so far as to justify the usage of "God" in a Hegelian *philosophical* context, "um auszudrücken, daß deren Subjekt in der Tat ein 'Subjekt' . . . ist." Prof. Wolfhart Pannenberg writes, "es zeigt sich hier, daß Hegels Logik des Begriffs in allem Ernst als Logik des Subjekts und zwar des absoluten Subjekts, Gottes, gelesen will." See his valuable article, "Die Bedeutung" 192. From the context of this quote in Pannenberg's article it would appear that he was there limiting consideration of logic as *logica divina* to the logic of the Concept, a position similar to that of Prof. Falk Wagner, *Der Gedanke der Persönlichkeit Gottes bei Fichte und Hegel* (Gütersloh: Mohn, 1971), concerning Trinity. See Ch. 1 n. 157 below. On Jaeschke's hesitation concerning Pannenberg's reference to "absolute Subject" in logic, see Ch. 1 nn. 133 and 147 below.

119. Again, note Ch. 1 n. 114 above.

120. Heede, "Die göttliche Idee" 55–57, with literature concerning this term on 55. He characterizes Hegel's philosophy of religion "*Phänomeno-theo-logik.*"

121. E.g., E § 1.

122. GW 9:45.36–46.5 (*Phen.* 40). See also Heede, "Die göttliche Idee" 53–54.

123. "Absolute" is for Hegel a particularly felicitous thought determination able to be used beyond its immediate logical context to indicate the inclusive totality, since the "Absolute" manifests or shows itself in "Attribute." See Ch. 1 n. 101 above.

124. On the more explicit reference to "God," see, e.g., on "Absolute" Ch. 1 n. 111 above.

125. E.g., GW 12:236.27–29/L 2:484 (GL 824–825). Also, e.g., E § 573R.

126. "formierte Materie," GW 11:301.13–302.19, esp. 302.6–9/L 2:75–76, esp. 76 (GL 455–456). See Ch. 1 n. 33 above.

127. On the problematic question of this identity of content between religion and philosophy see more generally, Falk Wagner, "Die Aufhebung der religiösen Vorstellung in dem philosophischen Begriff," *Neue Zeitschrift für systematische Theologie und Religionsphilosophie* 18 (1976) 44–73. Walter Jaeschke on the other hand stresses the "dialectical" identity of content between religion and philosophy and thus allows for the inclusion of difference even in the identity of content Hegel posits. "Speculative and Anthropological Criticism of Religion: A Theological Orientation to Hegel and Feuerbach," *The Journal of the American Academy of Religion* 48 (1980) 354.

128. The nuanced positions of certain philosophers as for example Heede, Theunissen, Lauer and Jaeschke form important exceptions. See briefly and more generally the remark by Walter Jaeschke, review of *Der Gottesbegriff der spekulativen Theologie*, by Klaus Krüger (Berlin: de Gruyter, 1972) in *Hegel-Studien* 10 (Bonn: Bouvier, 1975) 373.

It is not however merely a question of differing departmental and academic interests, but of a difference rooted in varied understandings of the nature and functioning of the movement of logical thought as Hegel envisioned it. For example, in "Bemerkungen zum Anfang von Hegels Logik," in *Seminar. Dialektik in der Philosophie Hegels*, ed. Rolf-Peter Horstmann (Frankfurt am Main: Suhrkamp, 1978) 203, Wolfgang Wieland argues that Hegel's logic consists in a movement from finite to infinite and not the self-positing of the infinite presented from the standpoint of the infinite. However, Hegel's logic in fact proposes to achieve this *Aufhebung* of finite to infinite precisely by means of and as a presentation (*Darstellung*) of the movement of divine self-positing thought. Hegel intended to combine ontological and cosmological proofs for the existence of God into one movement of divine self-thought raising negated finite thought to its level. See, e.g., BDG 85–86 (LPR 3:235–86 (LPR 3:235–236). Rüdiger Bubner, "Strukturprobleme dialektischer Logik, "in *Der Idealismus und seine Gegenwart. Festschrift für Werner Marx zum 65. Geburtstag*, ed. Ute Guzzoni, Bernhard Rang and Ludwig Siep (Hamburg: Felix Meiner, 1976) 51 n. 2 agrees with Wieland.

In the Russian philosopher Iwan Iljin's famous *Die Philosophie Hegels als kontemplative Gotteslehre* (Bern: Francke, 1946) the immediately relevant ninth chapter, "Die göttliche Logik," 203–230, speaks somewhat too unnuancedly of logic as the first, speculative epoch of divine life. In addition, note that Koch, *Differenz* 58–62 n. 67, esp. p. 61, has situated Iljin's unacceptable intuitionist understanding of Hegel within the context of a wider historical interpretation of Hegel's *Logic* as replacing formal logic with a material one whose content is derived from reality (*Weltwirklichkeit*). See also the observations from Puntel's particular interpretative point of view in his discussion with Iljin in *Darstellung* 101–109.

129. "die Wissenschaft nur des göttlichen Begriffs." GW 12:253.4–5/L 2:505 (GL 843). Puntel, *Darstellung* 108, emphasizes this quote's context, i.e., the relationship of logic to the other sciences. Granted the context, the descriptive reference "*göttliche*" remains, and "*nur*" qualifies not "divine" but "Concept." So "nur" does not denigrate "divine" but "Concept" in relation to the further development constituting the realphilosophical sciences.

130. "aber in der Idee bleibt sie [die *Form* ihrer Bestimmtheit, die *Äusserlichkeit*] an und für sich die Totalität des Begriffs und die Wissenschaft im Verhältnisse des göttlichen Erkennens zur Natur." GW 12:253.27–29/L 2:506 (GL 844 trans. amended).

131. E § 1; and, added to the second edition of the logic of being, "und das unbestrittenste Recht hätte *Gott*, daß mit ihm der Anfang gemacht werde." L 1:63 ("and *God* has the absolutely undisputed right that the beginning be made with him" GL 78).

132. E § 577. Traugott Koch first brought the importance of this quote's position to my attention.

133. For an analysis of Hegel's interpretation of Aristotle's νοήσισ νοήσεως from the point of view of Hegel's explicit concern with a theory of subjectivity, see Düsing, *Das Problem der Subjektivität* 305–313 with helpful literature cited. On Hegel's thought from logic through philosophy as speculative theology see Heede, "Die göttliche Idee" 62–64.

As indicated in Ch. 1 nn. 70, 104 and 112 above, Dr. Jaeschke proposes not to refer to logic and particularly to the absolute Idea at the end of the *Logic* as *absolute* subjectivity and *Subject*. Rather Jaeschke posits a specific difference between the absolute Idea at the end of the *Logic* and absolute subjectivity in the philosophy of Spirit. On the basis of this distinction (without of course for Jaeschke positing two subjectivities) Jaeschke stresses the difference between the "Aristotelian" speculative theology as developed by Hegel in the *Logic* and that of Hegel in the philosophy of religion. Then Jaeschke continues, "Und um dieser Differenz willen kann das aristotelische τοῦτο γὰρ ὁ θεός im prägnanter sinne von keinem der in der Logik entwickelten Begriffe ausgesagt werden, sondern erst vom Begriffe Gottes als absoluter Subjektivität." "Absolute Idee" 406, see also 407–408. The operative phrase in Jaeschke's position is "im prägnanter Sinne." Granted the Aristotle reference applies explicitly to Hegel's Concept of God and most adequately to the final encyclopedic level of philosophy, the Aristotle reference is still in clearly Hegelian fashion to be seen as qualifying each level in the encyclopedic system as appropriate to that specific level. In fact, philosophic thought as grounding return to the unity of the absolute Idea in logic and even therewith as return to the originary unity of being as first logical thought determination ultimately justifies the claim that Hegel makes in referring to logic as "divine." For additional references to Hegel's description of logic as divine, see Jaeschke, "Absolute Idee" 399, 404. On Jaeschke's understanding of logic as speculative theology *only* in an Aristotelian sense, see Ch. 1 n. 147 below.

134. "Das Sein selbst sowie die folgenden Bestimmungen nicht nur des Seins, sondern die logischen Bestimmungen überhaupt können als Definitionen des Absoluten, als die *metaphysischen Definitionen Gottes* angesehen werden; . . . Denn Gott metaphysisch definieren heißt, dessen Natur in *Gedanken*, als solchen ausdrücken; die Logik aber umfaßt alle Gedanken, wie sie noch in der Form von Gedanken sind." E § 85 (SL § 85). Puntel, *Darstellung* 73 n. 39, cites other important references: E §§ 87R, 112, 181R, 194R, 213R.

135. See Hegel's argumentation later on in E § 85. Wieland recalls the inadequacy of the form of definition qua definition to grasp the Absolute. "Bemerkungen zum Anfang" in *Seminar. Dialektik in der Philosophie Hegels* 205.

136. GW 12:210.4–214.39/L 2:451–458 (GL 795–800).

137. Hegel's treatment of definition falls within his presentation of the Idea of knowing (*Die Idee des Erkennens*) which constitutes the second chapter of the *Logic*'s final section entitled "the Idea" (*Die Idee*).

138. GW 12:210.17–211.6, 214.27–214.39/L 2:452–453, 457–458 (GL 795–796, 800).

139. The constitutive moments of definition are themselves those of the Concept: universality; particularity; individuality. GW 12:210.6–16/L 2:451–452 (GL 795).

140. From his particular perspective, Puntel on the other hand argues that these "definitions of the divine" are references (*Hinweise*) not to be understood purely internally, that is, not in reference to logical thought itself but to the "realphilosophical dimension," to the manifestation of the Absolute in the sphere of religion. *Darstellung* 72–73, see 90–91, 115. It would be more Hegel's mind however to understand these definitions as referring *both* to the moments of logical thought *and* through them to particular manifestations analyzed in the philosophy of religion. Michael Theunissen tentatively proposes an understanding parallel to this latter position. See his *Sein und Schein. Die kritische Funktion der Hegelschen Logik* (Frankfurt am Main: Suhrkamp, 1978) 62.

141. "Die Definition *des Absoluten*, daß es die *Idee ist*, ist nun Selbst absolut. Alle bisherigen Definitionen gehen in diese zurück." E § 213R ("The definition, which declares *the Absolute* to be the *Idea* is itself absolute. All former definitions come back to this." SL § 213R trans. amended). It is almost as if Hegel uses "definition" both in a negatively critical sense and in a less technical but more positive way.

142. E § 85. See also L 1:125 (GL 137). Jaeschke sheds further light on Hegel's distinction of first and third determinations from second determinations in any logical triadic. Jaeschke hypothesizes "ob diese Unterscheidung ihre Wurzeln nicht lediglich in dem von Hegel sonst kritisierten Verfahren der natürlichen Theologie habe, Gott allein die Realitäten und nicht die Negationen bzw. die bloß abgeleiteten Realitäten zuzusprechen." "Absolute Idee" 402.

143. "Es folgte hieraus die zweite Definition des Absoluten, daß es das *Nichts* ist." E § 87R ("Hence was derived the second definition of the Absolute; the Absolute is the Nought." SL § 87R). Though it could technically be argued that Hegel was earlier speaking of definitions of God and here refers only to the Absolute, such a distinction would not in view of E § 85 and, with everything considered, be tenable here. See also Koch, *Differenz* 92–93 with nn. 35 and 36.

144. "So in Gott selbst enthält die Qualität, *Tätigkeit, Schöpfung, Macht* usf. wesentlich die Bestimmung des Negativen,—sie sind ein Hervorbringen eines *Anderen.*" L 1:70 ("Thus in God self Quality [*activity, creation, power* and so forth] involves the determination of the negative—they are the bringing forth of an *other*." GL 85 trans. amended); GW 11:45.34–46.6/L 1:69 (GL 84–85).

145. Léonard's explanation, "c'est seulement avec le devenir qu'on a la première pensée concrete, le premier Concept et par là, la première véritable détermination logique," *Commentaire* 47 n. 2, fails to address directly Hegel's considering *Nichts* an important definition of the Absolute.

146. GW 12:246.14–15 with 18–23/L 2:496 (GL 835).

147. In a manner sensitive to Hegel's texts and with a series of important distinctions Jaeschke in "Absolute Idee" (esp. 398–405) briefly but forcefully presents perhaps the best alternative to the somewhat Pannenbergian position espoused here concerning logical thought as for Hegel a movement of the divine self-positing Subject. While it is not possible to present all of Jaeschke's argumentation, it will be of value to indicate that Jaeschke practically speaking delineates and critiques, in the context of his discussion on ways absolute logic might be seen as establishing the personhood of God, four possible ways ("noch mehrer konkurrierende Modelle einer logischen Begründung der Erkenntnis der Persönlichkeit Gottes" 398) in which logic could be referred to as *Gottesbegriff*: 1) a general challenge to any theological dimension to the *Logic*; 2) the *Logic* as presuming the personhood of God; 3) stressing that only some of the logical thought determinations are suitable to establish a knowledge of God; 4) the totality of theological determinations as culminating in the absolute Idea would constitute a *Gottesbegriff* (398). In agreement with Jaeschke it must be said that the first three options are not tenable interpretations of Hegel's thought. Jaeschke likewise rejects the fourth position, since for him the logical thought determinations are finite (402). To the extent that this fourth position or approach might involve the surreptitious constitution of a supposedly absolute Subject modeled on a finite Subject Jaeschke (402–405) rightly warns against any interpretation claiming Hegel presupposes a Subject underlying the movement of logical thought. Likewise he correctly warns against any uncritical transfer from Christian theology in interpreting Hegel's logic as "speculative theology." Then Jaeschke proposes to turn for a concept of God from logic to philosophy of religion (397, 405–416), since according to him it is inappropriate to speak of Subject or absolute Subject in reference to the subjectivity Hegel establishes in the *Logic* (405–406, 407–408; see Ch. 1 n. 104 above). Finally Jaeschke would propose to describe logic only as a movement of subjectivity and distinguishes between absolute Idea in logic and absolute subjectivity in the philosophy of Spirit (e.g., 406–407, 408–410, also see quote in Ch. 1 n. 133 above). Jaeschke would speak of Hegel's logic as speculative theology only in an "Aristotelian sense" (404–405). Though this present sketch is by its very brevity naturally unfair to Jaeschke's nuanced, wider position involving as well Hegel's philosophy of religion and the differing forms in which logic and philosophy of religion establish for Hegel a concept of God, nevertheless it does now allow for a summary response. First of all, Jaeschke's references to the position of Christian theology and ecclesial teaching (e.g., 405, 410–411, 416) as distinguished from Hegel's speculative theology's being supposedly more akin to that of Aristotle would appear to presuppose too homogeneous a Christian theological tradition. Second, it would be important to give more attention to Hegel's notion of totality (*das Ganze*) in relation to logic as a whole, to

each thought determination and to concrete universal, all with their nominalist thrust. They surely call for usage of a reconstructed understanding of Subject. Reference to Hegel's logic as movement of divine self-positing subjectivity as Subject is to be understood for Hegel as the appropriate *logical* reformulation of "God." Absolute Idea as definition of God does not exclude but presupposes that all other thought determinations are likewise in their own way definitions of God. It should be possible without equivocation on the basis of a common structure to refer both to the absolute Idea at the end of the *Logic* and to "God" in the philosophy of religion varyingly as divine Subject while acknowledging that each reference is conditioned by its "location" in Hegel's system. This would give emphasis to the dynamic unity of Hegel's encyclopedic system. A final observation. Dr. Jaeschke's objections to considering logic as *Gottesbegriff* or *Gotteslehre* are in the last analysis apparently rooted in the desire to avoid the philosophically clothed reestablishment of a being merely over against finitude (e.g., 407–410), an "existent" Subject. This legitimate concern indicates the regular need in interpreting Hegel to recall Hegel's thorough reconstruction and reformulation of the notion of God as truth and that Hegel's movement of logical thought is always to be conceived of as taking place in and through finite thought while grounding and sublating that thought.

Briefly again on Jaeschke's particular insistence on Hegel's logic nevertheless being a speculative theology, see Hogemann and Jaeschke, "Die Wissenschaft der Logik" 78–79.

For the best older literature on the question of divine subjectivity under the rubric of divine personhood see Jaeschke, "Absolute Idee" 387 n. 5.

148. Note especially regarding the *Logic*: Staudenmaier, *Darstellung*; touching on the *Logic*, Hessen, *Hegels Trinitätslehre*; Bruaire, *Logique et Religion* 65–131; Splett, *Trinitätslehre* 77–81; Falk Wagner, *Der Gedanke* esp. 223–254 with important references and remarks on Fichte and Strauß.

149. GW 12:247.7–248.4/L 2:497–498 (GL 836–837). See Splett, *Trinitätslehre* 77–78. On Hegel interpreters such as Kroner who claim Hegel's was a tetradically structured dialectical method, see Heede, "Die göttliche Idee" 227–231, esp. 229. On the difficulty with such an understanding see further Ch. 2 n. 82 below. See also Ch. 1 n. 95 above.

150. For example, Hegel's remarks on the moments of the Absolute, GW 11:371.12–16/L 2:158 (GL 530).

151. E § 162R. Recall that beginnings are as yet unposited totalities, GW 12:240.20–241.251L 2:489–490 (GL 828–830).

152. GW 12:16.16, 32.16–29/L 2:219, 239 (GL 582, 600); E § 160.

153. See Ch. 3 Subsection 2a below.

154. "Jedes Moment des Begriffs ist selbst der ganze Begriff (§ 160) aber die Einzelheit, das Subjekt, ist der als Totalität *gesetzte* Begriff." E § 163R (SL § 163R but my trans.).

155. "Moment as totality" also points to the absence of any underlying Self or substratum and to the continuing sublated presence of preceding thought determinations in the one under consideration.

156. This of course in the context of all that has been presented so far in this chapter. On the immediate Kantian background to Hegel's logical form of "immanent" Trinity and the appropriateness of locating "immanent" Trinity in the realm of pure thought where form and content are first adequate to one another, see Wagner, *Der Gedanke* 223–229. Splett, *Trinitätslehre* 145–148 and esp. n. 2, Kern, "Dialektik und Trinität in der Religionsphilosophie Hegels. Ein Beitrag zur Diskussion mit L. Oeing-Hanhoff," *Zeitschrift für Katholische Theologie* 102 (1980) 150–151 and Ludger Oeing-Hanhoff, "Hegels Trinitätslehre. Zur Aufgabe ihrer Kritik und Reception," *Theologie und Philosophie* 52 (1977) 378–407, argue only to a "diunity" (*Zweieinigkeit*) in Hegel's thought. Kern writes, "Der Heilige Geist verliere, als Name für die Einheit von Vater und Sohn, seine eigene Personalität, die von den beiden anderen göttlichen Personen verschiedene Subsistenz" (151). The overall weakness in Kern's interpretation of Hegel lies in the failure to acknowledge Hegel's absolute logic as itself reformulated "immanent" Trinity (see even Kern's own remark alluding to this, p. 137 n. 27). More basically the weakness in these critiques lies in the inadequate attention given to Hegel's dialectical method in the *Logic*. There Hegel establishes a third, which as negation of negation is renewedly positive, a logical advance over the first two terms of any triadic.

157. In *Der Gedanke* at least Wagner limits consideration of Trinity to the logic of the Concept, since there the posited difference between God and other (*Anderssein* 235) is sublated (*aufgehoben*). "Der allgemeine Begriff, der in seinem Unterschied nur als mit sich identisch ist, stellt spekulativ-logisch den Ort dar, wo Gott als dreieiniger Gott gedacht werden kann" (234). He claims, "daß die Trinität nicht in der Logizität des Wesens erfaßt werden kann, habe ich in dem Aufsatz: Der Gedanke der Persönlichkeit Gottes bei Ph. Marheineke, bes. 73ff., gezeigt," (234–235 n. 125; see also 230–231 n. 123). See "Der Gedanke der Persönlichkeit Gottes bei Ph. Marheineke," *Neue Zeitschrift für systematische Theologie und Religionsphilosophie* 10 (1968) 44–88. For a critique of this position of Wagner's see Jaeschke, "Absolute Idee" 400–403, 412 n. 41.

158. Recall again E § 163 R.

159. Intended as a negative critique, J. Hessen writes, "Hegels Trinitätslehre ist im Grunde genommen nichts anders als die mit dem panlogischen Grundprinzip gegebene dialektische Methode, der 'Dreischlag des Begriffes Begriffes.'" *Hegels Trinitätslehre* 38.

160. That is, not necessary in order to qualify Hegel's logic as intended reformulation of Trinity. And that is all that is of present concern. Whether Hegel's presentation of "immanent" Trinity would as it stands be a valid refor-

mulation compatible with the various Christian traditions is another question to be answered only if it has first been established that Hegel's theory is itself viable, given the conditions he himself establishes for its successful establishment.

Additionally, stating that Hegel's appropriation of Trinity does not correspond to Church dogmatics too easily presumes a unified and homogeneous Christian tradition. J. Hessen makes such a claim despite his acknowledgement of Hegel's good intentions in *Hegels Trinitätslehre* 36. Overall Hessen's critique remains external and married by a number of misunderstandings (see Hessen, 32–43). Concerning this presumption of a unified Christian tradition, see L. Bruno Puntel, who makes a similar criticism of Splett, "Die Trinitätslehre G. W. F. Hegels. Zur gleichnamigen Buch von Jörg Splett," *Zeitschrift für katholische Theologie* 89 (1967) 203–213. Note Kern's more nuanced remark in "Dialektik und Trinität" 151.

On the other hand, Wagner, *Der Gedanke* esp. 241–251, does treat of logically presented Trinity in terms of "tri-personal" unity. His section headings read: "Trinität als Einheit dreier Personen" (241); and, "Gott als immanent trinitarische Persönlichkeit" (249). But see Ch. 1 n. 164 here below. Pannenberg, "Die Bedeutung" 192–195, has recalled that Hegel uses "personhood" in two senses (recall also Hegel's at least double usage of subjectivity). Hegel speaks of personhood in negatively critical fashion as merely abstract, and in a positively approving sense as individual, inclusive and concrete.

161. On Hegel's often not too logically rigorous distinction of Person as "realized personality" see Wagner, *Der Gedanke* 249–250 with n. 146. See Hegel's texts indicated here in Ch. 1 n. 163 below.

162. Prof. Falk Wagner drew my attention to this in a private conversation. See also the remarks by Jaeschke, "Absolute Idee" 407–408 with nn. 35 and 36.

163. Note in the *Logic* the juxtaposed and parallel usages: GW 12:236.12–15, 246.23–27, 251.8–13/L 2:484, 496–497, 502 (GL 824, 835–836, 841).

164. Similarly, Karl Heinz Haag writes, "Dadurch, daß sich alle Bestimmungen—Sein und Nichts—lediglich in ihrer Beziehung aufeinander konstituieren, sind sie an sich selbst ein Werden, ein Übergehen ineinander." "Die Seinsdialektik bei Hegel und in der scholastischen Philosophie" (Ph. D. dissertation, Johann Wolfgang Goethe Universität, Frankfurt am Main, 1951) 20 n. 1, also 21–22, cited by Koch, *Differenz* 96 n. 47. Koch also cites GW 11:44.22–26/L 1:67 (GL 82–83).

On the other hand, Jaeschke, "Absolute Idee" e.g., 412–413, would argue against the possibility of establishing any tri-personally structured divine subjectivity directly and simply out of Hegel's logic. Jaeschke would apparently not allow for self-donation as such but only negation of negation, knowledge of the Self in the other as made explicit and thematic then being considered "personal" (see Jaeschke, 410–411, 414). It would appear that one of Jaeschke's underlying concerns is to avoid any crude notion of Person as "individual over against others" being introduced into the *Logic*.

Wagner and Pannenberg point out Fichte's and Spinoza's positing of the contradiction of applying the notion "Person" or "personhood" to God, since for Fichte and Spinoza Person included finitude in that it referred to an other. Both Wagner and Pannenberg bring out Hegel's overcoming of Fichte's objection by establishing Person as "going over into." See overall, Wagner, *Der Gedanke*, cited by Pannenberg, "Die Bedeutung" 194 n. 73. See also the following by Pannenberg: *Jesus—God and Man* (Philadelphia: Westminster, second ed. 1977) 181–182 with n. 155, cited according to the second edition; "Die Bedeutung" 192–194 with further references to Hegel's positing of the abstract and concrete personhood of God; *Das Glaubensbekenntnis ausgelegt und verantwortet von den Fragen der Gegenwart* (Hamburg: Siebenstern Taschenbuch, 1972) 35–37.

Jaeschke, "Absolute Idee" 401, gives further precision by recalling that Hegel both profits from and criticizes Fichte's understanding.

165. Wagner, *Der Gedanke* 241–249, develops these thoughts, but only on the level of the logic of the Concept.

166. See Bruaire, *Logique et religion* 91–92. Wagner argues within his own context to a necessarily "tri-personal" movement of three Persons on the basis of individuality inclusive of universality and particularity. *Der Gedanke* 249–251. Wagner concludes (250–251) against Hegel: "Darin, daß Gottes Persönlichkeit als manifeste Einheit von Allgemeinheit und Besonderheit einerseits zur Konstitution der innertrinitarischen Personengemeinschaft vorausgesetzt werden muß, aber andererseits Gott sich in der Gemeinschaft der innertrinitarischen Personen als Person erinnert, besteht allerdings die Grenze der Hegelschen Trinitätslehre . . . Hegel setzt sonach die Wirklichkeit der innertrinitarischen Personen, deren Gott bedarf, um in der Hingabe an sie zur immanenten Selbsterfüllung seiner Persönlichkeit zu gelange, voraus, ohne zeigen zu können, wie es zu dieser Unterschied Gottes in sich gekommen ist. Das besagt nichts anders, als daß auch Hegels Darstellung der Trinität in der Form des reinen Denkens 'nur den Wert eines hinter dem Geheimnis der göttlichen Wirklichkeit zurückbleibenden Gleichnisses haben.' (147). W. Pannenberg: *Grundzüge der Christologie* (Gütersloh: Mohn, 1976) 329 Anm. 89, kann." For a critical response both to such an understanding of divine personhood and to such a critique of Hegel by Wagner, see Jaeschke, "Absolute Idee" esp. 22–24, whose philosophically more purist response in effect is that this understanding and critique of Wagner's, and indirectly of Pannenberg's perhaps as well, involve a Church-theological contamination of Hegel's thought.

167. See GW 12:25.29–33/L 2:231 (GL 592).

168. Briefly on Hegel's dialectical identification of "inner" Trinity and logic, see ILT 525.13–14 and 29, 527.1–16 and 23–24/AR 56.32–33 and 40, 57.1–16 (CR 67, 67–68).

With careful qualification of the distinction between "immanent" and "economic" Trinity, and recognizing that Hegel treats of "immanent" Trinity both as logic and in its realphilosophical appearance in absolute religion, it could be said with Splett, "Die Logik als ganze ist also die Darstellung der spekulativen Wahrheit dessen, was die christliche Dogmatik als 'immanente Trinität' bezeichnet (wie das ganze System die der 'ökonomischen Trinität')." *Trinitätslehre* 78. Unfortunately Splett's more restricted treatment (77–81) of Hegel's *Logic* is less helpful than his other analyses. Despite his valuable contribution in surveying and gathering Hegel's teaching on Trinity, his evaluation of Hegel's Trinity as modalistic is in this respect correctly criticized by Wagner. Splett (145) claims: "Hegels Trinität ist also eine Zweiheit oder sich entfaltende Einheit, in einem Modalismus, dem die Zahl der Momente letztlich gleichgültig ist (Ph 538f.)." This fails adequately to consider triadicity and totality. See also Wagner, *Der Gedanke* 241 n. 130.

Similarly on the question of the relationship between logic and "immanent" Trinity: Bruaire, *Logique et religion* 61, cited as well by Heede, "Die göttliche Idee" 82, 188–189; Kimmerle, "Religion und Philosophie" 159; implicitly Wagner as cited in nn. 156, 157, 165 and 166 above; further in Bruaire, 65–81, 87, esp. 71 citing Hegel, AR 74 (CR 86), 96, "on peut dire aussi bien que la *Logique*, l'Idée logique, est le Père, le Royaume du Père au Trinité en laquelle les deux autres personnes jouent en fonction du Père pour sa particularisation et sa singularisation, *et* la structure complète de la Trinité avec les trois figures du syllogisme que nous aurons à decouvrir." With Heede this writer is however hesitant about Bruaire's and others' efforts to develop further and define beyond what Hegel himself has done at the end of the *Encyclopedia* (E §§ 574–577). This hesitation is primarily about extending beyond what Hegel has established rather than about interpreting what Hegel has in fact done. Heede, "Die göttliche Idee" 276–278, 280–284, 319, etc.

See Ch. 1 n. 112 above for a response to Jaeschke's position that "Was die Theologie 'immanente Trinität' nennt, ist nichts anderes als diese Idee, die aber erst hier, in der Philosophie des absoluten Geistes, als die im realen Inhalt Gewährte, absolut-konkrete und allgemeine Idee gewußt wird." "Absolute Idee" 25.

169. Most fundamentally in as Hegel clearly distinguishes logic and realphilosophical spheres.

As mentioned in Ch. 1 n. 113 above, Prof. Wolfhart Pannenberg in a more benign interpretation of Hegel vis-à-vis the pantheism charge and Hegel's positing of the necessitarian character of divine "economic" self-othering has brought renewed attention to this distinction in Hegel's thought. See "Die Bedeutung" 188–192, 194–195. See also in general Fackenheim, *The Religious Dimension*. Though Fackenheim speaks of "Trinities" in the plural, it would seem preferable to remain with the singular in interpreting Hegel's thought.

"Immanent" and "economic" are placed in quotes to recall that these expressions became popular after Hegel's time and do not easily clarify the distinctions necessary when referring to Hegel's thought.

170. See the discussion in Ch. 1 Subsection 3 of the present study.

171. Again see Ch. 1 Subsection 3 of the present study.

172. For a good summary presentation on the theological reaction to this necessity and a call to examine more closely Hegel's understanding of inner necessity as freedom, see Pannenberg, who identifies Müller as the first (1838) to focus on necessity as the systematic source of theological accusations of pantheism and non-personal deity lodged against Hegel. E.g.: Pannenberg, "Die Bedeutung" 195–197; also _____, "Die Subjektivität" 34–35. For a theological objection to Hegel's thought on the divine necessity or need for "economic" self-othering, see William J. Hill, O.P., "Presidential Address. Christian Panentheism. Orthopraxis and God's Action in History," *Proceedings of the Thirty-Fifth Annual Convention, June 11–14, 1980, The Catholic Theological Society of America*, 35 (June 11–14, 1980) 116.

173. Pannenberg, "Die Bedeutung" 198–199 ("The Significance" 172–173); _____, "Die Subjektivität" 35. See also Ch. 1 n. 53 above.

174. GW 12:252.25–253.34/L 2:504–506 (GL 842–844); E § 244.

175. Question raised by Prof. Dr. Ekkehard Mühlenberg during a historical-systematic seminar on Trinity, Claremont, California, Nov. 21, 1977. See also in general Koch, *Differenz* 71. Finitude and infinity are explicitly discussed in Ch. 6 Subsection 2 of the present study.

176. See Hegel's important remarks within the context of his critique of the theory of the immediate knowledge of objectivity, E §§ 74, 75 and the remarks on this text in Ch. 2 n. 122 below.

177. Any lesser linkage between the two would fail to acknowledge the development from within characteristic of Hegel's thought and argumentation.

178. Heede, "Die göttliche Idee" 266–268.

179. On Trinity as already philosophically interpreted, see Kimmerle, "Religion and Philosophie" 158, 162–163. Hegel's prolonged treatment of religion is a "philosophy of religion." Also see Heede, "Die göttliche Idee" 52. From the perspective of his treatment of the *Lectures* Heede remarks: "Auffallend ist, daß Hegel das *Reich des Vaters* und die *Logik* mit dem gleichen Characteristika versieht, daß die Logik mit Wendungen 'vorstellig' gemacht wird, die wir allesamt im Reich des Vaters wiederfinden." After citing a number of parallels, Heede continues: "Diese Parallelen legen die Deutung nahe, daß Hegel das Reich des Vaters als eine Logik in der Form der Vorstellung bestimmen will, so daß eben auch umgekehrt das Verständnis der Logik in ihrer Abstraktheit mit den konkreten Vorstellungsformen der ewigen Sphären des christlichen Gottes gefördert werden kann." "Die göttliche Idee" 188–189. See also Yerkes, *The Christology of Hegel* 290.

Hegel would not consider it a devastating critique if someone claimed his trinitarian thought was conditioned by logic or vice versa, so long as the proper transitions were allowed and reference were made to logic as pure thought. In their own way, as mentioned in Ch. 1 n. 106 above, Staudenmaier, *Darstellung*

752–753, Hessen, *Hegels Trinitätslehre* 8, 39, and Splett, *Trinitätslehre* 148 have made this critique that Hegel's trinitarian thought was conditioned by logic. On internal systematic grounds Hegel treats of religious dogmas and conceptualities from a philosophical perspective.

180. In so far as true philosophic thought is meant by Hegel to be an enriched return to the simplicity of the absolute Idea and to pure being (E §§ 574–577) it could be argued that Hegel treats of "immanent" Trinity in a third way as well.

For an overview of "immanent" Trinity in the realphilosophical spheres, in the *Encyclopedia* see Ch. 3 Subsection 2b below, in the *Phenomenology* see Ch. 4 Subsection 4 of the present study, and in the *Lectures* see Ch. 5 Subsection 2a of the present study.

181. Note Hegel's remark, "Man mag an Gott glauben,—bestimmen, wie man will, fehlt Persönlichkeit, so nicht genügend." G. W. F. Hegel, *Grundlinien der Philosophie des Rechts*, Philosophische Bibliothek, vol. 124a, ed. Johannes Hoffmeister (Hamburg: Felix Meiner, 1967) 324 § 35, cited by Pannenberg, "Die Bedeutung" 194 ("The Significance" 167 n. 73 cites p. 234) ("One may define believing in God how one will, but if personality is not there, the definition is inadequate." Translation as in Pannenberg, "The Significance" 167, since this text is, according to Pannenberg's English text, p. 167 n. 73, missing in the English translation of Hegel's *Outline of the Philosophy of Right*, trans. T. M. Knox (Oxford: Oxford University Press, 1952).

182. "Die Logik ist sonach als das System der reinen Vernunft, als das Reich des reinen Gedankens zu fassen. Dieses Reich ist die Wahrheit selbst, wie sie ohne Hülle an (und) für sich selbst ist; man kann sich deßwegen ausdrücken, daß dieser Inhalt die Darstellung Gottes ist, wie er in seinem ewigen Wesen, vor der Erschaffung der Natur und eines endlichen Geistes ist." Quoted from the first edition, GW 11:21.16–21 (GL 50 trans. amended). The second edition, L 1:31, contains considerable italicizing, which emphasizes the notions "truth" and "presentation of God." Jaeschke and Hogemann point out that the terms "God" and "before" (*vor*) are taken from the sphere of representation. "Die Wissenschaft der Logik" 79. See also Hegel's remarks at the beginning of his 1827 lectures on the philosophy of religion, BR 189.10–21.

On "presentation" (*Darstellung*) in a Hegelian context as the totality of the system, see Theunissen, *Sein und Schein* 13–19, esp. 13–14 and Puntel, *Darstellung* passim.

2. Hegel's Logic of Pure Thought

1. See Ch. 1 Subsection 1 of the present study. The present chapter generally presupposes the exposition in Ch. 1 of the present study and at the same time indirectly attempts further to ground the positions argued there.

2. Among many studies on the shaping of the modern mind, e.g.: sociologically, Peter L. Berger, Brigitte Berger and Hansfried Kellner, *The Homeless Mind, Modernization and Consciousness* (New York: Random, 1973); more historically, Benjamin Nelson, *Der Ursprung der Moderne. Vergleichende Studien zum Zivilisationsprozeß* (Frankfurt am Main: Suhrkamp, 1978); _____, *On the Roads to Modernity: Conscience, Science and Civilizations, Selected Writings* (Totowe, N.J.: Rowman and Littlefield, 1980).

3. See, e.g., Hegel's remark, GW 11:23.15–25.17/L 1:33–34 (GL 51–53).

4. This argumentation will be critically dependent on that of Traugott Koch in *Differenz und Versöhnung. Eine Interpretation der Theologie G. W. F. Hegels nach seiner "Wissenschaft der Logik"* (Gütersloh: Mohn, 1967).

5. On the logical moment as totality, see Ch. 1 Subsection 4 of the present study.

6. Succinctly stated, E § 162.

7. See Ch. 1 Subsections 1 and 2 of the present study.

8. See Hegel's warning concerning beginning, GW 12:240.24–28/L 2:489 (GL 829).

9. Behind this discussion lies the well-discussed question of whether to stress the importance of doing detailed studies on Hegel (the term used is learning "to spell" [*Buchstabieren*]) or the necessity to keep a wider view so as not to get lost in ambiguous detail. Theodor W. Adorno, *Drei Studien zu Hegel* (Frankfurt am Main: Suhrkamp Taschenbuch, 1971), can serve as representative of this latter. Among his many observations on interpreting Hegel, Adorno recalls the significance for Hegel of the whole (*das Ganze*) (86), the inherent ambiguity of specific Hegel texts (84) and the danger of simply paraphrasing (118). One of the first of those stressing *Buchstabieren* or detail study of Hegel is Hans-Georg Gadamer, *Hegels Dialektik. Fünf hermeneutischen Studien* (Tubingen: Mohr, 1971). Surely all would agree on the necessity to do both. It would appear that English-speaking students of Hegel presently, for the sake of accuracy and clarity, need the discipline of spending more time on the *Buchstabieren*.

10. Of primary interest here is the immediate treatment of *Etwas* L 1:101–103 (GL 114–116). In view of Hegel's numerous textual changes and clarifications, the discussion of *Etwas* and its wider logical context will generally follow Hegel's revised text. On Hegel's general reworking of the "Logic of Being" as an attempt to eliminate first edition argumentation based on external reflection, see Walter Jaeschke, "Äußerliche Reflexion und immanente Reflexion. Eine Skizze der systematischen Geschichte des Reflexionsbegriffs in Hegel's Logik-Entwürfen," *Hegel-Studien* 13 (Bonn: Bouvier, 1978) 85–117, esp. 112.

11. GW 12:90.1–126.11/L 2:308–352 (GL 664–704).

12. GW 11:327.1–337.33/L 2:105–119 (GL 484–496).

13. "nur der Anfang des Subjekts," L 1:102 (GL 115).

14. L 1:95, 102 (GL 109, 115) with what is said on ground (*Grund*) as later thought determination, GW 11:291.1–322.8/L 2:63–100 (GL 444–478). See the excellent study by Peter Rohs, *Form und Grund, Hegel-Studien*, Beiheft 6 (Bonn: Bouvier, 1969).

15. GW 11:43.20–44.29, 56.21–57.37/L 1:66–67, 92–93 (GL 82–83, 105–106).

16. Klaus Düsing, *Das Problem der Subjektivität in Hegels Logik, Hegel-Studien*, Beiheft 15 (Bonn: Bouvier, 1976) 268–269.

17. GW 12:133.3–7 and 27–28/L 2:359–360 (GL 711).

18. For an overview of syllogism in the *Logic* see Ch. 3 Subsection 2a of the present study.

19. L 1:101–103 (GL 114–116). Unless otherwise indicated this overview of *Etwas* is drawn from these pages.

20. As indicated somewhat by the meaning in English of "qualification" as "determination," with the negative note of limitation in the phrase "with this qualification" and positively stated "he has these qualifications." These nuances recall somewhat Hegel's use of reality (*Realität*) and negation (*Negation*) as the difference of quality in his revised logic-of-being text, L 1:97–101 (GL 111–114).

21. "Die Bestimmtheit ist die Negation als affirmativ gesetzt, ist der Satz des Spinoza: *Omnis determinatio est negatio.*" L 1:100 ("Determinateness is negation posited as affirmative and is the proposition of Spinoza: *omnis determinatio est negatio.*" GL 113). See briefly Ch. 2 n. 60 below.

22. Recall the critical function of logic for Hegel.

23. See Hegel's discussion of the Idea (*Idee*), GW 12:176.4–177.3/L 2:410–411 (GL 758–759).

24. E.g., being and nothing in *Dasein*, L 1:73 (GL 88); becoming, L 1:70, 103 (GL 85, 116). Along this line, Jan van der Meulen, *Hegel. Die gebrochene Mitte* (Hamburg: Felix Meiner, 1958) 45–46, although his remark that this first triad "ist nicht eigentlich die erste Stufe der Unmittelbarkeit, sondern deren Begründung," is rather unhegelian. For Hegel the first triad is both.

25. As with many aspects of Hegel's philosophy, the general question of the relationship of the first three categories to the rest of the *Logic* may remain forever disputed.

26. Wolfgang Wieland, "Bemerkungen zum Anfang von Hegels Logik," in *Seminar: Dialektik in der Philosophie Hegels*, ed. Rolf-Peter Horstmann (Frankfurt am Main: Suhrkamp, 1978) 195, 198–199.

27. Note Hegel's observation in L 1:1 (GL 39–40).

28.
"*Seyn, reines Seyn,*
—ohne alle weitere Bestimmung.
In seiner unbestimmten Unmittelbarkeit ist es

nur sich selbst gleich
und auch nicht ungleich gegen Anderes,
hat keine Verschiedenheit
innerhalb seiner
noch nach Außen.

Durch irgend eine Bestimmung oder Inhalt,
der in ihm unterschieden,
oder wodurch es als unterschieden von einem Anderen
gesetzt würde,
würde es nicht in seiner Reinheit festgehalten.

Es ist die reine Unbestimmtheit und Leere.

—Es ist *nichts* in ihm anzuschauen,
wenn von Anschauen hier gesprochen werden kann;
oder es ist nur diß reine, leere Anschauen selbst.
Es ist eben so wenig etwas in ihm zu denken,
oder es ist ebenso nur diß leere Denken.

Das Seyn, das unbestimmte Unmittelbare ist in der That *Nichts*
und nicht mehr
noch weniger
als Nichts."

Text unchanged in first and second editions: GW 11:43.20–44.6, L 1:66–67 (GL 82 trans. amended). Besides remarks on being and beginning scattered throughout the *Logic*, see particularly: in the discussion on method, GW 12:239.10–241.23, 249.8–252.24/L 2:487–490, 500–504 (GL 827–830, 838–842); Hegel's reflections, GW 11:33.3–40.29/L 1:51–64, 67–75, 77–79, 85–93 (GL 67–78, 83–90, 92–94, 99–106), and in the first edition, GW 11:51.37–53.11, cited, summarized and reflected on by Wieland, "Bemerkungen zum Anfang" 195ff; E §§ 84–86 with Remark, 238 with Remark. Traugott Koch provides a good summary of Hegel's understanding of being in *Differenz* 78–81. For helpful commentary, see André Léonard, *Commentaire littéral de la Logique de Hegel* (encyclopedic *Logic*) (Paris: Vrin, 1974) 37–46, 571–576. For further literature on being in Hegel's thought as well as the other, immediately following logical categories, see Michael Theunissen, *Sein und Schein. Die kritische Funktion der Hegelschen Logik* (Frankfurt am Main: Suhrkamp, 1978) 488–494, and on being/beginning see 130–131. See also John Burbidge, *On Hegel's Logic. Fragments of a Commentary* (Atlantic Highlands, N.J.: Humanities, 1981) esp.: 37–45, where he treats of Being/Nothing/Becoming.

29. Koch, *Differenz* 78–79 n. 2.
30. L 1:57–58 (GL 72–73).
31. E §§ 85, 86R. It is infinite as it is unrelated to an other. See L 1:70–71 (GL 85–86).
32. Koch, *Differenz* 79–80 with nn. 4–6 and especially the reminder in n. 5 that the being of finitude is not its own.
33. L 1:43 (GL 61); L 2:489 (GL 829); E § 84.
34. L 1:67–68, 70–71, 97 (GL 83, 86, 110).
35. Koch, *Differenz* 84, cites L 1:66, 85, L 2:489, 501 (GL 81, 99, 829, 839–840). See also L. Bruno Puntel, *Darstellung, Methode und Struktur. Untersuchungen zur Einheit der systematischen Philosophie G. W. F. Hegels, Hegel-Studien*, Beiheft 10 (Bonn: Bouvier, 1973) 234 n. 327, where he cites E § 238.
36. Wieland, "Bemerkungen zum Anfang" 209.
37. Theunissen on the other hand speaks of the speculative logic as not as yet having reached the level of absolute form. *Sein und Schein* 122. Yet he acknowledges that the separation between Subject and object is overcome (106, 107). Perhaps regarding absolute form he means the "explicit" level, since already on the level of being content (determinationlessness) is for Hegel already fully adequate to form.
38. But not beyond any distinction. See generally Ch. 1 Subsection 1 of the present study.
39. GW 12:239.21–27/L 2:488 (GL 827–828). On the ambiguity of the term "intuition" in Hegel's thought, see Meulen, *Hegel* 182–186. Meulen (186) identifies this ambiguity as a carryover from Schelling's notion of "intuition" as "non-reflected otherside" (*Jenseit*). For further discussion on "intuition," see Theunissen, *Sein und Schein*, 110.
40. "reiner Gedanke," L 1:74 (GL 88); E § 86.
41. Koch, *Differenz* 81.
42. See e.g., GW 11:21.6–18/L 1:30–31 (GL 49).
43. L 1:54 (GL 70). Already in the first edition, GW 11:33.29–30.
44. "das *Erste* im *Gange* des Denkens." L 1:52 (GL 68 trans. amended).
45. The "Begriff nur an *sich.*" E § 84.
46. GW 12:128.32–35/L 2:355 (GL 706); Koch, *Differenz* 80.
47. GW 11:33.22–30/L 1:54 (GL 70). For an overview see the helpful article by Hans Friedrich Fulda, "über den spekulativen Anfang," in *Subjektivität und Metaphysik. Festschrift für Wolfgang Cramer* (Frankfurt am Main: Klostermann, 1966) 109–127, esp. 114, 121–122; also Karin Schrader-Klebert, *Das Problem des Anfangs in Hegels Philosophie* (Vienna: Oldenbourg, 1969) 7–13.
48. Nevertheless, the difficulty of understanding how "the beginning begins," how this transition is made, is witnessed to by the admittance of non-understanding by so acknowledged a *Logic* scholar as Peter Rohs, review

of *Werden zu sich. Eine Untersuchung zu Hegels* "Wissenschaft der Logik," by Ute Guzzoni in *Hegel-Studien* 4 (Bonn: Bouvier, 1967) 254.

49. Koch, *Differenz* 85–86 with n. 19. On misunderstandings of how this transition from the contradiction already implicit in indeterminate being occurs, see Koch's excellent survey from the time of Schelling on, 86–88 n. 20

50. L 1:85 (GL 99).

51. The text on nothing: *"Nichts, das reine Nichts;* es ist einfache Gleichheit mit sich selbst, vollkommene Leerheit, Bestimmungs- und Inhaltlosigkeit; Ununterschiedenheit in ihm selbst.—Insofern Anschauen oder Denken hier erwähnt werden kann, so gilt es als ein Unterschied, ob etwas oder *nichts* angeschaut oder gedacht wird. Nichts Anschauen oder Denken hat also eine Bedeutung; beide werden unterschieden, so *ist* (existiert) Nichts in unserem Anschauen oder Denken; oder vielmehr ist es das leere Anschauen und Denken selbst und dasselbe leere Anschauen oder Denken als das reine Sein.—Nichts ist somit dieselbe Bestimmung oder vielmehr Bestimmungslosigkeit und damit überhaupt dasselbe, was das reine *Sein* ist." L 1:67 (*"Nothing pure nothing;* it is simply equality with itself, complete emptiness, absence of all determination and content—undifferentiatedness in itself. In so far as intuiting or thinking can be mentioned here, it counts as a distinction whether something or *nothing* is intuited or thought. To intuit or think nothing has, therefore, a meaning; both are distinguished and thus nothing *is* (exists) in our intuiting or thinking; or rather it is empty intuition and thought itself, and the same empty intuition or thought as pure being. Nothing is, therefore, the same determination, or rather absence of determination, and thus altogether the same as, pure *being*." GL 82). The first edition text differs slightly, GW 11:44.8–17. Besides remarks scattered throughout the *Logic*, see particularly on nothing: in the discussion on method, GW 12:241.24–247.6, 249.8–252.24, esp. 241.24–242.13, 244.29–246.17/L 2:490–497, 500–504, esp. 490–491, 494–496 (GL 830–836, 838–842, esp. 830–831, 833–835; Hegel's reflections L 1:67–75, 77–79, 85–93 (GL 83–90, 92–93, 99–106), GW 11:53.22–30; E §§ 87 with Remark, 88 with Remark, 239 with Remark, 240–242. See also Koch's summary and critique in *Differenz* 89–94, where he handles the initial presentation of nothing and that on method together. For helpful commentary, see Léonard, *Commentaire* (encyclopedic *Logic*) 47–53, 576–587. (Note, in E § 88, "Das *Nichts* ist als dieses unmittelbare" does not refer to the *"Unmittelbarkeit"* of being in L 1:66 (GL 82), but in view of E § 87 to the immediacy of transition from being to nothing. On several senses in which nothing is immediate, see Ch. 2 n. 86 below.

52. L 1:68 (GL 83).

53. See Koch, *Differenz* 89–91, and L 1:67, 88 (GL 82, 101–102).

54. Pierre Jean Labarrière, *Structures et mouvement dialectique dans la "Phénoménologie de l'Esprit" de Hegel* (Paris: Aubier-Montaigne, 1968), distin-

guishes *Nichts* already in the initial presentation as signifying *néant* and *rien*, non-existing and nothing as opposed to something.

55. "so *ist* (existiert) Nichts in unserem Anschauen und Denken selbst." L 1:67 (GL 82). The second edition quoted here stresses more than the first that nothing *is*.

56. L 1:68 (GL 83).

57. See E § 85.

58. Perhaps it would be better to say "unthematized." Koch, *Differenz* 93–94 n. 41, quotes from Meulen, *Hegel* 50: "Auf unserer Stufe des Seins ist dieser Widerspruch allerdings noch nicht als Widerspruch expliziert, sondern erst als die unmittelbare Beziehung von Sein und Nicht-sein. Aber schon hier kommt es darauf an, diese Beziehung aufzufassen, sie zu Ende zu denken und nicht sofort zum Nächsten weiterzueilen." A word of caution however is in order regarding the use of *"Beziehung"* and *"Nicht-sein"* at this point. Léonard observes that "être et néant sont ensuite l'opposition dans toute son immédiateté." *Commentaire* 52.

59. GW 12:246.3–17/L 2:496 (GL 835).

60. Hegel regularly distinguishes between the abstraction of being and nothing considered as the first two thought determinations, and the more concrete determinations from becoming on. E.g., L 1: 69–70, 85, 89–90 (GL 85, 99, 103). See Léonard's flourish of a commentary on the abstractness of nothing, especially in terms of nothing's "immediacy," *Commentaire* 48.

This sketching of nothing and the previous one on being are not meant to cover up the complexity and unfinished character of Hegel's thought. See remarks on the need for further development of the notion of negation in Walter Jaeschke and Friedrich Hogemann, "Die Wissenschaft der Logik," in *Hegel. Einführung in seine Philosophie*, ed. Otto Pöggeler (Freiburg: Alber, 1977) 87 and in Walter Jaeschke, "Äußerliche Reflexion und immanente Reflexion. Eine Skizze der systematischen Geschichte des Reflexionsbegriffs in Hegel's Logik-Entwürfen," in *Hegel-Studien* 13 (Bonn: Bouvier, 1978) 85–117.

A detailed, constructive analysis of Hegel's overall notion of negation would be beyond the scope of this study. But a gathering of several uses of the term in the sphere of logic and brief reference to the other philosophical spheres will give some idea of the complexity of this question and of the burden Hegel's notion of negation is made to bear. In the context of the discussion on method, the second moment or progression is referred to as the first or formal negation, the negation establishing otherness; the third moment is the negation of negation, i.e., the second negation or absolute negativity, which is positive, GW 12:247.10–11/L 2:497 (GL 836). This latter, as the highest form of *Nichts für sich*, is freedom, E § 87R. Negation taken as sheer lack would be nothing, L 1:98 (GL 111), and with the determination of *Nichtsein* is quality, etc. Regarding Spinoza's dictum, "Die Bestimmtheit ist die Negation als affirmativ gesetzt, ist der Satz des Spinoza: *Omnis determinatio est negatio*. Dieser Satz ist von unendlicher Wichtigkeit." L 1:100 (GL 113). In the first edition: "*Die Bestimmtheit überhaupt ist Negation*. (Determinatio est negatio) sagte *Spinoza*." GW 11:76.11–12. On several philosphy of history theses concerning the thinking of nothing, see Koch, *Differenz* 92 n. 35. Andries Sarlemijn speaks of the beginning of *The Phenomenology of Spirit* as a first negation and the beginning of the *Logic* as a second negation, *Hegelsche Dialektik* (Berlin: De Gruyter, 1971). On Hegel's notion of negation handled from a psychological point of view, see W. Ver Eecke, "Zur Negativität bei Hegel," in *Hegel-Studien* 4 (Bonn: Bouvier, 1967) 215–218, with reference to *The Phenomenology of Spirit*. See also Howard P. Kainz, *Hegel's Phenomenology*, Part I: *Analysis and Commentary* (University, Alabama: University of America Press, 1976); and, the larger study by Wolfgang Bonsiepen, *Der Begriff der Negativität in der Jenaer Schrifte Hegels*, *Hegel-Studien*, Beiheft 16 (Bonn: Bouvier, 1977).

61. E.g., L 1:67, 92 (GL 83, 105).

62. GW 12:245.27–35/L 2:495–496 (GL 834–835).

63. "jenes Übergehen ist noch kein Verhältnis." L 1:90 (GL 103).

64. L 1:68 (GL 83).

65. Logically and non-temporally of course.

66. More generally, "Sein ist Sein und Nichts ist Nichts nur in ihrer Unterschiedenheit voneinander; in ihrer Wahrheit aber, in ihrer Einheit, . . ." L 1:95 ("Being is being, and nothing is nothing, only in their contradistinction from each other; but in their truth, in their unity, . . ." GL 108).

67. Karl Heinz Haag, *Philosophischer Idealismus. Untersuchungen zur Hegelschen Dialektik mit Beispielen aus der "Wissenschaft der Logik"* (Frankfurt am Main: Europäische Verlagsanstalt, 1967) 43. Though Haag (44) misunderstands or at least does not grant significance to the move from implicit to explicit when he claims that Hegel could have started with either being or nothing.

68. Léonard, *Commentaire* 52.

69. For a brief survey and critique of various understandings of this arising, see Koch, *Differenz* 97–98 n. 52.

70. Texts on becoming: L 1:67, 92–93 (GL 82–83, 105–106). These second edition texts generally underscore the continuing distinction and yet inseparability of being and nothing in becoming more than the following first edition texts: GW 11:44.19–29, 56.22–57.37. Besides scattered remarks throughout the *Logic*, see particularly: in the discussion on method, GW 12:246.18–252.24/L 2:496–504 (GL 835–842); Hegel's reflections, L 1:68–71, 75–80, 89–92, 95 (GL 83–86, 90–94, 103–105, 108); E §§ 88 with Remark, 89 with Remark, 242. Also, Koch's summary and critique, *Differenz* 95–101. For helpful commentary, Léonard, *Commentaire* 48–62, 582–587.

71. L 1:82 (GL 96).

72. Koch, *Differenz* 96.

73. "*Das reine Sein und das reine Nichts ist also dasselbe.*" L 1:67 (GL 82). The speculative truth that being and nothing find their truth in becoming cannot for Hegel be adequately expressed in terms of a sentence, which always remains one-sided. On this and the limitations of the term "unity of being and nothing," see L 1:75–79 (GL 90–93).

74. L 1:92 (GL 105).

75. "Aber . . . ist die Wahrheit nicht ihre Ununterschiedenheit, sondern daß *sie nicht dasselbe*, daß sie *absolute unterschieden*, aber ebenso ungetrennt und untrennbar sind und unmittelbar *jedes in seinem Gegenteil verschwindet.*" L 1:67 (GL 83 trans. amended). First edition reads, "Aber . . . ist die Wahrheit nicht ihre Ununterschiedenheit, sondern daß sie absolute unterschieden sind, aber eben so unmittelbar jedes in seinem Gegentheil verschwindet." GW 11:44.24–26.

76. On identity and difference, see esp. GW 11:260.19–36, 265.28–270.18, 272.16–275.23/L 2:26, 32–38, 40–44 (GL 411–412, 417–421, 424–427).

77. L 1:78, 79 (GL 92, 93).

78. L 1:92 (GL 105).

79. "Sie [Sein, Nichts] heben sich nicht gegenseitig, nicht das eine äußerlich das andere auf, sondern jedes hebt sich an sich selbst auf und ist an ihm selbst das Gegenteil seiner." L 1:93 (GL 106).

80. "Das Werden ist eine haltungslose Unruhe, die in ein ruhiges Resultat zusammensinkt." L 1:93 (GL 106).

81. L 1:93 (GL 106).

82. John Ellis McTaggart had suggested reinterpreting becoming as "Transition into *Dasein*" (*Übergang in das Dasein*), *A Commentary on Hegel's Logic* (Cambridge, England: At the University Press, 1910) 17–21. Koch has criticized a similar correction proposed by Ernst Cassirer, "Transition to Determination" (*Übergang zur Bestimmung*) in *Das Erkenntnisproblem in der Philosophie und Wissenschaft der neueren Zeit*, vol. 3: *Die nachkantischen Systeme* (Berlin: Cassirer, 1920) 335. Koch correctly remarks, "Sie bringt das 'Affirmative' der Einheit nicht zum Ausdruck, was indessen nach Hegel zu geschehen hat." *Differenz* 97 n. 49. McTaggert's correction, cited by Cassirer, 335.

83. "Die Idee sich selbst *Frey entläßt*," GW 12:253.22/L 2:505 (GL 843).

84. In the third paragraph on becoming Hegel basically repeats four times in the paragraph's four subdivisions the transition from becoming to *Dasein*. See further on the relationship between becoming and *Dasein*, L 1:95, 96 (GL 108, 109). On Hegel's treatment of *Dasein* in the *Logic*'s first edition in the determination of nothing and in the second edition in the determination of being, see Theunissen, *Sein und Schein* 193–194. Though Theunissen is right in indicating the generally problematic character of the "transition" from becoming to *Dasein*, the details of his argumentation (187–196) on this "transition"

are not necessarily convincing. He seems (188 n. 1) unaware that the phrase *"Entstehen und Vergehen"* (rising and disappearing), which does not appear in Hegel's first edition (GW 11:56.22–23), was raised by the editor Lasson from the text itself to the title of Hegel's second paragraph on becoming in the second edition (see Lasson's own remark, L 1:401, concerning text p. 92 line 12 from the top). Somewhat more substantively, Hegel argues, GW 11:57.29–31/L 1:93 (GL 106), that the peaceful result into which becoming sinks is not nothing but the unity of being and nothing, a unity come to peaceful simplicity. For Theunissen (194–195) to refer to this argument in the following manner is not a fair account of the complexity of Hegel's thought: "Gemäß der zweifelhaften Maxime, nach der nicht sein kann, was nicht sein soll, sichert Hegel seine Behauptung, das Resultat, welches das Verschwinden des Verschwindens zeitigt, sei 'die zur ruhigen Einfachheit gewordene Einheit des Seins und Nichts,' gegen den Einwand, es ergebe sich daraus überhaupt nichts, durch die Bemerkung ab: 'so wäre es nur ein Rückfall in die eine der schon aufgehobenen Bestimmungen' (92.25/113). Die Replik entzieht sich rationaler Diskussion. Mag es sich um einen Rückfall handeln oder nicht—falsch ist jedenfalle die Schlußfolgerung Hegels, die Verhinderung des Rückfalls bedeute schon Fortschritt." Hegel had earlier argued to the simple unity of being and nothing on the basis of the mutually paralyzing *Entstehen* and *Vergehen*, and, whether his argument would hold up under scrutiny or not, even in view of Theunissen's previous remarks it is surely not a question of "should not be, therefore cannot be." See further in Theunissen, 119–120. On the transition from abstract to concrete, Schrader-Klebert, *Das Problem des Anfangs* 126–127. See the more developed critique in Ch. 4 Subsection 3b of the present study.

85. "Dieser Sachverhalt gilt in Hegels ganzer Logik: Der Fortgang des logischen Gedankens führt vertiefend und erhellend in den Anfang zurück. Das deduktive Fortgehen ist ein reduktives[55] Zurückkommen in das Anfängliche, weil der Fortschritt dialektische—in Negation sich vollziehende—Entwicklung[56] des Anfänglichen ist." Koch, *Differenz* 98, 100, see also 102 and 98–100 with the evaluative nn. 55, 56 and 57. On the general theme of speculative progression as return into ground, see John Ellis McTaggart, *Studies in the Hegelian Dialectic* (Cambridge, England: at the University Press, 1896) *passim*, cited by Reinhard Heede, "Die göttliche Idee und ihre Erscheinung in der Religion. Untersuchungen zum Verhältnis von Logik und Religionsphilosophie bei Hegel" (Ph.D. dissertation, Philosophical Faculty of the Westfälischen Wilhelms-Universität zu Münster/Westfalen, 1972) 315.

86. Immediacy is used in a slightly wider sense here covering being, nothing and becoming. Being is absolute immediacy. Nothing is immediacy in the following senses: immediately arising out of being, L 1:85 (GL 99), E § 88; indeterminate simplicity and abstract, immediate negation, L 1:67–68

(GL 83); as not yet *aufgehoben*, L 1:94 (GL 107). Becoming is immediacy in as it is the unity of the fully abstract determinations being and nothing as opposed to *Etwas* as unity of *Dasein* and quality, L 1:102–103 (GL 115–116).

87. E § 243.
88. Fulda, "über den spekulativen Anfang" 117.
89. GW 11:36.4–6/L 1:57 (GL 72).
90. L 1:29 (GL 48).
91. GW 11:36.5–6/L 1:57 (GL 72).
92. L 1:68 (GL 83); in general GW 12:244.33–245.9/L 2:494–495 (GL 834); note the interchangeability, "die Negation oder das Nichts," L 1:100 (GL 113).
93. Being's content is its contentlessness or determinationlessness. Nothing's content is posited contentlessness, determinationlessness which is.
94. Hegel remarks on mediation in general: "die Vermittlung ist ein Hinausgegangensein aus einem Ersten zu einem Zweiten und Hervergehen aus Unterschiedenen." E § 86R ("mediation is the condition of having gone out from a first to a second and a proceeding out of that which is different." SL § 86R, but my trans.).
95. Karl Heinz Haag speaks of being and nothing as *"werdend."* "Die Seinsdialektik bei Hegel und in der scholastischen Philosophie" (Ph.D. dissertation, Philosophical Faculty of the Johann Wolfgang Goethe-Universität, Frankfurt am Main, 1951) 21. Also, Ruth-Eva Schulz-Seitz, " 'Sein' in Hegels Logik: 'Einfache Beziehung auf sick,' " in *Wirklichkeit und Reflexion. Walter Schulz zum 60. Geburstag*, ed. Helmut Fahrenbach (Pfulligen: Neske, 1973) 365–383, esp. 382–383.
96. Koch, *Differenz* 101.
97. L 1:70 (GL 85). GW 11:46.3–6 is less explicit. For remarks placing Hegel's understanding of becoming within the context of the western philosophical tradition, see Haag, "Seinsdialektik" 20.
98. See Ch. 2 nn. 58 and 60 above.
99. Theunissen, *Sein and Schein* 120, provides a point of entry into the discussion as to whether the notion of transition might be applied to the very first thought determinations or not, a question more generally statable as the type of difference characteristic of being and nothing within the context of the movement of pure thought. He cites Hans-Georg Gadamer, *Hegels Dialektik* 60, as wanting to remove any thought of transition from the beginning of logic, and Schulz-Seitz, " 'Sein' in Hegels Logik" 378, as taking the opposite position. Schulz-Seitz in turn also refers back to Gadamer, and then to Dieter Henrich, *Hegel im Kontext* (Frankfurt am Main: Suhrkamp, 1967) 88. And so the discussion continues. Hegel would seemingly respond that the transition

from being to nothing is thematizable only in becoming, although each of the two categories is transition, a "having gone over into."

100. On being and nothing, L 1:69 (GL 84–85); on becoming, see Ch. 2 n. 97 above.

101. Note the use of "*Element*" concerning becoming in the quotation Ch. 2 n. 97 above.

102. Specifically on being, see Theunissen, *Sein and Schein* 118, citing L 1:56, 71 (GL 71, 86).

103. E.g., L 1:73 (GL 88) which, though it is in a "Remark," is typical. Examples are found scattered throughout the *Logic*,

104. Regarding becoming, the move is to restless mediation of positive and negative in a positive not yet explicitly for Hegel negation of negation. On positive and negative see esp. GW 11:273.4–285.15/L 2:41–56 (GL 424–438), where they are treated under opposition (*Gegensatz*) and contradiction (*Widerspruch*). In the encyclopedic *Logic* positive and negative are handled more directly under difference, E §§ 119, 120.

Most of these present pages could be exegeted from GW 12:244.29–245.9, 248.5–24/L 2:494–495, 498–499 (GL 833–834, 837–838).

105. On the similarity Koch in *Differenz* refers to Erich Heintel, *Hegel and die analogia entis* (Bonn: Bouvier, 1958).

106. Immanent meaning internal self-grounding development and not directly in the sense of immanence versus transcendence.

107. Hegel tends to use *an sich* and *für sich* somewhat loosely in his various writings.

108. See GW 11:265.32–35/L 2:32 (GL 417). E § 116 with Remark briefly stresses the particular form of otherness in the logic of essence where identity and difference are located and formally treated. For a brief resume of the structure and movement of the logic of essence, see Koch, *Differenz* 150–152 with 131–132 and n. 112 there.

109. "Die Bestimmtheit ist die Negation als affirmativ gesetzt." L 1:100 (GL 113).

110. In particular, GW 12:33.3–52.26/L 2:240–264 (GL 601–602); E §§ 163–165 with Remarks, and § 161, which recalls the particular form of transition characteristic of the logic of the Concept. On universality in the determination of being, GW 12:33.11–12/L 2:240 (GL 601); particularity in the determination of nothing (negativity), GW 12:38.19–21/L 2:246 (GL 607); individuality in the determination of becoming, GW 12:49.22–23/L 2:260 (GL 619). With certain reservations, as for example regarding his proposal to understand individuality through universality and not sufficiently vice versa, one might refer to Edwin Stuart Dalrymple II, "On Hegel's Doctrine of the Notion as Universality, Particularity and Individuality" (Ph. D. dissertation, Yale University, 1974) esp. 114–166, and Koch, who mixes presentation with

critique in *Differenz* 150–174. To use phrases more loosely borrowed from Hegel, universality is the Concept as simple relationship to itself, absolute (but unposited) negativity. Particularity is the Concept as differentiation, that is, as relation to its other (universality) and inclusive of that other. Individuality is the Concept as self-related determinateness, the determinate determinate, posited negation of negation.

    111. GW 12:32.20–21/L 2:239 (GL 600).

    112. GW 12:49.22–23/L 2:260 (GL 619).

    113. GW 12:246.14–15/L 2:496 (GL 835).

    114. See already Ch. 1 Subsection 1 above regarding logic as the realm of pure thought.

    115. "Noch ist die allgemeine Natur der *Form der Unmittelbarkeit* kurz anzugeben. Es ist nämlich diese Form selbst, welche, weil sie *einseitig* ist, ihren Inhalt selbst einseitig und damit endlich macht." E § 74 (SL § 74 trans. considerably amended).

    116. Hegel's response to an antinomic analysis of reality is likewise already evident here. Being and nothing are not equally acceptable starting points. There is progression from being to nothing. And being and nothing are then seen to be the same.

This necessary self-othering of the Concept in as it is absolute Idea is in the transition to the spheres of nature and finite Spirit of course described as free release (*frei entläßt*), free in the sense that the self-release is grounded in the immanent logical drive or impulse (*Trieb*) of the absolute Idea to other itself in the world in order to come to itself in philosophical thought as the enriched return of absolute Spirit.

Pierre-Jean Labarrière seems concerned that reference to "self-othering," and it would seem by implication various other forms of self-differentiating, presumes a pre-existent "Self" which then would other itself. His concern provides the occasion to stress that in Hegel's case of course the notion of "self-othering" is most basically a way of referring to an immanent movement "from" "to." The notion of "Self" here involved is simply the point of departure in the process which, in the case of logical thought, is not a subsistent Self but the logical movement of subjectivity as Hegel understands it. Hegel's thought is of course so much more radical in its formulation of a notion of the self-development of God in comparison with Barth's notion of divine self-revelation and Rahner's notion of divine self-communication. For ease of reference, one could note that Labarrière writes as follows: "Aux concepts de base de Barth et de Rahner—respectivement auto-révélation et auto-communication de Dieu—Schlitt substitue, s'agissant de Hegel, le concept d'auto-altération (*self-othering*); c'est supposer, de la façon la plus traditionnelle qui soit, un Dieu subsistant d'abord en lui-même, et méconnaître peut-être la transcendance réciproque du 'fondement' et ses 'conditions' d'existence; avec le danger de réduire la perspective de Hegel à un idéalisme 'subjectif.'" Review of Dale M. Schlitt, *Hegel's Trinitarian Claim: A Critical Reflection*. In *Archives de philosophie* 50 (1987) 318–319.

117. "So in Gott selbst enthält die Qualität, *Tätigkeit, Schöpfung, Macht* usf. wesentlich die Bestimmung des Negativen,—sie sind ein Hervorbringen eines *Andern*." L 1:70 (GL 85 trans. slightly amended). Compare first edition, GW 11:45.34–46.6.

118. "seiende Bestimmtheit," L 1:97 (GL 111).

119. "Dem *Allgemeinen* gibt sie [die Form der Unmittelbarkeit] die Einseitigkeit einer *Abstraction*, so daß Gott zum bestimmungslosen Wesen wird"; E § 74 ("It [the form of immediacy] gives to the universal the one-sidedness of an *abstraction*, so that God is made a being without determination." SL § 74 trans. amended).

120. "Geist aber kann Gott nur heißen, insofern er als *sich* in sich selbst mit sich vermittelnd gewußt wird. Nur so ist er *konkret*, lebendig und Geist." E § 74 ("but God can only be called Spirit when God is known as God self-mediating Self with Self. Only thus is God *concrete*, living, and Spirit." SL § 74 trans. amended). Note Hegel's statement is made here prior to a distinction between God as "immanent" Trinity and as "economic" Trinity. The statement is therefore in the context applicable to both aspects.

121. Walter Jaeschke, "Speculative and Anthropological Criticism of Religion. A Theological Orientation to Hegel and Feuerbach," *Journal of the American Academy of Religion* 48 (1980) 356.

122. Further on in E § 74 Hegel writes: "Für das Wahre aber kann nur ein Inhalt erkannt werden, insofern er nicht mit einem Andern vermittelt, nicht endlich ist, also sich mit sich selbst vermittelt, und so in Eins Vermittlung und unmittelbare Beziehung auf sich selbst ist." As is the case with Wallace's translation of this paragraph as a whole, his translation of this sentence loses much of the connotative force of Hegel's original. Wallace translates: "The only content which can be held to be the truth is one not mediated with something else, not limited by other things: or, otherwise expressed, it is one mediated by itself, where mediation and immediate reference–to–self coincide." SL § 74. Wallace captured the relationship content/truth. However, there is an extremely close tie between this sentence and the reference to God in the beginning of the paragraph. "*Das Wahre*" not only serves as modifier of content, but is a technical term in Hegel, "the True," see e.g., GW 11:29.20–22/L 1:41 (GL 59); GW 12:246.18–23/L 2:496 (GL 835). It is the true content of the name God. Secondly, in view of the context of a discussion on knowledge of God, the content which is mediated by an other posited by itself, a content which is non-finite, connotes if not outright denotes God who is Spirit. Hegel has managed to work into this sentence a fourfold reference: first, to what constitutes the true content of knowledge; second, in view of the context, to the mediated nature of all knowledge; third, at least indirectly to the structure of the True

as self-mediating; fourth, in view of the first third of the paragraph, a reference to God as Subject and Spirit. All of this is rooted in Hegel's being able to speak about a knowledge *of* God, with this genitive taken both objectively and subjectively. Both are united, in that divine self-knowledge occurs in and as sublated human thought.

123. E.g., on otherness as negation, see Ch. 2 n. 60 above.

124. See the remarks in Ch. 1 Subsection 3 of the present study.

125. See Ch. 1 n. 173 with further references there.

126. Again the question raised by Prof. Dr. Ekkehard Mühlenberg during a historical-systematic seminar on Trinity, Claremont, California, Nov. 21, 1977.

127. "Die beyden ersten Momente der Triplizität sind die *abstrakten*, unwahren Momente, die eben darum dialektisch sind und durch diese ihre Negativität sich zum Subjekte machen." GW 12:248.17–19/L 2:409 ("The first two moments of the triplicity are *abstract*, untrue moments which for that very reason are dialectical, and through this their negativity make themselves into the subject." GL 837 typographical error corrected).

128. That is, Hegel neither explicitly integrated nor in an adequate fashion thematically developed his notion of otherness as negativity, or more exactly, negation. Again, see Ch. 2 n. 60 above.

129. The question is raised in the context of the *Phenomenology* with a proposed alternative *Dialogik* by Johannes Heinrichs, *Die Logik der "Phänomenologie des Geistes"* (Bonn: Bouvier, 1974) 523–526.

130. Haag, *Philosophischer Idealismus* 43, writes of an idealistic presupposition that nonidentity has no content of its own. Independently of Haag, the use of "content" here in the text is less technical than Hegel's usage.

131. To correct such is a major plank in Koch's philosophical and theological program, *Differenz* 64 n. 71, p. 68 with n. 84, p. 71.

132. This critique and the overall position taken in Chapter Six below concerning the inclusive character of the true infinite *generally*, but without entering into detailed discussion, follow that of Koch, who in *Differenz* 24, sees Hegel's whole philosophy centered in the *Aufhebung* of the alienated, in the mediation of a self-contradictory opposition. Summarily stated: "Als erste These dieser Arbeit formulierte ich [Koch]: Hegel erkannte das fundamentale Problem der Entzweiung und sah, daß das Denken der Differenz als Differenz über diese hinaus zum Erkennen der Identität nötigt, denn Einseitiges könnte nicht sein, nicht bestehen, wäre es nicht durch das übergreifende 'Ganze' getragen und gehalten. Darum ist Hegels Grundthema die 'Aufhebung' der Entzweiung, die 'Vermittlung' der sich widersprechenden Gegensätze.—Nun dürfte deutlich geworden sein, daß sich die Kritik darauf zu richten hat, ob es Hegel gelingt, diesen Prozeß der Aufhebung in einem endgültigen Resultat zu vollenden. Als Leitsatz der Kritik diene die Frage—und das ist die zweite These dieser Arbeit—: Erreicht es Hegel, die identität so zu denken, daß *in* ihrem

Erfassen die Differenz und damit die Endlichkeit (auch des Denkens) vollgültig überwunden, 'aufgehoben' ist? Läßt sich das 'Ganze' ohne Einseitigkeit und damit ohne Rückfall in die Endlichkeit definierend erkennen?"

133. GW 11:21.5–9 and clearer in L 1:30–31 (GL 49).

134. GW 11:17.29–18.17/L 1:26–27 (GL 46). On *Verstand*, GW 11:17. 20–28 but clearer in L 1:26 (GL 45–46); E §§ 20R, 25. As commonly enough acknowledged, Hegel's reasoning thought is not a merely intellectualistic process because it contains subsumed love within it. E.g., Koch, *Differenz* 39 n. 31 with references, and p. 29 concerning Rudolf Bultmann as the first in the area of theology to bring out the distinction between a rationalistic and a Hegelian understanding of thought. See also GW 11:7.29–8.4/L 1:6–7 (GL 28).

135. In this line, Koch, *Differenz* 33–34 with n. 23.

136. GW 11:8.15–17/L 1:7 (GL 28). Also, e.g., GW 11:21.6–8/L 1:30 (GL 49); E § 38. *Denken* is the generic verb and substantive ordinarily used by Hegel.

137. "Das Unwahre ist das Unerreichbare." L 1:138 ("What is untrue is unattainable." GL 149 trans. amended).

138. Koch, *Differenz* 34–35, 37–38, 57.

139. Note Hegel's critique of understanding as opinion (*Meinung*). GW 11:17.26–28/L 1:26 (GL 45–46) and Hegel's reference to objective thought (*objectives Denken*), GW 11:21.11/L 1:31 (GL 49).

140. Hegel speaks of "Das *Denken*, oder bestimmter das *begreifende Denken*," GW 11:15.19–21/L 1:23 ("thinking, or more specifically *comprehensive* thinking." GL 43), "comprehensive" in the sense of "grasping" as the object handled within "logic." See also GW 12:239.25–240.19/L 2:488–489 (GL 828).

141. GW 11:20.5–7, 37–39/L 1:29–30 (GL 48–49). Hegel's view of the *Phenomenology* at the writing of the *Logic*. On Hegel's varying attitude to the *Phenomenology*, see the literature cited in Ch. 3 n. 149 below.

142. See, for example, L 1:16 (GL 37); GW 12:240.30–241.19/L 2:488–489 (GL 828).

143. See GW 11:58.1–29 with the somewhat expanded second edition text L 1:93–95 (GL 106–108). Pierre-Jean Labarrière and Gwendoline Jarezyk render *aufheben* in French by supprimer-conserver-élever, and the neologism sursumer in G. W. Hegel, *Science de la logique*. Premier Tom. Premier livre. *L'être, édition de 1812* (Paris: Aubier-Montaigne, 1972) 38 with n. 32, citing Pierre-Jean Labarrière, *Structures et mouvement dialectique dans la Phénoménologie de l'Esprit de Hegel* (Paris: Aubier-Montaigne, 1968) 309. "Sublate" is generally used in this present study to render *aufheben* and "sublation" to translate *Aufhebung*, as has become customary in English translations of Hegel.

144. On the manifold as moment of the universal, see Koch, *Differenz* 51–52 with these references: GW 11:29.12–22/L 1:1 (GL 59); E §§ 12, 14.

145. This of course does not mean making thought subjective. Rather, thought is where subjective thought finds its truth. Hegel's philosophy remains absolute idealism. On the taking up of human thought into absolute thought, see for example the discussion in L 1:14–16 (GL 35–37) and Hegel's discussion on Kant, GW 12:17.28–19.2/L 2:221–222 (GL 584–585).

146. Koch, *Differenz* 29–38, 52 n. 50 with several literature references. In the context of a critique of Koch's study, Puntel, *Darstellung* 116–117, recalls the necessity to understand the relationship between absolute thought and finite thought dialectically. But against Puntel, dialectically does not mean distinctively or better discreetly.

147. E § 2; L 1:110 (GL 123).

148. E.g., GW 11:25.4–17/L 1:35–36 (GL 54); also, L 1:18 (GL 39); GW 12:250.8–39/L 2:501–502 (GL 839–840). Implicitly this constitutes two uses of the term "content," i.e., as applied to the second and third dialectical moment moments in the movement of logic.

149. Note the brief discussion of method in terms of form and of content in Ch. 1 n. 73 above.

150. "Die Form so in ihre Reinheit herausgedacht, enthält es dann in sich selbst, sich zu bestimmen, d.i. sich Inhalt zu geben, und zwar denselben in seiner Notwendigkeit,—als System der Denkbestimmungen." L 1:46 (GL 63 trans. amended). Not found in GW 11.

Lothar Eley's important though quite critical review of Koch's *Differenz* in "Zum Problem des Anfangs in Hegels *Logik und Phänomenologie*," in *Hegel-Studien* 6 (Bonn: Bouvier, 1971) 267–283, strongly defends Hegel against Koch's critique. Koch argues perhaps too undifferentiatedly for a priority of form over content in Hegel's thought: "die absolute Form *setzt* ihren Inhalt selbst? . . . Damit ist eine Priorität der Form gegenüber dem Inhalt ausgesagt, die in ihrem Prae *vor* dem Inhalt auch gedacht werden soll, und in dem Gedanken von der setzenden Wirksamkeit der Form ja auch ausgedrückt ist." (63 further 64–65). Eley (274) recalls the reflexive in L 1:46 (GL 63) and continues to argue that Hegel did not mean any simple priority of form over content (274–277). Koch's somewhat undifferentiated statement could be traceable partially to his dependence at this point (see Koch, 58 nn. 66 and 67) on Meulen's (*Hegel* 47, 52) also inadequately nuanced but more general statement concerning form's positing of its content moment. Meulen's remark is somewhat better qualified on p. 61 though again more ambiguous elsewhere. Koch is quite aware of Hegel's statements on the determinate character of all thought (58), on the nature of form as content (57) and in particular of Hegel's insistence that the determination of pure being is its determinationlessness (84). On the content of pure being and of all logical beginnings as beginnings, GW 12:249.31–250.25/L 2:501–502 (GL 839–840). Nevertheless, even granting

Eley's somewhat corrective critique of Koch's formulation of a Hegelian priority of form over content, Koch's criticism finally stands or falls not with this initial generalized statement, but with his examination of the thought categories and determinations themselves (Koch, 70 n. 91). See further in Eley (278–283) where he continues his criticism of Koch's analysis. Puntel, *Darstellung* Section C III, proposes an alternative to Koch's understanding of the relationship between form and content.

151. Logical thought as such is abstract for Hegel in the sense that it is not the realization found in the realphilosophical spheres. Being and nothing are abstract moments of logical thought in comparison to the more concrete forms from becoming on. Yet logical thought as a whole is from its beginning concrete in the sense mentioned here in the text, or it could not be the self-positing of the Concept. "Die Form . . . enthält es dann in sich selbst, sich zu bestimmen" L 1:46 ("The form will have within itself the capacity to determine itself." GL 63). On being as the as yet unposited totality, see Hegel's remarks on universality as beginning, GW 12:240.29–31/L 2:489 (GL 829).

152. See the various phrases Hegel uses, phrases which taken together add up to "determinationlessness," GW 11:43.4–11, 20–44.2/L 1:66 with 85 (GL 81–82 with 99). Hegel does explicitly use the term *Bestimmungslosigkeit* to refer to nothing, GW 11:44.10/L 1:67 (GL 82). (Note that in this present study *Bestimmtheit* is translated by "determinateness" and *Bestimmung* by "determination." For Hegel's distinction see esp. GW 11:69.20–71.7, and in revised form esp. L 1:110 (GL 123).

153. On negation see Ch. 2 n. 51 above and in the *Logic* particularly L 1:97–101 (GL 111–114). Jaeschke and Hogemann, "Die Wissenschaft der Logik" 86, write, "Indem es, 'Bestimmtheit' zum Grundbegriff der Seinslogischen Kategorien macht, werden diese zu Formen der Negation; indem andereseits alle Realität Negation ist, wird der Inbegriff aller Realitäten—durch den die Metaphysik den Gottesbegriff dacht—zum Inbegriff aller Negationen, das ens realissimum Zugleich zum Nichts."

154. "omnis determinatio est negation." L 1:100 (GL 113). See also E § 50R. Léonard misses the complexity of Hegel's thought by introducing the terms "*finie*" and "*limitée*" into his commentary: "Toute détermination finie et limitée est en effet, en tant que finie et limitée, une négation." *Commentaire* 27.

155. This was earlier treated in the context of discussing the theological character and significance of the movement of pure thought in Ch. 1 Subsection 3 of the present study.

156. E.g., the section "Womit muß der Anfang der Wissenschaft gemacht werden?" GW 11:33.3–40.29/L 1:51–64 ("With What Must the Science begin?" GL 67–78). But Peter Rohs observes, "der Anfang der dialektischen Bewegung enthält nun einmal mehr Voraussetzungen, als Hegel zuzugeben beriet war," Review of *Werden zu sich. Eine Untersuchung zu Hegels "Wissenschaft der Logik"* by Ute Guzzoni in *Hegel-Studien* 4 (Bonn: Bouvier, 1967) 256–257.

157. GW 12:240.26–28/L 2:489 (GL 829). Granted for the sake of discussion of course the logically retroactive positing of being by Idea, it is still necessary to establish being as conceptually thinkable. In this sense Hegel's system is deductively dependent on the beginning in pure being.

Daniel Oscar Dahlstrom's observation that Hegel did not claim that the logical beginning is fully established at the beginning does not do justice to Hegel's concern and efforts. "Essence and Subjectivity in Hegel's *Science of Logic*" (Ph.D. dissertation, St. Louis University, 1978) 501. Dahlstrom gathers helpful information on the critique of Hegel's notion of the unique beginning of logic: various interpretations, 479 n. 136 with 480 n. 137; on Albrecht's interpretations, 485–492; on Trendelenburg's critique, 492–502. For a summary of the critiques of being as logical beginning, see Henrich, *Hegel im Kontext* 75–84.

158. See the presentation on pure being, Ch. 2 Subsection 2 of the present study.

159. Generally following Koch, whose criticism of Hegel's understanding and presentation of pure being is found in *Differenz* 81–86 with the remarks Ch. 2 n. 150 above. Koch (63) writes, "Aber der eine Begriff *ist* nie ohne Inhaltsbestimmung, er ist ohne das, 'was als Inhalt erscheint,' überhaupt nicht denkbar. Bei dem ersten Beginnen, irgend etwas von der logischen Form auszusagen, stellten sich inhaltliche Bestimmungen ein. Ohne diese wäre 'logische Form' ein sinnloser Laut."

It should be added that references to Koch are meant to indicate dependence of thought and not to give the impression of an adequate summary of his rich, carefully formulated thought. Michael Theunissen's questionable observation that Koch employs two different meanings in his positing of determinateness at "beginning" and "end" does not negate the real determinateness involved (and not just determinationlessness as determinateness of any beginning). *Hegels Lehre* 40. For Theunissen's overall critique of Koch, see in Theunissen, 39–42. For a somewhat different critique of the end or result as determinate, see briefly on becoming Ch. 4 Subsection 3b of the present study and on self-determining syllogistic mediation Ch. 5 Subsection 3b of the present study.

160. A summary reminder: "Das Erkennen ist aber begreiffendes Denken, sein Anfang daher auch *nur in Elemente des Denkens,—ein Einfaches* und *Allgemeines*." GW 12:239.25–27/L 2:488 ("But cognition is thinking by means of concepts, and therefore its beginning also is *only in the element of thought—it* is a *simple* and a *universal*." GL 828). It might be argued that "being" is a *Grenzbegriff* (meant more generally here as a concept in some way related to and bringing together two distinct realms of thought). However with Hegel being must stand or fall as the comprehensible beginning of logical thought, of absolute form.

Heinrich Fink-Eitel distinguishes "beginning in the sense of starting point" (*Ansatz*) and "beginning as initial moment" (*Anfang*). The former refers to being's constitution as negation of negation (out of the *Phenomenology*) and the latter to being's constituting the initial moment of the movement of logic. "Hegels phänomenologische Erkenntnistheorie als Begründung dialektischer Logik," *Philosophisches Jahrbuch* 85 (1978) 242–258, esp. 258. Though this distinction can be of help, it does not resolve the dilemma into which Hegel is systematically forced.

161. See Ch. 2 n. 152 above.

162. Trying to make pure being more available to thought by use of Hegel's expression, "relation to itself" (*Beziehung auf sich*), e.g., GW 12:128.32–33, 252.30–31/L 2:355, 504 (GL 706, 842) helps express the continuity between being and further logical moments, all of which are in their own way *Beziehung* or relation. See the argumentation by Ruth-Eva Schulz-Seitz, " 'Sein' in Hegels Logik" 365–383. But *Beziehung auf sich* must be interpreted in the light of the initial and normative presentation of being. For Hegel this phrase adds no determination, which Schulz-Seitz (370) would agree with, in that *Beziehung auf sich* as applied to being is not to be set over against progression.

Taken together, this and the following notes provide a representative survey of several attempts to defend Hegel's absolute logic in its initial moment. In this way these notes also form an introductory listing of alternatives to Koch's basic critique of Hegel's immanent dialectic (see Koch's thesis quoted Ch. 2 n. 132 above). Several alternatives: some sort of content within the framework of contentlessness; appeals to intuition or terms of reflection; distinctions between being and the determination being. In all but the last Hegel himself had already discussed these options.

On the older reception of Hegel's initial logical moment, see Fulda, "Über den spekulativen Anfang," 115–116 nn. 9, 10, p. 118 n. 17. Further surveys cited by Dahlstrom. See Ch. 2 n. 157 above.

163. E § 87R.

164. "Sichselbstgleichheit, Einfachheit, Reinheit, Unmittelbarkeit, das ganze Leere, das Allgemeinste, vollkommene Abstraktion, Unbestimmtheit," Koch, *Differenz* 82 (my trans.).

165. See the beginning of Ch. 2 Subsection 2 of the present study.

166. Koch, *Differenz* 82 n. 12 singles out Dieter Henrich, "Anfang und Methode der Logik," in *Heidelberger Hegel-Tage 1962, Hegel-Studien*, Beiheft 1 (Bonn: Bouvier, 1964) 24, 28, 34. Henrich tried to solve the problem of reference to being my means of determinations of reflection. Koch observes: "das Sein soll aber, dem ersten Satz der Seinslogik (L 1:66) zufolge, 'frei' sein 'von der Bestimmtheit gegen das Wesen,' gegen die Reflexionslogik." Henrich has widened his argumentation in "Hegels Logik der Reflexion. Neue Fassung," in *Die Wissenschaft der Logik und die Logik der Reflexion, Hegel-Tage Chantilly 1971, Hegel-Studien*, Beiheft 18 (Bonn: Bouvier, 1978) 203–324. Fulda, "Über den spekulativen Anfang" 126, approaches the question by giving a double role to determinations of reflection: an indicatory task; and, the job of moving forward from one content to the next.

167. "Die einfache Unmittelbarkeit ist selbst ein Reflexionsausdruck und bezieht sich auf den Unterschied von dem Vermittelten. In ihrem wahren Ausdrucke ist daher diese einfache Unmittelbarkeit das *reine Sein*." L 1:54 (GL 69). First edition, GW 11:33.16–19.
168. See again L 1:54 (GL 69).
169. "ein Unsagbares," E § 87R. See Koch, *Differenz* 81.
170. "Das *Seyn* ist einfaches, als *unmittelbares*; deswegen ist es ein nur *Gemeyntes* und kann man von ihm nicht sagen, was es ist." GW 12:33.27–29/L 2:241 (GL 601). To establish the relationship between initial moment of the Concept and its expression as unexpressible makes the initial moment unavailable.
171. "Seyn, reines Seyn," GW 11:43.20/L 1:66 (GL 82). See also the quote in Ch. 2 n. 167 above.
Wieland, "Bemerkungen zum Anfang" 196, cites GW 11:51.37–53.11 and proposes that on the basis of Hegel's argumentation by the "method of elimination" (*Exhaustionsmethode*) this beginning is plausible (198). But the difficulty with any argument by the process of elimination is that the process itself does not take its own method seriously enough. The very thing argued to must itself be submitted to the possibility of being eliminated. Hegel left this section out of the second edition of the *Logic*. Wieland further argues to being as a mere mentioning ("*allein mit der satzlosen Erwähnung*" 199) and merely nameable (*nennbar* 209, "*er [Anfang] kann immer nur gennant werden*" 210). This dovetails with Wieland's claim (204) that Hegel's logic is not developed from the standpoint of the Absolute.
Theunissen, *Sein und Schein*, works by means of a "correction" (103ff, 113) of Tugendhat, "Das Sein und das Nichts," in *Durchblicke. Martin Heidegger zum 80. Geburtstag*, ed. Vittorio Klostermann (Frankfurt am Main: Klostermann, 1970) 132–161, with a notion of intuition likewise to speak of being as the "content of intuition" (*Anschauungsinhalt*) and equally "intuition itself" (*das Anschauen selber*) (105, see 108). He refers to "the intuitional thinking of pure being" (*das anschauliche Denken des reinen Seins*) (107, see 108). Besides the fact that Hegel finally comes down not on the side of intuition but of thought, intuition is always intuition of something. Theunissen distinguishes: "Das 'reine Sein' ist nach der Konzeption Hegels nicht *nur* Gegenstand, sondern auch dasjenige, das es vergegenständlicht." This double notion of being is to be maintained by means of an act: "Die Vermittlung, der das Sein seine Entstehung verdankt, ist die Abstraktion von der Bestimmtheit alles Seienden" (114). Such abstraction Theunissen argues must be possible, "Andernfalls nämlich könnte sie nicht auch von denn in der logischen Wissenschaft tätigen Denken vollbracht werden" (115). But precisely this logical activity is in question. On Meulen, who had without reference to intuition similarly proposed pure being as the mere result of an act of sublation, see the summary and critique with references in Koch, *Differenz* 83–84 n. 15. Eley, "Zum Problem des Anfangs," 280–282,

rejects Koch's argumentation and opts for taking being nominally as a name. "Sein ist nominal Gemeintes, Sein hat seine Vergangenheit im einfachen Ausdruck, und das ist die Wahrheit des Namens" (280). But being is not just a name. It is the initial moment of the Concept. James Yerkes, *The Christology of Hegel* (Missoula, Montana: Scholars, 1978) 305 n. 112, appears to agree with Mumson and Iljin that Hegel's beginning is rooted in intuition.

172. "Jede Aussage verkehrt das Sein zu einem Bestimmten und Endlichen, und hat dies immer schon getan. Auch das abstrakteste 'Daß' beinhaltet immer bereits ein 'Was.'" Die Bestimmung Sein bringt also die absolute Einheit, den *einen* Begriff, nicht *als* Absolutes zu einem selbst-absoluten Ausdruck." Koch, *Differenz* 83.

173. Within the context of a reference to Parmenides Hegel writes, "Sein wäre überhaupt nicht der absolute Anfang, wenn es eine Bestimmtheit hätte; als dann hinge es von einem Andern ab und wäre nicht unmittelbar, nicht des Anfang." L 1:80 ("If being had a determinateness, then it would not be the absolute beginning at all; it would then depend on an other and would not be immediate, would not be the beginning. GL 94).

174. On nothing, see Ch. 2 Subsection 2 of the present study.

175. Hegel in fact needs to refer to *Etwas* (something) in order to establish *Nichts* (nothing) in thought. GW 11:44.11–14/L 1:67 (GL 82).

If the initial moment of being were truly establishable according to Hegel's own criteria, it could be argued that nothing is momentary totality dialectically containing its other. Then Koch's critique, "Für das 'Nichts' ist, so sehen wir, die Näherbestimmung 'das Andere' konstitutiv," would not touch Hegel's thought. Koch states his case by quoting Meulen, "'Das Nichts ist in der Tat immer ein konkret bestimmtes Nichts, das Nicht von Etwas.'" *Differenz* 93, quoted from *Hegel* 49.

In "Zum Problem des Anfangs" 282, Eley tries to respond to Koch's critique by distinguishing between temporally conditioned development and purely logical development. However, this distinction is of decisive value here only if pure being can be adequately established in thought. Again, to say as Eley does (282–283) that Koch falls back into a subjectivist idealism is likewise a valid critique only if the establishment of pure being in thought is first accepted.

176. E § 85R; GW 12:33.27–29/L 2:241 (GL 601).

177. On being as *Grenzbegriff*, see briefly Ch. 2 n. 160 above.

178. On becoming see esp. the last pages of Ch. 2 Subsection 2 of the present study.

179. In *Differenz* Koch refers to the insufficiency (*Insuffizienz* 105) and the immanent inadequacy of each determinateness ("Das immanente Ungenügen jeder Bestimmtheit" 102).

180. Koch, *Differenz* 102.

181. E § 80, where Hegel of course speaks as far as he is concerned only of understanding (*Verstand*).

182. This settling is critiqued from the point of view of result in the context of an examination of Hegel's notion of incarnational immediacy in Ch. 4 the second half of Subsection 3b of the present study.

183. The exposition in Ch. 1 Subsections 1 and 2 of the present study not only provides an introduction to Hegel's form of logic, a clarifying of how Hegel was being interpreted here and a sense of the whole and of Hegel's notion of subjectivity and Subject, but as well allows for taking into consideration the logically grounding presence of the absolute Idea.

184 *Dasein* can be taken here simply to mean the givenness of finitude, of finite thought or, if one were to work with a finite objective thought, the initial moment in that movement of finite objective thought. In the immediate context of this examination of Hegel's *Logic* reference is quite naturally made to thought. However, the reference to *Dasein* can be widened and made more formal.

185. For a fuller statement see Ch. 6 Subsection 2 of the present study.

186. In the context of a discussion on the *Phenomenology* see esp. Ch. 4 Subsection 4b of the present study. Note that Quentin Lauer, S.J., remarks concerning Hegel's view of thought, "Truly self-developing thought is itself concrete (from *concrescere*, a process of internal growth)." *Hegel's Concept of God* (Albany: State University of New York Press, 1982) 73.

187. Concerning the relationship of the movement of pure thought as a whole to these its initial moments, see Ch. 2 Subsection 1 of the present study and in general recall remarks made throughout concerning method, absolute form, the Concept's unity and the paradigmatic nature of the initial moments.

Concerning Hegel's attempt to work in the publicly arguable realm of discourse see briefly in Ch. 2 Subsection 4 and Ch. 2 n. 139 of the present study.

James Brouwer has responded very thoughtfully and at some length to my argumentation concerning the non-viability of Hegel's position especially on the beginning of pure or logical thought in being. His response consists, as I read it, in reaffirming strongly, insistently and very clearly what Hegel himself had written about, and meant concerning, a beginning in pure being. See his thesis, "The Conception of the Hegelian Dialectic" (M.A. Thesis, University of Ottawa, 1977) 16–26. Brouwer argues, in effect, that what I say about Hegel's presentation of pure being is correct, but that, in drawing the conclusion that Hegel cannot make pure being available as first moment in conceptual thought, I have in effect argued what he would say Hegel himself is affirming, namely, the unthinkableness of pure being. Brouwer speaks, for example, of "it [pure being] as thinkable in this its unthinkability" (18). One might, then, wonder whether in this case pure being would not be some sort of Kantian "thing in itself," and writes of pure being's "unthinkableness as implicitly thinkable" (19).

In a very thorough, most helpful recent study, *The Opening of Hegel's Logic. From Being to Finitude* (West Lafayette, IN: Purdue University Press, 2006), Stephen Houlgate has made a strong presentation in favor of the viability of Hegel's presentation of pure being and his argument in its favor as the first moment in the movement of logical thought. He writes often of the "thinking of being" (*passim*) and, at various times, of "thinking being" (e.g., 90). His focus is on pure being as indeterminate being (e.g., 34, 82–83, 263). He says, "For Hegel, pure thought is indeed the intellectual intuition of being" (125).

188. Paul Tillich is reportedly more generally to have criticized Hegel's defining of subjectivity in terms of lacking. See Kenan Osborne, *New Being. A Study on the Relationship between Conditioned and Unconditioned Being according to Paul Tillich* (The Hague: Nijhoff, 1969) 49.

189. GW 11:28.32–35/L 1:40 (GL 58).

190. See, e.g., Ch. 2 n. 152 above.

191. Koch writes, "Wir aber wissen anfänglich nur von Bestimmtheiten, Differenten," and continues, "für uns entscheidet sich alles daran, der Nötigung ansichtig zu werden, daß das Differente nicht sein kann ohne die absolute Identität, daß das Endliche selbst über sich hinaus zur Aufhebung ins Unendliche drängt." *Differenz* 71. In the second half of this quote Koch moves perhaps too quickly to an identity without which difference could not exist.

192. Hegel's dialectic itself is summarized in Ch. 2 Subsection 3 of the present study.

193. See esp. GW 11:258.1–290.8/L 2:23–62 (GL 409–443).

194. See the handy general overview in W. T. Stace, *The Philosophy of Hegel. A Systematic Exposition* (New York: Macmillan, 1924; reprint ed. New York: Dover, 1955) 43–49, and Hegel's own remarks, GW 11:17.20–19.37/L 1:26–29 (GL 45–48). Slight variations between the first edition (GW 11) and the second (L 1).

195. See Koch, *Differenz* 65–71. As Koch says explicitly, "Aber nach seiner [Hegels] Interpretation ist das Auftreten der Differenz, der Bestimmtheit, nicht das Geschick der Verkehrung, die sich unserem Denken und Reden von der absoluten Einheit ereignet, sondern Akt der Setzung, den die absolute Einheit ausführt" (68). But recall the distinctions made esp. in Ch. 2 n. 150 above. Koch speaks of inversion or reversal (*Verkehrung*) and more often of the loss (*Verlust*, e.g., 66, 67, 70, 71) of the identity Hegel proposed to attain in rational thought (*Vernunft*). It would be important to qualify the use of terms such as "loss" by recalling that from the beginning Hegel could not establish the initial identity as he had proposed to.

196. Abstraction here not in Hegel's sense of as yet undeveloped or unposited but in the sense of bracketed out or eliminated from.

197. See Ch. 6 Subsection 2 and the tentative revision in Ch. 6 Subsection 3 of the present study.

198. "Deductive" position or system is used here in the first instance to refer to any argumentation claiming to develop its position immanently

and consistently out of an initial moment which in its own realm requires no presuppositions to ground itself.

199. It is beyond the scope of this study to consider in detail many wider implications of this shifting from a beginning in the self-positing absolute to a finite beginning for a creative appropriation of Hegel's philosophy and its concerns and for philosophical theology in general. It will have to suffice here to hint at some of the wider implications of the recognition of the truly finite character of thought in that thought's beginning and further development: the possibility of a monological movement of differentiated concepts structuring the dialogical experience of self-consciousness; the possibility of a plurality of forms of objective thought, of rigorously formulated philosophies, which could form the basis of a dialog in the public realm; the reduction of the Enlightenment-posited gulf between thought as universal and history as particular or positive by here acknowledging the historically conditioned determinateness of thought itself; the nature of thought as itself a striving for and reaching (*Erreichen*) but never fully attaining or grasping (*Begreifen*) the truly universal, the infinite; a philosophically appropriate reformulation of the cosmological arguments as movement from finite to infinite; a restructuring of the relationship between Christology and theology in a strict sense of this latter. There in addition lies in the acknowledgement of the true and abiding finitude of thought the rootage of a new and more respectful reconciliation between philosophy and history, logic and contingency. As mentioned, this acknowledgement would provide as well the ontological basis for a plurality of thought systems while retaining a public realm of thought and discourse in view of the use of reflexively critiquable finite logical categories. The true strength of finite thought would lie not in its ability to comprehend the infinite, or more exactly, to be sublated into a movement of infinite thought. Rather, based on its own finitude, thought would show the capacity to argue beyond itself to that unity without which its own concrete existence and development could not be adequately explained.

200. To propose in response that epistemologically speaking any beginning may be finite but ontologically a beginning *in itself* could be infinite, would be an uncritical reversion to a pre-Kantian framework. The question here is of a beginning graspable in human thought. To posit a beginning outside of and not graspable in finite thought but from which finite thought would argue or progress would again simply presuppose the prior movement of thought from finitude to infinity. To oppose ontological and epistemological or noetic and then give a priority to the ontological would not escape presupposing a prior movement from finite beginning to proposed initial infinite. An ontologically prior starting point in infinity would always remain hypothetical.

3. Overview of Hegel's Explicit Trinitarian Thought and a Criterion for the *Phenomenology*

1. Again, see Ch. 1 n. 168 above for reservations regarding reference to Hegel's trinitarian thought's being expressed in terms of "immanent" and "economic."

2. Note the Encyclopedia's full title, *Enzyklopädie der philosophischen Wissenschaften im Grundrisse* (*Encyclopedia of the Philosophical Sciences in Outline*).

Prior to the third and last edition of 1830, Hegel had published the first edition in 1817 and an enlarged second edition in 1827. Briefly on the *Encyclopedia*'s pedagogical background, development and orientation, see Friedhelm Nicolin, "Pädagogik—Propädeutik—Enzyklopädie," in Otto Pöggeler, ed., *Hegel. Einführung in seine Philosophie* (Munich: Alber, 1977) 91–105, esp. 100–104 and initial bibliography 182–183. On the *Encyclopedia*'s nature and historical/pedagogical context, see Jürgen Henningsen, " 'Enzyklopädie.' Zur Sprach- und Deutungsgeschichte eines pädagogisches Begriffs," *Archiv für Begriffsgeschichte. Bausteine zu einem historischen Wörterbuch der Philosophie* 10 (1966) 271–362. Succinctly on what Hegel excludes and includes by the term "Encyclopedia of Philosophical Sciences," see Gary J. Percesepe, "Hegel's *Encyclopedia* and the Shift in the Self-understanding of Philosophy," *The St. Louis Journal of Philosophy* 1 (1981) 37–52, esp. 38–43.

3. See esp. E § 577 but also GW 9:10.34–36 (*Phen.* 2, 11).

4. The driving force of this argument derives from and pertains primarily to Hegel's conception of an encyclopedic system. It would be good to recall that "realphilosophical" applies strictly speaking to those texts in the *Encyclopedia* and to Hegel's various lecture texts and transcripts which go beyond the presentation of the movement of logical thought qua logical. Realphilosophical is used here however also in a wider sense to include Hegel's *Phenomenology of Spirit*, which admittedly could not as such be integrated without difficulties into Hegel's encyclopedic system. Nevertheless, not only on the basis of the need for a comprehensive treatment but also more substantively the *Phenomenology* must be considered in its own way as a realphilosophical text. As a finished work it does presuppose logic. As will be elaborated in the course of this second part of this present study, in the *Encyclopedia* texts on revealed religion, in Hegel's lecture texts (including student transcripts) on the absolute or consummate religion and in the *Phenomenology*'s treatment of revelatory religion, the syllogistic structure of Hegel's trinitarian thought remains consistent and constant from the 1807 *Phenomenology* on. It is this common underlying syllogistic structure which, despite differences between the *Phenomenology*'s development and that of the philosophy of religion lectures, justifies along with the *Encyclopedia*'s very nature an overview drawn from that *Encyclopedia*. On the general question of the relationship between specific logical categories and shapes of consciousness in

the *Phenomenology*, see Pierre-Jean Labarrière, *Structures et movement dialectique dans la "Phénoménologie de l'Esprit" de Hegel* (Paris: Aubier-Montaigne, 1968) 248–255 esp. 250–252. On this question regarding logic and philosophy of religion, see esp. Reinhard Heede, "Die göttliche Idee and ihre Erscheinung in der Religion. Untersuchungen zum Verhältnis von Logik and Religionsphilosophie bei Hegel" (Ph.D. dissertation, Philosophical Faculty of the Westfälischen Wilhelms-Universität zu Münster/Westfalen, 1972).

5. Recall that Heede has referred to the philosophy of religion as *Phänomeno-theo-logik*, "Die göttliche Idee" 56–57.

6. When referred to as a text, the philosophy of religion lectures will be abbreviated *Lectures*.

7. See briefly on God as Spirit, truth and totality, Ch. 1 n. 111 above.

8. E §§ 574–577.

9. On the different nuances see Albert Chapelle, *Hegel et la religion*, vol. 3: *La théologie et l'église* (Paris: Editions Universitaires, 1971) 50, 60, 84, 85, 98–105, who speaks with a certain sensitivity of the *Encyclopedia*'s conception of religion as "speculative theology" in contradistinction to the "ascetic theology" of the *Phenomenology* and the "positive theology" of the *Lectures;* Michael Theunissen, *Hegels Lehre vom absoluten Geist als theologisch-politischer Traktat* (Berlin: de Gruyter, 1970) 217–218; indirectly also Hodgson, "Introduction" in CR xxi–xxiii.

10. As mentioned in Ch. 3 n. 4 above, the exposition of the consistent and constant syllogistic structure undergirding Hegel's trinitarian thought is one of the tasks of this present Part Two of the present study.

11. The first copies of the *Phenomenology* were probably available at the beginning of April, 1807. Apparently Hegel began the *Phenomenology* at least by 1805 and sent the last manuscripts to the printer about January 10, 1807. For details see Wolfgang Bonsiepen and Reinhard Heede, "Editorischer Bericht," GW 9:462–463, 465.

12. Again, Jörg Splett, *Die Trinitätslehre G. W. F. Hegels* (Munich: Alber, 1965), has conveniently gathered pertinent Trinity references found throughout the Hegelian Corpus, including Hegel's lectures on the proofs for the existence of God. These lectures on the proofs are most appropriately handled according to Hegel in relation to logic. See in Ch. 6 n. 86 below. As Heede, "Die göttliche Idee" 64–66, points out, not only are the philosophy of religion texts representative of other lecture texts, but more fundamentally the treatment of religion in the other lectures is only by means of anticipation.

For a brief overview and comparison of the more significant Hegel texts on religion, see Albert Chapelle, *Hegel et la religion*, vol. 2: *La dialectique. A. Dieu et la création* (Paris: Editions Universitaires, 1967) 13–21. Some of Chapelle's details and conclusions based on the state of texts would require correction in view of subsequent studies. For a comparative outline of Hegel's more significant texts on religion, excluding transcripts of the 1824–1831 *Lectures*, see Albert Chapelle, *Hegel et la religion. Annexes. Les textes théologiques de Hegel* (Paris: Éditions Universitaires, 1967), and Chapelle refers to less important texts on religion on p. 7 n. 1.

13. "ein Kreis von Kreisen." E § 15 (SL § 15). E § 15 along with § 16 and § 16R summarize the typically Hegelian dynamic of a dialectically developed encyclopedic science in which each part is a necessary moment which on the basis of its own inner limitation grounds the transition to another more adequate sphere—in teleologically circular fashion. See Nicolin, "Pädagogik" 102–103.

Heede's rather novel and it would appear correct reading of E §§ 574–577 at the end of the *Encyclopedia* proposes that Hegel is presenting a triple syllogistic structuring of the *Encyclopedia*'s realphilosophical spheres. Heede writes: "Nach der These, die wir vertreten, thematisiert Hegel in den §§ 574–577 die vier Teile des philosophischen Systems—die Logik, die Naturphilosophie, die Philosophie des endlichen Geistes und die Philosophie des absoluten Geistes." "Die göttliche Idee" 280. Heede cites with reference to these same §§ 574–577 others who often with a somewhat more "religious" interest tend to speak simply of the three syllogisms of logic, nature and Spirit. For a detailed discussion of these "three" syllogisms in conjunction with Heede's bibliographical references and discussion of the explicitly religious questions, see "Die göttliche Idee" 269–351. Though Heede's interpretation of these last syllogisms in the *Encyclopedia* would appear to be consistent with his opting for a tetradic structure to Hegel's dialectic (see Heede, 227–230) this interpretation does not necessitate embracing a tetradically structured dialectic. Rather, it again merely highlights the doubled nature of the middle term in all of Hegel's thought. Here it is a question of doubling the second moment, whereas Heede's proposed tetradic dialectic would distinguish or rather divide the third moment into result and renewed immediacy.

For bibliography on the last three syllogisms in the *Encyclopedia* see Heede, 276–278. It might be helpful simply to list the authors Heede deals with, especially those who comment not only on the philosophical syllogisms, but more so in their relation to the syllogisms of revealed religion: Claude Bruaire, *Logique et religion chrétienne dans la philosophie de Hegel* (Paris: du Seuil, 1964); Chapelle, *Hegel et la religion*; Splett, *Trinitätslehre*; Hans Friedrich Fulda, *Das Problem einer Einleitung in Hegels "Wissenschaft der Logik"* (Frankfurt am Main: Klostermann, 1965); André Léonard, *La foi chez Hegel* (Paris: Desclés, 1970); Theunissen, *Hegels Lehre*; L. Bruno Puntel, *Darstellung, Methode and Struktur. Untersuchungen zur Einheit der systematischen Philosophie G. W. F. Hegels*, *Hegel-Studien*, Beiheft 10 (Bonn: Bouvier, 1973).

In view of the specific thesis being argued in this study, it would not be necessary to take a final stand on the interpretation of the last syllogisms in the *Encyclopedia*. What is of present and paramount importance is the fact that each totalizing moment is finally seen equally as totalizing syllogism and syllogistically structured moment of the inclusive syllogistic movement of absolute Spirit. In the last analysis the reason why it is not necessary to discuss at great length the intricacies of the various possible interpretations of Hegel's syllogistically structured *Encyclopedia* as well as various detailed readings of Hegel's syllogistically structured understanding of Trinity is that Hegel's theory of syllogism as he presents it is itself not viable. See Ch. 5 Subsection 3b of the present study.

14. E § 385 with § 553.

15. E § 554. For commentary see Theunissen's development of his thesis on the philosophy of history as philosophy of religion in *Hegels Lehre* 77–100 and 118–128, esp. 125–128. Theunissen recalls that religion is for Hegel ever the doubled movement of subjective Spirit to Absolute and, above all, of the objective self-positing of absolute Spirit.

See also Heede, "Die göttliche Idee" 64, where Heede speaks of logic as the last science in so far as it is the one to which philosophy returns and in so far as the science of religion (*Religionswissenschaft*) or the philosophy of absolute Spirit is the moment where "die logische Formen vollendete Wirklichkeit gewinnen."

16. Note Hegel's footnote on Tholuck, E p. 13 line 31 from top to p. 14 line 43 and briefly in William Wallace, "Bibliographical Notice on the Three Editions and Three Prefaces of the *Encyclopedia*," SL xxi.

17. "der denkend erkannte *Begriff* der Kunst und Religion." E § 572 (PM § 572 trans. amended).

18. E §§ 564–571, explicitly on syllogisms §§ 567–571.

19. And, as Walter Jaeschke warns, without any trivial or simplistic identification of the reformulation of "God" in logic and in the philosophy of Spirit, that is, rather with a dialectical identification taking into consideration the differences between Hegel's logic and philosophy of Spirit. "Absolute Idee—absolute Subjektivität. Zum Problem der Persönlichkeit Gottes in der Logik und in der Religionsphilosophie," *Zeitschrift für philosophische Forschung* 35 (1981) e.g., 408–409.

20. As interpreted by Heede Hegel states explicitly in the *Encyclopedia* of 1817 (§ 17R) that the philosophy of absolute Spirit is speculative theology. Hegel is quoted by Heede, "Die göttliche Idee" 63. See also Heede, 69, on Hegel's philosophy as a whole as speculative theology.

21. Benoît Garceau has proposed a similar procedure regarding an approach to Hegel's Christology. "Hegel et la christologie," *Église et Théologie* 4 (1973) 352, a critical review of Hans Küng, *Menschwerdung Gottes. Eine Einführung in Hegels theologisches Denken als Prolegomena zu einer künftigen Christologie* (Freiburg: Herder, 1970).

Hegel's major texts on syllogism are: GW 12:90.1–126.11/L 2:308–352 (GL 664–704); and for present purposes esp. E §§ 181–193. See also Hegel's

"Zur Lehre von den Schlüssen" ("On the Theory of Syllogisms"), GW 12:299.1–309.27, dated 1809 by Friedrich Hogemann and Walter Jaeschke, "Editorischer Bericht," GW 12:333 (not indicated by line).

Studies upon which the present summary draws, which also elaborate points not brought out here such as the presuppositional interrelationship of the syllogisms and which manifest a surprising consensus of interpretation as to what Hegel meant by syllogism: Jan van der Meulen, *Hegel. Die gebrochene Mitte* (Hamburg: Felix Meiner, 1958) 9–144, esp. 9–97; Hermann Schmitz, *Hegel als Denker der Individualität* (Meisenheim/Glan: Hain, 1957) 90–168, esp. 94–103; Fulda, *Das Problem einer Einleitung*; Theunissen, *Hegels Lehre* 256 n. 84, is on syllogism dependent on Betty Heimann, *System und Methode in Hegels Philosophie* (Leipzig: Felix Meiner, 1927) 354–377; Wolfgang Krohn, *Die formale Logik in Hegels "Wissenschaft der Logik." Untersuchungen zur Schlußlehre* (Munich: Hanser, 1972); André Léonard, *Commentaire littéral de la logique de Hegel* (Paris: Vrin, 1974) 390–433, providing an excellent introductory overview; Klaus Düsing, *Das Problem der Subjektivität in Hegels Logik*, Hegel-Studien, Beiheft 15 (Bonn: Bouvier, 1976) esp. 266–288; John Burbidge, *On Hegel's Logic. Fragments of a Commentary* (New York: Humanities, 1981) 158–192. See further brief bibliography in Michael Theunissen, *Sein und Schein. Die kritische Function der Hegelschen Logik* (Frankfurt am Main: Suhrkamp, 1978) 18 n. 5.

This is of course not to deny the importance of a study of the development of Hegel's thought even in the area of syllogism and its varied realization in the realphilosophical spheres, but to focus on one specific question for present purposes.

In general on syllogism see Schmitz, *Hegel als Denker* 94, and on the development of Hegel's thought on syllogism until its mature flowering in the *Phenomenology*, Schmitz, 118–146. One might consult the schematic table in Düsing, *Das Problem der Subjektivität* 274, a table applicable to Hegel's *Logic*, and to the various editions of the *Encyclopedia*. See also the as yet cruder language of Hegel's various attempts to develop an explicit theory of syllogism in 1809, "Zur Lehre von den Schlüssen," GW 12:299.1–309.27, where there is however already the order of the clearly established progression of middle terms characteristic of Hegel's mature system.

22. Schmitz, *Hegel als Denker*, was one of the first to observe this.

23. E § 181; GW 12:90.3–4/L 2:308 (GL 664).

24. Léonard, *Commentaire* 390, where Léonard also discusses the way judgement as singular Subject and universal predicate remain in sublated form in syllogism. See in this line E § 181.

25. GW 12:31.16–20, 126.4–5/L 2:238, 352 (GL 599, 704); see in this line E § 181 with § 193. See also Meulen, *Hegel* 9.

26. On the importance of the positioning of syllogism vis-à-vis Hegel's theory of subjectivity in the *Logic*, see briefly esp. Ch. 2 n. 17 above. Based as well on E § 192.

27. E § 180; GW 12:89.14–19, 90.7–9/L 2:308 (GL 663, 664). Meulen, *Hegel* 94.

28. But of course not three sentences or judgements in any merely formal syllogistic sense since the form of the syllogism is its own content, GW 12:94.33–35, 95.20–22/L 2:314 (GL 669). Hegel's primary concern was however not with the formulation of premises and conclusion, important as they are to establish syllogism's inferential process, but with the development of the middle term of concrete universal inclusive of extremes. On Hegel's evaluation of syllogism's middle term as essential to the syllogism in that it distinguishes syllogism from judgement, see GW 12:111.8–10/L 2:334 (GL 687). See also Düsing, *Das Problem der Subjektivität* 272–273.

On judgement as "particularization" (*Besonderung*) of the Concept, see Léonard, *Commentaire* 341–343, and on Hegel's use of the German *Urteil* (judgement) in the sense of division with reference to an originary unity see Léonard, 342 n. 1. See also Düsing, *Das Problem der Subjektivität* 251–266.

29. Major and minor referring both to the two premises and to the term related to the middle term in each of these two premises.

30. Krohn, *Die formale Logik* 179.

31. "ein Zusammenschließen des Subjekts nicht mit *Anderem*, sondern mit *aufgehobenem* Andern, *mit sich selbst.*" E § 192 (SL § 192 trans. amended). See also E §§ 191, 192; GW 12:125.11–15/L 2:351 (GL 703).

32. E § 193. "Erst in der Schlußlehre konzipiert Hegel also nicht nur, sondern demonstriert er die logische Beziehungsstruktur des vermittelten Selbstverhältnisses der Subjektivität." Düsing, *Das Problem der Subjektivität* 270.

Note from the point of view of the last syllogism, that of disjunction, Hegel also speaks of the "Subjektivität des Schlusses," GW 12:125.7–8/L 2:351 ("subjectivity of the syllogism" GL 702), to indicate the incompleteness of the prior syllogisms.

33. "Der schluß ist das *Vernünftige* und *Alles* Vernünftige." E § 181 (SL § 181 italics added); see GW 12:90.10–11, 14–15/L 2:308 (GL 664). Syllogism is for Hegel this level's definition of the Absolute, so that "*Alles ist ein Schluß.*" E § 181R ("Everything is a syllogism" SL § 181R italics added). See Schmitz, *Hegel als Denker* 98–101.

34. See Hegel's summary description of the structure of syllogism, e.g., GW 12:91.9–15, 125.29/L 2:309, 351 (GL 665, 703); E § 181R with § 192. See also Meulen, *Hegel* 10–11 and Léonard, *Commentaire* 391.

35. E § 192 with §§ 181 and 193. See Krohn, *Die formale Logik* 174–180, esp. 175; Léonard, *Commentaire* 428–429; and an especially well nuanced summary of Hegel's conception of subjectivity in terms of syllogism, Düsing, *Das Problem der Subjektivität* 266–273, 287–288.

36. GW 12:111.9–10/L 2:334 (GL 687). Again, as Hegel here observes, it is the middle term which distinguishes syllogism from judgement. See also GW 12:125.16–19/L 2:351 (GL 703).

37. The intention here is simply to give a taste of Hegel's theory of syllogism. The further detail necessary for a critique of the disjunctive syllogism will be introduced as appropriate where the critique itself is made in Ch. 5 Subsection 3 of the present study.

For an outline of the various syllogisms, see Düsing, *Das Problem der Subjektivität* 274. For more detailed commentary on each of the individual syllogisms, see Krohn, *Die formale Logik* 20–77, 128–173; Léonard, *Commentaire* 398–426; Düsing, *Das Problem der Subjektivität* 273–288.

38. GW 12:125.18/L 2:351 (GL 703). Heede speaks of "types of syllogisms" (*Schlußarten* or *-gattungen*) and "syllogism figures" (*Schlußfiguren*) to distinguish respectively between the wider groupings of syllogisms and the various individual syllogisms, e.g., "Die göttliche Idee" 320–321. Heede remarks that Hegel himself "einen klassifikatorischen 'conceptus communis' beharrlich vermeidet" (309). This is correct if by "classificatory" one understands formalistically classificatory." Hegel did himself speak of "Die verschiedenen Gattungen der Schlüsse." GW 12:125.18/L 2:351 (GL 703). The underlying reason why Hegel would not speak of a formalistic classification of syllogisms is of course that, typical of Hegel's thought, there is finally no underlying thinker thinking these syllogisms. The individual syllogisms themselves are the movement of pure or absolute thought as these specific thought determinations.

39. GW 12:93.3/L 2:311 (GL 667). Or alternatively A-B-E in view of the flexibility in Hegel's handling of extremes. See esp. Ch. 3 nn. 49–51 below.

40. In fact four, but the fourth or mathematical syllogism, A-A-A, where two things equal to a third are equal to one another, does not involve a truly mediating third. See GW 12:104.21–33/L 2:326 (GL 679–680).

41. "hiemit sind die Extreme ebensosehr gegeneinander wie gegen ihre Mitte *gleichgültig für sich* bestehend gesetzt." E § 182 (SL § 182). "In dem Formalen Schlusse wird die Mitte nur dadurch als Totalität gesetzt, daß alle Bestimmtheiten, aber jede *einzeln*, die Function der Vermittlung durchlauffen." GW 12:125.19–21/L 2:351 ("In the formal syllogism the middle term is posited as totality only in such a way that all the determinations, but each *singly*, go through the function of mediation." GL 703 trans. amended). "Au niveau du syllogisme qualitatif, cette totalisation de chaque terme n'est encore qu'une exigence ou un devoir-être dès lors que c'est seulement *séparément* que chaque moment isolé devient successivement moyen-terme et unifie ainsi abstraitement les deux autres ([E] §§ 182 et 189)." Léonard, *Commentaire* 427.

42. GW 12:118.18–19/L 2:343 (GL 695).

43. "Nunmehr ist sie [die Mitte] gesetzt als die *Totalität* der Bestimmungen; so ist sie die *gesetzte* Einheit der Extreme." GW 12:110.32–34/L 2:333 (GL 686 trans. amended). "In den Schlüssen der Reflexion ist die Mitte als die, die Bestimmungen der Extreme *äusserlich* zusammenfassende Einheit." GW 12:125.21–23/L 2:351 ("In the syllogisms of reflection the middle term appears

as the unity that gathers together *externally* the determinations of the extremes." GL 703); see E § 190. "La totalisation qui apparaît dans le syllogisme de la réflexion est déjà plus concrète dans la mesure où chaque moment joue successivement le rôle d'un moyen-terme qui rassemble réflexivement les déterminations des extrêmes ([E] §§ 189b et 190)." Léonard, *Commentaire* 427.

Note that in the *Logic* Hegel speaks rather of the difference between the mediation or the presence of the extremes in the middle term in the syllogisms of *Dasein* and reflection respectively as "posited" (*gesetzt*) GW 12:91.37/L 2:310 (GL 666) and "posited as mediated" (*die [Bestimmungen] als "vermittelte" gesetzt sind*) GW 12:92.3/L 2:310 (GL 666).

44. GW 12:118.20–23/L 2:343 (GL 695).

45. E § 191; GW 12:120.1–2/L 2:345 (GL 697). On the categorical syllogism in general, see E § 191; GW 12:119.13–121.15/L 2:344–346 (GL 696–698). Note that within each of the three genera of syllogism, namely those of *Dasein*, reflection and necessity, the order of the individual syllogism figures, E-B-A, B-E-A (A-E-B), E-A-B (B-A-E) is the same, when the interchangeability of extremes is taken into consideration (on this latter, see Ch. 3 nn. 49–51 below).

46. E § 191; GW 12:123.34–35/L 2:349 (GL 701). On the hypothetical syllogism in general, see E § 191; GW 12:121.16–123.31/L 2:346–349 (GL 698–701).

47. E § 191; GW 12:123.35–36/L 2:349 (GL 701). On the disjunctive syllogism in general, see E § 191; GW 12:123.34–126.11/L 2:349–352 (GL 701–704).

48. "Die Mitte ist aber die *mit der Form erfüllte Allgemeinheit*; sie hat sich als die *Totalität*, als *entwickelte* objektive Allgemeinheit. Der Medius Terminus ist daher sowohl Allgemeinheit, als Besonderheit und Einzelnheit." GW 12:123.36–124.2/L 2:349 (GL 701). Heede conveniently summarizes some of the characteristics of the full Hegelian syllogism, a summary particularly applicable to the syllogism of necessity and especially the disjunctive syllogism: "Ein vollkommener Schluß ist für Hegel eine Beziehung von drei Termen in der Weise, daß jeder Term einmal die anderen beiden Terme mit einander vermittelt." "Die göttliche Idee" 278. See also Léonard, *Commentaire* 425–426.

49. As Hegel observes in discussing judgement in the context of the hypothetical syllogism. GW 12:121.35–122.4/L 2:347 (GL 699).

50. Note Hegel's change of the second formal or qualitative syllogism from B-E-A in the *Logic* to A-E-B in the *Encyclopedia* and the third qualitative syllogism from E-A-B in the *Logic* to B-A-E in the *Encyclopedia*. See Düsing, *Das Problem der Subjektivität* 274–275, and Léonard, *Commentaire* 406 briefly in n. 3.

51. As Theunissen points out, even the *Logic* itself is not totally unified in its disposition of extremes, *Hegels Lehre* 254 n. 84. However as Heede remarks,

"Gelegentlich stellt Hegel auch die Zusatzbedingung, daß jeder Term einmal vorderes und einmal hinteres Extrem sein müsse." "Die göttliche Idee" 278.

The exchange could be made most justifiably in the case of the syllogisms of necessity in view of the various characteristics Hegel attributes to each term and to each mediating moment.

52. Note, for example, how Hegel speaks of the disjunctive syllogism as being "überhaupt in der Bestimmung der *Allgemeinheit*." GW 12:124.39–125.1/ L 2:350 ("in general in the determination of *universality*," GL 702).

53. As Hegel does in a specific formulation concerning revealed religion, E §§ 567–569.

These different points of view and perspectives on the middle terms allow for a reconciliation of Hegel's specific ordering of the syllogisms according to middle terms (B-E-A) with the overall development of his thought (A-B-E). B-E-A provides Hegel's intended immediate structural movement of mediating middle terms. A-B-E provides the global structure of Hegel's thought. In his interpretation of Trinity, Bruaire, *Logique et religion* 60–61, works on the basis of both former and latter ordering and identification of syllogisms. Heede, "Die göttliche Idee" e.g., 314–316, objects, on the basis of the former identification, to Bruaire's interpretation. In this particular instance and in this one question both Bruaire and Heede are correct from their respective points of view, though Bruaire's is more inclusive. Theunissen, whose interpretation is followed in this present study, is dependent on Bruaire, but does a more *Encyclopedia* text oriented exegesis, *Hegels Lehre* 254. Theunissen separates (more clearly than Bruaire does) the presentation of E §§ 567–571 from the question of the relationship between syllogisms of revealed religion and syllogisms of philosophy.

54. An application of Hegel's theory of method. See Ch. 1 Subsection 2 of the present study. And for example in regard to revealed religion, see the expressions used by Hegel in E § 566.

55. Explicitly regarding judgment in Hegel's treatment of revealed religion, E § 568, implicitly concerning the first and third syllogisms in E §§ 567 and 569.

Theunissen recalls that Hegel's ability to link so many points of view is rooted in the fact that Hegel is developing a theory of subjectivity, *Hegels Lehre* 276. It should be added that this is so because Hegel is proposing a theory of subjectivity in which Concept and Subject are ultimately identified.

56. By establishing the mediated within that which mediates Hegel sublates mediation itself, e.g., GW 12:125.13–15/L 2:351 (GL 703), and thus moves from subjectivity to objectivity in the *Logic*, GW 12:125.28, 126.10–11/ L 2:351, 352 (GL 703, 704), and in the *Encyclopedia* to object, E § 193, with all the connotations of independence and otherness in German of object (*Objekt*) vis-à-vis *Gegenstand*. See Léonard, *Commentaire* 430–431. Hegel moves in the

Logic from the disjunctive syllogism's middle term as "objective universality" (*objektive Allgemeinheit*), GW 12:125.11–12/L 2:351 (GL 703), to objectivity. See also briefly on "concrete universality" as Concept, Klaus Düsing, review of *Die formale Logik in Hegels "Wissenschaft der Logik"* by Wolfgang Krohn in *Hegel-Studien* 10 (Bonn: Bouvier, 1975) 328.

57. The intention here is not in any way to touch on all aspects of Hegel's dense summary of revealed religion, but rather only to gather elements of his thought helpful to an overview of the syllogistic structure of Hegel's understanding of "immanent" and "economic" Trinity.

For a summary of the dangers and difficulties in this delicate question of trying to elaborate a syllogistic structure in Hegel's presentations of the absolute, revealed, revelatory religion, and especially on the danger of schematism, see Walter Jaeschke, *Die Religionsphilosophie Hegels* (Darmstadt: Wissenschaftliche Buchgesellschaft, 1983) the last section, 3.6.

58. There are no essential differences concerning the trinitarian structure of revealed religion among the 1817, 1827 and 1830 editions of the *Encyclopedia*.

59. E §§ 564–571. For an overall "exegesis" see Theunissen, *Hegels Lehre* 216–297, which forms the general background for this summary paragraph. Specifically regarding trinitarian syllogistic subjectivity Theunissen is in turn originally dependent on Bruaire, *Logique et religion* esp. 60–61, 83–112. See in Theunissen, e.g., 270 with n. 113, and his remarks on pp. 236 and 254 as interpreted by Heede, "Die göttliche Idee" 309 and by Johannes Heinrichs, *Die Logik der "Phänomenologie des Geistes"* (Bonn: Bouvier, 1974) 453 n. 283. Also on the religion texts in the *Encyclopedia*, see Chapelle, *La théologie et l'église* 84–111 and Splett, *Trinitätslehre* 81–90.

60. "Es liegt wesentlich im Begriff der wahrhaften Religion, d.i. derjenigen, deren Inhalt der absolute Geist ist, da sie *geoffenbart*, und zwar *von Gott* geoffenbart sei." E § 564 (PM § 564 trans. amended).

61. Apparently Hegel was the first so to insist on the currently usually accepted position that any divine revelation must be self-revelation. On Hegel's stance already in the 1807 *Phenomenology* see Ch. 4 n. 34 below.

62. E § 564.

63. "der Form nach ist er [der absolute Geist] zunächst für das subjektive Wissen der Vorstellung." E § 565 (PM § 565 trans. amended).

Recall the earlier remarks on Hegel's proposal of identity of content but difference of form and the two proposed resolutions to the difficulty of such a position, either a dialectical identity of content (Jaeschke) or in fact a change of content (Wagner). See Ch. 1 n. 127 above. In his exegesis of these revealed religion texts Theunissen spends a great deal of time on the question of true content but unfortunately does not directly address the type of identity of content between true religion and philosophy, *Hegels Lehre*. Note also Quentin

Lauer, S.J., "Hegel on the Identity of Content in Religion and Philosophy," in *Essays in Hegelian Dialectic* (New York: Fordham, 1977) 153–168.

On representation in Hegel's thought in general, see Malcolm Clark, *Logic and System. A Study of the Transition from "Vorstellung" to Thought in the Philosophy of Hegel* (The Hague: Nijhoff, 1971) 50–218. More specifically on religious representation see on the *Phenomenology* Ch. 4 n. 121 below and on the philosophy of religion *Lectures* Ch. 5 n. 34 below.

64. E § 565.

65. E § 566.

66. Theunissen, *Hegels Lehre*, incorrectly limits representation (*Vorstellung*) to the second sphere, that of particularity, and speaks of the other two spheres in terms of thought. Rather, Hegel posits the whole movement of revealed religion as occurring in the form of religious representation with the proviso of course that the second sphere is where representation is most properly spoken of.

67. E §§ 567–570.

68. "In dieser Form der Wahrheit ist die Wahrheit der Gegenstand der Philosophie." E § 571 (PM § 571), taken with E § 577.

69. Schmitz, *Hegel als Denker* 99.

70. "Aber das Konkrete ist, daß Gott ein Schluß ist, der sich mit sich selbst zusammenschließt." *Sämtliche Werke. Jubiläumsausgabe in zwanzig Bänden*, ed. Hermann Glockner, vol. 18: *Vorlesungen über die Geschichte der Philosophie*, vol. 2 (Stuttgart: Frommann, 1928) 253 (*Lectures on the History of Philosophy*, trans. E. S. Haldane and F. H. Simson, vol. 2 [New York: Humanities, 1955] 76, but translated from the second Friends edition of 1840. The present trans. is my own) cited by Schmitz, *Hegel als Denker* 99. In the context of a discussion of Plato's philosophy of nature, Hegel is recorded as reflecting on the nature of the syllogism, so that this quote is an expression of his own understanding of God and not merely a remark on Plato's thought. See in the *Jubiläumsausgabe* vol. 18 pp. 252–254 on syllogism, and pp. 248–269 on Plato's philosophy of nature.

In the *Jubiläumsausgabe* Glockner reproduces the generally longer and apparently preferable text of the first edition of Hegel's *Lectures on the History of Philosophy*. See Glockner's remarks, "Vorwort zur Jubiläumsausgabe," in G. W. F. Hegel, *Sämtliche Werke, Jubiläumsausgabe in zwanzig Bänden*, vol. 1: *Aufsätze aus dem kritischen Journal der Philosophie und andere Schriften aus der Jenenser Zeit* (Stuttgart: Frommann, 1927) xi, and vol. 17: *Vorlesungen über die Geschichte der Philosophie*, vol. 1 (Stuttgart: Frommann, 1928) 14. See also Carl Ludwig Michelet, "Vorwort des Herausgebers zur zweiten Ausgabe," in G. W. F. Hegel, *Werke, Vollständige Ausgabe durch einen Verein von Freunden des Verewigten*, second ed., vol. 13: *Vorlesungen über die Geschichte der Philosophie*, ed. Carl Ludwig Michelet (Berlin: Duncker und Humblot, 1840) xvii–xviii.

On texts and the respectful approach used by Michelet in editing these lectures, see Michelet's "Vorwort [des Herausgebers zur ersten Ausgabe]," in *Jubiläumsausgabe*, vol. 17 pp. 1–14. In view of Michelet's remark (9) that the earlier Jena lectures (1805–1806) often presented the briefer and more abstract statement, it might provisionally be argued that the first edition quote here in question might be the older and yet perduring mature lecture view of Hegel on God as syllogism.

71. "Schluß der absoluten Vermittlung mit sich, den drei Schlüsse ausmachen." Review of "Über die hegelsche Lehre oder: absolutes Wissen und moderner Pantheismus," 2. "Über Philosophie überhaupt und Hegels *Enzyklopädie* der philosophischen Wissenschaften insbesondere. Ein Beitrag zur Beurteilung der Letzteren. Von Dr. K. E. Schubarth und Dr. L. Carganico," in *Berliner Schriften 1818–1831*, Philosophische Bibliothek, vol. 240, ed. Johannes Hoffmeister (Hamburg: Felix Meiner, 1956) 352 (my trans.), cited by Schmitz, *Hegel als Denker* 99.

72. E §§ 569–570.

73. E §§ 567–570.

74. "Diese drei Schlüsse, die den einen Schluß der absoluten Vermittlung des Geistes mit sich selbst ausmachen, sind die Offenbarung desselben, welche dessen Leben in der Kreislaufe konkreter Gestalten der Vorstellung explizirt." E § 571 (PM § 571 trans. slightly amended). This reference of Hegel's remains admittedly ambiguous. Depending on the significance and interpretation given the individual words and their context, Hegel could refer first only to the three syllogisms making up the moment of individuality alone, E §§ 569–570, or second, to the movement from universality to particularity to individuality, E §§ 567–570, or third, to both of the above as here opted for. The ambiguity cannot be resolved on the basis of an analysis of E § 571 alone, but must be handled by a consideration of the words in their context as revealed religion's last paragraph, which serves as transition to philosophy. Theunissen, *Hegels Lehre* 291–292, provides a partial clarification in asserting that the transition to philosophy would not be justified if "three syllogisms" did not refer primarily to E §§ 567–570. However, Theunissen does not explicitly enough bring out the interpretational significance of the tri-syllogistic structure of the final moment or sphere, individuality, vis-à-vis the other two spheres. Given the ever-present recapitulative role of the final moment or sphere of individuality in Hegel's thought, any reference to that moment should be interpreted to refer as well to the moments or spheres out of which it arises.

On the other hand, with more sensitivity to text than to overall context and on the basis of "concrete shapes" (*konkreter Gestalten*) and the sentences immediately following this quote in § 571, Heede, "Die göttliche Idee" 270–276, would limit this reference concerning three syllogisms to the last moment of revealed religion, to §§ 569–570. Heede (273) cites Schmitz and Chapelle as being in apparent agreement with him. Upon examination, Schmitz, *Hegel als Denker* 99, does not appear even to recognize the contradiction involved in restricting the reference in E § 571 to E §§ 569–570 while acknowledging Hegel's description of Trinity in terms of syllogism. Over against Bruaire, and by extension Theunissen, Chapelle succinctly presents and defends his position in *La théologie et l'église* 104–105 n. 14. However, in this same volume, p. 90 n. 32, Chapelle indicates his "accord de fond" with Theunissen's emphasis on "la portée de la form syllogistique dans la théologie de *l'Encyclopédie*." It has not been possible for the present writer to check Chapelle's later writings to follow up on this apparent ambiguity (note the reference to "pages" in Chapelle's footnote 32 should be to numbered paragraphs in the *Encyclopedia*). Heede (274) is well aware of Hegel's explicit claims concerning the syllogistic structure of his thought on Trinity, but proposes on the basis of an analysis of the various editions of the *Encyclopedia* to distinguish between what Hegel says (*Rede*) and Hegel's actual working out (*tatsächlicher Struktur des Textes*) of his thought on Trinity. Despite Heede's distinction between Hegel's intention and the factual text, and despite Heede's reference to *konkreter Gestalten*, which could admittedly, if interpreted without full consideration of the overall role of E § 571, be seen to refer only to E §§ 568–570 or to E §§ 569–570 while excluding either the abstract moment of universality in E § 567 or that plus the moment or sphere of particularity in E § 568, Heede gives no finally convincing reason why Hegel could not refer to the last moment or sphere, that of individuality, E §§ 569–570, and through that moment to the trinitarian syllogistic structure of revealed religion as a whole, E §§ 567–570. Both last moment and overall movement are tri-syllogistically structured with the last as recapitulative return from the otherness of particularity to individuality as concrete universality. As Theunissen, *Hegels Lehre* 291–292, points out, each of the three spheres is in its own way already revelation. Finally, Heede's (272–276, 309–319) proposal to limit Hegel's syllogism reference to E §§ 569–570 is too limited a reading of Hegel's observation in the last and therefore hermeneutically important § 571 of the section of the *Encyclopedia* on revealed religion. However, in view of certain contradictions and exaggerations in what Heede identifies as textually unwarranted amplifications on Hegel's text, it is wise to use the more "theologically" oriented syllogistic interpretations and/or extrapolations with care.

Heede's specific treatment of E §§ 566–571 and his negative critique of Bruaire's, Theunissen's and Chapelle's (see texts cited Ch. 3 n. 13 above) syllogistic interpretations of Hegel's presentation of revealed religion can be found in "Die göttliche Idee" 309–319. The points so far made in this introductory overview on syllogism and the corrections and clarifications now to be made concerning the syllogistic interpretations of E §§ 566–571 are made with the intention of rendering the interpretation presented here not susceptible to Heede's specific objections. Heede (313) basically proposed that syllogistic figures (*Schlußfigur*) should not and could not be used to structure and interpret revealed religion in the *Encyclopedia* because (a) that presupposes a false identification of Hegel's reference to syllogism with the three spheres of revealed religion and (b) because of the minimal security with which he felt one could identify the theological content of specific extremes and middle terms.

In any case, the critique of Hegel's explicitly syllogistically structured trinitarian subjectivity is going to be handled in Ch. 5 below in terms of the third or inclusive moment, which Heede himself (272, 276) and commentators in general agree is by Hegel at least generally intentionally syllogistically structured. Unfortunately it is not here possible to summarize further Heede's helpful and detailed discussion of issues and of pertinent literature.

75. E §§ 567–570.
76. Note of course a certain flexibility or variation in the extremes.
77. E §§ 564–566.
78. As mentioned in the course of Ch. 1 Subsection 4 of the present study.
79. GW 12:25.29–33/L 2:231 (GL 592). Note that the transition from Hegel's own expression concerning logic in relation to the concrete sciences and the application here to the relation between specific thought determinations and realizations in the realphilosophical spheres is justified by the characteristic of both thought determinations and of these realizations on the level of religion as "momentary totalities." There remains much research to be done in determining the wider relationship of the *Logic* to the rest of Hegel's work and of the *Encyclopedia* to Hegel's various lecture series.
80. As for example done by Chapelle, who speaks though only of the syllogistic structure of the sphere of individuality (E §§ 569–570). Though Chapelle speaks once (*La théologie et l'église* 95–96) of the wider syllogistic types of *Dasein*, reflection and necessity, he unreflectively employs only the structure and Hegel's discussion of the first three syllogisms of *Dasein*, perhaps because of their exemplary character. See *La théologie et l'église* esp. 95–98, and Albert Chapelle, *Hegel et la religion. Annexes. Les textes théologiques de Hegel* (Paris: Éditions universitaires, 1967) 91–92, 97. Chapelle himself had called for paying *close attention* to the formal structure of *specific* syllogisms, *La théologie et l'église* 95–96 n. 61. To the extent that the syllogisms of *Dasein* are exemplary, Chapelle's analysis remains instructive.
81. As Theunissen does, *Hegels Lehre* e.g., 254, 292. Heede's critique of Theunissen is justified to the extent that Theunissen has employed the wider types of syllogisms rather than the specific syllogisms of necessity. Heede, "Die göttliche Idee" 309. Johannes Heinrichs, *Die Logik* 453 n. 282, briefly provides several reasons for not accepting Theunissen's reference to the syllogisms of

Dasein, reflection and necessity, though he excuses Theunissen's reference to these syllogisms a bit too easily.

82. Generally following Heinrichs, *Die Logik* 452–460, esp. 453 n. 282, who interprets Hegel's thought on "immanent" and "economic" Trinity in the *Phenomenology* as a movement of the three syllogisms of necessity.

Chapelle himself does of course acknowledge each moment or element's serving as totality in the *third* sphere. *La théologie et l'église* 95.

For further discussion of the positions of Falk Wagner, Claude Bruaire and Albert Chapelle, see Heinrichs, 452–453 nn. 281, 282.

83. GW 12:123.36–124.2/L 2:349 (GL 701).

84. See concerning the *Phenomenology* Ch. 4 Subsection 2 of the present study, building on Heinrichs, *Die Logik* 452–560, and concerning the 1827 *Lectures* Ch. 5 Subsections 2a–c of the present study.

85. On Hegel's understanding of universality, particularity and individuality see briefly Ch. 2 n. 110 above.

86. "sich der absolute Inhalt darstellt, a) als in seiner Manifestation bei sich selbst bleibender, ewiger Inhalt." E § 566 (PM § 566 trans. amended).

87. On the categorical syllogism, see texts referred to in Ch. 3 n. 45 above. The more detailed study of the specific characteristics of one determinate syllogism, the disjunctive syllogism, will be more directly handled in the critique in Ch. 5 Subsection 3b of the present study. It will suffice for the present to point out that in the categorical syllogism universality functions as middle term, "—das Allgemeine gesetzt als in sich wesentlich bestimmt. Zunächst ist 1) das Besondre in der Bedeutung der bestimmten *Gattung* oder Art die vermittelnde Bestimmung,—im *kategorischen* Schlusse," E § 191 ("—the universal expressly put as in its very nature intrinsically determinate. In the first place (1) the particular with the meaning of the determinate *genus* or *species* is the mediating determination—in the categorical syllogism." SL § 191 trans. amended). On *bestimmten* (determinate) modifying *Gattung* (genus) rather than *Art* (species), see Léonard, *Commentaire* 423 n. 1.

88. Bruaire, *Logique et religion*, on p. 60 retains the order E-B-A found in the *Logic* and *Encyclopedia* but A-B-E on p. 94. His interpretation on p. 60 would at first sight appear to make clearer the dynamic transition to the sphere of particularity in that the second extreme (A) in the sphere of universality would serve as first extreme in the sphere of particularity. However A-B-E better reflects the actual content as expressed in E § 567 and the structuring role of the first sphere. In addition and more importantly the transition to the second sphere occurs finally on the basis of second extreme in the first sphere becoming not first extreme but middle term in the second sphere. In this way the doubled grounding of the transition to the sphere of particularity is united (the doubled movement being the transition to externalized particularity on the basis both of the self-othering as Son in the sphere of universality and that sphere's third moment or resultant return to immediacy as individuality).

This inversion of extremes to A-B-E is in agreement with the analyses by Theunissen, *Hegels Lehre* 254–255, and by Heinrichs concerning the *Phenomenology*, *Die Logik* 454. Note that Heinrichs (454) warns against the appearance of a *petitio principii* in his use of *Encyclopedia* texts to illuminate briefly the structure of *Phenomenology* texts. In fact, the argumentation here and in Heinrichs is based on the specific texts standing on their own.

89. "in dieser ewigen Sphäre . . . nur *sich selbst* als seinen *Sohn* erzeugt." E § 567 (PM § 567 trans. amended).

90. "sich ewig aufhebt und [da-]durch die erste Substanz wesentlich als *konkrete Einzelheit* und Subjektivität,—der *Geist* ist." E § 567 (PM § 567 trans. amended).

91. E § 568.

92. "als Unterscheidung des ewigen Wesens von seiner Manifestation, welche durch diesen Unterschied die Erscheinungswelt wird, in die der Inhalt tritt." E § 566 (PM § 566 trans. amended). It might be of interest to point out the similarity with Karl Rahner's position concerning creation as necessary condition for the sending of the Son. See Karl Rahner, *The Trinity* (London: Burns and Oates, 1970) 89. On similarities between Hegel and Rahner in general, see Winfried Corduan, "Elements of the Philosophy of G. W. F. Hegel in the Transcendental Method of Karl Rahner" (Ph.D. dissertation, Rice University, 1977).

93. In full agreement with Heinrichs, *Die Logik* 456; in agreement with Theunissen, *Hegels Lehre* 267, in so far as identification of extremes and middle terms (A-E-B) and their general content are concerned. In agreement as well with Bruaire, *Logique et religion* 60, in so far as identification of extremes and middle terms as A-E-B are concerned (note that Bruaire, 101, inverts the extremes in view of his concern to relate the syllogisms of philosophy to those of religion).

On the hypothetical syllogism, see texts referred to in Ch. 3 n. 46 above. Note that in the hypothetical syllogism universality functions as middle term "—das Allgemeine gesetzt als in sich wesentlich bestimmt . . . 2) das *Einzelne* in der Bedeutung des unmittelbaren Seins, daß es ebenso vermittelnd als vermittelt sei,—im *hypothetischen* Schlusse." E § 191 ("—the universal expressly put as in its very nature intrinsically determinate . . . [i.e.] (2) the individual with the meaning of immediate, so that it is as much mediating as mediated,—in the *hypothetical* syllogism." SL § 191 trans. amended).

94. Theunissen, *Hegels Lehre* 272, correctly refers to this as characteristic of the second syllogism of reflection, that of induction. See GW 12:113.16–115.17/L 2:337–339 (GL 689–692). Here, however, Hegel's position is being extended to include individuality as middle term in the hypothetical syllogism.

95. Recall even that "nothing is."

96. "On voit que chaque syllogisme présuppose les autres." Bruaire, *Logique et religion* 60. See also concerning trinitarian syllogisms presupposing

one another especially with reference to E §§ 569–570, Theunissen, *Hegels Lehre* 277.

97. "Dies konkrete ewige Wesen [ist] das Vorausgesetzte." E § 568 (PM § 568).

98. "das Zerfallen . . . des ewigen Sohnes, in den selbständigen Gegensatz, einerseits . . . der . . . konkreten Natur, andererseits . . . des *endlichen Geistes.*" E § 568 (PM § 568 trans. greatly amended). Here the more explicitly representational terms have been cited. They are of course in the text (E § 568) accompanied by Concept-oriented terms and further elaboration.

99. For an excellent discussion of the ambiguities and options allowed by Hegel's text, see Theunissen, *Hegels Lehre*. Ironically, Heede, "Die göttliche Idee" 311, accuses Theunissen of such ambiguities.

100. "und durch seine damit gesetzte eigene Natürlichkeit [der endlichen Geist] ist, in dieser als denkend zugleich auf das Ewige gerichtet." E § 568 (PM § 568 trans. amended).

101. Again, E § 566.

102. E § 569.

103. E §§ 569–570. Note at this point a difference between on the one hand the *Encyclopedia* and on the other hand the *Phenomenology* and *Lectures* from 1824 on concerning the religious representation expressed in the moment of particularity's middle term and second extreme. Here in the *Encyclopedia* explicit reference to Incarnation, death and resurrection of the Mediator is reserved for the moment of individuality (E §§ 569–570), whereas in the *Phenomenology* and *Lectures* such is introduced already in the moment of particularity's middle term and second extreme. In both cases, the syllogistic structure of the moment of particularity (A-E/E-B) remains the same. More generally on the distribution of content in Hegel's variously perspectived "theologies," see Chapelle, *La théologie et l'église* 105–109.

104. "c) als unendliche Rückkehr und Versöhnung der entäußerten Welt mit dem ewigen Wesen, das Zurückgehen desselben aus der Erscheinung in die Einheit seiner Fülle." E § 566 (PM § 566 trans. amended).

105. "c) Im Momente der *Einzelheit* als solcher, nämlich der Subjektivität und des Begriffes selbst, als des in seinen *identischen Grund* zurückgekehrten Gegensatzes der Allgemeinheit und Besonderheit." E § 569 ("c) In the moment of *individuality* as such, namely of subjectivity and of the Concept itself, as the opposition of universality and particularity—an [opposition] having gone back into its *identical ground*" PM § 569 trans. amended).

106. This moment of individuality as absolute Spirit is presupposed by the initial moment of universality or "inner" Trinity. E § 567. Bruaire, *Logique et religion* 60.

107. Similarly, Bruaire, *Logique et religion* 60.

108. Briefly on the triple realization of individuality, each involving respectively the characteristic of Concept, judgement and syllogism in E §§ 569–570, see Theunissen, *Hegels Lehre* 274–276.

109. "als *Voraussetzung* die *allgemeine* Substanz . . . zum *einzelnen* Selbstbewußtsein verwirklicht." E § 569 (PM § 569 trans. amended).

110. "Diese . . . sinnliche Existenz . . . sich in das Urteil setzend und in den Schmerz der *Negativität* ersterbend." E § 569 (PM § 569 trans. amended).

111. "Es [das absolut Konkrete] als unendliche Subjektivität identisch mit sich, . . . als *absolute Rückkehr* . . . *für sich* geworden ist,—die Idee des als ewigen, aber lebendigen und in der Welt gegenwärtigen Geistes." E § 569 (PM § 569 trans. amended).

This syllogism expressed more typically theologically: "C'est d'abord le mouvement de l'Incarnation particulière, de la Mort et de la Résurrection du Fils éternel qui est, en son unicité, principe universel de vérité." Chapelle, *La théologie et l'église* 94. This is explicitly and specifically the syllogism of "redemptive Incarnation." Chapelle, 99.

This delineation of extremes, middle terms and the theological content of E § 569 c/1 is in agreement with that of Chapelle, *La théologie et l'église* 91–92, 94, 96, 99–101, who concerning E §§ 569–570 elaborates in detail minor and major promises and conclusion. See also Chapelle, *Annexes* 91. On the other hand, for a negatively critical summary of Chapelle's position, see Heede, "Die göttliche Idee" 319. This present delineation is also in general agreement with Theunissen, *Hegels Lehre* 277–284, except for his positing this as a syllogism of *Dasein* (277) and except for his unnecessary exchange of extremes (277). In agreement with Bruaire, *Logique et religion* 60 (with inverted extremes indicated p. 104 in view of the syllogism of philosophy), and with Heinrichs, *Die Logik* 457–458. On the basis of the text itself this delineation is in opposition to Heede, who shys away from a syllogistic interpretation of this first realization of the third moment (individuality). "In den beiden ersten Phasen der *dritten Sphäre* ist dann allerdings von der 'Allgemeinheit' und der 'Einzelheit' die Rede, aber wohl kaum als in einem Schluß fungierend." "Die göttliche Idee" 312. Earlier in his study (273) Heede had acknowledged at least the basic syllogistic structure of the three stages of this moment of individuality (see Ch. 3 n. 74 above).

112. "Diese objektive Totalität [die Idee des . . . ewigen, aber . . . gegenwärtigen Geistes] ist die an sich seiende *Voraussetzung* für die *endliche* Unmittelbarkeit des einzelnen Subjekts, für dasselbe . . . ein *Anderes* und *Angeschautes*, aber die Anschauung der an *sich* seienden Wahrheit." E § 570 (PM § 570 trans. amended).

113. Individuality or the individual of course taken to be the multiplicity of individuals characteristic of finite individuality and appropriate to the middle term in the hypothetical syllogism.

114. "Es wegen seiner unmittelbaren Natur zunächst sich für sich als das Nichtige und Böse bestimmt, und weiter nach dem Beispiel seiner Wahrheit, vermittelst des Glaubens auch die Bewegung ist, seiner unmittelbaren Naturbestimmtheit . . . sich zu entäußern und . . . in dem Schmerze der Negativität sich zusammenzuschließen." E § 570 (PM § 570 trans. amended).

115. "so als vereint mit dem Wesen sich zu erkennen," E § 570 (PM § 570 trans. amended).

This syllogism expressed more typically theologically: "La vérité de sa [du Fils incarné] transfiguration en gloire se manifeste dans l'abnégation croyante qui identifie négativement ses fidèles à son Unicité spirituelle." Chapelle, *La théologie et l'église* 94. This is "le syllogisme de la vie chrétienne," Chapelle, 99.

This delineation of extremes, middle terms and theological content of them in E § 570 c/2 is in agreement with that of Chapelle, *La théologie et l'église* 92, 94, 96–97, 99–101, who elaborates major and minor premises and conclusion. See also Chapelle, *Annexes* 92. In *general* agreement also with Theunissen, *Hegels Lehre* 284–287, except for his positing of this as a syllogism of reflection (277, 285). On Bruaire Ch. 3 n. 116 immediately below.

116. Bruaire, *Logique et religion* 60, introduces elements (e.g., *Église universelle*) from the third syllogism of the moment of individuality in order to characterize this moment as universality and thus establish the overall syllogism B-A-E (the third syllogism in the third figure) for the moment of individuality as a whole. In a sense this characterization is permissible in that it is the movement of concrete universality which occurs in and through finite individuals. Nevertheless, it seemed textually speaking preferable here to reserve the realization of the disjunctive syllogism for E § 570 c/3 and not try to take a final position concerning the identification of E §§ 569–570 as a whole likewise as a specifically disjunctive syllogism with the attendant difficulty of trying to reconcile the overall determining middle term of individuality with disjunctive syllogism's requirement of universality as determining middle term. A similar difficulty would arise with regard to E § 570 c/3. However, in the *Phenomenology* (see Ch. 4 Subsection 2 of the present study) and in the 1827 *Lectures* (see Ch. 5 Subsection 2c of the present study) the overall third moment is constructed as a disjunctive syllogism.

117. Concerning the disjunctive syllogism see Ch. 3 n. 47 above. Also Theunissen, *Hegels Lehre* 276–277, 287–288.

118. "durch diese Vermittlung." E § 570 (PM § 570).

119. "welches [Wesen] . . . sich als inwohnend im Selbstbewußtsein bewirkt." E § 570 (PM § 570).

120. "welches [Wesen] . . . die wirkliche Gegenwärtigkeit des an and für sich seienden Geistes als des allgemeinen ist." E § 570 (PM § 570 trans. amended).

This delineation of extremes, middle term and their theological content in E § 570 c/3 is in agreement with that of Chapelle, *La théologie et l'église* 93, 94, 97, 99–101, who elaborates major and minor premises and conclusion. See also, Chapelle, *Annexes* 92. In *general* agreement also with Theunissen, *Hegels Lehre* 287–290.

121. This syllogism expressed more typically theologically: "Il [l'Esprit] se révèle par-là comme l'Universel concret et le lien substantiel de la communauté où la conscience finie se trouve unie à la subjectivité de l'Esprit." Chapelle, *La théologie et l'église* 94. This is "le syllogisme de la Communauté." Chapelle 99. This specific identification of the last moment as properly and explicitly "syllogism of community" does not of course militate against interpreting the whole of Hegel's philosophy of religion as a philosophy of community, as done by Trutz Rendtorff, *Kirche and Theologie. Die systematische Funktion des Kirchenbegriffs in der neueren Theologie* (Gütersloh: Mohn, 1966) 63–113.

122. At this point since it is a question of concrete universality as totality, the overall characterization could equally be that of individuality, as in Bruaire, *Logique et religion* 61, though Bruaire unnecessarily and incorrectly introduces a reference to the historical ("au terme de l'histoire"). In the sense of universality as individuality, this study's interpretation is also in agreement with Heinrichs, *Die Logik* 457–458.

123. Implicit in the sense that the syllogistic structure has not yet been developed as it will be in Hegel's explicitation of the simple content of the revelatory religion as "immanent" and "economic" Trinity. Implicit as well in as incarnational immediacy thus constitutes the condition for the possibility of the development of Trinity as available to religious consciousness for Hegel in the *Phenomenology*.

Recall that in the *Encyclopedia* Hegel refers to the perception of the "finite" Subject in question as "die Anschauung der *an sich* seienden Wahrheit." E § 570 ("the intuition of truth existing *in itself*" PM § 570 trans. amended).

At the end of this encyclopedic overview it is helpful to recall that working with Hegel's *Encyclopedia* presentation of "immanent" and "economic" Trinity in the realphilosophical spheres does not mean that there are not significant differences as to the way in which Hegel "distributes" the representational content of revelatory, revealed, absolute and consummate religion in the *Phenomenology*, the *Encyclopedia* and the philosophy of religion *Lectures*. There are even shifts in distribution of theological content between the 1821 and later lectures (see overall Ch. 5 of the present study). Furthermore, as Falk Wagner in *Der Gedanke der Persönlichkeit Gottes bei Fichte and Hegel* (Gütersloh: Mohn, 1971) 202, indicates, whereas in the *Phenomenology* religion and religious representation function to elevate the natural consciousness to the point of view of absolute knowledge, in the *Lectures* religion and religious representation (*Vorstellung*) are treated more positively as vehicle in their own right making truth available to all (see E § 573R, cited by Wagner, 202). Nevertheless, there is first of all from 1807 on a sufficient overall coherence to Hegel's distinction between logic and realphilosophical spheres and to his understanding of the role of logical thought determinations as "structuring" the realizations of the realphilosophical spheres to posit a valid encyclopedic overview of the syllogistic structure of Hegel's realphilosophical trinitarian thought. In addition, that syllogistic structure itself remains surprisingly consistent from 1807 to 1831. Wagner's (287–288) positing of a more radical distinction between the *Phenomenology* as representing a God coming to Self first in human self-consciousness and the *Encyclopedia* and *Lectures* as presenting a God now tri-personal and therefore eternal self-consciousness would not, even if so radically accepted, obviate the common syllogistic structure of Hegel's realphilosophical trinitarian thought. In fact the consistent underlying syllogistic structures would militate against Wagner's more radical dichotomy between *Phenomenology* and *Lectures*. (In a more general way the exaggerated distinction Wagner makes was brought to this writer's attention in a letter from Walter Jaeschke, May 12, 1981.)

124. These Subsections 3 and 4 in this present Ch. 3 are more directly dependent on the following recommended studies. For an overview of Trinity in the *Phenomenology*, Splett, *Trinitätslehre* 52–72. For information concerning the *Phenomenology's* composition and history of interpretation, see the following articles by Otto Pöggeler: "Zur Deutung der *Phänomenologie des Geistes*," in *Hegel-Studien* 1 (Bonn: Bouvier, 1961) 255–294; "Die Komposition der *Phänomenologie des Geistes*," in *Hegel-Tage Royaumont 1964, Hegel-Studien*, Beiheft 3, ed. Hans-Georg Gadamer (Bonn: Bouvier, 1966) 27–74; "Hegels Phänomenologie des Selbstbewußtseins," in Otto Pöggeler, *Hegels Idee einer Phänomenologie des Geistes* (Munich: Alber, 1973) 231–298. Concerning the overall structural unity of the *Phenomenology*, Labarrière, *Structures et mouvement*. Especially on the Preface and Introduction, Werner Marx, *Hegel's "Phenomenology of Spirit." Its Point and Purpose—A Commentary on the Preface and Introduction* (New York: Harper, 1975). For an analysis of the *Phenomenology* chapter on religion and in particular on the revelatory or Christian religion as well as concerning the significance of this chapter on religion for the *Phenomenology* as a whole, Francis Guibal, *Dieu selon Hegel. Essai sur la problématique de la "Phénoménologie de l'Esprit"* (Paris: Aubier-Montaigne, 1975). On the logical dynamic underlying Hegel's explicit remarks as well as regarding all the aspects mentioned so far here in this footnote, Johannes Heinrichs, *Die Logik*.

Important studies on the *Phenomenology* are gathered in the following more specific bibliographies: for older works of this century, Jean Hyppolite, *Genèse et structure de la "Phénoménologie de l'Esprit" de Hegel* (Paris: Montaigne, 1946) 586–587; Hans Friedrich Fulda and Dieter Henrich, eds., *Materialien zu Hegels "Phänomenologie des Geistes"* (Frankfurt am Main: Suhrkamp, 1973)

429–433; Walter Kern, S.J., "(Neue) Hegel-Bücher. 1961–1971. Register," *Theologie und Philosophie* 51 (1976) 568, where reference is made to books reviewed by Kern over a number of years; Otto Pöggeler, ed., *Hegel. Einführung in seine Philosophie* (Munich: Alber, 1977) 180–181; for several English works, Robert E. Innis, "Reading Hegel Rightly: A Review Discussion of Some Recent Hegelians," *The New Scholasticism* 52 (1978) 110–129; on the history of French Hegelian scholarship with special emphasis on the *Phenomenology*, see John Heckman, "Introduction," in Jean Hyppolite, *Genesis and Structure of Hegel's "Phenomenology of Spirit,"* trans. Samuel Cherniak and John Heckman (Evanston: Northwestern, 1974) xv–xli. Entries in these bibliographies in turn contain almost innumerable further references.

125. Less strongly stated by Labarrière, *Structures et mouvement* 27–28 n. 32 and p. 145. See also Guibal, *Dieu Selon Hegel* 23; Heinrichs, *Die Logik* 495, 502; and, despite his dependence on Haering's outmoded theory of the *Phenomenology* as a divided or broken work, Meulen, *Hegel* 289–293 (see also Ch. 3 n. 128 below).

126. "Wissenschaft der Erfahrung des Bewußtseyns." GW 9:61.29–30 (*Phen.* 56).

127. "Dies Werden der *Wissenschaft* überhaupt oder des *Wissens* ist es, was diese *Phänomenologie* des Geistes darstellt. Das Wissen, wie es zuerst ist, oder der *unmittelbare Geist* ist das Geistlose, das *sinnliche Bewußtsein*. Um zum eigentlichen Wissen zu werden, oder das Element der Wissenschaft, das ihr reiner Begriff selbst ist, zu erzeugen, hat es durch einen langen Weg sich hindurch zu arbeiten." GW 9:24.1–6, but quoted according to the text eliminating the reference to "first part of the system" in *Phän.* 26 (*Phen.* 15).

128. Though Hegel speaks of absolute knowledge arguably as "figure of consciousness" (*Gestalt des Bewußtseyns*) GW 9:423.6–9 (*Phen.* 480), and clearly as "figure of Spirit" (*Gestalt des Geistes*), GW 9:427.28–31 (*Phen.* 485), it is a figure *sui generis*: the final inclusive figure no longer characterized by opposition.

Already in the Introduction Hegel spoke of both a "science of the experience of consciousness" (*Wissenschaft der Erfahrung des Bewußtseyns*) and of a "science of Spirit" (*Wissenschaft des Geistes*) GW 9:61.29–30, 62.4 (*Phen.* 56, 57).

In opposition to Haering's now classic positing of an internal contradiction in the *Phenomenology* (see also Heinrichs, *Die Logik* 502), Labarrière argues in *Structures et mouvement* 48–63 generally convincingly by an analysis of various parallel references in the *Phenomenology* to basic underlying logical structures founding the *Phenomenology*'s fundamental unity as a written work (17–21, explicitly 20–21, 28–30). This position and way of approaching the *Phenomenology* have been accepted as valid and built upon in their own way by Puntel, *Darstellung*; Guibal, *Dieu selon Hegel* 16, 18, 43 n. 1; Heinrichs, *Die Logik* 78–79 with n. 55, whose logico-systematic approach is generally compatible with Labarrière's structural approach.

As André Léonard observes, "Avec un peu plus de nuances, c'est aussi la position [Haering's] de Pöggeler, suivant lequel le projet hégélien s'est modifié en cours de route et a emporté Hegel au delà de ce qu'il visait à l'origine, au point que la petite 'science de l'expérience de la conscience' qui devait précéder les cours de logique et de métaphysique serait devenue progressivement l'immense 'phénoménologie de l'esprit' que nous connaissons aujourd'hui.

"Les récents travaux de Labarrière et de Heinrichs renversent ces interprétations hâtive et, par des voies différentes, rétablissent l'unité du project systématique de Hegel." "Pour une exégèse renouvelée de la *Phénomélogie de l'Esprit* de Hegel," *Revue Philosophique de Louvain* 74 (1976) 574. Again concerning Labarrière, without effectively denying his major contribution in arguing to the *Phenomenology*'s basic unity, Wim van Dooren does raise important questions especially concerning religious presuppositions possibly leading to an exaggeration of the role of religion in the *Phenomenology*. For such hesitations concerning Labarrière's philological study see Wim van Dooren's "Zwei Methoden, die *Phänomenologie des Geistes* zu interpretieren," in *Hegel-Studien* 7 (Bonn: Bouvier, 1972) 298–301.

Though Labarrière's position, and that of the others here cited arguing to the real resultant unity which is the *Phenomenology*, is accepted here in this chapter, Pöggeler's work still performs the continuing valuable function of recalling the real roughness and ambiguities, the developmental character, of Hegel's "first systematic work."

Approaching the question similarly to Pöggeler (that is, historically, for references see Ch. 3 n. 124 above), but arguing against a basic shift (*keine umfassende Änderung*) not just in the finished work but in Hegel's original intention concerning the *Phenomenology*, Johann Heinrich Trede, "Phänomenologie und Logik. Zu den Grundlagen einer Diskussion," in *Hegel-Studien* 10 (Bonn: Bouvier, 1975) 173–194, esp. 194.

Werner Marx argues independently to a unified work on the basis of an examination of the *Phenomenology*'s Introduction and Preface. *Hegel's Phenomenology* xii, 53, 62–64. W. Marx rightly concludes (98) that the principle, "self-consciousness," with Self as conceptual in nature is the "idea" unifying the *Phenomenology*. However, it would be better to mention explicitly "absolute self-consciousness" in view of the Preface.

To the question of internal unity belong also the difficulties surrounding Hegel's change of title and double subdivision of the text. For a very brief summary of a number of the now classical interpretations of unity and/or diversity of the *Phenomenology*, see Henri Niel, *De la médiation dans la philosophie de Hegel* (Paris: Aubier-Montaigne, 1945) 111–112.

Finally, note also Hegel's own logical interpretation of the *Phenomenology*'s movement as a whole, GW 9:422.29–428.3 (*Phen.* 480–486).

129. Heinrichs, *Die Logik* 463.

130. See Labarrière, *Structures et mouvement* 13, 265–266. On the geometrical increase in length of the *Phenomenology*'s subdivisions in the course of its composition see Pöggeler, "Die Komposition" 31.

Among the *Phenomenology*'s characteristics as a "first work" its handling of negativity as yet in various forms and not radically sublated into the logical category of *das Nichts* (see on several forms of negativity in the *Phenomenology*, Howard P. Kainz, *Hegel's "Phenomenology," Part I: Analysis and Commentary* [University, Alabama: The University of Alabama Press, 1976]); its being Hegel's most "personal" text, i.e., the one making most easily available the route of Hegel's intellectual journey (Labarrière, *Structures et mouvement* 28); its complexity; its attempt to accomplish too much in one work by at least in principle referring to the totality of the history of consciousness; its many ambiguities as witnessed to by the history of its interpretation; the brilliance and availability of insights developed by other, later thinkers; perhaps exaggerated statement of distinctions such as the difference between religion and philosophy and the question of the more passing nature of religion.

131. Pöggeler writes concerning Hegel's own situation and remarks, "Die Ruhe und Muße zur Ausarbeitung, die SCHELLING dem Freund [Hegel] gewünscht hatte, waren ausgeblieben. Hegel entschuldigte sich: das Werk bedürfe noch mannifacher Überarbeitung; was die 'größere Unform der letztem Partien' betreffe, so möge der Freund ihm zugutehalten, daß er, Hegel, die Redaktion 'in der Mitternacht vor der schlacht bei Jene geendigt habe.'" "Zur Deutung der *Phänomenologie*" 255, where Pöggeler refers to letters between Hegel and Schelling, *Briefe von und an Hegel*, vol. 1, ed. Johannes Hoffmeister (Hamburg: Felix Meiner, 1952) 132, 134, 161. In Pöggeler's article see also pp. 271–292.

132. Along this line see Wolfgang Bonseipen, *Der Begriff der Negativität in der jenaer Schrifte Hegels*, *Hegel-Studien*, Beiheft 16 (Bonn: Bouvier, 1977) 14 with 18, 182. On the concepts of "negation" and of "negativity" in the *Phenomenology* see Bonsiepen, 127–192, with important references from the *Phenomenology* cited 201–204. For an exhaustive listing of various forms of negation and the negative, see the appropriate terms listed in Joseph Gauvin, *Wortindex zu Hegels "Phänomenologie des Geistes," Hegel-Studien*, Beiheft 14 (Bonn: Bouvier, 1977). The *Wortindex* is referred to in this chapter by *Formnummer* (Form number).

See also Alexandre Kojève, *Introduction à la lecture de Hegel. Leçons sur la "phénoménologie de l'esprit"* (Paris: Aubier, 1946), cited along with Karl Marx by Wolfgang Bonsiepen, "Phänomenologie des Geistes," in Hegel, *Einführung in seine Philosophie*, ed. Otto Pöggeler (Munich: Alber, 1977) 60.

On the unfinished character in general of Hegel's writing on negativity, see Ch. 2 n. 60 above. Also, W. Ver Eecke's brief article cited there, "Zur Negativität bei Hegel," in *Hegel-Studien* 4 (Bonn: Bouvier, 1967) 215–218.

133. In agreement with Heinrichs, *Die Logik* 452 with n. 281, where Heinrichs disagrees with the position that Hegel had first to work out his concept of the individual in the *Logic*. This latter position is taken by Wagner, *Der Gedanke* 259, cited by Heinrichs. Heinrichs also speaks then of a "breakthrough" (*Durchbruch*) text (468 and see also 475). Particularly concerning syllogism: "In der 'Phänomenologie' finden wir den Schluß zu seinen dialektisch-spekulativen Form und Bedeutung ausgereift." Schmitz, *Hegel als Denker* 138, and on the history of the development of Hegel's understanding of syllogism up to the *Phenomenology*, Schmitz, 118–138; on the concept and significance of syllogism in Hegel's thought in general, Schmitz, 94–103. Note Hegel's reference to syllogism in GW 9:423.1–5 (*Phen.* 480).

134. In this sense Hegel's famous dictum, "Es kommt nach Felix Meiner Einsicht, . . . , alles darauf an, das Wahre nicht als *Substanz*, sondern eben so sehr als *Subjekt* aufzufassen und auszudrücken." GW 9:18.3–5 ("In my view, . . . , everything turns on grasping and expressing the True, not only as *Substance*, but equally as *Subject*." *Phen.* 9–10). Rudolf Haym's observation, quoted by Walter Kaufmann, *Hegel: A Reinterpretation* (New York: Doubleday, 1965) 1, can also be interpreted in this direction: "It is not saying too much when I claim that anyone understands Hegel's philosophy if he completely masters the meaning of this preface."

See also Klaus Düsing, *Das Problem der Subjektivität in Hegels Logik* with subtitle *Systematische und entwicklungsgeschichtliche Untersuchungen zum Prinzip des Idealismus und zur Dialektik* e.g., 205–208 with references to Hegel, and 201, 202 with n. 149 citing *Phän.* 20, 22 (*Phen.* 10, 12); Heinrichs, *Die Logik* 453, 461–468, esp. 467.

135. E.g., GW 9:20.11–25, 430.29–31 (*Phen.* 12, 489). See Bonsiepen, *Der Begriff der Negativität* 124, 176–177, 182, 194; on the new triadic and tetradic structure, Heinrichs, *Die Logik* 463, 495, 498–499 and 495 on Hegel's "Durchbruch zur dreigliedrigen Logik" (in the *Phenomenology* as well as in the contemporaneous lectures of 1805–1806), 498.

136. Niel, *De la médiation* 112–114.

137. See Ch. 1 Subsection 2 of the present study. See also Heinrichs, *Die Logik* 35–36.

138. "Das Nichts ist aber nur, genommen als das Nichts dessen, woraus es herkömmt, in der That das wahrhafte Resultat; es ist hiemit selbst ein *bestimmtes* und hat einen *Inhalt*. . . . Indem . . . das Resultat, wie es in Wahrheit ist, aufgefaßt wird, als *bestimmte* Negation, so ist damit unmittelbare eine neue Form entsprungen." GW 9:57.9–16 (*Phen.* 51 trans. amended).

139. Hindering in the sense of inhibiting as well as facilitating progression to absolute knowledge. Representation in the *Phenomenology* hinders even while at the same time being the very means of transition to absolute knowledge.

On the presence of true content in revelatory religion, GW 9:408.17–29, 418.16–421.18, esp. 420.9–421.18, 427.18–27 (*Phen.* 463, 475–478, esp. 477–478, 485).

140. Incarnation beginning with GW 9:403.17 (*Phen.* 457). Note, Guibal, *Dieu selon Hegel* 119, and Heinrichs, *Die Logik* 445, agree on where this treatment begins in Hegel, but differ as to further subdividing.

On Trinity, GW 9:409.37–421.18 (*Phen.* 464–478). Again here Guibal and Heinrichs divide the passages somewhat differently.

141. "Diese letzte Gestalt des Geistes, der Geist, der seinem vollständigen und wahren Inhalte zugleich die Form des Selbsts gibt, und dadurch seinen Begriff ebenso realisiert, als er in dieser Realisierung in seinem Begriffe bleibt, ist das absolute Wissen; es ist der sich in Geistgestalt wissende Geist oder das *begreifende Wissen*." GW 9:427.28–31 (*Phen.* 485 trans. amended).

142. See the beginning of Ch. 1 of the present study with references to Günter Rohrmoser in Ch. 1 n. 2 above.

143. Pöggeler writes, "Unter Hegels Büchern ist die *Phänomenologie* dasjenige, welches zum wirkungsmächtigsten, berümtesten, und umstrittensten der Hegelschen Werke geworden ist—zwar noch nicht zu Hegels Lebzeiten, aber doch in den Jahrzehnten nach seinem Tode und dann wieder in unserem Jahrhundert." "Hegels Phänomenologie des Selbstbewußtseins" 231.

144. Regarding the *Phenomenology*'s systematic development against the background of Hegel's earlier works, see the specific studies by Bonsiepen, *Der Begriff der Negativität*, and by Düsing, *Das Problem der Subjektivität*. As point of entry into the discussion concerning the *Phenomenology*'s historic-societal origins, see Rohrmoser, *Subjektivität und Verdinglichung* esp. 107–114. On the history of the *Phenomenology*'s composition, Hyppolite, *Genèse et structure* esp. 54–62; Pöggeler, "Die Komposition" esp. 35–62; with emphasis on the history of the *Phenomenology*'s printing, Bonsiepen and Heede, "Editorische Bericht" 456–464. On the unity of the *Phenomenology* see also Ch. 3 n. 128 above.

145. For an overview, Bonsiepen, *Der Begriff der Negativität* 127–135; W. Marx, *Hegel's Phenomenology* xvii–xxiii.

146. To enter into the question of the *Phenomenology* both as part of the System and as preparation for scientific or philosophical knowledge, one could well begin with Fulda, *Das Problem einer Einleitung* 79–115, cited by Düsing, *Das Problem der Subjektivität* 208 n. 176. See also Labarrière, *Structures et mouvement* 19–21, 35, 250–255; for the specific position taken by Puntel, *Darstellung*, see Ch. 1 n. 14 above; and especially Heinrichs, *Die Logik* 71–76, whose position particularly regarding the relationship of the *Phenomenology* to Hegel's understanding of logic in 1805–1806 is referred to in Ch. 3 n. 158 below.

147. For literature see Ch. 3 n. 128 above.

148. Rohrmoser, *Subjektivität and Verdinglichung*, provides excellent sketches of three partial and therefore inadequate interpretations. Hegel's phenomenological dialectic is not reducible to: the total societal processes of production—Lukács (101–102); the dynamic between *Herrschaft* and *Knechtschaft*, a historical dialectic reaching its climax in the Napoleonic universal state and ending in atheism—Kojève (102–105); the liberation of thought from the dominance of metaphysics by way of an abstraction from the historico-societal origins of the *Phenomenology*'s interests (despite the real value of seeing the abstract one-sidedness of a consciousness embraced by Lukács and Kojève)—Heidegger (105–106). See also Rohrmoser's summary remarks on these three thinkers (107–108). Pöggeler provides an overview of the history of attempts to understand the *Phenomenology*, "Zur Deutung der *Phänomenologie*" esp. 256–271 and "Die Komposition" 31–35; also briefly, Bonsiepen, "Phänomenologie des Geistes" 59–62. On the basically false distinction between Hegel as living thinker of the *Phenomenology* and systematician see Heinrichs, *Die Logik* 515–517 with n. 325.

149. Starting already with Hegel's own *Selbstanzeige* or published announcement, GW 9:446.2–447.6, in late Fall, 1807. See Bonsiepen, "Phänomenologie des Geistes" 59, 72–74; schematically, Heinrichs, *Die Logik* 510.

150. Recall again that "realphilosophical" refers to all Hegel's systematic philosophical texts other than the *Logic*.

151. Note the general methodological dependence on Pöggeler, Labarrière, W. Marx and Heinrichs, all cited Ch. 3 n. 124 above. See esp. Heinrichs, *Die Logik* 4. Splett, *Trinitätslehre* 52 with 56 and n. 76, on the other hand treats the *Phenomenology* additionally in relation to Hegel's later *Geistesphilosophie*.

152. See briefly Bonsiepen, "Phänomenologie des Geistes" 74.

153. "Eigentümliche frühere Arbeit, nicht Umarbeiten,—auf die damalige Zeit der Abfassung bezüglich—in Vorrede: *das abstrakte Absolute* herrschte damals." GW 9:448.11–14, found also in Johannes Hoffmeister, "Zur Feststellung des Textes," in *Phän.* 578. On preparations for a second edition, see GW 9:472–478.

Referring to the *Phenomenology* as a first systematic work and first love indicates Hegel's long-range attitude to it and is not meant to downplay the *Phenomenology*'s intrinsic philosophical significance as stressed by Labarrière, *Structures et mouvement* 265–266.

154. See Ch. 1 Subsection 4 of the present study.

155. See Ch. 2 Subsection 4 of the present study.

156. Note already in the *Phenomenology*'s last chapter, "das Selbst führt das Leben des absoluten Geistes durch." GW 9:426.19–20 ("the Self accomplishes the life of absolute Spirit." *Phen.* 484). In the Preface see GW 9:24.1–6 (*Phen.* 15).

157. Heinrichs, *Die Logik* 61 citing GW 9:29.14–17, 432.25–27 (*Phen.* 21, 491).

158. Labarrière, *Structures et mouvement* 250–255, and Heinrichs, *Die Logik* 58–62, both with references. In discussing absolute knowledge Hegel writes, "Umgekehrt entspricht jedem abstrakten Momente der Wissenschaft eine Gestalt des erscheinenden Geistes überhaupt." GW 9:432.23–25 ("Conversely, to each abstract moment of Science corresponds a shape of manifest Spirit as such." *Phen.* 491).

On the basis of his structural analysis Labarrière speaks of and restricts his remarks to "une correspondence de principe entre les moments divers de la *Phénoménologie* et ceux de la *Logique*" (250). On the basis of his speculative-logical analysis Heinrichs speaks of and carries through a study of the correspondence between specific logical moments and shapes of consciousness (for specific *Phenomenology* quotes see Heinrichs, 59 with n. 41).

On the problematic surrounding the discussion of the relation between logic and phenomenology prior to Heinrichs's study, see Johann Heinrich Trede, "Phänomenologie and Logik, zu den Grundlagen einer Diskussion," in *Hegel-Studien* 10 (Bonn: Bouvier, 1975) 195–209. For a generally negative critique of Heinrichs's book, see Johann Heinrich Trede's review article, "Die endgültige Lösung einer Diskussion?" in *Hegel-Studien* 11 (Bonn: Bouvier, 1976) 228–234. For a very positive reception of Heinrichs's work, Léonard, "Pour une exégèse renouvelée" 572–593. Léonard stresses the value of Heinrichs's proposal to interpret the *Phenomenology* on the basis of its logical structures as they appear in Hegel's logic of 1805–1806 and then modified in the course of the *Phenomenology's* being written. Trede stresses Heinrichs' emphasis on the logic of 1805–1806 as underlying structural framework. He sees Heinrichs as not taking adequately into consideration the development of Hegel's logic during the writing of the *Phenomenology* itself, although Trede does mention (233 citing Heinrichs, 493ff) Heinrichs's acknowledgement of a new conception of logic over against that by Hegel of 1804–1805. In fact Heinrichs takes both aspects (relation to the then current logic of Hegel's and development beyond it) into consideration (461–468, 495, 497–498, 515). Heinrichs's insistence on the *Phenomenology's* dependence on Hegel's 1804–1805 logic and metaphysics for its basic logical structuring coupled with Heinrichs's (e.g., 406–407) added insistence on Hegel's development beyond them would appear to remain quite valid. However Heinrichs's tentative statements especially early in the book are not formulated so as to emphasize development (for an example of such formulations see Heinrichs, 103). Heinrichs's analyses and conclusions are more precise than his initial thesis formulations or hypotheses.

For an English overview of Heinrichs's argument that the logical categories of Hegel's 1805–1806 logic and modifications thereof are concretized in the *Phenomenology*'s shapes of consciousness, see William Maker, Review of *Die Logik der "Phänomenologie des Geistes"* by Johannes Heinrichs, *The Owl of Minerva* 9 (June 1978) 2–3. Maker's brief critique (5) that Heinrichs's thesis presupposes Hegel's logical forms to be empty over against content fails to distinguish between the realm of pure thought in which form and content are truly the same and the realization of these logical forms in the "realphilosophical" spheres, where it is fully Hegelian and appropriate to speak of self-realization or self-concretization of the Concept. See then Heinrichs, *Die Logik* 61, 85, 517, and GW 9:432.23–30 (*Phen.* 491).

Unfortunately Heinrichs's fine study of Hegel's thought is marred by his interpreting of the immanent and consistent dialectical development of pure thought in the *Logic* as a dialogical relationship between knowing and intuition. See Heinrichs, 65–76 esp. 68. Such a position grounds Heinrichs's argument that *at the time* of the *Phenomenology*'s writing Hegel held to the equally originary character of *Phenomenology* and *Logic* (73) and (73–74 n. 51) against Puntel's positing of several equally originary presentations of the whole by Hegel. See on Puntel Ch. 1 n. 14 above.

159. GW 9:61.18–30 (*Phen.* 56). On the various points of view or instances of consciousness in the *Phenomenology*, see Ch. 3 Subsection 4a of the present study.

160. GW 9:61.31–37 (*Phen.* 56). See W. Marx, *Hegel's Phenomenology* esp. pp. 67–69, but also 3 with pp. 5–6 n. 2 and Hermann Schmitz's article cited there, "Der Gestaltbegriff in Hegels *Phänomenologie* [sic] *des Geistes* und seine geistesgeschichtliche Bedeutung," in *Gestaltprobleme der Dichtung. Festschrift für Günther Müller* (Bonn: Bouvier, 1957) 315–334; Labarrière, *Structures et mouvement* 41–44; Heinrichs, *Die Logik* 61.

161. For an exhaustive counting of Hegel's use of the various forms of *Moment* in the *Phenomenology*, see Gauvin, *Wortindex*, form numbers 5815–5818.

162. See already in the Introduction GW 9:61.31–37 (*Phen.* 56) and then in the Preface arguably concerning the *Phenomenology* GW 9:24.1–12 (*Phen.* 15–16); also GW 9:427.23–27 (*Phen.* 485).

Totalisations successives is Labarrière's expression. He continues, "chacune des figures, dans sa singularité propre, est l'expression du mouvement universel dans une structure particulière, et sa relation aux autres figures est commandée par cette résurgence en elles du sens unitare qui la constitue elle-même comme figure determinée." *Structures et mouvement* 65, further 43. Heinrichs, *Die Logik* 102–103 with n. 70, adapts this term in his own way as well. In this present study all figures are considered "successive totalisations."

163. See Ch. 1 Subsection 1 of the present study. Prof. John N. Findlay recalls that Hegel borrowed the term *Moment* from mechanics (Lecture, "Hegel Colloquium. Hegel as Theologian," April 9, 1980, Boston University).

164. Broadly speaking, here "content" refers to "what is thought" and "form" to "the way in which content is thought." See explicitly GW 9:432.14–19 (*Phen.* 491).

165. E.g., GW 9:427.28–31 (*Phen.* 485); see also GW 9:425.18–22 (*Phen.* 483).

166. On Hegel's attitude in 1812 see Ch. 1 n. 30 above. In the quote cited there Hegel speaks of the "opposition of consciousness" (*Gegensatz des Bewußtseyns*). See also GW 11:24.38–25.17/L 1:35–36 (GL 53–54).

167. See Labarrière, *Structures et mouvement* 49. After the *Phenomenology* itself Hegel begins more clearly to distinguish between Self, subjectivity (logic) and absolute Spirit (philosophy), with Subject or subjectivity being the structuring of Selfhood and absolute Spirit its realization and thereby final inclusive totality. Both occur in and through the finite Self and in its sublation. See further W. Marx, *Hegel's "Phenomenology"* 54–62.

168. Heinrichs, *Die Logik* 7–76, makes this distinction between hermeneutic and systematic-logical treatments. He speaks of the two points of view as "moments of method" (*Methodenmoment*) (4). Though his distinction is drawn too neatly, its basic insight is both valid and helpful.

The second half of the Introduction: GW 9:58.10–62.5 (*Phen.* 52–57). These remarks on the Introduction are dependent particularly on the following: Labarrière, *Structures et mouvement* 31–48; W. Marx, *Hegel's Phenomenology* esp. 65–77; and especially Heinrichs's more critically detailed *Die Logik* 7–43, esp. 19–43. Despite clear differences, both Introduction and Preface follow generally parallel developments of thought. In both of them the first half of the text treats of the *Idee des Werkes* (the work's conception and purpose) and the second half treats of method (Heinrichs, 45). Regrettably the fine detail of these three studies cannot be reproduced here. Only what is essential to the question at hand is included.

169. Note too that in the Preface Hegel writes of the "universal individual" (*das allgemeine Individuum*) or the "world Spirit" (*der Weltgeist*) GW 9:24.13–15 (*Phen.* 16).

170. "Dieses [Bewußtsein] *unterscheidet* nemlich etwas von sich, worauf es sich zugleich *bezieht*." GW 9:58.25–26 (*Phen.* 52 trans. amended). Note the typically Hegelian concern with that which relates itself and is related.

171. GW 9:63.2–70.29 (*Phen.* 58–66).

172. *Bewußtseinsinstanzen*, Heinrichs's term, *Die Logik* 13.

173. "der jeweilige Repräsentant der Bildungsstufe einer Epoche," Heinrichs, *Die Logik* 12, where he attributes this clarification to the convincing presentation by W. Marx in *Hegel's Phenomenology*. Heinrichs (49) speaks of *ein reflektierendes Bewußtsein*.

174. E.g., "Nur diese Nothwendigkeit selbst, oder die *Entstehung* des neuen Gegenstandes, der dem Bewußtseyn, ohne zu wissen, wie ihm geschieht,

sich darbietet, ist es, was für uns gleichsam hinter seinem Rücken vorgeht. Es kommt dadurch in seine Bewegung ein Moment des *an sich* oder für *uns seyns*, welches nicht für das Bewußtseyn, das in der Erfahrung selbst begriffen ist, sich darstellt; der *Inhalt* aber dessen, was uns entsteht, ist *für es*, und wir begreiffen nur das formelle desselben, oder sein reines Entstehen; *für es* ist diß entstandene nur als Gegenstand, *für uns* zugleich als Bewegung und Werden." GW 9:61.19–27 ("But it is just this necessity itself, or the *arising* of the new object, that presents itself to consciousness without its understanding how this happens, which proceeds for us, as it were, behind the back of consciousness. Thus in the movement of consciousness there occurs a moment of *being-in-itself* or *being-for-us* which is not present to the consciousness comprehended in the experience itself. The *content*, however, of what presents itself to us does exist *for it*; we comprehend only the formal aspect of that content, or its pure arising. For it, what has thus arisen exists only as an object; *for us*, it appears at the same time as movement and becoming." *Phen.* 56 trans. amended).

175. Heinrichs, *Die Logik* 13, 18–19, 25. Note Hegel's own claim that specific logical thought determinations are realized in particular figures of consciousness. GW 9:432.23–25 (*Phen.* 491).

176. Heinrichs, *Die Logik* 39, 41–42.

177. Heinrichs, *Die Logik* 13, 19.

178. Heinrichs, *Die Logik* 25. Note the parallel with Hegel's 1812 position on pure being as immediate unity in the realm of pure thought.

179. Stated generally, GW 9:58.25–27 (*Phen.* 52); explicitly concerning sense certainty, GW 9:63.30–33, 64.3–7 (*Phen.* 59). Were the intention of this study simply a negative critique of Hegel's trinitarian claim rather than an additionally reconstructive argument, it would be sufficient to argue against the availability to thought of this primordially unified sense certainty. And this along lines drawn in the earlier negative critique of the possibility of grasping pure being in logical thought. See Ch. 2 Subsection 4 of the present study.

180. GW 9:58.26–29 (*Phen.* 52). Hegel uses "for it" (*für es, für sich*) to refer interrelatedly to the movement of natural consciousness (see Ch. 3 n. 174 above), directly to the second dialectical moment in the overall structure of the movement of consciousness and to the second moment as related to consciousness. E.g., GW 9:59.9–10, 60.24, 27–32 (*Phen.* 53, 55).

181. "für ein Bewußtseyn," "für ein anderes." GW 9:58.28–29 (*Phen.* 52).

182. GW 9:58.25–31 (*Phen.* 52–53); Heinrichs, *Die Logik* 20. On Hegel's inconsistent usage of *an sich* see briefly Walter Kaufmann, *Hegel. Text and Commentary* (Notre Dame, IN: Notre Dame, 1977) 31 n. 10.

183. "An und für sich" appears already in the Introduction, GW 9:59.25 (*Phen.* 54).

Heinrichs, *Die Logik* 20–21, points out this double usage of "truth." Hegel is cleverly setting up the discussion using terms favorable to his position.

See also text cited in Ch. 3 n. 187 below. Note the use of "knowledge" (*Wissen*) for "object" and for the final figure or shape of consciousness, "absolute knowledge" (*das absolute Wissen*).

Hegel further argues to an "in itself" (*an sich*) and "for itself" (*für es*) of that which is related to the *an sich* of consciousness (i.e., *Wissen*). See GW 9:59.9–11 (*Phen.* 53).

184. "Das Bewußtseyn gibt seinem Maßstab an ihm selbst, und die Untersuchung wird dadurch eine Vergleichung seiner mit sich selbst seyn; denn die Unterscheidung, welche so eben gemacht worden ist, fällt in es." GW 9:59.5–8 (*Phen.* 53); also GW 9:59.20–25 (*Phen.* 53–54). Note the structural parallel with Hegel's position and argumentation in the 1812–1816 *Logic*. See Ch. 1 Subsection 1 above. The distinction is said to fall within "knowledge" (*Wissen*) GW 9:59.22 (*Phen.* 53).

185. Heinrichs, *Die Logik* 20.

186. Heinrichs, *Die Logik* 20–22 with n. 14 where he cites Klaus Hartmann, "Das Realitätsproblem" in *Lebendiger Realismus. Festschrift für J. Thyssen*, ed. Klaus Hartmann (Bonn: Bouvier, 1962) 115–130. Given the framework within which Hegel is working and this present study's specific interests, it is not necessary to take a final stance here on the success or failure of Hegel's argumentation concerning the problem of truly knowing "reality."

187. In complex argumentation the epistemological question and that of the role of phenomenologist are brought together: GW 9:59.4–60.14 (*Phen.* 53–55). Heinrichs, *Die Logik* 23–25.

188. For further remarks on Hegel's relatively sparse but significant use of the term "dialectic" (*dialektisch*) in the *Phenomenology* and for references see Heinrichs, *Die Logik* 26–28 with n. 16. See also Gauvin, *Wortindex* Form numbers 2045–2048.

189. "Diese *dialektische* Bewegung, welche das Bewußtseyn an ihm selbst, sowohl an seinem Wissen, als an seinem Gegenstande ausübt, *in sofern ihm der neue wahre Gegenstand daraus entspringt*, ist eigentlich dasjenige, was *Erfahrung* genannt wird." GW 9:60.15–18 (*Phen.* 55 trans. amended).

Rohrmoser, *Subjektivität und Verdinglichung* 105, summarizes Heidegger's valuable interpretation of Hegel's concept of experience: "die dialektische Bewegung, die das Bewußtsein an sich selbst vollzieht und in der es sich als ein Mehr gegenüber dem erfährt, als was es sich weiß." See Martin Heidegger, "Hegels Begriff der Erfahrung," in *Holzwege* (Frankfurt am Main: Klostermann, 1950) 105–192.

For a Marxist interpretation of this dialectical experience, see Oskar Nekt, "Zum Problem der Aktualität Hegels," in *Aktualität und Folgen der Philosophie Hegels*, ed. Oskar Negt (Frankfurt am Main: Suhrkamp, 1970) esp. 18–19.

190. "Der Fortgang zum wahren Wissen." Hoffmeister's title, *Phän.* 69. The text is quoted in Ch. 3 n. 138 above. The quote should here be extended

to include: "Indem . . . das Resultat, wie es in Wahrheit ist, aufgefaßt wird, als *bestimmte* Negation, so ist damit unmittelbar eine neue Form entsprungen, und in der Negation der Ubergang gemacht, wodurch sich der Fortgang durch die vollständige Reihe der Gestalten von selbst ergibt." GW 9:57.14–17 ("When . . . the result is conceived as it is in truth, as *determinate* negation, a new form has thereby immediately arisen, and in the negation the transition is made through which the progress through the complete series of shapes comes about of itself." *Phen.* 51 trans. amended).

191. GW 9:61.7–18 (*Phen.* 56). This could be called "transcendental experience." Heinrichs, *Die Logik* 29 with nn. 19 and 20 citing Richard Kroner, *Von Kant bis Hegel*, vol. 2 (Tübingen: Mohr, 1924) 366.

192. See Ch. 1 n. 43 above.

193. Labarrière speaks of "l'auto-mouvement du content." *Structures et mouvement* esp. 44–48.

194. Explicitly stated by Hegel. See Ch. 3 n. 190 above.

195. See Ch. 3 n. 184 above. Heinrichs, *Die Logik* 68, obfuscates the immanence of this auto-development of consciousness. See Ch. 3 n. 158 above.

196. "das reine Zusehen," GW 9:59.26–30, 61.22–27 (*Phen.* 54–56). W. Marx goes too far in describing the role of phenomenologist as initiator: "The phenomenologist—so we found—is in the *first* place he who 'takes' phenomenal knowledge 'along on the road.' *Secondly*, he is the initiator of the movement of the history of experience, and hence also that of the dialectical history of experience. *Thirdly*, by means of his superior knowledge, the phenomenologist surveys the dialectical movement of experience and the category of necessity underlying it, which makes possible the exoteric presentation, and hence the 'justification' vis-à-vis natural consciousness. *Fourthly*, as a result of the foregoing history of experience, there arises for the phenomenologist the synthesis positively apprehended as principle. *Fifthly*, he can act as a 'guide' for phenomenal knowledge." *Hegel's Phenomenology* 91–92. See also Werner Marx, "Dialectic and the Role of the Phenomenologist," *The Owl of Minerva* 11 (December 1979) 1–4, esp. 4.

197. Preface: GW 9:9.1–49.30 (*Phen.* 1–45). The Preface is discussed here only with a view to distilling internal criteria with which to evaluate the success of Hegel's trinitarian argument. On the Preface in general see despite limitations in his Hegel interpretation Kaufmann, *Hegel. Text and Commentary*; Heinrichs, *Die Logik* 46–76, esp. 57–76. Unless otherwise mentioned reference to the Preface is hereafter meant to be understood to include the *Phenomenology*'s last chapter as well.

198. With reference to the *Phenomenology* see in the Preface e.g.: consciousness as that which distinguishes and relates, or more exactly, as characterized by opposition, GW 9:23.9–11, 29.14–15 (*Phen.* 15, 21); figures of consciousness as successive totalizations (the reference arguably concerning the *Phenomenology*), GW 9:25.18–22 (*Phen.* 17); these figures as realizations of

logical moments, see Ch. 3 n. 201 below; the self-othering of consciousness as internal to itself, GW 9:24.6–8 (*Phen.* 15–16); the dialectical movement of consciousness called experience, GW 9:29.8–28 (*Phen.* 21).

199. Heinrichs, *Die Logik* 46–76, esp. 57–76.

200. Regarding terminology, "form" and "content" are used only a few times by Hegel in the Introduction, but "form" occurs 44 times and "content" 76 times in the Preface. See Gauvin, *Wortindex* Form numbers 3300, 5020–5022, 5026.

201. GW 9:29.15–17 (*Phen.* 21) with GW 9:24.1–6, 432.11–30 (*Phen.* 15, 491), and Heinrichs, *Die Logik* 60.

Of concern in this study are precisely logical forms in as they arise within and structure specific shapes of consciousness, and not the more general question of the specific relationship between the *Phenomenology* and Hegel's various individual "logics."

202. GW 9:29.14–17 (*Phen.* 21).

203. Already in the *Phenomenology*'s last chapter "configuration of Spirit" (*Gestaltung des Geistes*), GW 9:425.19 with 35, 427.27–28 (*Phen.* 483, 485). Note in the Preface GW 9:25.1–3, 29.14–17 (*Phen.* 16, 21). Labarrière, *Structures et mouvement* 41, 43.

204. GW 9:427.28–31 (*Phen.* 485).

205. E.g., GW 9:432.31–37 (*Phen.* 491).

206. Perhaps the clearest example of this movement in the *Phenomenology* is the way in which *Itzt* (*Jetzt*, "now") is argued by Hegel to be, always already to have been (*gewesen*) and nevertheless again "is." See GW 9:67.33–68.7 (*Phen.* 63). In general, the best way to get a sense of the movement of Hegel's argumentation in the *Phenomenology* is a close reading of the first two or three chapters.

207. See Ch. 1 Subsection 1 of the present study.

208. See remarks in Ch. 2 Subsection 4 of the present study. See also concerning "science," GW 9:428.11–15 (*Phen.* 486).

209. Note already in the Introduction the reference to the *determinate* side (*die bestimmte Seite*) of the relation of opposition constitutive of consciousness, GW 9:58.27–28 (*Phen.* 52). Note Hegel's apposition of object and content, GW 431.17–19 (*Phen.* 490), though Hegel here inadequately parallels "object" and "objectivity."

210. Note Hegel's apposition of figure (*Gestalt*) and content (*Inhalt*), GW 9:24.7 (*Phen.* 15). W. Marx, *Hegel's "Phenomenology"* 68, had correctly pointed out in discussing the Introduction that Hegel failed to distinguish adequately between "object" (*Gegenstand*) and "objectivity" (*Gegenständlichkeit*).

211. GW 9:427.35–36 with 57.14–17 (*Phen.* 485 with 51). See also Ch. 3 nn. 183 and 138 above.

212. E.g., GW 9:427.28–31 (*Phen.* 485). Considered from the point of view of absolute knowledge, the development of consciousness to self-conscious-

ness as a whole can also be referred to as content, giving in a sense a fourth way of speaking of content in relation to consciousness. True content was already truly present but inadequately formulated prior to absolute knowledge also in the revelatory religion.

213. In fact, for Hegel all reality as grasped in thought is finally Self since it is taken up into and is the self-expression of absolute Spirit.

Note the more ambiguous use of form in GW 9:57.9–16 (*Phen.* 51). Even in that quote it would appear arguable that Hegel is not using form only coextensively with "figure" but possibly also in reference to consciousness "in itself."

214. E.g., negatively stated GW 9:425.23–26 (*Phen.* 483); positively GW 9:427.28–31 (*Phen.* 485). Hegel also more loosely refers to "figure" as "form." See Ch. 3 n. 213 immediately above. He apparently does this especially in the last chapter and in the Preface under the influence of his concern for and discussion on absolute knowledge, science and logic. E.g., GW 9:25.23–26.2 (*Phen.* 17), or more generally GW 9:425.34–35 (*Phen.* 483).

215. GW 9:29.29–30 (*Phen.* 21).

216. See, e.g., Ch. 1 n. 33 above.

217. Note the juxtaposition of "content" (*Inhalt*) and "figure" (*Gestalt*) in GW 9:24.7 (*Phen.* 15).

218. This is simply to restate in terms of form and content what Hegel has argued concerning determinate negation in the *Phenomenology* and concerning negation of negation in the *Logic*. See Heinrichs, *Die Logik* 35–36.

219. In the Introduction, GW 9:55.32–39, 56.18–21, 57.18–22 (*Phen.* 49, 50, 51); concerning the Preface, "Die Erhebung in dasselbe [Element des Wissens] ist die Phänomenologie des Geistes," subtitle Hegel gives to one section of the Preface, GW 9:5.6–7 ("The elevation into the same [the element of knowledge] is the Phenomenology of Spirit." *Phen.* xxxiii trans. amended), and the text itself esp. GW 9:24.1–12 (*Phen.* 15–16).

220. Discursive thought, i.e., on the level of understanding (*Verstand*) and not yet on what is for Hegel the level of reason (*Vernunft, begreiffendes Denken*).

221. GW 9:61.19–27 (*Phen.* 56).

222. Again, GW 9:61.19–27 (*Phen.* 56).

223. It can already here be indicated that Jaeschke raises the question in principle as to whether it would be possible for the understanding which merely separates to elevate itself to rational speculation without reference to an underlying speculative logic. "Äußerliche Reflexion und immanente Reflexion. Eine Skizze der systematischen Geschichte des Reflexionsbegriffs in Hegels Logikentwürfen," *Hegel-Studien* 13 (Bonn: Bouvier, 1978) 99.

224. A movement for Hegel of consciousness qua consciousness and taking place as the progressive sublation of finite consciousness.

225. Not simply a question of whether Hegel himself accomplishes what he intended, but whether it can be done at all as he proposes to do it.

226. Hegel integrates determinate negation, syllogism and Trinity.

227. Hegel consistently elaborates a progression of middle terms (B-E-A) in a series of three syllogisms, categorical, hypothetical and disjunctive, structured respectively A-B-E/A-E-B/B-A-E (A = universality, B = particularity, E = individuality). Allowing of course for the fact that Hegel develops the moment of individuality in the *Encyclopedia* (E §§ 569–570) as a movement of three syllogisms, whereas in the *Phenomenology* and in the philosophy of religion *Lectures* the moment of individuality is given a more straightforward disjunctive syllogistic structure. On the *Encyclopedia* see Ch. 3 Subsection 2b of the present study. On the *Phenomenology* see Ch. 4 Subsection 2 of the present study. On the 1827 philosophy of religion *Lectures* see Ch. 5 Subsection 2 of the present study.

4. The Incarnational Immediacy of Trinitarian Reconciliation in The *Phenomenology*

1. E.g., in a general way, David Tracy in *Blessed Rage for Order* (New York: Seabury, 1975) and *The Analogical Imagination. Christian Theology and the Culture of Pluralism* (New York: Crossroad, 1981) has based his approach to "classic texts" in fundamental theology on the work of Paul Ricoeur.

2. In Ch. 2 Subsection 1 of the present study.

3. GW 9:363.1–421.18 (*Phen.* 410–478). *Phen.* sometimes cited also with line from the top. At times the Hoffmeister edition, *Phän.*, is also cited, often with line from the top.

4. GW 9:422.1–434.9 (*Phen.* 479–493).

5. "Die offenbare Religion," GW 9:400.1–421.18 (*Phen.* 453–478).

6. GW 9:323.23–24 (*Phen.* 263). Also, GW 9:425.19–21 (*Phen.* 482). The *Phenomenology*'s Ch. 6: GW 9:323.22–362.29 (*Phen.* 263–409). On this double reconciliation in consciousness and self-consciousness, in morality and in religion, see also Heinrichs, *Die Logik der "Phänomenologie des Geistes"* (Bonn: Bouvier, 1974) 363–402, 473–481, related 402–407. The earlier reconciliation (Ch. 5) results in the finite Idea (*die endliche Idee*) and is therefore not of direct interest here. Heinrichs, *Die Logik* 256, 447–448.

7. GW 9:361.22–25 (*Phen.* 408), where Hegel speaks of "the existing Spirit" (*der daseyende Geist);* for "actual Spirit" (*wirklicher Geist*) see, e.g., GW 9:367.27–28 (*Phen.* 415). On actual Spirit interpreted as "for itself" (*für sich*) from Hegel's point of view in the chapter on absolute knowledge, see GW 9:425.10–15 (*Phen.* 482).

8. GW 9:362.12–16 (*Phen.* 409), cited by Heinrichs, *Die Logik* 400. Also GW 9:367.27–28 (*Phen.* 415). For more detail concerning Hegel's shift to a logic of self-manifestation (*Erscheinungslogik*) in the transition from actual Spirit to religious Spirit, see *Die Logik* 410–413.

9. GW 9:425.10–12 (*Phen.* 482).

10. GW 9:425.23–25 (*Phen.* 483). For a structural comparison of actual Spirit and religious Spirit, see "Zur dialektischen Einheit von wirklichem und religiösem Geist," Schema 2 in Heinrichs, *Die Logik* (unnumbered end foldout). See also Heinrichs, 413–430, 473–481 and related thereto 402–407.

On the implications of religion's being *an sich* the reconciliation of actual Spirit and religious Spirit for the significance of Ch. 7, "Religion," in the overall structure of the *Phenomenology* see Heinrichs, *Die Logik* 410–430. On the other hand, Johann Heinrich Trede, Phänomenologie und Logik. Zu den Grundlagen einer Diskussion," in *Hegel-Studien* 10 (Bonn: Bouvier, 1975) 173–209, maintains that Heinrichs exaggerates the importance of Ch. 7.

11. Heinrichs develops the opposition "*an sich*/theoretical/religious" and "*für sich*/practical/actual" in conjunction with his discussion on actual Spirit and religious Spirit. See Ch. 4 n. 10 immediately above.

12. Natural religion: GW 9:369.1–399.35 (*Phen.* 416–424).

13. Art religion: GW 9:376.1–399.35 (*Phen.* 424–453). On revelatory religion as synthesis: GW 9:368.26–31 (*Phen.* 416). See also Francis Guibal, *Dieu selon Hegel. Essai sur la problématique de la "Phénoménologie de l'Esprit"* (Paris: Aubier-Montaigne, 1975) 53.

14. GW 9:420.19–22, 421.15–18 (*Phen.* 477, 478).

15. GW 9:425.19–22 (*Phen.* 483). Note that just prior to this quote Hegel had shifted his references for *an sich* and *für sich*. For further details see Heinrichs, *Die Logik* 473, where in n. 296 he also cites Pierre-Jean Labarrière, *Structures et mouvement dialectique dans la "Phénoménologie de l'Esprit" de Hegel* (Paris: Aubier-Montaigne, 1968) 189–190. From another, phenomenologically earlier perspective Hegel is able to consider religion as *für sich* reconciliation.

16. As mentioned in Ch. 3 Subsection 1 of the present study.

17. In agreement with Heinrichs, *Die Logik* 452–458, explicitly 452, 454, 456 n. 284.

18. Mentioned in Ch. 2 Subsection 1 of the present study.

19. See the references to Heinrichs in Ch. 4 nn. 6 and 10 above.

20. Guibal, *Dieu selon Hegel* 10–11.

21. These paragraphs are dependent on and generally paraphrase Heinrichs's excellent outline. The summary of the progression of Hegel's thought itself is based on Guibal's helpful and detailed analysis, *Dieu selon Hegel*, with outlines on pp. 101–102, 119–121, 131–133, 141–142, 170–172, 194–197 (Guibal's valuable work is marred by page or line printing errors on pp. 101, 119 and 194). It is unfortunately not possible but also here not necessary to reproduce the rich detail of their studies.

Heinrichs, *Die Logik* 550, develops a fourfold subdivision, whereas Guibal, *Dieu selon Hegel* 94 with n. 2, works with a threefold outline: recapitulative introduction; reflection on the simple Concept; the developed Concept. However, Heinrichs's delineation of a section between Incarnation and Trinity better highlights Hegel's transition from simple to developed "Concept."

Other outlines differing somewhat from Heinrichs's in subdivision or amount of material covered: a very detailed breakdown differing from that of Heinrichs in a number of particulars, Albert Chapelle, *Hegel et la religion. Annexes. Les textes théologiques de Hegel* (Paris: Éditions universitaires, 1967) 61–85, 96, and Albert Chapelle, *Hegel et la religion*, vol. 3: *La théologie et l'église* (*La dialectique, deuxième partie*) (Paris: Éditions Universitaires, 1971) 68–79. On the publisher's outline appearing in the first two editions of the *Phenomenology*, see *Phän.* 565, 573–574.

Exposition from varying points of view and containing commentaries and/or analyses: negatively critical, Franz Anton Staudenmaier, *Darstellung und Kritik des Hegelschen Systems. Aus dem Standpunkte der christlichen Philosophie* (Mainz: Kupferberg, 1844; reprint ed. Frankfurt am Main: Minerva, 1966) 817–836; Günter Rohrmoser, *Subjektivität und Verdinglichung. Theologie und Gesellschaft im Denken des jungen Hegels* (Gütersloh: Mohn, 1961) 101–114; Splett, *Die Trinitätslehre G. W. F. Hegels* (Munich: Alber, 1965) 57–68; Labarrière, *Structures et mouvement* 174–183 (on the first third of Chapter Seven); Falk Wagner, *Der Gedanke der Persönlichkeit Gottes bei Fichte und Hegel* (Gütersloh: Mohn, 1971); Heinrichs, *Die Logik* 442–460; Guibal, *Dieu selon Hegel* 94–219 (an in-depth study); A. V. Miller, "Analysis of the Text," in G. W. F. Hegel, *Hegel's Phenomenology of Spirit*, trans. A. V. Miller (New York: Oxford University Press, 1977) 584–589; Chapelle, *La théologie et l'église* 66–84, containing brief comparisons with the *Lectures on the Philosophy of Religion*.

22. "Der entwickelte Inhalt des sich offenbarenden Geistes," Heinrichs, *Die Logik* 550.

23. GW 9:400.3–403.16/*Phän.* 521.3–525.23 (*Phen.* 453.6–457.2). These very general. remarks are simply meant to give an overall sense of the movement of Hegel's thought in Chapter Seven. Specific, representative texts explicitly elaborating Hegel's argumentation will be treated in more detail in the following critique.

24. See Labarrière, *Structures et mouvement* 182.

25. "—die Einfachheit des reinen Begriffs, der jene Gestalten als seine Momente enthält." GW 9:403.16 (*Phen.* 457 trans. amended). The conditions for revelation are summarized in GW 9:402.34–403.16 (*Phen.* 456.18–457.2). Heinrichs, *Die Logik* 443–444; Guibal, *Dieu selon Hegel* 102.

26. GW 9:403.17–407.13/*Phän.* 525.24–530.28 (*Phen.* 457.3–461.29).

27. GW 9:403.17–35 (*Phen.* 457.3–25).

28. "als diese ihre Einheit ins Daseyn tritt." GW 9:403.35 (*Phen.* 457).

29. "das unmittelbare Seyn selbst," GW 9:404.25–26 (*Phen.* 458).

30. "es der *Glauben der Welt* ist, daß der Geist als ein Selbstbewußtseyn d.h. als ein wirklicher Mensch *da ist*, daß er für die unmittelbare Gewißheit ist, daß das glaubende Bewußtseyn diese Göttlichkeit *sieht* und *fühlt* und *hört*." GW 9:404.3–37 ("this now appears as the *belief of the world* that Spirit is *immediately* present as a self-conscious Being, that is, as an *actual human being*,

that Spirit exists for immediate certainty, the believer *sees* and *feels and hears* this divinity." *Phen.* 458 trans. amended).

31. "Diese Menschwerdung des göttlichen Wesens, oder daß es wesentlich und unmittelbar die Gestalt des Selbstbewußtseyns hat, ist der einfache Inhalt der absoluten Religion." GW 9:405.14–16 (*Phen.* 459).

32. Although the term "Christian" does not appear here in the *Phenomenology*.

33. And not without a play on words. "Sein Offenbarseyn besteht offenbar darin, daß gewußt wird, was es [das göttliche Wesen] ist." GW 9:405.23–24 ("Its being revealed obviously [*offenbar*] consists in this, that what it [the divine essence] is, is known." *Phen.* 459).

34. GW 9:405.16–25 (*Phen.* 459). In this quote (specifically GW 9:405.19–22) Hegel argues that in the Incarnation substance has become Subject. This recalls Hegel's insistence on the importance of conceiving the True not only in terms of substance but also as Subject, GW 9:18.3–5 (*Phen.* 9–10). This insistence is a philosophical formulation of Hegel's trinitarian claim.

Wolfhart Pannenberg has observed that it was Hegel who first developed the thought of God's revelation as necessarily a self-revelation. See Pannenberg's *Revelation as History* (London: Macmillan, 1968) 4–5. Guibal reflects briefly on Pannenberg's correct reading of Hegel's conception of universal history as divine self-revelation. According to Guibal, both Hegel and Pannenberg pose the question "à quelles conditions un événement singulier peut-il être reconnu comme ayant une signification absolue pour le tout de la réalité? Mais la réponse est assez différente [for the two], dans la mesure où Hegel ne place pas l'aspect décisif de l'Événement-Jésus-Christ dans la résurrection qui anticipe la fin de l'histoire (Pannenberg), mais dans la manifestation de Dieu et de l'homme comme esprit." *Dieu selon Hegel* 123–124 n. 50.

On Hegel's understanding of divine revelation as self-revelation forming the background and source of the doctrine ultimately adapted by the Second Vatican Council, see Henri Bouillard, "Le Concept de révélation de Vatican I à Vatican II," in *Révélation de Dieu et langage des hommes* (Paris: Cerf, 1972) 44–46, reference indicated by Prof. Jacques Gagné, O.M.I.

35. GW 9:407.14–409.36/*Phän.* 530.29–534.4 (*Phen.* 461.30–464.1).

36. Guibal, *Dieu selon Hegel* 120. Guibal stresses this aspect of the text here under consideration and consequently links most of this section, i.e., GW 9:407.14–408.29 (*Phen.* 461.30–463.19), with the previous treatment of Incarnation and GW 9:408.30–409.36 (*Phen.* 463.20–464.36) as introduction to the Chapter Seven's last subsection on Trinity (Guibal, 120–121, 131–133).

37. Due to present concern with Hegel's progressive argument forward to absolute knowledge, Heinrichs's gathering of the material in question into a specific subdivision is being followed here. In view of its richness and perhaps ambiguity Hegel's material is often enough open to multiple structuring or

subdividing. Heinrichs's outline is used here but without necessarily adapting in all its details his positing of an exact parallel between Chapter Five on reason and this segment of Chapter Seven. For the details of Heinrichs' further breakdown of this third larger section or subdivision of revelatory religion see *Die Logik* 550.

38. With the chapter on religion, and concerning revelatory religion in particular, Hegel's writing becomes increasingly marked by the use of more distinctly logical terms and expressions.

39. GW 9:409. 10–25 (*Phen.* 464.1–21). Guibal, *Dieu selon Hegel* 131.

40. Guibal, *Dieu selon Hegel* 131.

41. GW 9:409.10–25 (*Phen.* 426.1–21).

42. In the second half of the *Phenomenology*'s Introduction and also in its Preface but above all in the *Logic*, where reflection on method forms the last moment of absolute thought.

43. "Der Geist ist Inhalt seines Bewußtseyns zuerst in der Form der reinen *Substanz*, oder ist Inhalt seines reinen Bewußtseyns. Diß Element des Denkens ist die Bewegung, zum Daseyn oder der Einzelheit herunter zu steigen." GW 9:409.10–12 (*Phen.* 464 trans. amended). This is an encapsulated restatement of what had been detailed in GW 9:407.14–407.32 (*Phen.* 461.30–462.13).

44. "Die Mitte zwischen ihnen [Denken, Einzelheit] ist ihre synthetische Verbindung, das Bewußtseyn des Anderswerden oder das Vorstellen als solches." GW 9:409.12–14 (*Phen.* 464 trans. amended). A restatement of what had been detailed in GW 9:407.33–409.9 (*Phen.* 462.14–463.40).

45. "die synthetische Verbinding der sinnlichen Unmittelbarkeit, und ihrer Allgemeinheit oder des Denkens." GW 9:408.15–16 (*Phen.* 464). See also on representation GW 9:409.21–25 (*Phen.* 464). Hegel treats representation twice at greater length in Chapter Seven.

46. "die Rückkehr aus der Vorstellung und dem Anderssseyn oder das Element des Selbstbewußtseyns selbst." GW 9:409.14–15 (*Phen.* 464).

47. GW 9:409.16 (*Phen.* 464).

48. "Substanz *im Elemente des reinen Denkens*." GW 9:409.37 (*Phen.* 464 trans. amended).

49. GW 9:410.1 (*Phen.* 464).

50. The fourth subdivision: GW 9:409.3–421Schluß/*Phän.* 534.5–548; Schluß (*Phen.* 464, 37–478).

51. GW 9:409.37–411.39 (*Phen.* 464.37–467.15). The first two paragraphs, GW 9:409.37–410.28 (*Phen.* 464.37–465.30) present the basic development of "immanent" Trinity.

52. At this point Hegel uses eternal essence to refer both to the abstract moment of "inner" Trinity as a whole, e.g., GW 9:410.1 (*Phen.* 464.39), and as first moment within "inner" Trinity, e.g., GW 9:410.14 (*Phen.* 465.13). Note again, "abstract" not in the sense of "abstracted from" but of "as yet not

explicitated." See also Michael Theunissen, *Hegels Lehre vom absoluten Geist als theologisch-politischen Traktat* (Berlin: de Gruyter, 1970) 261.

53. Note Hegel's not untypical tendency to use the same term to express two different though related meanings. The same holds for "essence," Ch. 4 n. 52, immediately above.

54. GW 9:410.18–20 (*Phen.* 465).

55. See in Ch. 3 Subsection 4a of the present study.

56. "das *Wissen* des *Wesens seiner selbst*," GW 9:410.22–23 (*Phen.* 465).

57. E.g., "die Momente der Bewegung, die der Geist ist, für isolirte nicht wankende Substanzen oder Subjekte, statt für übergehende Momente zu nehmen,—" GW 9:411.9–10 ("the standpoint which takes the moments of the movement which Spirit is, as isolated unmovable Substances or Subjects, instead of transient moment—" *Phen.* 466). Note Hegel argues the movement of "immanent" Trinity with logical terms even here in the religious realm of representation.

58. GW 9:411.30–34 (*Phen.* 467).

59. "diese in sich kreisende Bewegung." GW 9:410.28 (*Phen.* 465).

60. Heinrichs, *Die Logik* 454. On the categorical syllogism see briefly Ch. 3 nn. 45 and 87 above. See also Ch. 5 n. 63 below.

61. Concerning the *Encyclopedia* see Ch. 3 Subsection 2b of the present study.

62. "*erschafft* also eine *Welt*." GW 9:412.2–3 (*Phen.* 467).

63. "Seyn für anderes," GW 9:412.10 (*Phen.* 467).

64. GW 9:412.15–19 (*Phen.* 467).

65. GW 9:412.1–417.5 (*Phen.* 467.16–473.23).

66. See further referrals in Ch. 3 n. 94 above.

67. "der sich selbst entgegengesetzte Gedanke des *Guten* und *Bösen*." GW 9:412.30–31 (*Phen.* 468).

68. GW 9:415.38–39 (*Phen.* 472).

69. GW 9:413.2 (*Phen.* 468).

70. GW 9:416.9 (*Phen.* 472).

71. GW 9:413.2–3 (*Phen.* 468).

72. "wie das Böse nichts anderes ist, als das Insichgehen des natürlichen Daseyns des Geistes, umgekehrt das Gute in die Wirklichkeit tritt und als ein daseyendes Selbstbewußtseyn erscheint." GW 9:414.5–8 (*Phen.* 469–470).

73. GW 9:414.16–20 (*Phen.* 470).

74. GW 9:414.35–38 (*Phen.* 470). Also, GW 9:415.38–417.5 (*Phen.* 472–473).

75. "das Einfache als das Wesen gilt, ist es, das sich selbst entäussert, in den Tod geht, und dadurch das absolute Wesen mit sich selbst versöhnt. Denn in dieser Bewegung stellt es sich als *Geist* dar; das abstrakte Wesen ist sich entfremdet, es hat natürliches Daseyn und selbstische Wirklichkeit; diß sein

Andersseyn oder seine sinnliche Gegenwart wird durch das zweyte Anderswerden zurückgenommen, und als aufgehobne, als *allgemeine* gesetzt; . . . dieser *Tod* ist daher sein Erstehen als Geist." GW 9:415.2–10 (*Phen.* 471).

76. "Dieser Schluß A-E-B läßt sich durchaus als *hypothetischer* Schluß bezeichnen und formulieren: Wenn Gott Geist ist, dann muß er sich zum *wirklichen* Anderen seiner selbst bestimmen und aus ihm geistig zurückgewinnen. Nun aber ist die bloße immanente Andersheit noch abstrakt und unwirklich (536, 30ff), wirklich dagegen sind Welt, endliches Fürsichsein, Böses und die menschlichen Natur des Erlösers. Daher gewinnt Gott sich in der Überwindung des natürlichen Fürsichseins bis zum Tod als dieser Wirklichkeit als Geist zurück und erlöst dann die menschliche und sonstige Natur zum geistigen Dasein." Heinrichs, *Die Logik* 456.

On the hypothetical syllogism see briefly in Ch. 3 nn. 46 and 93 above. See also Ch. 5 n. 94 below.

77. Perhaps Josiah Royce develops this theme and draws upon Hegel at this point or from parallel texts in his theory on atonement in *The Problem of Christianity* (Chicago: Chicago University Press, 1968) 179–186. Royce did this of course in terms of his own unique synthesis of intellect and will as act of loyalty.

78. Heinrichs, *Die Logik* 455.

79. GW 9:415.11–16 (*Phen.* 471).

80. "Der Geist ist also in dem dritten Elemente, im *allgemeinen Selbstbewußtseyn* gesetzt; er ist seine *Gemeinde*." GW 9:417.6–7 (*Phen.* 473).

81. The text for this third element: GW 9:417.6–420.8 (*Phen.* 473.24–477.15); GW 9:415.11–16 (*Phen.* 471.16–24) should be included here as well.

82. GW 9:419.31–38 (*Phen.* 476–477).

83. GW 9:417.7–11 (*Phen.* 473).

84. GW 9:417.6–420.8 (*Phen.* 473.24–477.15).

85. A linguistic allusion by Hegel to the middle term (*Mitte*) in a syllogism. E.g., GW 9:419.8 (*Phen.* 476).

86. See again GW 9:407.14–409.36/*Phän.* 530.29–534.4 (*Phen.* 461.30–464.1). And in this regard, GW 9:417.6–8 with 419.31–38 (*Phen.* 473 with 476–477).

87. As Guibal writes, "le rôle de la communauté ecclésiale telle qu'elle apparaît ici: elle est le milieu de formation des consciences croyantes à la vie spirituelle." *Dieu selon Hegel* 182.

88. Referring directly to the developed second moment of the divine trinitarian self-othering but also to the earlier statement of implicit divine self-revelation. See Ch. 4 Subsection 2 of the present study.

89. GW 9:417.17 (*Phen.* 473).

90. GW 9:417.20–25 (*Phen.* 474).

91. GW 9:417.36–418.6 (*Phen.* 474).

92. GW 9:418.16–25 (*Phen.* 475); Heinrichs, *Die Logik* 458–459.
93. "vielmehr als ein *besonderer.*" GW 9:418.36 (*Phen.* 475).
94. GW 9:418.35–419.2 (*Phen.* 475).
95. "der in seiner Gemeine lebt, in ihr täglich stirbt und aufersteht." GW 9:418.33–34 (*Phen.* 475 trans. amended).
96. GW 9:419.8–13 with 31–38 (*Phen.* 476).
97. Ch. 4 Subsection 2 of the present study.
98. Heinrichs, *Die Logik* 457–458, a particularly succinct and helpful elaboration with references to the later *Logic.* On the disjunctive syllogism, see briefly Ch. 3 n. 47 above and Ch. 5 Subsection 3b of the present study.
99. "Der vom Selbst ergrieffne Tod des Mittlers ist das Aufheben seiner *Gegenständlichkeit* oder seines *besondren Fürsichseyns*; diß *besondre* Fürsichseyn ist allgemeines Selbstbewußtseyn geworden." GW 9:419.8–11 (*Phen.* 476 trans. amended).
100. "Die Einigung des Gläubigen mit dem Mittler (Christus) ist das Allgemeinwerden des letzteren selbst sowie des einzelnen Gläubigen. Anderseits wird das allgemeine Selbstbewußtsein der Gemeinde durch die Vereinigung des einzelnen Gläubigen mit dem Mittler selbst vermittelt. Dies, daß die *vermittelnde* (allgemeine) Mitte durch die Extreme selbst *vermittelt* wird, die sich *gegenseitig* zur Allgemeinheit vermitteln, kennzeichnet den vollendeten Schluß der Notwendigkeit, den disjunktiven Schluß, 'der aus diesem Grunde ebensosehr *kein Schluß* mehr ist' (L II 350)." Heinrichs, *Die Logik* 457. The nature of the mediation making up this disjunctive syllogism provides the reason in logic why the Mediator must remain "other" and therefore why consciousness of Incarnation and Trinity remain in the realm of representation. See Heinrichs, 458.
101. GW 9:419.19–22 (*Phen.* 476).
102. On these terms see again Ch. 3 Subsection 4a of the present study.
103. "Er ist diß, indem er die drey Elemente seiner Natur durchlaufft; diese Bewegung durch sich selbst hindurch mach seine Wirklichkeit aus;—was sich bewegt, ist er, er ist das Subjekt der Bewegung, und er ist ebenso *das Bewegen* selbst, oder die Substanz, durch welche das Subjekt hindurchgeht." GW 9:419.35–38 (*Phen.* 476–477 trans. amended).
104. GW 9:421.14–18 (*Phen.* 478); Heinrichs, *Die Logik* 459.
105. GW 9:420.31–32 (*Phen.* 478).
106. GW 9:420.19–22 (*Phen.* 477).
107. GW 9:420.37–421.2 (*Phen.* 478).
108. Heinrichs, *Die Logik* 459–460, quoting GW 9:419.19–30 (*Phen.* 476). Hegel does not so easily work here in the *Phenomenology* with the mediation of mediation and consequent renewed immediacy as the result of the disjunctive syllogism. See on the *Lectures,* e.g., Ch. 5 Subsection 2c of the present study.
109. However, Labarrière, *Structures et mouvement* 182–183, reflects on the implications of Hegel's apparently no longer so explicitly and rigorously

developed parallels in revelatory religion with earlier shapes of consciousness in the *Phenomenology*.

110. GW 9:420.9–421Schluß (*Phen.* 477.16–478end). A brief summary of Hegel's moves: "C'est cette limite représentative que met fortement en lumière le paragraphe sur lequel s'achève l'ensemble de la section 'Religion': après avoir énoncé le principe général de cette limitation, Hegel montre comment elle se traduit de façon conséquente dans la triple relation à Dieu, à la temporalité et à l'effectivité mondaine; il conclut alors en indiquant comment cet enchaînement de contradictions appelle de lui-même son dépassement dans le Savoir Absolu.

"Le principe général de la critique est simple, et il avait d'ailleurs déjà été annoncé: la représentation, au lieu de se trouver comprise par la conscience de soi, reste comme un élément d'opacité qui forme obstacle à la transparence conceptuelle." Guibal, *Dieu selon Hegel* 191. Guibal, 191–194, 195, 215–219, provides an excellent analysis of and reflection on this paragraph.

111. Reinhard Heede, "Die göttliche Idee und ihre Erscheinung in der Religion. Untersuchungen zum Verhältnis von Logik und Religionsphilosophie bei Hegel" (Ph. D. dissertation, Philosophical Faculty of the Westfälische Wilhelms-Universität zu Münster/Westfalen, 1972) 187; Paul Ricoeur, "Hegel Colloquium. The Status of *Vorstellung* in Hegel's Philosophy of Religion: a Twentieth Century Appraisal," Lecture at Boston University, April 9, 1980, Photocopied text. These two speak of Hegel's later and more appreciative evaluation of *Vorstellung* in the *Lectures on the Philosophy of Religion*. Ricoeur points out though that there is little change in Hegel's "characterization of religious discourse as 'figurative,'" (lecture text p. 2) from the earlier to the later Hegel.

112. GW 9:420.9–13 (*Phen.* 477). The statement is made directly concerning pure thought's being so burdened. Also GW 9:420.36–37 (*Phen.* 478). Ricoeur treats in more detail of this impeding side to representation in his lecture, "The Status of *Vorstellung*" 21–24.

113. GW 9:420.15–16 (*Phen.* 477). Examples of such representations are summarized by Guibal, Ch. 4 n. 110 above.

114. GW 9:420.16–22 (*Phen.* 477).

115. "Das Thun des Selbst behält . . . diese negative Bedeutung gegen es [das religiöse Bewußtseyn], weil die Entäusserung der Substanz von ihrer Seite ein *Ansich* für jenes ist, das es nicht ebenso erfaßt und begreift, oder nicht in *seinem* Thun als solchem findet." GW 9:420.28–31 (*Phen.* 478 trans. amended).

116. GW 9:420.34–37 (*Phen.* 478).

117. Guibal, *Dieu selon Hegel* 192 n. 135, speaks of Hegel's accenting the power and force of the Self conscious of itself as radical negativity. Recall the general movement in the *Phenomenology* to a higher shape of consciousness on the basis of the arising of a new object of consciousness.

118. GW 9:421.7–8 (*Phen.* 478). Ricoeur speaks of the "inner dynamism" moving representation to absolute knowledge. "The Status of *Vorstellung*" 4. It would seem preferable while speaking as yet directly at this point of

revelatory religion rather than of absolute knowledge to refer to a "longing" or sense of non-accomplishment in order to account for and better acknowledge the reappearance of the unhappy consciousness at this moment.

119. GW 9:421.15–18 (*Phen.* 478).

120. On representation in the *Phenomenology* see further Heede, "Die göttliche Idee" 185–187; Guibal, *Dieu selon Hegel* 119, 191–194, 195, 215–219.

121. GW 9:408.15–16 (*Phen.* 463).

122. Here it is only a question of religion. There is no need now to discuss other areas of philosophy treated by Hegel as *Vorstellung*. By the *Phenomenology*'s Preface Hegel links *Vorstellung* and *Verstand* (understanding) and thus widens the applicability of *Vorstellung*. See also E § 20R.

123. GW 9:409.21–25 (*Phen.* 464); Heinrichs, *Die Logik* 457.

124. Again, Hegel's distinction of the same content but different form must be understood in terms of a dialectical identity of content.

For more general critical questioning of Hegel's understanding of representation in the *Phenomenology* see Heinrichs, *Die Logik* 456 n. 284; Guibal, *Dieu selon Hegel* 135, 215–219.

125. GW 9:403.17–407.13 but esp. 403.17–35 (*Phen.* 457.3–461.29 but esp. 453.3–25). This incarnational immediacy is to be distinguished from Hegel's second treatment of Incarnation within the context of the divine self-othering or second moment of developed trinitarian self-revelation.

Despite his overly brief treatment of religion in the *Phenomenology*, Joseph L. Navickas correctly indicates that "Hegel's principal argument hinges on the theme of Incarnation—that is *Menschwerdung*." *Consciousness and Reality: Hegel's Philosophy of Subjectivity* (The Hague: Nijhoff, 1976) 272 and see 272–274.

126. E.g., GW 9:417.6–420.8 (*Phen.* 473.24–477.15).

127. See Ch. 3 Subsection 5 of the present study.

128. This last also earlier referred to as the "point of view of the author of the *Phenomenology*," the vantage point of absolute knowledge.

129. "Menschwerdung des göttlichen Wesens," GW 9:405.14 (*Phen.* 459).

130. GW 9:405.14–16 (*Phen.* 459).

131. "[17] Er [Geist] hat die zwey Seiten an ihm, die oben als die beyden umgekehrten Sätze [18] vorgestellt sind; die eine ist diese, daß die *Substanz* sich ihrer selbst entäussert [19] und zum Selbstbewußtseyn wird, die andre umgekehrt, daß das *Selbstbewußtseyn* [20] sich seiner entäussert und zur Dingheit oder zum allgemeinen Selbst macht. [21] Beyde Seiten sind sich auf diese Weise entgegen gekommen, und hierdurch ihre [22] wahre Vereinigung entstanden. Die Entäusserung der Substanz, ihr Werden zum [23] Selbstbewußtseyn drückt den Uebergang ins Entgegengesetzte, den bewußtlosen [24] Uebergang der *Nothwendigkeit*, oder diß aus, daß sie *an sich* Selbstbewußtseyn [25] ist.

Umgekehrt, die Entäusserung des Selbstbewußtseyns diß, daß es *an sich* [26] das allgemeine Wesen ist, oder weil das Selbst das reine Fürsichseyn ist, das [27] in seinem Gegentheile bey sich bleibt, diß, daß für *es* es ist, daß die Substanz [28] Selbstbewußtseyn, und ebendadurch Geist ist. Es kann daher von diesem Geiste, [29] der die Form der Substanz verlassen, und in der Gestalt des Selbstbewußtseyns [30] in das Daseyn tritt, gesagt werden,—wenn man sich der aus der natürlichen Zeugung [31] hergonemmenen Verhältnisse bedienen will,—da er eine *wirkliche* [32] Mutter, aber einen ansichseyenden Vater hat; denn die *Wirklichkeit* oder [33] das Selbstbewußtseyn, und das *Ansich* als die Substanz sind seine beyden Momente, [34] durch deren gegenseitige Entäusserung, jedes zum andern werdend, er [35] als diese ihre Einheit ins Daseyn tritt." GW 9:403.17-35 (*Phen.* 457.3-25). Numbers in brackets indicate lines from the top in the German text of GW 9. These same line indications have been inserted into the English text from *Phen.* 457 to the extent that language structures would allow. Bracketed line indications were placed at the end of words hyphenated at the ends of lines in GW 9.

132. GW 9:412.1–417.5 (*Phen.* 467.16–473.23). Note that Jan van der Meulen weakens his treatment of Incarnation by indiscriminately interweaving Hegel's two presentations. *Hegel. Die gebrochene Mitte* (Hamburg: Felix Meiner, 1958) 329–332.

133. GW 9:403.32–35 (*Phen.* 457). See Guibal, *Dieu selon Hegel* 119.

134. GW 9:403.13–15 (*Phen.* 456–457). On the relation of opposition between happy or comic consciousness and the unhappy consciousness with the latter as fulfillment of the former, see GW 9:401.27–29 (*Phen.* 454). See further Heinrichs, *Die Logik* 441–442.

135. Meulen, *Hegel* 328, recalls that this *an sich* unity in revelatory religion is one of content.

136. Summarily stated, GW 9:405.17–19 (*Phen.* 459).

137. Guibal, *Dieu selon Hegel* 112 n. 30.

138. As for example when Hegel claims that the only way to avoid the Incarnation's being mere subjective imagination (*Einbildung*) (à la Feuerbach) is to realize that the Incarnation is *an sich* equally a movement of the Concept from itself as substance to itself as self-consciousness. GW 9:403.36–404.4 (*Phen.* 457).

139. As Hegel reminds the reader, GW 9:406.28–31 (*Phen.* 460–461).

140. "Er [Geist] als diese ihre Einheit ins Daseyn tritt." GW 9:403.34–35 (*Phen.* 457).

141. GW 9:403.17–35 (*Phen.* 457.3–25) quoted in Ch. 4 n. 131 above.

142. E.g., GW 9:407.18–24 (*Phen.* 461–462).

143. "*ein wirklicher einzelner Mensch.*" GW 9:405.12–13 (*Phen.* 459). Also GW 9:404.35–36, 406.15–16, 407.33 (*Phen.* 458, 461, 462).

144. "das glaubende Bewußtseyn . . . *sieht* und *fühlt* und *hört*. So ist es nicht Einbildung, sondern es ist *wirklich* an dem." GW 9:404.36–405.1 (*Phen.* 458).

145. "Er [dieser einzelne Mensch] ist der *unmittelbar* gegenwärtige Gott; dadurch geht sein Seyn in *Gewesenseyn* über." GW 9:407.34–36 ("He [this individual man] is the *immediately* present God; consequently, his '*being*' passes over into '*having been.*'" *Phen.* 462).

146. GW 9:408.11 (*Phen.* 462).

147. GW 9:404.24–26 (*Phen.* 458).

148. Consciousness arising out of an originary unity, and being that which distinguishes and relates.

149. GW 9:18.3–5 (*Phen.* 9–10).

150. See Ch. 4 Subsection 2 of the present study.

151. GW 9:402.17–35 (*Phen.* 457.3–25).

152. As immediate arising to the reader and from the point of view of the author of the *Phenomenology*.

153. An immediate arising as immediate appearance to natural consciousness. GW 9:405.13, 406.9–10, 407.12–13, 20–22, 408.1–2 (*Phen.* 459, 461, 461, 461). In the Introduction Hegel had used the term "*das formelle*" slightly differently to indicate the first of the three uses of immediacy distinguished here. See GW 9:61.19–27 (*Phen.* 56).

154. "weder als gedachtes oder vorgestelltes noch hervorgebrachten." GW 9:405.10 (*Phen.* 459).

155. "Das Selbst des daseyenden Geistes." GW 9:405.8–9 (*Phen.* 459).

156. "*einfaches* positives Selbst." GW 9:405.6–7 (*Phen.* 459).

157. "hat dadurch die form der vollkommenen Unmittelbarkeit." GW 9:405.9–10 (*Phen.* 459).

158. GW 9:405.6, 8, 15 (*Phen.* 459).

159. GW 9:405.19–22 with 406.2–5 (*Phen.* 459 with 460).

160. GW 9:407.18–32 (*Phen.* 461–462).

161. GW 9:404.17–22 (*Phen.* 458).

162. "Er [Geist] wird gewußt als Selbstbewußtseyn und ist diesem unmittelbar offenbar, denn er ist dieses selbst; die göttliche Natur ist dasselbe, was die menschliche ist, und diese Einheit ist es, die angeschaut wird." GW 9:406.7–10 (*Phen.* 460).

163. "Diese Menschwerdung des göttlichen Wesens, oder daß es wesentlich und unmittelbar die Gestalt des Selbstbewußtseyns hat, ist der einfache Inhalt der absoluten religion." GW 9:405.14–16 (*Phen.* 459).

164. By way of example, GW 9:406.11–27 (*Phen.* 460).

165. *das unmittelbare Bewußtseyn* 404.15; *der seyende Gegenstand* 404.15–16; *der sich selbst wissende Geist* 404.16–17; *Begriff* 404.17; *das unmittelbare Ansich* 404.23; *das unmittelbare Ansich des Geistes* 404.28; *die seyende Notwen-*

digkeit 404.23–24; *Wissen von sich* 404.30; *Wahrheit* 404.31; *die Gestalt des Selbstbewußtseyns 'an sich'* 404.33; *ein wirklicher Mensch* 404.35–36; *diese Göttlichkeit* 404.37; *das Selbst des daseyenden Geistes* 405.9; *die Form der vollkommen Unmittelbarkeit* 405.9–10; *dieser Gott* 405.12; *Selbstbewußtseyn* 405.13; *Wesen/ Geist* 405.16–19; *Subjekt oder Selbst* 405.22; *die untrennbare Einheit mit sich* 405.32; *das unmittelbar allgemeine* 405.32–33; *der reine Begriff, das reine Denken, Fürsichseyn, das unmittelbar Seyn, Seyn für anderes, das Wahrhaft und allein offenbare* 405.33–36; *diese reine Allgemeine* 406.2; *das offenbare* 406.5–6; *die göttliche Natur ist dasselbe, was die menschliche ist, und diese Einheit ist est, die angeschaut wird* 406.8–10; *dieses Seyn* 406.13–14; *das absolute Wesen* 406.14–15; *die absolute Abstraction* 406.18–19; *die reine Einzelheit des Selbsts* 406.19–20; *das Unmittelbare* 406.20; *Seyn* 406.20; *ein seyender Selbstbewußtseyn* 406.24–25; *das unmittelbare Daseyn* 406.28; *die Unmittelbarkeit* 406.29; *das rein gedachten oder absoluten Wesen* 406.31; *die Einheit des Seyns und Wesens, des Denkens* 406.33; *der Gedanke dieses religiöses Bewußtseyn* 406.34; *vermitteltes Wissen* 406.34–35; *unmittelbares Wissen* 406.35; *die Einheit des Seyns und Denkens* 406.35–36; *die gedachte Einheit* 406.36–37; *Denken* 407.4; *reines Wesen* 407.4; *Daseyn* 407.5; *die Negativität seiner selbst* 407.5; *Selbst, dieses, allgemeines Selbst* 407.6; *Offenbarung* 407.8; *Geist* 407.13. Page and line references are to GW 9 (*Phen.* 457.3–461.29).

166. GW 9:403.21–22 (*Phen.* 457).

167. "Die Entäusserung der Substanz, ihr Werden zum Selbstbewußtseyn drückt den Uebergang ins Entgegengesetzte, den Bewußtlosen Uebergang der *Nothwendigkeit*, oder diß aus, daß sie *an sich* Selbstbewußtseyn ist." GW 9:403.22–25 (*Phen.* 457 trans. amended). It can equally be said that the opposite movement is one of necessity since it too bears the structure of development from implicit to explicit. GW 9:403.25–29, (*Phen.* 457). The statement is made by Hegel explicitly concerning the first of the two externalizations.

See also in the context of Hegel's argument against mere imagination, GW 9:404.14, 16, 19 (*Phen.* 458).

168. "nach eben der Nothwendigkeit des Begriffes . . . , als *das Seyn* oder die *Unmittelbarkeit*, die der innhaltslose Gegenstand des sinnlichen Bewußtseyns ist, sich seiner entäussert, und Ich für das Bewußtseyn wird." GW 9:404.19–22 (*Phen.* 458).

169. "Erkennen der Nothwendigkeit"/"die seyende Nothwendigkeit." GW 9:404.22–24 (*Phen.* 458).

170. "das Werden der *angeschauten Nothwendigkeit*." GW 9:404.26–27 (*Phen.* 458).

171. On Hegel's goal of uniting the three "logicities" (immediate, phenomenological and speculative) see Ch. 3 Subsection 4a of the present study.

172. GW 9:403.17–35 (*Phen.* 457.3–25), quoted Ch. 4 n. 131 above. On several meanings to Hegel's use of *Dasein*, see Ch. 4 n. 239 below.

173. "das *Werden*, den *Begriff*, oder das *ansichseyende* Hervorgehen desselben [des seiner als Geist selbstbewußten Geistes]." GW 9:402.35–36 (*Phen.* 456 trans. amended).

174. GW 9:403.18–22 (*Phen.* 457).

175. GW 9:403.22–28 (*Phen.* 457).

176. GW 9:403.32–35 with 16–18 (*Phen.* 457).

177. Recall that religion, and especially revelatory religion, is the *an sich* reconciliation of actual Spirit and religious Spirit in the *Phenomenology*.

178. "jedes zum andern werdend," "er [Geist] als diese ihre Einheit ins Daseyn tritt." GW 9:403.34–35 (*Phen.* 457).

179. With more inclusive terms Heinrichs observes, "In der Gestalt des menschgewordenen Gottes sind die Reflexionslogik des 'Denkens' und die Unmittelbarkeit des 'Seins' (529.30) unmittelbar vereinigt. . . . Die Ineinssetzung von Wesentlichkeit und Unmittelbarkeit ist nur eine durch das Selbstbewußtsein des Geistes, also begriffslogisch, vermittelte!" *Die Logik* 445–446. Granted it was Hegel's intention to unite the logic of reflection and the immediacy of being through the logic of the Concept as self-consciousness of Spirit, the question remains whether Hegel was able to accomplish this as he intended. The logically later logic of reflection is here structurally dependent upon and reproduces in advanced form the logically earlier movement of becoming settling into concrete existence. Hence the underlying structural movement here is that of *Werden im Dasein* (becoming to concrete existence). Though Hegel's *Phenomenology* was conceived by him as being structured in relationship to his "earlier" logic, he has by this stage in the *Phenomenology* developed a new *Erscheinungslogik* whose structure is clearly that of the later, basic movement developed by Hegel in the *Logic*. On Hegel's later, fuller developed logic of appearance (*Erscheinungslogik*) see esp. GW 11:341.1–352.35/L 2:122–136 (GL 499–511). On becoming settling in concrete existence, see Ch. 2 Subsection 2 above and the quotes in Ch. 4 n. 249 below. Note however that here in the *Phenomenology* Hegel uses the preposition *in* with the accusative, *ins Dasein*, which stresses transition into, whereas Hegel also uses *in* with the dative, e.g., L 1:140 (GL 150).

180. For further reflections on theological questions see Guibal, *Dieu selon Hegel* 111–127.

181. E.g., GW 9:403.36–404.32 (*Phen.* 457–458). See also Guibal, *Dieu selon Hegel* 112–115; Heinrichs, *Die Logik* 445.

182. Consciousness as that which distinguishes and relates, GW 9:58.25–26 (*Phen.* 52), and as beginning in an originary unity, GW 9:63.29–33 (*Phen.* 58–59).

183. The term is Chapelle's, "la re-présentation de la présence." *Hegel et la religion*. Vol. 1: *La problématique* (Paris: Éditions Universitaires, 1964) 25,

cited by Heede, *Die göttliche Idee* 187. However Chapelle is speaking of "religion" rather than more specifically of reconciliation in Christ as Heede claims.

184. GW 9:412.15–19 (*Phen.* 467).

185. GW 9:403.8–16 (*Phen.* 457).

186. E.g., here on the level of representation.

187. From the perspective of the writer of the *Phenomenology*, that is, from the perspective of absolute knowledge out of which the writer works.

188. "Er [Geist] als diese ihre [die zwei Entäusserungen] Einheit ins Daseyn tritt." GW 9:402.34–35 (*Phen.* 457). In the paragraph which ends with this phrase Hegel asserted the entrance of absolute essence into existence three times.

189. "weder als gedachtes oder vorgestelltes noch hervorgebrachtes." GW 9:405.10 (*Phen.* 459). Hegel continues, "dieser Gott wird unmittelbar als Selbst, als ein wirklicher einzelner Mensch, sinnlich angeschaut; so nur *ist* er Selbstbewußtseyn." GW 9:405.12–13 ("this God is sensuously and directly beheld as a Self, as an actual individual man; only so *is* this God self-consciousness." *Phen.* 459).

190. "Er [Geist] wird gewußt als Selbstbewußtseyn und ist diesem unmittelbar, denn er ist dieses selbst; die göttliche Natur ist dasselbe, was die menschliche ist, und diese Einheit ist es, die angeschaut wird." GW 9:406.7–10 (*Phen.* 460).

191. Note for example Hegel's mixture of categories in the assertion, "daß das glaubende Bewußtseyn diese Göttlichkeit *sieht* und *fühlt* und *hört*." GW 9:404.36–37 ("that the believing consciousness *sees* and *feels* and *hears* this divinity." *Phen.* 458 trans. amended).

192. In their own way, each of these three aspects of critique concretizes Hegel's own characterization of consciousness as that which distinguishes and relates. On this characteristic, see again GW 9:58.25–26 (*Phen.* 52).

193. As pointed out in a more general way already by Jean Hyppolite, *Genèse et structure de la "Phénomenologie de l'Esprit" de Hegel* (Paris: Montaigne, 1946) 540.

As also indicated by Walter Jaeschke's interpretation of "God-man" more specifically with references to Hegel's philosophy of religion *Lectures*. "It is crucial for the proper understanding of the Concept of free subjectivity that one interpret the notion God-man not through a doctrine of two natures but as the expression, at the level of representation, of the Concept of absolute Spirit. The foundation of the representation God-man is the inseparability of subjectivity and its other, objectivity: God is no longer opposed to the Subject as a mere other but rather as the other of the Subject itself; and in this other the Subject has its self-consciousness." "Christianity and Secularity in Hegel's Concept of the State," *The Journal of Religion* 61 (April 1981) 135. For Hegel, however, this dialectical unity with the acknowledgement of mediation as implied by Jaeschke is not what must be revealed at this point if the structure of the *Phenomenology* is to succeed at this point in the *Phenomenology*'s movement.

194. Again, recall GW 9:403.17–35 (*Phen.* 457.3–25). The two becomings are retained as "moments."

195. GW 9:406.7–10 (*Phen.* 460).

196. See in Ch. 4 this Subsection 3b of the present study.

197. Recall again the general remarks in Ch. 3 Subsections 4a and b of the present study.

198. GW 9:403.32–35 with 425.23–25 (*Phen.* 457 with 483). See also Ch. 4 n. 10 above.

199. "Er [dieser einzelner Mensch] ist der *unmittelbar* gegenwärtige Gott." GW 9:407.33–35 ("He [this individual man] is the *immediately* present God." *Phen.* 462). Hegel's terminology is not always so clear, consistent and insistent. When stressing sense immediacy as with this quote, Hegel speaks of an immediately present God. When he argues concerning structure and movement, he underscores the intuited unity of human and divine, as for example GW 9:406.7–10 (*Phen.* 460). Again, in trying from the point of view of consciousness to stress immediate objectivity Hegel can write, "Das Bewußtseyn geht dann nicht aus *seinem* Innern von dem Gedanken aus, and schließt in *sich* den Gedanken des Gottes mit dem Daseyn zusammen, sondern es geht von dem unmittelbaren gegenwärtigen Daseyn aus, and erkennt den Gott in ihm." GW 9:405.1–4 ("Consciousness, then, does not start from *its* inner life, from thought, and unite *within itself* the thought of God with existence; on the contrary, it starts from an existence that is immediately present and recognizes God therein." *Phen.* 458). The structural demands of Hegel's *Phenomenology* require however that this last quote be taken in the light of Hegel's texts stressing intuited unity. Were Hegel able to stick solely with this last quote, and were he able to develop its implications, he would have produced a considerably different and more viable structuring of the experience of the divine.

200. See esp. Ch. 4 n. 165 above.

201. Again on the divine-human unity, GW 9:406.7–10 (*Phen.* 460).

202. In line with his program as sketched in Ch. 3 Subsection 4a of the present study.

203. See also Ch. 3 n. 169 above.

204. See the beginning of Ch. 3 Subsection 4a of the present study.

205. GW 9:29.14–17 (*Phen.* 21).

206. Recall Ch. 3 Subsection 5 of the present study and especially Ch. 3 n. 221 above.

207. It might be helpful to recall the basic unity of the *Phenomenology* (see Ch. 3 n. 128 above) and in its Preface Hegel's reiteration of positions taken earlier in the Introduction (see Ch. 3 n. 198 above). These two points justify

a continuing application of Hegel's programmatic observation as found in the Introduction to this later part of the *Phenomenology* as well.

208. E.g., GW 9:403.28-30 (*Phen.* 459). In general on the question of this Self as object of consciousness, see GW 9:405.14-406.10 (*Phen.* 459-460).

209. Along with the citations in n. 208 immediately above, see also the overviews in Ch. 4 Subsections 2 and 3a of the present study.

210. GW 9:404.33-37 (*Phen.* 458).

211. For specific references see Ch. 4 nn. 131 and 165 above.

212. E.g., E § 147R. On Hegel's conception of the infinite as inclusive totality and truth, see Ch. 6 Subsection 2 of the present study.

213. "Diese Einheit der Möglichkeit und Wirklichkeit ist die *Zufälligkeit*." GW 11:383.36/L 2:173 ("This unity of possibility and actuality is *contingency*." GL 545). See also Ch. 4 n. 214 immediately below.

214. For the sake of clarity and brevity, one might express Hegel's position simply by quoting from the *Logic* where Hegel writes concerning "formal" actuality, possibility and necessity, "Diese Einheit der Möglichkeit und Wirklichkeit ist die *Zufälligkeit*. . . . Diese *absolute Unruhe* des *Werdens* dieser beyden Bestimmungen ist die *Zufälligkeit*. Aber darum weil jede unmittelbar in die entgegengesetzte umschlägt, so *geht* sie in dieser ebenso schlechthin *mit sich* selbst zusammen, und diese *Identität* derselben, einer in der andern, ist die *Notwendigkeit*." GW 11:383.36 and 384.31-34/L 2:173-174 ("This unity of possibility and actuality is *contingency*. . . . This *absolute unrest* of the *becoming* of these two determinations is *contingency*. But just because each immediately turns into its opposite, equally in this other it simply *unites with itself*, and this identity of both, of one in the other, is *necessity*." GL 545).

215. Recall even Hegel's moves to overcome a projectionist view of the appearance of the divine, of essence, GW 9:403.36-404.32 (*Phen.* 457-458).

216. See again the quote in Ch. 4 n. 214 here above, a quote in which Hegel sublates contingency in necessity, with necessity as the identity of the double becoming of possibility and actuality constituting contingency.

217. It was the *an sich* reconciliation of actual Spirit and religious Spirit in the divine-human Self which Hegel needed on structural and systematic bases to establish and which he tried to make available as divine-human Self.

218. That is of course in its structure and not merely as the psychological perception of an object by a specific individual.

219. See again the remarks in Ch. 4 Subsection 3a of the present study.

220. With one qualification. In his need to achieve the *an sich* reconciliation attained in the divine-human Self Hegel stresses again and again the *immediate* appearance of this object. However, in his initial treatment of sense certainty, Hegel had spoken more explicitly of sense certainty or consciousness as both immediate and mediated. "Diesen Unterschied des Wesens und des Beyspiels, der Unmittelbarkeit und der Vermittlung, machen nicht wir, sondern

wir finden ihn an der sinnlichen Gewißheit selbst." GW 9:64.12–14 ("It is not just we who make this distinction between essence and instance, between immediacy and mediation; on the contrary, we find it within sense-certainty itself." *Phen.* 59). Also, GW 9:64.1–22 (*Phen.* 59).

221. GW 9:63.1–70.29 (*Phen.* 58–67). The comparison could in its own way, though need not here, be carried through to include the *Phenomenology's* Chapter Two on perception (*Wahrnehmung*) GW 9:71.1–81.14 (*Phen.* 67–79).

222. As a general conclusion against the background of Hegel's distinctions in the *Phenomenology's* Introduction taken with his distinction of the object (*Gegenstand*) of immediate consciousness on the basis of example (*Beispiel*), GW 9:64.1–28 (*Phen.* 59).

223. As Hegel describes the very dialectic of sense certainty: "*Sie* [die sinnliche Gewißheit] ist also selbst zu fragen: *Was ist das Diese?* Nehmen wir es in der gedoppelten Gestalt seines Seyns, als das *Itzt* und als das *Hier*, so wird die Dialektik, die es an ihm hat, eine so verständliche Form erhalten, als es Selbst ist." GW 9:64.29–31. ("It is, then, sense-certainty itself that must be asked: 'What is the *This*?' If we take the 'This' in the twofold shape of its being, as 'Now' and as 'Here,' the dialectic it has in it will receive a form as intelligible as the 'This' itself is." *Phen.* 59–60).

224. "Was das sinnliche Bewußtseyn gennant wird, ist eben diese reine *Abstraction*, es ist diß Denken, für welches das *Seyn*, das *Unmittelbare ist.*" GW 9:406.21–22 ("What is called sense–consciousness is just this pure *abstraction*, it is this thinking for which *being* is the *immediate*." *Phen.* 460).

225. GW 9:406.7–10 (*Phen.* 460).

226. One cannot respond that Hegel argues to essence available merely *as* a finite consciousness, since Hegel claims and must claim the immediate presence to consciousness of a divine-human unity. Recall that "simple immediacy," GW 9:63.28–30 (*Phen.* 58–59), or "immediacy," GW 9:406.21–22 (*Phen.* 460), is the proper and essential characteristic directly correlative to sense certainty.

227. I.e., in the first half of the present Ch. 4 Subsection 3b.

228. It might be of additional help to recall again that sense consciousness is a form of thought. GW 9:406.21–22 (*Phen.* 460). And thought for Hegel always involves mediation, e.g., GW 9:406.33–35 (*Phen.* 461).

229. GW 9:58.25–26 (*Phen.* 52). That Hegel was apparently not interested in the inner condition of the divine-human mediator does not in any way absolve that self-consciousness from the conditioning requirements of the structure of developing self-consciousness as such. Hegel could absolve the proposed divine-human Self from the limitations of consciousness, that is, claim that it is the immediate unity of a divine-human self-consciousness, only if he were to presuppose, and more, to argue from the nature of absolute knowledge. To do so would, however, violate the canons of his own program. As indicated

here in the text, such a move to absolve would equally fall behind the level of religious consciousness already to have been arrived at.

230. The *locus* of consciousness as consciousness and for Hegel the *Dasein* of absolute Spirit.

231. As a general statement, see GW 9:61.19–27 (*Phen.* 56).

232. GW 9:403.17–35 (*Phen.* 457.3–25).

233. "nach eben der Nothwendigkeit des Begriffes . . . , als das *Seyn* oder die *Unmittelbarkeit*, die der innhaltslose Gegenstand des sinnlichen Bewußtseyns ist, sich seiner entäussert, und Ich für das Bewußtseyn wird." GW 9:404.19–22 (*Phen.* 458 trans. amended).

In his treatment of the *Phenomenology*'s first four chapters, Howard P. Kainz had spoken of at least five different forms of necessity discoverable in Hegel's *Phenomenology*. *Hegel's "Phenomenology," Part I: Analysis and Commentary* (University, Alabama: The University of Alabama Press, 1976). These five are summarized by James L. Marsh as "logical, not in a traditional sense but in a sense involving non-identity and opposition; natural, hypothetical, general, and transcending." Review of *A Reading of Hegel's "Phenomenology of Spirit"* by Quentin Lauer, S.J., in *The Owl of Minerva* 12 (September 1980) 2. Hegel's use of necessity as that of the Concept would be the foundation for any other types of necessity distinguishable in the *Phenomenology*.

234. On formal necessity, GW 11:383.36 and 384.31–34/L 2:173–174 (GL 545). Concerning real necessity, GW 11:390.7–11/L 2:181 (GL 551); on absolute necessity, "Die absolute Notwendigkeit ist also die Wahrheit, in welche Wirklichkeit und Möglichkeit überhaupt, sowie die formelle und reale Notwendigkeit zurückgeht." GW 11:391.5–7/L 2:182 ("Absolute necessity is, therefore, the truth into which actuality and possibility as such, and formal and real necessity withdraw." GL 552). In general, see GW 11:380.1–392.31/L 2:169–184 (GL 541–553). On the difficulty involved in the conception of necessity, see E § 147R.

235. E.g., GW 9:403.17–35 (*Phen.* 457.3–25).

236. In this critique, Ch. 4 Subsection 3b of the present study, so far.

237. Were the focus of this study more directly the *Phenomenology* itself, it would be profitable to pursue in detail the question as to how Hegel tries to move from comic consciousness and unhappy consciousness by means of a logico-ontological generalization of these constructs to the concreteness of a divine-human unity. The problem would be whether these two can be argued to constitute and be interrelated in a structure of determinate negation.

238. Very generally stated, Hegel could not assert phenomenologically that the incarnational immediacy of a divine-human unity of self-consciousness was the simple content of revelatory religion if he did not presuppose the goal of an identity of Concept and Self in absolute knowledge. Were Hegel's

phenomenological project successfully arguable in terms of its own inner consistency as well as immanent and consistent development, then Hegel could justify presuppositions concerning the grounding reality of absolute knowledge.

239. And here as a concrete existent. *Dasein* or concrete existence functions for Hegel in the *Logic* as thought determination, especially L 1:95–97 (GL 109–111), and in the *Phenomenology* text in question, GW 9:403.17–35 (*Phen.* 457.3–25), as concrete existence. It comes as well to mean a concrete existent when the *Dasein* is considered a specific self-consciousness. In this present discussion *Dasein* will be used to refer to "thought determination" unless otherwise indicated.

240. Reaching its mature expression in the *Logic* and of course here worked out by Hegel as a development from his 1804–1805 logic.

241. GW 9:403.34–35 (*Phen.* 457).

242. Note again GW 9:403.17–35 (*Phen.* 457.3–25). The term, *Werden im Dasein*, is Hegel's, L 1:140 (GL 150).

243. Unless otherwise indicated, references are to GW 9:403.17–25 (*Phen.* 451.3–25).

244. L 1:67, 92–93 (GL 82–83, 105–106). See Ch. 2 Subsection 2 of the present study.

245. At the end of Ch. 2 Subsection 4 of the present study.

246. L 1:92–93 (GL 105–106).

247. "Beide [Entstehen, Vergehen] sind dasselbe, Werden, und auch als diese so unterschiedenen Richtungen durchdringen und paralysieren sie sich gegenseitig. . . . Das Werden ist eine haltungslose Unruhe, die in ein ruhiges Resultat zusammensinkt." L 1:92–93 (GL 106).

248. "Das Werden ist die Ungetrenntheit des Sein and Nichts, . . . als Einheit des *Seins* and *Nichts* ist es diese *bestimmte* Einheit, oder in welcher sowohl Sein als Nichts *ist*." L 1:92 ("Becoming is the unseparatedness of being and nothing, . . . as the unity of being and nothing it is this *determinate* unity in which there *is* both being and nothing." GL 105). See also the text in Ch. 4 n. 249 immediately below.

249. "Das Werden ist eine haltungslose Unruhe, die in ein ruhiges Resultat zusammensinkt." L 1:93 ("Becoming is an unstable unrest which settles into a stable result." GL 106). Hegel tries to cover the double result by a singular "this result" (*Dies Resultat*) L 1:93 (GL 106). Again, though in another context and with different considerations, Hegel covers with "Das Dritte oder das Vierte ist überhaupt die Einheit des ersten and zweyten Moments, des Unmittelbaren and des Vermittelten." GW 12:247.18–20/L 2:498 ("The third or the fourth is in general the unity of the first and second moments, of the immediate and the mediated." GL 836).

250. And according to the very dynamic of Hegel's own dialectic.

251. L 1:96 (GL 109).

252. "paralysieren sie sich gegenseitig." L 1:92–93 (GL 106 trans. amended).

253. The famous discussion about whether Hegel's thought is triadic or tetradic can in one sense be resolved into the question of the relationship between becoming and *Dasein*. On this problematic see the stimulating study by Meulen, *Hegel*. However, Meulen's position on the structural "brokenness" or division in the *Phenomenology* would need to be nuanced in view of the later studies by Labarrière and Heinrichs. See Ch. 3 n. 128 above.

But as Hegel himself in another context observes, counting is to him unimportant, GW 12:247.7–26/L 2:497–498 (GL 836–837). In fact this argument over triadic versus tetradic in Hegel can best be resolved by a careful analysis of the "transition" from becoming to *Dasein*, where Hegel bridges the gap between becoming and *Dasein* with an additional, though camouflaged triadic. It is then not simply a question of the triadic versus tetradic interpretations of this instantiation of Hegel's dialectic.

It has come to the attention of this writer that John Burbidge proposes, beyond Meulen's tetradic analysis, his own interpretation of the movement from being to *Dasein*, an interpretation involving "five operations: understanding, dialectic, synthesis, mediation, and speculative unity." *On Hegel's Logic. Fragments of a Commentary* (Atlantic Highlands, NJ: Humanities, 1981) 58, further 246 n. 8, and 42–45. In view of Prof. Burbidge's statement that "concepts are signs for the dynamic activity of intelligence" (56), it would be important to explore whether he is proposing a pentadic structure to the movement of Hegel's overall dialectic of pure thought.

254. Becoming thematizes the dialectical identity of being and nothing, but not thereby resultant restful identity as enriched return to immediacy.

255. Abstraction in the sense of left behind and not in the properly Hegelian sense of not as yet having been made explicit.

256. As concluded in Ch. 2 Subsection 5 of the present study.

257. A reduplication of becoming on the basis of a second appeal to being and nothing, that is, then a reduplication both of becoming and of the appeal to being and nothing, L 1:92–93 (GL 105–106). Note a comparison of the first edition, GW 11:56.21–57.37, and second edition, L 1:92–93 (GL 105–106), on the move from becoming to *Dasein* would reveal various attempts by Hegel to clarify this "transition."

258. L 1:96 (GL 109).

259. It is in this doubled synthesis of becoming and *Dasein* that Meulen finds the paradigm for what he terms "the broken middle" ("*eine in sich gebrochene Mitte*"), *Hegel* 52.

260. See Ch. 4 n. 257 here above. Hegel argues in a similar vein regularly enough throughout the *Logic* by reduplicating his appeal to or recalling the prior moments of a newly established thought determination. In regard to the

transition from becoming to *Dasein* this procedure is unacceptable first because Hegel is here uniquely dealing with an attempt to move from determinationless *Sein* to *Dasein* and second because Hegel is obliged to set up a further triadic negation of negation in order to move from becoming to *Dasein*. In other logically later moves, on the other hand, where Hegel's result is an immediately doubled set of thought determinations, e.g., *Etwas* and *Anderes*, L 1:103 (GL 116), this procedure would be more acceptable since Hegel is there not trying by a further negation of negation to establish what should have already arisen. Also, in view of the critique so far presented here, Hegel's logic is neither a movement from the totally indeterminate nor is there any longer a need to cover the brokenness of becoming in its later logical formulation by a further triadic negation of negation.

261. GW 11:44.24/L 1:67 (GL 83).

262. GW 11:44.22–29/L 1:67 (GL 82–83).

263. "Das Werden ist auf diese Weise in gedoppelter Bestimmung; in der einen ist das Nichts als unmittelbar, d.h., sie ist anfangend vom Nichts, das sich auf das Sein bezieht, d.h. in dasselbe übergeht, in der anderen ist das Sein als unmittelbar, d.i. sie ist anfangend vom Sein, das in das Nichts übergeht,— *Entstehen* und *Vergehen*. Beide sind dasselbe, Werden." L 1:92 (GL 105–106). Hegel lists coming-to-be and ceasing-to-be as "moments of becoming," which nevertheless were to function for him as transition to *Dasein*. However, Hegel is either trapped in becoming or must establish another triadic to get to *Dasein*, neither of which alternatives he wanted or could admit to. Hegel had tried to hide the necessary second movement of determinate negation in the *Logic* by stressing that *Entstehen* and *Vergehen* were each becoming. However, in the *Phenomenology* Hegel needed to highlight the two as respectively the movements from substance to self-consciousness (comic consciousness) and from self-consciousness to universal essence (unhappy consciousness). It is this need of Hegel to highlight the distinctiveness of these two in the *Phenomenology* which provides the occasion here for a clearer critique.

264. It would be interesting to explore whether or not all philosophical and theological arguments from infinity to finitude do not in some way or other include a parallel second appeal or usage to compensate for the unexpressed original move from finitude to infinity.

265. In a sense there are then three presentations of "Incarnation" in the chapter on revelatory religion: incarnational immediacy; reflection on the limitations thereof; the developed content of divine self-othering.

266. "Dieser einzelne Mensch also, als welcher das absolute Wesen offenbar ist, vollbringt an ihm als Einzelnem die Bewegung des *sinnlichen Seins*. Er ist der *unmittelbar* gegenwärtige Gott." GW 9:407.33–35 (*Phen.* 462 trans. amended).

267. See Ch. 4 Subsection 3b of the present study.

268. As also in the *Logic*. See on the *Phenomenology*, Guibal, *Dieu selon Hegel* 112. Hegel's reference to "the world's faith" (*Glauben der Welt*), GW 9:404.33–405.4 (*Phen.* 458), cannot be appealed to in order to weaken this public stance. This for several reasons, including: Hegel's intention to elevate natural consciousness; Hegel's emphasis on sense intuition; the *Phenomenology*'s beginning in the unity of sense certainty.

269. In *any* theory because the arguments presented concern the finitude of consciousness and thought as such.

270. A commonly enough accepted position in Christology today. See e.g., Lucien Richard, *What Are They Saying about Christ and World Religions* (New York: Paulist, 1981) 58.

271. Divine and infinite taken very generally here.

272. To be seen against the background of Hegel's inadequate understanding of negativity.

In *Dieu selon Hegel* Guibal underscores Hegel's intention to establish the facticity of the Incarnation (311). But Guibal wonders if there is not more of importance to the reality of the Mediator than the simple event or appearance (284, also 124) and if the Mediator should not stand out more sharply and clearly (311). Unfortunately in spite of a valuable exposition of Hegel's thought on religion in the *Phenomenology* Guibal generally stays more or less and in too mild a manner on the outside without engaging Hegel directly enough from within Hegel's thought (271–272, see also 286, 310, 314, 335).

273. See Guibal, *Dieu selon Hegel* 94.

274. Or compared or integrated.

275. Meulen's interweaving of Hegel's two major presentations of Incarnation confuses the structure of this implicit syllogism of incarnational immediacy. Meulen speaks of E-A-B (individuality/universality/particularity) in *Hegel* 330. It would seem preferable not to try to interpret incarnational immediacy in such an explicit syllogistic formulation. Admittedly, this looser term "implicit syllogism" is not Hegel's. It could be said that "judgement" is the more appropriate referent. However, with the Incarnation as immediate appearance of a divine-human Self, Hegel is in the *Phenomenology* beyond "mere judgement." See also Ch. 3 n. 123 above.

276. Splett speaks more generally of incarnational immediacy as *Ausgangspunkt*, *Trinitätslehre* 65. Guibal speaks of incarnational immediacy as "le présupposé fondamental qui la [la communauté spirituelle] rend possible." *Dieu selon Hegel* 122.

277. "In ihre [der absoluten religion] wird das Wesen als Geist gewußt, oder sie ist sein Bewußtseyn über sich, Geist zu seyn. Denn der Geist ist das Wissen seiner selbst in seiner Entäusserung." GW 9:405.16–18 ("In this absolute religion the divine Being is known as Spirit, or this religion is the consciousness of the divine Being that it is Spirit. For Spirit is the knowledge

of oneself in the externalization of oneself." *Phen.* 459 trans. amended). Also GW 9:405.22–25 (*Phen.* 459).

278. Recall again the statement of Hegel's trinitarian claim in the Introduction to this study.

279. On "absolute knowledge" (the *Phenomenology's* Chapter 7) see Labarrière's phenomenological and structural analysis, *Structures et mouvement* 185–263, and Heinrichs's more logical analysis, *Die Logik* 469–490.

280. GW 9:425.23–26 (*Phen.* 483).

281. See the beginning of Ch. 1 Subsection 1 of the present study, and especially the references in Ch. 1 n. 2 above.

282. "Der seiner selbst gewiße Geist." One of Hegel's titles, GW 9:323.23 (*Phen.* 364).

283. GW 9:425.26–426.14 (*Phen.* 483–484).

284. GW 9:422.10–28, 427.18–23 (*Phen.* 479–480, 485).

285. "Diese Versöhnung des Bewußtseyns mit dem Selbstbewußtseyn zeigt sich hiemit von der gedoppelten Seite zu Stande gebracht, das einemal im religiösen Geiste, das anderemal im Bewußtseyn selbst als solchem [dem seiner selbst gewißen Geist]. Sie unterscheiden sich beyde so voneinander, daß jene diese Versöhnung in der Form das *Ansichseyns*, diese in der Form des *Fürsichseyns* ist. . . . Die Vereinigung beyder Seiten ist noch nicht aufgezeigt; sie ist es, welche diese Reihe der Gestaltungen des Geistes beschließt; denn in ihr kommt der Geist dazu, sich zu wissen nicht nur wie er *an sich*, oder noch seinem absoluten Inhalte, noch nur wie er für *sich* nach seiner inhaltslosen Form oder nach der Seite des Selbstbewußtseyns, sondern wie er an und *für sich* ist." GW 9:425.10–14, 18–22 (*Phen.* 482–483 trans. amended. It may be helpful to indicate that Miller translates *an und für sich* as "both *in essence and in actuality*, or *in and for itself*").

Both Labarrière, *Structures et mouvement* 189–190, and Heinrichs, *Die Logik* 473 esp. n. 296, underscore Hegel's shifting from a more expected consideration of religion as *für sich* and actual Spirit as *an sich*. Heinrichs situates and roots the possibility of this "shift" within the perspective of absolute knowledge where objectivity has become transparent. That this is a much less radical shift than either Labarrière or Heinrichs would tend to imply is indicated by Hegel's regular reference already prior to absolute knowledge to religion as the an *sich* reconciliation of actual Spirit and religious Spirit as well as the *fürsichseinde, selbstbewußte Geist*. Hegel's usage of certain key terms is marked by a certain flexibility.

286. As Hegel reminds the reader, GW 9:426.16–18 (*Phen.* 484).

287. GW 9:427.28–428.3 (*Phen.* 485–486).

288. GW 9:423.1–16 (*Phen.* 480). Note Hegel speaks of the second moment as *Bestimmung* (determination) rather than his later regular use of *Besonderheit* (particularity).

289. GW 9:429.31–32, 432.31–37 (*Phen.* 488, 491). In Hegel's mature thought and here specifically in the *Phenomenology* absolute knowledge was intended to be the grounding return to the originary unity, here of sense certainty and to the divine-human unity to have been established in revelatory religion. However, as with the *Logic* Hegel's forward moving deductive argumentation cannot be supplemented or replaced by this grounding return. To do so would be to presuppose the validity of Hegel's argument.

290. GW 9:427.28–428.3 with 431.36–432.30 (*Phen.* 485–486 with 490–491).

291. See Ch. 2 Subsections 4 and 5 of the present study.

292. GW 9:58.25–26 (*Phen.* 52).

293. Positions excellently elaborated by Labarrière and Heinrichs against Haering and those following Haering's lead. See Ch. 3 n. 128 above. This is surely what W. Marx meant in arguing that self-consciousness is the principle which unifies the *Phenomenology*. Again see Ch. 3 n. 128 above.

This present critique's implications for a discussion as to whether the *Phenomenology* itself despite Hegel's intention and the underlying logical structure can still be claimed to be a unified work is beyond the scope of this present study. Nevertheless this critique certainly implies a partially new approach to a possible rupture in the text as text, as was briefly mentioned concerning Meulen's theory, Ch. 4 n. 253 above.

294. Argued in Ch. 4 Subsection 3b of the present study.

295. E.g., GW 9:426.14, 427.28–30 (*Phen.* 484, 485). This helps to explain the moves underlying Hegel's identification of Concept and Subject, an identification Wolfhart Pannenberg has so insightfully objected to. See Ch. 1 n. 53 above.

296. See GW 9:425.32, 426.10–14, 427.28–428.15, 431.36–432.30 esp. 432.14–23 (*Phen.* 483, 485–486, 490–491 esp. 491).

297. "*Wissen* des *unmittelbaren* oder *Seyenden*," GW 9:63.5–6 (*Phen.* 58). The movement from originary unity to differentiation takes place already in GW 9:63.1–64.11 (*Phen.* 58–59). A specific and fuller critique of Hegel's notion of the originary unity of sense certainty would follow lines of thought developed in the earlier critique of the beginning of pure thought in pure being, as carried through in Ch. 2 Subsection 4 of the present study but here appropriately adapted.

298. "Sie [diese sinnliche Gewißheit] sagt von dem, was sie weiß, nur diß aus: es *ist*; und ihre Wahrheit enthält allein das *Seyn* der Sache; das Bewußtseyn seinerseits ist in dieser Gewißheit nur als reines Ich; oder Ich bin darin nur als reiner *dieser*, und der Gegenstand nur als reines dieses." GW 9:63.17–20 (*Phen.* 58 trans. amended).

299. GW 9:63.20–30 (*Phen.* 58–59).

300. "Eine wirklich sinnliche Gewißheit ist nicht nur diese reine Unmittelbarkeit, sondern ein Beyspiel derselben." GW 9:64.3–4 (*Phen.* 59).

301. Though Hegel's explicit reason for such reference was of course merely to correct a possibly inaccurate reading by the reader. Hegel claims that it is the reflection brought by the reader which contributes the appearance of any such distinction within the originary unity of sense certainty. GW 9:64.8–11 (*Phen.* 59). Though as with pure being, Hegel is likewise here forced for the sake of consistency to posit a beginning to consciousness not publicly available to that consciousness, which even here is *thought* in the form of sense consciousness. In so far as this sense certainty is available to thought, there is always already a distinction present.

302. Logically unfounded on the basis of Hegel's inability to establish pure being as beginning of pure thought and absolute knowledge as grounding result of the phenomenological movement of consciousness.

303. As concluded in Ch. 2 Subsection 5 of the present study.

304. GW 9:38.25–26 (*Phen.* 52).

305. It is from this point of finite becoming that any more directly Christological reflection on the divinity of the Mediator or Redeemer would begin. Such a Christology could be elaborated in critical dialogue with any number of other Christologies, including ones as diverse as those by Wolfhart Pannenberg, Edward Schillebeeckx and John Cobb. Though this would form the topic of another study, could it not nevertheless be asked even here whether such an approach would not be a better carrying out of Hegel's proposal than his own system was: "So ist es nicht Einbildung, sondern es ist *wirklich an dem*. Das Bewußtseyn geht dann nicht aus *seinem* Innern, von dem Gedanken aus, und schließt *in sich* den Gedanken des Gottes mit dem Daseyn zusammen, sondern es geht von dem unmittelbaren gegenwärtigen Daseyn aus, und erkennt den Gott in ihm." GW 9:404.37–405.4 ("Thus this self-consciousness is not imagination, but is *actual* in the believer. Consciousness, then, does not start from *its* inner life, from thought, and unite *within itself* the thought of God with existence; on the contrary, it starts from an existence that is immediately present and recognizes God therein." *Phen.* 458).

306. GW 11:28.32–35/L 1:40 (GL 58).

307. GW 11:19.24–37/L 1:28–29 (GL 47).

308. Puntel had spoken of a parallel development of various total formulations of the Hegelian systematic. However, he proposed to interpret correctly Hegel's own mature systematic thought, whereas here there is proposed a tentative reconstruction of Hegel's concerns and dynamic as a movement from finite to true infinite. See Ch. 1 n. 14 above. Note also that this reference to a monologically structured movement of finite qualitative increment, becoming, merely makes explicit what is contained in Ch. 2 Subsection 5 of the present study, namely, that any beginning in the public realm is necessarily finite.

309. The in principle establishable progressively richer movement of finite logical thought would be a focusing on the monologically developed structure

of the dialogical phenomenology of finite self-consciousness. This in contradistinction to the tentative proposal by Heinrichs, *Die Logik* 523, to develop a "dia-logic" (*Dia-logik*) when he asks, "Oder wäre solche *Dialogik*, wie man eine Kategorienlehre im Ausgang vom intersubjektiven Verhältnis nennen könnte, ein Rückfall in eine Anthropologie des unmittelbaren, unbegriffenen Hinnehmens?" (525).

In theory there could be any number of formulations of "finite objective thought," and though this might at first seem objectionable, in reality the formulation of such "finite objective thought developments" would provide a particularly clear basis for dialog among cultures and religious traditions.

310. Recall Hegel's initial reference in the *Phenomenology* to the interplay between Subject and object in consciousness as one of "opposition" (*Gegensatz*). See esp. Ch. 3 n. 198 above. Recall also the earlier mentioned (Ch. 2 n. 60 above) "undeveloped" character of Hegel's presentation of negativity.

311. See variants on this in Heinrichs, *Die Logik* 523–526, with literature and helpful questions concerning the relationships among negativity, otherness and novelty; also Werner Flach, *Negation and Andersheit. Ein Beitrag zur Problematik der Letztimplikation* (Munich: Reinhardt, 1959).

One might recognize a residual indication of the co-constitutive character of the relationship of object to Subject as negative and positive in Hegel's determination of quality (*Qualität*) as "reality" (*Realität*) and "negation" (*Negation*), L 1:98 (GL 111). In the *Phenomenology* recall the double reality of finite Spirit as evil and good.

312. Any prioritization would be the result of cultural and societal conditioning and not the result of an intrinsic interrelationship between otherness as negation and positive.

313. The specific argument is sketched in Ch. 6 Subsection 3 of the present study.

5. Trinitarian Reconciliation in Hegel's Philosophy of Religion *Lectures*

1. Though Hegel rewords, clarifies and develops these lectures through the years, they are all very generally speaking divided into a brief "Introduction" and longer "Concept of Religion," then "Determinate Religions" and finally "Absolute Religion."

On the lecture texts themselves, their availability, reliability and ordering, see esp. Walter Jaeschke, "Der Aufbau und bisherigen Editionen von Hegels Vorlesungen über Philosophie der Religion" (unpublished M.A. thesis, Die Freie Universität Berlin, 1971) 4–10, 40–90 with subsequent revisions conveyed orally or in correspondence by Dr. Jaeschke. Also, Reinhard Heede, "Die göttliche

Idee und ihre Erscheinung in der Religion. Untersuchungen zum Verhältnis von Logik und Religionsphilosophie bei Hegel" (Ph.D. dissertation, Philosophical Faculty of the Westfälische Wilhelms-Universität zu Münster/Westfalen, 1972) 88–109; Reinhard Heede, "Hegel Bilanz: Hegels Religionsphilosophie als Aufgabe und Problem der Forschung," in *Hegel-Bilanz. Zur Aktualität und Inaktualität der Philosophie Hegels*, ed. Reinhard Heede and Joachim Ritter (Frankfurt am Main: Klostermann, 1973) 44–49, 54–58; Karl-Heinz Ilting, "Zur Edition," in G. W. F. Hegel, *Religionsphilosophie*, vol. 1: *Die Vorlesung von 1821*, ed. Karl-Heinz Ilting (Naples: Bibliopolis, 1978) 737–765; with particular concern for the lecture sections on the absolute religion, Peter C. Hodgson, "Editor's Introduction," in *The Christian Religion* (Ann Arbor, Michigan: Scholars, 1979) vii–xxxi; Walter Jaeschke, "Hegel's Philosophy of Religion: the Quest for a Critical Edition," *The Owl of Minerva* 11 (March 1980) 4–8, (June 1980) 1–6; Walter Jaeschke, "Probleme der Edition der Nachschriften von Hegels Vorlesungen," *Allgemeine Zeitschrift für Philosophie* 3 (1980) 51–63. On the currently rapidly developing lecture text situation, see Robert F. Brown, "Hegel's Lectures on the Philosophy of Religion: A Progress Report on the New Edition," *The Owl of Minerva* 14/3 (1983) 1–6. Identification of transcriber and dating of texts for the philosophy of religion lectures follows Jaeschke and in particular for the absolute religion Hodgson, who has incorporated then recent research including that done by Jaeschke. See also in the Introduction n. 1 above. On editions and content of Hegel's *Lectures*, see Dale M. Schlitt, *Divine Subjectivity. Understanding Hegel's Philosophy of Religion* (Scranton, PA: University of Scranton Press, 2009) 3–121.

Beyond the briefest of remarks in this "Introduction and Context," for a more nuanced and complete study of the outline and composition of Hegel's various lectures on the philosophy of religion see Jaeschke, "Aufbau" 11–39; with discussion of the relevant literature, Heede, "Die göttliche Idee" 110–189; Falk Wagner, *Der Gedanke der Persönlichkeit Gottes bei Fichte und Hegel* (Gütersloh: Mohn, 1971) 205–206.

For bibliographic references concerning Hegel's philosophy of religion lectures, besides those *in Hegel Bibliography-Bibliographie. Background Material on the International Reception of Hegel within the Context of the History of Philosophy/Materialien zur Geschichte der internationalen Hegel-Rezeption und zur Philosophie-Geschichte*, compiled by Kurt Steinhauer, two volumes (Munich: Saur, 1980, 1998), see especially the references with their own further bibliographic indications in Walter Kern, "Dialektik und Trinität in der Religionsphilosophie Hegels. Ein Beitrag zur Diskussion mit Oeing-Hanhoff," *Zeitschrift für katholische* Theologie 102 (1980) 133 n. 19. Also BR 329–340; Otto Pöggeler, ed., *Hegel. Einführung in seine Philosophie* (Munich: Alber, 1977) 185–186, and bibliographies in the works cited immediately below in this note.

Helpful secondary literature forming the background to this present chapter, some of which however have become relatively less helpful in view of progress by Jaeschke, Heede and Hodgson in distinguishing Hegel's four lecture series: (while studies which do not fully distinguish the various lecture series do provide a valuable overview of Hegel's thought, it would be unfair to Hegel to argue against him from such overviews) especially now for the 1821 lectures, Albert Chapelle, *Hegel et la religion* (Paris: Éditions Universitaires), vol. 1: *La problématique* (1963); vol. 2: *La dialectique. A. Dieu et la création* (1967); vol. 3: *La théologie et l'église* (*La dialectique, deuxième partie*) (1971); *Annexes. Les textes théologiques de Hegel* (1967). Also, more generally, Claude Bruaire, *Logique et religion chrétienne dans la philosophie de Hegel* (Paris: du Seuil, 1964); Jörg Splett, *Die Trinitätslehre G. W. F. Hegels* (Munich: Alber, 1965) 116–136; Jaeschke, "Aufbau"; Wagner, *Der Gedanke* 200–288; Heede, "Die göttliche Idee"; Heede, "Hegel-Bilanz" 41–89; Wolfhart Pannenberg, "Die Subjektivität Gottes und die Trinitätslehre. Ein Beitrag zur Beziehung zwischen Karl Barth und die Philosophie Hegels," *Kerygma und Dogma* 23 (1977) 25–40; James Yerkes, *The Christology of Hegel* (Missoula, Montana: Scholars, 1978) esp. 71–244; Peter C. Hodgson, "Appendix. Commentary on the Text," in CR 313–350; Walter Jaeschke, "Absolute Idee—absolute Subjektivität. Zum Problem der Persönlichkeit Gottes in der Logik und in der Religionsphilosophie," *Zeitschrift für philosophische Forschung* 35 (1981) esp. 405–416; O. Kern Luther and Jeff L. Hoover, "Hegel's Phenomenology of Religion," *The Journal of Religion* 61 (1981) 229–241; Quentin Lauer, S.J., *Hegel's Concept of God* (Albany, NY: State University of New York, 1982); Walter Jaeschke, *Die Religionsphilosophie Hegels* (Darmstadt: Wissenschaftliche Buchgesellschaft, 1983); Peter Koslowski, "Hegel—'der Philosoph der Trinität'? Zur Kontroverse um seine Trinitätslehre," *Theologische Quartalschrift* 162 (1982) 105–131. See also Ch. 5 n. 32 below.

2. Note more generally E § 554 with Remark. Recall Chapelle's more specific description of the last syllogism in the *Encyclopedia* as "le syllogisme de la Communauté." See Ch. 3 n. 121 above. On Hegel's philosophy of religion as a philosophy of community see the well-presented study by Trutz Rendtorff, *Kirche und Theologie. Die systematische Funktion des Kirchenbegriffs in der neuem Theologie* (Gütersloh: Mohn, 1966) 63–113, explicitly, e.g., 76, 87, 95–96, cited in general and approvingly by Wagner, *Der Gedanke* 224 n. 108. See also especially concerning absolute religion the article by John E. Smith, "Hegel's Reinterpretation of the Doctrine of Spirit and Religious Community," in *Hegel and the Philosophy of Religion*, ed. Darrel E. Christensen (The Hague: Nijhoff, 1970) 158–177 with further comment 178–185.

Note further that Chapelle interestingly refers to the presentation of revealed religion in the *Encyclopedia* as "speculative theology," that in the *Phenomenology* as "ascetical theology" and now that in the philosophy of religion

Lectures as "positive theology." *La théologie et l'église* 50 with references in nn. 5 and 6.

3. GW 9:63.4–8, 64.1–11 (*Phen.* 58, 59).

4. GW 11:43.20–44.6/L 1:66–67 (GL 82); E § 86 with R.

5. "a. Begriff der Religion überhaupt. a.) Dieser Begriff aus der Vorstellung—wissen wir zunächst—daß Religion *Bewußtseyn von Gott überhaupt*— . . . [aber] Der Gegenstand den wir betrachten ist—die *Religion* selbst;—in ihr aber treffen wir sogleich die 2 Momente an;—[a)] den *Gegenstand* IN der Religion und b.) das Bewußtseyn *Subject—Mensch—der* sich zu ihm verhält—die religiöse Empfindung Anschauung, u.s.f." ILT 65.7–9, 12–16/BR 156.3–6, 9–13 (my trans. based on additions in BR). With the joining of these two moments Hegel reacts to natural theology, which he perceived as isolating the object of religion, and against the then current view, which Hegel considered as reducing religion to the subjective aspect. See ILT 65.17–85.10 (Hegel's manuscript text found only on odd numbered pages)/BR 156.14–162.22. For a more detailed presentation of religion as "Einheit von Gott und Bewußtsein Gottes" see Wagner, *Der Gedanke* 206–208.

6. "die *unendliche Negativität*, das affirmative Bewußtsein, das nur ist als Negation des Endlichen als eines Negativen." BR 149.17–18 (my trans.).

7. "Of God as this inclusive infinite" is a sort of short-hand reference to Hegel's identification, in the 1824 lectures, of religion as "die Idee des Geistes, der sich zu sich selbst verhält, das *Selbstbewußtsein des absoluten Geistes*." BR 150.36–38 ("the Idea of Spirit, which relates itself to itself, the *self-consciousness of absolute Spirit*" [my trans.]). And "gerade ist darin [in der Bewegung des Göttlichen sich zum Menschlichen zu verendlichen] das Einzelne aufgehoben und die Religion Wissen des göttlichen Geistes von sich durch vermittlung des endlichen Geistes." BR 151.28–30 ("it is exactly therein [in the movement of the divine to make itself finite in the human] that the individual is sublated and religion is through the mediation of finite Spirit the divine Spirit's knowledge of itself." my trans.) 1824.

On the need in the transition from finite to infinite to shift from the posture of observer to that of "die Bewegung der 'Sache selbst,'" ("the movement of the 'reality itself,'") see Jaeschke, "Aufbau" 17.

8. BR 188.23–33, 1824, cited by Jaeschke, "Aufbau" 18.

9. Jaeschke, "Aufbau" 18.

10. BR 67.13–37, 1824; Jaeschke, "Aufbau" 25. For the 1824 lecture section on cult in the "Concept of Religion," see e.g., BR 237.16–238.21, 1824.

11. On the general lack of specifically identifiable 1831 lecture texts on the "Concept of Religion" and the presupposition that in 1831 Hegel followed the 1827 lectures closely, see Jaeschke, "Aufbau" 22, and Heede, "Die göttliche Idee" 143.

12. Jaeschke, "Aufbau" 20, 21.

13. Jaeschke, "Aufbau" 20–22, with Jaeschke's identification on p. 22 of the subdivisions and pages in BR constituting the 1827 version of the "Concept of Religion."

14. "erst die Religionsphilosophie ist die wissenschaftliche Entwicklung, Erkenntnis dessen, was Gott ist, wodurch man erst auf erkennende Weise erfährt, was Gott ist." BR 189.4–6 (my trans.) 1827.

15. From 1821 ILT 63.21–23/BR 75.7–9. Hegel refers to the Christian religion as the religion of revelation, truth, reconciliation and freedom, ILT 495.4–499.30/AR 32.6–35.4 (CR 11–13) 1821, and as the religion of Spirit, ILT 665.18–21/AR 181.1–6 (CR 237) 1821. See also AR 227.27–31 (CR 291) 1827. In this regard see Rendtorff, *Kirche und Theologie* 75 with n. 26, where he traces the understanding of Hegel's philosophy of religion as a philosophy of Christianity to Joachim Ritter. See further Rendtorff, 109–111.

In a review of G. W. F. Hegel, *The Christian Religion*, ed. and trans. Peter C. Hodgson in *The Owl of Minerva* 11 (June 1980) 9, Stephen Crites observes regarding Hodgson's admittedly somewhat surprising but also further qualified choice of the title *The Christian Religion* for Hegel's *Die absolute Religion* that "the Christian-apologetic reading of these lectures . . . is at least as plausible as the opposite reading, according to which Hegel was a witting or unwitting enemy of Christianity." The question of concern here is however that, against Crites's own apparent orientation, Hegel's philosophy is indeed meant by him to be the adequate philosophical reformulation of the true content of the absolute religion as that content has appeared historically in the Christian religion. Whether such a reformulation is then an "apologetic" is another question.

16. Note for example, Ignatius Viyagappa, S.J., *G. W. F. Hegel's Concept of Indian Philosophy* (Rome: Università Gregoriana, 1980).

17. By way of brief example, see on "immanent" Trinity on the level of absolute religion ILT 527.3–16, 23–24 /AR 57.1–16 (CR 67–68). See in more detail the summary in Ch. 5 Subsection 2 of the present study.

18. That is, absolute Subject inclusive of object. AR 10.38–11.16 (CR 31) 1827. See also Jaeschke, "Absolute Idee" 385–386.

19. Note the references in Ch. 5 n. 5 above.

20. Heede, "Die göttliche Idee" 181–182. As Heede (182) points out, Hegel came to distinguish the absolute religion in such a way from the determinate religions since in the absolute religion God was never conceived without being present to the human Spirit, whereas in the determinate religions the elevation of finite Spirit to God occurred first in cult. Jaeschke reflects on the advantages and disadvantages of this structural shift in "Aufbau" 29–31. See BR 65.7–13, 1827.

21. BR 64.33–65.13, 1827, and BR 66.1–16, probably 1831, reflecting Hegel's intention as well regarding the 1827 structure. See also Jaeschke's remarks on the 1827 "Concept of Religion structured according to the logical

moments of the Concept, "Aufbau" 20–22, and Wagner, *Der Gedanke* 205–206, whom Kern, "Dialektik und Trinität" 134–135, follows.

22. BR 66.1–16, probably 1831, reflecting the 1827 lectures as well.

23. Explicitly probably in 1831 concerning the triads "universality—particularity—individuality" and "Concept—judgment—syllogism" BR 66.1–16.

24. Regarding the triads indicated from the logic of being and the logic of the Concept, see Heede, "Die göttliche Idee" 110–112. Note his qualification: "Von einer 'operativen' kategorialen Verwendung zu sprechen ist sicher inadäquat, da in der Religionsphilosophie diese Kategorien ja solche des Gegenstandes selbst sein sollen, und nicht etwa von einem 'tabellarischer Verstand' nur an den Gegenstand herangetragen. Aber entscheidend ist, daß Hegel die religionsphilosophischen Strukturen mit Termini benennt, die in ihrer Provenienz aus der Logik und in ihrer dortigen Stelle eindeutig identifizierbar sind und insofern dann im religionsphilosophischen Kontext as transponierte 'operative' Bestimmungen auftreten" (111).

25. Explicitly probably in 1831 with reference to the "three moments of the Concept" and concerning the triad "Concept—judgment—syllogism" in the spheres of universality, particularity and individuality. BR 65.35–66.16.

26. ILT 85.11–21 and 87.1–16/BR 162.24–163.13, 1821; see also NR 201.11–25. For a fuller discussion see Heede, "Die göttliche Idee" 157–162. This characteristic of "totality" grounds Hegel's claim that each sphere and each religion contains in its own way (externally or internally) all of the determinations.

27. Jaeschke, "Aufbau" 28, 38 and 39. Jaeschke, 31–37, provides a section by section comparison of the various lecture series on the absolute religion. Heede, "Die göttliche Idee" 181–185, does underscore what he calls "essential" differences between the 1821 and later lectures concerning the way religious representational content is distributed in the second sphere.

28. In absolute religion's three main divisions in the 1821 lectures Hegel followed the structure of his presentation of the various determinate religions. See Jaeschke, "Aufbau" 28, 30; Heede, "Die göttliche Idee" 181–183; schema in Hodgson, CR xxx.

29. Jaeschke, "Aufbau" 28–31; Heede, "Die göttliche Idee" 182–185, 187–189; schema in Hodgson, CR xxxi plus 102 n. 20 and "Commentary on the Text" 321–324. See these authors for further pertinent remarks on Hegel's shift from 1821 to 1824.

30. Heede, "Die göttliche Idee" 183, 184–189; Wagner, *Der Gedanke* 223–224. On the revelatory religion in the *Phenomenology* see the overview in Ch. 4 Subsection 2 of the present study and on Hegel's 1827 presentation on the absolute religion Ch. 5 Subsections 2a–c of the present study.

31. Jaeschke, "Aufbau" 28.

32. E.g., ILT 63.14–21/BR 74.38–75.6, 1821; BR 74.10–14, 26–29, 1824; BR 19.14–25, 74.23–26, 1827. On the absolute religion as religion of absolute subjectivity, see Ch. 5 n. 18 above.

For a general survey discussion of the content of Hegel's lectures on the absolute religion in addition to references in Ch. 5 n. 1 above, see more specifically the following. A brief discussion on literature: Heinz Kimmerle, "Religion und Philosophie als Abschluß des Systems," in *Hegel. Einführung in seine Philosophie*, ed. Otto Pöggeler (Munich: Alber, 1977) 150–153. Older critical attitudes: Ferdinand Christian Baur, *Die christliche Lehre von der Dreieinigkeit und Menschwerdung Gottes in ihrer geschichtlichen Entwicklung. Drittes Theil. Die neuere Geschichte des Dogma, von der Reformation bis in die neueste Zeit* (Tübingen: Osiander, 1843) 886–936; Franz Anton Staudenmaier, *Darstellung und Kritik des Hegelschen Systems. Aus dem Standpunkte der christlichen Philosophie* (Mainz: Kupferberg, 1844) 817–836. From the point of view of the 1821 lectures: Chapelle, *La dialectique. A. Dieu et la création*; _____, *La théologie et l'église* 7–60, 113–139; _____, *Annexes* 37–60, 97; André Léonard, *La foi chez Hegel* (Paris: Desclée, 1970) 195–196, 209–322. On the lectures taken together but unfortunately without the currently preferred attention to the specific structures of the various lecture series: Henri Niel, *De la médiation dans la philosophie de Hegel* (Paris: Aubier, 1945) 339–351; Splett, *Trinitätslehre* 126–136; Rendtorff, *Kirche und Theologie* 75–87; Wagner, *Der Gedanke* 219–254, 260–270, 273–285. Working with the differing lecture series, Jaeschke, *Die Religionsphilosophie Hegels*.

33. E.g., ILT 161.4–11/BR 280.1–9, 1821. Note Hegel's distinction between "picture" (*Bild*) as sensible or sentient (*sinnlich*) and "representation" (*Vorstellung*) as "das Bild in seine *Allgemeinheit* erhoben, Gedanke, gedankenvoll, Form auch für Gedanken." ILT 169.10–12/BR 284.30–32 ("the picture raised up into its *universality*, thought, filled with thought, form likewise for thought." my trans.). The mixed nature of representation allows Hegel to treat of religion primarily as philosophy of religion. Hodgson, CR 42 n. 28.

On Hegel's interest in a *philosophy* of religion see briefly BR 28.29–29.25 with the distinction, "Indem wir überhaupt über Religion philosophieren, denken wir die Religion." BR 68.28–29 ("In as we at all philosophize over religion, we *think* religion." my trans.) 1827. Of course the Concept of religion does for Hegel give rise to a series of religions as a history of religion philosophically treated, BR 72. 14–27, 1827 Introduction. See also on the history of religion BR 72.27–73.15, 1824.

34. "die Religion ist die Wahrheit *für alle Menschen*." E § 573R (PM § 573R trans. amended). See BR 69.10–18, 1827, and note Hegel's openness to a variety of ways in which truth can be manifested through the positive character of the absolute religion, AR 23.5–15 (CR 21) 1827. See also Hegel's positive stress on the presence of truth in religion, ILT 189.15–26/BR 299.3–14, 1821.

On representation in the philosophy of religion *Lectures* see in particular Chapelle, *La problématique* 118–121; Léonard, *La foi* 231–235; Yerkes, *Christology* 89–117, 149–155; Hodgson, CR xxv–xxvi with xxix n. 20; Paul Ricoeur, "Hegel Colloquium. The Status of 'Representation' in Hegel's Philosophy of

Religion: A Twentieth Century Appraisal," Lecture, Boston University, April 9, 1980, photocopied text.

35. "Gott ist *Geist*, d.i. das, was wir *dreyeinigen* Gott heißen;[58]—Gott ist Geist—die *absolute Thätigkeit actus pursus—d.i. Subjectivität—unendliche Persönlichkeit—unendlich*—Unterscheidung *seiner von sich selbst—Erzeugung—aber* dieses Unterschiedene ist *im ewigen Begriffe*[59] d.i. [in] *Allgemeinheit* als *absoluter Subjectivitiit*, gehalten, . . . [58] Rein *speculativer* Inhalt, d.i. MYSTERIUM Gottes[59] Sich gegenständlich—sich objective Göttlichkeit–[35]" ILT 527.3–9 and 23–24/AR 57.1–9 (CR 67–68 trans. amended). Note Ilting places marginal notes in footnotes. Hodgson's translation (CR) indicates them by + ... + and incorporates them thus in the text.

As Hodgson, CR 103 n. 32, observes, Hegel generally reserves the term "triune" for what would be referred to as "inner" or "immanent" Trinity.

36. "Gott ist der wahre Gott, Geist, indem er nicht bloß Vater und so verschlossen, sondern indem er Sohn ist, das Andere wird und dies Andere aufhebt. Diese Negation ist angeschaut als Moment der göttlichen Natur; darin sind alle versöhnt." AR 165.13–17 (CR 210 trans. amended). See also the basically parallel statement of 1821, ILT 647.1–16, 17/AR 163.29–164.5 (CR 208).

37. "So ist die Gemeinde selbst der existierende Geist, der Geist in seiner Existenz, Gott als Gemeinde existierend. Das Erste ist die Idee in ihrer einfachen Allgemeinheit für sich, die zum Urteil, Anderssein noch nicht fortgeschritten, aufgeschlossen ist,—der Vater. Das Zweite ist das Besondere, die Idee in der Erscheinung,—der Sohn. Sofern das Erste konkret ist, ist allerdings das Anderssein schon darin enthalten; die Idee ist ewiges Leben, ewiges Hervorbringen. Das Zweite aber ist die Idee in der Außerlichkeit, so daß die äußerliche Erscheinung umgekehrt wird zum Ersten, gewußt wird als göttliche Idee, die Identität des Göttlichen und Menschlichen. Das Dritte ist dann dies Bewußtsein Gottes als Geistes. Dieser Geist als existierend und sich realisierend ist die Gemeinde." AR 198.19–31 (CR 256–257). See also the text following this quote, AR 198.32–199.18 (CR 257). Note that in view of AR 29.35–37 (CR 37) the third element or community is to be identified as individuality or the individual.

38. Note also BR 150.14–151.9, 1824.

39. Hegel generally says "Spirit *for* Spirit," as in AR 35.21–22 (CR 13) 1824. See also AR 35.22–26, 36.1–9 (CR 13–14) 1824, where Hegel recalls that this revelation or existence of Spirit for Spirit is finally through sublation absolute Spirit, that is, Spirit relating itself to itself.

40. Chapelle, *La problématique* 232; also Heede, "Die göttliche Idee" 125.

41. Specifically regarding the absolute religion, AR 27.3–15 (CR 25–26) 1827; on religion in general, BR 151.31–152.40, 1824. See Heede, "Die göttliche Idee" 52, 55; Hodgson, CR 42 n. 28.

42. Heede, "Die göttliche Idee" 56–57. Of further interest note Heede's description of the philosophy of religion's being for Hegel a totality, an *Encyclopedia in nuce* (115).

43. Jaeschke, "Aufbau" 3–4, indicates (beyond the more specific question of development in Hegel's trinitarian thought) the importance of Hegel's continuing overall development during the Berlin period and according to Hotho especially from 1823 to 1827 (Jaeschke, 95).

44. On the formal relations between the various lecture series, see Jaeschke, "Aufbau" 38–39, who proposes that the 1827 lectures are dependent on the 1821 manuscript only by way of the 1824 Griesheim text (see also Jaeschke, 21), and Hodgson, CR vii–xiii.

Jaeschke, 93–96, and Heede, "Die göttliche Idee" 124–125, have correctly argued to the value of the 1821 manuscript while at the same time likewise correctly not wanting to give it a hermeneutical priority over the later lecture materials. For another view from a particular perspective, Luther, "Hegel's Phenomenology of Religion" 235–237.

In his earlier and now somewhat relativized work, Chapelle, *La problématique* 231, and *Annexes* 12–13, opted for such a hermeneutical priority to the 1821 manuscript, given the state of the texts at the time of his study. For further remarks on Chapelle's immense program, see Heede, 123–124.

Some of the research (1980 or so) on Hegel's philosophy of religion lectures is available in Jaeschke, *Die Religionsphilosophie Hegels*.

45. Jaeshke, "Aufbau" 34, 36, 38; Hodgson, CR x.

46. See briefly Ch. 5 n. 63 below. Though of course particularly with regard to the second overall moment or "element" this distribution of content has varied between the 1821 and the later lecture series. (Note that "content" is used here more loosely to refer to the way in which Hegel has "allotted" various theologoumena to the second and third overall moments or "elements." "Content" in this looser sense does not as such refer to Hegel's technical usage of "true content" as absolute Spirit present representationally in religion.)

Another formal indication of the basic continuity in Hegel's thought concerning the overall structural development of trinitarian subjectivity can be found in the basic agreement among the 1817, 1827 and 1830 editions of the *Encyclopedia*'s presentation of "immanent" and "economic" Trinity.

47. Jaeschke, "Aufbau" 5. Lasson's ordering of the text must be corrected in line with and following Jaeschke's analyses in "Aufbau" and for the absolute religion according to Hodgson in CR (see Ch. 5 n. 1 above). Jaeschke's harsh criticism of Lasson's text as "simply unusable" (*einfach unbrauchbar*, 89) refers to the Lasson text as it stands. With Jaeschke's corrections it becomes especially for the absolute religion usable until a critical edition of the 1827 transcripts is made available. Where deemed important the Lasson texts have been compared

with parallels in the Friends' second edition, that of 1840, as made available in WS. This in lieu of a truly critical edition of the 1827 lectures.

Jaeschke speaks of the Lasson text in general as "relatively more complete" (89). On the value of the overall 1827 student transcripts which agreed basically among themselves and were integrated in Lasson, see Jaeschke, 5–6. Also Chapelle, *La problématique* 229–232; Hodgson, CR xv–xvii; and the wider references in Ch. 5 n. 1 above. In conversation March 28–30, 1982, Dr. Jaeschke indicated that several then recently discovered student transcripts of the 1827 lectures confirm the basic reliability of the Lasson text, though these transcripts do raise some questions concerning a few specific passages in Lasson.

48. AR 29.35–37 (CR 37) and AR 198.19–31 (CR 256–257). On the 1824 lectures see AR 65.19–28 (CR 65).

49. See Heede, "Die göttliche Idee" 188–189. Texts on the first major section of the absolute religion lecture transcripts of Hegel's 1827 lectures, as identified and sequenced in Jaeschke, "Aufbau" 35 with xv–xvi (slightly modified in view of research utilized in CR and with smaller units grouped together here): AR 74.12–77.5, 47.11–48.10, 77.6–84.7 (CR 85–99 with 1827 lecture transcripts indicated by superscripts b ... b); also AR 237.13–14.

Hegel's development of thought is directly carried forward in AR 74.12–75.29, 47.11–48.10, 77.6–19, 81.12–28, 81.38–82.1 (CR 85–87, 89–90, 95–96). See also the overview in AR 28.9–19, 30.4–5 (CR 35, 37).

50. AR 80.6–81.11 (CR 94–95). Similarly in the 1821 manuscript, ILT 537.1–539.4/AR 60.29–61.17 (CR 71–72).

51. "in seiner ewigen Idee . . . noch im abstrakten Elemente des Denkens überhaupt, abstrakte Idee des Denkens, nicht des Begreifens." AR 74.22–24 (CR 86).

52. AR 75.28 (CR 87). And in the 1821 manuscript ILT 525.26–27/AR 56.26–28 (CR 63).

53. "was die heilige *Dreieinigkeit* heißt; das ist Gott selbst, ewig dreieinig." AR 74.26–28 (CR 86).

54. AR 74.31–32 (CR 86).

55. AR 48.11–12 (CR 89). On the correspondence of this first element to Concept (*Begriff*) also in the 1821 manuscript, see the brief mention in ILT 527.14/AR 57.14 (CR 68).

56. AR 47.34–48.1 (CR 89–90).

57. AR 77.13–14 (CR 90).

58. AR 81.12–14 (CR 95).

59. "In diesem Urteil ist das Andere, das dem Allgemeinen Gegenüberstehende, das Besondere Gott als das von ihm Unterschiedene, aber so, daß dies Unterschiedene seine ganze Idee ist an und für sich, so daß diese zwei Bestimmungen auch füreinander dasselbige, diese Identität, das Eine sind." AR 74.32–37 (CR 86).

Characteristically Hegel will refer to this first element to exemplify and explain further developments. In the second element see AR 140.21–29 (CR 179–180). In the third element see AR 203.37–39 (CR 265).

60. "ein Spiel des Unterscheidens," AR 75.24 (CR 87 trans. amended).

61. AR 47.18–48.1 (CR 89–90).

62. AR 74.32–35 (CR 86). On the immediacy of transition, AR 93.25–27 (CR 117).

63. Structurally identical to but more loosely formulated than the sphere of universality in the *Encyclopedia* and to the moment of thought in the *Phenomenology*. Note the parallel structure and identical content "God—Son/difference—absolute unity" interpretable as A-B-E but not explicitly so identified by Hegel in the 1821 manuscript, ILT 527.3–16 and 23–24/AR 57.1–16 (CR 67–68). In the 1821 manuscript Hegel speaks explicitly of this self-contained process as taking place "*im ewigen Begriffe*, d.h. [in] *Allgemeinheit als absoluter Subjektivität.*" ILT 527.7–8/AR 57.7–10 ("within the eternal concept, i.e. [within] universality as absolute subjectivity." CR 67–68). For a succinct comparison of the 1821, 1824 and 1827 lectures on this first major section of absolute religion, see Jaeschke, "Aufbau" 34–35. For an overview of Hegel's 1821 manuscript on the material corresponding to this first element of the 1827 lectures, see Chapelle, *Annexes* 40; _____, *La dialectique* 55–109.

On the categorical syllogism see briefly Ch. 3 nn. 45 and 87 above.

64. AR 81.38–82.1 (CR 96).

65. Texts on the second and largest major section of the absolute religion lecture transcripts of Hegel's 1827 lectures, as identified and sequenced in Jaeschke, "Aufbau" 36 with xvi–xx (modified in view of research incorporated in CR and with smaller units grouped together here): AR 92.16–95.19 [WS 17:252.16–24 not in Lasson, 1827 or 1831?], 112.36–121.24, 126.38–129.40, 138.36–142.29, 154.7–155.21, 150.31–151.11, 151.22–24, 151.34–152.15, 153.12–154.6, 169.4–15, 170.26–172.32, 173.20–174.24 (CR 116–120, 137–142, 147–152, 158–161, 177–182, 193–199, 214–221 with 1827 lecture transcripts indicated by superscripts b . . . b); also AR 237.15–16.

Hegel is recorded in these gathered transcripts as carrying forward the progression of his thought practically speaking throughout the texts indicated here. See also and note the emphasis on the division of nature and Spirit in the overview in AR 28.20–29.16, 30.6–16 (CR 35–37).

66. AR 92.16–17 (CR 116).

67. Summarized in AR 94.17–27 (CR 118–119).

68. AR 29.36–37 (CR 37). The 1821 equivalent of this second element is likewise referred to as "objectivity," AR 95.23–32 (CR 122).

69. AR 93.39–94.2 (CR 118). The equivalent of the second element referred to in terms of "judgement" in the 1821 manuscript, ILT 547/AR 85.10–19 (CR 109). And in terms of *für sich*, AR 96.13–14 (CR 122).

70. AR 92.16–17 (CR 116).
71. Much less formalized in the 1821 manuscript.
72. "sofern sie [die Idee] aus ihrer Allgemeinheit, Unendlichkeit heraustritt in die Bestimmung der Endlichkeit." AR 92.18–19 (CR 116 trans. amended).
73. AR 92.30–36 (CR 116).
74. AR 92.37–93.38 (CR 116–118).
75. AR 92.14–16 (CR 118).
76. AR 113.1–17 (CR 137–138). As Jaeschke, "Aufbau" 36, observes, in the 1824 lectures Hegel is reported as speaking of the need for reconciliation. In the 1827 lectures the stress here and especially then in the *third* main section of Hegel's treatment of absolute religion is on the need for and reconciliation with truth. An indication of Hegel's increasingly speculative interpretation of the Christian religion.
77. AR 28.22–27, 30.6–10 (CR 35, 37).
78. AR 112.36–116.32, 116.37–121.24 (CR 137–142, 147–152).
79. AR 138.36–139.5 (CR 177–178).
80. AR 138.36–139.12 (CR 177–178).
81. This statement is the conflation of two differing sets of claims by Hegel: first, the two sides to the sublation of the opposition in question, AR 139.13–19 (CR 178); and as the two conditions for the appearance of the God-man, AR 142.11–15 (CR 182).
82. "die Einheit der göttlichen und menschlichen Natur in *einem Mensch*." AR 141.29–30 (CR 181). There is no intention here of summarizing all of Hegel's Christology as found in the 1827 lecture transcripts.
83. On the *Phenomenology* see Ch. 4 Subsections 2 and then 3a of the present study.
84. AR 141.9–28 (CR 180–181).
85. AR 171.35 (CR 218). Hegel also refers to the death of Christ as "middle point" (*Mittelpunkt*) of consciousness, AR 170.1–2 (CR 215), and of reconciliation, AR 171.23–24 (CR 217).
86. AR 170.37–38 (CR 217).
87. AR 172.12–14, 174.19–24 (CR 218, 221).
88. AR 173.20–32 (CR 220).
89. AR 171.36–172.1 (CR 218).
90. AR 171.32–172.3 with 173.20–25 (CR 218 with 220).
91. Note the typical preference for present perfect tense as found in the student transcript, AR 173.25–27 (CR 220).
92. "Dies ist für die Gemeinde die Geschichte der Erscheinung Gottes; diese Geschichte ist göttliche Geschichte, wodurch sie zum Bewußtsein der Wahrheit gekommen ist. Daraus bildete sich das Bewußtsein, das Wissen, daß

Gott der Dreieinige ist. Die Versöhnung, an die geglaubt wird in Christo, hat keinen Sinn, wird Gott nicht als der Dreieinige gewußt, wird nicht erkannt, daß er *ist*, aber auch *als das Andere*, als das sich Unterscheidende [ist] so daß dieses Andere *Gott selbst* ist, an sich die göttliche Natur an ihm hat, und daß das Aufheben dieses Unterschieds, Andersseins, diese Rückkehr, diese Liebe der Geist ist. In diesem Bewußtsein ist es enthalten, daß der Glaube nicht Verhältnis zu etwas anderem, sondern *Verhältnis zu Gott selbst* ist." AR 173.33–174.4 but quoted here according to WS 17:298.18–31 (CR 220 trans. amended).

93. It is striking to read again in the *Logic* on the hypothetical syllogism, GW 12:121.18–123.31/L 2:346–349 (GL 698–701), and recall the emphasis there on negativity after reading Hegel's presentation of the second element in the 1827 lectures.

94. Reflected succinctly in AR 174.17–24 (CR 221).

Syllogistically structured identical to the sphere of particularity in the *Encyclopedia* and to the moment of *representation* in the *Phenomenology*. However, whereas the *Phenomenology* and the 1827 lectures are in basic agreement regarding distribution of theologoumena, in the *Encyclopedia* Hegel establishes only an implicit reconciliation in the moment of particularity and addresses explicit reconciliation in Christ only in the moment of individuality. As indicated by Jaeschke, "Aufbau" 31, Hegel could have brought his encyclopedic representation into correspondence with that of the 1824, 1827 and 1831 lectures by shifting E § 569 to the sphere of particularity.

Note in the 1821 manuscript the parallel structure and generally speaking identical "distribution" of content "God—real self-othering in nature and finite Spirit—objective reconciliation in Christ" interpretable as A-E/E-B but not explicitly so identified, ILT 647.17–649.23/AR 164.6–36 (CR 208–209). In the 1821 manuscript there is somewhat less stress on this process as being the life and history of God Self, though this is at least so indicated. For a succinct comparison of the 1821, 1824, and 1827 lectures on this second major section of absolute religion, see Jaeschke, "Aufbau" 35–36. For an overview and partial commentary on Hegel's 1821 manuscript on the material corresponding to this second element in the 1827 lectures, see Chapelle, *Annexes* 41–51, and Chapelle, *La dialectique* 113–237.

On the hypothetical syllogism see briefly Ch. 3 nn. 46 and 93 above.

95. Texts on the third major section of the absolute religion lecture manuscripts of Hegel's 1827 lectures, as identified and sequenced in Jaeschke, "Aufbau" 37 with xxi–xxiii (modified in view of research incorporated in CR): AR 194.27–196.18, 198.19–199.18, 202.18–204.34, 205.15–206.25, 207.29–208.19, 214.19–215.12, 216.28–219.5, 225.16–228.31, 232.8–17 (CR 254–257, 263–268, 275–276, 278–281, 287–289, 291–293, with the 1827 lecture transcripts indicated by superscripts b . . . b); also AR 237.17–26 and the

overview in AR 29.18–25, 30.17–20 (CR 36, 37). See John E. Smith's analysis, but without distinction of the various lecture series, in "Hegel's Reinterpretation" 162–174, cited by Hodgson, CR 350 n. 16.

96. AR 199.6–11 (CR 257).

97. "für die Empfindung . . . , für die Subjektivität and in der Subjektivität des Geistes, im Innersten des subjektiven Geistes." AR 29.19–21 (CR 36 trans. amended).

98. AR 28.2–29.35 and esp. 29.17–21 and 26–35, 198.32–199.11 (CR 35–37 and esp. 36–37, 257).

99. AR 28.2–8 (CR 35).

100. AR 29.37–30.28 (CR 36–37).

101. AR 199.10–11, 203.9–10 (CR 257, 264).

102. AR 194.31–34, 199.12–18 (CR 254, 257). On Hegel's philosophically informed notion of community see in general, Rendtorff, *Kirche und Theologie* 63–113. Also John E. Smith, "Hegel's Reinterpretation" 157–177.

103. "Das Dritte ist dann dies Bewußtsein Gottes als Geistes. Dieser Geist als existierend und sich realisierend ist die Gemeinde." AR 198.29–31 (CR 257). Compare a parallel but more reserved wording in the 1821 manuscript, ILT 669.2–9/AR 182.4–12 (CR 238). This identification of finite Spirit and absolute Spirit is of course for Hegel always dialectical.

104. AR 29.21–23, 198.19–20 (CR 36, 256).

105. AR 30.17–20 (CR 37).

106. Jaeschke, "Aufbau" 29–30, and concerning the parallel in the 1821 manuscript see the remarks in Ch. 5 n. 29 above.

107. AR 29.37 (CR 37). Similarly in the 1821 manuscript, ILT 649.5–6/AR 164.20–21 (CR 209).

108. AR 28.2–8 with 30.23–24 (CR 35 with 27).

109. On absolute religion in general as religion of absolute subjectivity, see AR 10.38–11.16 (CR 31) 1827. On absolute religion's third element in particular, see for example the wording in AR 199.12–18 (CR 257) 1827, a phraseology parallel to that of AR 10.38–11.16 (CR 31) 1827.

Concerning the self-consciousness of freedom in the absolute religion in general, "Das Selbstbewußtsein der Freiheit" and "die Freiheit des Selbstbewußtseins," AR 14.10–15.11 and specifically 14.19–20 and 14.34 (CR 4–5) 1824. Note that this is an explicitation of Hegel's proposal of religion as an originary unity of religious consciousness and God (see Ch. 1 n. 5 above).

For a brief, wider overview, see Walter Jaeschke, "Christianity and Secularity in Hegel's Concept of the State," *The Journal of Religion* 61 (1981) 127–145. As Niel correctly observes regarding religion in general, "On ne saurait trop insister sur ce fait que, pour Hegel, la catégorie fondamentale du religieux est la catégorie de libération." *De la médiation* 340.

110. "*die Realisierung des Geistigen der Gemeinde zur allgemeinen Wirklichkeit.*" AR 237.13–26 (CR xxxi and 278). Compare this with the doubled presentation of the second element. See Ch. 5 Subsection 2b of the present study.

111. AR 237.17–20, 194.27–196.18 (CR 254–256).

112. AR 195.5–8 (CR 255). The historical representation is the only source of certainty, AR 195.13–21 (CR 255).

113. AR 196.4–6 (CR 256).

114. "die Ausgießung des heiligen Geistes." AR 194.28 (CR 254).

115. "eine sinnliche, menschliche Erscheinung." AR 195.23 (CR 255).

116. AR 195.22–25 (CR 255). Also AR 194.29–30, 195.26–27 (CR 254, 255). Note the parallel but less clear emphasis on "spiritual totality" (*geistige Totalität*) in the 1821 manuscript, ILT 683.21–29, 685.1–5, 20–21/AR 188.19–33 (CR 245).

117. AR 194.34–36 (CR 255).

118. AR 195.26–27, 196.16–18 (CR 255, 256).

119. In the 1821 manuscript Hegel treats faith twice, that is, in both the third element's first subsection (the origin of the community) out of a discussion on miracles, ILT 677.13–24, 679.1–21, 681.1–20, 683.1–23, 685.1–5/ AR 186.7–188.33 (CR 243–245), and in the third element's second subsection (the realization of the community) as first point followed by doctrine and Church, ILT 685.16–19, 687.1–23/AR 199.19–200.10 (CR 258). As here in the 1827 lectures so also in the 1824 lectures and there at greater length but less rigorously Hegel handles faith systematically speaking more appropriately in the first subsection of the third element, AR 190.27–193.15 (CR 247–250) 1824. Then Hegel does not refer to faith in the first part of the second subsection (the realization of the community) in the 1824 lectures, AR 202.1–17, 204.35–205.14, 206.26–207.28 (CR 260–263), and in the 1827 lectures he refers to faith as a presupposition, AR 202.24–28, 203.9–16 (CR 263, 264). This simplification from 1824 on constitutes an improvement in that it allows for a clearer delineation of the first part of the second subsection in terms of the otherness of doctrine and institutional Church. This first moment (here, the origin of the community) is always for Hegel that of immediacy and the second (here, the realization of the community) that of otherness.

120. AR 203.11–13 (CR 264).

121. AR 237.21–22, 198.19–199.18, 202.18–204.34, 205.15–206.25, 207.29–208.19, 214.19–215.12 (CR 256–257, 263–268, 275–276). AR 198.19–199.18 (CR 256–257) forms an overview of Hegel's triadically structured project in the 1827 lectures on the absolute or consummate religion and a summary of what has been discussed so far in the third element.

122. AR 203.9–16 (CR 264).

123. "ernstliche Wille," AR 203.17–25 (CR 264). Finally, however, of course still on the level of religious representation.

124. "gefühltes, blitzähnliches Zeugnis des Geistes." AR 202.25–26 (CR 263). Note that Hegel is speaking of teaching (*Lehre*) as faith.

125. AR 202.18–37 (CR 263–264). The relationship of development from *Glauben* to *Glaubenslehre* is not indicated in the 1821 manuscript (texts cited Ch. 5 n. 119 above) so clearly. Rather, the community explicates its faith out of the Spirit. ILT 685.16–17/AR 199.19–20 (CR 258).

126. AR 202.37–203.8, 203.40–204.17 (CR 264–265).

127. "notwendig zuerst als *Autorität*." AR 204.18–19 (CR 265).

128. AR 204.20–34, 205.15–23 (CR 265–266).

129. "Angewöhnung an das Gute und Vernünftige." AR 205.30–31 (CR 266). Overall, AR 205.23–31 (CR 266).

130. "an sich Nichtiges." AR 205.40 (CR 267). Overall, AR 205.31–206.2 (CR 266–267). Repentance (*Reue*) and penitence (*Buße*) signify that the individual Subject recognizes truth in contrast to evil and wills the good. AR 206.3–8 (CR 267).

131. AR 206.12–25 (CR 267).

132. "Die reale Gemeinde ist das, was wir im allgemeinen die *Kirche* nennen." AR 207.30–31 (CR 267–268). Compare the similar position but with closer identification of Church and kingdom of God in the 1821 manuscript, ILT 689.14–15, 691.1–4/AR 201.10–15 (CR 260).

133. AR 214.26 (CR 275); Hodgson, CR 343.

134. "dem sich Erhalten der Gemeinde der Genuß der Gegenwart Gottes." AR 215.11–12 (CR 276). Overall, AR 207.31–208.19, 214.19–215.12 (CR 268, 275–276). Note that Hegel does not relate the three interpretations of eucharistic presence dialectically in terms of negation of negation.

135. Similarly in the 1821 manuscript, ILT 693.13–14, 695.1–8 and 11–16/AR 209.15–25 (CR 269–270).

136. "die Realisierung des Geistigen der Gemeinde zur allgemeinen Wirklichkeit." AR 237.23–26 (CR 278).

The texts making up this third subsection are AR 237.23–26, 216.28–219.5, 225.16–228.31, 232.8–17 (CR 278–281, 287–289, 291–293).

137. In the 1821 manuscript Hegel merely alludes to some elements in this development, ILT 699.10–19 and 27–31, 701.1–29, 703.1–24/AR 211.23–213.10 (CR 272–274). He ends with the famous but rather cryptic "passing of the community" which forms the conclusion of the 1821 manuscript and is not repeated in the 1824 or 1827 lectures, ILT 705.7–31, 707.1–34, 709.1–35/AR 229.2–231.32 (CR 294–297 with pp. 308–311 notes 88–100, correcting the arrangement in AR). Walter Jaeschke states that Hegel's attempt at a reconciliation of state, religion and philosophy in ethical life "constitutes Hegel's 'last word' on this subject; his last word is not the supposed confession

of the failure of his 'political Protestantism' in the chapter on the 'passing of the community' at the end of his lectures on the philosophy of religion of 1821. The conclusion to those lectures is only a reflection of the *Philosophy of Right*, which appeared in the same year and mentions Protestantism as a political principle only in the preface." "Christianity and Secularity in Hegel's Concept of the State," *The Journal of Religion* 61 (1981) 133.

In the 1824 texts Hegel refers to the triple objective realization culminating in ethical life only with reference to and out of the subjective forms of Spirit (immediate heart, abstract understanding and the Concept), AR 215.14–216.27, 219.6–224.5 (CR 276–278, 281–287, 289–291). In the presently considered 1827 transcripts Hegel elaborates these objective realizations in their own right and then proceeds to handle the "ideal" side as a development into philosophy, into the Concept. Jaeschke, "Aufbau" 37. John E. Smith, "Hegel's Reinterpretation" 168–171 with notes pp. 176–177 bases his analysis upon a mixed citing of 1824 and 1827 texts, though apparently structurally speaking principally upon the 1824 presentation.

138. AR 237.23–26, 216.28–217.22 (CR 278–279).

139. AR 216.28–35 (CR 278). Here Hegel concludes that since this reconciliation occurs as the enjoyment of the presence of God in the pure heart, it is as such the attainment of the enjoyment of the pure heart itself's being reconciled.

140. "die Wahrheit für das Weltliche ist das Geistige." AR 217.3 (CR 278 trans. amended).

141. AR 217.4–19 (CR 278–279).

142. "Diese Freiheit, die den Trieb und die Bestimmtheit hat, sich zu realisieren, ist die Vernünftigkeit." AR 217.19–21 (CR 279).

143. AR 217.23–219.5 (CR 279–281).

144. AR 217.23–38 (CR 279).

145. AR 217.37–38 (CR 279).

146. AR 217.39–218.28 (CR 279–280).

147. "wo eins über das andere herrscht und also die Versöhnung gerade nicht da ist." AR 218.3–4 (CR 280).

148. AR 218.6–7 (CR 280).

149. AR 218.24 (CR 280).

150. "der absolute Widerspruch des Geistigen in sich selbst." AR 218.27–28 (CR 280).

151. Note however Hodgson's hesitations on the interpretation of this section, CR 344.

152. AR 218.29–219.2 (CR 280–281).

153. AR 218.29–31 (CR 280).

154. "die konkret gewordene Freiheit, der vernünftige Wille ist." AR 218.33–34 (CR 281).

155. AR 203.17–25 (CR 264).

156. AR 219.3–5 (CR 281).

157. As Hodgson, CR 344, remarks, it would seem Hegel was rushing to cover his lecture material at the end of the term. Nevertheless, Hegel is progressing by a certain discernible though not always worked out inner logic.

158. AR 225.16–17 (CR 287). The pertinent texts for this third step are AR 225.16–228.31, 232.8–17 (CR 287–289, 291–293). Note however that Hegel had spoken of the "three real stages" (*drei reale Stufen*) constituting the objective side of realized reconciliation. AR 219.3–5 (CR 281).

159. Note that Hegel's principle that the truth for the worldly is the spiritual also underlies this treatment of real and then ideal realizations of reconciliation. See AR 217.2–3 (CR 278). Note in the *Encyclopedia* Hegel's more developed presentation of ethical life as third moment of objective Spirit and as such then transition to that knowing which is absolute Spirit, E §§ 513, 552.

160. AR 225.20 (CR 287).

161. AR 216.35–38 (CR 278).

162. "Das Innere weiß sich eben in diesem Versöhntsein des Geistes mit sich als bei sich seiend, und dies Wissen, bei sich selbst zu sein, ist eben das Denken." AR 225.17–19 (CR 287).

163. AR 225.20–21 (CR 287).

164. AR 225.21–30 (CR 287).

165. AR 225.30–226.14 (CR 287–288).

166. AR 225.32–34 (CR 287).

167. AR 226.12–14 (CR 288). This Enlightenment thinking consequently finds itself opposed to any thought of God as Trinity, as self-relating, AR 225.35–40 (CR 287).

168. AR 226.15–40 (CR 288–289). In the text Hegel makes the transition from first to second form of abstract thought on the basis of an analysis of the first form's denial of determination in God and on the second's developing determination only out of the Subject's own natural impulses and tendencies, AR 225.40–226.18 (CR 288).

169. AR 226.30–32 (CR 288).

170. AR 226.18–28 (CR 288).

171. AR 226.28–36 (CR 288–289).

172. "zwei Extreme . . . gegeneinander in der Fortbildung der Gemeinde." AR 227.2–3 (CR 289). As Smith underscores, it is the inability of these two extremes themselves to sustain community which in this context makes Hegel so critical of them. "Hegel's Reinterpretation" 172.

173. AR 227.20–22, 227.5 with 232.10–11 (CR 291, 289 with 293).

174. "Das Dritte ist dann, daß die Subjektivität zwar aus sich, aber nach der Notwendigkeit den Inhalt entwickelt, daß sie einen Inhalt als notwendig und diesen notwendigen Inhalt als objektiv, an und für sich seiend weiß und

anerkennt. Das ist der Standpunkt der *Philosophie*, daß sich der Inhalt in den Begriff flüchtet und durch das Denken seine Rechtfertigung erhält." AR 227.7–13 (CR 291). Note that in the 1824 transcript by Griesheim it is explicitly this third, philosophy, which is to establish the relation to the prior two stages (*Stufe*), AR 224.18–19 (CR 289).

175. "sich zu seiner Totalität, zur Idee bestimmt." AR 227.15–16 (CR 291 trans. amended).

176. AR 227.16–17 (CR 291).

177. AR 227.22–25 (CR 291).

178. AR 227.25–228.16 (CR 291–292).

179. AR 227.31–228.2 (CR 291–292).

180. "diesen Gegensatz durchzumachen, bis er zur Versöhnung kommt." AR 228.19–20 (CR 293 trans. amended).

181. AR 228.3–11 (CR 292).

182. "die Philosophie ist insofern Theologie." AR 228.21–22 (CR. 293). John E. Smith points out a possible ambiguity as to whether this is to mean philosophy in a specific function is theology or philosophy as such is theology. In agreement with Smith it would seem that Hegel meant the latter, while of course not excluding the former to the extent that philosophy qua philosophy functions thus for Hegel. See Smith, "Hegel's Reinterpretation" 177 n. 37. Note however a somewhat different formulation of the text in WS 342.10–15.

183. "Diese Versöhnung ist dann der Friede Gottes." AR 228.27 (CR 293).

184. Hegel's operative principle in this third stage: "Der Geist aber ist dies, sich zu entwickeln, sich zu unterscheiden bis zur Wirklichkeit." AR 217.37–38 ("But the very nature of Spirit is to develop itself, to differentiate itself until it attains the worldly realm." CR 279).

185. For texts see Ch. 5 n. 136 above.

186. Though these points are not essential to the following critique of Hegel's trinitarian thought, there are enough textual indications and specific characteristics to warrant identifying the structural movement of these two realizations according to the overall dynamic of Hegel's dialectic. On Hegel's Concept as universal, particular and individual, see again GW 12:32.1–52.26/L 2:239–264 (GL 600–622).

187. That is, a double movement from universal to particular to individual.

188. AR 227.7–16 (CR 291). Rendtorff, *Kirche and Theologie* 103, remarks that pure subjectivity becomes for Hegel in the philosophy of religion lectures the "presence of God." And, it should be added, vice versa.

189. AR 29.37 (CR 37). Note that this corresponds directly to the end result in the *Encyclopedia*, E § 570. In the *Phenomenology* Hegel dwells more on the failure of religion itself finally to achieve reconciliation and uses this failure precisely as a means of transition to absolute knowledge.

190. "die Realisierung des Geistigen der Gemeinde zur allgemeinen Wirklichkeit." AR 237.23–26 (CR 278).

191. Texts cited in Ch. 5 n. 111 above.

192. Texts cited in Ch. 5 n. 121 above.

193. In this sense the mediating presence of God is the communal consciousness, and so parallel to Hegel's position in the *Encyclopedia*, and parallel to the presentation in the *Phenomenology*.

194. Texts cited in Ch. 5 n. 136 above.

195. Recall that for Hegel the extremes in a syllogism are interchangeable, as Hegel in effect observes in discussing judgement in the context of the hypothetical syllogism, GW 12:121.35–122.4/L 2:347 (GL 699). In the *Logic* Hegel identifies the overall pattern of the disjunctive syllogism as E-A-B (individuality-universality-particularity), GW 12:123.35–36/L 2:349 (GL 701), whereas here there is a question of working with B-A-E. On the disjunctive syllogism see the pertinent Hegel texts cited in Ch. 3 n. 47 above.

Though Hegel illustrates his discussion of the disjunctive syllogism in the *Logic* with formulated premises and conclusions, it is clear that his concern is with the role and nature of the middle term and with the overall dynamic interrelationship of terms and middle. It is therefore not necessary here to elaborate specific sentences as major and minor premises and conclusion.

In the 1821 lectures Hegel speaks so famously of the disappearance of the spiritual community, ILT 705.1–709.35/AR 229.1–231.32 (CR 294–297). On the transitional nature of Hegel's opinion on this point in the 1821 lectures, see Ch. 5 n. 137 above. The question as to how the 1821 lectures exhibit the structure of a disjunctive syllogism would be beyond the scope of the present primary concern with the 1827 lectures.

196. Recall that in the 1821 lectures Hegel treats of the absolute religion as the last of the determinate religions, whereas from 1824 on he presents the absolute religion more clearly as the fulfillment of the determinate religions.

197. See Ch. 5 n. 47 above.

198. As Klaus Düsing more generally recalls concerning syllogism, the truth of the syllogism lies in its being a triplicity of syllogisms where each moment of the Concept necessarily plays the role of middle term. *Das Problem der Subjektivität in Hegels Logik*, *Hegel-Studien*, Beiheft 15 (Bonn: Bouvier, 1976) 443. This is to use the term "truth of the syllogism" somewhat differently than Hegel's technical usage of this term to describe the disjunctive syllogism as last and culminant syllogism in which the syllogistic form of mediation itself is overcome.

199. The more straight-forwardly triadic structure of "immanent" and "economic" trinitarian reconciliation in the *Phenomenology* and *Lectures* especially from 1824 on gives more prominence to the moment of community, whereas Hegel's *Encyclopedia* version highlights objective reconciliation implicitly already in the arising of finite Spirit and explicitly in the death of the Mediator.

200. See Ch. 4 Subsection 2 of the present study.

201. See Ch. 3 Subsection 2b of the present study.

202. Theologically stated, these three examinations and critiques can be seen as touching upon and having implications respectively for theology, Christology and ecclesiology or grace. Note that Wolfhart Pannenberg's theses on ecclesiology can be seen as a theological reflection on Hegel's "third element" or absolute religion, though without an explicit distinction of Hegel's various lecture series. *Thesen zur Theologie der Kirche* (Munich: Claudius, 1974).

203. Recall that the structural movement of this "third element" is at least logically speaking constant and consistent as disjunctive syllogism in Hegel's thought from the *Phenomenology* on. Therefore a critique of this third element of absolute religion in the 1827 philosophy of religion lectures is as well at least a critique of the logical structure of Hegel's various presentations of the spiritual community.

204. ILT 63.14–23/BR 74.38–75.6 and 7–9, 1821.

205. BR 65.7–13, 1827.

206. AR 237.23–26 (CR 278) 1827.

207. From the already accomplished objective reconciliation in Christ by means of the subjective reconciliation of the individual with this objective reconciliation.

208. See taken together, AR 28.2–10, 30.23–24, 198.29–31, 29.21–23, 198.19–20 (CR 35, 27, 257, 36, 256) 1827.

209. In general, AR 14.10–15.11 (CR 4–5) 1824.

210. AR 14.12–22 (CR 4) 1824.

211. It will be helpful again to underscore that the absolute religion is the consummate religion in that it realizes in thematic fashion the unity of God and of the consciousness of God Hegel had originally proposed as the Concept of religion and consequently the object of a philosophy of religion. See briefly Ch. 5 n. 5 above.

212. AR 217.8–22, 225.16–30 and 35–40, 227.15–16 (CR 278–279, 287, 291) 1827. On the consummate or revelatory religion in general, see AR 6.3–12.35 (CR 26–33) 1827.

213. AR 217.19–21 (CR 279) 1827. See also AR 218.29–34, 225.16–30 (CR 280–281, 287) 1827. On freedom in philosophy and religion as the process of thinking itself as such, see AR 25.35–37 (CR 24) 1827.

John E. Smith has somewhat more externally without distinction of the various lecture series and more restrictedly concerning the transition to ethical life but quite correctly observed: Hegel "made the task easier for himself by reducing the content of reconciliation or the substantial truth of the revealed religion to the freedom of reason so that the problem is solved as soon as we have passed from the abstract form of this freedom to its concrete realization in ethical life which, as an expression of Spirit in accord with the Concept, is the secular counterpart of the religious community." "Hegel's Reinterpretation" 171.

Smith's incisive remark turns attention to the movement of self-determining thought Hegel proposes, but the point of application needs to be widened by recalling that from the beginning of the philosophy of religion and specifically from the first sentences on the third element of absolute religion, e.g., AR 194.34–36 (CR 254) 1827, Hegel has spoken of religion in terms of various types of thought.

214. "Die Freiheit des Selbstbewußtseins ist der Inhalt der Religion, and dieser Inhalt ist selbst Gegenstand der christlichen Religion, d.h. der Geist ist sich selbst Gegenstand." AR 14.34 and 15.2 (CR 5) 1824. Note Lasson's text incorrectly reads "spiritual religion" (*geistigen Religion*) for Griesheim's "Christian Religion." See CR 40 n. 10.

215. AR 227.7–13 with 16–18 and 29–30 (CR 291) 1827.

216. E § 2 with R.

217. AR 14.22–25 (CR 4) 1824.

218. Hegel speaks of freedom as the law of human rationality, AR 20.38–39 (CR 18) 1827.

219. See briefly the end of Ch. 4 Subsection 4b, of the present study, with nn. 216 and 217 above.

220. According to Hegel everything rational is in some sense a syllogism. More exactly, "Der Schluß ist das *Vernünftige* und *Alles* Vernünftige," E § 181 ("The Syllogism is the reasonable, and everything reasonable." SL § 181).

221. On the third element as syllogistically structured, recall by way of shorthand reference E §§ 570 (Subsection 3) and 571. Note the identical wording of the text itself as well in the 1817 edition of the *Encyclopedia*, G. W. F. Hegel, *Enzyklopädie der philosophischen Wissenschaften im Grundrisse, Jubiläumsausgabe*, vol. 6, ed. Hermann Glockner (Stuttgart: Frommann, 1927) § 470/c, and in the 1827 edition, _____, *Enzyclopädie der philosophischen Wissenschaften im Grundrisse* (Heidelberg: Oßwald, 1827) § 570/3.

222. GW 12:92.8–10/L 2:310 (GL 666).

223. GW 12:124.28–29/L 2:350 (GL 702).

224. GW 12:124.29–30, 125.11–15/L 2:350, 351 (GL 702, 703).

225. The extremes are inverted here. In the *Logic* Hegel speaks of the disjunctive syllogism as E-A-B.

On syllogism in general, see Ch. 3 Subsection 2a of the present study. Hegel treats of the disjunctive syllogism in GW 12:123.32–126.11/L 2:349–352 (GL 701–704); E § 191/3. See as background the syllogism of *Dasein* in the third figure, GW 12:102.33–104.20/L 2:324–325 (GL 678–679); E § 187.

Helpful secondary literature on the disjunctive syllogism: Betty Heimann, *System und Methode in Hegels Philosophie* (Leipzig: Felix Meiner, 1927) 354–377; Wolfgang Krohn, *Die formale Logik in Hegels "Wissenschaft der Logik." Untersuchungen zur Schlußlehre* (Munich: Hanser, 1972) 165–168; Düsing, *Das Problem der Subjektivität* 286–287 with further bibliography 287 n. 238; John Burbidge,

On Hegel's Logic. Fragments of a Commentary (Highlands, NJ: Humanities, 1981) 186–188, 191–192.

It will be helpful to recall that logic is for Hegel the movement of pure thought as absolute form. Each moment is the momentary totality of that self-positing and self-determining thought.

226. "A ist entweder B oder C oder D
A ist aber B
Also ist A nicht C noch D." GW 12:124.12–14/L 2:350 (GL 701). Hegel provides a second formulation, "A ist entweder B oder C oder D/A ist aber nicht C noch D/Also ist es B." GW 12:124.16–18/L 2:350 ("A is either B or C or D, But A is neither C nor D, Therefore A is B." GL 702). The first of Hegel's formulations will serve sufficiently for present purposes.

227. Hegel's turn of phrase is more technical than need be reproduced here in this present paragraph.

228. GW 12:124.19–30 with lines 2–11/L 2:350 with 349–350 (GL 702 with 701).

229. GW 12:123.36–124.34/L 2:349–350 (GL 701–702).

230. GW 12:123.36–124.11/L 2:349–350 (GL 701).

231. GW 12:124.12–18/L 2:350 (GL 702).

232. GW 12:124.19–34/L 2:350 (GL 702).

233. GW 12:124.19–24/L 2:350 (GL 702).

234. GW 12:124.25–34/L 2:350 (GL 702).

235. GW 12:124.19–24/L 2:350 (GL 702).

236. GW 12:124.2–3/L 2:349 (GL 701).

237. GW 12:124.8–11/L 2:349 (GL 701). On individuality as such see GW 12:49.1–51.9/L 2:259–262 (GL 618–621), and on this point explicitly GW 12:43.14–19/L 2:253 (GL 612).

238. Again, GW 12:124.8–11/L 2:349–350 (GL 701).

239. "die in die Totalität ihrer Arten besonderte *allgemeine* Sphäre." GW 12:124.20–21/L 2:350 (GL 702). On particularity as such see GW 12:37.6–43.19/L 2:245–253 (GL 605–612), and on this point esp. GW 12:37.14–38.9/L 2:245–246 (GL 605–606).

240. See GW 12:12–14/L 2:350 (GL 701). On the importance of the predicate of the first premise in disjunctive inference see Burbidge, *On Hegel's Logic* 187.

241. Recall that the third step of the third subsection of the third element or spiritual community in the 1827 philosophy of religion lectures contains two developments interpretable as a movement A/B/E. See Ch. 5 Subsection 2c of the present study. In the *Logic* this discussion by Hegel of the self-determining of universality as particularity and individuality can be seen in its own way as an enriched return to and recollection of the first syllogism of *Dasein* in the first figure of the syllogism, GW 12:93.3/L 2:311 (GL 667). Note that here

in the disjunctive syllogism Hegel does not speak of universality "through" particularity but *as* particularity.

242. [123.36] "Die Mitte ist aber die *mit der Form erfüllte* [37] *Allgemeinheit;* sie hat sich als die *Totalität*, als *entwickelte* objective [124.1] Allgemeinheit bestimmt. Der Medius Terminus ist daher sowohl Allgemeinheit, [2] als Besonderheit und Einzelheit. Als jene ist er erstlich die substantielle Identität [3] der Gattung, aber zweytens als eine solche, in welche die *Besonderheit*, [4] aber *als ihre gleich, aufgenommen* ist, also als allgemeine Sphäre, die ihre [5] totale Besonderung enthält,—die in ihre Arten zerlegte Gattung; *A* welches *sowohl* [6] *B als C als D* ist. Die Besonderung ist aber als Unterscheidung ebensosehr [7] das *Entweder Oder* des *B, C* und *D, negative* Einheit, das *gegenseitige* [8] Ausschliessen der Bestimmungen.—Diß Ausschliessen ist nun ferner nicht [9] nur ein gegenseitiges und die Bestimmung bloß eine relative, sondern ebensosehr [10] wesentlich sich *auf sich beziehende* Bestimmung; das Besondere als *Einzelnheit* [11] mit Ausschliessung der *andern*." GW 12:123.36–124.11/L 2:349–350 (GL 701). Bracketed numbers in the English translation and in the German text indicate the page and subsequently the beginnings of new text lines according to GW 12. In the German text page and line indications have been inserted at the end of a word if that word was hyphenated in GW 12. In the English text the page and line indications have been inserted as close to the original (GW 12) as possible.

243. Cited here in parentheses by page and line according to GW 12:123.36–124.11 but found also in L 2:349–350 with the English translation in GL 701.

244. GW 12:37.6–43.19, 49.1–51.9/L 2:245.253, 259–262 (GL 605–612, 618–621).

245. GW 12:80.14–83.36/L 2:297–301 (GL 653–657).

246. Note "therefore" (*daher*) in GW 12:124.1/L 2:349 (GL 701).

247. Compare on the disjunctive judgement, GW 12:81.1–2/L 2:298 (GL 654).

248. The only possible way Hegel could justify positing particularity as he first tries to would be to presume pure being's availability as initial moment of pure thought. That has already been argued against in Ch. 2 above. Even if such were possible, Hegel would still be faced with the question of a collapse of "either B, C or D" into mutually related and therefore finite others.

There does of course occur an exclusion as well between the subject A and "C and D," which exclusion Hegel terms "exclusive individuality." However this exclusion is clearly logically subsequent in the disjunctive syllogism to and dependent upon the exclusion among "B and C and D."

249. "wesentlich sich *auf sich beziehende* Bestimmung; das besondere als *Einzelheit* mit Ausschliessung der andern." L 2:350 (GL 701). Notice how Hegel shifts from the plural "determinations" ("*Bestimmungen*") to the singular "determination" ("*Bestimmung*").

250. "Im Schlußsatz ist es [A] als die ausschliessende, *einzelne* Bestimmtheit gesetzt.—Oder auch ist es schon im Untersatze als ausschliessende Einzelnheit, und im Schlußsatze als das Bestimmte, was es ist, positiv gesetzt." GW 12:124.22–24/L 2:350 ("In the conclusion it (A) is posited as the exclusive, *individual* determinateness. Or again, it already appears in the minor premise as exclusive individuality and is positively posited in the conclusion as the determinate which it is." GL 702). On the determination of the Concept as individual, see again esp. GW 12:49.1–51.9/L 2:259–262 (GL 618–621). For an overview of Hegel's understanding of individuality, see Traugott Koch, *Differenz and Versöhnung* (Gütersloh: Mohn, 1967) 163–169. On the relationships among universality, particularity and individuality as Hegel intended them in the disjunctive syllogism, see Krohn, *Die formale Logik* 169.

To use phrases loosely borrowed from Hegel, universality is the Concept as simple relationship to itself, absolute (but unposited) negativity. Particularity is the Concept as differentiation, that is, as relation to its other (universality) and inclusive of that other. Individuality is the Concept as self–related determinateness, the determinate determinate, posited negation of negation.

251. GW 12:124.28–29/L 2:350 (GL 702).

252. GW 12:126.7–8/L 2:352 (GL 704).

253. Whereas here the collapse in the self-positing of universality is posited already at the moment of particularity, Jan van der Meulen, *Hegel. Die gebrochene Mitte* (Hamburg: Felix Meiner, 1958) esp. 94–97, would identify the collapse of Hegel's understanding of self-mediation with the renewed immediacy of objectivity and the shift from mediation to immediacy. Very generally stated, Koch, *Differenz* 159–163, critiques Hegel earlier in the *Logic* by proposing that particularity's being other to universality inevitably constitutes particularity as finite. Koch gives in a sense a lead into the presently stated critique of Hegel's conception of particularity as "mere summing up" (*"bloße Summation"* 160). For Koch's critique of Hegel's notion of "exclusive individuality," see 163–168, 172.

According to Düsing, *Das Problem der Subjektivität* 287 n. 238, John Ellis McTaggart in *A Commentary on Hegel's Logic* (Cambridge, England: at the University Press, 1896) 237–240, "kritisiert, daß Hegel die Selbstdifferenzierung des Begriffs als konkrete Allgemeinheit in ihrer Möglichkeit im disjunktiven Schluß nicht bewiesen habe."

On Adolf Trendelenburg, *Logische Untersuchungen*, two volumes (Leipzig: Hirzel, 1870) and his critique of Hegel's logic of syllogism on the basis of formal logic, see Klaus Düsing, review of *Die formale Logik* by Wolfgang Krohn in *Hegel-Studien* 10 (Bonn: Bouvier, 1975) 326 with n. 3; and more generally Düsing, *Das Problem der Subjektivität* 34–35, 275–276, 279, 283; Koch, *Differenz* 52–54 n. 51.

For a more general analysis of what is actually taking place in Hegel's proposal, see Ch. 2 Subsection 5 of the present study.

254. See briefly in this regard Pannenberg, *Thesen zur Theologie der Kirche* theses 58–61.

Most European and Latin American liberation theologies would appear to be reacting either unconsciously or more explicitly against positions subsumable under this interpretation of Hegel's understanding of community and freedom.

255. See this study's general Introduction above.

256. "ein Hinausgegangensein aus einem Ersten zu einem Zweiten und Hervorgehen aus Unterschiedenen." E § 86R (SL § 86R but my trans.).

257. See overall E §§ 573–577, esp. 577.

258. Even Hegel's *Phenomenology* finally presupposed this logically graspable self-mediation for its own argumentation.

259. "Pour Hegel cette notion [médiation] s'entend de toute unification des opposés dans le bon (bonne positivité) et le mauvais sens (mauvaise positivité). Très vite cette notion s'entendra uniquement de la bonne unification. Elle désignera l'intériorité spirituelle des différents moments à l'intérieur d'un tout qui les englobe." Niel, *De la médiation* 70 n. 10.

260. See Ch. 4 Subsection 4b of the present study.

261. Again, see Ch. 4 Subsection 4b of the present study.

262. See briefly Ch. 1 Subsection 1 of the present study.

263. See briefly Ch. 4 Subsection 4b of the present study.

264. In a sense Hegel had attempted to define otherness more complexly than as negation in that the second moment of any dialectical progression was to be the thinking of contradiction. GW 12:246.13–15/L 2:496 (GL 835). Note that for Hegel "nothing is," GW 11:44.13–15/L 1:67 (GL 82). Nevertheless otherness is for Hegel logically speaking first of all negation.

See in general Werner Flach, *Negation and Andersheit. Ein Beitrag zur Problematik der Letztimplikation* (Munich: Reinhardt, 1959).

265. The term "encounter" is here assiduously avoided since it bears such heavy existentialist baggage with it and since its application is more restricted to a merely dialogical context.

266. This co-constitutively negative and positive character of otherness further insures that this formal treatment of becoming has a built in guarantee against a Polyanna view of reality.

267. Against the background of a more explicit reference to the theological concept of freedom's being for him the Concept of the trinitarian history of God, Jürgen Moltmann has identified possible relationships between Subject and object or Subject and Subject or again Subject and project in terms of possible formulations of freedom respectively as "dominance" (*Freiheit als Herrschaft*), "community" (*Freiheit als Gemeinschaft*) and "creative initiative" (*schöpferische Initiative*). *Trinität and Reich Gottes. Zur Gotteslehre* (Munich: Kaiser, 1980) 230–239, esp. 232–235. This present study's concern whether at this point or

in Chapter Six below is, in a sense, with a question prior to these perspectives sketched by Moltmann.

A more developed discussion beyond this present "prior question" would have to take into consideration Moltmann's critique of Hegel, a critique developed more directly in relation to the trinitarian thought of Karl Barth and Karl Rahner. See *Trinität and Reich Gottes* 30–31, 154–166. Here this present "prior question" is still posed before Moltmann's distinction between monological and communitarian or social models of Trinity (33–35). In saying that the question of subjectivity has lost its power and significance for today, Moltmann distinguishes in too facile a fashion between Hegel's understanding of absolute Spirit and Moltmann's own concerns.

268. It could also but not with such immediate necessity be said that a community does grow and develop, friendships do deepen, a person does grow and become stronger psychologically and emotionally.

269. "Otherness" here includes connotations indicated by two German words, *Andersheit* and *Anderssein*.

270. By way of illustration, when Hegel's elaboration of the transition in the *Logic* from *Dasein* on is freed from the constraints of a self-positing pure thought, there could be sketched a development from *Dasein* as the expression of the givenness of initial Selfhood as beginning and the determination of otherness as co-constitutively quality (*Qualität*) as reality (*Realität*) and quality as negation (*Negation*). The thought interrelationship between *Dasein* as initial Selfhood and quality as otherness would give rise to *Etwas* as enriched Selfhood renewedly initial Selfhood over against and related to recurrent otherness (*das Andere*). For Hegel's original elaboration see L 1:95–103 (GL 109–116).

271. Recall E §§ 12R, 86R.

6. From Finite to Infinite

1. See the present study's general Introduction above.

2. On the necessitarian character of this transition, see Ch. 1 nn. 106, 113, 169, 172 above.

3. E.g., AR 47 (CR 89–90) 1827.

4. "so ist über das Herausgehen des Endlichen aus dem Unendlichen zu sagen, das Unendliche gehe zur Endlichkeit *heraus*, darum weil es keine Wahrheit, kein Bestehen an ihm, wie es als abstrakte Einheit gefaßt ist, hat; so umgekehrt geht das Endliche aus demselben Grunde seiner Nichtigkeit in das Unendliche *hinein*." L 1:144 (GL 154). Here Hegel is speaking in a Remark concerning his formulation of finitude and infinity as thought categories in the movement of pure thought. See further Ch. 6 Subsection 2 of the present study.

In the context of his discussion on the true infinite Hegel insists that it does not matter whether one begins with the finite or the infinite, L 1:142–145 (GL 152–154). However, there Hegel is not speaking of the *beginning of his system as such*, which beginning can for him only be made in pure being, inclusive momentary totality constituting the absolute beginning of the movement of pure thought. Note also in Hegel's critique of Kant on the cosmological proofs for the existence of God, BDG 155.

5. L 1:102 (GL 115).

6. It has unfortunately not as yet been possible for this writer to do follow-up reading on Robert Scharlemann's observation at the end of his study on Tillich, "The [ontological] structure is constituted not by the self-world polarity but by a self-world—other-self triad; the basic structure is not subject and object only, but subject, object and parasubject." *Reflection and Doubt in the Thought of Paul Tillich* (New Haven: Yale, 1969) 201. Scharlemann indicates he obtained the term "parasubject" from Gotthard Günther, *Idee und Grundriß einer nicht-aristotelischen Logik*, vol. 1 (Hamburg: Felix Meiner, 1959).

7. GW 11:33.22–30/text reworked in the second ed. L 1:54 (GL 70). See in general on "beginning" GW 11:33.3–40.29/second edition L 1:51–64 (GL 67–78).

8. L 1:101–103 (GL 114–116).

9. See Ch. 2 Subsection 1 of the present study.

10. "nur der Anfang des Subjekts." L 1:101 (GL 115).

11. GW 11:59.1–85.12.

12. GW 11:60.15–35.

13. GW 11:65.24–66.2.

14. L 1:95–146 (GL 109–156).

15. Compare GW 11:82.1–83.9 with the more elaborated L:132–140 (GL 143–150). Though too much should not be made of the point, on the one hand in the first edition when push comes to shove Hegel spoke of "finitude" (*Endlichkeit*) and "infinity" (*Unendlichkeit*). On the other hand in the second edition Hegel tends to speak more concretely of "the finite" (*das Endliche*) and "the infinite" (*das Unendliche*). Compare the climactic phrases "the true infinity" (*die wahre Unendlichkeit*) of GW 11:82.32 with the "true infinite" (*wahrhaft Unendliches*) of L 1:138 (GL 148).

16. For example, L 1:138 (GL 148).

17. It would be of interest on another occasion to analyze in detail the presentation of finite and infinite in the 1817, 1827 and 1830 editions of the *Encyclopedia*, though their merely schematic presentations do prove generally more problematic in any attempt to trace the changes in Hegel's presentation of finitude and infinity.

Helpful secondary literature on either the full *Logic* or the smaller, encyclopedic *Logic's* treatments of finite and infinite: W. T. Stace, *The Philosophy of Hegel. A Systematic Exposition* (New York: Macmillan, 1924) 138–149, tends to give a confused view of the progressive ordering of Hegel's *Encyclopedia* categories; Karl Heinz Haag, "Die Seinsdialektik bei Hegel und in der scholastischen Philosophie," (Ph.D. dissertation, Philosophical Faculty of the Johann Wolfgang Goethe-Universität, Frankfurt am Main, 1951) 35–51; Traugott Koch, *Differenz und Versöhnung. Eine Interpretation der Theologie G. W. F. Hegels nach seinem "Wissenschaft der Logik"* (Gütersloh: Mohn, 1967) 106–130 containing excellent overview especially of finitude and infinity with critique and with a discussion of much significant literature in the footnoting; André Léonard, *Commentaire littéral de la logique de Hegel* (Paris: Vrin, 1974) 62–81, a helpful detailed commentary on the 1830 encyclopedic *Logic* with references to the larger *Science of Logic;* John Burbidge, *On Hegel's Logic. Fragments of a Commentary* (Atlantic Highlands, N.J.: Humanities, 1981) esp. 46–59 and 246–248, whose clear analyses present the forward movement of Hegel's thought and will therefore allow here for a briefer summary.

18. Again, for a summary of Hegel's presentation of *Etwas*, especially in respect to the thought determinations for Hegel logically prior to it, see Ch. 2 Subsection 1 of the present study.

19. "Das Negative des Negativen ist als *Etwas* nur der Anfang des Subjekts." L 1:102 (GL 115 trans. amended).

20. "welche die konkrete, *absolute* Negativität, wie jene erste dagegen nur die *abstrakte* Negativität ist." L 1:103 (GL 116).

21. "nun Dasein und weiter Daseiendes." L 1:103 (GL 116).

22. "ein *Daseiendes*, aber als Negatives des Etwas bestimmt,—ein *Anderes*." L 1:103 (GL 116).

23. L 1:103–104 (GL 116). For difficulties involved in this transition see the critique in terms of "becoming to *Dasein*" (*Werden im Dasein*) in Ch. 4 Subsection 3b of the present study.

24. See the brief discussion in Haag, "Seinsdialektik" 50–51.

25. L 1:103–125 (GL 116–127).

26. "Etwas und ein Anderes." L 1:104 (GL 117 trans. amended).

27. L 1:106 (GL 118–119).

28. L 1:106–107 (GL 119–120).

29. L 1:106 (GL 119).

30. L 1:107–110 (GL 120–122).

31. L 1:110 (GL 122).

32. "Bestimmung, Beschaffenheit und Grenze." L 1:110–116 (GL 122–129).

33. L 1:110 (GL 123).

34. L 1:111 (GL 124).

35. "Das Etwas selbst ist weiter bestimmt, und die Negation als ihm immanent gesetzt, als sein entwickeltes *Insichsein*." L 1:112 (GL 125 trans. amended).

36. L 1:113 (GL 125–126).

37. See further in Burbidge, *On Hegel's Logic* 50–51.
38. L 1:114 (GL 126).
39. "*ist* Etwas zugleich durch seine Grenze." L 1:114 (GL 126 trans. amended).
40. L 1:114 (GL 126–127).
41. "Sie [die Grenze] ist die Vermittlung, wodurch Etwas und Anderes *sowohl ist* als *nicht ist*." L 1:114 (GL 127 trans. amended).
42. L 1:114 (GL 127).
43. "über sich hinaus auf sein Nichtsein weist und dies als sein Sein ausspricht." L 1:115 (GL 127).
44. L 1:115 (GL 128).
45. "Etwas mit seiner immanenten Grenze gesetzt als der Widerspruch seiner selbst, durch den es über sich hinausgewiesen und getrieben wird, ist das *Endliche*." L 1:116 (GL 129 trans. amended).
46. GW 11:44.24/L 1:67 (GL 83) with E §§ 161, 240.
47. L 1:104 (GL 117).
48. L 1:116 (GL 129). See Burbidge, *On Hegel's Logic* 51.
49. See L 1:116–117 (GL 129).
50. 1:119 (Gl 131–132).
51. L 1:119–120 (GL 132).
52. L 1:120 (GL 132).
53. "Was sein soll, *ist* und zugleich *ist nicht*." L 1:120 (GL 132).
54. L 1:121 (GL 133).
55. "Das Endliche ist so der Widerspruch seiner in sich." L 1:124 (GL 136).
56. "Diese *Identität mit sich*, die Negation der Negation, ist affirmatives Sein, so das Andere des Endlichen, als welches die erste Negation zu seiner Bestimmtheit haben soll; jenes Andere ist *das Unendliche*." L 1:125 (GL 137).
57. Note Hegel's statement of purpose, L 1:125–126 (GL 137).
58. "Was *ist*, ist nur das *Unendliche*." L 1:126 (GL 138).
59. "zugleich die *Negation* eines *Andern*, des Endlichen." L 1:127 (GL 138 trans. slightly amended).
60. "in qualitativer *Beziehung* als außer einander *bleibende*." L 1:127 (GL 138).
61. "das unbestimmte Leere, das Jenseits des Endlichen." L 1:128 (GL 139).
62. L 1:128 (GL 139).
63. L 1:128–131 (GL 140–143).
64. L 1:129 (GL 140).
65. "Aber diese ihre Einheit ist in dem qualitativen Anderssein derselben *verborgen*." L 1:129 (GL 141).
66. "und so fort ins Unendliche." L 1:130 (GL 141).

67. "Die Unendlichkeit des unendlichen Progresses bleibt mit dem Endlichen als solchem behaftet, ist dadurch begrenzt und selbst *endlich*." L 1:131 (GL 142). See also L 1:133, 140, 141 (GL 144, 150, 151).
68. L 1:132, 134, 137 (GL 143, 145, 147).
69. "ist die Wahrheit [des unendlichen Progresses] an sich schon *vorhanden*, und es bedarf nur des Aufnehmens dessen, was vorhanden ist." L 1:132 (GL 143 trans. amended).
70. L 1:132 (GL 143).
71. "die Negation seiner an ihm selbst, welche die Unendlichkeit ist." L 1:132 (GL 143).
72. L 1:132 (GL 143).
73. L 1:132–133 (GL 143–144).
74. "welche das Unendliche sein soll." L 1:133 (GL 144).
75. This is somewhat of a simplification since Hegel speaks of the common element in the context of their separateness. L 1:133 (GL 144).
76. L 1:133 (GL 144).
77. L 1:134 (GL 145).
78. L 1:134 (GL 145).
79. L 1:135 (GL 145–146).
80. "sein Sichaufheben im Endlichen ist ein Zurückkehren aus der leeren Flucht, *Negation* des Jenseits, das ein *Negatives* an ihm selbst ist." L 1:135 (GL 146).
81. L 1:135 (GL 146).
82. L 1:135–136 (GL 146).
83. "die vollständige, sich selbst schließende Bewegung, die bei dem angekommen, das den Anfang machte." L 1:136 (GL 147).
84. L 1:136 (GL 147).
85. "daß sie darin nur als Momente eines Ganzen vorkommen." L 1:137 (GL 147).
86. L 1:137 T (GL 148). Here Hegel is speaking of points of departure and not of the absolute beginning of his system, which for him must be pure being. Systematically speaking, Hegel's argument remains a movement from infinite to finite.

It would be appropriate at this point to enter into a discussion of Hegel's lectures on the proofs for the existence of God. Note Hegel's repeated reference to logic: BDG 22, 85, 91, 109, 150 (LPR 3:171, 235, 270, 293, ___). In principle, discussion of the *Logic* and of the *Lectures on the Philosophy of Religion* has treated of the content of these lectures on the proofs for the existence of God.

87. "als Negation jener Endlichkeit beider mit Wahrheit das Unendliche." L 1:137 (GL 148). For a handy brief summary of Hegel's double usage of finite and infinite, see L 1:137–138 (GL 148).

88. L 1:138 (GL 148).
89. L 1:138 (GL 148).
90. "In-sich-Zurückgekehrtsein, Beziehung seiner auf sich selbst." L 1:138 (GL 148).
91. L 1:138–139 (GL 149).
92. L 1:139 (GL 149–150).
93. As Hegel had written earlier concerning the infinite as moment in infinite progression, "als *nur* Eines der beiden ist es [das Unendliche] selbst endlich, est ist nicht das Ganze, sondern nur eine Seite." L 1:133 ("as *only* one of the two it [the infinite] is itself finite, it is not the whole, but only *one* side." GL 144 trans. amended).
94. See Ch. 1 Subsection 4 of the present study.
95. Hegel's references to seeing what is at hand ring vaguely of his position in the *Phenomenology* that the phenomenologist need not contribute as such to the process of the elevation of natural consciousness but merely observe. See Ch. 3 Subsection 4a of the present study. Here in the context of the *Logic* Hegel surely means "to think through."
96. The viability of such a self-sublation is questioned by Koch, *Differenz* 114–122, 124, explicitly concerning the bad infinite.
97. It is here not so much a question of arguing these points concerning finite and infinite in any detail as simply one of summarizing the generally valid contours of finitude and infinity arising out of Hegel's analysis. A renewed, yet preliminary argumentation will be proposed in Ch. 6 Subsection 3 of the present study.
98. L 1:116 (GL 129).
99. Note the structure of philosophy, i.e., its Concept and Idea, as summarized by Hegel in E §§ 574, 577.
100. As Koch states succinctly in connection with the necessity of thought to refer to and reach but not to grasp the infinite, "Hat das Denken, genötigt durch die Widersprüchlichkeit des Endlichen, sich zum Unendlichen erhoben und es als das, was est ist, *erreicht*, so hat das Denken in diesem Erreichen des Unendlichen—das Unendliche immer schon *verloren*." *Differenz* 120.
101. See on the value of Hegel's inclusive infinite Koch, *Differenz* 128 with 130 and 173. See also Ch. 6 n. 105 below.
102. L 1:135 with 136–137 and 139 (GL 146 with 147 and 149).
103. L 1:138 with 139 (GL 148 with 149–150).
104. Stated more religiously, the world could not be seen as a unity if it were not conceived of as being "contained" in God.
105. John Hutchison Stirling's unfairly maligned proposal to have discovered the secret of Hegel in Hegel's elaboration of the concrete universal emphasizes this point in its own way. Stirling wrote, "The secret of Hegel may be indicated at shortest then: as Aristotle—with considerable assistance from

Plato—made *explicit* the *abstract* Universal that was *implicit* in Socrates, so Hegel—with less considerable assistance from Fichte and Schelling made *explicit* the *concrete* Universal that was *implicit* in Kant." *The Secret of Hegel*, revised ed. (New York: G. P. Putnam's Sons, 1898) xxii.

106. Ch. 5 Subsection 4 of the present study.
107. See Ch. 6 Subsection 2 of the present study.
108. See Ch. 5 Subsection 4 of the present study.
109. See Ch. 6 Subsection 2 of the present study.
110. See Koch's somewhat parallel remarks using the terms "identity" and "difference," *Differenz* 173–174; also Wolfhart Pannenberg, "Speaking about God in the Face of Atheist Criticism," in *The Idea of God and Human Freedom* (Philadelphia: Westminster, 1973) 110 with n. 4 citing Traugott Koch, "Gott—der Grund der Freiheit," *Pastoraltheologie* 57 (1968) 45–56.
111. The specific terms "Subject" and "Person" have been bracketed out of this more provisional reformulation of Hegel's trinitarian claim so as not to prejudice further discussion of particular questions.
112. In his review of the hardback edition of this study, in *Gregorianum* 66 (1985) 571, John O'Donnell indicates that as a theologian he feels "a certain dissatisfaction with the whole notion of postulating the Trinity as a means of reconciling the self-contradictions of finitude." He continues, "Perhaps there is a place for this type of transcendental deduction, but this approach seems to give far too little attention to the Christological moment, i.e. the wholly unpredictable event of Jesus Christ, which, historically speaking, was the driving force which led the church to reformulate the doctrine of God in specifically trinitarian terms." Perhaps as a sort of first response to this remark it could be helpful to note that one is here first and foremost trying to work out a philosophical understanding of the relationship between finitude and infinity. Of course one of the further purposes here would be to establish a philosophically expressed framework permitting one to confirm the idea as such that the philosophical notion of a triadically structured inclusive infinite can be seen as reasonable and compatible with more specifically theological affirmations concerning Incarnation and Trinity. It could be hoped as well that what is here worked out on a more formal level might contribute in some way to further reflection on Trinity, whether from a philosophical or a theological perspective. In this regard, see the Postscript to the present study. Also, when one is here speaking of "need," one is not saying that God is Trinity because of finitude's need, but that for finitude to be fully comprehensible in its self-contradiction one would need to refer to a triadically structured inclusive infinite.

As a theologian, O'Donnell also wonders: ". . . he [Schlitt] says that limit pertains to the essence of true Infinity (p. 266). Does this mean that the Infinite requires the limit to be itself? Such an idea seems to make the creation necessary to God, a doctrine which theologians have traditionally criticized in

Hegel's philosophical vision." It may be that the phrase "pertains to the essence of true Infinity" needs further nuance. On p. 266 of the hardback edition being reviewed by O'Donnell, one does read, ". . . limit as such, given finitude, pertains to the essence of true infinity." So, if hypothetically there were no finitude, then limit, at least as characteristic of finitude, would of course not pertain to true infinity. I would, however, think one could and should argue that distinction as such (and, from a theological perspective, of Persons) would still, in such a hypothetical case were there were no finitude, pertain to the essence of true infinity.

Postscript: From Thought to Experience

1. In what is, from the perspective of someone interested in Hegel's thought and its possible relevance, a fascinating and even inspiring brief text, Slavoj Žižek speaks of the various directions thought has taken after the death of Hegel. See "Preface. Hegel's Century," in *Hegel and the Infinite. Religion, Politics, and Dialectic*, ed. Slavoj Žižek, Clayton Crockett and Creston Davis (New York: Columbia University Press, 2011) ix–xi, where Žižek writes, ". . . the time of Hegel still lies ahead—Hegel's century will be the twenty-first" (xi). He is here speaking not of the Hegel of 1831, but the Hegel who would confront our "age of extremes."

Perhaps one could note at this point an example I came upon recently of a very interesting study of Troeltsch's seemingly sympathetic and yet quite critical attitude toward Hegel with regard to the philosophy of history. See George J. Yamin, Jr., *In the Absence of Fantasia. Troeltsch's Relation to Hegel* (Gainsville, FL: University Press of Florida, 1993). Yamin writes, for example, "Despite the sustained criticism of Hegel's thought found throughout his corpus, however, Troeltsch accepted, at least in modified form, certain key elements of the Hegelian paradigm" (11).

2. Hans-Georg Gadamer, *Wahrheit und Methode*, second edition (Tübingen: J. C. B. Mohr, 1965) 329–344, and also of interest 52–66, 449–452/*Truth and Method*, second revised edition, translation revised by Joel Weinsheimer and Donald G. Marshall (New York: Crossroad, 1990) 346–362, and also of interest 55–70, 474–477. This revised translation is based on *Gesammelte Werke*, vol. 1: *Hermeneutik I. Wahrheit und Methode* (Tübingen: J. C. B. Mohr [Paul Siebeck], 1986).

3. Josiah Royce, *The Problem of Christianity. Lectures Delivered at the Lowell Institute in Boston, and at Manchester College, Oxford*, two volumes (New York: Macmillan, 1913; reprinted two volumes in one, Hamdon, CN: Archon, 1967). *The Problem of Christianity* has been republished with a new Introduction by John E. Smith, (Chicago: The University of Chicago Press, 1968).

4. John Dewey, *Experience and Nature. The Later Works, 1925–1953*, vol. 1: *1925*, ed. Jo Ann Boydston with associate textual editors, Patricia Baysinger and Barbara Levine (Carbondale, IL: Southern Illinois University Press, 1981, first edition originally published 1925, second edition 1929). Dewey and the others here noted did not, to my knowledge, identify themselves as following such a trajectory from Hegel on.

5. See, for example, John E. Smith, *The Analogy of Experience* (New York: Harper, 1973).

6. Here I have not been in a position to give sufficient credit to the work of Alfred North Whitehead, who himself had worked out a universalizing understanding of experience. In a sense, there would seem to be three more easily identifiable general families of "metaphysical" options before us today, namely, those rooted in and arising out of the thought of Thomas Aquinas, of Whitehead and of Hegel. Perhaps the secret to more successful longer-term philosophical reflection will lie in bringing together elements of each of these three on the basis of an embracing of one or the other as fundamental overall orientation capable of bringing such elements together in a coherent way.

For further remarks on these and other points mentioned in this Postscript, see Dale M. Schlitt, *Experience and Spirit. A Post-Hegelian Philosophical Theology* (New York: Peter Lang, 2007). For an example of a more concrete reflection on the notion of enriching experience, see Dale M. Schlitt, *Generosity and Gratitude. A Philosophical Psalm* (New York: Peter Lang, 2011).

7. It would surely seem, for example, that in a Christian theological context one would be ready to speak of the triune God's experience of finitude and of us, given the thought that whatever is done to the least among us is done to the risen One and given belief in the resurrection of the dead.

8. In a particularly helpful and insightful review of the first publication of *Hegel's Trinitarian Claim*, in *Theologie und Philosophie* 61 (1986) 133–135, Jörg Splett ends his review by remarking that Trinity does not present us with a theme of becoming (though this theme can surely be a way to Trinity), but with the theme of being: as Being-for ("Trinität stellt uns nicht das Thema des Werdens [mag dieses Thema auch durchaus ein Weg zu ihr sein], sondern des Seins: als Sein-für"). Here in the text of the present study the reference to three instances of "being-for" is an effort, however initial, to bring together the dynamic traditionally implied by the notion of God as *ipsum esse subsistens* ("subsistent being" or, perhaps better, "the subsistent 'to be'") with the further dynamic of divine Persons understood as subsistent relations in one dynamic movement identified as "becoming." This parallels somewhat Hegel's ability to speak of the moments of divine self-development without Hegel's needing to work at two levels, so to speak, namely, on the one hand, that of being and, on the other hand, that of relation. Hegel speaks simply of a movement of inclusive divine subjectivity.

We need, furthermore, to take note of the fact that when we move from a more formal notion of becoming and its structured movement to a more concrete consideration of experience, the latter is a form of becoming, but not a form necessarily occurring as a strictly mono-subjectivally structured movement of becoming with resultant Selfhood being a return to initial Selfhood. Indeed, whenever we speak of God we find that the very words used and their meanings are modified in that speaking. In this specific case of reference to Trinity as a movement of experience, that movement is unique and unrepeatable. This reference to God as movement of experience, then, helps us, in our further discussion of finite experiences, to see that even these experiences are more than a simple, formal movement of becoming.

Bibliography

A helpful list of primary and secondary electronic resources for the study of Hegel and his thought can be found at http://www.hegel.net/en/etexts. htm. This site was accessed on August 21, 2011.

1. G. W. F. Hegel's Works

a. Published by Hegel

PHENOMENOLOGY OF SPIRIT

Gesammelte Werke. Vol. 9: *Phänomenologie des Geistes.* Edited by Wolfgang Bonsiepen and Reinhard Heede. Hamburg: Felix Meiner, 1980. Abbreviated GW 9.
Phänomenologie des Geistes. Philosophische Bibliothek. Vol. 114. Edited by Johannes Hoffmeister. Hamburg: Felix Meiner, 1952. Abbreviated *Phän.*
Phenomenology of Spirit. Translation of *Phän.* by A. V. Miller. New York: Oxford University Press, 1977. Abbreviated *Phen.*

SCIENCE OF LOGIC

Gesammelte Werke. Vol. 11: *Wissenschaft der Logik. Erster Band. Die objektive Logik (1812–1813).* Abbreviated GW 11. Vol. 12: *Wissenschaft der Logik. Zweiter Band. Die subjektive Logik (1816).* Abbreviated GW 12. Vol. 21: *Wissenschaff der Logik. Erster Teil. Die objektive Logik. Erster Band. Die Lehre vom Sein (1832).* Edited by Friedrich Hogemann and Walter Jaeschke. Hamburg: Felix Meiner, 1978, 1981, 1985.
Wissenschaft der Logik. Philosophische Bibliothek. Vols. 56 and 57. Edited by Georg Lasson. Hamburg: Felix Meiner, 1975. Abbreviated L 1, 2.
Hegel's Science of Logic. Translation of L 1 and 2 by A. V. Miller. New York: Humanities, 1969. Abbreviated GL.

OUTLINE OF THE PHILOSOPHY OF RIGHT

Grundlinien der Philosophie des Rechts. Philosophische Bibliothek. Vol. 124a. Edited by Johannes Hoffmeister. Hamburg: Felix Meiner, 1967.
Gesammelte Werke. Vols. 14/1, 14/2, 14/3: *Grundlinien der Philosophie des Rechts.* Edited by Klaus Grotsch and Elisabeth Weisser-Lohmann. Hamburg: Felix Meiner, 2009, 2010, 2011.
Outline of the Philosophy of Right. Translated by T. M. Knox. Oxford: Oxford University Press, 1952.
Elements of the Philosophy of Right. Edited by Allen W. Wood. Translated by H. B. Nisbet. Cambridge: Cambridge University Press, 1991.

ENCYCLOPEDIA

Sämtliche Werke. *Jubiläumsausgabe in zwanzig Bänden.* Edited by Hermann Glockner. Vol. 6: *Enzyklopädie der philosophischen Wissenschaften im Grundrisse und andere Schriften aus der Heidelberger Zeit.* First original edition 1817. Stuttgart: Frommann, 1927.
Encyclopädie der philosophischen Wissenschaften im Grundrisse. Second original edition 1827. Heidelberg: Oßwald, 1827.
Enzyklopädie der philosophischen Wissenschaften im Grundrisse. Third original edition 1830. Philosophische Bibliothek. Vol. 33. Edited by Friedhelm Nicolin and Otto Pöggeler. Hamburg: Felix Meiner, 1969. Abbreviated E.
Gesammelte Werke. Vol. 13: *Enzyklopädie der philosophischen Wissenschaften im Grundrisse (1817).* Edited by Wolfgang Bonsiepen and Klaus Grotsh, with Hans-Christian Lucas and Udo Rameil. Vol. 19: *Enzyklopädie der philosophischen Wissenschaften im Grundrisse (1827).* Edited by Wolfgang Bonsiepen and Hans-Christian Lucas. Vol. 20: *Enzyklopädie der philosophischen Wissenschaften im Grundrisse (1830).* Edited by Wolfgang Bonsiepen and Hans-Christian, with Udo Rameil. Hamburg: Felix Meiner, 2001, 1989, 1992.
Hegel's Logic. Translation of E, Part One, by William Wallace. Oxford: Clarendon, 1975. Abbreviated SL.
The Encyclopedia Logic. Translation of the 1830 *Encyclopedia*, Part One, by T. F. Geraets, W. A. Suchting, and H. S. Harris. Indianapolis, IN: Hackett, 1991.
Hegel's Philosophy of Nature. Three volumes. Translation of the 1830 *Encyclopedia*, Part Two, by M. J. Petry. New York: Humanities, 1970.
Hegel's Philosophy of Mind. Translation of E, Part Three, by William Wallace. Oxford: Clarendon, 1971. Abbreviated PM.
Hegel's Philosophy of Subjective Spirit. Translation of the 1830 *Encyclopedia*, the first section of Part Three, by M. J. Petry. Dordrecht: Riedel, 1979.

REVIEW ARTICLES

Review of "Über die hegelsche Lehre oder: absolutes Wissen und moderner Pantheismus," 2. "Über Philosophie überhaupt und Hegels Enzykloplädie der philosophischen Wissenschaften insbesondere. Ein Beitrag zur Beurteilung der Letzteren. Von Dr. K. E. Schubarth und Dr. L. Carganico." In *Berliner Schriften 1818–1831*. Philosophische Bibliothek. Vol. 240 pp. 339–402. Edited by Johannes Hoffmeister. Hamburg: Felix Meiner, 1956.

b. Manuscripts and Transcripts Posthumously Published

LECTURES ON THE HISTORY OF PHILOSOPHY

Sämtliche Werke. Jubiläumsausgabe in zwanzig Bänden. Edited by Hermann Glockner. Vols. 17 and 18: *Vorlesungen über die Geschichte der Philosophie*. Stuttgart: Frommann, 1928. Reproduces the first Friends edition text.
Werke. Vollständige Ausgabe durch einen Verein von Freunden des Verewigten. Second edition. Vols. 13 and 14: *Vorlesungen über die Geschichte der Philosophie*. Edited by Carl Ludwig Michelet. Berlin: Duncker und Humblot, 1840.
Vorlesungen. Ausgewählte Nachschriften und Manuskripte. Vol. 6: *Vorlesungen über die Geschichte der Philosophie. Teil 1: Einleitung. Orientalische Philosophie.* Vol. 7: *Vorlesungen über die Geschichte der Philosophie. Teil 2: Griechische Philosophie I. Thales bis Kyniker.* Vol. 8: *Vorlesungen über die Geschichte der Philosophie. Teil 3: Griechische Philosophie II. Plato bis Proklos.* Vol. 9: *Vorlesungen über die Geschichte der Philosophie. Teil 4: Philosophie des Mittelalters und der neueren Zeit.* Edited by Pierre Garniron and Walter Jaeschke. Hamburg: Felix Meiner, 1994, 1989, 1996, 1986.
Lectures on the History of Philosophy. Three volumes. Translated by K. S. Haldane and F. H. Simson. New York: Humanities Press, 1955, 1963.
Lectures on the History of Philosophy (1825–1826). Vol. 1: *Introduction and Oriental Philosophy, Together with the Introductions from the Other Series of These Lectures.* Edited by Robert F. Brown. Translated by Robert F. Brown and J. M. Stewart with the assistance of H. S. Harris. Vol. 2: *Greek Philosophy.* Edited and translated by Robert F. Brown. Vol. 3: *Medieval and Modern Philosophy.* Edited by Robert F. Brown. Translated by Robert F. Brown and J. M. Stewart with the assistance of H. S. Harris. New York: Oxford University Press, 2009, 2006, 2009.

LECTURES ON THE PHILOSOPHY OF HISTORY

Vorlesungen über die Philosophie der Weltgeschichte. Auf Grund der Handschriften herausgegeben. Vol. 1: *Die Vernunft in der Geschichte.* Philosophische

Bibliothek. Vol. 171a. Edited by Johannes Hoffmeister. Vols. 171b–d. Edited by Georg Lasson. Hamburg: Felix Meiner, 1970, 1976.

Vorlesungen. Ausgewählte Nachschriften und Manuskripte. Vol. 12: *Vorlesungen über die Philosophie der Weltgeschichte*. Edited by Karl-Heinz Ilting, Karl Brehmer and Hoo Nam Seelmann. Hamburg: Felix Meiner, 1996.

Lectures on the Philosophy of History. Translated by John Sibree. New York: Dover, 1956.

LECTURES ON THE PHILOSOPHY OF RELIGION

Werke. Vollständige Ausgabe durch einen Verein von Freunden des Verewigten. Vols. 11–12: *Vorlesungen über die Philosophie der religion. Nebst einer Schrift über die Beweise vom Daseyn Gottes*. Edited by Philipp Marheineke. Berlin: Duncker und Humblot, 1832.

Werke. Vollständige Ausgabe durch einen Verein von Freunden des Verewigten. Second edition. Vols. 11–12: *Vorlesungen über die Philosophie der Religion. Nebst einer Schrift über die Beweise vom Daseyn Gottes*. Edited by Philipp Marheineke [and Bruno Bauer]. Berlin: Duncker und Humblot, 1840.

Vorlesungen über die Philosophie der Religion. Philosophische Bibliothek. Vols. 59, 60, 61, 63 bound in two volumes. Edited by Georg Lasson. Hamburg: Felix Meiner, 1925, reprinted 1974. Vols. 59, 60, 61 and 63 abbreviated respectively BR, NR, GI, AR.

Werke. Theorie Werkausgabe. Edited by Eva Moldenhauer and Karl Markus Michel. Vols. 16 and 17: *Vorlesungen über die Philosophie der Religion*. Frankfurt am Main: Suhrkamp, 1969. Abbreviated WS 16, 17.

Religionsphilosophie. Edited by Karl-Heinz Ilting. Vol. 1: *Die Vorlesung von 1821*. Naples: Bibliopolis, 1978. Abbreviated ILT.

Vorlesungen. Ausgewählte Nachschriften und Manuskripte. Vol. 3: *Vorlesungen über die Philosophie der Religion. Teil 1: Einleitung. Der Begriff der Religion*. Vol. 4: *Vorlesungen über die Philosophie der Religion. Teil 2: Die bestimmte Religion*. a: *Text*. b: *Anhang*. Vol. 5: *Vorlesungen über die Philosophie der Religion. Teil 3: Die vollendete Religion*. Edited by Walter Jaeschke. Hamburg: Felix Meiner, 1983, 1985, 1984. Abbreviated V 3, 4, 5.

Gesammelte Werke. Vol. 17: *Vorlesungsmanuskripte I (1816–1831)*. Edited by Walter Jaeschke. Hamburg: Felix Meiner, 1987.

The Christian Religion. Lectures on the Philosophy of Religion. Part Three. The Revelatory, Consummate, Absolute Religion. Translation of AR by Peter C. Hodgson. Ann Arbor, MI: Scholars, 1979. Abbreviated CR.

The Christian Religion. Lectures on the Philosophy of Religion, Part III: The Revelatory, Consummate, Absolute Religion. Translated and edited by Peter C. Hodgson. Missoula, MT: Scholars Press, 1979.

Lectures on the Philosophy of Religion. Vol. 1: *Introduction and The Concept of Religion*. Vol. 2: *Determinate Religion*. Vol. 3: *The Consummate Religion*.

Edited by Peter C. Hodgson. Translated by R. F. Brown, P. C. Hodgson, and J. M. Stewart with the assistance of J. P. Fitzer (L 1) and H. S. Harris. Berkeley: University of California Press, 1984, 1987, 1985; paperback editions: Oxford: Oxford University Press, 2007.

Lectures on the Philosophy of Religion. One-volume edition. *The Lectures of 1827.* Edited by Peter C. Hodgson. Translation of materials from V 3, 4, and 5 by R. F. Brown, P. C. Hodgson, and J. M. Stewart with the assistance of H. S. Harris. Berkeley: University of California Press, 1988; paperback edition: Oxford: Oxford University Press, 2006.

LECTURES ON THE PROOFS OF THE EXISTENCE OF GOD

Vorlesungen über die Beweise vom Dasein Gottes. Philosophische Bibliothek. Vol. 64. Edited by Georg Lasson. Hamburg: Felix Meiner, 1973. Abbreviated BDG.

Lectures on the Philosophy of Religion. Vol. 3. Translation of BDG, according to the second Friends edition, by E. B. Speirs and J. Burdon Sanderson. New York: Humanities, 1962. Abbreviated LPR 3.

Lectures on the Proofs of the Existence of God. Edited and translated by Peter C. Hodgson. New York: Oxford University Press, 2007.

LETTERS

Briefe von und an Hegel. Edited by Johannes Hoffmeister. Vol. 1: *1785–1812.* Philosophische Bibliothek. Vol. 235. Hamburg: Felix Meiner, 1952.

Briefe von und an Hegel. Four volumes. Edited by Johannes Hoffmeister and J. Nicolin. Third edition. Hamburg: Felix Meiner, 1969–1981.

Hegel: The Letters. Translated by Clark Butler and Christiane Seiler with commentary by Clark Butler. Bloomington: Indiana University Press, 1984.

2. Secondary Literature

Adorno, Theodor W. *Drei Studien zu Hegel.* Frankfurt am Main: Suhrkamp, 1971.

Ahlers, Rolf. Review of *Die Idee als Ideal: Trias und Tripliziät bei Hegel,* by Katharina Comoth. In *The Owl of Minerva* 19 (1988) 194–200.

Albert, Hans. *Glauben und Denken: Hegelkritik als Anfange an das Selbstverständnis heutigen Theologie.* Regensburg; Verlag Friedrich Pustet, 1983.

Apostel, Pavel. "Wie ist die Entwicklung einer 'Logica Humana' im Rahmen der Darlegung der 'Logica Divina' in Hegels *Wissenschaft der Logik* möglich?" In *Die Wissenschaft der Logik und die Logik der Reflexion. Hegel-Tage*

Chantily 1971. Hegel-Studien. Beiheft 18 pp. 37–39. Edited by Dieter Henrich. Bonn: Bouvier, 1978.

Atherton, J. Patrick. "The Neoplatonic 'One' and the Trinitarian 'APXH.'" In *The Significance of Neoplatonism.* Pp. 173–185. Edited by R. Baine Harris. Norfolk, VA: International Society for Neoplatonic Studies, Old Dominion University, 1976.

Baur, Ferdinand Christian. *Die christliche Lehre von der Dreieinigkeit und Menschwerdung Gottes in ihrer geschichtlichen Entwicklung.* Vol. 3: *Die neuere Geschichte des Dogma, von der Reformation bis in die neueste Zeit.* Tübingen: Osiander, 1843.

Benson, Peter. "Hegel and the Trinity." *Philosophy Now. A Magazine of Ideas* 42 (2003) 23–25. Available online at http://www.philosophynow.org/issue42/Hegel_and_the_Trinity. Accessed on August 21, 2011.

Berger, Peter, Brigitte Berger and Hansfried Kellner. *The Homeless Mind. Modernization and Consciousness.* New York. Random, 1973.

Bernasconi, Robert. "'The Ruling Categories of the World': The Trinity in Hegel's Philosophy of History and the Rise and Fall of Peoples." In *A Companion to Hegel.* Edited by Stephen Houlgate and Michael Baur. Pp. 313–331. Malden, MA: Wiley-Blackwell, 2011.

Bonsiepen, Wolfgang. *Der Begriff der Negativität in den Jenaer Schriften Hegels, Hegel-Studien,* Beiheft 16. Bonn: Bouvier, 1977.

———. "Phänomenologie des Geistes." In *Hegel. Einführung in seine Philosophie.* Pp. 59–74. Edited by Otto Pöggeler. Munich: Alber, 1977.

Bonsiepen, Wolfgang, and Reinhard Heede. "Editorischer Bericht." In G. W. F. Hegel. *Gesammelte Werke.* Vol. 9: *Phänomenologie des Geistes.* Pp. 453–479. Edited by Wolfgang Bonsiepen and Reinhard Heede. Hamburg: Felix Meiner, 1980.

Bouillard, Henri. "Le concept de révélation de Vatican I à Vatican II." In J. Auginet and others. *Révélation de Dieu et langage des hommes.* Pp. 35–49, 131. Paris: Cerf, 1972.

Brewer, James. "The Conception of the Hegelian Dialectic." M.A. Thesis, University of Ottawa, 1997.

Brito, Emilio. *La christologie de Hegel. Verbum crucis.* Paris: Beauchesne, 1983.

———. *Hegel et la tâche actuelle de la christologie.* Paris: Lethielleux, 1979.

———. "The Holy Spirit according to Hegel." *Ephemerides Theologicae Lovaniensis. Louvain Journal of Theology and Canon Law* 85 (2009) 423–438.

———. Review of *Hegel's Trinitarian Claim,* by Dale M. Schlitt. In *Revue théologique de Louvain* 17 (1986) 368–369.

Brown, Robert F. "Hegel's Lectures on the *Philosophy of Religion*: A Progress Report on the New Edition." *The Owl of Minerva* 14/3 (1983) 1–6.

Bruaire, Claude. *Logique et religion chrétienne dans la philosophie de Hegel.* Paris: du Seuil, 1964.

Bubner, Rüdiger. "Strukturprobleme dialektischer Logik." In *Der Idealismus und seine Gegenwart. Festschrift für Werner Marx zum 65. Geburtstag.* Pp. 36–52. Edited by Ute Guzzoni, Bernhard Rang and Ludwig Siep. Hamburg: Felix Meiner, 1976.

Bubner, Rüdiger. *Zur Sache der Dialektik.* Stuttgart: Reclam, 1980.

Burbidge, John W. *Hegel on Logic and Religion. The Reasonableness of Christianity.* Albany, NY: State University of New York Press, 1992.

———. *On Hegel's Logic. Fragments of a Commentary.* New York: Humanities, 1981.

———. "The Syllogisms of Revealed Religion or the Reasonableness of Christianity." Workshop Lecture given at the Bilingual Hegel Symposium, "The Meaning of Absolute Spirit," Ottawa University, Nov. 7, 1981. Published as "The Syllogisms of Revealed Religion, or the Reasonableness of Christianity." *The Owl of Minerva* 18 (1986) 29–42.

Butler, Clark. "Commentary." In G. W. F. Hegel. *Hegel: The Letters.* Translated by Clark Butler and Christiane Seiler with commentary by Clark Butler. Bloomington: Indiana University Press, 1984.

Calton, Patricia Marie. *Hegel's Metaphysics of God. The Ontological Proof as the Development of a Trinitarian Divine Ontology.* Aldershot, England: Ashgate, 2001.

Cassirer, Ernst. *Das Erkenntnisproblem in der Philosophie und Wissenschaft der neueren Zeit.* Second edition. Vol. 3: *Die nachkantischen Systeme.* Berlin: Cassirer, 1920.

Chapelle, Albert. *Hegel et la religion.* Three volumes. Paris: Éditions Universitaires, 1964–1971. Vol. 1: *La problématique,* 1964. Vol. 2/1: *La dialectique. A. Dieu et la création,* 1967. Vol. 2/2 (3): *La dialectique. B. La théologie et l'église,* 1971. Annexes. *Les textes théologiques de Hegel,* 1967.

Cisco, Giuliano. "Recenti studi italiani sulla filosofia della religione de Hegel." *Verifiche* 26 (1997) 209–235.

Clark, Malcolm. *Logic and System. A Study of the Transition from "Vorstellung" to Thought in the Philosophy of Hegel.* The Hague: Nijhoff, 1971.

Coda, Piero. *Il negative e la Trinità: imposti su Hegel.* Rome: Città nuova, 1987.

Comoth, Katharina. "Hegels 'Logik' und die spekulative Mystik." In *Hegel-Studien.* Vol. 19 pp. 65–93. Bonn: Bouvier, 1984.

———. *Die Idee als Ideal. Trias und Triplizität bei Hegel.* Heidelberg: Carl Winter Universitätsverlag, 1986.

Corduan, Winfried. "Elements of the Philosophy of G. W. F. Hegel in the Transcendental Method of Karl Rahner." Ph.D. dissertation, Rice University, 1977.

Crites, Stephen. Review of *The Christian Religion,* by G. W. F. Hegel. Edited and translated by Peter C. Hodgson. *The Owl of Minerva* 11 (June 1980) 7–9.

Crouter, Richard. "Hegel and Schleiermacher at Berlin: A Many-sided Debate." *Journal of the American Academy of Religion* 48 (1980) 19–43.
Dahlstrom, Daniel Oscar. "Essence and Subjectivity in Hegel's *Science of Logic*." Ph.D. dissertation, St. Louis University, 1978.
Dalrymple, Edwin Stuart. "On Hegel's Doctrine of the Notion as Universality, Particularity and Individuality." Ph.D. dissertation, Yale University, 1974.
Declève, Henri. "Schöpfung, Trinität und Modernität bei Hegel." *Zeitschrift für katholische Theologie* 107 (1985) 187–198.
Desmond, William. *Beyond Hegel and Dialectic. Speculation, Cult, and Comedy.* Albany, NY: State University of New York Press, 1992.
———. *Hegel's God. A Counterfeit Double?* Aldershot, Hants: Ashgate, 2003.
Dewey, John. *Experience and Nature. The Later Works, 1925–1953.* Vol. 1: *1925*. Edited by Jo Ann Boydston with associate textual editors, Patricia Baysinger and Barbara Levine. Carbondale, IL: Southern Illinois University Press, 1981. First edition originally published 1925, second edition 1929.
Dierken, Jörg. "Gott als Geist. Theo-logik und religionsvollzug in Hegels Religions-Philosophie." In *Wahrheit und Versöhnung*. Edited by Dietrich Korsch and Hartmut Ruddies. Gütersloh: G. Mohn, 1989.
Dooren, Willem van. "Zwei Methoden, die *Phänomenologie des Geistes* zu interpretieren." In *Hegel-Studien*. Vol. 7 pp. 298–302. Bonn: Bouvier, 1972.
Düsing, Klaus. "Hegels Begriff der Subjektivität in der *Logik* und in der Philosophie des subjektiven Geistes." In *Hegels philosophische Psychologie. Hegel-Tage Santa Margherita. Hegel-Studien.* Beiheft 19 pp. 201–214. Edited by Dieter Henrich. Bonn: Bouvier, 1979.
———. *Das Problem der Subjektivität in Hegels Logik. Hegel-Studien.* Beiheft 15. Bonn: Bouvier, 1976.
———. Review of *Die formale Logik in Hegels "Wissenschaft der Logik." Untersuchungen zur Schlußlehre*, by Wolfgang Krohn. In Hegel-Studien. Vol. 10 pp. 326–328. Bonn: Bouvier, 1975.
Eecke, W. ver. "Zur Negativität bei Hegel." In *Hegel-Studien*. Vol. 4 pp. 215–218. Bonn: Bouvier, 1967.
Eley, Lothar. "Zum Problem des Anfangs in Hegels *Logik* und *Phänomenologie*." In *Hegel-Studien*. Vol. 6 pp. 267–283. Bonn: Bouvier, 1971.
Fackenheim, Emil L. *The Religious Dimension in Hegel's Thought*. Bloomington: Indiana University Press, 1967.
Findlay, John N. *Hegel. A Re-Examination*. London: George Allen and Unwin, 1958.
———. "Hegel Colloquium. Hegel as Theologian." Lecture at Boston University, April 9, 1980.
———. "Hegel's Concept of Subjectivity." In *Hegels philosophische Psychologie. Hegel-Tage Santa Margherita. Hegel-Studien.* Beiheft 19 pp. 13–26. Edited by Dieter Henrich. Bonn: Bouvier, 1979.

Fink-Eitel, Hinrich. "Hegels phänomenologische Erkenntnistheorie als Begründung dialektischer Logik." *Philosophisches Jahrbuch* 85, second half-volume (1978) 242–258.

Flach, Werner. *Negation und Andersheit. Ein Beitrag zur Problematik der Letztimplikation.* Munich: Reinhardt, 1959.

Flasch, Kurt. Review of *Die Trinitätslehre G. W. F. Hegels*, by Jörg Splett. In *Philosophisches Jahrbuch* 73 (1965–1966) 422–425.

Fornari, Fabrizio. "Le prove di Dio in Hegel." *Rivista di Teoretica* 1 (1985) 9–42, 107–144.

Fulda, Hans Friedrich. *Das Problem einer Einleitung in Hegels "Wissenschaft der Logik."* Frankfurt am Main: Klostermann, 1965.

———. "Über den spekulativen Anfang." In *Subjektivität und Metaphysik. Festschrift für Wolfgang Cramer.* Pp. 109–127. Edited by Dieter Henrich and Hans Wagner. Frankfurt am Main: Klostermann, 1966.

Fulda, Hans Friedrich and Henrich, Dieter, eds. *Materialien zu Hegels "Phänomenologie des Geistes."* Frankfurt am Main: Suhrkamp, 1973.

Gadamer, Hans-Georg. *Hegels Dialektik. Fünf hermeneutische Studien.* Tübingen: Mohr, 1971. English translation: *Hegel's Dialectic.* Translation by P. Christopher Smith. New Haven: Yale University Press, 1976.

———. *Gesammelte Werke.* Vol. 1: *Hermeneutik I. Wahrheit und Methode.* Tübingen: J. C. B. Mohr [Paul Siebeck], 1986. English translation: *Truth and Method.* Second revised edition. Translation revised by Joel Weinsheimer and Donald G. Marshall. New York: Crossroad, 1990.

———. *Wahrheit und Methode.* Second edition. Tübingen: J. C. B. Mohr, 1965.

Garceau, Benoît. "Hegel et la christologie." *Église et Théologie* 4 (1973) 349–358.

Gauvin, Joseph. *Wortindex zu Hegels "Phänomenologie des Geistes." Hegel-Studien.* Beiheft 14. Bonn: Bouvier, 1977.

Glockner, Hermann. "Vortwort zur Jubiläumsausgabe." In G. W. F. Hegel. *Sämtliche Werke. Jubiläumsausgabe in zwanzig Bänden.* Vol. 1: *Aufsätze aus dem kritischen Journal der Philosophie und andere Schriften aus der Jenenser Zeit.* Pp. v–xiv. Edited by Hermann Glockner. Stuttgart: Frommann, 1927.

Günther, Gotthard. *Idee und Grundriß einer nicht-aristotelischen Logik.* Vol. 1. Hamburg: Felix Meiner, 1959.

Guibal, Francis. *Dieu selon Hegel. Essai sur la problématique de la "Phénoménologie de l'Esprit."* Paris: Aubier-Montaigne, 1975.

Guzzoni, Ute. *Werden zu sich. Eine Untersuchung zu Hegels "Wissenschaft der Logik."* Munich: Alber, 1963.

Guzzoni, Ute, Rang, Bernhard and Siep, Ludwig, eds. *Der Idealismus und seine Gegenwart. Festschrift für Werner Marx zum 65. Geburtstag.* Hamburg: Felix Meiner, 1976.

Haag, Karl Heinz. *Philosophischer Idealismus. Untersuchungen zur Hegelschen Dialektik mit Beispielen aus der "Wissenschaft der Logik."* Frankfurt am Main: Europäische Verlagsanstalt, 1967.

———. "Die Seinsdialektik bei Hegel und in der scholastischen Philosophie." Ph.D. dissertation, Philosophical Faculty of the Johann Wolfgang Goethe-Universität, Frankfurt am Main, 1951.

Harris, Errol E. Review of *Lectures on the Philosophy of Religion*. Vol. 3: *The Consummate Religion*, by G. W. F. Hegel. Edited by Peter C. Hodgson. In *The Owl of Minerva* 20 (1998) 101–105.

Harris, H. S. *Hegel's Development. Toward the Sunlight, 1770–1801*. Oxford: Clarendon, 1972.

———. *Hegel's Development. Night Dreams, Jena 1801–1806*. Oxford: Clarendon, 1983.

Hartmann, Klaus. "Das Realitätsproblem." In *Lebendiger Realismus. Festschrift für Johannes Thyssen*. Pp. 115–130. Edited by Klaus Hartmann. Bonn: Bouvier, 1962.

Heckman, John. "Introduction." In Jean Hyppolite. *Genesis and Structure of Hegel's "Phenomenology of Spirit."* Pp. xv–xli. Translated by Samuel Cherniak and John Heckman. Evanston: Northwestern University Press, 1974.

Hedwig, Klaus. "Trinität und Triplizität. Eine Untersuchung zur Methode der Augustinischen und Hegelschen Metaphysik." Ph.D. dissertation, Philosophical Faculty of the Albert-Ludwigs-Universität zu Freiburg im Breisgau, 1968.

Heede, Reinhard. "Die göttliche Idee und ihre Erscheinung in der Religion. Untersuchungen zum Verhältnis von Logik und Religionsphilosophie bei Hegel." Ph.D. dissertation, Philosophical Faculty of the Westfälischen Wilhelms-Universität zu Münster/Westfalen, 1972.

———. "Hegel-Bilanz: Hegels Religionsphilosophie als Aufgabe und Problem der Forschung." In *Hegel-Bilanz. Zur Aktualität und Inaktualität der Philosophie Hegels*. Pp. 41–89. Edited by Reinhard Heede and Joachim Ritter. Frankfurt am Main: Klostermann, 1973.

Heede, Reinhard and Ritter, Joachim, eds. *Hegel-Bilanz. Zur Aktualität und Inaktualität der Philosophie Hegels*. Frankfurt am Main: Klostermann, 1973.

Heidegger, Martin. "Hegels Begriff der Erfahrung." In *Holzwege*. Pp. 105–192. Frankfurt am Main: Klostermann, 1957.

Heimann, Betty. *System und Methode in Hegels Philosophie*. Leipzig: Felix Meiner, 1927.

Heinrichs, Johannes. *Die Logik der "Phänomenologie des Geistes."* Bonn: Bouvier, 1974.

Heintel, Erich. *Hegel und die analogia entis*. Bonn: Bouvier, 1958.

Henningsen, Jürgen. "'Enzyklopädie.' Zur Sprach- und Deutungsgeschichte eines pädagogischen Begriffs." *Archiv für Begriffsgeschichte. Bausteine zu einem historischen Wörterbuch der Philosophie* 10 (1966) 271–362.

Henrich, Dieter. "Anfang und Methode der Logik." In *Heidelberger Hegel-Tage 1962. Hegel-Studien*. Beiheft 1 pp. 19–35. Edited by Hans-Georg Gadamer. Bonn: Bouvier, 1964.

———. *Hegel im Kontext*. Frankfurt am Main: Suhrkamp. 1967.

———. "Hegels Logik der Reflexion. Neue Fassung." In *Die Wissenschaft der Logik und die Logik der Reflexion. Hegel-Tage Chantilly 1971. Hegel-Studien.* Beiheft 18 pp. 203–324. Edited by Dieter Henrich. Bonn: Bouvier, 1978.

Hessen, Johannes. *Hegels Trinitätslehre. Zugleich eine Einführung in Hegels System.* Freiburg in Breisgau: Herder, 1922.

Hill, William, O.P. "Presidential Address. Christian Panentheism: Orthopraxis and God's Action in History." *Proceedings of the Thirty-Fifth Annual Convention. The Catholic Theological Society of America. San Francisco, California* 35 (June 11–14, 1980) 113–123.

Hodgson, Peter C. "Editorial Introduction." In G. W. F. Hegel. *Lectures on the Philosophy of Religion.* Vol. 1: *Introduction and The Concept of Religion.* Pp. 1–81. Edited by Peter C. Hodgson. Berkeley: University of California Press, 1984.

———. "Editorial Introduction." In G. W. F. Hegel. *Lectures on the Philosophy of Religion.* Vol. 2: *Determinate Religion.* Pp. 1–90. Edited by Peter C. Hodgson. Berkeley: University of California Press, 1987.

———. "Editorial Introduction." In G. W. F. Hegel. *Lectures on the Philosophy of Religion.* Vol. 3: *The Consummate Religion.* Pp. 1–57. Edited by Peter C. Hodgson. Berkeley: University of California Press, 1985.

———. "Editorial Introduction." In G. W. F. Hegel. *Lectures on the Philosophy of Hegel.* One-volume edition. *The Lectures of 1827.* Pp. 1–71. Edited by Peter C. Hodgson. Berkeley: University of California Press, 1988.

———. "Editor's Introduction," "Comparative Analysis of the Structure of the Text," "Glossary," Key to Signs," "Appendix: Commentary on the Text." In G. W. F. Hegel. *The Christian Religion. Lectures on the Philosophy of Religion. Part III. The Revelatory, Consummate, Absolute Religion.* Pp. vii–xxxvii, 313–350. Translated and edited by Peter C. Hodgson. Ann Arbor, MI: Scholars, 1979.

———. *Hegel and Christian Theology. A Reading of the Lectures on the Philosophy of Religion.* Oxford: Oxford University Press, 2005, paperback 2007.

———. "Hegel's Approach to Religion: The Dialectic of Speculation and Phenomenology." *The Journal of Religion* 64 (1984) 158–172.

———. "Hegel's Christology: Shifting Nuances in the Berlin Lectures." *Journal of the American Academy of Religion* 53 (1985) 23–40.

———. "Logic, History, and Alternative Paradigms in Hegel's Interpretation of the Religions." *The Journal of Religion* 68 (1988) 1–20.
———. "Plans for Completing the English Study Edition of Hegel's Lectures on the Philosophy of Religion." *The Owl of Minerva* 11, 4 (1980) 6–7.
———. "A Reply to Professor Harris." *The Owl of Minerva* 20 (1989) 252–256.
———. Review of *Religionsphilosophie*. Vol. 1: *Die Vorlesung von 1821*, by G. W. F. Hegel. Edited by Karl-Heinz Ilting. In *The Owl of Minerva* 11, 2 (1979) 4–7.
Hoffmeister, Johannes. "Zur Feststellung des Textes." In G. W. F. Hegel. *Phänomenologie des Geistes*. Philosophische Bibliothek. Vol. 114 pp. 575–581. Edited by Johannes Hoffmeister. Hamburg: Felix Meiner, 1952.
Homann, Karl. "Zum Begriff 'Subjektivität' bis 1802." *Archiv für Begriffsgeschichte* 11 (1967) 184–205.
Horstmann, Rolf-Peter, ed. *Seminar: Dialektik in der Philosophie Hegels*. Frankfurt am Main: Suhrkamp, 1978.
Houlgate, Stephen. *The Opening of Hegel's Logic. From Being to Infinity*. West Lafayette, IN: Purdue University Press, 2006.
Huber, Herbert. *Idealismus und Trinität, Pantheon und Götterdämmerung. Grundlagen und Grundzüge der Lehre von Gott nach dem Manuscript Hegels zur Religionsphilosophie*. Weinheim: Acta humaniora, 1984.
———. "Zum Vorlesungsmanuskript von 1821. Bemerkungen zur Edition von K.-H. Ilting." In *Die Flucht in den Begriff*. Pp. 159–162. Edited by Friedrich Wilhelm Graf and Falk Wagner. Stuttgart: Klett-Cotta, 1982.
Hyppolite, Jean. *Genèse et structure de la "Phénoménologie de l'Esprit" de Hegel*. Paris: Montaigne, 1946. English translation: *Genesis and Structure of the Hegel's "Phenomenology of Spirit."* Translated by Samuel Chemiak and John Heckman. Evanston, IL: Northwestern University Press, 1974.
Iljin, Iwan. *Die Philosophie Hegels als kontemplative Gotteslehre*. Bern: Francke, 1946.
Ilting, Karl-Heinz. "Zur Edition." In G. W. F. Hegel. *Religionsphilosophie*. Vol. 1: *Die Vorlesung von 1821*. Pp. 737–765. Edited by Karl-Heinz Ilting. Naples: Bibliopolis, 1978.
Innis, Robert E. "Reading Hegel Rightly. A Review Discussion of Some Recent Hegeliana." *The New Scholasticism* 52 (1978) 110–129.
Inwood, Michael. *A Hegel Dictionary*. Oxford: Blackwells, 1992.
Jaeschke, Walter. "Absolute Idee—absolute Subjektivität. Zum Problem der Persönlichkeit Gottes in der Logik und in der Religionsphilosophie." *Zeitschrift für philosophische Forschung* 35 (1981) 385–416.
———. "Der Aufbau und die bisherigen Editionen von Hegels Vorlesungen über Philosophie der Religion." M.A. dissertation, Die freie Universität Berlin, 1970–1971.

———. "Äußerliche Reflexion und immanente Reflexion. Eine Skizze der systematischen Geschichte des Reflexionsbegriffs in Hegels Logikentwürfen." In *Hegel-Studien*. Vol. 13 pp. 85–117. Bonn: Bouvier, 1978.

———. "Christianity and Secularity in Hegel's Concept of the State." *The Journal of Religion* 61 (1981) 127–145.

———. "Die Flucht vor dem Begriff: Ein Jahrzehnt Literatur zur Religionsphilosophie (1971–1981)." In *Hegel-Studien*. Vol. 18 pp. 295–354. Bonn: Bouvier, 1983.

———. "Die Geburt Gottes aus dem reinen Wissen. Zur Inversion der Relation von Gottesgedanke und Intersubjektivität." *Archivio di Filosofia* 69 (2001) 1–3, 149–155.

———. *Hegel-Handbuch. Leben—Werk—Schule*. Stuttgart: Metzler, 2003, 2010.

———. "Hegel's Last Year in Berlin." In *Hegel's Philosophy of Action*. Pp. 31–48. Edited by Lawrence S. Stepelevich and David Lamb. Atlantic Highlands, NJ: Humanities, 1983.

———. "The History of Religion and the Absolute Religion." In *Thought and Faith in the Philosophy of Hegel*. Pp. 9–27. Edited by John Walker. Dordrecht: Kluwer Academic, 1991.

———. "Zur Logik der Bestimmten Religion." In *Hegels Logik der Philosophie. Religion und Philosophie in der Theorie des absoluten Geistes*. Pp. 172–188. Stuttgart: Klett-Cotta, 1984.

———. "Philosophy of Religion: The Quest for a Critical Edition." *The Owl of Minerva* 11/3 (March 1980) 4–8, and 11/4 (June 1980) 1–6.

———. "Probleme der Edition der Nachschriften von Hegels Vorlesungen." *Allgemeine Zeitschrift für Philosophie* 3 (1980) 51–63.

———. *Die Religionsphilosophie Hegels*. Darmstadt: Wissenschaftliche Buchgesellschaft, 1983.

———. Review of *Darstellung, Methode und Struktur. Untersuchungen zur Einheit der systematischen Philosophie G. W. F. Hegels*, by L. Bruno Puntel. In *Hegel-Studien*. Vol. 12 pp. 210–214. Bonn: Bouvier, 1977.

———. Review of *Der Gottesbegriff der spekulativen Theologie*, by Klaus Krüger, and *Gottesbeweise im deutschen Idealismus. Die modal-theoretische begründung des Absoluten dargestellt an Kant, Hegel und Weiße*, by Harold Knudsen. In *Hegel-Studien*. Vol. 10 pp. 373–382. Bonn: Bouvier, 1975.

———. "Speculative and Anthropological Criticism of Religion: A Theological Orientation to Hegel and Feuerbach." *Journal of the American Academy of Religion* 48 (1980) 345–364.

———. *Die Vernunft in der Religion*. Stuttgart-Bad Cannstatt: frommann-holzboog, 1986. English translation: *Reason in Religion. The Foundations of Hegel's Philosophy of Religion*. Berkeley: University of California Press, 1990.

———. "Vorwort des Herausgebers." In G. W. F. Hegel. *Vorlesungen. Ausgewählte Nachschriften und Manuskripte*. Vol. 3: *Vorlesungen über die Philosophie der Religion*. Teil 1: Einleitung. Der Begriff der Religion. Pp. ix–lxxxvi. Edited by Walter Jaeschke. Hamburg: Felix Meiner, 1983.

Jaeschke, Walter and Hogemann, Friedrich. "Editorischer Bericht." In G. W. F. Hegel. *Gesammelte Werke*. Vol. 12: *Wissenschaft der Logik. Zweiter Band. Die subjektive Logik* (1816). Pp. 318–336. Edited by Walter Jaeschke and Friedrich Hogemann. Hamburg: Felix Meiner, 1981.

———. "Die Wissenschaft der Logik." In *Hegel. Einführung in seine Philosophie*. Pp. 75–90. Edited by Otto Pöggeler. Freiburg: Alber, 1977.

Jüngel, Ebehard. *Gott als Geheimnis der Welt*. Second edition. Tübingen: Mohr, 1977.

Kainz, Howard P. *Hegel's "Phenomenology."* Part I: *Analysis and Commentary*. University, Alabama: University of Alabama Press, 1976.

Kaufmann, Walter. *Hegel: A Reinterpretation*. New York: Doubleday, 1965.

———. *Hegel: Text and Commentary*. Notre Dame, Indiana: Notre Dame, 1977.

Kern, Walter. "Dialektik und Trinität in der Religionsphilosophie Hegels. Ein Beitrag zur Discussion mit L. Oeing-Hanhoff." *Zeitschrift für katholische Theologie* 102 (1980) 129–155.

———. "Fragen an Hegels Religionsphilosophie anhand neuer Publikationen." *Zeitschrift für katholische Theologie* 107 (1985) 271–286.

———. "(Neue) Hegel-Bücher. Ein Literaturbericht für die Jahre 1958–1960." *Scholastik* 37 (1962) 85–114, 550–578; vol. 38 (1963) 62–90.

———. "Hegel-Bücher 1961–1966. Ein Auswahlbericht." *Theologie und Philosophie* (formerly *Scholastik*): Parts 1 and 2. Vol. 42 (1967) 79–88 and 402–418; Part 3. Vol. 44 (1969) 245–267; Part 4. Vol. 46 (1971) 71–87; Part 5. Vol. 47 (1972) 245–276; Part 6. Vol. 48 (1973) 389–409; Part 7. Vol. 49 (1974) 72–92; Part 8. Vol. 50 (1975) 565–581; Part 9. Vol. 51 (1976) 93–114; Part 10. Vol. 51 (1976) 559–570 (includes index for Parts 1–10).

———. Review of *Hegel's Trinitarian Claim*, by Dale M. Schlitt. In *Zeitschrift für katholische Theologie* 107 (1985) 277–278.

Kimmerle, Heinz. "Hegels 'Wissenschaft der Logik' als Grundlegung seines Systems der Philosophie. Über das Verhältnis von 'Logik' und 'Realphilosophie.'" In *Die Logik des Wissens und das Problem der Erziehung*. Pp. 52–60. Edited by Wilhelm Raimund Beyer. Hamburg: Felix Meiner, 1982.

———. "Religion und Philosophie als Abschluß des Systems." In *Hegel. Einführung in seine Philosophie*. Pp. 150–171. Edited by Otto Pöggeler. Munich, Alber, 1977.

Koch, Traugott. *Differenz und Versöhnung. Eine Interpretation der Theologie G. W. F. Hegels nach seiner "Wissenschaft der Logik."* Gütersloh: Mohn, 1967.

———. "Gott—der Grund der Freiheit. Überlegungen zum christlichen Gottesgedanken." *Pastoraltheologie* 57 (1968) 45–56.

Kojève, Alexandre. *Introduction à la lecture de Hegel. Leçons sur la "Phénoménologie de l'Esprit."* Paris: Aubier, 1946. English translation: *Introduction to the Reading of Hegel*. Translated by James H. Nichols. New York: Basic Books, 1969.

Koslowski, Peter. "'Hegel—der Philosoph der Trinität'? Zur Kontroverse um seine Trinitätslehre." *Theologische Quartalschrift* 162 (1982) 105–131.

Krohn, Wolfgang. *Die formale Logik in Hegels "Wissenschaft der Logik." Untersuchungen zur Schlußlehre*. Munich: Hanser, 1972.

Kroner, Richard. *Von Kant bis Hegel*. Two volumes. Tübingen: Mohr, 1921–1924; second edition, Tübingen: Mohr, 1961.

Krüger, Klaus. *Der Gottesbegriff der spekulativen Theologie*. Berlin: de Gruyter, 1972.

Küng, Hans. *Menschwerdung Gottes. Eine Einführung in Hegels theologisches Denken als Prolegomena zu einer künftigen Christologie*. Freiburg: Herder, 1970. English translation: *The Incarnation of God. An Introduction to Hegel's Theological Thought as a Prolegomena to a Future Christology*. Translated by J. R. Stephenson. New York: Crossroad, 1987.

Labarrière, Pierre-Jean. *Structures et mouvement dialectique dans la "Phénoménologie de l'Esprit" de Hegel*. Paris: Aubier-Montaigne, 1968.

———. Review of *Hegel's Trinitarian Claim*, by Dale M. Schlitt. In *Archives de Philosophie* 50 (1987) 318–319.

Labarrière, Pierre Jean and Jarezyk, Gwendoline, trans. *Science de la logique. Premier tom. Premier livre. L'être, édition de 1812*. Paris: Aubier-Montaigne, 1972.

Lämmermann, Godwin. "Redaktion und Redaktionsprinzipien der Vorlesungen über Religionsphilosophie in ihrer zweiten Ausgabe." In *Die Flucht in den Begriff*. Pp. 140–158. Edited by Friedrich Wilhelm Graf and Falk Wagner. Stuttgart: Klett-Cotta, 1982.

Lasson, Georg. "Zur Feststellung des Textes." In G. W. F. Hegel. *Wissenschaft der Logik*. Vol. 1 pp. 399–402. Edited by Georg Lasson. Hamburg: Felix Meiner, 1975.

Lauer, Quentin, S.J. *Essays in Hegelian Dialectic*. New York: Fordham University Press, 1977.

———. "Hegel on the Identity of Content in Religion and Philosophy." In *Essays in Hegelian Dialectic*. Pp. 153–168. New York: Fordham University Press, 1977.

———. *Hegel's Concept of God*. Albany, New York: State University of New York Press, 1982.

———. *A Reading of Hegel's "Phenomenology of Spirit."* New York: Fordham, 1976.

Léonard, André. *Commentaire littéral de la logique de Hegel*. Paris: Vrin, 1974.

---. *La foi chez Hegel.* Paris: Desclée, 1970.

---. "Pour une exégèse renouvelée de la *Phénoménologie de l'Esprit* de Hegel." *Revue philosophique de Louvain* 74 (1976) 572–593.

Luther, O. Kern and Jeff L. Hoover. "Hegel's Phenomenology of Religion." *The Journal of Religion* 61 (1981) 229–241.

McCarthy, Vincent A. *Quest for a Philosophical Jesus. Christianity and Philosophy in Rousseau, Kant, Hegel, and Schelling.* Macon, GA: Mercer University Press, 1986.

McTaggart, John Ellis. *A Commentary on Hegel's Logic.* Cambridge, England: University Press, 1910.

---. *Studies in the Hegelian Dialectic.* Cambridge, England: University Press, 1896.

Maker, William. Review of *Die Logik der "Phänomenologie des Geistes,"* by Johannes Heinrichs. In *The Owl of Minerva* 9 (June 1978) 2–5.

Marheineke, Philipp. *Die Grundlehren der christlichen Dogmatik.* Berlin: F. Dümmler, 1819.

---. *Die Grundlehren der christlichen Dogmatik als Wissenschaft.* Berlin: Duncker und Hümblot, 1827.

Marsh, James L. Review of *A Reading of Hegel's "Phenomenology of Spirit,"* by Quentin Lauer. In *The Owl of Minerva* 12 (September 1980) 1–3.

Marx, Werner. "Dialectic and the Role of the Phenomenologist." *The Owl of Minerva* 11 (December 1979) 1–4.

---. *Hegels "Phenomenology of Spirit." Its Points and Purpose—a Commentary on the Preface and Introduction.* New York: Harper, 1975.

Melica, Claudia. "*Il concetto di Dio nella prima parte delle lezioni sulla filosofia della religione di Hegel del 1824 et del 1827. Sviluppi e cambiamenti.*" Research doctorate in Philosophy, La Sapienza University, Rome, 1994.

Merklinger, Philip M. *Philosophy, Theology and Hegel's Berlin Philosophy of Religion 1821–1827.* Albany, NY: State University of New York Press, 1993.

Meulen, Jan van der. *Hegel. Die gebrochene Mitte.* Hamburg: Felix Meiner, 1958.

Michelet, Carl Ludwig. "Vorwort [des Herausgebers zur ersten Ausgabe]." In G. W. F. Hegel. *Sämtliche Werke. Jubiläumsausgabe in zwanzig Bänden.* Vol. 17: *Vorlesungen über die Geschichte der Philosophie.* Vol. 1 pp. 1–14. Edited by Hermann Glockner. Stuttgart: Frommann, 1928.

---. "Vorwort des Herausgebers zur zweiten Ausgabe." In G. W. F. Hegel. *Werke. Vollständige Ausgabe durch einen Verein von Freunden des Verewigten.* Second Edition. Vol. 13: *Vorlesungen über die Geschichte der Philosophie.* Edited by Carl Ludwig Michelet. Berlin: Duncker und Humblot, 1840.

Miller, A. W. "Analysis of the Text." In G. W. F. Hegel. *Hegel's Phenomenology of Spirit.* Pp. 495–591. Trans. by A. V. Miller. New York: Oxford, 1977.

Min, Anselm K. "Hegel's Absolute: Transcendent or Immanent?" *The Journal of Religion* 56 (1976) 61–87.

———. "The Trinity and the Incarnation: Hegel and Classical Approaches." *The Journal of Religion* 66 (1986) 173–193.
Moltmann, Jürgen. *Trinität und Reich Gottes. Zur Gotteslehre.* Munich: Kaiser, 1980. English translation: *The Trinity and the Kingdom.* New York: Harper and Row, 1981.
Mueller, Gustav E. *Hegel: The Man, His Vision and Work.* New York: Pageant, 1968.
Navickas, Joseph L. *Consciousness and Reality: Hegel's Philosophy of Subjectivity.* The Hague: Nijhoff, 1976.
Nekt, Oskar. "Zum Problem der Aktualität Hegels." In *Aktualität und Folgen der Philosophie Hegels.* Pp. 7–20. Edited by Oskar Nekt. Frankfurt am Main: Suhrkamp, 1970.
Nelson, Benjamin. *On the Roads to Modernity: Conscience, Science and Civilizations. Selected Writings.* Totowe, New Jersey: Rowman and Littlefield, 1980.
———. *Der Ursprung der Moderne. Vergleichende Studien zum Zivilisationsprozeß.* Frankfurt am Main: Suhrkamp, 1978.
Nicolin, Friedhelm. "Pädagogik-Propädeutik-Enzyklopädie." In *Hegel. Einführung in seine Philosophie.* Pp. 91–105. Edited by Otto Pöggeler. Munich: Alber, 1977.
Niel, Henri. *De la médiation dans la philosophie de Hegel.* Paris: Aubier-Montaigne, 1945.
O'Donnell, John. Review of *Hegel's Trinitarian Claim*, by Dale M. Schlitt. In *Gregorianum* 66 (1985) 571.
Oeing-Hanhoff, Ludger. "Hegels Trinitätslehre. Zur Aufgabe ihrer Kritik und Reception." *Theologie und Philosophie* 52 (1977) 378–407.
Olson, Alan M. *Hegel and the Spirit. Philosophy as Pneumatology.* Princeton, NJ: Princeton University Press, 1992.
O'Regan, Cyril. *The Heterodox Hegel.* Albany, NY: State University of New York Press, 1994.
The Owl of Minerva 36 (2005) 1–200.
The Owl of Minerva 37 (2005–2006) 1–182.
Osborne, Kenan B. *New Being. A Study on the Relationship between Conditioned and Unconditioned Being according to Paul Tillich.* The Hague: Nijhoff, 1969.
Ottmann, Henning. *Individuum und Gemeinschaft bei Hegel.* Vol. 1: *Hegel im Spiegel der Interpretationen.* Berlin: de Gruyter, 1977.
Pannenberg, Wollhart. "Die Bedeutung des Christentums in der Philosophie Hegels." In *Stuttgarter Hegel-Tage 1970. Hegel-Studien.* Beiheft 11 pp. 175–202. Edited by Hans-Georg Gadamer. Bonn: Bouvier, 1974. English translation: "The Significance of Christianity in the Philosophy of Hegel." In Wollhart Pannenberg. *The Idea of God and Human Freedom.* Pp. 144–177. Philadelphia: Westminster, 1973.

———. *Das Glaubensbekenntnis ausgelegt und verantwortet von den Fragen der Gegenwart*. Hamburg: Siebenstern Taschenbuch, 1972.
———. *Grundzüge der Christologie*. Gütersloh: Mohn, 1976. English translation: *Jesus—God and Man*. Philadelphia: Westminster, 1968; second edition Philadelphia: Westminster, 1977.
———. *Revelation as History*. London: Macmillan, 1968.
———. Review of *Subjektivität und Verdinglichung*, by Günter Rohrmoser. In *Theologische Literaturzeitung* 88 (1963) cols. 294–296.
———. "Speaking about God in the Face of Atheist Criticism." In Wolfhart Pannenberg. *The Idea of God and Human Freedom*. Pp. 99–115. Philadelphia: Westminster, 1973.
———. "Die Subjektivität Gottes und die Trinitätslehre. Ein Beitrag zur Beziehung zwischen Karl Barth und die Philosophie Hegels." *Kerygma und Dogma* 23 (1977) 25–40.
———. *Thesen zur Theologie der Kirche*. Second edition. Munich: Claudius, 1974.
Percesepe, Gary, J. "Hegel's *Encyclopedia* and the Shift in the Self-understanding of Philosophy." *The St. Louis Journal of Philosophy* (1981) 37–52.
Pöggeler, Otto. "Zur Deutung der *Phänomenologie des Geistes.*" In *Hegel-Studien*. Vol. 1 pp. 255–294. Bonn: Bouvier, 1961.
———. *Hegels Idee einer "Phänomenologie des Geistes."* Munich: Alber, 1973.
———. "Hegels Phänomenologie des Selbstbewußtseins." In Otto Pöggeler. *Hegels Idee einer "Phänomenologie des Geistes."* Pp. 231–298. Munich: Alber, 1973.
———. "Die Komposition der *Phänomenologie des Geistes.*" In *Hegel-Tage Royaumont 1964. Hegel-Studien*. Beiheft 3. Edited by Hans-Georg Gadamer. Bonn: Bouvier, 1966.
Pöggeler, Otto, ed. *Hegel. Einführung in seine Philosophie*. Munich: Alber, 1977.
Powell, Samuel M. *The Trinity in German Thought*. Cambridge: Cambridge University Press, 2000.
Puntel, L. Bruno. *Darstellung, Methode und Struktur. Untersuchungen zur Einheit der systematischen Philosophie G. W. F. Hegels. Hegel-Studien.* Beiheft 10. Bonn: Bouvier, 1973.
———. "Die Trinitätslehre G. W. F. Hegels. Zur gleichnamigen Buch von Jörg Splett." *Zeitschrift für katholische Theologie* 89 (1967) 203–213.
Rahner, Karl. *The Trinity*. London: Burns and Oates, 1970.
———. "Trinity, Divine." In *Sacramentum Mundi. An Encyclopedia of Theology*. Vol. 6 pp. 295–303. Edited by Karl Rahner and others. New York: Herder, 1970.
Rendtorff, Trutz. *Kirche und Theologie. Die systematische Funktion des Kirchenbegriffs in der neueren Theologie*. Gütersloh: Mohn, 1966.
Richard, Lucien. *What Are They Saying about Christ and World Religions?* New York: Paulist, 1981.

Ricoeur, Paul. "Hegel Colloquium. The Status of 'Representation' in Hegel's Philosophy of Religion: A Twentieth Century Appraisal." Boston University, April 9, 1980, photocopied text. Published as: "The Status of *Vorstellung* in Hegel's Philosophy of Religion." In *Meaning, Truth, and God.* Pp. 70–88. Edited by Leroy S. Rouner. Notre Dame: University of Notre Dame Press, 1982.

Rocker, Stephen. *Hegel's Rational Religion. The Validity of Hegel's Argument for the Identity in Content of Absolute Religion and Absolute Philosophy.* London: Associated University Presses, 1995.

Rohrmoser, Günter. *Subjektivität und Verdinglichung. Theologie und Gesellschaft im Denken des jungen Hegel.* Gütersloh: Mohn, 1961.

———. "Die theologische Bedeutung von Hegels Auseinandersetzung mit der Philosophie Kants und dem Prinzip der Subjektivität." *Neue Zeitschrift für systematische Theologie* 1 (1962) 87–111.

Rohs, Peter. *Form und Grund. Hegel-Studien.* Beiheft 6. Bonn: Bouvier, 1969.

———. Review of *Werden zu sich. Eine Untersuchung zu Hegels "Wissenschaft der Logik*," by Ute Guzzoni. In *Hegel-Studien*. Vol. 4 pp. 251–257. Bonn: Bouvier, 1967.

Rosen, Stanley. *G. W. F. Hegel. An Introduction to the Science of Wisdom.* New Haven: Yale, 1974.

Royce, Josiah. *The Problem of Christianity. Lectures Delivered at the Lowell Institute in Boston, and at Manchester College, Oxford.* Two volumes. New York: Macmillan, 1913; reprinted two volumes in one. Hamdon, CN: Archon, 1967.

———. *The Problem of Christianity.* "Introduction by John E. Smith." Chicago: University of Chicago Press, 1968.

Sarlemijn, Andries. *Hegelsche Dialektik.* Berlin: de Gruyter, 1971.

Saß, Hans-Martin. "Untersuchungen zur Religionsphilosophie in der Hegelschule 1830–1850." Ph.D. dissertation, Westfälischen Wilhelms-Universität zu Münster/Westfahlen, 1963.

Schadel, Erwin, ed., with the co-operation of Dieter Brünn and Peter Müller. *Bibliotheca Trinitariorum. International Bibliography of Trinitarian Literature.* Vol. 1: *Author Index.* Vol. 2: *Indices and Supplementary List.* Munich: K. G. Saur, 1984, 1988.

Scharlemann, Robert P. *Reflection and Doubt in the Thought of Paul Tillich.* New Haven: Yale, 1969.

Schlitt, Dale M. *Divine Subjectivity. Understanding Hegel's Philosophy of Religion.* Scranton, PA: University of Scranton Press, 1990, 2009.

———. *Experience and Spirit. A Post-Hegelian Philosophical Theology.* New York: Peter Lang, 2007.

———. *Generosity and Gratitude. A Philosophical Psalm.* New York: Peter Lang, 2011.

———. "Hegel, Georg Wilhelm Friedrich [1770–1831]." In *Dictionary of Fundamental Theology*. Edited by René Latourelle and Rino Fisichella. English-language edition edited by René Latourelle. Pp. 407–414. New York: Crossroad and Middlegreen, Slough, United Kingdom: St. Paul's, 1994.

———. "Hegel's Reconceptualization of Trinity. Further Reflections." In *Sein— Erkennen—Handeln. Interkulturelle, ontologische und ethische Perspektiven. Festschrift für Heinrich Beck zum 65. Geburtstag*. Edited by Erwin Schadel and Uwe Voigt. Pp. 559–565. Frankfurt am Main: Peter Lang, Europäischer Verlag der Wissenschaften, 1994.

———. Review of *Hegel and the Spirit. Philosophy as Pneumatology*, by Alan M. Olson. In *International Journal for Philosophy of Religion* 35 (1994) 62–64.

———. Review of *Hegel's Critique of Metaphysics*, by Béatrice Longuenessee. In *The Review of Metaphysics* 63 (2009) 486–488.

———. Review of *Die Idee als Ideal. Trias und Triplizität bei Hegel*, by Katharina Comoth. In *The Review of Metaphysics* 41 (1988) 822–824.

———. Review of *Reason in Religion. The Foundations of Hegel's Philosophy of Religion*, by Walter Jaeschke. In *Journal of the American Academy of Religion* 60 (1992) 341–344.

———. Review of *Reason in Religion. The Foundations of Hegel's Philosophy of Religion*, by Walter Jaeschke. In *The Heythrop Journal* 34 (1993) 110–111.

Schmitz, Hermann. "Der Gestaltbegriff in Hegels *Phenomenologie* [sic] *des Geistes* und seine geistesgeschichtliche Bedeutung." In *Gestaltprobleme der Dichtung. Festschrift für Günter Müller*. Pp. 315–334. Bonn: Bouvier, 1957.

Schmidt, Erik. "Hegel und die kirchliche Trinitätslehre." *Neue Zeitschrift für systematische Theologie und Religionsphilosophie* 24 (1982) 241–260.

Schmidt, J., Review of *Idealismus und Trinität*, by Herbert Huber. In *Theologie und Philosophie* 61 (1986) 131–133.

———. *Hegel als Denker der Individualität*. Meisenheim/Glan: Hain, 1957.

Schrader-Klebert, Karen. *Das Problem des Anfangs in Hegels Philosophie*. Vienna: Oldenbourg, 1969.

Schultz, Michael. "Warum das Christentum die absolute Religion ist. Zu Hegels trinitätsphilosophischer Begründung." *Münchner Theologische Zeitschrift* 47 (1996) 365–384.

Schulz-Seiz, Ruth-Eva. "'Sein' in Hegels Logik: Einfache Beziehung auf sich." In *Wirklichkeit und Reflexion. Walter Schulz zum 60. Geburtstag*. Pp. 365–383. Edited by Helmut Fahrenbach. Pfullingen: Neske, 1973.

Smith, John E. *The Analogy of Experience*. New York: Harper, 1973.

———. "Hegel's Reinterpretation of the Doctrine of Spirit and the Religious Community." In *Hegel and the Philosophy of Religion*. Pp. 157–177. Edited by Darrel E. Christensen. The Hague: Nijhoff, 1970.

Splett, Jörg. Review of *Hegel's Trinitarian Claim*, by Dale M. Schlitt. In *Theologie und Philosophie* 61 (1986) 133–135.

———. *Die Trinitätslehre G. W. F. Hegels*. Munich: Alber, 1965.

Stace, W. T. *The Philosophy of Hegel. A Systematic Exposition.* New York: Macmillan, 1924; reprint edition New York: Dover, 1955.
Staudenmaier, Franz Anton. *Darstellung und Kritik des Hegelschen Systems. Aus dem Standpunkte der christlichen Philosophie.* Mainz: Kupferberg, 1844; reprint edition Frankfurt am Main: Minerva, 1966.
Steinhauer, Kurt, compiler. *Hegel Bibliography-Bibliographie. Background Material on the International Reception of Hegel within the Context of the History of Philosophy/Materialien zur Geschichte der internationalen Hegel-Rezeption und zur Philosophie-Geschichte.* Two volumes. Munich: Saur, 1980 [revised 2008], 1998. In addition, there are growing numbers of electronic bibliographies of works by and about Hegel available online.
Stirling, John Hutchison. *The Secret of Hegel.* Revised edition. New York: G. P. Putnam's Sons, 1898.
Tawny, Peter. *Die Zeit der Dreieinnigkeit. Untersuchungen zur Trinität bei Hegel und Schelling.* Würzburg: Königshausen & Neumann, 2002.
Taylor, Charles. *Hegel.* Cambridge: Cambridge University Press, 1975.
Theunissen, Michael. *Hegels Lehre vom absoluten Geist als theologisch-politischer Traktat.* Berlin: de Gruyter, 1970.
———. *Sein und Schein. Die kritische Funktion der Hegelschen Logik.* Frankfurt am Main: Suhrkamp, 1978.
Tracy, David. *The Analogical Imagination. Christian Theology and the Culture of Pluralism.* New York: Crossroad, 1981.
———. *Blessed Rage for Order. The New Pluralism in Theology.* New York: Crossroad, 1975.
Trede, Johann Heinrich. "Die endgültige Lösung einer Diskussion?" In *Hegel-Studien.* Vol. 11 pp. 228–234. Bonn: Bouvier, 1976.
———. "Phänomenologie und Logik. Zu den Grundlagen einer Diskussion." In *Hegel-Studien.* Vol. 10 pp. 173–209. Bonn: Bouvier, 1975.
Trendelenburg, Adolf. *Logische Untersuchungen.* Two volumes. Third edition. Leipzig: Hirzel, 1870.
Tugendhat, Ernst. "Das Sein und das Nichts." In *Durchblicke. Martin Heidegger zum 80. Geburtstag.* Pp. 132–161. Edited by Vittorio Klostermann. Frankfurt am Main: Klostermann, 1970.
Viellard-Baron, Jean-Louis. *L'idée logique, l'idée de la philosophie et la structure théologico-historique de la pensée de Hegel.* In *Hegel-Studien.* Vol. 38 pp. 61–83. Hamburg: Felix Meiner, 2003.
Viviano, Benedict. "The Spirit in John's Gospel. A Hegelian Perspective." *Freiburger Zeitschrift für Philosophie und Theologie* 43 (1996) 368–387.
Viyagappa, Ignatius, S.J. *G. W. F. Hegel's Concept of Indian Philosophy.* Rome: Università Gregoriana, 1980.
Wagner, Falk. "Die Aufhebung der religiösen Vorstellung in den philosophischen Begriff." *Neue Zeitschrift für systematische Theologie und Religionsphilosophie* 18 (1976) 44–73.

———. "Bibliographie zu Hegels Religionsphilosophie." In *Die Flucht in den Begriff. Materialien zu Hegels Religionsphilosophie*. Pp. 309–345. Edited by Friedrich Wilhelm Graf and Falk Wagner. Stuttgart: Klett-Cotta, 1982.

———. *Der Gedanke der Persönlichkeit Gottes bei Fichte und Hegel*. Gütersloh: Mohn, 1971.

———. "Der Gedanke der Persönlichkeit Gottes bei Ph. Marheineke." *Neue Zeitschrift für systematische Theologie und Religionsphilosophie* 10 (1968) 44–88.

———. "Religiöser Inhalt und logischer Form. Zum Verhältnis von Religionsphilosophie und 'Wissenschaft der Logik' am Beispiel der Trinitätslehre." In: *Die Flucht in den Begriff*. Pp. 196–227. Edited by Friedrich Wilhelrn Graf and Falk Wagner. Stuttgart: Klett-Cotta, 1982.

Walker, John, "Comment on The History of Religion and the Absolute Religion." Pp. 29–37. In Walker, John, ed. *Thought and Faith in the Philosophy of Hegel*. Dordrecht: Kluwer Academic, 1991.

Walker, John, ed. *Thought and Faith in the Philosophy of Hegel*. Dordrecht: Kluwer Academic, 1991.

Wallace, William. "Bibliographical Notice on the Three Editions and Three Prefaces of the *Encyclopedia*." In G. W. F. Hegel. *Hegel's Logic*. Pp. xxxi–xliii. Translated by William Wallace. Oxford: Clarendon, 1975.

Westphal, Merold. "Hegel, Hinduism, and Freedom." *The Owl of Minerva* 20 (1989) 193–204.

———. Review of *Hegel's Trinitarian Claim*, by Dale M. Schlitt. In *Journal of the American Academy of Religion* 58 (1990) 312–314.

Wieland, Wolfgang. "Bemerkungen zum Anfang von Hegels Logik." In *Seminar: Dialektik in der Philosophie Hegels*. Pp. 194–212. Edited by Rolf-Peter Horstmann. Frankfurt am Main: Suhrkamp, 1978.

Williams, Robert R. *Recognition. Fichte and Hegel on the Other*. Albany, NY: State University of New York Press, 1992.

Williamson, Raymond Keith. *Introduction to Hegel's Philosophy of Religion*. Albany, NY: State University of New York Press, 1984.

Yarmin, George J., Jr. *In the Absence of Fantasia. Troeltsch's Relation to Hegel*. Gainsville, FL: University Press of Florida, 1993.

Yerkes, James. *The Christology of Hegel*. Missoula, Montana: Scholars, 1978; Albany, NY: State University of New York Press, 1983.

Žižek, Slavoj. "Preface. Hegel's Century." In *Hegel and the Infinite. Religion, Politics, and Dialectic*. Pp. ix–xi. Edited by Slavoj Žižek, Clayton Crockett and Creston Davis. New York: Columbia University Press, 2011.

Zeller, Eduard. "Hegel's Vorlesungen über die Philosophie der Religion (Zweite Auflage, Berlin, 1840)." In *Die Flucht in den Begriff*. Pp. 114–139. Edited by Friedrich Wilhelrn Graf and Falk Wagner. Stuttgart: Klett-Cotta, 1982.

Index of Names

*Excluding Hegel, traditional religious names for the divine and listings in the "List of Abbreviations" and the "Bibliography of Works Cited."

Adorno, Theodor W., 228 n. 9
Albrecht, 245 n. 157
Anselm of Canterbury, 215 n. 115
Apostel, Pavel, 215 n. 114
Aquinas, Thomas, 347 n. 6
Aristotle, 17, 218 n. 133, 220 n. 147, 344 n. 105
Augustine of Hippo, 128

Barth, Karl, xix, 194 nn. 2 and 3, 206 n. 53, 239 n. 116, 315 n. 1, 339 n. 267
Baysinger, Patricia, 347 n. 4
Berger, Birgitte, 228 n. 2
Berger, Peter L., 228 n. 2
Bonsiepen, Wolfgang, 234 n. 60, 253 n. 11, 275 n. 132, 276 n. 135, 277 nn. 144 and 145, 278 nn. 148, 149 and 152
Bouillard, Henri, 290 n. 34
Boydston, Jo Ann, 347 n. 4
Brito, Emilio, xii, 193 n. 5
Brouer, James, 249 n. 187
Brown, Robert F., 314 n. 1
Bruaire, Claude, 210 n. 95, 221 n. 148, 224 n. 166, 225 n. 168, 254 n. 13, 260 n. 53, 261 n. 59, 264 n. 74, 266 nn. 84 and 88, 267 nn. 93 and 96, 268 nn. 106 and 107, 269 n. 111, 270 nn. 115 and 116, 271 n. 122, 315 n. 1
Bubner, Rüdiger, 217 n. 128
Burbidge, John. W., 213 n. 106, 230 n. 28, 256 n. 21, 307 n. 253, 334 n. 225, 335 n. 240, 341 n. 17, 342 nn. 37 and 48

Carganico, L., 263 n. 71
Cassirer, Ernst, 235 n. 82
Chapelle, Albert, 213 n. 106, 253 n. 9, 253–254 n. 12, 254 n. 13, 261 n. 59, 264 n. 74, 265 n. 80, 266 n. 82, 268 n. 103, 269 n. 111, 270 n. 115, 271 nn. 120 and 121, 289 n. 21, 300–301 n. 183, 315 nn. 1 and 2, 319 nn. 32 and 34, 320 n. 40, 321 n. 44, 322 n. 47, 323 n. 63, 325 n. 94
Cherniak, Samuel, 273 n. 124
Christensen, Darrel E., 315 n. 2
Clark, Malcolm, 262 n. 63
Cobb, John. B., 312 n. 305
Corduan, Winfried, 267 n. 92
Cramer, Wolfgang, 201 n. 16, 231 n. 47
Crites, Stephen, 317 n. 15

Crockett, Clayton, 346 n. 1
Crouter, Richard, 197 n. 21

Dahlstrom, Daniel Oscar, 245 n. 157, 246 n. 162
Dalrymple, Edwin Studart III, 238 n. 110
Davis, Creston, 346 n. 1
Descartes, René, 186
Desmond, William, xi, 193 n. 2
Dewey, John, 187, 189, 347 n. 4
Dooren, Wim van, 274 n. 128
Düsing, Klaus, 206 n. 54, 207 nn. 65, 68 and 69, 208 nn. 72 and 73, 218 n. 133, 229 n. 16, 256 n. 21, 257 nn. 28, 32 and 35, 258 n. 37, 259 n. 50, 261 n. 56, 276 n. 134, 277 nn. 144 and 146, 332 n. 198, 334 n. 225, 337 n. 253

Eecke, W. Ver, 234 n. 60, 275 n. 132
Eley, Lothar, 243–244 n. 150, 247 n. 171, 248 n. 175

Fackenheim, Emil L., 199 n. 2, 225 n. 169
Fahrenbach, Helmut, 137 n. 95
Feuerbach, Ludwig, 216 n. 127, 240 n. 121, 297 n. 138
Fichte, Johann Gottlieb, 3, 5, 10, 20, 50, 185, 186, 210
Findlay, John N., 207 n. 69, 280 n. 163
Fink-Eitel, H., 245 n. 60
Flach, Werner, 313 n. 311, 338 n. 264
Flasch, Kurt, 198 n. 33
Fulda, Hans Friedrich, 201 n. 16, 231 n. 47, 237 n. 88, 246 nn. 162 and 166, 254 n. 13, 256 n. 21, 272 n. 124, 277 n. 146

Gadamer, Hans-Georg, 187, 189, 215 n. 113, 228 n. 9, 237 n. 99, 272 n. 124, 346 n. 2
Gagné, Jacques, 290 n. 34
Garceau, Benoît, 255 n. 21
Gauvin, Joseph, 206 n. 58, 275 n. 132, 280 n. 161, 283 n. 188, 285 n. 200
Glockner, Hermann, 262 n. 70, 334 n. 221
Griesheim, Karl Gustav von, 194 n. 1, 321 n. 44, 331 n. 174, 334 n. 214
Günther, Gotthard, 340 n. 6
Guibal, Francis, 272 n. 124, 273 nn. 125 and 128, 277 n. 140, 288 nn. 13 and 20, 288–289 n. 21, 289 n. 25, 290 nn. 34 and 36, 291 nn. 39 and 40, 293 n. 87, 295 nn. 110, 113 and 117, 296 nn. 120 and 124, 297 nn. 133 and 137, 300 nn. 180 and 181, 309 nn. 268, 272, 273 and 276
Guzzoni, Ute, 215 n. 116, 217 n. 128, 232 n. 48, 244 n. 156

Haag, Karl Heinz, 223 n. 164, 234 n. 67, 237 nn. 95 and 97, 241 n. 130, 341 nn. 17 and 24
Haering, Theodor Lorenz, 273 n. 125, 273–274 n. 128, 311 n. 293
Hartmann, Klaus, 283 n. 186
Hausen, Gitta, 198 n. 31
Heckman, Hohn, 273 n. 124
Hedwig, Klaus, 198 n. 33
Heede, Reinhard, ix, 198 n. 31, 199 n. 2, 204 n. 42, 210 n. 95, 216 nn. 118, 120, 122 and 128, 218 n. 133, 221 n. 149, 225 n. 168, 226 nn. 178 and 179, 236 n. 85, 253 nn. 4, 5, 11 and 12, 254 n. 13, 255 nn. 15 and 20, 258 n. 38,

259 nn. 48 and 51, 260 n. 53, 261 n. 59, 263–265 n. 74, 265 n. 81, 268 n. 99, 269 n. 111, 277 n. 144, 295 n. 111, 296 n. 120, 301 n. 183, 313–315 n. 1, 316 n. 11, 317 n. 20, 318 nn. 24 and 26–30, 320 nn. 40 and 41, 321 nn. 42 and 44, 322 n. 49
Heidegger, Martin, 247 n. 171, 278 n. 148, 283 n. 189
Heimann, Betty, 156 n. 21, 334 n. 225
Heinrichs, Johannes, 201 n. 14, 214 n. 111, 241 n. 129, 261 n. 59, 265 n. 81, 266 nn. 82 and 84, 267 nn. 88 and 93, 269 n. 111, 271 n. 122, 272 nn. 214 and 125, 273–274 n. 128, 274 n. 129, 276 nn. 133–135 and 137, 277 nn. 140 and 146, 278 nn. 148, 149 and 151, 279 n. 157, 279–280 n. 158, 280 nn. 160 and 162, 281 nn. 168, 172 and 173, 282 nn. 175–178, 182 and 183, 282 nn. 185–188, 284 nn. 191, 195 and 197, 285 nn. 199 and 201, 288–289 n. 21, 289 nn. 22 and 25, 290–291 n. 37, 292 n. 60, 293 nn. 76 and 78, 294 nn. 92, 98, 100, 104 and 108, 296 nn. 123 and 124, 297 n. 134, 300 nn. 179 and 181, 307 n. 253, 310 nn. 279 and 285, 311 n. 293, 313 nn. 309 and 311
Heintel, Erich, 238 n. 105
Henningsen, Jürgen, 252 n. 2
Henrich, Dieter, 201 n. 16, 237 n. 99, 245 n. 157, 246 n. 166, 272 n. 124
Hessen, Johannes, xxii, 198 n. 32, 213 n. 106, 221 n. 148, 222 n. 159, 223 n. 160, 227 n. 179

Hill, William J., 226 n. 172
Hodgson, Peter C., ix, x, 194 n. 1, 204 n. 4, 253 n. 9, 314–315 n. 1, 317 n. 15, 318 nn. 28 and 29, 319 nn. 33 and 34, 320 nn. 35 and 41, 321 nn. 44 and 45, 321–322 n. 47, 326 n. 95, 328 n. 133, 329 n. 151, 330 n. 157
Hoffmeister, Johannes, 196 nn. 7 and 10, 227 n. 181, 263 n. 71, 275 n. 131, 278 n. 153, 283 n. 190, 287 n. 3
Hogemann, Friedrich, 201 n. 18, 206 n. 54, 215 n. 114, 221 n. 147, 227 n. 182, 233 n. 60, 244 n. 153, 256 n. 21
Homann, Karl, 207 n. 69
Hoover, Jeff L. 315 n. 1
Horstmann, Rolf-Peter, 217 n. 128, 229 n. 26
Hotho, Heinrich Gustav, 321 n. 43
Houlgate, Stephen, 193 n. 4, 249 n. 187
Hyppolite, Jean, 272–273 n. 124, 277 n. 144, 301 n. 193

Iljin, Iwan, 217 n. 128
Ilting, Karl-Heinz, 314 n. 1
Innis, Robert E., 273 n. 124

Jaeschke, Walter, ix, x, 194 n. 1, 199–200 n. 2, 201 nn. 14 and 18, 204 n. 43, 206 nn. 53 and 54, 207–208 n. 70, 211–212 n. 104, 214 nn. 110 and 112, 215 n. 114, 216 n. 118, 216 nn. 127 and 128, 218 n. 133, 219 n. 142, 220–221 n. 147, 222 n. 157, 223 n. 162, 223–224 n. 164, 224 n. 166, 225 n. 168, 227 n. 182, 228 n. 10, 233 n. 60, 240 n. 121, 244 n. 153, 255 n. 19, 256 n. 21, 261

Jaeschke, Walter *(continued)*
nn. 57 and 63, 272 n. 123, 286 n. 223, 301–302 n. 193, 313–315 n. 1, 316 nn. 7–12, 317 nn. 13, 18, 20 and 21, 318 nn. 27–29 and 31, 319 n. 32, 321 nn. 43–45, 321–322 n. 47, 322 n. 49, 323 nn. 63 and 65, 324 n. 76, 325 nn. 94 and 95, 326 nn. 106 and 107, 329 n. 137
Jarezyk, Gwendoline, 242 n. 143
Jüngel, Ebehard, 194 n. 2

Kant, Immanuel, xii, 3, 5, 10, 42, 185, 186, 193 n. 4, 199 n. 2, 202 n. 5, 243 n. 145, 284 n. 191, 340 n. 4, 345 n. 105
Kaufmann, Walter, 276 n. 134, 282 n. 182, 284 n. 197
Kellner, Hansfried, 228 n. 2
Kern, Walter, 198 nn. 31 and 33, 200 n. 12, 222 n. 156, 223 n. 160, 273 n. 124, 314 n. 1, 318 n. 21
Kierkegaard, Søren, xiii, 128, 186
Kimmerle, Heinz, 199 n. 2, 215 n. 115, 225 n. 168, 226 n. 179, 319 n. 32
Klostermann, Vittorio, 277 n. 171
Knox, T. M., 227 n. 181
Koch, Traugott, 200 n. 12, 201 n. 18, 210 n. 95, 213 n. 106, 215 nn. 113 and 114, 217 nn. 128 and 132, 219 n. 143, 223 n. 164, 226 n. 175, 228 n. 4, 230 n. 28, 231 nn. 29, 32, 35, 41 and 46, 232 nn. 49, 51 and 53, 233 n. 58, 234 nn. 60, 69, 70 and 72, 235 nn. 82 and 85, 237 n. 96, 238 nn. 105, 108 and 110, 241 nn. 131 and 132, 242 nn. 134, 135, 138 and 144, 243 n. 146, 243–244 n. 150, 245 n. 159, 246 nn. 162, 164 and 166, 247 n. 169, 247–248 n. 171, 248 nn. 172, 175, 179 and 180, 250 nn. 191 and 195, 337 nn. 250 and 253, 341 n. 17, 344 nn. 96, 100 and 101, 345 n. 110
Kojève, Alexandre, 275 n. 132, 278 n. 148
Koslowski, Peter, 315 n. 1
Krohn, Wolfgang, 256 n. 21, 257 nn. 30 and 35, 258 n. 37, 261 n. 56, 334 n. 225, 337 nn. 250 and 253
Kroner, Richard, 221 n. 149, 284 n. 191
Krüger, Klaus, 216 n. 128
Küng, Hans, 255 n. 21

Labarrière, Pierre-Jean, xiii, 194 n. 9, 206 n. 58, 232 n. 54, 239 n. 116, 242 n. 143, 253 n. 4, 272 n. 124, 273 n. 125, 273–274 n. 128, 275 n. 130, 277 n. 146, 278 nn. 151 and 153, 279 n. 158, 280 nn. 160 and 162, 281 nn. 167 and 168, 284 n. 193, 285 n. 203, 288 n. 15, 289 nn. 21 and 24, 294 n. 109, 307 n. 253, 310 nn. 279 and 285, 311 n. 293
Lasson, Georg, ix, 126, 131, 140, 194 n. 1, 195 n. 4, 196 n. 6
Lauer, Quentin, S.J., 214 nn. 110 and 111, 216 n. 128, 249 n. 186, 262 n. 63, 305 n. 233, 315 n. 1
Leibniz, Gottfried Wilhelm, 211 n. 101
Léonard, André, 201 n. 18, 210 n. 99, 215 n. 117, 219 n. 145, 230 n. 28, 232 n. 51, 233 nn. 58 and 60, 234 nn. 68 and 70, 244 n. 154, 254 n. 13, 256 nn. 21 and 24, 257 nn. 28, 34 and 35, 258

nn. 37 and 41, 259 nn. 43, 48 and 50, 260 n. 56, 266 n. 87, 274 n. 128, 279 n. 158, 319 nn. 32 and 34, 341 n. 17
Levine, Barbara, 347 n. 4
Lukács, György, 278 n. 148
Luther, O. Kem, 315 n. 1, 321 n. 44

McTaggart, John Ellis, 235 n. 82, 236 n. 85, 337 n. 253
Maker, William, 280 n. 158
Marsh, James L., 305 n. 233
Marshall, Donald G., 346 n. 2
Marx, Karl, 186, 275 n. 132
Marx, Werner, 217 n. 128, 272 n. 124, 274 n. 128, 277 n. 145, 278 n. 151, 280 n. 160, 281 nn. 167, 168 and 173, 284 n. 196, 285 n. 210, 311 n. 293
Meulen, Jan van der, 200 n. 12, 207 n. 69, 210 n. 95, 229 n. 24, 231 n. 39, 233 n. 58, 243 n. 150, 247 n. 171, 248 n. 175, 256 nn. 21 and 25, 257 nn. 27 and 34, 273 n. 125, 297 nn. 132 and 135, 307 nn. 253 and 259, 309 n. 275, 311 n. 293, 337 n. 253
Michelet, Carl Ludwig, 262–263 n. 70
Miller, A. V., 195 n. 4, 202 n. 31, 203 n. 35, 289 n. 21, 310 n. 285
Min, Anselm K., 212 n. 106
Moltmann, Jürgen, 194 n. 2, 196 n. 6, 338–339 n. 267
Mühlenberg, Ekkehard, 194 n. 3, 226 n. 175, 241 n. 126
Müller, Ch., 226 n. 172
Müller, Günther, 280 n. 160
Mueller, Gustav E., 199 n. 2
Mumson, Ch., 248 n. 171

Navickas, Joseph L., 296 n. 125

Nekt, Oskar, 283 n. 189
Nelson, Benjamin, 228 n. 2
Nicolin, Friedhelm, 252 n. 2, 254 n. 13
Niel, Henri, 274 n. 128, 276 n. 136, 319 n. 32, 326 n. 109, 338 n. 259

O'Donnell, John, 345–346 n. 112
Oeing-Hanhoff, Ludger, 198 n. 33, 222 n. 156, 314 n. 1
Osborn, Kenan B., 250 n. 188
Ottmann, Henning, 199 n. 2

Pannenberg, Wolfhart, 194 n. 2, 198 n. 33, 199 n. 2, 205–206 n. 53, 215 n. 113, 216 n. 118, 223 n. 160, 224 nn. 164 and 166, 225 n. 169, 226 nn. 172 and 173, 227 n. 181, 290 n. 34, 311 n. 295, 312 n. 305, 315 n. 1, 333 n. 202, 338 n. 254, 345 n. 110
Parmenides, 248 n. 173
Peirce, Charles Sanders, 187
Percesepe, Gary J., 252 n. 2
Plato, 262 n. 70, 345 n. 105
Pöggeler, Otto, 199 n. 2, 201 n. 18, 233 n. 60, 252 n. 2, 272 n. 124, 273 n. 124, 274 n. 128, 275 nn. 130–132, 277 nn. 143 and 144, 278 nn. 148 and 151, 314 n. 1, 319 n. 32
Puntel, L. Bruno, 198 n. 33, 201 nn. 14 and 20, 206 n. 58, 210 n. 95, 215 n. 114, 217 nn. 128 and 129, 218 n. 134, 219 n. 140, 223 n. 160, 227 n. 182, 231 n. 35, 243 n. 146, 244 n. 150, 254 n. 13, 273 n. 128, 277 n. 146, 280 n. 158, 312 n. 308

Rahner, Karl, xix, 194–195 n. 3, 239 n. 116, 267 n. 92, 339 n. 267

Rang, Bernhard, 217 n. 128
Rendtorff, Trutz, 271 n. 121, 315 n. 2, 317 n. 15, 319 n. 32, 326 n. 102, 331 n. 188
Richard, Lucien, 309 n. 270
Ricoeur, Paul, 287 n. 1, 295 nn. 111, 112 and 118, 319 n. 34
Ritter, Joachim, 314 n. 1, 317 n. 15
Rohrmoser, Günter, 199 n. 2, 277 nn. 142 and 144, 278 n. 148, 283 n. 189, 289 n. 21
Rohs, Peter, 203 n. 33, 215 n. 116, 229 n. 14, 231 n. 48, 244 n. 156
Rosen, Stanley, 200 n. 11
Royce, Josiah, 187, 189, 293 n. 77, 346 n. 3

Sarlemijn, Andries, 234 n. 60
Saß, Hans-Martin, 199 n. 33
Scharlemann, Robert, 340 n. 6
Schelling, Friedrich W. J., 50, 231 n. 39, 232 n. 49, 275 n. 131, 345 n. 105
Schillebeeckx, Edward, 312 n. 305
Schleiermacher, Friedrich, 197 n. 21
Schlitt, Dale M., 193 nn. 4, 5 and 7, 239–240 n. 116, 314 n. 1, 345 n. 112, 347 n. 6
Schmitz, Hermann, 256 nn. 21 and 22, 257 n. 33, 262 nn. 69 and 70, 263 n. 71, 264 n. 74, 276 n. 133, 280 n. 160
Schrader-Klebert, Karin, 231 n. 47, 236 n. 84
Schubarth, K. E., 263 n. 71
Schulz, Walter, 237 n. 95
Schulz-Seitz, Ruth-Eva, 237 nn. 95 and 99, 246 n. 162
Siep, Ludwig, 217 n. 128
Smith, John. E., 187, 189, 315 n. 2, 326 nn. 95 and 102, 329 n. 137, 330 n. 172, 331 n. 182, 333–334 n. 213, 346 n. 3, 347 n. 5

Socrates, 345 n. 105
Spinoza, Baruch, 38, 44, 211 n. 101, 224 n. 164, 229 n. 21, 233–234 n. 60
Splett, Jörg, xxii, 194 n. 1, 195 nn. 3 and 5, 196 n. 10, 198 nn. 32 and 33, 199 n. 34, 213 n. 106, 221 nn. 148 and 149, 222 n. 156, 223 n. 160, 225 n. 168, 227 n. 179, 253 n. 12, 254 n. 13, 261 n. 59, 272 n. 124, 278 n. 151, 289 n. 21, 309 n. 276, 315 n. 1, 319 n. 32, 347 n. 8
Stace, W. T., 205 n. 47, 250 n. 194, 340 n. 17
Staudenmaier, Franz Anton, 196 n. 17, 213 n. 106, 221 n. 148, 226 n. 179, 289 n. 21, 319 n. 32
Steinhauer, Kurt, 198 n. 31, 314 n. 1
Stirling, John Hutchison, 344 n. 105
Strauß, David Friedrich, 221 n. 148

Theunissen, Michael, 199 n. 2, 216 n. 128, 219 n. 140, 227 n. 182, 230 n. 28, 231 nn. 37 and 39, 235–236 n. 84, 237 n. 99, 238 n. 102, 245 n. 159, 247 n. 171, 253 n. 9, 254 n. 13, 255 n. 15, 256 n. 21, 259 n. 51, 260 nn. 53 and 55, 261 nn. 59 and 63, 262 n. 66, 263–264 n. 74, 265–266 n. 81, 267 nn. 88, 93 and 94, 268 nn. 96 and 99, 269 nn. 108 and 111, 270 nn. 115 and 117, 271 n. 120, 292 n. 52
Tholuck, August, 255 n. 16
Thyssen, J., 283 n. 186
Tillich, Paul, 250 n. 188, 340 n. 6
Tracy, David, 287 n. 1
Trede, Johann Henrich, 274 n. 128, 279 n. 158, 288 n. 10
Trendelenburg, Adolf, 201 n. 18, 245 n. 157, 337 n. 253

Troeltsch, Ernst, 346 n. 1
Tugendhat, Ernst, 247 n. 171

Viyagappa, Ignatius, S.J., 317 n. 16

Wagner, Falk, 201 n. 16, 216 nn. 118 and 127, 221 n. 148, 222 nn. 156 and 157, 223 nn. 160 and 162, 224 nn. 164–166, 225 n. 168, 261 n. 63, 266 n. 82, 271–272 n. 123, 276 n. 133, 289 n. 21, 314–315 n. 1, 316 n. 5, 318 nn. 21 and 30, 319 n. 32
Wagner, Hans, 201 n. 16

Wallace, William, 240 n. 122, 255 n. 16
Weinsheimer, Joel, 346 n. 2
Westphal, Merold, xiii, 193 n. 7
Whitehead, Alfred North, 186
Wieland, Wolfgang, 217 n. 128, 218 n. 135, 229 n. 26, 230 n. 28, 231 n. 36, 247 n. 171

Yamin, George J., Jr., 346 n. 1
Yerkes, James, 199 n. 2, 226 n. 179, 248 n. 171, 315 n. 1, 319 n. 34

Žižek, Slavoj, 346 n. 1

www.ingramcontent.com/pod-product-compliance
Lightning Source LLC
Chambersburg PA
CBHW020120240426

43673CB00038B/541